BRIEF CONTENTS

Management 9e

BICENTENNIAL
1807
⊛WILEY
2007
BICENTENNIAL

THE WILEY BICENTENNIAL–KNOWLEDGE FOR GENERATIONS

*E*ach generation has its unique needs and aspirations. When Charles Wiley first opened his small printing shop in lower Manhattan in 1807, it was a generation of boundless potential searching for an identity. And we were there, helping to define a new American literary tradition. Over half a century later, in the midst of the Second Industrial Revolution, it was a generation focused on building the future. Once again, we were there, supplying the critical scientific, technical, and engineering knowledge that helped frame the world. Throughout the 20th Century, and into the new millennium, nations began to reach out beyond their own borders and a new international community was born. Wiley was there, expanding its operations around the world to enable a global exchange of ideas, opinions, and know-how.

For 200 years, Wiley has been an integral part of each generation's journey, enabling the flow of information and understanding necessary to meet their needs and fulfill their aspirations. Today, bold new technologies are changing the way we live and learn. Wiley will be there, providing you the must-have knowledge you need to imagine new worlds, new possibilities, and new opportunities.

Generations come and go, but you can always count on Wiley to provide you the knowledge you need, when and where you need it!

WILLIAM J. PESCE
PRESIDENT AND CHIEF EXECUTIVE OFFICER

PETER BOOTH WILEY
CHAIRMAN OF THE BOARD

Management

9e

JOHN R. SCHERMERHORN, JR.

John Wiley & Sons, Inc.

ASSOCIATE PUBLISHER Judith R. Joseph
SENIOR ACQUISITIONS EDITOR Jayme Heffler
ASSOCIATE EDITOR Jennifer Conklin
EDITORIAL ASSISTANT Carissa Marker
MARKETING MANAGER Christopher Ruel
SENIOR PRODUCTION EDITOR Sandra Dumas
CREATIVE DIRECTOR Harry Nolan
SENIOR DESIGNER Madelyn Lesure
SENIOR PHOTO EDITOR Hilary Newman
PHOTO RESEARCHER Teri Stratford
PHOTO EDITOR Hilary Newman
OUTSIDE PRODUCTION SERVICE Ingrao Associates
BICENTENNIAL LOGO DESIGN Richard J. Pacifico
COVER/CHAPTER OPENER PHOTO © Lightscapes/SuperStock/AgeFotostock

This book was set in 10/12 Garamond Book by Prepare and printed and
bound by Von Hoffman Corporation. The cover was printed by Lehigh Press.
This book is printed on acid-free paper. ∞

The paper in this book was manufactured by a mill whose forest management
programs include sustained yield harvesting of its timberlands. Sustained
yield harvesting principles ensure that the number of trees cut each year does
not exceed the amount of new growth.

ISBN-13: 978-0470-07835-8
Printed in the United States of America
10 9 8 7 6 5 4 3 2

To my sons John Christian and Charles Porter

While you played
I wrote.
But always,
I was listening
and loving
you.
■ *1984*

It's later now.
Don't worry.
Time
means love shared,
by you
and me.
■ *1986*

Think
of all the fun
we have.
Here, there, everywhere,
doing things
together.
■ *1989*

Home,
now and forever,
will always be
wherever
I can be
with you.
■ *1992*

Time
has its ways,
doesn't it?
Not enough,
not enough,
I often say.
■ *1996*

Hurry home
when you can.
Come laughing, sons.
Tell us
your
wonderful stories.
■ *1999*

Songs riding winds.
Mimi,
Uncle George,
Uncle Nelson.
Whispers and choirs.
Silence speaks.
■ *2002*

On the mountain,
by Irish lakes,
find beauty and
peace.
Fairies dance
there.
■ *2004*

Mom loves
us, cats
and rainy days.
Nana and Poppy
loved us
too.
■ *2007*

ABOUT THE AUTHOR

Dr. John R. Schermerhorn, Jr. is the Charles G. O'Bleness Professor of Management in the College of Business at Ohio University, where he teaches graduate and undergraduate courses in management. Dr. Schermerhorn earned a Ph.D. in organizational behavior from Northwestern University, an MBA (with distinction) in management and international business from New York University, and a BS in business administration from the State University of New York at Buffalo. He has taught at Tulane University, the University of Vermont, and Southern Illinois University at Carbondale, where he also served as Head of the Department of Management and Associate Dean of the College of Business Administration.

Highly dedicated to serving the needs of practicing managers, Dr. Schermerhorn focuses on bridging the gap between the theory and practice of management in both the classroom and in his textbooks. Because of his commitment to instructional excellence and teaching innovation, Ohio University has named Dr. Schermerhorn a University Professor. This is the university's highest campus-wide honor for excellence in undergraduate teaching.

Dr. Schermerhorn's international experience also adds a unique global dimension to his teaching and textbooks. He holds an honorary doctorate from the University of Pécs in Hungary. He has served as a Visiting Professor of Management at the Chinese University of Hong Kong, as on-site Coordinator of the Ohio University MBA and Executive MBA programs in Malaysia, and as Kohei Miura visiting professor at the Chubu University of Japan. Presently he is Adjunct Professor at the National University of Ireland at Galway, a member of the graduate faculty at Bangkok University in Thailand, and advisor to the Lao-American College in Vientiane, Laos.

An enthusiastic scholar, Dr. Schermerhorn is a member of the Academy of Management, where he served as chairperson of the Management Education and Development Division. In addition, educators and students alike know him as author of *Exploring Management* (Wiley, 2008), *Management 8e* (Wiley, 2005) and senior co-author of *Organizational Behavior 9/e* (Wiley, 2005) and *Core Concepts of Organizational Behavior* (Wiley, 2004). Dr. Schermerhorn has also published numerous articles, including ones in the *Academy of Management Journal*, *Academy of Management Review*, *Academy of Management Executive*, *Organizational Dynamics*, *Asia-Pacific Journal of Management*, the *Journal of Management Development*, and the *Journal of Management Education.*

Dr. Schermerhorn serves as a guest speaker at colleges and universities, lecturing on developments in higher education for business and management, as well as on manuscript development, textbook writing, and instructional approaches and innovations.

PREFACE

From the beautiful cover of this book to the realities of organizations today, great accomplishments are very much inspired works of art. Whether one is talking about arranging stones or bringing together people and other resources in organizational systems, it is a balancing act. But the results can be absolutely spectacular when goals and talent combine to create a lasting and positive impact.

Just as artists find inspiration in all the senses that bring our world to life, managers find inspiration in daily experiences, from the insights of management scholars, through relationships with other people, and among the goals that guide organizations in service of an ever more demanding society. And like artists, managers must master challenges as they strive to create the future from the resources of the present. Those challenges are many.

Without any doubt we live in a time rich with the forces of cultural pluralism, globalization, high technology and significant change. But just as a beautiful formation of natural stone can offer the beholder a mix of forms balanced together in a compelling masterpiece, so too does a well managed workplace build, mix and integrate with great success the beauties of human talent and organizational understanding. This capacity for positive impact is the goal bound into the pages of *Management 9/E*. It is an opportunity to gain knowledge, find inspiration and engage practices that can prepare each of us to help build the organizations we need to forge a better world.

MANAGEMENT 9/E PHILOSOPHY

Today's students are tomorrow's leaders and managers. They are the hope of the 21st century. Just as the workplace in this new century will be vastly different from today's, so too must our teaching and learning environments be different from days gone by. Management educators must confidently move students forward on paths toward an uncertain future. New values and management approaches are appearing; the nature of work and organizations is changing; the age of information is not only with us, it is transforming our lives.

Management 9/e is part of the same transformation. This edition has been extensively revised with a sincere commitment to learning in today's complex environment. It is based on four constructive balances that I believe remain essential to the agenda of higher education for business and management.

- **The balance of research insights with formative education.** As educators we must be willing to make choices when bringing the theories and concepts of our discipline to the attention of the introductory student. We cannot do everything in one course. The goal should be to make good content choices and to set the best possible foundations for lifelong learning.
- **The balance of management theory with management practice.** As educators we must understand the compelling needs of students to learn and appreciate the applications of the material they are reading and thinking about. We must continually bring to their attention good, interesting, and recognizable examples.

- **The balance of present understandings with future possibilities.** As educators we must continually search for the directions in which the real world of management is heading. We must select and present materials that can both point students in the right directions and help them develop the confidence and self-respect needed to best proceed with them.

- **The balance of what "can" be done with what is, purely and simply, the "right" thing to do.** As educators we are role models; we set the examples. We must be willing to take stands on issues like managerial ethics and corporate social responsibility. We must be careful not to let the concept of "contingency" betray the need for positive "action" and "accountability" in managerial practice.

Today, more than ever before, our students have pressing needs for direction as well as suggestion. They have needs for application as well as information. They have needs for integration as well as presentation. Our instructional approaches and materials must deliver on all of these dimensions and more. My goal is to put into your hands and into those of your students a learning resource that can help meet these needs. *Management 9/e* and its supporting websites are my contributions to the future careers of your students and mine.

MANAGEMENT 9/E HIGHLIGHTS

Management 9/e introduces the essentials of management as they apply within the contemporary work environment. The subject matter is carefully chosen to meet AACSB accreditation guidelines while still allowing extensive flexibility to fit various course designs and class sizes. There are many new things to look for in this edition. Along with updates of core material, *Management 9/e* offers a number of changes in the organization, content, and design that respond to current themes and developments in the theory and practice of management.

Organization

- ***Part 1: Management***—focuses on understanding managers, what they do, the exciting new workplace, lessons of the past and present, and ethics and social responsibility.
- ***Part 2: Environment***—explores the contemporary environment in terms of competition, diversity, organization cultures, globalization, cross-cultural management, entrepreneurship, and small business.
- ***Part 3: Planning***—addresses how managers use information, information technology, and decision making for planning and in the process of strategic management.
- ***Part 4: Organizing***—reviews traditional and new developments in organization structures, organizational design contingencies, as well as human resource management, innovation and change.
- ***Part 5: Leading***—presents the major models and current perspectives on leadership, individual behavior and performance, teams and teamwork, communication and interpersonal skills, and change leadership.
- ***Part 6: Controlling***—addresses how managers use information for controlling, and in the processes of operations management and services.

Chapter Features

A most important feature of *Management 9/e* is the use of an integrated learning model to help guide students as they read and study for exams. This edition emphasizes visual and active learning, with many opportunities for critical thinking and reflection tied to core management concepts and issues. Look for the following features in each chapter.

Planning Ahead—
- Study Questions and learning objectives
- *The Topic* – opening vignette with dialog and point-counter point discussion

In Text—
- Visual Chapter Preview linking study questions to an overall chapter guide
- Learning Checks for reviewing each major text section
- Management Smarts – boxed feature summarizing practical guidelines and suggestions
- Research Brief – summary of recent journal article relevant to chapter topics
- Insights – photo enhanced positive example highlighting chapter themes
- Issues & Viewpoints – timely issues posed for further thought and discussion
- Real Ethics – examples and situations raising ethical questions for debate
- Kaffeeklatsch – simulated coffee table conversations about management news and worker concerns

End-of-Chapter Study Guide—
- Study Question *Summary* in bullet list format
- Key Terms Review for major concepts
- Chapter Self-Test with multiple-choice, short-answer, essay questions

End-of-Chapter Study Applications—
- Case feature based on developments with an organization and its management
- Team Project – describing a suggested research and presentation activity on chapter content
- Personal Management feature encouraging self reflections for personal skills development
- Next Steps guide to self-assessments and experiential exercises in the Management Learning Workbook.

Management Learning Workbook

The end-of-text *Management Learning Workbook* provides students and instructors with a rich variety of suggested learning activities.

- Experiential Exercises—30 exercises for in-class and out-of-class use
- Self-Assessments—30 personality and self-reflection instruments

MANAGEMENT, 9TH EDITION: TEACHING AND LEARNING RESOURCES

Instructor's Resource Manual

Prepared by Dr. Molly Pepper of Gonzaga University, the Instructor's Resource Manual offers helpful teaching ideas, advice on course development, sample assignments, and chapter-by-chapter text highlights, learning objectives, lecture outlines, class exercises, lecture notes, answers to end-of-chapter material, and tips on using cases.

Test Bank

Prepared by Dr. Brian Maruffi of Fordham University, this comprehensive Test Bank (available on the instructor portion of the website) will consist of over 200 questions per chapter. Each chapter will have true/false, multiple choice, and short answer questions. The questions are designed to vary in degree of difficulty to challenge your Management students. *The **Computerized Test Bank,** for use on a PC running Windows, is from a test-generating program that allows instructors to modify and add questions to the test Bank, and to customize their exams.*

Web Quizzes

An online study guide with quizzes of varying levels of difficulty designed to help your students evaluate their individual progress through a chapter. It is available on the student portion of the Schermerhorn, *Management, 9th* edition website.

Pre- and Post-Lecture Quizzes

Prepared by Amy Sevier of The University of Southern Mississippi and included in **WileyPLUS**, the Pre- and Post-Lecture Quizzes consist of questions varying in level of detail and difficulty. They focus on the key terms and concepts within each chapter, so that professors can evaluate their students' progress from before the lecture to after it.

Personal Response System

The Personal Response System questions (PRS or "Clickers") for each chapter of the Schermerhorn, *Management, 9th* edition textbook are designed to spark discussion/debate in the Management classroom. For more information on PRS, please contact your local Wiley sales representative.

PowerPoints

Prepared by Jim LoPresti of the University of Colorado at Boulder, this robust set provides lecture/interactive PowerPoints for each chapter to enhance your students' overall experience in the management classroom. The PowerPoint slides can be accessed on the instructor portion of the Schermerhorn, *Management, 9th* edition website and include lecture notes to accompany each slide.

Videos

Lecture Launcher: Short video clips tied to the major topics and developed from CBS source materials, are available on DVD. They provide an excellent starting point for lectures or for general class discussion. Teaching notes for using the video clips are available on the Instructor's portion of the Web site.

Movies and Music

For those interested in integrating popular culture and the humanities into their management courses, the special teaching supplement—*Art Imitates Life*, prepared by Robert L. Holbrook of Ohio University, offers a world of options. Dr. Holbrook provides innovative teaching ideas and scripts for integrating movies and music into day-to-day classroom activities. Available exclusively for adopters, this popular supplement is praised for its insights for increasing student involvement and enthusiasm for learning.

MP3 Downloads

A complete play list of MP3 downloads is available for all text chapters. The MP3 downloads provide easy-to-access and ever ready audio files that overview key chapter topics, terms and potential test materials.

Student Portfolio Builder

This special guide to building a student portfolio is complete with professional résumé and competency documentations. It can be found on the student companion site.

Companion Website

The text's website at http://www.wiley.com/college/schermerhorn contains a myriad of tools and links to aid both teaching and learning, including resources described above.

Business Extra Select Online Courseware System
http://www.wiley.com/college/bxs

Wiley has launched this program that provides an instructor with millions of content resources from an extensive database of cases, journals, periodicals, newspapers, and supplemental readings. This courseware system lends itself extremely well to the integration of real-world content that helps instructors to convey the relevance of the course content to their students.

WileyPLUS

WileyPLUS provides an integrated suite of teaching and learning resources, along with a complete online version of the text, in one easy-to-use Web site. **WileyPLUS** will help you create class presentations, create assignments, and automate the assigning and grading of homework or quizzes, track your students' progress and administer your course. It also includes mp3 downloads of the key chapter topics, providing students with audio chapter overviews, team evaluation tools, experiential exercises, student self assessments, flashcards of key terms, and more! For more information, go to http://www.wiley.com/college/wileyplus.

ACKNOWLEDGMENTS

Management 9/e was initiated and completed with the support of my inspiring editor Jayme Heffler and ever helpful associate editor Jennifer Conklin, along with a talented Wiley team that includes Judith Joseph (associate publisher), Don Foley (publisher), Madelyn Lesure (designer), Hilary Newman (photo research), Suzanne Ingrao (Ingrao Associates), Sandra Dumas (production), Chris Ruel (marketing), and with the help of Teri Stratford (photos).

Writing and revising *Management 9/e* came during trying times in our family as we managed elder-care, new jobs and schooling as well as the challenges of geographical dispersion. I remain grateful to Ann, Christian, and Porter for allowing me to once again continue this project. I sincerely hope the results meet their expectations. I am also grateful to my colleagues at Ohio University, especially Lenie Holbrook and Will Lamb, for being continuing sources of teaching inspiration.

I thank the following colleagues whose help with this book at various stages of its life added to my understanding. Carl Adams, *University of Minnesota*; Allen Amason, *University of Georgia*; Lydia Anderson, *Fresno City College*; Hal Babson, *Columbus State Community College*; Marvin Bates, *Benedictine University*; Joy Benson, *University of Wisconsin–Green Bay*; Peggy Brewer, *Eastern Kentucky University*; Jim Buckenmyer, *Southeast Missouri State University*; William Clark, *Leeward Community College*; Jeanie Diemer, *Ivy Tech State College*; Richard Eisenbeis, *Colorado State University–Pueblo*; Phyllis Flott, *Tennessee State University*; Shelly Gardner, *Augustana College*; Tommy Georgiades, *DeVry University*; Marvin Gordon, *University of Illinois–Chicago*; Carol Harvey, *Assumption College*; Lenie Holbrook, *Ohio University*; Kathleen Jones, *University of North Dakota*; Marvin Karlins, *University of South Florida*; John Lipinski, *University of Pittsburgh*; Beverly Little, *Western Carolina University*; Kristie Loescher, *University of Texas*; Kurt Martsolf, *California State University–Hayward*; Brian Maruffi, *Fordham University*; Brenda McAleer, *University of Maine at Augusta*; Donald Mosley, *University of South Alabama*; Behnam Nakhai, *Millersville University of Pennsylvania*; Robert Nale, *Coastal Carolina University*; John Overby, *The University of Tennessee–Martin*; Javier Pagan, *University of Puerto Rico–Piedras*; Diana Page, *University of West Florida*; Richard Pena, *University of Texas, San Antonio*; Wendy Pike, *Benedictine University*; Newman Pollack, *Florida Atlantic University*; Jenny Rink, *Community College of Philadelphia*; Joseph Santora, *Essex County College*; Rajib Sanyal, *The College of New Jersey*; Roy Shin, *Indiana University*; Shanthi Srinivas, *California State Polytechnic University–Pomona*; Howard Stanger, *Canisius College*; Jerry Stevens, *Texas Tech University*; William Stevens, *Missouri Southern State College*; Chuck Stubbart, *Southern Illinois University*; Harry Stucke, *Long Island University*; Thomas Thompson, *University of Maryland*; Judy Thompson, *Briar Cliff University*; Michael Troyer, *University of Wisconsin–Green Bay*; Jeffrey Ward, *Edmonds Community College*; Marta White, *Georgia State University*; James Whitney, *Champlain College*; Garland Wiggs, *Radford University*; Eric Wiklendt, *University of Northern Iowa*; Greg Yon, *Florida StateUniversity*; Yichuan Zhao, *Dalian Maritime University*.

BRIEF CONTENTS

CONTENTS

PART TWO ■ ENVIRONMENT

CHAPTER **4**

Environment and Organizational Culture   81

THE TOPIC Fit In or Stand Out?   82

CHAPTER **5**

Global Dimensions of Management   105

THE TOPIC Down the Block and Around
the World   106

PART THREE ■ PLANNING

PART FOUR ■ ORGANIZING

PART FIVE ■ LEADING

CHAPTER 17
Communication, Conflict, and Negotiation   421

THE TOPIC Building Up or Breaking Down?   422

THE COMMUNICATION PROCESS   424

PART SIX ■ CONTROLLING

CHAPTER 18
Controlling–Processes and Systems   449

THE TOPIC Who Has Control?   450

WHY AND HOW MANAGERS CONTROL   452

MANAGEMENT LEARNING WORKBOOK

Introducing Management

1

Planning Ahead

Putting Progress into Practice

Do big ideas drive best practices? Or do the needs of business ultimately dictate the where and when of creative propositions? Web-auction powerhouse

eBay has no shortage of big ideas, and it has an excellent track record of putting them into play.

"Build a better mousetrap, and the world will beat a path to your door."—*Ralph Waldo Emerson*

Emerson has a great line; but, if we take it too quickly we may only get half the point. Being creative and inventing something is great, but it isn't a sure fire guarantee of success. In the real world, after you build a better mousetrap you have to sell it.

Whether we're talking about a new business idea, product, or just a new way of doing something, the lesson is the same. Coming up with the idea is one thing, realizing the benefits when it is put into use is another.

Management today is focused on *innovation* as the process of both creating new ideas and putting them into practice. This involves a combination of insight and creativity, what some call *invention*, with actual *implementation*. The best performers, individuals, groups, and organizations all have a great capacity to both generate new ideas and put them into practice.

What *They* Think

"*You are constantly taking in new information, constantly changing the prism through which you view your business.*"
Meg Whitman, CEO of eBay.

INNOVATION: "*Just as energy is the basis of life itself, and ideas the source of innovation, so is innovation the vital spark of all human change, improvement and progress.*"
Ted Levitt, marketing guru.

IMPLEMENTATION: "*So if you're a customer today, the same person who came in to demonstrate the technology for you and helped you architect the solution before you bought it is likely going to be leading the team to help you do the implementation.*"
Sanjay Kumar, former Chairman & CEO of Computer Associates International; current co-owner of the NHL's New York Islanders.

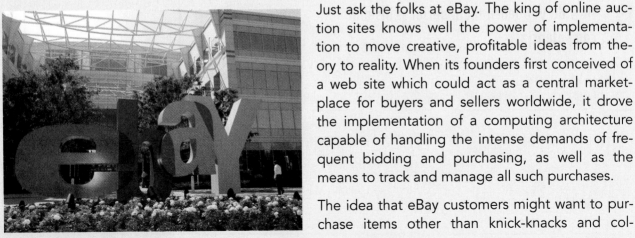

Just ask the folks at eBay. The king of online auction sites knows well the power of implementation to move creative, profitable ideas from theory to reality. When its founders first conceived of a web site which could act as a central marketplace for buyers and sellers worldwide, it drove the implementation of a computing architecture capable of handling the intense demands of frequent bidding and purchasing, as well as the means to track and manage all such purchases.

The idea that eBay customers might want to purchase items other than knick-knacks and collectibles led to the implementation of their highly successful specialty stores. One innovation was eBay Motors. In a recent year, eBay Motors handled more than $3 billion in automotive-related purchases.[1] The idea that eBay might attract even more customers by straying from its model of frenzied bidding thrived as well. It lead to the firm's purchase of Half.com, a site where sellers try to attract buyers on the strength of a fixed price.

According to Meg Whitman, CEO of eBay, innovation means keeping a dynamic frame of reference. "You are constantly taking in new information," she said, "constantly changing the prism through which you view your business."[2]

But sometimes necessity is the mother of invention, and competition drives a business to innovate for either success or survival. To keep with ever-growing demands on its Web site, eBay has upgraded and remodeled its server system multiple times in order to keep transactions smooth and avoid service outages.[3]

One company's successes can compel another to continuously innovate as a means of improving its products and services. Such was the case when fledgling online payment company PayPal offered its services to eBay. The rest was history, with eBay incorporating PayPal in 2002 for $1.5 billion.[4] About the advantages of competition, Whitman says: "we believe that when a company is out in front of the competition and you have an opportunity to acquire such a company, it's a great thing to do."

Will eBay continue its track record of combining innovative ideas with the business acumen and discipline necessary to implement them? Log on and see.

The Numbers

Annual eBay Net Revenues (in millions) Upon Key Innovations or Acquisitions

Founding of eBay (1997)	$0.2
Addition of PayPal (1999)	$224.7
Acquisition of Half.com (2000)	$431.4
Acquisition of Latin American auction sites Mercado Libre, Lokau, and iBazar (2001)	$748.8
Acquisition of PayPal (2002)	$1,214.1
Acquisition of 25% of Craigslist (2004)	$3,271.3
Acquisition of Skype (2005)	$4,552.4

Quick Facts

* Power Sellers—users who make all or a substantial portion of their living on eBay—account for about 29 percent of eBay's sales.[5]
* The most expensive item ever sold on eBay was a Grumman Gulfstream II jet for $4.9 million.[6]
* eBay went public on September 24, 1998 at an IPO split adjusted price of $0.75.[7]
* Adam Ginsberg, one of eBay's most successful sellers, sold over $20 million of merchandise on the site between 2001–2004.[8]
* An innovative restructuring of eBay's computer servers helped it reduce the number of servers by 71%.[9]

What Do *You* Think?

1. Given eBay's strength in the online auction market, does it need to innovate still more? Can you suggest an innovation that would benefit either eBay or its customers?
2. What difference does a leader make in terms of an organization's propensity to be innovative?

Introducing Management				
Study Question 1	**Study Question 2**	**Study Question 3**	**Study Question 4**	**Study Question 5**
Working Today	**Organizations**	**Managers**	**The Management Process**	**Learning How to Manage**
■ Intellectual capital ■ Globalization ■ Technology ■ Diversity ■ Ethics ■ Careers	■ What is an organization? ■ Organizations as systems ■ Organizational performance ■ Changing nature of organizations	■ What is a manager? ■ Levels of managers ■ Types of managers ■ Managerial performance ■ Changing nature of managerial work	■ Functions of management ■ Managerial activities and roles ■ Managerial agendas and networking	■ Essential managerial skills ■ Skill and outcome assessment
Learning Check 1	**Learning Check 2**	**Learning Check 3**	**Learning Check 4**	**Learning Check 5**

We are dealing with a new workplace, one in which everyone must adapt to a rapidly changing society with constantly shifting demands and opportunities. Learning and speed are in; habit and complacency are out. Organizations are fast changing, as is the nature of work itself. The economy is global, driven by innovation and technology. Even the concept of success, personal and organizational, is evolving as careers are transformed. The editors of *Fast Company* magazine have called this a time of "unparalleled opportunity and unprecedented uncertainty," where smart people and smart organizations create their own futures.[10]

In the quest for the future the best employers share an important commitment—they value people! They offer supportive work environments that reward and respect people, allowing their talents to be fully utilized. The themes of the day are "respect," "participation," "empowerment," "involvement," "teamwork," "self-management." You probably know them well. What you also need to remember is that the best employers are not just extremely good at attracting and retaining talented employees. They also excel at creating high-performance settings in which talented people achieve great results—individually and collectively.

After studying high-performing companies, management scholars Charles O'Reilly and Jeffrey Pfeffer concluded that success is achieved because they are better than their competitors at getting extraordinary results from the people working for them. "These companies have won the war for talent," they say, "not just by being great places to work—although they are that—but by figuring out how to get the best out of all of their people, every day."[11] This, in large part, is what *Management 9/e* and your management course are all about. Both are designed to introduce you to the concepts, themes, and directions that are consistent with career success and organizational leadership in today's high-performance work settings.

WORKING TODAY

There is no doubt that our new economy is ripe with challenges, uncertainty, and great possibilities. Expectations for organizations and their members are very high; our society is demanding nothing but the best from all its

ISSUES AND SITUATIONS

Talent Wars

Scene: Executive conference room at a *Fortune* 500 corporation.

Action: The vice president for human resource development is convening an important staff meeting.

"Welcome everyone. The purpose of today's meeting is to get everyone's attention focused on a fundamental issue, one that may well determine the future of our company. I'm speaking about TALENT, the lifeblood of any organization. And I'm concerned about the implications of facts on this Power Point slide.

> **Facts:**
> - *About 50% of senior management at America's largest firms will depart in the next six years.*
> - *The country has 77 million baby boomers set to retire; just 46 million "Xers" are ready to replace them.*
> - *Only 25% of large employers now consider their talent pools to be sufficient.*

Now, here's the task. Each year we hire many newcomers into the firm; we also make a fair number of offers that are rejected. Think about our college recruiting and the management of newcomers. Think of everything that you believe we can and should be doing in order to attract, hold, nurture, and develop the most talented workforce possible. Jot down your ideas as two lists: List A for college recruiting, and List B for managing newcomers.

Tell me what you think we need to do in order to win what some people are starting to call the 'war for talent'."

Critical Response

Project yourself into the conference room. Respond to the VP's charge by preparing A and B lists that would allow this firm to satisfy based on your needs, aspirations, and situation. Include insights based on your friends and acquaintances, and the insightful conversations and experiences you share with them.

---

institutions. Organizations are expected to continuously excel on performance criteria that include concerns for ethics and social responsibilities, innovativeness, and employee development, as well as more traditional measures of profitability and investment value. When they fail, customers, investors, and employees are quick to let them know. For individuals, there are no guarantees of long-term employment. Jobs are increasingly earned and re-earned every day through one's performance accomplishments. Careers are being redefined in terms of "flexibility," "free agency," "skill portfolios," and "enterpreneurship."

Career success today takes lots of initiative and discipline, as well continuous learning. It's your own arena for innovation—good ideas and plans that are well implemented. There is no other way to stay in charge of your own career destiny. Are you ready for the challenges ahead?

INTELLECTUAL CAPITAL

At Herman Miller, the innovative manufacturer of designer furniture, respect for employees is a rule of thumb. The firm's core values include this statement: "Our greatest assets as a corporation are the gifts, talents and abilities of our employee-owners. . . . When we as a corporation invest in developing people, we are investing in our future." Former CEO Max DePree says, "At Herman Miller, we talk about the difference between being successful and being exceptional. Being successful is meeting goals in a good way— being exceptional is reaching your potential."[12]

The point of these examples is that people—what they know, what they learn, and what they do with it—are the ultimate foundations of organizational performance. They represent **intellectual capital**, the collective

■ **Intellectual capital** is the collective brainpower or shared knowledge of a workforce.

■ A **knowledge worker** is someone whose mind is a critical asset to employers.

brainpower or shared knowledge of a workforce that can be used to create value.[13] Indeed, the ultimate elegance of any organization is its ability to combine the talents of many people, sometimes thousands of them, to achieve unique and significant results.

If you want a successful career, you must be a source of intellectual capital as someone willing to reach for the heights of personal competency and accomplishment. This means being a self-starter willing to continuously learn from experience. And it means becoming a valued **knowledge worker**— someone whose mind is a critical asset to employers and who adds to the intellectual capital of the organization. About knowledge workers, the late management guru Peter Drucker once said: "Knowledge workers have many options and should be treated as volunteers. They're interested in personal achievement and personal responsibility. They expect continuous learning and training. They will respect and want authority. Give it to them."[14]

GLOBALIZATION

Japanese management consultant Kenichi Ohmae suggests that the national boundaries of world business have largely disappeared.[15] Can you state with confidence where your favorite athletic shoes or the parts for your personal computer were manufactured? More and more products are designed in one country, while their components are sourced and final assembly is contracted in others, all for sale in still others. Top managers at Starbucks, IBM, Sony, and other global corporations have little need for the word "overseas" in everyday business vocabulary. They operate as global businesses that are equidistant from customers and suppliers, wherever in the world they may be located.

■ **Globalization** is the world-wide interdependence of resource flows, product markets, and business competition.

This is part of the force of **globalization**, the worldwide interdependence of resource flows, product markets, and business competition that characterizes our new economy.[16] It is described as a process in which "improvements in technology (especially in communications and transportation) combine with the deregulation of markets and open borders to bring about vastly expanded flows of people, money, goods, services, and information."[17]

In our globalized world, countries and peoples are increasingly interconnected through the news, in travel and lifestyles, in labor markets and employment patterns, and in business dealings. Government leaders now worry about the competitiveness of nations just as corporate leaders worry about business competitiveness.[18] The world is increasingly arranged in regional economic blocs, with Asia, North and Latin America, and Europe as key anchors, and with Africa fast emerging to claim its economic potential. Just as any informed citizen, you, too, must understand the forces of globalization.

TECHNOLOGY

Who hasn't been affected by the Internet and the explosion in communication technologies? For better or worse, we now live in a technology-driven world increasingly dominated by bar codes, automatic tellers, e-mail, instant messaging, text messaging, Web blogs, online media, electronic commerce, and more.

INSIGHTS

Smart People Create Their Own Futures

Monster.com is still an exemplar among the growing field of online job placement services available on the Web. Monster's founder, Jeff Taylor, describes its birth this way: "One morning I woke up at 4 A.M., and wrote an idea down on a pad of paper I keep next to my bed. I had this dream that I created a bulletin board called the Monster Board. That became the original name for the company. When I got up, I went to a coffee shop, and from 5:30 A.M. until about 10:00 A.M. I wrote the user interface for what today is Monster.com."

You don't need to create your own company the way Jeff Taylor did to achieve career success, although you could. What you must do, however, is discover the learning "monster" within yourself and commit it to academic success and career development.

Monster.com is a top destination for job seekers and one of the most visited domains on the Internet. Job candidates search the site for job postings, interviewing advice, company information, and even moving tips. The site represents itself as a "lifelong career network" that serves everyone from recent college graduates all the way up to seasoned executives. There's no complacency here, no becoming comfortable with success. The "Monster" keeps changing as its markets develop. Headquartered in Maynard, Massachusetts, Monster.com is the flagship brand of the Interactive Division of TMP Worldwide Inc., one of the world's largest search and selection agencies. Its clients include almost all the *Fortune* 500 companies.

From the small retail store to the large multinational firm, technology is an indispensable part of everyday operations—whether one is checking inventory, making a sales transaction, ordering supplies, or analyzing customer preferences. And when it comes to communication in organizations, geographical distances hardly matter anymore. Computer networking can bring together almost anyone from anywhere in the world at the mere touch of a keyboard. In "virtual space," people hold meetings, access common databases, share information and files, make plans, and solve problems together—all without ever meeting face-to-face. More and more people are "telecommuting" instead of reporting to an office everyday.

As the pace and complexity of technological change continue to accelerate, we have to keep up. The demand for knowledge workers with the skills to best utilize technology is increasing; computer literacy must be mastered and continuously updated as a foundation for career success.

DIVERSITY

The term **workforce diversity** describes the composition of a workforce in terms of differences among people on gender, age, race, ethnicity, religion, sexual orientation, and able-bodiedness.[19] The diversity trends of changing workforce demographics are well recognized: more seniors, women, minorities, and immigrants are in the workforce. And the changes continue: minorities are projected to be at least one third the population of the United States by 2016; Hispanics are the largest minority group in America (14.5% in 2005) and the fastest growing (up 21% from 2000–2005); retired baby boomers are a growing proportion of the population (already 12+%).[20]

The *Wall Street Journal* is among the voices calling diversity a "business imperative," meaning that today's increasingly diverse and multicultural workforce should be an asset that, if tapped, creates opportunities for performance gains. A female vice president at Avon once posed the

■ **Workforce diversity** describes differences among workers in gender, race, age, ethnicity, religion, sexual orientation, and able-bodiedness.

diversity challenge this way: "Consciously creating an environment where everyone has an equal shot at contributing, participating, and most of all advancing."[21] But consultant R. Roosevelt Thomas says that too many employers still address diversity with the goal of "making their numbers" in respect to workforce composition. He advises that truly managing diversity means moving beyond this mindset to make the most of a diverse workforce.[22]

Unfortunately, positive diversity messages don't always reflect work realities. How can we explain research in which résumés with white-sounding first names, like Brett, received 50 percent more responses from potential employers than those with black-sounding first names, such as Kareem?[23] The fact that these résumés were created with equal credentials suggests diversity bias. **Prejudice**, or the holding of negative, irrational opinions and attitudes regarding members of diverse populations, sets the stage for such bias. It becomes active **discrimination** when minority members are unfairly treated and denied the full benefits of organizational membership. A subtle form of discrimination is called the **glass ceiling effect**, an invisible barrier or "ceiling" that prevents women and minorities from rising above a certain level of organizational responsibility.[24]

Scholar Judith Rosener suggests that the loss caused by discriminatory practices is "undervalued and underutilized human capital."[25] Recent reports show women holding 50.3% of managerial jobs, 16.4% of *Fortune* 500 corporate officer jobs, and 8% of top management jobs.[26] In wage comparisons, women earn about 76 cents for each $1 earned by men; African American women earn 71 cents and Hispanic women earn 59 cents. And, a study by the research organization Catalyst found that 66 percent of minority women in management are dissatisfied with their career advancement opportunities.[27]

> ■ **Prejudice** is the display of negative, irrational attitudes toward members of diverse populations.
>
> ■ **Discrimination** actively denies minority members the full benefits of organizational membership.
>
> ■ The **glass ceiling effect** is an invisible barrier limiting career advancement of women and minorities.

ETHICS

When Jeffrey Skilling was sentenced to 24+ years in jail for crimes committed during the sensational collapse of Enron Corporation, the message was crystal clear. There is no excuse for senior executives in any organization to act illegally and to tolerate management systems that enrich the few while damaging the many. The harm done at Enron affected company employees who lost retirement savings, and stockholders who lost investment values, as well as customers and society at large who paid the price as the firm's business performance deteriorated.[28]

The issue raised here is **ethics**—a code of moral principles that sets standards of what is "good" and "right" as opposed to "bad" or "wrong" in the conduct of a person or group. And even though ethical failures like those at Enron are well publicized and should be studied, there are a plethora of positive cases and ethical role models to be studied as well. You will find in this book many people and organizations that are exemplars of ethical behavior and whose integrity is unquestioned. They meet the standards of a new ethical reawakening and expectations for ethical leadership at all levels in an organization. They also show respect for such things as sustainable development and protection of the natural environment, protection of consumers through product safety and fair practices, and protection of human rights in all aspects of society, including employment.

One of the concerns linked to the rash of business ethics failures is the role of **corporate governance**, the active oversight of management decisions and company actions by boards of directors.[29] Businesses by law must have boards of directors that are elected by stockholders to represent their inter-

> ■ **Ethics** set moral standards of what is "good" and "right" in one's behavior.

> ■ **Corporate governance** is oversight of a company's management by a board of directors.

REAL ETHICS

$100 Laptops

"When you have both Intel and Microsoft on your case, you know you're doing something right," says Nicholas Negroponte. He's a professor at MIT and head of One Laptop Per Child, a nonprofit association. Negroponte wants to build and distribute laptops for $100 to the world's children. He's convinced that this is a way to vastly improve the quality of their educations and life opportunities. Once children are given laptops, Negroponte believes they will be naturally drawn into learning how to learn. "The speed with which this child will acquire the knowledge to use the device," he says, "is so astonishing, you risk thinking it is genetic."

The One Laptop Per Child project is backed by Google, chip maker AMD, and Linux software distributor Red Hat to the tune of over $29 million. But technology giants Microsoft and Intel are tossing out criticisms from the sidelines. From Microsoft one hears that the hard drive is too small; Intel suggests it's just a gadget. In the meantime Negroponte has raised $29 million and hopes to be distributing some 5 to 10 million of the devices within two years. He says: "I hope that in 10 years every child on the planet will be connected."

FURTHER INQUIRY

Does this initiative make sense to you? Why isn't a project like this something that any firm, Microsoft and Intel included, would support automatically? As you think about Negroponte's idea, consider a broader question: Is cooperation or competition the best way to rally the world's greatest businesses around positive social change and development in the world's poorest nations?

---

ests. Many argue that boards and corporate governance failed in cases like Enron. The result is more emphasis today on restoring the strength of corporate governance. The expectation is that board members will hold management accountable for ethical and socially responsible behavior by the businesses they are hired to lead.

CAREERS

The new economy and the challenges of change make personal initiative and self-renewal critical career skills. British scholar Charles Handy suggests the analogy of the Irish shamrock to describe and understand the new employment patterns characteristic of this dynamic environment.[30]

Each of a shamrock's three leaves has a different career implication. In one leaf are the core workers. These full-time employees pursue traditional career paths. With success and the maintenance of critical skills, they can advance within the organization and may remain employed for a long time. In the second leaf are contract workers. They perform specific tasks as needed by the organization and are compensated on a fee-for-services basis rather than by a continuing wage or salary. They sell a skill or service and contract with many different employers over time. In the third leaf are part-time workers hired only as needed and for only the number of hours needed. Employers expand and reduce their part-time staffs as business needs rise and fall. Part-time work can be a training ground or point of entry to the core when openings are available.

You must be prepared to prosper in any of the shamrock's three leaves. Not only must you be prepared to change jobs and employers over time, but your skills must be portable and always of current value in the employment markets. Skills aren't gained once and then forgotten; they must be carefully maintained and upgraded all the time. One career consultant describes this career scenario with the analogy of a surfer: "You're always moving. You can expect to fall into the water any number of times, and you have to get back up to catch the next wave."[31] Handy's advice is that you maintain a "portfolio of skills" that is always up-to-date and valuable to potential employers.

Learning Check 1

Be sure you can ■ describe how intellectual capital, ethics, diversity, globalization, technology, and the changing nature of careers influence working in the new economy ■ define the terms intellectual capital, workforce diversity, and globalization ■ explain how prejudice, discrimination, and the glass ceiling effect can hurt people at work

ORGANIZATIONS IN THE NEW WORKPLACE

In his article "The Company of the Future," Robert Reich says: "Everybody works for somebody or something—be it a board of directors, a pension fund, a venture capitalist, or a traditional boss. Sooner or later you're going to have to decide who you want to work for."[32] In order to make good employment choices and perform well in a career, you need a fundamental understanding of the nature of organizations in the new workplace. *Management Smarts 1.1* provides a first look at some of the critical survival skills that you should acquire to work well in the organizations of today . . . and tomorrow.[33]

WHAT IS AN ORGANIZATION?

▨ An **organization** is a collection of people working together to achieve a common purpose.

An **organization** is a collection of people working together to achieve a common purpose. It is a unique social phenomenon that enables its members to perform tasks far beyond the reach of individual accomplishment. This description applies to organizations of all sizes and types, from large corporations, to the small businesses that make up the life of any community, to nonprofit organizations such as schools, government agencies, and community hospitals.

All organizations share a broad purpose—providing goods or services of value to customers and clients. A clear sense of purpose tied to "quality products" and "customer satisfaction" is an important source of organizational strength and performance advantage; it creates a platform for growth and long-term success. At Skype (now owned by eBay), founders Niklas Zennstrom and Janus Friis began with a straightforward and compelling sense of purpose: they want the whole world to be able to talk by telephone for free. That sense of purpose helps align their growing workforce with the common goal of attracting an ever-growing and loyal batch of customers.

MANAGEMENT SMARTS 1.1

Critical survival skills for the new workplace

- *Mastery:* You need be good at something; you need to be able to contribute something of value to your employer.
- *Contacts:* You need to know people; links with peers and others within and outside the organization are essential to get things done.
- *Entrepreneurship:* You must act as if you are running your own business, spotting ideas and opportunities and stepping out to embrace them.
- *Love of technology:* You have to embrace technology; you don't have to be a technician, but you must be willing and able to fully utilize Information Technology.
- *Marketing:* You need to be able to communicate your successes and progress, both yours personally and those of your work group.
- *Passion for renewal:* You need to be continuously learning and changing, always updating yourself to best meet future demands.

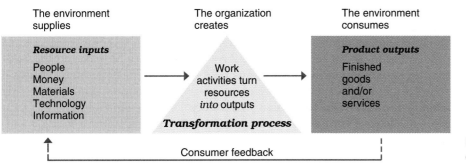

Figure 1.1 Organizations as open systems.

ORGANIZATIONS AS SYSTEMS

All organizations are complex systems whose many interrelated parts should function together so that a common purpose is achieved.[34] They are also **open systems** that interact with their environments in the continual process of obtaining resource inputs and transforming them into product outputs in the form of finished goods and/or services.

As shown in *Figure 1.1*, the external environment is both a supplier of resources and the source of customers. Feedback from the environment indicates how well an organization is doing. When customers stop buying a firm's products, it will be hard to stay in business for long unless something soon changes for the better. Anytime you hear or read about bankruptcies, remember that they are stark testimonies to this fact of the marketplace: without loyal customers, a business can't survive.

▨ An **open system** transforms resource inputs from the environment into product outputs.

ORGANIZATIONAL PERFORMANCE

For an organization to perform well, its resources must be well utilized and its customers must be well served. This is a process of *value creation*. If operations add value to the original cost of resource inputs, then (1) a business organization can earn a profit—that is, sell a product for more than the cost of making it, or (2) a nonprofit organization can add wealth to society—that is, provide a public service that is worth more than its cost (e.g., fire protection in a community).

A common way to describe how well an organization is performing overall is **productivity**. It measures the quantity and quality of work outcomes relative to the cost of resources used. Productivity can be measured at the individual and group as well as organizational levels. And as *Figure 1.2* shows, productivity involves success on two other common performance measures: effectiveness and efficiency.

▨ **Productivity** is the quantity and quality of work performance, with resource utilization considered.

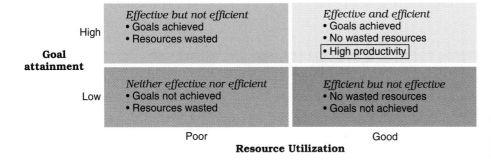

Figure 1.2 Productivity and the dimensions of organizational performance.

■ **Performance effectiveness** is an output measure of task or goal accomplishment.

■ **Performance efficiency** is an input measure of resource cost associated with goal accomplishment.

Performance effectiveness is an output measure of task or goal accomplishment. If you are working as a software engineer for a computer game developer, performance effectiveness may mean that you meet a daily production target in terms of the quantity and quality of lines of code written. By so doing, you help the company as a whole maintain its production schedule and meet customer demands for timely delivery and high-quality gaming products. **Performance efficiency** is a measure of the resource costs associated with goal accomplishment. Returning to the gaming example, the most efficient software production is accomplished at a minimum cost in materials and labor. If you were producing fewer lines of code in a day than you were capable of, this amounts to inefficiency. Likewise, if you made a lot of mistakes that required extensive rewrites, this is also inefficient work.

CHANGING NATURE OF ORGANIZATIONS

Change is a continuing theme of this book, and organizations are certainly undergoing dramatic changes today. Among recent trends, the following organizational transitions are especially relevant to your study of management:[35]

- *Belief in human capital:* Demands of the new economy place premiums on high-involvement and participatory work settings that rally the knowledge, experience, and commitment of all members.
- *Demise of "command-and-control":* Traditional hierarchical structures with "do as I say" bosses are proving too slow, conservative, and costly to do well in today's competitive environments.
- *Emphasis on teamwork:* Today's organizations are less vertical and more horizontal in focus; they are increasingly driven by teamwork that pools talents for creative problem solving.
- *Pre-eminence of technology:* New opportunities appear with each new development in computer and information technology; they continually change the way organizations operate and how people work.
- *Embrace of networking:* Organizations are networked for intense, real-time communication and coordination, internally among parts and externally with partners, contractors, suppliers, and customers.
- *New workforce expectations:* A new generation of workers brings to the workplace less tolerance for hierarchy, more informality, and more attention to performance merit than to status and seniority.
- *Concern for work-life balance:* As society increases in complexity, workers are forcing organizations to pay more attention to balance in the often-conflicting demands of work and personal affairs.
- *Focus on speed:* Everything moves fast today; in business those who get products to market first have an advantage, and in any organization work is expected to be both well done and timely.

Learning Check 2

Be sure you can ■ describe how organizations operate as open systems ■ explain productivity as a measure of organizational performance ■ distinguish between performance effectiveness and performance efficiency ■ list several ways in which organizations are changing today

MANAGERS IN THE NEW WORKPLACE

In an article entitled "Putting People First for Organizational Success," Jeffrey Pfeffer and John F. Veiga argue forcefully that organizations perform better when they treat their members better. They describe an important distinguishing characteristic of high-performing organizations: Their "managers" don't consider people as costs to be controlled but rather as valuable strategic assets to be carefully nurtured.[36]

WHAT IS A MANAGER?

You find them in all organizations. They work with a wide variety of job titles—team leader, department head, supervisor, project manager, dean, president, administrator, and more. They always work directly with other persons who rely on them for critical support and assistance in their own jobs. We call them **managers**, people in organizations who directly support, supervise, and help activate the work efforts and performance accomplishments of others.

> ■ A **manager** is a person who supports and is responsible for the work of others.

For those serving as managers, the job is challenging and substantial. Any manager is responsible not just for her or his own work but for the overall performance accomplishments of a team, work group, department, or even organization as a whole. Whether they are called direct reports, team members, work associates, or subordinates, these "other people" are the essential human resources whose contributions represent the real work of the organization. And as pointed out by management theorist Henry Mintzberg, being a manager in this sense is an important and socially responsible job:[37]

> *No job is more vital to our society than that of the manager. It is the manager who determines whether our social institutions serve us well or whether they squander our talents and resources. It is time to strip away the folklore about managerial work, and time to study it realistically so that we can begin the difficult task of making significant improvement in its performance.*

LEVELS OF MANAGERS

At the highest levels of organizations, common job titles are chief executive officer (CEO), president, and vice president. These **top managers** are responsible for the performance of an organization as a whole or for one of its larger parts. They pay special attention to the external environment, are alert to potential long-run problems and opportunities, and develop appropriate ways of dealing with them. They create and communicate long-term vision, and ensure that strategies and objectives are consistent with the organization's purpose and mission.

> ■ **Top managers** guide the performance of the organization as a whole or of one of its major parts.

Top managers should be future-oriented, strategic thinkers who make many decisions under highly competitive and uncertain conditions. Before retiring as Medtronics' CEO, for example, Bill George repositioned the firm as a client-centered deliverer of medical services. The hours were long and the work demanding, but he loved his job, saying: "I always dreamed . . . of being head of a major corporation where the values of the company and my own values were congruent, where a company could become kind of a symbol for others, where the product that you represent is doing good for people."[38]

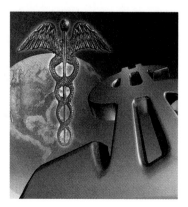

■ **Middle managers** oversee the work of large departments or divisions.

■ **Team leaders** or **supervisors** report to middle managers and directly supervise nonmanagerial workers.

■ **Line managers** directly contribute to the production of the organization's basic goods or services.

■ **Staff managers** use special technical expertise to advise and support line workers.

■ **Functional managers** are responsible for one area of activity, such as finance, marketing, production, personnel, accounting, or sales.

■ **General managers** are responsible for complex, multi-functional units.

■ An **administrator** is a manager in a public or nonprofit organization.

Reporting to top managers are **middle managers** who are in charge of relatively large departments or divisions consisting of several smaller work units. Examples are clinic directors in hospitals; deans in universities; and division managers, plant managers, and branch sales managers in businesses. Middle managers work with top managers and coordinate with peers to develop and implement action plans to accomplish organizational objectives.

Even though most people enter the workforce as technical specialists, sooner or later they advance to positions of initial managerial responsibility. A first job in management typically involves serving as a **team leader** or **supervisor**—someone in charge of a small work group composed of nonmanagerial workers. Job titles for these *first-line managers* vary greatly but include such designations as department head, group leader, and unit manager. For example, the leader of an auditing team is considered a first-line manager, as is the head of an academic department in a university.

Management Smarts 1.2 offers advice for team leaders and other first-line managers.[39] And, these positions are very important. Bill George's repositioning goals at Medtronics could only be met with the contributions of people like Justine Fritz, who led a 12-member Medtronics team to launch a new product. She says: "I've just never worked on anything that so visibly, so dramatically changes the quality of someone's life," while noting that the demands are also great. "Some days you wake up, and if you think about all the work you have to do it's so overwhelming, you could be paralyzed." That's the challenge of managerial work at any level. Justine says, "You just have to get it done."[40]

TYPES OF MANAGERS

In addition to serving at different levels of authority, managers work in different capacities within organizations. **Line managers** are responsible for work that makes a direct contribution to the organization's outputs. For example, the president, retail manager, and department supervisors of a local department store all have line responsibilities. Their jobs in one way or another are directly related to the sales operations of the store. **Staff managers**, by contrast, use special technical expertise to advise and support the efforts of line workers. In a department store, again, the director of human resources and chief financial officer would have staff responsibilities.

In business, **functional managers** have responsibility for a single area of activity, such as finance, marketing, production, human resources, accounting, or sales. **General managers** are responsible for activities covering many functional areas. An example is a plant manager who oversees many separate functions, including purchasing, manufacturing, warehousing, sales, personnel, and accounting.

Finally, it is common for managers working in public or nonprofit organizations to be called **administrators**. Examples include hospital administrator, public administrator, and city administrator.

MANAGERIAL PERFORMANCE

All managers help people, working individually and in groups, to perform. They do this while being held personally "ac-

MANAGEMENT SMARTS 1.2

Nine responsibilities of team leaders

1. Plan meetings and work schedules.
2. Clarify goals and tasks, and gather ideas for improvement.
3. Appraise performance and counsel team members.
4. Recommend pay increases and new assignments.
5. Recruit, train, and develop team members.
6. Encourage high performance and teamwork.
7. Inform team members about organizational goals.
8. Inform higher levels of team needs and accomplishments.
9. Coordinate activities with other teams.

KAFFEEKLATSCH

Evidence-Based Management

First Cup

"How do you know if a management practice really works? Just because you read about something in the *Wall Street Journal*, *Business Week* or *Fortune*, does that make it a 'benchmark' for the rest of us to blindly follow? Sometimes I wonder: are we chasing fads when we should be focusing on our own situations?"

Studying the Grounds

■ A book by Stanford scholars Jeffrey Pfeffer and Robert I. Sutton, *Hard Facts: Dangerous Half-Truths & Total Nonsense*, questions the conventional wisdom behind some popular management practices. The authors want business practice to emulate medical practice and become more "evidence-based."

■ Jack Welch, former CEO of GE, popularized "forced ranking" in performance appraisals (20% top, 70% middle, 10% bottom). Those at the bottom were largely targeted for removal. Pfeffer and Sutton say it's practiced by as many as a third of companies today, even though human resource managers using the approach believe it lowers morale, teamwork, and productivity.

Double Espresso

"I think Pfeffer and Sutton have a point. Who knows when the next new 'fad' might hit home . . . hard? I just read something in the *Wall Street Journal* that has me worried. It was an article describing the CEO of Freedom Communications, Scott Flanders, as telling 'his managers that they can't afford to constantly offer advice and guidance to their staffs.' Flanders seems to believe managers don't have the time for such activities.

Would a 'quick read' of the WSJ article lead one to conclude that mentoring by managers isn't worth the time it takes? Or, is there another side to the issue? In fact, the end of the article offers a counterpoint example of Tom Mattia, senior vice president of worldwide communications at Coca-Cola. He has 90 direct reports but tries to 'mentor on the go' and 'make every interaction I have with someone on my team a teaching experience'."

Your Turn

What is your take on management fads and fashions? Who would you prefer to work for—Mattia or Flanders?

---

countable" for results achieved. **Accountability** is the requirement of one person to answer to a higher authority for performance results in his or her area of work responsibility. The team leader is accountable to a middle manager, the middle manager is accountable to a top manager, and even the top manager is accountable to a board of directors.

But what actually constitutes managerial performance; when is a manager "effective"? A good answer is that effective managers are those who successfully help others to achieve *both* high performance and satisfaction in their work. This dual concern for performance and satisfaction is represented in the concept of **quality of work life**, an indicator of the overall quality of human experiences in the workplace. A "high-QWL" workplace offers such things as fair pay, safe working conditions, opportunities to learn and use new skills, room to grow and progress in a career, protection of individual rights, and pride in the work itself and in the organization. [41] Would you agree that performance, satisfaction, and a high-quality work life can and should go hand in hand?

■ **Accountability** is the requirement to show performance results to a supervisor.

■ **Quality of work life** is the overall quality of human experiences in the workplace.

CHANGING NATURE OF MANAGERIAL WORK

Many trends and emerging practices in organizations require new thinking from those who serve as managers. We are in a time when the best managers are known more for "helping" and "supporting" than for "directing" and "order giving." There is less and less tolerance in today's organizations for managers who simply sit back and tell others what to do. The words

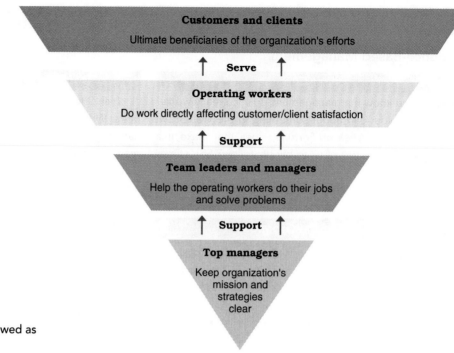

Figure 1.3 The organization viewed as an upside-down pyramid.

"coordinator," "coach," and "team leader" are heard as often as "supervisor" or "boss." The best managers are well informed regarding the needs of those reporting to or dependent on them. They can often be found providing advice and developing the support needed for others to peform to the best of their abilities.

The concept of the "upside-down pyramid" reflects these changes in managerial work. Shown in *Figure 1.3*, it offers an alternative and suggestive way of viewing organizations and the role played by managers within them. The operating workers are at the top of the upside-down pyramid, just below the customers and clients they serve. They are supported in their work efforts by managers below them. These managers clearly aren't just order-givers; they are there to mobilize and deliver the support others need to do their jobs best and serve customer needs. The whole organization is devoted to serving the customer, and this is made possible with the support of managers.

Learning Check 3	*Be sure you can* ■ describe the various types and levels of managers ■ define the terms accountability and quality of work life, and explain their importance to managerial performance ■ discuss how managerial work is changing today ■ explain the role of managers in the upside-down pyramid view of organizations

THE MANAGEMENT PROCESS

The ultimate "bottom line" in every manager's job is to help an organization achieve high performance by best utilizing its human and material resources. If productivity in the form of high levels of performance effectiveness and efficiency is a measure of organizational success, managers are largely responsible for its achievement.

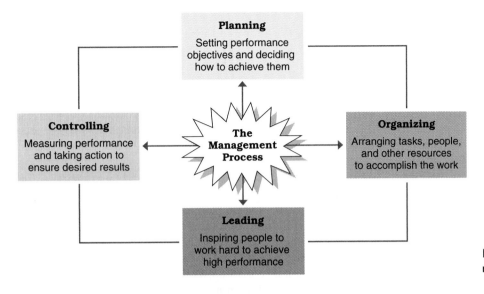

Figure 1.4 Four functions of management.

FUNCTIONS OF MANAGEMENT

The process of **management** involves planning, organizing, leading, and controlling the use of resources to accomplish performance goals. These four management functions and their interrelationships are shown in *Figure 1.4*. All managers, regardless of title, level, type, and organizational setting, are responsible for the four functions. However, they are not accomplished in linear, step-by-step fashion. The reality is that these functions are continually engaged as a manager moves from task to task and opportunity to opportunity in his or her work.

▪ **Management** is the process of planning, organizing, leading, and controlling the use of resources to accomplish performance goals.

Planning

In management, **planning** is the process of setting performance objectives and determining what actions should be taken to accomplish them. Through planning, a manager identifies desired results and ways to achieve them.

Take, for example, an Ernst & Young initiative that was developed to better meet the needs of the firm's female professionals.[42] Top management grew concerned about the firm's retention rates for women and by a critical report from the research group Catalyst. Chairman Philip A. Laskawy, who personally headed Ernst & Young's Diversity Task Force, responded by setting a planning objective to reduce turnover rates for women. Rates at the time were running some 22 percent per year and costing the firm about 150 percent of each person's annual salary to hire and train new staff.

▪ **Planning** is the process of setting objectives and determining what should be done to accomplish them.

Organizing

Even the best plans will fail without strong implementation. Success begins with **organizing**, the process of assigning tasks, allocating resources, and coordinating the activities of individuals and groups to implement plans. Through organizing, managers turn plans into actions by defining jobs, assigning personnel, and supporting them with technology and other resources.

At Ernst & Young, Laskawy organized to meet his planning objective by first creating a new Office of Retention and then hiring Deborah K. Holmes to head it. As retention problems were identified in various parts of the firm, Holmes convened special task forces to tackle them and recommend

▪ **Organizing** is the process of assigning tasks, allocating resources, and coordinating work activities.

location-specific solutions. A Woman's Access Program was started to give women access to senior executives for mentoring and career development.

Leading

> ■ **Leading** is the process of arousing enthusiasm and inspiring efforts to achieve goals.

In management, **leading** is the process of arousing people's enthusiasm to work hard and inspiring their efforts to fulfill plans and accomplish objectives. Through leading, managers build commitments to a common vision, encourage activities that support goals, and influence others to do their best work on the organization's behalf.

At Ernst & Young, Deborah Holmes identified a core problem: work at the firm was extremely intense, and women were often stressed because their spouses also worked. She became a champion for improved work-life balance and pursued it relentlessly. Although admitting that "there's no silver bullet" in the form of a universal solution, new initiatives from her office supported and encouraged better balance. She started "call-free holidays," when professionals did not check voice mail or e-mail on weekends and holidays. She also started a "travel sanity" program that limited staffers' travel to four days a week so that they could get home for weekends.

RESEARCH BRIEF

Worldwide study identifies success factors in global leadership

Recognizing both the importance and complexity of global leadership, Robert J. House and colleagues developed a network of 170 researchers to study leadership around the world. Over a ten-year period they investigated cultural frameworks, cultural differences, and their leadership implications as part of Project GLOBE. The results are summarized in the book *Culture, Leadership and Organizations: The Globe Study of 62 Societies* (Sage, 2004).

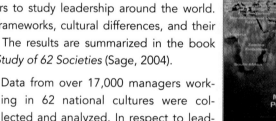

> *Universal facilitators of leadership effectiveness –*
> * *Trustworthy, honest, just*
> * *Foresight, ability to plan ahead*
> * *Positive, dynamic, encouraging, motivating*
> * *Communicative, informed, integrating*
>
> *Universal impediments to leadership effectiveness –*
> * *Loner, asocial, self-protective*
> * *Non-cooperative, irritable*
> * *Dictatorial and autocratic*

Data from over 17,000 managers working in 62 national cultures were collected and analyzed. In respect to leadership effectiveness, the researchers found that the world's cultures share certain universal facilitators and impediments to leadership success, while also having some unique cultural contingencies. In terms of leadership development, the GLOBE researchers conclude that global mindsets, tolerance for ambiguity, cultural adaptability, and flexibility are essential as leaders seek to influence persons whose cultural backgrounds are different from their own. Personal aspects that seemed most culturally sensitive in terms of leadership effectiveness were being individualist, being status conscious, and being risk taking.

QUESTIONS & APPLICATIONS

Take a survey of workers at your university, place of employment or a local organization. Ask them to describe their best and worst leaders. Use the results to answer the question: How closely do local views of leadership match with findings of the GLOBE study?

As informative as the GLOBE project is, don't you agree that we still have a lot more to learn about how leadership success is viewed in the many cultures of the world? The links between culture and leadership seem particularly important not only in a business context, but also as governments try to work together both bilaterally and multilaterally in forums such as the United Nations.

Reference: Robert J. House, P.JU. Hanges, Mansour Javidan, P. Dorfman and V. Gupta (Editors), *Culture, Leadership and Organizations: The GLOBE Study of 62 Societies* (Thousand Oaks, CA: Sage Publications, Inc., 2004); and, Mansour Javidan, Peter W. Dorfman, Mary Sully de Luque and Robert J. House, *Academy of Management Perspective*, Vol. 20 (2006), pp. 67–90

Controlling

The management function of **controlling** is the process of measuring work performance, comparing results to objectives, and taking corrective action as needed. Through controlling, managers maintain active contact with people in the course of their work, gather and interpret reports on performance, and use this information to plan constructive action and change. In today's dynamic times, such control and adjustment are indispensable. Things don't always go as anticipated, and plans must be modified and redefined for future success.

At Ernst & Young, Laskawy and Holmes both knew what the retention rates were when they started the new program, and they were subsequently able to track improvements. Through measurement they were able to compare results with objectives and track changes in work-life balance and retention rates. They continually adjusted the program to improve it.

■ **Controlling** is the process of measuring performance and taking action to ensure desired results.

MANAGERIAL ACTIVITIES AND ROLES

Although the management process may seem straightforward, things are more complicated than they appear at first glance. In his classic book *The Nature of Managerial Work,* Henry Mintzberg describes the daily work of corporate chief executives as follows: "There was no break in the pace of activity during office hours. The mail . . . telephone calls . . . and meetings . . . accounted for almost every minute from the moment these executives entered their offices in the morning until they departed in the evenings."[43] Today, we would have to add ever-present e-mail and instant messages to Mintzberg's list of executive preoccupations.

In trying to systematically describe the nature of managerial work and the demands placed on those who do it, Mintzberg identified the set of 10 roles depicted in *Figure 1.5.* The roles involve managing information, people, and action.[44] In this framework, a manager's *informational roles* involve the giving, receiving, and analyzing of information. The *interpersonal roles* involve interactions with people inside and outside the work unit. The *decisional roles* involve using information to make decisions to solve problems or address opportunities.

Mintzberg is careful to note that the manager's day is unforgiving in the intensity and pace of these role requirements. The managers he observed had little free time because unexpected problems and continuing requests for meetings consumed almost all the time that became available. Their workdays were hectic, and the pressure for continuously improving performance was all encompassing. Says Mintzberg: "The manager can never be free to forget the job, and never has the pleasure of knowing, even temporarily, that there is nothing else to do. . . . Managers always carry the nagging suspicion that they might be able to contribute just a little bit more. Hence they assume an unrelenting pace in their work."[45]

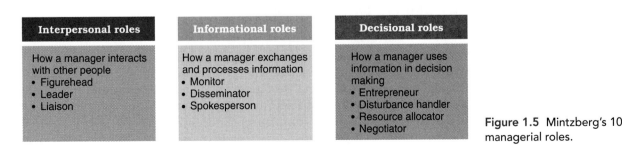

Interpersonal roles	Informational roles	Decisional roles
How a manager interacts with other people • Figurehead • Leader • Liaison	How a manager exchanges and processes information • Monitor • Disseminator • Spokesperson	How a manager uses information in decision making • Entrepreneur • Disturbance handler • Resource allocator • Negotiator

Figure 1.5 Mintzberg's 10 managerial roles.

Without any doubt, managerial work is busy, demanding, and stressful for all levels of responsibility in any work setting. A summary of research on the nature of managerial work offers this important reminder.[46]

- Managers work long hours.
- Managers work at an intense pace.
- Managers work at fragmented and varied tasks.
- Managers work with many communication media.
- Managers accomplish their work largely through interpersonal relationships.

MANAGERIAL AGENDAS AND NETWORKING

On his way to a meeting, a GM bumped into a staff member who did not report to him. Using this opportunity, in a two-minute conversation he (a) asked two questions and received the information he needed; (b) reinforced their good relationship by sincerely complimenting the staff member on something he had recently done; and (c) got the staff member to agree to do something that the GM needed done.

This brief incident provides a glimpse of an effective general manager (GM) in action.[47] It portrays two activities that management consultant and scholar John Kotter considers critical to a general manager's success: agenda setting and networking. Through *agenda setting*, good managers develop action priorities that include goals and plans spanning long and short time frames. These agendas are usually incomplete and loosely connected in the beginning, but they become more specific as the manager utilizes information continually gleaned from many different sources. The agendas are kept always in mind and are "played out" whenever an opportunity arises, as in the preceding quotation.

Good managers implement their agendas by working with a variety of people inside and outside the organization. This is made possible by *networking*, the process of building and maintaining positive relationships with people whose help may be needed to implement one's work agendas. In Kotter's example, the GM was getting things done through a staff member who did not report directly to him. His networks would also include relationships with peers, a boss, higher-level executives, subordinates, and members of their work teams, as well as with external customers, suppliers, and community representatives.

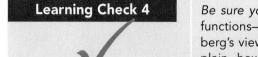

Learning Check 4

Be sure you can ■ define and give examples of each of the management functions—planning, organizing, leading, and controlling ■ explain Mintzberg's view of what managers do, including the key managerial roles ■ explain how managers use agendas and networks to fulfill their work responsibilities

LEARNING HOW TO MANAGE

Today's turbulent times present an ever-shifting array of problems, opportunities, and performance expectations for organizations and their members. Change is a way of life, and the quest for high performance is relentless; workers everywhere are expected to find ways to achieve high productivity under new, dynamic, and sometimes stressful conditions. All of this, of course, means that your career success depends on a real commitment to learning. And, it's not just formal learning in the classroom that counts, but also **lifelong learning**—the process of continuously learning from our daily experiences and opportunities.

Lifelong learning is continuous learning from daily experiences.

ESSENTIAL MANAGERIAL SKILLS

A **skill** is the ability to translate knowledge into action that results in desired performance. Obviously, many skills are required to master the challenging nature of managerial work. Harvard scholar Robert L. Katz has classified the essential or baseline skills of managers into three categories: technical, human, and conceptual.[48] He suggests that their relative importance tends to vary by level of managerial responsibility, as shown in *Figure 1.6.* This figure should offer some interesting personal development insights.

A **technical skill** is the ability to use a special proficiency or expertise to perform particular tasks. Accountants, engineers, market researchers, financial planners, and systems analysts, for example, possess technical skills. These skills are initially acquired through formal education and are further developed by training and job experience. Figure 1.6 shows that technical skills are very important at career entry levels. The critical question to be asked and positively answered by you in this respect and in preparation for any job interview comes down to this simple test: "What can I really do for an employer?"

The ability to work well in cooperation with other persons is a **human skill**. It emerges in the workplace as a spirit of trust, enthusiasm, and genuine involvement in interpersonal relationships. A manager with good human skills will have a high degree of self-awareness and a capacity to understand or empathize with the feelings of others. An important aspect of the essential human skills is **emotional intelligence**. Discussed more in Chapter 13 for its leadership implications, "EI" is defined by scholar and consultant Daniel Goleman as the "ability to manage ourselves and our relationships effectively."[49] Given the highly interpersonal nature of managerial work, human skills and emotional intelligence are consistently important across all the managerial levels. Again, a straightforward question puts your interpersonal skills and emotional intelligence to the test: "How well do you work with others?"

The ability to think critically and analytically is a **conceptual skill**. It involves the capacity to break problems into smaller parts, to see the relations between the parts, and to recognize the implications of any one problem for others. In the classroom we often call this "critical thinking." As people assume ever-higher responsibilities in organizations, they are called upon to deal with more ambiguous problems that have many complications and

A skill is the ability to translate knowledge into action that results in desired performance.

A technical skill is the ability to use expertise to perform a task with proficiency.

A human skill is the ability to work well in cooperation with other people.

Emotional intelligence is the ability to manage ourselves and our relationships effectively.

A conceptual skill is the ability to think analytically and solve complex problems.

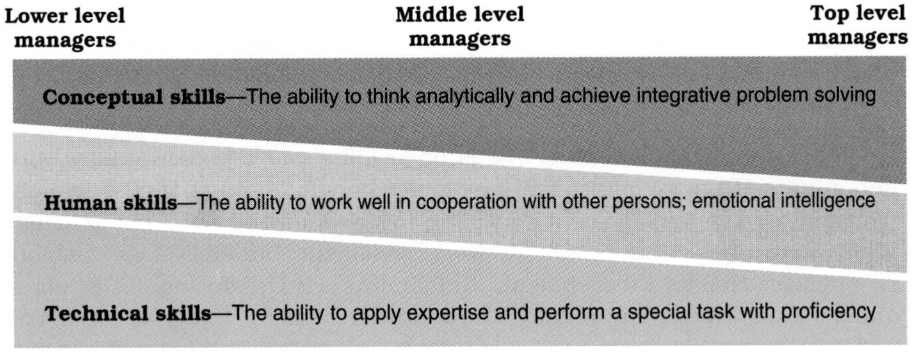

Lower level managers	Middle level managers	Top level managers

Conceptual skills—The ability to think analytically and achieve integrative problem solving

Human skills—The ability to work well in cooperation with other persons; emotional intelligence

Technical skills—The ability to apply expertise and perform a special task with proficiency

Figure 1.6 Katz's essential managerial skills.

longer-term consequences. This is why Figure 1.6 shows that conceptual skills gain in relative importance for top managers. At this point, you should ask: "Am I developing the critical-thinking and problem-solving capabilities I will need for long-term career success?"

SKILL AND OUTCOME ASSESSMENT

Katz's notion of the essential managerial skills meshes with the observations expressed by futurist and best-selling author Daniel Pink in his book *A Whole New Mind*.[50] Pink believes conceptual and human skills are of paramount importance today since we are moving from an information age into a new *conceptual age*. In this setting the demands on each of us are for right brain skills that are both *high concept*—ability to see the big picture, identify patterns and combine ideas, and *high touch*—ability to empathize and enjoy others in the pursuit of a purpose.

These ideas pose quite a learning challenge for all of us, managers included. And business and management educators are increasingly interested in helping people acquire the skills and competencies needed for managerial success. A **managerial competency** is a skill-based capability that contributes to high performance in a management job.[51] A number of these competencies have been implied in the previous discussion of the management process, including those related to planning, organizing, leading, and controlling. Competencies are also implicit in the information, interpersonal, and decision-making demands of managerial roles, as well as in agenda setting and networking as managerial activities.

As you ponder your career readiness, here is a quick checklist of basic skills and personal characteristics management educators emphasize as foundations for continued professional development and career success.

■ A **managerial competency** is a skill-based capability for high performance in a management job.

- *Communication*—Ability to share ideas and findings clearly in written and oral expression—includes writing, oral presentation, giving/receiving feedback, technology utilization.
- *Teamwork*—Ability to work effectively as a team member and team leader—includes team contribution, team leadership, conflict management, negotiation, consensus building.
- *Self-management*—Ability to evaluate oneself, modify behavior, and meet performance obligations—includes ethical reasoning and behavior, personal flexibility, tolerance for ambiguity, performance responsibility.
- *Leadership*—Ability to influence and support others to perform complex and ambiguous tasks—includes diversity awareness, global understanding, project management, strategic action.
- *Critical thinking*—Ability to gather and analyze information for creative problem solving—includes problem solving, judgment and decision making, information gathering and interpretation, creativity/innovation.
- *Professionalism*—Ability to sustain a positive impression, instill confidence, and maintain career advancement—includes personal presence, personal initiative, and career management.

The focus in *Management 9/e* is on helping you become familiar with important skills and competencies by better understanding the practical implications of key management concepts, theories, and terms. The six major parts of the book are presented in a systematic building-block fashion: (1) Management, (2) Environment, (3) Planning, (4) Organizing, (5) Leading, and (6) Controlling. The chapters are written with an integrated learning pedagogy that makes it easier for you to do well on assignments and exami-

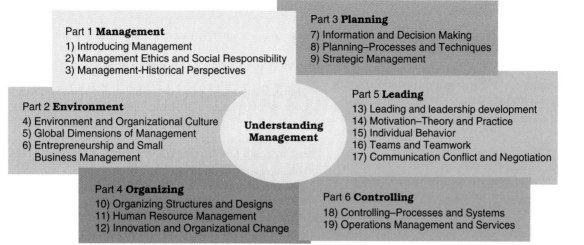

Figure 1.7 Understanding management from theory to practice.

nations. From the chapter-opening study questions, to the visual learning preview, to the embedded learning checks, through the many examples, to the end-of-chapter study guide with its summary, key terms review, and self-test, you have the opportunity to learn as you read. If you allow the pedagogy to work for you, the learning opportunities summarized in *Figure 1.7* should pay off in solid understanding and enhanced course performance.

Be sure you can ▪ define three essential managerial skills—technical, human, and conceptual skills ▪ explain Katz's view of how these skills vary in importance across management levels ▪ define emotional intelligence as an important human skill ▪ list and give examples of personal characteristics important for managerial success

Learning Check 5

CHAPTER 1 STUDY GUIDE

STUDY QUESTIONS SUMMARY

1 What are the challenges of working today?

▪ Work in the new economy is increasingly knowledge based, and people, with their capacity to bring valuable intellectual capital to the workplace, are the ultimate foundation of organizational performance.

▪ The forces of globalization are bringing increased interdependencies among nations and economies, as customer markets and resource flows create intense business competition.

▪ Ever-present developments in information technology and the continued expansion of the Internet are reshaping organizations, changing the nature of work, and increasing the value of knowledge workers.

▪ Organizations must value the talents and capabilities of a workforce whose members are increasingly diverse with respect to gender, age, race and ethnicity, able-bodiedness, and lifestyles.

▪ Society has high expectations for organizations and their members to perform with commitment to high ethical standards and in socially responsible ways, including protection of the natural environment and human rights.

▪ Careers in the new economy require great personal initiative to build and maintain skill "portfolios" that are always up-to-date and valuable to employers challenged by the intense competition and the information age.

2 What are organizations like?

- Organizations are collections of people working together to achieve a common purpose.
- As open systems, organizations interact with their environments in the process of transforming resource inputs into finished goods and services as product outputs.
- Productivity is a measure of the quantity and quality of work performance, with resource costs taken into account.
- High-performing organizations are both performance effective, in terms of goal accomplishment, and performance efficient, in terms of resource utilization.

3 Who are managers, and what do they do?

- Managers directly support, supervise, facilitate, and help activate the work efforts of other people in organizations.
- Top managers scan the environment, create vision, and emphasize long-term performance goals; middle managers coordinate activities in large departments or divisions; team leaders and supervisors support performance at the team or work-unit level.
- Functional managers work in specific areas such as finance or marketing; general managers are responsible for larger, multifunctional units; administrators are managers in public or nonprofit organizations.
- Managers are held accountable for performance results that the manager depends on other persons to accomplish.
- The upside-down pyramid view of organizations shows operating workers at the top serving customer needs while being supported from below by various levels of management.

- The changing nature of managerial work emphasizes being good at "coaching" and "supporting" others, rather than simply "directing" and "order giving."

4 What is the management process?

- The management process consists of the four functions of planning, organizing, leading, and controlling.
- Planning sets the direction; organizing assembles the human and material resources; leading provides the enthusiasm and direction; controlling ensures results.
- Managers implement the four functions in daily work that can be intense and stressful, involving long hours and continuous performance pressures.
- Managerial success in this demanding context requires the ability to perform well in interpersonal, informational, and decision-making roles.
- Managerial success also requires the ability to utilize interpersonal networks to accomplish well-selected task agendas.

5 How do you learn managerial skills and competencies?

- Career success in the new economy requires taking full advantage of lifelong learning in all aspects of our daily experience and job opportunities.
- Skills considered essential for managers are broadly described as technical—ability to use expertise; human—ability to work well with other people; and conceptual—ability to analyze and solve complex problems.
- Skills and outcomes considered as foundations for managerial success include communication, teamwork, self-management, leadership, critical thinking, and professionalism.

KEY TERMS REVIEW

Accountability (p. 15)
Administrators (p. 14)
Conceptual skill (p. 21)
Controlling (p. 19)
Corporate governance (p. 8)
Discrimination (p. 8)
Emotional intelligence (p. 21)
Ethics (p. 8)
Functional managers (p. 14)
General managers (p. 14)
Glass ceiling effect (p. 8)
Globalization (p. 6)
Human skill (p. 21)

Intellectual capital (p. 5)
Knowledge worker (p. 6)
Leading (p. 18)
Lifelong learning (p. 21)
Line managers (p. 14)
Management (p. 17)
Manager (p. 13)
Managerial competency (p. 22)
Middle managers (p. 14)
Open system (p. 11)
Organization (p. 10)
Organizing (p. 17)
Performance effectiveness (p. 12)

Performance efficiency (p. 12)
Planning (p. 17)
Prejudice (p. 8)
Productivity (p. 11)
Quality of work life (p. 15)
Skill (p. 21)
Staff managers (p. 14)
Supervisor (p. 14)
Team leader (p. 14)
Technical skill (p. 21)
Top managers (p. 13)
Workforce diversity (p. 7)

MULTIPLE-CHOICE QUESTIONS:

1. The process of management involves the functions of planning, _____, leading, and controlling.

    (a) accounting   (b) creating   (c) innovating   (d) organizing

2. An effective manager achieves both high-performance results and high levels of _____ among people doing the required work.

    (a) turnover   (b) effectiveness   (c) satisfaction   (d) stress

3. Performance efficiency is a measure of the _____ associated with task accomplishment.

    (a) resource costs   (b) goal specificity   (c) product quality   (d) product quantity

4. The requirement that a manager answer to a higher-level boss for results achieved by a work team is called _____.

    (a) dependency   (b) accountability   (c) authority   (d) empowerment

5. Productivity is a measure of the quantity and _____ of work produced, with resource utilization taken into account.

    (a) quality   (b) cost   (c) timeliness   (d) value

6. _____ pay special attention to the organization's external environment, looking for problems and opportunities and finding ways to deal with them.

    (a) Top managers   (b) Middle managers   (c) Team leaders   (d) Supervisors

7. The accounting manager for a local newspaper would be considered a _____ manager, whereas the publisher in charge of everything would be considered a _____ manager.

    (a) general, functional   (b) middle, top   (c) staff, line   (d) senior, junior

8. When a team leader clarifies desired work targets and deadlines for a work team, he or she is fulfilling the management function of _____.

    (a) planning   (b) delegating   (c) controlling   (d) supervising

9. The process of building and maintaining good working relationships with others who may help implement a manager's work agendas is called _____.

    (a) governance   (b) networking   (c) authority   (d) entrepreneurship

10. In Katz's framework, top managers tend to rely more on their _____ skills than do lower-level managers.

    (a) human   (b) conceptual   (c) decision-making   (d) technical

11. The research of Mintzberg and others concludes that managers _____.

    (a) work at a leisurely pace   (b) have blocks of private time for planning   (c) always live with the pressures of performance responsibility   (d) have the advantages of short workweeks

12. When someone with a negative attitude toward minorities makes a decision to deny advancement opportunities to a Hispanic worker, this is an example of _____.

    (a) discrimination   (b) emotional intelligence   (c) control   (d) prejudice

13. Among the trends in the new workplace, one can expect to find _____.

    (a) more order giving   (b) more valuing people as human assets   (c) less teamwork   (d) reduced concern for work-life balance

14. The manager's role in the "upside-down pyramid" view of organizations is best described as providing _____ so that operating workers can directly serve _____.

    (a) direction, top management   (b) leadership, organizational goals   (c) support, customers   (d) agendas, networking

15. The management function of _____ is being performed when a retail manager measures daily sales in the dress department and compares them with daily sales targets.

    (a) planning   (b) agenda setting   (c) controlling   (d) delegating

SHORT-RESPONSE QUESTIONS:

16. List and explain the importance of three pressures of ethics and social responsibility that managers must be prepared to face.

17. Explain how "accountability" operates in the relationship between (a) a manager and her subordinates, and (b) the same manager and her boss.

18. Explain how the "glass ceiling effect" may disadvantage newly hired African American college graduates in a large corporation.

19. What is "globalization," and what are its implications for working in the new economy?

APPLICATION QUESTION:

20. You have just been hired as the new supervisor of an audit team for a national accounting firm. With four years of experience, you feel technically well prepared for the assignment. However, this is your first formal appointment as a "manager." Things are complicated at the moment. The team has 12 members, of diverse demographic and cultural backgrounds, as well as work experience. There is an intense workload and lots of performance pressure. How will this situation challenge you to develop and use essential managerial skills and related competencies to successfully manage the team to high levels of auditing performance?

CHAPTER 1 APPLICATIONS

CASE 1

Virgin Group, Ltd.: Reaching for the Sky in a New Economy

Sir Richard Branson has assembled a collection of companies under the umbrella brand of "Virgin." Branson has repeatedly confounded analysts with his ability to spot emerging trends and profit from them. One senior executive at Virgin describes the company as a "branded venture-capital firm."[52] Branson has continually redefined Virgin's business operations, branching out into a variety of ventures but always capitalizing on his exuberant entrepreneurial spirit.

Richard Branson: Young Entrepreneur

Born in 1950, Branson began his first entrepreneurial venture when he was a 16-year-old boarding school student—a magazine called *Student* which addressed issues of the time, such as the Vietnam War and the Paris student uprising. While raising about $6,000 over a six-month period to fund the magazine, Branson recruited well-known celebrities—like Jean-Paul Sarte and Vanessa Redgrave, among others—to be interviewed in or to write for the publication.[53] Branson, with his brashness, extraordinary ambition, and passion for success, went on to become a billionaire entrepreneur.

The magazine was followed in 1970 with a venture into discount records. Branson and Company ran ads in a mail-order catalog, and an increasing number of individuals purchased discounted records from it. Then his group from the magazine found an old shop, cleaned it up, and started a discount record store. Searching for a name for the business, they came up with three options: "Slipped Disc," "Student," and "Virgin." Since they were all virgins at business, the name Virgin was selected.[54] It quickly became the largest discount music megastore chain in the world.

In 1972 Branson branched out into the music recording business with Virgin Records. His first recording artist, Mike Oldfield (a multi-instrumentalist whose music was featured in *The Exorcist*), released *Tubular Bells,* which went on to sell more than 5 million copies. As punk rock began to swell out of back-alley pubs and basement parties, Branson signed the Sex Pistols, a group no other record label would touch. Other groups signing to Virgin included Genesis, Simple Minds, Culture Club, Phil Collins, and the Rolling Stones.

Moving on to Other Ventures

Although other people might have been content with such early success, Richard Branson has never been known to say "enough." Running his business interests out of a houseboat on the Thames River, he launched Virgin Airways in 1984 (now Virgin Atlantic) with a single jumbo jet. Taking on British Airways, he sued them for alleged dirty tricks and won. The airline is famous for its offbeat perks, including massages and premium first-class service.

Branson also refuses to follow the industry leaders. As many airlines drop fares and cut service in order to compete for passengers, Branson keeps Virgin Atlantic focused on reasonable fares and unique customer service, including ice cream with movies, private bedrooms, showers, and exercise facilities.

"The conventional wisdom is you should specialize in what you know and never stray from that, but no other brand has become a way-of-life brand the way Virgin has," Branson says. "And it wasn't us setting out to become a way-of-life brand, it was me continually being interested in learning new things."[55] Branson's business objectives from the start have been to be noticed, have fun, and make money by constantly starting new firms.[56]

Over the years, Virgin Group Ltd. has created more than 200 new businesses, employing more than 25,000 people, with revenues exceeding $7.2 billion annually.[57] Though the Virgin brand is becoming increasingly well-known in the U.S., many Americans would be surprised to discover that the corporation only does 10% of its business there. And many of its major investments—like Virgin Atlantic—succeed without ever becoming American brands. Virgin Group Ltd. currently has business interests in planes, trains, finance, soft drinks, music, mobile phones, holidays, cars, wines, publishing, bridal wear—and more.[58] Virgin doesn't represent a business so much as it represents a business-making machine.[59]

When Virgin starts a new business, it is based on solid research and analysis. The company reviews the industry and puts itself in the customer's shoes. Virgin executives ask several fundamental questions: "Is this an opportunity for restructuring a market and creating

competitive advantage? What are the competitors doing? Is the customer confused or badly served? Is this an opportunity for building the Virgin brand? Can we add value? Will it interact with our other businesses? Is there an appropriate trade-off between risk and reward?"[60] The notion of value is especially important to Virgin because it's the primary concept used to tie together so many disparate brands.

Not everything touched by Branson turns to gold. He was forced in the early 1990s to sell his beloved Virgin Records to Thorn EMI to secure the survival of his Virgin Airlines. As a result, Branson now employs a strategy of using wealthy partners to provide the bulk of the cash necessary to run a business, with Virgin providing the brand-name recognition in exchange for a controlling interest in the venture. Rather than mixing with investment bankers, he has a habit of keeping his companies private—preferring to sell off chunks of his empire to fund new business startups. The sale of a 49 percent share of Virgin Atlantic to Singapore Airlines for $979 million provided him the needed cash to plow into his Internet ventures.[61]

Although Virgin represents a late arrival to the Internet, Branson has attacked the venture with the same enthusiasm displayed in his previous business startups. Many of his business interests already had a presence on the Web, including Thetrainline.com, a joint venture with the British transport company Stagecoach. The site sells tickets for Britain's 23 train operators, has more than 1.8 million users and purchases of more than $2.5 million weekly, and is adding 55,000 new users each week.[62] By transferring an airline-type reservation system onto the Net, Virgin earns 9 percent of every ticket booked. Virgin will sell competitors' services right alongside its own. What

Branson is hoping to do is leverage his presence into a "cyberbrand" with a premium presence on the Web.

"Virgin's approach to the Net has been very clever," claims Simon Knox, professor of brand marketing at the Cranfield University School of Management in Bedford, UK. "Each launch of a new business builds upon the one before, rather than developing isolated branded businesses."[63] Others, like Michael Arnbjerg, with the market research firm IDC in Copenhagen, disagree. He argues that "Virgin can leverage its brand in certain market sectors, but that's not enough to become a major player."[64]

Expanding the Business Portfolio

The Virgin Group's main focus is on providing services rather than on producing products. To help fuel its services growth, Virgin actively seeks business proposals from the public via its website. "If you have a fantastic idea for us, then we're all ears! We're always on the lookout for fresh ideas to improve our current companies and to create brand new ones."[65]

In soliciting proposals, the company emphasizes that "Virgin is famous for its down-to-earth good value and service, so all new ideas will need to reflect these values. We also have a great sense of fun, and we like to do things just a little bit differently from the rest." Virgin asks people who submit business proposals to address the following issues: the nature of the product or service idea; the business sector into which this idea fits; the idea or project's current stage of development; the proposal submitter's involvement in the project, as well as the role he/she/they would like to maintain; the reason for approaching Virgin and the anticipated role of Virgin in the project; and an assessment of the venture's potential.

Virgin says that it respects the intellectual property rights of all new business proposals that it receives. The company notes, however, that it receives "hundreds of proposals which are often similar to those suggested by others, or to ideas which we have developed internally." Although only a few submitted proposals actually move forward in the business development process, the ones that are most likely to be successful are already well developed, have large-scale potential, and can be implemented quickly.[66]

What does the future hold for Sir Richard and the Virgin Group? If history is any predictor, the company's portfolio will continue to embrace a wide range of businesses that have the potential for providing quality service in a fun and different way.

REVIEW QUESTIONS

1. How would you describe the managerial skills and competencies of Richard Branson?
2. What are the main advantages and disadvantages associated with Virgin's solicitation of business proposals from the public to help grow the firm?
3. As the stable of Virgin brands grows increasingly diverse, what management challenges must Virgin executives meet to stay successful with the corporate strategy?

TEAM PROJECT

Diversity Lessons—
"What Have We
Learned?"

R. Roosevelt Thomas, head of the American Institute for Managing Diversity, has written four books on diversity and consulted with numerous corporations and nonprofits on the subject. In an interview with *The Wall Street Journal*, he said: ". . . companies tend to define diversity as representation. . . Most organizations define diversity as having the right racial composition, or 'making their numbers'. . .the assumption is that once you get representation, people will assimilate."

Question: What are the current "facts" in terms of progress for minorities and women in the workplace? What lessons of diversity have been learned? What are the "best" employers doing to take full advantage of the opportunities offered by a diverse workforce?

Research Directions:

■ Examine case studies of employers reported as having strong diversity programs. What do they have in common? What do they do differently?

■ Find out what we know about how well people work together when they come from different racial, ethnic, gender, life-style, and generational backgrounds.

■ Find and analyze for the implications data on how the "glass ceiling" affects the careers of women and minorities in various occupational settings.

■ Take a critical look at the approaches of diversity training programs. What do these programs try to accomplish, and how? Are they working or not, and how do we know?

■ What have we learned that helps break what Thomas calls the "assimilation myth" and get on with effectively managing diversity?

PERSONAL MANAGEMENT

Self Awareness

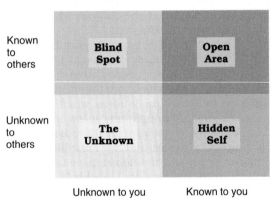

SELF AWARENESS is one of those concepts that is easy to talk about but very hard to master. What do you really know about yourself? How often do you take a critical look at your attitudes, behaviors, skills, and accomplishments? Do you ever realistically assess your personal strengths and weaknesses—both as you see them and as others do? A high degree of self awareness is essential for personal adaptibility, to be able to grow and develop in changing times. This figure, called the Johari Window, offers a way of comparing what we know about ourselves with what others know about us. Our "open" areas are often small, while the "blind spot," "the unknown," and the "hidden" areas can be quite large. Think about the personal implications of the Johari Window. Are you willing to probe the unknown, uncover your blind spots, and discover talents and weaknesses that may be hidden? As your self awareness expands, you will find many insights for personal growth and development.

Building the Brand Called "You" Ask friends, family members and co-workers to comment on your skills and weaknesses in management. Write a self-reflection statement in which you (1) summarize your scores on the recommended assessments and what others say about you, (2) identify where you agree and disagree with the feedback, and (3) state the implications for your continued personal and professional development.

NEXT STEPS: MANAGEMENT LEARNING WORKBOOK

Self-Assessments

■ 21st-Century Manager (#1)

■ Emotional Intelligence (#2)

Experiential Exercises

■ My Best Manager (#1)

■ What Managers Do (#2)

■ The Future Workplace (#14)

Management Ethics and Social Responsibility

2

Chapter 2 Study Questions

1 What is ethical behavior?

2 How do ethical dilemmas complicate the workplace?

3 How can high ethical standards be maintained?

4 What is social responsibility and governance?

Is There a Right Way to Make Money?

In an era in which CEOs are widely thought to exemplify unscrupulous greed, is it true that profits and principles are mutually exclusive? Although increasing quarterly profits is the goal of almost every corporate leader, a growing number of them, such as Burt's Bees co-founder Roxanne Quimby, are insisting that those earnings should not compromise the integrity of their beliefs.

"In the end, all business operations can be reduced to three words: people, product, and profits."—*Lee Iacocca, former chairman of Chrysler Corporation.*

Is this really it? Can all matters of commerce be simply boiled down to these three elements? While few would doubt Iacocca's business acumen, perhaps there is another component to this mix, one that may be equally as influential.

To illustrate the point, consider Burt's Bees. The manufacturer of all-natural health and beauty products has grown into a tremendous force in the cosmetics market, achieving annual sales of $225 million.[1]

Growing from a two-person operation in rural Maine to a multimillion dollar business, Burt's Bees's

What *They* Think

"The disappointing thing was leaving my employees, mostly moms who'd been on welfare. But I never lost sight of the fact that the business needs were most important, that we needed to go to somewhere more business-friendly."
Roxanne Quimby, founder of Burt's Bees.

PROFITS: "Profits are the driving force of the market economy. The greater the profits, the better the needs of the consumers are supplied. . . . He who serves the public best, makes the highest profits."
Ludwig von Mises, economist and social philosopher.

PRINCIPLES: " 'Tis the business of little minds to shrink; but he whose heart is firm, and whose conscience approves his conduct, will pursue his principles unto death."
Thomas Paine, author of *Common Sense* and *Crisis*.

success is largely owed to the energy and initiative of its figurehead and co-founder, Roxanne Quimby, who ran the organization almost exclusively on her terms.

"I tend to be very uncompromising," Quimby said. "My dad was a despot, and I got that from him. Though I used to see it as an attribute, I'm trying to modify this 'my way or the highway' attitude."[2]

As Quimby suggests, it was impossible for her to separate her pursuit of profits from the *principles* that guide her. But Quimby is quick to draw on both positive and negative examples of how her adherence to her principles has shaped the growth of Burt's Bees.

Conventional logic dictates that both product and retail packaging should be bulky, wasteful, and laden with unrecyclable plastics. Not so, says Quimby. Her demand for eco-friendly packaging publicly demonstrated her—and her company's—commitment to environmental sustainability; moreover, the emphasis garnered praise from both customers and market analysts. It proved Quimby was willing to put her money where her mouth was.

Quimby followed her heart, and two of Iacocca's three central notions, when she decided to move Burt's Bees from its longtime headquarters in Maine to the more business-friendly North Carolina. While earnestly following her principles, her pursuit of profit led to some unintended consequences. "In Maine we paid 8% unemployment tax," Quimby said. "In North Carolina, it's 1%. But I didn't anticipate one big difference. In Maine, I'd start people at $5 an hour. In North Carolina, nobody would work for less than $10 an hour."

Despite the initial economic challenges, the human cost made her momentarily question her decision. "The disappointing thing was leaving my employees, mostly moms who'd been on welfare," she said. "But I never lost sight of the fact that the business needs were most important, that we needed to go to somewhere more business-friendly."[3]

What's next for Quimby? Well, some want her to run for public office. She may be considering it. But in the meantime she's started another company, Happy Green Bee. It sells children's clothes made from organic cotton. Quimby believes this is good for both the kids—benefitting from the soft fibers—and for the environment—benefitting from the absence of chemical pesticides. Still committed to her principles, Quimby says: "I'm going to see if lightning can strike twice."[4]

In the end, Quimby values corporate profits as much as the next CEO. Yet she's only willing to pursue them by means that suit her principles of environmental friendliness. Quimby sold a majority share in Burt's Bees to a New York-based private equity company. Under the new leadership, Burt's Bees continues to grow profitably in North Carolina, sticking to the core mission— to *make natural products available to everyone, everywhere.*

The Numbers

Percentage of Post-Consumer Recycled (PCR) Materials in Burt's Bees Packaging

Boxes	30% PCR cardboard
Plastic Bottles	90% or more PCR plastic
Plastic Squeeze Tubes	40% or more PCR plastic
Corrugated Shipping Containers	100% PCR paper (printed with water-based inks)
Printed Materials	50% or more PCR paper (printed with vegetable-based inks)

Quick Facts

* Roxanne Quimby purchased over 40,000 acres of Maine wilderness with her own money in order to keep the area from being developed.
* Quimby sold 80% of her share of Burt's Bees to AEA Investors in 2004 for $177 million.[5]
* 48% of workers in a survey by Carez said they would take less pay to work for a socially responsible company.[6]
* 78% of respondents over age 60 in the Carez survey said it was "very important" to work for a socially responsible company; only 47% of those under 18 said so.[7a]
* Academic research reports 56% of MBA students admit cheating; 47% of non-business graduate students admit it also.[7b]

What Do *You* Think?

1. When Roxanne Quimby decided to move the Burt's Bees headquarters to North Carolina, did she put profits ahead of principles?
2. Business owners who follow their principles may earn the respect of some shareholders and analysts, but are they forgetting that business is inherently a for-profit enterprise?

Management Ethics and Social Responsibility			
Study Question 1	**Study Question 2**	**Study Question 3**	**Study Question 4**
What Is Ethical Behavior?	**Ethics in the Workplace**	**Maintaining High Ethical Standards**	**Social Responsibility and Governance**
■ Laws, values, and ethical behavior ■ Alternative views of ethics ■ Cultural issues in ethical behavior	■ Ethical dilemmas at work ■ Rationalizations for unethical behavior ■ Factors influencing ethical behavior	■ Ethics training ■ Whistleblower protection ■ Ethical role models ■ Codes of ethical conduct ■ Moral management	■ Stakeholder issues and analysis ■ Perspectives on corporate social responsibility ■ Evaluating corporate social performance ■ Role of corporate governance
Learning check 1	**Learning check 2**	**Learning check 3**	**Learning check 4**

sn't it time for you to get serious about the moral aspects and social implications of decision making in organizations? In your career and in the work of any manager, wouldn't you agree that performance goals must always be achieved through ethically and socially responsible action?

The opening example of Roxanne Quimby and her decisions at Burt's Bees should be thought provoking, and other cases of people and organizations operating in socially responsible ways—pursuing profits with principles, are out there. But let's not forget the underlying foundations for such behavior—it is people, individuals like you and me, which make and implement decisions ethically or not. And nowhere is this point more significant than in respect to the great range of decisions that managers make daily and the many people whose lives are affected by them. As we move into the issues of management ethics and social responsibility in this chapter, the following reminder from Desmond Tutu, archbishop of Capetown, South Africa, and winner of the Nobel Peace Prize, is well worth consideration.[8]

You are powerful people. You can make this world a better place where business decisions and methods take account of right and wrong as well as profitability. . . . You must take a stand on important issues: the environment and ecology, affirmative action, sexual harassment, racism and sexism, the arms race, poverty, the obligations of the affluent West to its less-well-off sisters and brothers elsewhere.

WHAT IS ETHICAL BEHAVIOR?

■ **Ethics** sets standards of good or bad, or right or wrong, in one's conduct.

■ **Ethical behavior** is "right" or "good" in the context of a governing moral code.

For our purposes, **ethics** is defined as the code of moral principles that sets standards of good or bad, or right or wrong, in one's conduct.[9] Ethics provides principles to guide behavior and help people make moral choices among alternative courses of action. In practice, **ethical behavior** is that which is accepted as "good" and "right" as opposed to "bad" or "wrong" in the context of the governing moral code.

LAWS, VALUES, AND ETHICAL BEHAVIOR

It makes sense that anything legal should be considered ethical. Yet slavery was once legal in the United States, and laws once permitted only men to vote.[10] That doesn't mean the practices were ethical. Furthermore, just because an action is not strictly illegal doesn't make it ethical. Living up to the "letter of the law" is not sufficient to guarantee that one's actions will or should be considered ethical.[11] Is it truly ethical, for example, for an employee to take longer than necessary to do a job? To make personal telephone calls on company time? To call in sick to take a day off for leisure? To fail to report rule violations by a co-worker? None of these acts are strictly illegal, but many people would consider them unethical.

Most ethical problems in the workplace arise when people are asked to do or find themselves about to do something that violates their personal beliefs. For some, if the act is legal, they proceed with confidence. For others, the ethical test goes beyond the legality of the act alone. The ethical question extends to personal **values**—the underlying beliefs and attitudes that help determine individual behavior. To the extent that values vary among people, we can expect different interpretations of what behavior is ethical or unethical in a given situation.

> ■ **Values** are broad beliefs about what is appropriate behavior.

The psychologist Milton Rokeach makes a popular distinction between "terminal" and "instrumental" values.[12] **Terminal values** are preferences about desired ends, such as the goals one strives to achieve in life. Examples of terminal values considered important by managers include self-respect, family security, freedom, inner harmony, and happiness. **Instrumental values** are preferences regarding the means for accomplishing these ends. Among the instrumental values held important by managers are honesty, ambition, courage, imagination, and self-discipline. The value pattern for any one person is very enduring, but terminal and instrumental values vary from one person to the next. This variation is a reason why people respond quite differently to situations and their ethical challenges.

> ■ **Terminal values** are preferences about desired end states.
>
> ■ **Instrumental values** are preferences regarding the means to desired ends.

ALTERNATIVE VIEWS OF ETHICS

Figure 2.1 shows four views of ethical behavior that philosophers have discussed over the years.[13] Behavior that would be considered ethical from the **utilitarian view** delivers the greatest good to the greatest number of people. Founded in the work of 19th-century philosopher John Stuart Mill, this results-oriented point of view tries to assess the moral implications of decisions in terms of their consequences. Business decision makers, for example, are inclined to use profits, efficiency, and other performance criteria to judge what is best for the most people. A manager may make a utilitarian decision to cut 30 percent of a plant's workforce in order to keep the plant profitable and save the remaining jobs.

> ■ In the **utilitarian view** ethical behavior delivers the greatest good to the most people.

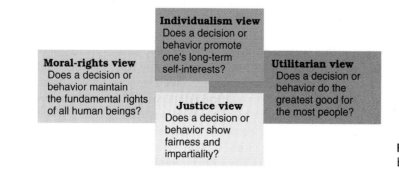

Figure 2.1 Four views of ethical behavior.

▓ In the **individualism view** ethical behavior advances long-term self-interests.

The **individualism view** of ethical behavior is based on the belief that one's primary commitment is long-term advancement of self-interests. People supposedly become self-regulating as they pursue long-term individual advantage. For example, lying and cheating for short-term gain should not be tolerated. If one person does it, everyone will do it, and no one's long-term interests will be served. The individualism view is supposed to promote honesty and integrity. But in business practice it may result in a *pecuniary ethic*, described by one executive as the tendency to "push the law to its outer limits" and "run roughshod over other individuals to achieve one's objectives."[14]

▓ In the **moral-rights view** ethical behavior respects and protects fundamental rights.

Ethical behavior under a **moral-rights view** is that which respects and protects the fundamental rights of people. From the teachings of John Locke and Thomas Jefferson, for example, the rights of all people to life, liberty, and fair treatment under the law are considered inviolate. In organizations, this concept extends to ensuring that employees are always protected in rights to privacy, due process, free speech, free consent, health and safety, and freedom of conscience. The issue of *human rights,* a major ethical concern in the international business environment, is central to this perspective. The United Nations, for example, stands by the Universal Declaration of Human Rights passed by the General Assembly in 1948.

▓ In the **justice view** ethical behavior treats people impartially and fairly.

▓ **Procedural justice** is concerned that policies and rules are fairly applied.

▓ **Distributive justice** is concerned that people are treated the same regardless of personal characteristics.

▓ **Interactional justice** is the degree to which others are treated with dignity and respect.

Finally, the **justice view** of moral behavior is based on the belief that ethical decisions treat people impartially and fairly, according to legal rules and standards. This approach evaluates the ethical aspects of any decision on the basis of whether it is "equitable" for everyone affected.[15] **Procedural justice** involves the degree to which policies and rules are fairly administered. For example, does a sexual harassment charge levied against a senior executive receive the same full hearing as one made against a first-level supervisor? **Distributive justice** involves the degree to which outcomes are allocated without respect to individual characteristics based on ethnicity, race, gender, age, or other particularistic criteria. For example, does a woman with the same qualifications and experience as a man receive the same consideration for hiring or promotion? **Interactional justice** involves the degree to which others are treated with dignity and respect. For example, does a bank loan officer take the time to fully explain to an applicant why he or she was turned down for a loan?[16]

CULTURAL ISSUES IN ETHICAL BEHAVIOR

The influence of culture on ethical behavior is a timely topic in this time of globalization. Corporate and government leaders must master difficult challenges when operating across borders that are cultural as well as national. Former Levi CEO Robert Haas once said that an ethical dilemma "becomes even more difficult when you overlay the complexities of different cultures and values systems that exist throughout the world."[17]

▓ **Cultural relativism** suggests there is no one right way to behave; ethical behavior is determined by its cultural context.

▓ **Universalism** suggests ethical standards apply absolutely across all cultures.

Those who believe that behavior in foreign settings should be guided by the classic rule of "when in Rome, do as the Romans do" reflect an ethical position of **cultural relativism**.[18] This is the belief that there is no one right way to behave, and that ethical behavior is always determined by its cultural context. An American international business executive guided by rules of cultural relativism, for example, would argue that the use of child labor is okay in another country as long as it is consistent with local laws and customs.

Figure 2.2 contrasts cultural relativism with the alternative of **universalism**. This is an absolutist ethical position suggesting that if a behavior or practice is not okay in one's home environment, it is not acceptable practice anywhere else. In other words, ethical standards are universal and should apply absolutely across cultures and national boundaries. In the former example,

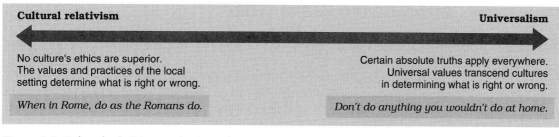

Figure 2.2 Cultural relativism and universalism in international business ethics. *Source:* Developed from Thomas Donaldson, "Values in Tension: Ethics Away from Home," *Harvard Business Review,* vol. 74 (September–October 1996), pp. 48–62.

the American executive would not do business in a setting where child labor was used, since it is unacceptable at home. Critics of such a universal approach claim that it is a form of **ethical imperialism**, or the attempt to externally impose one's ethical standards on others.

Business ethicist Thomas Donaldson has discussed the debate between cultural relativism and ethical imperialism. Although there is no simple answer, he finds fault with both extremes. He argues instead that certain fundamental rights and ethical standards can be preserved, while values and traditions of a given culture are respected.[19] The core values or "hypernorms" that should transcend cultural boundaries focus on human dignity, basic rights, and good citizenship. With a commitment to core values creating a transcultural ethical umbrella, Donaldson believes international business behaviors can be tailored to local and regional cultural contexts. In the case of child labor, again, the American executive might ensure that any children working in a factory under contract to his or her business would be provided schooling as well as employment.[20]

> ■ **Ethical imperialism** is an attempt to impose one's ethical standards on other cultures.

Be sure you can ■ define ethics ■ list and explain four views of ethical behavior ■ differentiate between cultural relativism and universalism in international business ethics

Learning Check 1

✓

ETHICS IN THE WORKPLACE

The real test of ethics occurs when you or anyone encounters a situation that challenges personal ethical beliefs and standards. Often ambiguous and unexpected, these ethical challenges are inevitable, and everyone has to be prepared to deal with them, even students.

A college student may get a job offer and accept it, only to get a better offer two weeks later. Is it right for her to renege on the first job to accept the second? A student knows that in a certain course his roommate submitted a term paper purchased on the Internet. Is it right for him not to tell the instructor? One student tells another that a faculty member promised her a high final grade in return for sexual favors. Is it right for him not to vigorously encourage her to inform the instructor's department head?

ETHICAL DILEMMAS AT WORK

■ An **ethical dilemma** is a situation that offers potential benefit or gain and is also unethical.

An **ethical dilemma** is a situation that requires a choice regarding a possible course of action that, although offering the potential for personal or organizational benefit, or both, may be considered unethical. It is often a situation in which action must be taken but for which there is no clear consensus on what is "right" and "wrong." The burden is on the individual to make good choices. An engineering manager speaking from experience sums it up this way: "I define an unethical situation as one in which I have to do something I don't feel good about."[21] Some problem areas and the types of ethical dilemmas managers can get caught in include:[22]

- *Discrimination*—denying promotion or appointment to a job candidate because of the candidate's race, religion, gender, age, or other non-job-relevant criterion.
- *Sexual harassment*—making a co-worker feel uncomfortable because of inappropriate comments or actions regarding sexuality; requesting sexual favors in return for favorable job treatment.

INSIGHTS

Help Make the World a Better Place

You know the ice cream for sure—who hasn't tasted a Ben & Jerry's Cherry Garcia® cone or delighted with a scoop of Chunky Monkey® banana ice cream? But do you really know the company? Ben & Jerry's earned its reputation not just from great ice cream but also from the concept of "linked prosperity," sharing prosperity with its employees and the communities in which it operates.

Flash back to 1977 when two friends, Ben Cohen and Jerry Greenfield, moved

from Long Island to Burlington, Vermont. Needing a source of income, they took a correspondence course on ice cream making from Pennsylvania State University. Fast forward to 1978, when Ben & Jerry's Homemade, on a $12,000 investment, sold its first ice cream cones from a con-

> *You have to appreciate what Ben Cohen and Jerry Greenfield accomplished at Ben & Jerry's. It isn't just that they were able to forge a well-regarded global company from a small startup. It's the nature of the company they developed, one with a commitment to ethical behavior and social responsibility, that is the true hallmark. The lesson is profits with principles; business performance, ethical behavior, and social responsibility can go hand in hand.*

verted gas station in downtown Burlington. It was a "different" ice cream store right from the start. In 1979 the first Free Cone Day—free ice cream all day— was held to celebrate the store's first anniversary.

Fast forward to 1985, when the company, with $9 million in annual sales, established the Ben & Jerry's Foundation to fund community-oriented projects. Financially, 7.5 percent of the company's annual pretax profits are pledged annually to support the foundation. Fast forward to 1988, when the firm, with $47 million in annual sales, received the Corporate Giving Award from the Council on Economic Priorities for its foundation's philanthropy. Fast forward to 1989—sales were $59 million, and the company introduced Rainforest Crunch® ice cream, with sales helping to support rainforest preservation efforts.

Fast forward to today—what do we find? The now-global company is owned by Unilever and has sales outlets in Europe, the Middle East, Latin America, and Asia. But it remains distinguished by a mission statement devoted to linked prosperity. The firm declares its commitments are to quality products, sustainable value for stakeholders, the welfare of employees, and innovation to improve the quality of life in its communities and around the world. The Ben & Jerry's foundation remains committed to "creative problem solving for hopefulness."

- *Conflicts of interest*—taking a bribe or kickback or extraordinary gift in return for making a decision favorable to the gift giver.
- *Customer confidence*—giving to another party privileged information regarding the activities of a customer.
- *Organizational resources*—using official stationery or a company e-mail account to communicate personal opinions or make requests from community organizations.

A survey of *Harvard Business Review* subscribers showed an interesting pattern in the ethical dilemmas reported by managers. Many of the dilemmas involved conflicts with superiors, customers, and subordinates.[23] The most frequent issues involved dishonesty in advertising and communications with top management, clients, and government agencies. Problems in dealing with special gifts, entertainment, and kickbacks were also reported. Significantly, the managers' bosses sometimes pressured them to engage in such unethical activities as supporting incorrect viewpoints, signing false documents, overlooking the boss's wrongdoings, and doing business with the boss's friends.

RATIONALIZATIONS FOR UNETHICAL BEHAVIOR

Why do otherwise reasonable people try to justify their unethical acts? Think back to earlier examples of ethical dilemmas and to those from your experiences. Consider also the possibility of being asked to place a bid for a business contract using insider information, paying bribes to obtain foreign business, falsifying expense account bills, and so on. "How," you should be asking, "do people explain doing things like this?"

In fact, there are at least four common rationalizations that may be used to justify misconduct in these and other ethical dilemmas.[24]

- Convincing yourself that the behavior is not really illegal.
- Convincing yourself that the behavior is in everyone's best interests.
- Convincing yourself that nobody will ever find out what you've done.
- Convincing yourself that the organization will "protect" you.

After doing something that might be considered unethical, a rationalizer says: *"It's not really illegal."* This expresses a mistaken belief that one's behavior is acceptable, especially in ambiguous situations. When dealing with shady or borderline situations in which you are having a hard time precisely determining right from wrong, the advice is quite simple: when in doubt about a decision to be made or an action to be taken, don't do it.

Another common statement by a rationalizer is *"it's in everyone's best interests."* This response involves the mistaken belief that because someone can be found to benefit from the behavior, the behavior is also in the individual's or the organization's best interests. Overcoming this rationalization depends in part on the ability to look beyond short-run results to address longer-term implications, and to look beyond results in general to the ways in which they are obtained. For example, in response to the question "How far can I push matters to obtain this performance goal?" the best answer may be, "Don't try to find out."

Sometimes rationalizers tell themselves that *"no one will ever know about it."* They mistakenly believe that a questionable behavior is really "safe" and will never be found out or made public. Unless it is discovered, the argument implies, no crime was really committed. Lack of accountability, unrealistic pressures to perform, and a boss who prefers "not to know" can all reinforce such thinking. In this case, the best deterrent is to make sure that everyone knows that wrongdoing will be punished whenever it is discovered.

ISSUES AND SITUATIONS

Ethics Training

Lots of organizations provide some form of ethics training for employees. At Lockheed Martin, employees watch DVD scenes involving ethically suspect actions. In one scene a manager gives a bad assignment to a direct report who had earlier criticized her behavior in a staff meeting. The scenes are discussed for their ethical implications.

> **Ethics Resource Center Report**
>
> • *3,015 U.S. workers surveyed*
>
> • *69% work for employers providing ethics training*
>
> • *About 50% observed unethical behavior in the past 12 months at work*
>
> • *The most common unethical actions were*
>
>   *21% Abusive or intimidating behavior toward employees*
>
>   *19% Lying to employees, customers, vendors, public*
>
>   *16% Misreporting actual time worked*
>
>   *12% Race, sex, or other discrimination*
>
>   *11% Theft*
>
>   *9% Sexual harassment*

Like other employers that invest in ethics training, the assumption is that such exercises will raise ethical awareness and confidence, creating a more ethical workplace. But does ethics training really work? The Ethics Resource Center finds that no more than 55 percent of persons who observe unethical acts actually report them.

Critical Response

Put yourself in the shoes of someone observing questionable practices at work. How would you respond? Now, put your own shoes back on. Suppose you learn of someone who turns in a term paper to your instructor that was downloaded from the Internet. Or, suppose you spot someone during an exam using a cell phone to take photos of test questions and send those photos to someone who is text messaging back answers. What do you do?

Conduct a brief survey of friends and acquaintances. Ask them about unethical practices in their work settings, and about what they and others do about them. Ask whether or not they have had ethics training at work and, if so, what it covered and what it meant in terms of personal impact.

Finally, rationalizers may proceed with a questionable action because of a mistaken belief that *"the organization will stand behind me."* This is misperceived loyalty. The individual believes that the organization's best interests stand above all others. In return, the individual believes that top managers will condone the behavior and protect the individual from harm. But loyalty to the organization is not an acceptable excuse for misconduct; it should not stand above the law and social morality.

FACTORS INFLUENCING ETHICAL BEHAVIOR

It is really too easy to confront ethical dilemmas from the safety of a textbook or a classroom discussion. In real life we are challenged to choose ethical courses of action in situations where the pressures are often unexpected, perhaps contradictory, and typically quite intense. Some 56 percent of U.S. workers in one survey reported feeling pressured to act unethically in their jobs. Sadly, the same survey revealed that 48 percent had committed questionable acts within the past year.[25]

Increased awareness of typical influences on ethical behavior can help you better deal with future ethical pressures and dilemmas. *Figure 2.3* shows these influences as coming from personal, organizational, and environmental factors.

Manager as a person	Employing organization	External environment
• Family influences • Religious values • Personal standards and needs	• Policies, codes of conduct • Behavior of supervisors, peers • Organizational culture	• Government regulations • Norms and values of society • Ethical climate of industry

Ethical managerial behavior

Figure 2.3 Factors influencing ethical managerial behavior— the person, organization, and environment.

The Person

Family influences, religious values, personal standards, and personal needs, financial and otherwise, will help determine a person's ethical conduct in any given circumstance. Managers who lack a strong and clear set of personal ethics will find that their decisions vary from situation to situation as they strive to maximize self-interests. Those with solid *ethical frameworks*, personal rules or strategies for ethical decision making, will be more consistent and confident. Their choices are guided by a stable set of ethical standards. Personal values that give priority to such virtues as honesty, fairness, integrity, and self-respect provide *ethical anchors* that help people make correct decisions even when circumstances are ambiguous and situational pressures are difficult.

It isn't always easy to stand up for what you believe in as a person, especially in a social context full of contradictory or just plain bad advice. Consider these words from a commencement address delivered a few years ago at a well-known school of business administration. "Greed is all right," the speaker said. "Greed is healthy. You can be greedy and still feel good about yourself." The students, it is reported, greeted these remarks with laughter and applause. The speaker was Ivan Boesky, once considered the "king of the arbitragers."[26] It wasn't long after his commencement speech that Boesky was arrested, tried, convicted, and sentenced to prison for trading on inside information.

The Organization

The organization is another important influence on ethics in the workplace. We noted earlier that bosses can have a major impact on their subordinates' behaviors. Just exactly what a supervisor requests, and which actions are rewarded or punished, can certainly affect an individual's decisions and actions. The expectations and reinforcement provided by peers and group norms are likely to have a similar impact. Formal policy statements and written rules are also helpful. They support and reinforce the ethical climate for the organization as a whole.

At The Body Shop, known along with Burt's Bees as a "profits with principles" firm, founder Anita Roddick created an 11-point charter to guide the company's employees: "Honesty, integrity and caring form the foundations of the company and should flow through everything we do— we will demonstrate our care for the world in which we live by respecting fellow human beings, by not harming animals, by preserving our forests." The fact that the Body Shop still gets occasional ethical criticisms demonstrates the inadequacy of formal policies alone to guarantee consistent ethical behavior.[27]

The Environment

Organizations operate in competitive environments influenced by government laws and regulations as well as social norms and values. Laws interpret social values to define appropriate behaviors for organizations and their members; regulations help governments monitor these behaviors and keep them within acceptable standards. For example, the Enron and Arthur Andersen scandals led to new legislation that attempts to substitute for any lack of ethical leadership at the firm and industry levels in U.S. business. The *Sarbanes-Oxley Act* of 2002 now makes it easier for corporate executives to be tried and sentenced to jail for financial misconduct. It also created the Public Company Accounting Oversight Board and set a new standard for auditors to verify reporting processes in the companies they audit.

The climate of competition in an industry also sets a standard of behavior for those who hope to prosper within it. Sometimes, the pressures of competition contribute to the ethical dilemmas of managers. Former American Airlines president Robert Crandall once telephoned Howard Putnam, then president of the now-defunct Braniff Airlines. Both companies were suffering from money-losing competition on routes from their home base of Dallas. A portion of their conversation follows:[28]

Putnam:	Do you have a suggestion for me?
Crandall:	Yes. . . . Raise your fares 20 percent. I'll raise mine the next morning.
Putnam:	Robert, we—
Crandall:	You'll make more money and I will, too.
Putnam:	We can't talk about pricing.
Crandall:	Oh, Howard. We can talk about anything we want to talk about.

The U.S. Justice Department disagreed. It alleged that Crandall's suggestion of a 20 percent fare increase amounted to an illegal attempt to monopolize airline routes. The suit was later settled when Crandall agreed to curtail future discussions with competitors about fares.

Learning Check 2

✓

Be sure you can ■ define an ethical dilemma ■ list at least three ethical problem areas common in the workplace ■ list four common rationalizations for unethical behavior ■ explain how ethics are influenced by the person, the organization, the environment

---

MAINTAINING HIGH ETHICAL STANDARDS

We all know that news from the corporate world is not always positive when it comes to ethics. Some items that quickly come to mind—*Item:* Firm admits lowering phone contract bid after receiving confidential information from an insider that an initial bid "was not good enough to win." *Item:* Company admits overcharging consumers and insurers more than $13 million for repairs to damaged rental cars. *Item:* Two Tyco executives found guilty; former CEO Dennis Kozlowski convicted on 22 counts of grand larceny, fraud, conspiracy, and falsifying business records. *Item:* U. S. lawmakers charge that BP was negligent in inspecting Alaskan pipelines and that workers complained of excessive cost-cutting and pressures to falsify maintenance records.

Yes, the problems are out there. But as quick as we are to recognize the bad news and problems about ethical behavior in organizations, we shouldn't forget that there is a lot of good news too. There are many organizations, like Burt's Bees, whose leaders and members set high ethics standards for themselves and others. Tom's of Maine, the chapter case, is another good example. You'll find that organizations like these engage a variety of methods to encourage consistent ethical behaviors by everyone they employ.

ETHICS TRAINING

Ethics training takes the form of structured programs to help participants understand the ethical aspects of decision making. It is designed to help people incorporate high ethical standards into their daily behaviors. Many, if not most, college curricula now include course work on ethics, and seminars on this topic are popular in the corporate world. But it is important to keep ethics training in perspective. An executive at Chemical Bank once put it this way: "We aren't teaching people right from wrong—we assume they know that. We aren't giving people moral courage to do what is right—they should be able to do that anyhow. We focus on dilemmas."[29]

Management Smarts 2.1 presents a seven-step checklist for dealing with an ethical dilemma. It offers an important reminder to double-check decisions *before* taking action. The key issue in the checklist may well be Step 6: the risk of public disclosure. Asking and answering the "spotlight" questions is a powerful way to test whether a decision is consistent with your personal ethical standards. They're worth repeating: "How will I feel about this if my family finds out, or if it's reported in the local newspaper?"

> **MANAGEMENT SMARTS 2.1**
>
> ### Checklist for dealing with ethical dilemmas
>
> Step 1. Recognize the ethical dilemma.
> Step 2. Get the facts.
> Step 3. Identify your options.
> Step 4. Test each option: Is it legal? Is it right? Is it beneficial?
> Step 5. Decide which option to follow.
> Step 6. Double-check with the *spotlight questions:* "How will I feel if my family finds out about my decision?" "How will I feel about this if my decision is reported in the local newspaper?"
> Step 7. Take action.

■ **Ethics training** seeks to help people understand the ethical aspects of decision making and to incorporate high ethical standards into their daily behavior.

WHISTLEBLOWER PROTECTION

Agnes Connolly pressed her employer to report two toxic chemical accidents; Dave Jones reported that his company was using unqualified suppliers in the construction of a nuclear power plant; Margaret Newsham revealed that her firm was allowing workers to do personal business while on government contracts; Herman Cohen charged that the ASPCA in New York was mistreating animals; Barry Adams complained that his hospital followed unsafe practices.[30] They were all **whistleblowers**, persons who expose the misdeeds of others in organizations in order to preserve ethical standards and protect against wasteful, harmful, or illegal acts.[31] They were also fired from their jobs.

Indeed, whistleblowers face the risks of impaired career progress and other forms of organizational retaliation, up to and including termination. Today, federal and state laws increasingly offer whistleblowers some defense against "retaliatory discharge." But although signs indicate that the courts are growing more supportive of whistleblowers, legal protection can still be

■ A **whistleblower** exposes the misdeeds of others in organizations.

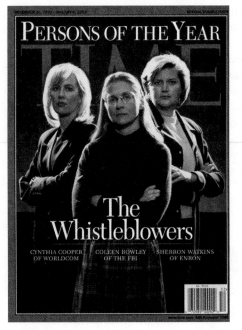

inadequate. Laws vary from state to state, and federal laws mainly protect government workers. Even with legal protection, potential whistleblowers may find it hard to expose unethical behavior in the workplace. Some organizational barriers to whistleblowing include a *strict chain of command* that makes it hard to bypass the boss; *strong work group identities* that encourage loyalty and self-censorship; and *ambiguous priorities* that make it hard to distinguish right from wrong.[32]

A survey by the Ethics Resource Center has found that some 44 percent of workers in the United States still fail to report the wrongdoings they observe at work. The top reasons for not reporting are "(1) the belief that no corrective action would be taken and (2) the fear that reports would not be kept confidential."[33]

ETHICAL ROLE MODELS

Gabrielle Melchionda, a young entrepreneur in Portland, Maine, started Mad Gab's Inc., an all-natural skin care business, while a college student. After her sales had risen to over $300,000, an exporter offered her a deal—sell $2 million of her products abroad. She turned it down. Why? The exporter also sold weapons, and that was against her values; principles trumped the allure of profits. Melchionda's values are reflected in other business decisions, from having an employee profit-sharing plan to hiring disabled adults to using only packaging designs that minimize waste.[34]

Top managers, in large and small enterprises, have the power to shape an organization's policies and set its moral tone. They also have a major responsibility to use this power well by serving as ethical role models. Not only must their day-to-day behavior be the epitome of high ethical conduct, but they must also create ethical cultures and communicate similar expectations throughout the organization.

Even though top managers bear a special responsibility for setting the ethical tone of an organization, all managers should act as ethics role models, and both expect and support ethical behavior by others. The important supervisory act of setting goals and communicating performance expectations is a good case in point. A surprising 64 percent of 238 executives in one study, for example, reported feeling stressed to compromise personal standards to achieve company goals. A *Fortune* survey also reported that 34 percent of its respondents felt a company president can create an ethical climate by setting *reasonable* goals "so that subordinates are not pressured into unethical actions."[35]

CODES OF ETHICAL CONDUCT

■ A **code of ethics** is a formal statement of values and ethical standards.

A **code of ethics** is a formal statement of an organization's values and ethical principles. It offers guidelines on how to behave in situations susceptible to ethical dilemmas. Such codes are important anchor points in professions such as engineering, medicine, law, and public accounting. In organizations, they identify expected behaviors in such areas as general citizenship, the avoidance of illegal or improper acts in one's work, and good relationships with customers. Specific guidelines are often set for bribes and kickbacks, political contributions, honesty of books or records, customer–supplier relationships, and confidentiality of corporate information.

At Gap Inc., global manufacturing is governed by a formal Code of Vendor Conduct.[36] The document specifically deals with *discrimination*—

REAL ETHICS

Résumé Lies

From the *Wall Street Journal*—Employers are looking for résumé lies; senders beware! Don't assume that because so many résumés are in the stack for a position that the employer won't bother to check details. They do. The Society for Human Resource Management surveyed 2,500 of its members, and 96 percent said that they checked up on references and/or stated credentials. When ResumeDoctor.com checked résumés submitted for its review by job hunters, 42.7 percent had at least one inaccuracy and 12.6 percent had more. One of the most common lies is the *out-of-work cover-up*: people try to hide periods of unemployment. Michael Worthington of ResumeDoctor.com says that "people are lying when they don't have to. Companies understand that being out of work can be the norm." Another lie is the *inflated credential*—job title or education. Elaine Hahn of Hahn Capital Management says

that "someone says they're a senior research analyst, but they're really an associate." At her firm that's cause for automatic rejection.

FURTHER INQUIRY

Although it may be tempting to "beef up" one's résumé, it's the wrong thing to do—unethical and potentially hazardous to a career. Go through your résumé and get it up to date for a serious internship or new job search. But before you send it out, check it again. This time look for "resume lies" or anything that may be viewed by a potential employer as of questionable accuracy. Remember the advice from ResumeDoctor.com: there is only one standard in résumé writing—100 percent truthfulness.

"Factories shall employ workers on the basis of their ability to do the job, not on the basis of their personal characteristics or beliefs"; *forced labor—*"Factories shall not use any prison, indentured or forced labor"; *working conditions—*"Factories must treat all workers with respect and dignity and provide them with a safe and healthy environment"; and *freedom of association—*"Factories must not interfere with workers who wish to lawfully and peacefully associate, organize or bargain collectively."

Although codes of ethical conduct are now common and helpful, codes alone cannot guarantee ethical conduct. Ultimately, the value of any ethics code still rests on the human resource foundations of the organization. There is no replacement for effective hiring practices that staff organizations with honest people. And there is no replacement for leadership by committed managers who set positive examples and always act as ethical role models.

MORAL MANAGEMENT

Management scholar Archie Carroll makes a distinction between amoral, immoral, and moral managers.[37] The **immoral manager** chooses to behave unethically. He or she does something purely for personal gain and intentionally disregards the ethics of the action or situation. The **amoral manager** also disregards the ethics of an act or decision, but does so unintentionally. This manager simply fails to consider the ethical consequences of his or her actions. In contrast to both prior types, the **moral manager** considers ethical behavior as a personal goal. He or she makes decisions and acts always in full consideration of ethical issues.

Think about these three types of managers and how common they might be in the real world of work. Although it may seem surprising, Carroll suggests that most of us act amorally. Although well intentioned, we remain mostly uninformed or undisciplined in considering the ethical aspects of our behavior.

■ An **immoral manager** chooses to behave unethically.

■ An **amoral manager** fails to consider the ethics of her or his behavior.

■ A **moral manager** makes ethical behavior a personal goal.

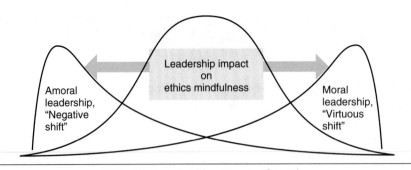

Figure 2.4 Moral management and the ethics center of gravity in organization. *Source:* Developed from Terry Thomas, John R. Schermerhorn Jr., and John W. Dienhart, "Strategic Leadership of Ethical Behavior in Business," *Academy of Management Executive,* vol. 18 (May 2004), pp. 56–66.

■ **Ethics mindfulness** is enriched awareness that leads to consistent ethical behavior.

Think also about how management morality can influence organizations. *Figure 2.4* shows this influence as reflected in the "ethics center of gravity" of the organization as a whole. The key is **ethics mindfulness**—a state of enriched awareness that causes a person to behave ethically from one situation to the next.[38] Moral managers are leaders with ethics mindfulness. By communicating ethical values and serving as ethics role models, they can help move the ethics center of gravity of the whole organization in a positive direction, contributing to a virtuous shift. Of course, amoral and immoral leaders can be just as influential, but their impact on the ethics center of gravity is largely negative rather than positive.

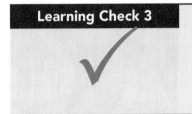

Learning Check 3

Be sure you can ■ define the term whistleblower ■ list three organizational barriers to whistleblowing ■ compare and contrast ethics training, codes of ethical conduct, and ethical role models as methods for encouraging ethical behavior in organizations ■ differentiate between amoral, immoral, and moral management ■ describe ethics mindfulness and how moral management can shift an organization's ethics center of gravity

SOCIAL RESPONSIBILITY AND GOVERNANCE

■ **Social responsibility** is the obligation of an organization to serve its own interests and those of society.

Our interest in ethical behavior also applies at the level of the organization as a whole. **Social responsibility** is an obligation of an organization to act in ways that serve both its own interests and the interests of society at large.

STAKEHOLDER ISSUES AND ANALYSIS

■ **Organizational stakeholders** are directly affected by the behavior of the organization and hold a stake in its performance.

Figure 2.5 describes the environment of a typical business firm as a network of **organizational stakeholders**—those persons, groups, and other organizations directly affected by the behavior of the organization and holding a stake in its performance.[39] In this perspective, the organization has a social responsibility to serve the interests of its many stakeholders, including:

■ *Employees*—employees and contractors who work for the organization.

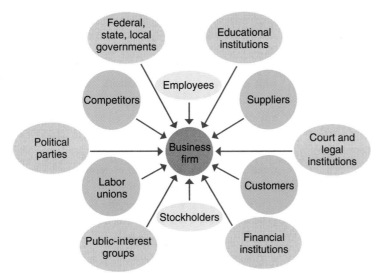

Figure 2.5 Multiple stakeholders in the environment of an organization.

- *Customers*—consumers and clients that purchase the organization's goods and/or use its services.
- *Suppliers*—providers of the organization's human, information, material, and financial resources.
- *Owners*—stockholders, investors, and creditors with claims on assets and profits of the organization.
- *Competitors*—other organizations producing the same or similar goods and services.
- *Regulators*—the local, state, and national government agencies that enforce laws and regulations.
- *Interest groups*—community groups, activists, and others representing interests of citizens and society.

Respect for stakeholders is evident at Tom's of Maine, whose founders Tom and Kate Chappell clearly state: "When we founded the company, it was our goal to make a different kind of business, one where people, the environment and animals are seen as inherently worthy and deserving of respect. We remain committed to this mission, now more than ever."[40] It's also present in the values of Ben Cohen, of Ben & Jerry's fame. He started Hot Fudge, a venture capital fund devoted to community development.[41] The fund supports small business development in depressed communities with the goal of building local economies. And it's found at Timberland Company where each full-time employee gets 40 hours of paid time per year for community volunteer work. "Timberland's motto is 'when you come to work in the morning, don't leave your values at the door.'"[42]

Stakeholders, consumers, activist groups, nonprofit organizations, and governments are often vocal and influential in directing organizations toward socially responsible practices. In today's information age, business activities are increasingly transparent. Irresponsible practices are difficult to hide for long, wherever in the world they take place. Not only do news organizations find and disseminate the information, activist organizations also lobby, campaign, and actively pressure organizations to respect and protect everything from human rights to the natural environment. Some investment funds only own shares in businesses that they evaluate as performing in socially responsible ways.[43]

KAFFEEKLATSCH

Day of Reckoning

First Cup

"I need to bring up the Enron case just one more time. Did Skilling get what he deserved?"

Studying the Grounds

■ Enron was once ranked by *Fortune* as "the most innovative company in America."

■ In August 2001, Jeffrey Skilling resigned as CEO and former CEO Kenneth Lay stepped in to take charge.

■ On December 2, 2001, Enron filed for Chapter 11 bankruptcy protection.

■ Lay resigned as CEO on January 23, 2002.

■ January 14, 2004: Andrew Fastow, former finance chief, pleaded guilty to conspiracy.

■ May 25, 2006: Lay and Skilling were found guilty on charges of conspiracy and fraud.

■ July 4, 2006: Lay dead of heart attack.

■ October 23, 2006: Skilling sentenced to 24+ years in prison.

Double Espresso

"You bet he got what he deserved. Think of it: both men left before the firm's financial collapse was publicly known, and sold lots of company stock in the process. While Enron's employees lost pensions and savings, with careers and livelihoods in many cases destroyed, they made off with millions. Enron's investors and customers also lost. How can there be any doubt?"

"I don't know. I keep wondering: Were they really bad people? Ken Lay's dead now; think about his family and what they're left to deal with."

"I'm sorry for Lay's family, but the fact is that he did wrong. Frankly, I don't think the financial penalties and sentences were harsh enough. Remember what the prosecutor said:"

■ They felt if they could just hold on, if they could just lie a bit longer and get to the next quarter and the next quarter and the next year, everything would be fine.

■ They figured the market wouldn't understand. They were arrogant, and they decided what the market heard and what the market didn't hear.

Your Turn

Kenneth Lay and Jeffrey Skilling found out the hard way that an executive office is no shield for wrongdoing. Does this mean they were inherently "bad" people who went into their jobs with the goals of defrauding employees and investors? Or, was something else going on here that we should also understand and be on guard against—both personally and as citizens?

Look at the Enron case from multiple perspectives: Lay and Skilling, other top managers, investors, employees, customers. What are the lessons here?

PERSPECTIVES ON CORPORATE SOCIAL RESPONSIBILITY

Two contrasting views of corporate social responsibility have stimulated debate in academic and public-policy circles.[44] The *classical view* holds that management's only responsibility in running a business is to maximize profits. In other words, "the business of business is business," and the principal concern of management should always be to maximize shareholder value. This view is supported by Milton Friedman, a respected economist and Nobel Laureate. He says, "Few trends could so thoroughly undermine the very foundations of our free society as the acceptance by corporate officials of social responsibility other than to make as much money for their stockholders as possible."[45]

The *arguments against corporate social responsibility* include fears that its pursuit will reduce business profits, raise business costs, dilute business purpose, give business too much social power, and do so without business accountability to the public.

By contrast, the *socioeconomic view* holds that management of any organization must be concerned within the broader social welfare and not just with corporate profits. This broad based stakeholder perspective is supported by Paul Samuelson, another distinguished economist and Nobel Laureate. He states, "A large corporation these days not only may engage in social responsibility, it had damn well better try to do so."[46]

Among the *arguments in favor of corporate social responsibility* are that it will add long-run profits for businesses, improve the public image of businesses, and help them avoid government regulation. Furthermore, businesses have the resources and ethical obligation to act responsibly.

There is little doubt today that the public at large wants businesses and other organizations to act with genuine social responsibility. Stakeholder expectations are increasingly well voiced and include demands that organizations integrate social responsibility into their core values and daily activities. Research indicates that social responsibility can be associated with strong financial performance; at worst it has no adverse financial impact.[47] The argument that acting with a commitment to social responsibility will negatively affect the "bottom line" is hard to defend. Indeed, evidence points toward a *virtuous circle* in which corporate social responsibility leads to improved financial performance for the firm, and this in turn leads to more socially responsible actions in the future.[48]

EVALUATING CORPORATE SOCIAL PERFORMANCE

If we are to get serious about social responsibility, we need to get rigorous about measuring corporate social performance and holding business leaders accountable for the results. A **social responsibility audit** can be used at regular intervals to report on and systematically assess an organization's performance in various areas of corporate social responsibility.

The social performance of business firms and other organizations can be described as driven by *compliance*—acting to avoid adverse consequences—or by *conviction*—acting to create positive impact.[49] Obviously, those of us who highly value corporate social responsibility believe that organizations should act with both.

Figure 2.6 links compliance and conviction with four criteria of social responsibility identified by Archie Carroll—economic, legal, ethical, and discretionary.[50] An audit of corporate social performance might include questions posed for each criterion: (1) Is the organization's *economic responsibility* met—is it profitable? (2) Is the organization's *legal responsibility* met—does it obey the law? (3) Is the organization's *ethical responsibility* met—is it doing the "right" things? (4) Is the organization's *discretionary responsibility* met—does it contribute to the broader community?

An organization is meeting its economic responsibility when it earns a profit through the provision of goods and services desired by customers. Legal responsibility is fulfilled when an organization operates within the law and according to the requirements of various external regulations. An organization meets its ethical responsibility when its actions voluntarily conform not only to legal expectations but also to the broader values and moral expectations of society. The highest level of social performance comes

■ A **social responsibility audit** assesses an organization's accomplishments in areas of social responsibility.

Zone of Compliance   **Zone of Conviction**

Economic Responsibility: *Be Profitable* → Legal Responsibility: *Obey the Law* → Ethical Responsibility: *Do What Is Right* → Discretionary Responsibility: *Contribute to Community*

Figure 2.6 Criteria for evaluating corporate social performance.

Figure 2.7 Four strategies of corporate social responsibility—from obstructionist to proactive behavior.

through the satisfaction of discretionary responsibility. Here, the organization voluntarily moves beyond basic economic, legal, and ethical expectations to provide leadership in advancing the well-being of individuals, communities, and society as a whole.

Figure 2.7 describes these tendencies on a continuum of four corporate social responsibility strategies. Note that the commitment to social performance increases as the strategy shifts from "obstructionist" at the lowest end to "proactive" at the highest.[51]

An **obstructionist strategy** ("Fight the social demands") reflects mainly economic priorities; social demands lying outside the organization's perceived self-interests are resisted. If the organization is criticized for wrongdoing, it can be expected to deny the claims. A **defensive strategy** ("Do the minimum legally required") seeks to protect the organization by doing the minimum legally necessary to satisfy expectations. Corporate behavior at this level conforms only to legal requirements, competitive market pressure, and perhaps activist voices. If criticized, intentional wrongdoing is likely to be denied.

Organizations pursuing an **accommodative strategy** ("Do the minimum ethically required") accept their social responsibilities. They try to satisfy economic, legal, and ethical criteria. Corporate behavior at this level is congruent with society's prevailing norms, values, and expectations. But it may be so only because of outside pressures. An oil firm, for example, may be willing to "accommodate" with cleanup activities when a spill occurs but remain quite slow in taking actions to prevent spills in the first place. The **proactive strategy** ("Take leadership in social initiatives") is designed to meet all the criteria of social performance, including discretionary performance. Corporate behavior at this level takes preventive action to avoid adverse social impacts from company activities, and it takes the lead in identifying and responding to emerging social issues.

An obstructionist strategy avoids social responsibility and reflects mainly economic priorities.

A defensive strategy seeks protection by doing the minimum legally required.

An accommodative strategy accepts social responsibility and tries to satisfy economic, legal, and ethical criteria.

A proactive strategy meets all the criteria of social responsibility, including discretionary performance.

ROLE OF CORPORATE GOVERNANCE

Corporate governance is the oversight of top management by a board of directors.

In Chapter 1, **corporate governance** was defined as oversight of the top management of an organization by a board of directors. Governance most typically involves hiring, firing, and compensating the CEO; assessing strategy; and verifying financial records.[52] One board member describes the responsibilities of corporate governance as "it's really about setting and maintaining high standards."[53]

It is tempting to think that corporate governance is a clear-cut way to ensure that organizations behave with social responsibility and that their leaders behave ethically. But even though its purpose is clear, there is a lot

RESEARCH BRIEF

Issue management pacesetters influence pharmaceutical industry's response to AIDS in Africa

Writing in *Business & Society*, Cedric E. Dawkins describes an *issues management pacesetter* as a company in an industry that addresses an external issue in a unique and different way. His article first develops a pacesetters model and then applies it to case studies of responses by global pharmaceutical firms to the AIDS crisis in Africa over a three-year period. In his words, the article analyzes "the confrontation between the mainline pharmaceutical industry and AIDS activists and stakeholders over access to AIDS medications in Africa."

Dawkins views organizational decision making as a process of negotiation between external normative and competitive pressures. Issues pacesetters are firms that change in response to pressures from external stakeholders and then stimulate further changes by other industry firms.

In the article, Dawkins examines two pacesetting pharmaceuticals that initiated pressures for change in Africa—one by substantially lowering prices of AIDS drugs, and the other by freeing patents on these drugs. Both pacesetters were responding to stakeholder views that were consolidating around a new set of expectations. He concludes that the pacesetters model is accurate in explaining the industry events, and that the perceptions of organizational decision makers of stakeholder interests and demands are a critical factor in the process. He also suggests that stakeholder groups that understand how firms make decisions will be able to gain more influence over firm behavior.

Abbreviated Issues Pacesetters Model

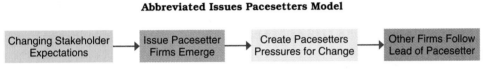

In a postscript to the article, Dawkins also notes increased cooperation among countries in the fight against AIDS. But he also points out that, in Africa and elsewhere, more still needs to be done to "widen access to HIV medicines and technologies."

QUESTIONS & APPLICATIONS

Can you come up with other examples or cases where the issues pacesetters model helps explain how organizations deal with stakeholder issues and concerns? Can this model explain why some firms might follow obstructionist or defensive social responsibility strategies?

Identify a social issue that is being voiced in your community. Study the issue, the stakeholders, and the businesses or other organizations whose products or services are in question. Test how well the issues pacesetters model helps to explain events to date and predict what might happen in the future.

Reference: Cedric E. Dawkins, "First to Market: Issue Management Pacesetters and the Pharmaceutical Industry Response to AIDS in Africa," *Business & Society* (September, 2005), pp. 244–282.

---

of concern that corporate governance can be inadequate and in some cases ineffectual. For example, the news contains critical reports that CEO pay is both too high and too often high when firms perform poorly; we also read about continuing accounting scandals that reveal misuse of corporate assets and wrongful financial reporting.

When governance is weak and corporate scandals occur, you will sometimes see government stepping in to try and correct things for the future. Laws are passed and regulating agencies are put in place in an attempt to better control and direct business behavior. The Sarbanes-Oxley Act, discussed briefly in Chapter 1, is one example. Passed by Congress in 2002 in response to public outcries over major ethics and business scandals, its goal is to ensure that top managers properly oversee the financial conduct of their organizations.

A *Wall Street Journal* survey suggests that business executives are starting to embrace corporate governance reform. They also see its value in terms of enhanced corporate reputations.[54] Importantly, the responsibilities

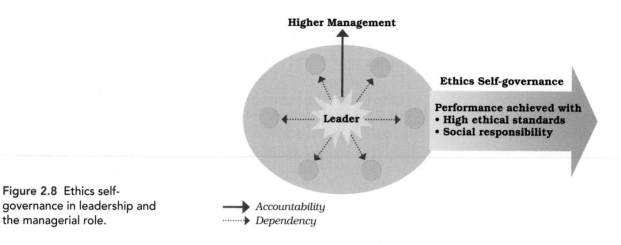

Figure 2.8 Ethics self-governance in leadership and the managerial role.

of "governance" in day-to-day managerial control are being better communicated throughout organizations. All managers must accept personal responsibility for doing the "right" things. Decisions must be made and problems solved with ethical considerations standing side-by-side with performance objectives.

Figure 2.8 brings this notion down to the level of the individual. It highlights each of our personal responsibilities, managers included, for ethics *self-governance*. While working to fulfill our accountability for achieving performance objectives, we must be certain to do so in an ethical and socially responsible manner. The full weight of this responsibility holds in every organizational setting, from small to large and from private to nonprofit. It holds also at every managerial level, top to bottom. There is no escaping the ultimate reality—being a manager is a very socially responsible job!

Learning Check 4

Be sure you can ■ define the term social responsibility ■ summarize arguments for and against corporate social responsibility ■ identify four criteria for measuring corporate social performance ■ explain four possible social responsibility strategies ■ define corporate governance and discuss its importance in organization–society relationships

CHAPTER 2 STUDY GUIDE

STUDY QUESTIONS SUMMARY

1 What is ethical behavior?

- Ethical behavior is that which is accepted as "good" or "right" as opposed to "bad" or "wrong."
- Because an action is not illegal does not necessarily make it ethical in a given situation.
- Because values vary, the question "What is ethical behavior?" may be answered differently by different people.
- The utilitarian, individualism, moral-rights, and justice views offer alternative ways of thinking about ethical behavior.
- Cultural relativism argues that no culture is ethically superior to any other; universalism argues that certain ethical standards apply everywhere.

2 How do ethical dilemmas complicate the workplace?

- Ethical managers can have a positive impact on other people at work and on the social good performed by organizations.
- An ethical dilemma occurs when someone must decide whether to pursue a course of action that, although offering the potential for personal or organizational benefit or both, may be unethical.
- Managers report that their ethical dilemmas often involve conflicts with superiors, customers, and subordinates over such matters as dishonesty in advertising and communications, as well as pressure from bosses to do unethical things.
- Common rationalizations for unethical behavior include believing the behavior is not illegal, is in everyone's best interests, will never be noticed, or will be supported by the organization.

3 How can high ethical standards be maintained?

- Ethics training can help people better deal with ethical dilemmas in the workplace.

- Whistleblowers expose the unethical acts of others in organizations, even while facing career risks for doing so.
- Top management sets an ethical tone for the organization as a whole, while all managers are responsible for acting as positive models of ethical behavior.
- Written codes of ethical conduct formally state what an organization expects of its employees regarding ethical behavior at work.
- Amoral managers disregard the ethics of their actions or decisions; immoral managers intentionally choose to behave unethically.
- Moral managers consider ethical behavior a personal goal; their actions can shift the ethics center of gravity in organizations in a positive direction and strengthen ethics mindfulness by others.

4 What is social responsibility and governance?

- Social responsibility is an obligation of the organization to act in ways that serve both its own interests and the interests of its many stakeholders.
- An organization's social performance can be evaluated on how well it meets economic, legal, ethical, and discretionary responsibilities.
- Corporate strategies in response to demands for socially responsible behavior include obstruction, defense, accommodation, and proaction, with more progressive organizations taking proactive stances.
- Corporate governance is the responsibility of a Board of Directors to oversee the performance by top management of a firm.
- Managers should exercise ethical self-governance by making sure that performance is achieved with commitments to high ethical standards and by socially responsible means.

KEY TERMS REVIEW

Accommodative strategy (p. 48)

Amoral manager (p. 43)

Code of ethics (p. 42)

Corporate governance (p. 48)

Cultural relativism (p. 34)

Defensive strategy (p. 48)

Distributive justice (p. 34)

Ethical behavior (p. 32)

Ethical dilemma (p. 36)

Ethical imperialism (p. 35)

Ethics (p. 32)

Ethics mindfulness (p. 44)

Ethics training (p. 41)

Immoral manager (p. 43)

Individualism view (p. 34)

Instrumental values (p. 33)

Interactional justice (p. 34)

Justice view (p. 34)

Moral manager (p. 43)

Moral-rights view (p. 34)

Obstructionist strategy (p. 48)

Organizational stakeholders (p. 44)

Proactive strategy (p. 48)

Procedural justice (p. 34)

Social responsibility (p. 44)

Social responsibility audit (p. 47)

Terminal values (p. 33)

Universalism (p. 34)

Utilitarian view (p. 33)

Values (p. 33)

Whistleblower (p. 41)

SELF-TEST 2

MULTIPLE-CHOICE QUESTIONS:

1. Values are personal beliefs that help determine whether a behavior will be considered ethical or unethical. An example of terminal value is _____.

   (a) ambition (b) self-respect (c) courage (d) imagination

2. Under the _____ view of ethical behavior, a business owner would be considered ethical if she reduced a plant's workforce by 10 percent in order to cut costs and be able to save jobs for the other 90 percent.

   (a) utilitarian (b) individualism (c) justice (d) moral-rights

3. A manager's failure to enforce a late-to-work policy the same way for all employees is an ethical violation of _____ justice.

   (a) ethical (b) moral (c) distributive (d) procedural

4. The Sarbanes-Oxley Act of 2002 makes it easier for corporate executives to _____.

   (a) protect themselves from shareholder lawsuits (b) sue employees who commit illegal acts (c) be tried and sentenced to jail for financial misconduct (d) shift blame for wrongdoing to boards of directors

5. Two "spotlight" questions for conducting the ethics double-check of a decision are (a) "How would I feel if my family found out about this?" and (b) "How would I feel if _____?"

   (a) my boss found out about this (b) my subordinates found out about this (c) this was printed in the local newspaper (d) this went into my personnel file

6. Research on ethical dilemmas indicates that _____ is/are often the cause of unethical behavior by people at work.

   (a) declining morals in society (b) lack of religious beliefs (c) the absence of whistleblowers (d) pressures from bosses and superiors

7. Customers, investors, employees, and regulators are examples of _____ that are important in the analysis of corporate social responsibility.

   (a) special-interest groups (b) stakeholders (c) ethics advocates (d) whistleblowers

8. A(n) _____ is someone who exposes the ethical misdeeds of others.

   (a) whistleblower (b) ethics advocate (c) ombudsman (d) stakeholder

9. Two employees are talking about their employers. Sean says that ethics training and codes of ethical conduct are worthless; Maura says these are the best ways to ensure ethical behavior in the organization. Who is right and why?

   (a) Sean—no one cares. (b) Maura—only the organization can influence ethical behavior. (c) Neither Sean nor Maura—training and codes can aid but never guarantee ethical behavior. (d) Neither Sean nor Maura—only the threat of legal punishment will make people act ethically.

10. A proponent of the classical view of corporate social responsibility would most likely agree with which of these statements?

    (a) Social responsibility improves the public image of business. (b) The primary responsibility of business is to maximize business profits. (c) By acting responsibly, businesses avoid government regulation. (d) Businesses can and should do "good" while doing business.

11. An ammoral manager_____.

    (a) always acts in consideration of ethical issues (b) chooses to behave unethically (c) makes ethics a personal goal (d) acts unethically but unintentionally

12. An organization that takes the lead in addressing emerging social issues is being _____, showing the most progressive corporate social responsibility strategy.

    (a) accommodative (b) defensive (c) proactive (d) obstructionist

13. The criterion of _____ responsibility identifies the highest level of conviction by an organization to operate in a responsible manner.

    (a) economic (b) legal (c) ethical (d) discretionary

14. Which ethical position has been criticized as a source of "ethical imperialism"?

    (a) individualism (b) absolutism (c) utilitarianism (d) relativism

15. A manager supports an organization's attempts at self-governance when he or she always tries to achieve performance objectives in ways that are _____.

    (a) performance effective (b) cost efficient (c) quality oriented (d) ethical and socially responsible

SHORT-RESPONSE QUESTIONS:

16. Explain the difference between the individualism and justice views of ethical behavior.
17. List four common rationalizations for unethical managerial behavior.
18. What are the major arguments in the socioeconomic view of corporate social responsibility?
19. What decisions should a Board of Directors oversee in order to fulfill its governance responsibilities?

APPLICATION QUESTION:

20. A small outdoor clothing company has just received an attractive offer from a business in Bangladesh to manufacture its work gloves. The offer would allow for substantial cost savings over the current supplier. The company manager, however, has read reports that some Bangladeshi businesses break their own laws and operate with child labor. How would differences in the following corporate responsibility strategies affect the manager's decision regarding whether to accept the offer: obstruction, defense, accommodation, and proaction?

CHAPTER 2 APPLICATIONS

CASE 2

Tom's of Maine: At Tom's, "Doing Business" Means "Doing Good"

Tom's of Maine was one of the first natural health care companies to distribute its products beyond the normal channels of health food stores. With its continued growth, owners Tom and Kate Chappell still emphasize the values that got them started more than three decades ago. The experiences of Tom and Kate in meeting their challenges provide considerable insight into how a small firm can stay true to its founding principles and continue to grow in a fiercely competitive environment.

Getting Tom's of Maine Going

For its first 15 years, Tom's of Maine looked a lot like many other new businesses. Tom and Kate Chappell had an idea they believed in—creating a line of all-natural, environmentally friendly household products—and felt others would buy into as well. Based on this idea, and with financing from a small loan, the Chappells started the company in 1970. As is the case with many startups, the company's first product was not successful. Its phosphate-free detergent was environmentally friendly, but according to Tom Chappell, "it didn't clean so well."[55] Consumers did appear to be interested in "green," or environmentally friendly, products, however, and the fledgling company's next products, toothpaste and soap, were more successful.

Tom's of Maine products were made with all-natural ingredients and were packaged using recycled materials whenever possible. New personal care products, including shampoo and deodorant, were developed while avoiding the controversial practice of animal testing.[56] This refusal to succumb to what is otherwise the industry standard caused Tom's to wait seven years and spend about ten times the usual sum to get the American Dental Association's seal of approval for its fluoride toothpastes.

In 1992, Tom's deodorant accounted for 25 percent of its business. Chappell reformulated the product for ecological reasons, but the new formulation "magnified the human bacteria that cause odor" in half its customers. After much agonizing, he ordered the deodorant taken off the shelves at a cost of $400,000, or 30 percent of the firm's projected profits for the year. Dissatisfied consumers were sent refunds for the new product, along with a letter of apology.

Tom's of Maine recovered from this experience, but founder Tom Chappell was not happy. The company's products were a success in health food stores, and Chappell was beginning to think in terms of national distribution. He had hired a team of marketing people with experience at major companies. At the same time, he felt that something was missing; he was tired of simply "creating new brands and making money."[57]

One pivotal event for Tom's was the introduction of its baking soda toothpaste. The product was gritty and didn't have the sweet flavor typical of commercial toothpastes, and the marketing manager told Chappell, "In all candor, I don't know how we're going to sell it."[58] Chappell insisted that the product be test marketed. It proved to be a best seller and was quickly copied by Arm and Hammer and Procter & Gamble.[59] It also appeared that the new product's sales potential had become more important to the company than the qualities of the product itself. "We were working for the numbers, and we got the numbers. But I was confused by success, unhappy with success" said Chappell.[60] He later wrote, "I had made a real go of something I'd started. What more could I do in life except make more money? Where was the purpose and direction for the rest of my life?"[61] As a

Founders Tom Chappell and his wife, Kate.

result of this line of thinking, successful businessman Tom Chappell entered Harvard Divinity School in the fall of 1986.[62]

Sharpening the Company's Focus

The years that Chappell spent as a part-time student at the divinity school brought him to a new understanding of his role. "For the first time in my career, I had the language I needed to debate my bean counters" he explained.[63] He realized that his company was his ministry. "I'm here to succeed. But there's a qualifier. It's not to succeed at all costs, it's to succeed according to my principles."[64]

One tangible result was the development of a mission statement for the company that reflected both the company's business aspirations and its commitment to social responsibility. This document spelled out the values that would guide the company in the future. It covered the types of products ordered and the need for natural ingredients and high quality. It also included respect for employees and the need for meaningful work as well as fair pay. It pointed out the need to be concerned with the community and even the world. Finally, it called for Tom's of Maine "to be a profitable and successful company, while acting in a socially responsible manner."[65] Some of the company's programs were the result of decisions made by top management. The company began donating 10 percent of its pretax profits to charities ranging from arts organizations to environmental groups.

The company also urged its employees to get involved in charitable causes. It set up a program that allowed employees to donate 5 percent of their work time to volunteer activities. Employees enthusiastically took advantage of the opportunity. When one employee began teaching art classes for emotionally disturbed children, others became interested, until almost all of the company's employees were involved.[66] Other employees worked in soup kitchens and homeless shelters. Employees formed their own teams to work on projects or used the company's matching service. Tom's even created the position of vice president of community life.

The volunteer program did have its costs, however. Other employees had to pitch in to cover volunteers' absences, which amounted to the equivalent of 20 days a month. However, Colleen Myers, the vice president of community life, believed that the volunteer activities were valuable to the company as well as the community. "After spending a few hours at a soup kitchen or a shelter, you're happy to have a job. It's a morale booster, and better morale translates pretty directly into better productivity."[67] Sometimes the company even benefited directly from these activities. Chappell explained, "The woman who headed up those art classes—she discovered she's a heck of a project manager. We found that out, too."[68]

Employee benefits were not strictly psychological. The company offered flexible four-day scheduling and subsidized day care. Even coffee breaks were designed with employee preferences in mind, providing them with fresh fruit. The company also helped individual employees earn their high school equivalency degrees and develop skills for new positions.[69]

Even as Tom's product distribution expanded nationwide, the company's marketing strategy was low key. Katie Shisler, vice president of marketing, says: "We just tell them our story. We tell them why we have such a loyal base of consumers who vote with their dollars every day. A number of trade accounts appreciate our social responsibility and are willing to go out on a limb with us."[70] Tom Chappell agreed: "We're selling a lot more than toothpaste; we're selling a point of view—that nature is worth protecting."[71]

All the time, Tom's of Maine was facing increasing pressures from its national competitors. Tom Chappell didn't worry; he believed that "you have to understand from the outset that they have more in the marketing war chest than you. That's not the way you're going to get market share, you're going to get it by being who you are."[72]

Tom explains his philosophy this way: "A small business obviously needs to distinguish itself from the commodities. If we try to act like commodities, act like a toothpaste, we give up our souls. Instead, we have to be peculiarly authentic in everything we do."[73] This authenticity is applied to both ingredients and advertising decisions. "When you start doing that customers are very aware of your difference. And they like the difference."[74]

A Different Kind of Company?

Tom's of Maine distinguishes itself from other companies by stressing the "common good" in all of its endeavors. The company is passionately concerned about corporate wellness, customer wellness, product wellness, community and environmental wellness, and employee wellness. Among other customer-oriented activities, Tom's utilizes the services of a wellness advisory council and provides wellness education. The company also practices stewardship through its commitment to natural, sustainable, and responsible ingredients, products, and packaging.

Throughout its growth Tom's of Maine has been repeatedly recognized for providing a model of ethical business standards for others to follow. Among other awards, Tom and Kate Chappell have received the Corporate Conscience Award for Charitable Contributions from the Council of Economic Priorities, the New England Environmental Leadership Award, and the Governor's Award for Business Excellence.[75] Clearly, Tom's of Maine demonstrates that "common-good capitalism" can work, and that businesses can be operated to simultaneously earn a profit and serve the common good. In an effort to pass these lessons on to other businesspeople, Tom Chappell has authored two books, *The Soul of a Business: Managing for Profit and the Common Good* and *Managing Upside Down: Seven Intentions for Values-Centered Leadership*, and has created the Saltwater Institute, a nonprofit organization that provides training in the Seven Intentions.[76]

Chappell's Seven Intentions for seeking and achieving a values–profits balance are

1. Connect with goodness. Nonwork discussions with an upbeat spin usually draw people to common ground, away from hierarchical titles.
2. Know thyself, be thyself. Discovering and tapping people's passions, gifts, and strengths generates creative energy.
3. Envision your destiny. The company is better served if its efforts are steered by strengths instead of following market whims.
4. Seek counsel. The journey is long, and assistance from others is absolutely necessary.
5. Venture out. The success of any business hinges on pushing value-enhanced products into the market.
6. Assess. Any idea must be regularly reviewed and refined if necessary.
7. Pass it on. Since developing and incorporating values is a trial-and-error process, sharing ideas and soliciting feedback allow for future growth.[77]

Into the Future

In embracing the philosophy of "doing well by doing good," Tom's has continued to produce impressive business results that attest to an ongoing stream of corporate wellness. Annual sales for Tom's have exceeded $ 50 million, which directly reflects the continued strengthening of its various product lines.[78]

Following the lead of other natural health product companies, including Burt's Bees, Tom's of Maine was purchased by a conglomerate, the Colgate-Palmolive Company. For approximately $100 million dollars— 84% of outstanding shares—Colgate will have the opportunity to compete in the Natural category of oral care brands. Tom's leads that niche, holding 60% of the market share. Tom Chappell remained on board to lead the company, which continues to be based in Kennebunk, Maine.[79]

Tom's of Maine is a rare instance of a company that has found continued financial success by sticking to its principles and ethics, even in the face of pessimistic analysts and naysayers. What others might call idealism, Tom Chappell has put to work as simple pragmatism. But has acquisition by Colgate-Palmolive tainted the company's commitment to environmental and ethical standards which may conflict with a large corporation's quest for profits? Or can a little company from the Northeast teach a cosmetics giant a thing or two about corporate responsibility?

REVIEW QUESTIONS

1. Which way of thinking about ethical behavior best describes Tom's of Maine and its founder, Tom Chappell?
2. How important were Tom Chappell's personal views in helping Tom's of Maine to be successful?
3. Define which "strategy" for social responsibility Tom Chappell seems to follow. Explain your answer.

TEAM PROJECT

Cheating On Campus

A student's prize winning essay for a Rotary Club contest contained this confession: "I came into high school strong, proud and ready to take on the new challenges that I faced. By my third year I was weak, desperate and ready to do whatever it took to keep myself ahead. I cheated." A survey by the Josephson Institute of Ethics found a disturbing pattern among high school students— 35% had copied material from the Internet, 62% had cheated on a test, and 83% had copied someone else's homework.

Question: What is the status of cheating on your campus? What does this say about the likely ethics of today's students in their future jobs and careers?

Research Directions:

- Design a research instrument—survey or interview—to find out what is taking place on your campus regarding cheating on examinations, homework, and assignments.
- Look for insights on what is considered "cheating" and what isn't, how much cheating takes place and of what types. Ask if students are willing to turn in others who are cheating, and if they cheat. Determine how students cheat, how often they get caught, what the penalties are for cheating, and what encourages or discourages cheating on this campus.
- Conduct the research with a good-sized sample of students on your campus.
- Push the research a bit further by also surveying or interviewing faculty members to get their perspectives on the cheating issue and their experiences with it.
- Analyze all your data and compile the results as a written report and an oral presentation for the instructor and/or class.
- Engage the class in a discussion of what the data suggest about the future ethics of students when they move into positions of responsibility in organizations during their careers.

PERSONAL MANAGEMENT

Individual Character

INDIVIDUAL CHARACTER is a foundation for all that we do. It establishes our integrity and provides an ethical anchor for our behavior in the workplace and in life overall. Persons of high integrity can always be confident in the self-respect it provides, even in the most difficult of situations. Those who lack it are destined to perpetual insecurity, acting inconsistently, and suffering not only in self-esteem but also in the esteem of others. How strong is your personal character? How well prepared are you to deal with the inevitable ethical dilemmas and challenges in work and in life? Can you give specific examples showing how your behavior lives up to these Six Pillars of Character identified by the Josephson Institute of Ethics?

- *Trustworthiness*—Honesty, integrity, reliability in keeping promises, loyalty
- *Respect*—Civility, courtesy and decency, dignity, tolerance, and acceptance
- *Responsibility*—Sense of accountability, pursuit of excellence, self-restraint
- *Fairness*—Commitment to process, impartiality, equity
- *Caring*—Concern for others, benevolence, altruism
- *Citizenship*—Knowing the law, being informed, volunteering

Building the Brand Called "You"   Make a list of at least three incidents that you have been involved in and that pose ethical dilemmas. Put yourself in the position of being your parent, a loved one, or just a good friend. Using their vantage points, write a letter to yourself that critiques your handling of each incident and summarizes the implications in terms of your individual character.

NEXT STEPS: MANAGEMENT LEARNING WORKBOOK

Self-Assessments
- Terminal Values (#5)
- Instrumental Values (#6)
- Diversity Awareness (#7)
- Internal/External Control (#26)

Experiential Exercises
- Confronting Ethical Dilemmas (#6)
- What Do You Value in Work? (#7)
- Case of the Contingency Workforce (#22)

Management— Historical Perspectives

3

Planning Ahead

Chapter 3 Study Questions

1 What can be learned from classical management thinking?

2 What insights come from the behavioral management approaches?

3 What are the foundations of modern management thinking?

The Dawn of a New Age

Just when you thought that we were firmly entrenched in the Information Age, a leading thinker is suggesting that our culture has already moved beyond its infatuation with raw information and now prizes those who can make sense of all that knowledge.

For some time, scholars, essayists, and pundits have heralded the arrival of the Information Age. Advances in computing power, they said, brought our culture to a new point where information was the new currency and the economy would be dominated by companies specializing in collecting, analyzing, or redistributing data.

But the truth was, the information age had arrived a long time before. Our economy had been traditionally led by individuals and corporations adept in the traditional fields of information moving—doctors, lawyers, financial analysts, even programmers.

Nonetheless, as the pace of technology quickened, certain companies distinguished themselves through their ability to combine new, desired information with traditional goods or services. Just ask Jeff Bezos, founder and CEO of Amazon.com, Inc.

Amazon began life rather modestly as an online bookstore, launched in Seattle, Washington, in 1995. It has grown into the world's largest online retailer, with 40 million customers and a most interesting story line.

What *They* Think

"We are willing to go down a bunch of dark passage-ways, and occasionally we find something that really works."
Jeffrey P. Bezos, Amazon.com founder and CEO

INFORMATION AGE: *"The Information Age offers much to mankind, and I would like to think that we will rise to the challenges it presents. But it is vital to remember that information—in the sense of raw data—is not knowledge, that knowledge is not wisdom, and that wisdom is not foresight. But information is the first essential step to all of these."*
Arthur C. Clarke, science-fiction author and inventor

CONCEPTUAL AGE: *"Want to get ahead today? Forget what your parents told you. Instead, do something foreigners can't do cheaper. Something computers can't do faster. And something that fills one of the nonmaterial, transcendent desires of an abundant age."*
Daniel Pink, author of A Whole New Mind

As Amazon grew from book seller to stock CDs and DVDs, the company quickly found ways to distinguish its otherwise generic service by providing information about products. One of the most enduring and successful has been its Spotlight Reviews, in which Amazon shoppers offer honest, sometimes blunt reviews. The service has become so well known that Amazon has become a destination for shoppers to research products that they may have no intention of purchasing on Amazon.

Bezos has been very good at building on Amazon's expertise and successful retail heritage. Amazon is extending as it grows. Did you know that Amazon has been running e-commerce for other large retailers, Target and Borders, among them, or that Fulfillment by Amazon gives smaller retailers access to its warehouse and distribution system? Of course, these initiatives seem to "fit the model," the types of things you might expect from the world's biggest Internet department store. But if you look closer, another Amazon is emerging from Bezos' creative business mind. And, according to author Daniel Pink, that's just where Amazon should be.

In his book *A Whole New Mind*, Pink advocates that our culture is shifting away from its traditional reliance on "left-brain" skills—calculation, analysis—and entering a time when "right brain" territory creativity, empathy, emotion—will dominate our economy. "Left-brain skills are still absolutely necessary in our complex world," Pink says. "They're just not sufficient anymore."[1]

Left brain and right brain are center stage in the new Amazon. Among recent initiatives there's Simple Storage Service—a way for small start-ups to use Amazon computers to store data and run programs. There's Alexa Internet Services—a source for Web site traffic rankings. There's Elastic Compute Cloud—a provider of on-demand computer power over the Internet. And, if you look again, you'll probably find something else newly arrived.

Bezos is always creating, coming up with new ideas, trying to find ways to use Amazon's great technologies in novel, business worthy ways. He says: "We are willing to go down a bunch of dark passageways, and occasionally we find something that really works."[2]

Is this really the beginning of the Conceptual Age? Only time will tell. But to just to be sure, it wouldn't hurt to get your left brain in shape!

The Numbers

Computer Science as Probable Major for Freshmen

1995	2.2%
1997	3%
1999	3.7%
2001	3.35%
2003	1.7%
2005	1.2%

Quick Facts

* The first incarnation of Amazon.com consisted of CEO Jeff Bezos selling books out of his garage.
* Some maintain that the information age era actually began in 1837, when Samuel Morse invented the telegraph.[3]
* ENIAC (Electrical Numerical Integrator and Computer), an early supercomputer developed by the military, was so large that it stretched around the walls of a 30-by 50-foot room.[4]
* U.S. colleges are projected to produce only one-half the graduates needed to fill computer and information jobs in 2012.[5]

What Do *You* Think?

1. Do you agree with Daniel Pink that our culture has entered a new conceptual age that prizes creativity over analysis?
2. Can you identify at least three new "Conceptual Age" careers that offer opportunities for your skills and knowledge?

Management—Historical Perspectives		
Study Question 1	**Study Question 2**	**Study Question 3**
Classical Management Approaches	**Behavioral Management Approaches**	**Modern Management Foundations**
■ Scientific management ■ Administrative principles ■ Bureaucratic organization	■ Follett on Organizations as Communities ■ The Hawthorne studies ■ Maslow's theory of human needs ■ McGregor's Theory X and Theory Y ■ Argyris's theory of adult personality	■ Decisions and operations management ■ Organizations as systems ■ Contingency thinking ■ High-performance organizations ■ Learning organizations
Learning Check 1	**Learning Check 2**	**Learning Check 3**

In *The Evolution of Management Thought*, Daniel Wren traces management as far back as 5000 B.C., when ancient Sumerians used written records to assist in governmental and commercial activities.[7] Management was important to the construction of the Egyptian pyramids, the rise of the Roman Empire, and the commercial success of 14th-century Venice. By the time of the Industrial Revolution in the 1700s, great social changes had helped prompt a great leap forward in the manufacture of basic staples and consumer goods. Industrial development was accelerated by Adam Smith's ideas of efficient production through specialized tasks and the division of labor. At the turn of the 20th century, Henry Ford and others were making mass production a mainstay of the emerging economy. Since then, the science and practices of management have been on a rapid and continuing path of development.

Not too long ago Harvard University Press released *Mary Parker Follett— Prophet of Management: A Celebration of Writings from the 1920s*. The book reminds us of the wisdom of history.[8] Although Follett wrote in a different day and age, her ideas are rich with foresight. She advocated cooperation and better horizontal relationships in organizations, taught respect for the experience and knowledge of workers, warned against the dangers of too much hierarchy, and called for visionary leadership. Today we pursue similar themes while using terms like "empowerment," "involvement," "flexibility," and "self-management."

The lessons regarding the history of management thought are clear. Rather than naively believe that we are always reinventing management practice today, it is wise to remember the historical roots of many modern ideas and admit that we are still trying to perfect them.

CLASSICAL MANAGEMENT APPROACHES

Our study of management begins with the classical approaches: (1) scientific management, (2) administrative principles, and (3) bureaucratic organization.[9] *Figure 3.1* associates each with a prominent person in the history of management thought. Their names are still widely used in management conversations today. The figure also shows that the classical approaches share a common assumption: People at work act in a rational manner that is primarily driven by economic concerns. Workers are expected to rationally consider opportunities made available to them and to do whatever is necessary to achieve the greatest personal and monetary gain.[10]

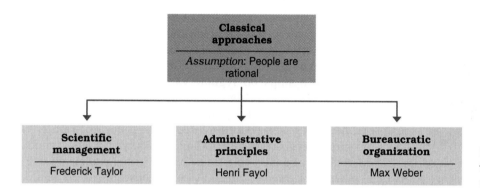

Figure 3.1 Major branches in the classical approach to management.

SCIENTIFIC MANAGEMENT

In 1911 Frederick W. Taylor published *The Principles of Scientific Management*, in which he made the following statement: "The principal object of management should be to secure maximum prosperity for the employer, coupled with the maximum prosperity for the employee."[11] Taylor, often called the "father of scientific management," noticed that many workers did their jobs their own way and without clear and uniform specifications. He believed this caused them to lose efficiency and perform below their true capacities. He also believed that this problem could be corrected if workers were taught and then helped by supervisors to always perform their jobs in the right way.

Taylor's goal was to improve the productivity of people at work. He used the concept of "time study" to analyze the motions and tasks required in any job and to develop the most efficient ways to perform them.[12] He then linked these job requirements both with training for the worker and with support from supervisors in the form of proper direction, work assistance, and monetary incentives. The lessons from his efforts are found in *Management Smarts 3.1*. Taylor's approach is known as **scientific management** and includes these four guiding action principles.

1. Develop for every job a "science" that includes rules of motion, standardized work implements, and proper working conditions.

> ### MANAGEMENT SMARTS 3.1
>
> **Practical lessons from scientific management**
>
> Step 1. Make results-based compensation a performance incentive.
>
> Step 2. Carefully design jobs with efficient work methods.
>
> Step 3. Carefully select workers with the abilities to do these jobs.
>
> Step 4. Train workers to perform jobs to the best of their abilities.
>
> Step 5. Train supervisors to support workers so they can perform to the best of their abilities.

■ **Scientific management** emphasizes careful selection and training of workers and supervisory support.

2. Carefully select workers with the right abilities for the job.
3. Carefully train workers to do the job and give them the proper incentives to cooperate with the job "science."
4. Support workers by carefully planning their work and by smoothing the way as they go about their jobs.

■ **Motion study** is the science of reducing a task to its basic physical motions.

Mentioned in Taylor's first principle, **motion study** is the science of reducing a job or task to its basic physical motions. Two contemporaries of Taylor, Frank and Lillian Gilbreth, pioneered motion studies as a management tool. In one famous study they reduced the number of motions used by bricklayers and tripled their productivity.[13] The Gilbreths' work established the foundation for later advances in the areas of job simplification, work standards, and incentive wage plans—all techniques still used in the modern workplace.

An example of the continuing influence of Taylor and the Gilbreths can be seen at United Parcel Service (UPS), where workers are guided by carefully calibrated productivity standards. At regional centers, sorters are timed according to strict task requirements and are expected to load vans at a set number of packages per hour. Delivery stops on regular van routes are studied and carefully timed, and supervisors generally know within a few minutes how long a driver's pickups and deliveries will take. Industrial engineers devise precise routines for drivers, who are trained to knock on customers' doors rather than spend even a few seconds looking for the doorbell. Handheld computers further enhance delivery efficiencies. At UPS, savings of seconds on individual stops add up to significant increases in productivity.

ADMINISTRATIVE PRINCIPLES

In 1916, after a career in French industry, Henri Fayol published *Administration Industrielle et Générale*.[14] The book outlines his views on the proper management of organizations and of the people within them. It identifies the following five "rules" or "duties" of management, which closely resemble the four functions of management—planning, organizing, leading, and controlling—that we talk about today:

1. *Foresight*—to complete a plan of action for the future.
2. *Organization*—to provide and mobilize resources to implement the plan.
3. *Command*—to lead, select, and evaluate workers to get the best work toward the plan.
4. *Coordination*—to fit diverse efforts together and to ensure information is shared and problems solved.
5. *Control*—to make sure things happen according to plan and to take necessary corrective action.

Importantly, Fayol believed that management could be taught. He was very concerned about improving the quality of management and set forth a number of "principles" to guide managerial action. A number of them are still part of the management vocabulary. They include Fayol's *scalar chain principle*—there should be a clear and unbroken line of communication from the top to the bottom in the organization; the *unity of command principle*—each person should receive orders from only one boss; and the *unity of direction principle*—one person should be in charge of all activities that have the same performance objective.

INSIGHTS

Practice Makes Perfect

"Googol" is a mathematical term standing for the number 1 followed by 100 zeros. That's a real big number. It's also symbolic of the reach and impact achieved by Google. The firm's origins trace to the day when Larry Page and Sergey Brin met as students at Stanford University. Their conversations led to collaboration on a search engine they called BackRub. It became so popular on campus that they kept refining and expanding the service as they worked in Larry's dormitory room.

> *Just as a Google search churns through billions of Web sites, Google's founders and staffers strive to learn from past experience and apply their expertise to continuously improving the company. Google couldn't have been created without the knowledge made available by the full history of research and development in computer science.*

Google Inc. was hatched in 1998 with this goal: "to organize the information overload of the Internet in a transparent and superior way." It hasn't stopped running, or growing, since. The Google mission is now described as: "To organize the world's information and make it universally accessible and useful." And if want to talk about success, take a look at its corporate information and stock price.

What is the Google difference? How did it gain such runaway popularity? The answer is performance excellence based on speed, accuracy, and ease of use. These have been the guiding performance criteria from the beginning, the basis for generating user appeal and competitive advantage in the marketplace. Page and Brin want to create a "perfect search engine" that "understands exactly what you mean and gives you back exactly what you want," says Page. With such goals, talent and motivation drive the system.

In the continuing search for innovation, the firm sticks to its historical roots—an informal culture with a small-company feel. At Google creative and happy people, diverse in backgrounds, skills, and interests, come together to build an ever-better search engine. The company Websites describe its approach to talent this way: "Google's hiring policy is aggressively non-discriminatory, and favors ability over experience. The result is a staff that reflects the global audience the search engine serves. Many different languages are spoken by Google staffers—from Turkish to Telugu. Outside of the office, 'Googlers' pursue interests from cross-country cycling to wine tasting, from flying to Frisbee."

BUREAUCRATIC ORGANIZATION

Max Weber was a late–19th-century German intellectual whose insights have had a major impact on the field of management and the sociology of organizations. His ideas developed somewhat in reaction to what he considered to be performance deficiencies in the organizations of his day. Among other things, Weber was concerned that people were in positions of authority not because of their job-related capabilities, but because of their social standing or "privileged" status in German society. For this and other reasons, he believed that organizations largely failed to reach their performance potential.

At the heart of Weber's thinking was a specific form of organization he believed could correct the problems just described—a **bureaucracy**.[15] For him it was an ideal, intentionally rational, and very efficient form of organization founded on principles of logic, order, and legitimate authority. The defining characteristics of Weber's bureaucratic organization are as follows:

■ A **bureaucracy** is a rational and efficient form of organization founded on logic, order, and legitimate authority.

- *Clear division of labor:* Jobs are well defined, and workers become highly skilled at performing them.
- *Clear hierarchy of authority:* Authority and responsibility are well defined for each position, and each position reports to a higher-level one.
- *Formal rules and procedures:* Written guidelines direct behavior and decisions in jobs, and written files are kept for historical record.
- *Impersonality:* Rules and procedures are impartially and uniformly applied, with no one receiving preferential treatment.
- *Careers based on merit:* Workers are selected and promoted on ability and performance, and managers are career employees of the organization.

Weber believed that organizations would perform well as bureaucracies. They would have the advantages of efficiency in utilizing resources and of fairness or equity in the treatment of employees and clients. In his words:[16]

> *The purely bureaucratic type of administrative organization . . . is, from a purely technical point of view, capable of attaining the highest degree of efficiency . . . . It is superior to any other form in precision, in stability, in the stringency of its discipline, and in its reliability. It thus makes possible a particularly high degree of calculability of results for the heads of the organization and for those acting in relation to it. It is finally superior both in intensive efficiency and in the scope of its operations and is formally capable of application to all kinds of administrative tasks.*

This is the ideal side of bureaucracy. However, the terms "bureaucracy" and "bureaucrat" are now often used with negative connotations. The *possible disadvantages of bureaucracy* include excessive paperwork or "red tape," slowness in handling problems, rigidity in the face of shifting customer or client needs, resistance to change, and employee apathy. These disadvantages are most likely to cause problems for organizations that must be flexible and quick in adapting to changing circumstances—a common situation today. Current trends in management include many innovations that seek the same goals as Weber but with different approaches to how organizations can be structured.

Learning Check 1

Be sure you can ■ list the principles of Taylor's scientific management ■ list three of Fayol's "principles" for guiding managerial action ■ list the key characteristics of bureaucracy and explain why Weber considered it an ideal form of organization ■ identify possible disadvantages of bureaucracy in today's environment

BEHAVIORAL MANAGEMENT APPROACHES

During the 1920s an emphasis on the human side of the workplace began to influence management thinking. Major branches in the behavioral or human resource approaches to management are shown in *Figure 3.2*. They include Follett's notion of organizations as communities, the famous Hawthorne studies and Maslow's theory of human needs, as well as theories generated from these foundations by Douglas McGregor, Chris Argyris, and others. The behavioral approaches maintain that people are social and self-actualizing. People at work are assumed to seek satisfying social relationships, respond to group pressures, and search for personal fulfillment.

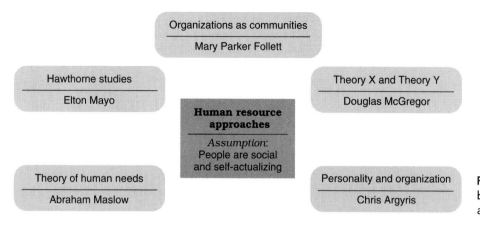

Figure 3.2 Foundations in the behavioral or human resource approaches to management.

FOLLETT ON ORGANIZATIONS AS COMMUNITIES

The work of Mary Parker Follett, briefly mentioned earlier, was part of an important transition from classical thinking into behavioral management. She was eulogized upon her death in 1933 as "one of the most important women America has yet produced in the fields of civics and sociology."[17]

In her writings, Follett views organizations as "communities" in which managers and workers should labor in harmony, without one party dominating the other and with the freedom to talk over and truly reconcile conflicts and differences. For her, groups were mechanisms through which diverse individuals could combine their talents for a greater good. And she believed it was the manager's job to help people in organizations cooperate with one another and achieve an integration of interests.

Follett's emphasis on groups and her commitment to human cooperation are still highly relevant themes today.[18] Follett believed that making every employee an owner in a business would create feelings of collective responsibility. *Today,* we address the same issues under such labels as "employee ownership," "profit sharing," and "gainsharing plans." Follett believed that business problems involve a wide variety of factors that must be considered in relationship to one another. *Today,* we talk about "systems" when describing the same phenomenon. Follett believed that businesses were services and that private profits should always be considered vis-a-vis the public good. *Today,* we pursue the same issues under the labels "managerial ethics" and "corporate social responsibility."

THE HAWTHORNE STUDIES

In 1924 the Western Electric Company commissioned a research program to study individual productivity at the Hawthorne Works of the firm's Chicago plant.[19] The initial "Hawthorne studies" had a scientific management perspective and sought to determine how economic incentives and the physical conditions of the workplace affected the output of workers. An initial focus was on the level of illumination in the manufacturing facilities; it seemed reasonable to expect that better lighting would improve performance. After failing to find this relationship, however, the researchers concluded that unforeseen "psychological factors" somehow interfered with their illumination experiments. This finding and later Hawthorne studies directed research attention toward human interactions in the workplace and ultimately had a major influence on the field of management.

ISSUES AND SITUATIONS

Management Candor

To: Sales Team List
From: Heather
Subject: Management Training Workshop

Dear Team Members:

We have scheduled a management development workshop for Thursday of next week. It will be a half-day session (1–4:30 P.M.) in the 4th floor seminar room for our entire sales management team.

I apologize for the short notice but it is the only day this month that we could get Prof. Holbrook from Corporate U to be with us. His reputation is really great, and we're hoping that the workshop will stimulate everyone to work together and really improve our managerial performance.

Prof. Holbrook wants everyone, including me, as national sales manager, to do the preworkshop homework attached to this e-mail. I'm sure you can identify with this. Be sure to bring your responses to his questions on Thursday.

I'm looking forward to the workshop and hope you will also. Thanks. /electronically signed Heather

Critical Response

Answer the activity questions based on your own personal experiences, and about managers for whom you have actually worked. Then, consider the differences between the two lists. How well do your lists fit what might be predicted by management theories?

Preworkshop Activity: "My Best Manager"

Think back to all the managers you have worked for in your career. Make a list of behaviors and characteristics that answer the following questions:

1. *What are the things that describe your "best" manager?*

2. *What are the things that describe your "worst" manager?*

Now assume Heather is the manager of your sales management team. The lists you just prepared may be perceived as reflecting on her.

- Would you have any reservations about sharing your lists in open discussion with Heather and other members of the sales team?

- Put yourself in Heather's shoes. As Heather, how would you take items on team members' "worst" manager lists as personal criticisms?

- Be the professor and consultant. What could you do to conduct this management workshop to make sure that it is positive and developmental for everyone?

Relay Assembly Test-Room Studies

A team led by Harvard's Elton Mayo began more research to examine the effect of worker fatigue on output. Care was taken to design a scientific test that would be free of the psychological effects thought to have confounded the earlier illumination studies. Six workers who assembled relays were isolated for intensive study in a special test room. They were given various rest pauses, as well as workdays and workweeks of various lengths, and production was regularly measured. Once again, researchers failed to find any direct relationship between changes in physical working conditions and output. Productivity increased regardless of the changes made.

Mayo and his colleagues concluded that the new "social setting" created for workers in the test room accounted for the increased productivity. Two factors were singled out as having special importance. One was the *group atmosphere*; the workers shared pleasant social relations with one another and wanted to do a good job. The other was more *participative supervision*. Test-room workers were made to feel important, were given a lot of information, and frequently were asked for their opinions. This was not the case in their regular jobs back in the plant.

Employee Attitudes, Interpersonal Relations, and Group Processes

Mayo's research continued until the worsening economic conditions of the Depression forced their termination in 1932. By then, interest in the human factor had broadened to include employee attitudes, interpersonal relations, and group dynamics. In one study over 21,000 employees were interviewed to learn what they liked and disliked about their work environment. "Complex" and "baffling" results led the researchers to conclude that the same things (e.g., work conditions or wages) could be sources of satisfaction for some workers and of dissatisfaction for others.

The final Hawthorne study was conducted in the bank wiring room and centered on the role of the work group. A surprise finding here was that people would restrict their output in order to avoid the displeasure of the group, even if it meant sacrificing pay that could otherwise be earned by increasing output. The researchers concluded that groups can have strong negative, as well as positive, influences on individual productivity.

> ■ The **Hawthorne effect** is the tendency of persons singled out for special attention to perform as expected.
>
> ■ The **human relations movement** suggested that managers using good human relations will achieve productivity.
>
> ■ **Organizational behavior** is the study of individuals and groups in organizations.

Lessons of the Hawthorne Studies

As scholars now look back, the Hawthorne studies are criticized for poor research design, weak empirical support for the conclusions drawn, and the tendency of researchers to overgeneralize their findings.[20] Yet their significance as turning points in the evolution of management thought remains intact. The studies helped shift the attention of managers and researchers away from the technical and structural concerns of the classical approach and toward social and human concerns as keys to productivity. They brought visibility to the notions that people's feelings, attitudes, and relationships with coworkers affected their work, and that groups were important influences on individuals. They also identified the **Hawthorne effect**—the tendency of people who are singled out for special attention to perform as anticipated because of expectations created by the situation.

The Hawthorne studies contributed to the emergence of the **human relations movement,** which influenced management thinking during the 1950s and 1960s. This movement was largely based on the viewpoint that managers who used good human relations in the workplace would achieve productivity. Importantly, this movement set the stage for what evolved into the field of **organizational behavior,** the study of individuals and groups in organizations.

MASLOW'S THEORY OF HUMAN NEEDS

The work of psychologist Abraham Maslow in the area of human "needs" has had a major impact on management.[21] He described a **need** as a physiological or psychological deficiency a person feels the compulsion to satisfy, suggesting that needs create tensions that can influence a person's work attitudes and behaviors. He also placed needs in the five levels shown in *Figure 3.3.* From lowest to highest in order, they are physiological, safety, social, esteem, and self-actualization needs.

> ■ A **need** is a physiological or psychological deficiency that a person wants to satisfy.

According to Maslow, people try to satisfy the five needs in sequence. They progress step by step from the lowest level in the hierarchy up to the highest. Along the way, a deprived need dominates individual attention and determines behavior until it is satisfied. Then, the next-higher-level need is activated. At the level of self-actualization, the deficit and progression principles cease to operate. The more this need is satisfied, the stronger it grows.

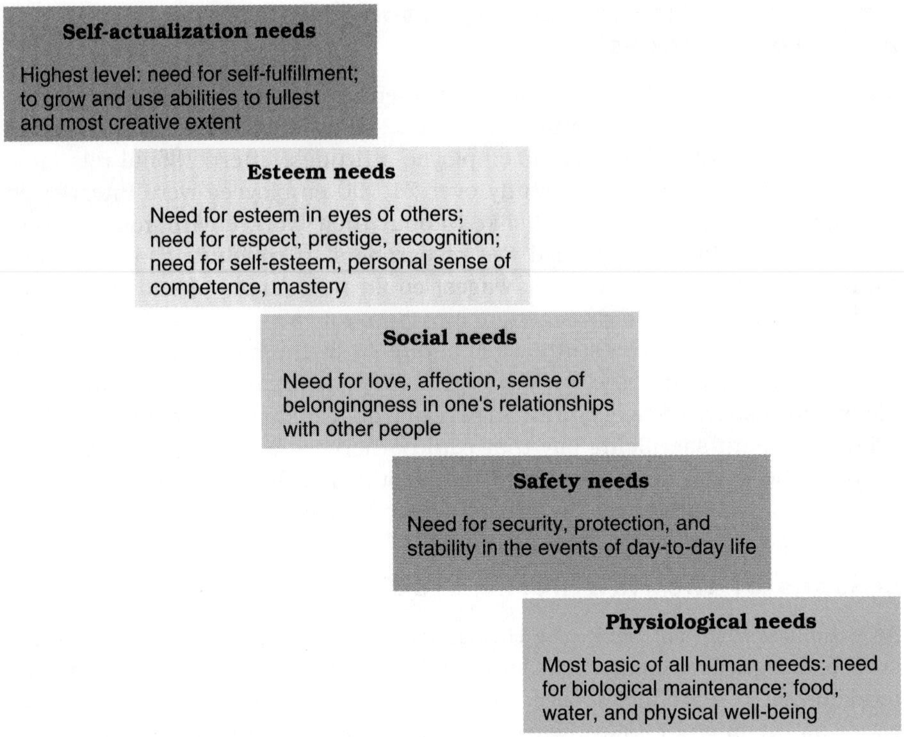

Figure 3.3 Maslow's hierarchy of human needs.

Maslow's theory is based on two underlying principles. The first is the *deficit principle*—a satisfied need is not a motivator of behavior. People act to satisfy "deprived" needs, those for which a satisfaction "deficit" exists. The second is the *progression principle*—the five needs exist in a hierarchy of "prepotency." A need at any level is only activated when the next-lower-level need is satisfied.

Consistent with human relations thinking, Maslow's theory implies that managers who understand and help people satisfy their important needs at work will achieve productivity. Although scholars now recognize that things are more complicated than this, Maslow's ideas are still relevant. Consider, for example, the case of volunteer workers who do not receive any monetary compensation. Managers in nonprofit organizations have to create jobs and work environments that satisfy the many different needs of volunteers. If their work isn't fulfilling, the volunteers will lose interest and probably redirect their efforts elsewhere.

MCGREGOR'S THEORY X AND THEORY Y

Douglas McGregor was heavily influenced by both the Hawthorne studies and Maslow. His classic book, *The Human Side of Enterprise*, advances the thesis that managers should give more attention to the social and self-actualizing needs of people at work.[22] McGregor called upon managers to shift their view of human nature away from a set of assumptions he called "Theory X" and toward ones he called "Theory Y."

According to McGregor, managers holding **Theory X** assumptions approach their jobs believing that those who work for them generally dislike work, lack ambition, are irresponsible, are resistant to change, and prefer to be led rather than to lead. McGregor considers such thinking inappropriate. He argues instead for the value of **Theory Y** assumptions, in which the manager believes people are willing to work, are capable of self-control, are

■ **Theory X** assumes people dislike work, lack ambition, are irresponsible, and prefer to be led.

■ **Theory Y** assumes people are willing to work, accept responsibility, and are self-directed and creative.

KAFFEEKLATSCH

Why Get an MBA?

First Cup

"I've been out of college now for three years. A lot of my friends are either starting MBA programs or talking about the possibility. So, I've been thinking about it also. But, I'm doing pretty well here—two promotions in 3 years, and an MBA would be costly both financially and in lost career time."

Studying the Grounds

In the article "Is the MBA Overrated?" *Business Week* reports:

■ In a study of 500 top executives at S&P companies, only 146 had MBAs.

■ Executives with MBAs outearn their non-MBA counterparts; the MBA "pay premium" is +19 percent.

■ Only 1 out of 4,000 graduates of top-tier MBA programs ranked among the highest-paid executives.

Double Espresso

"That *Business Week* article is offering up good food for thought. Perhaps the notion that just having an MBA will guarantee a pathway to the top slots and to the top pay is false. Maybe the decision to pursue an MBA or not should be made on other grounds. I guess the real questions for

me might be these: What doors would an MBA open that aren't otherwise available to me? What can I learn in an MBA that would help me grow professionally and personally in ways that I can be proud of?"

"By the way, here's two interesting cases from the same article."

■ David K. Zweiner graduated with a master's from Northwestern University's Kellogg School of Management. Even though he became an executive VP at Hartford Financial Services Group Inc., he says: "[An MBA] opens the first door for you. After that it's up to you."

■ Peter D. Crist, head of the executive search firm Crist Associates, says this about executive success: "Pedigrees mean nothing. It's instinct, it's hard work and it's raw intelligence."

Your Turn

Without a doubt, the decision whether or not to pursue an MBA is a big one. There are lots of personal issues involved, including questions of personal and family sacrifice, as well as potential career gains. There's also the choice of what type of MBA program is best for you: full-time, part-time, or executive? And then there's the question of how much institutional prestige counts; must you go to a top-tier school in order to benefit from an MBA?

---

willing to accept responsibility, are imaginative and creative, and are capable of self-direction.

An important aspect of McGregor's ideas is his belief that managers who hold either set of assumptions can create **self-fulfilling prophecies**—that is, through their behavior they create situations where others act in ways that confirm the original expectations. *Managers with Theory X assumptions*, for example, act in a very directive "command-and-control" fashion that gives people little personal say over their work. These supervisory behaviors create passive, dependent, and reluctant subordinates, who tend to do only what they are told to or required to do. This reinforces the original Theory X viewpoint.

In contrast, *managers with Theory Y perspectives* behave in "participative" ways that allow subordinates more job involvement, freedom, and responsibility. This creates opportunities to satisfy esteem and self-actualization needs, and workers tend to perform as expected with initiative and high performance. The self-fulfilling prophecy thus becomes a positive one. Theory Y thinking is consistent with developments in the new workplace and its emphasis on valuing workforce diversity. It is also central to the popular notions of employee participation, involvement, empowerment, and self-management.[23]

A **self-fulfilling prophecy** occurs when a person acts in ways that confirm another's expectations.

ARGYRIS'S THEORY OF ADULT PERSONALITY

Ideas set forth by the well-regarded scholar and consultant Chris Argyris also reflect the belief in human nature advanced by Maslow and McGregor. In his book *Personality and Organization*, Argyris contrasts the management practices found in traditional and hierarchical organizations with the needs and capabilities of mature adults.[24] He concludes that some practices, especially those influenced by the classical management approaches, are inconsistent with the mature adult personality.

Consider these examples. In scientific management, the principle of specialization assumes that people will work more efficiently as tasks become better defined. Argyris believes that this may inhibit self-actualization in the workplace. In Weber's bureaucracy, people work in a clear hierarchy of authority, with higher levels directing and controlling lower levels. Argyris worries that this creates dependent, passive workers who feel they have little control over their work environments. In Fayol's administrative principles, the concept of unity of direction assumes that efficiency will increase when a person's work is planned and directed by a supervisor. Argyris suggests that this may create conditions for psychological failure; conversely, psychological success occurs when people define their own goals.

Like McGregor, Argyris believes that managers who treat people positively and as responsible adults will achieve the highest productivity. His advice is to expand job responsibilities, allow more task variety, and adjust supervisory styles to allow more participation and promote better human relations. He believes that the common problems of employee absenteeism, turnover, apathy, alienation, and low morale may be signs of a mismatch between management practices and mature adult personalities.

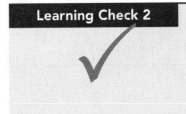

Learning Check 2

Be sure you can ■ explain Follett's concept of organizations as communities ■ define the term Hawthorne effect ■ explain how the Hawthorne findings influenced the development of management thought ■ explain how Maslow's hierarchy of needs operates in the workplace ■ distinguish between Theory X and Theory Y assumptions, and explain why McGregor favored Theory Y ■ explain Argyris's criticism that traditional organizational practices are inconsistent with mature adult personalities

MODERN MANAGEMENT FOUNDATIONS

The concepts, models, and many accumulating insights discussed so far helped set the stage for continuing developments in management thought. The many themes reflected throughout *Management 9/e* build from foundations that include the use of quantitative techniques, a systems view of organizations, use of contingency thinking, commitment to quality and focus on high performance, and the importance of learning organizations.

DECISION SCIENCES AND OPERATIONS MANAGEMENT

About the same time that some scholars were developing human resource approaches to management, others were investigating how quantitative techniques could improve managerial decision making. The foundation of these analytical decision sciences approaches is the assumption that mathematical techniques can be used for better problem solving. Today these applications are increasingly supported and driven by computer technology and software programs.

The terms *management science* and *operations research* are often used interchangeably to describe the scientific applications of mathematical techniques to management problems. A typical quantitative approach proceeds as follows. A problem is encountered, it is systematically analyzed, appropriate mathematical models and computations are applied, and an optimum solution is identified. There are a variety of management science applications that can be used in this way.

Mathematical forecasting helps make future projections that are useful in the planning process. *Inventory modeling* helps control inventories by mathematically establishing how much to order and when. *Linear programming* is used to calculate how best to allocate scarce resources among competing uses. *Queuing theory* helps allocate service personnel or workstations to minimize customer waiting time and service cost. *Network models* break large tasks into smaller components to allow for better analysis, planning, and control of complex projects, *Simulations* create models of problems so different solutions under various assumptions can be tested.

An important counterpart to the management science approaches is **operations management** which focuses on how organizations produce goods and services efficiently and effectively. The emphasis is on the study and improvement of operations, the transformation process through which goods and services are actually created. As discussed in Chapter 19 on operations management and services, the applications include such things as business process analysis, workflow designs, facilities layouts and locations, work scheduling and project management, production planning, inventory management, and quality control.

▪ **Operations management** is the study of how organizations produce goods and services.

REAL ETHICS

Employment Agreements

Nelsonville, Ohio—Rocky Brands chief executive Mike Brooks announced that his company had filed a suit in Athens County Common Pleas Court against Joe P. Marciante, former regional vice president for sales. Marciante had resigned from Rocky and Brooks believed Marciante was going to work for a competitor, Ariat International of Union City, California.

The suit claims Marciante is in violation of a noncompete agreement he had signed, stipulating he would not go to work for a competitor for one year after leaving Rocky Brands. The court is being asked to enforce the one-year waiting period and require that Marciante return all materials in his possession that provide inside information on Rocky Brands. Rocky also seeks $25,000 in compensatory damages.

Marciante's attorney says: "Right now, we're involved in a concerted effort to settle."

FURTHER INQUIRY

What ethics message does this case send? Assuming that the facts are as stated in this case, is Marciante justified in taking a sales job with Ariat? Is Mike Brooks doing the right thing in filing a lawsuit against him? Are there any other ways that this situation could be handled and still protect Rocky's interests?

Noncompete and nondisclosure agreements are increasingly common in today's knowledge-driven economy. Chances are that you will be asked to sign one someday. Share this case with your friends, co-workers, and family; ask for their views and even their personal experiences. What advice about employment agreements is available from the professionals, perhaps from your college or campus placement services?

■ **Total quality management** is a process of making a commitment to quality part of all operations.

Within operations management, the term **total quality management** (TQM) describes a process of applying quality principles to all aspects of operations and striving to meet customers' needs by doing things right the first time. Quality is emphasized right from resource acquisition and supply chain management through production processes and into the distribution of finished goods and services. This commitment to quality involves an emphasis on **continuous improvement**—always looking for new ways to improve on current performance. The notion is that one can never be satisfied; something always can and should be improved on.

■ **Continuous improvement** is a process of always looking for new ways to improve.

ORGANIZATIONS AS SYSTEMS

■ A **system** is a collection of interrelated parts working together for a purpose.

One of the centerpoints of operations management is understanding an organization as a **system**, a collection of interrelated parts that function together to achieve a common purpose. This includes the roles of subsystems, or smaller components of a larger system.[25]

One of the earliest management writers to adopt a systems perspective was Chester Barnard. His 1938 ground-breaking book, *Functions of the Executive*, was based on years of experience as a telephone company executive.[26] Like Mary Parker Follett, Barnard described organizations as cooperative systems that achieve great things by integrating the contributions of many individuals to achieve a common purpose. Importantly, Barnard considered cooperation a "conscious, deliberate, and purposeful" feature of organizations. He believed an executive's primary responsibility was to use communication to make this cooperation happen.

■ An **open system** interacts with its environment and transforms resource inputs into outputs.

Figure 3.4 builds on the systems view of organizations described in Chapter 1. It first depicts the larger organization as an **open system** that interacts with its environment in the continual process of transforming inputs from suppliers into outputs for customers. Within the total system of the organization, any number of critical subsystems take part in the transformation process. In the figure, the operations and service management subsystems are a central point. They provide the integration among other subsystems, such as purchasing, accounting, sales, and information, that are essential to the work of the organization. Importantly, and as suggested by Barnard, high performance by the organization as a whole occurs only when each subsystem both performs its tasks well and works well in cooperation with

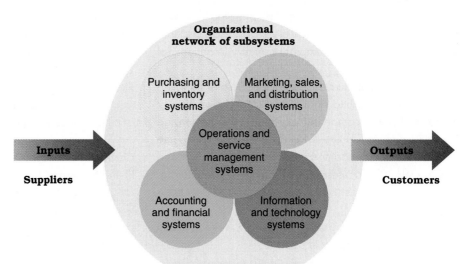

Figure 3.4 Organizations as complex networks of interacting subsystems.

others. It is the job of managers throughout the organization to make this coordinated action possible.

CONTINGENCY THINKING

Modern management is situational in orientation; that is, it attempts to identify practices that are the best fit with the unique demands of a situation. It utilizes **contingency thinking** that tries to match managerial responses with the problems and opportunities specific to different settings, particularly those posed by individual and environmental differences. In modern management approaches, there is no expectation that one can or should find the "one best way" to manage in all circumstances. Rather, the contingency perspective tries to help managers understand situational differences and respond to them in ways appropriate to their unique characteristics.[27]

■ **Contingency thinking** tries to match management practices with situational demands.

Contingency thinking is an important theme in this book, and its implications extend to all of the management functions—from planning and controlling for diverse environmental conditions, to organizing for different strategies, to leading in different performance situations. Consider again the concept of bureaucracy. Weber offered it as an ideal form of organization. But from a contingency perspective, the strict bureaucratic form is only one possible way of organizing things. What turns out to be the "best" structure in any given situation will depend on many factors, including environmental uncertainty, an organization's primary technology, and the strategy being pursued. The strict bureaucracy works best only when the environment is relatively stable and operations are predictable. In other situations, alternative and more flexible structures are needed.

HIGH-PERFORMANCE ORGANIZATIONS

A book published by Tom Peters and Robert Waterman in 1982, *In Search of Excellence: Lessons from America's Best-Run Companies*, helped kindle research interest in the attributes of organizations that achieve performance excellence.[28] Peters and Waterman highlighted things like "closeness to customers," "bias toward action," "simple form and lean staff," and "productivity through people."

■ A **high-performance organization** consistently achieves excellence while creating a high-quality work environment.

Today we have moved beyond these generalized impressions of excellence to talk more specifically about the characteristics of **high-performance organizations**—ones that consistently achieve high-performance results while also creating high quality-of-work-life environments for their employees.[29] High-performance organizations are often described as:

- *People oriented*—they value people as human assets, respect diversity, empower members to fully use their talents, and are high in employee involvement.
- *Team oriented*—they achieve synergy through teamwork, emphasize collaboration and group decisions, and allow teams to be self-directing.
- *Information oriented*—they mobilize the latest information technologies to link people and information for creative problem-solving.
- *Achievement oriented*—they are focused on the needs of customers and stakeholders, and committed to quality operations and continuous improvement.
- *Learning oriented*—they operate with an internal culture that respects and facilitates learning, innovation, and constructive change.

RESEARCH BRIEF

The great companies make the leap from doing good to doing great, while the others do not

That's one of the messages in Jim Collins's best-selling book *Good to Great*. He opens the book with this sentence: "Good is the enemy of great." He goes on to describe an extensive study that compares companies that had moved to and then sustained "great" performance in cumulative stock returns over a 15-year period with those that hadn't. The study started by examining the records of 1,435 companies; only 11 made the final cut, joining the good-to-great set. The basic question addressed by Collins and his team of 21 researchers was "What did the good-to-great companies share in common that distinguishes them from the comparison companies?"

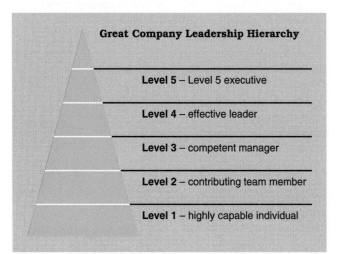

Great Company Leadership Hierarchy

Level 5 – Level 5 executive
Level 4 – effective leader
Level 3 – competent manager
Level 2 – contributing team member
Level 1 – highly capable individual

One of the major findings was that great companies demonstrate a unique form of leadership that Collins calls "Level 5." He says it is *not* leadership by celebrity, or leadership driven by compensation, or leadership based on a perfect strategy. Rather, Level 5 leadership *is focused on people*—getting the right people in, getting the wrong ones out; *ambitious*—wanting the best for the company and for the long term; *resolute*—showing a determination to succeed in creating a great firm; *modest*—not taking personal credit but recognizing the contributions of others. Collins summarizes it as a combination of personal will and humility, stating that Level 5 leaders want to build "something larger and more lasting than themselves." While the comparison leaders were seeking fame, fortune, and power, the great company leaders were trying to create and contribute.

QUESTIONS & APPLICATIONS

Collins and his team studied highly successful businesses. Would their findings on Level 5 leadership hold true in government or in nonprofit organizations? Is Level 5 leadership alone sufficient to create long-term organizational greatness? Identify organizations in your community that have reputations for great performance. Conduct your own study: interview the leaders and samples of persons working in one or more of these organizations. See how well they fit Collins's model.

Reference: Jim Collins, *Good to Great: Why Some Companies Make the Leap . . . and Others Don't* (New York: Harper Business, 2001).

LEARNING ORGANIZATIONS

■ A **learning organization** continuously changes and improves, using the lessons of experience.

Along with the high-performance focus, the change and uncertainty in today's environment have given rise to an emphasis on creating **learning organizations.** These organizations are able to continually learn and adapt to new circumstances. They become successful because they are uniquely capable of improving themselves by learning from experience.

Consultant Peter Senge popularized the concept of the learning organization in his book *The Fifth Discipline*, and he identifies the following as its core ingredients:[30]

1. Mental models—everyone sets aside old ways of thinking.
2. Personal mastery—everyone becomes self-aware and open to others.
3. Systems thinking—everyone learns how the whole organization works.
4. Shared vision—everyone understands and agrees to a plan of action.
5. Team learning—everyone works together to accomplish the plan.

Organizations that meet Senge's criteria for learning organizations offer work settings in which members develop their abilities to learn and are encouraged to make that learning continuously available to everyone else. They have value-driven organizational cultures that emphasize information sharing, teamwork, empowerment, participation, and learning. Importantly, the leaders of learning organizations set an example by embracing change and communicating enthusiasm for solving problems and growing with new opportunities.

Be sure you can ■ ■ define the terms system, subsystem, and open system ■ apply these concepts to describe the operations of an organization in your community ■ define the term contingency thinking ■ explain how contingency thinking might influence a manager's decision to use or not use a bureaucratic approach to organization structure ■ list characteristics of high-performance organizations and of learning organizations	**Learning Check 3** ✓

CHAPTER 3 STUDY GUIDE

STUDY QUESTIONS SUMMARY

1 What can be learned from classical management thinking?

■ Frederick Taylor's four principles of scientific management focused on the need to carefully select, train, and support workers for individual task performance.

■ Henri Fayol suggested that managers should learn what are now known as the management functions of planning, organizing, leading, and controlling.

■ Max Weber described bureaucracy with its clear hierarchy, formal rules, and well-defined jobs as an ideal form of organization.

2 What insights come from the behavioral management approaches?

■ The behavioral approaches to human resource shifted management attention toward the human factor as a key element in organizational performance.

■ Mary Parker Follett describes organizations as communities within which people combined talents to work for a greater good.

■ The Hawthorne studies suggested that work behavior is influenced by social and psychological forces and that work performance may be improved by better "human relations."

■ Abraham Maslow's hierarchy of human needs introduced the concept of self-actualization and the potential for people to experience self-fulfillment in their work.

■ Douglas McGregor urged managers to shift away from Theory X and toward Theory Y thinking, which views people as independent, responsible, and capable of self-direction in their work.

■ Chris Argyris pointed out that people in the workplace are adults and may react negatively when constrained by strict management practices and rigid organizational structures.

3 What are the foundations of modern management thinking?

■ Advanced quantitative techniques in decision sciences and operations management can help managers solve complex problems.

■ Organizations are complex open systems that interact with their external environments to transform resource inputs into product outputs.

■ Organizations are composed of many internal subsystems that must work together in a coordinated way to support the organization's overall success.

■ Contingency thinking avoids "one best way" arguments, recognizing the need to understand situational differences and respond appropriately to them.

■ High-performance organizations are able to consistently achieve excellent results while creating high-quality work environments for their members.

■ Changing times place great value on learning organizations, ones that are able to continually learn and adapt themselves to changing circumstances.

KEY TERMS REVIEW

Bureaucracy (p. 63)
Contingency thinking (p. 73)
Continuous improvement (p. 72)
Hawthorne effect (p. 67)
High-performance organization
  (p. 73)
Human relations movement (p. 67)

Learning organization (p. 74)
Motion study (p. 62)
Need (p. 67)
Open system (p. 72)
Operations management (p. 71)
Organizational behavior (p. 67)

Scientific management (p. 61)
Self-fulfilling prophecies (p. 69)
System (p. 72)
Theory X (p. 68)
Theory Y (p. 68)
Total quality management (p. 72)

SELF-TEST 3

MULTIPLE-CHOICE QUESTIONS:

1. The assumption that people are complex with widely varying needs is most associated with the _____ management approaches.
   (a) classical   (b) neoclassical   (c) behavioral   (d) modern

2. The father of scientific management is _____.
   (a) Weber   (b) Taylor   (c) Mintzberg   (d) Katz

3. When the registrar of a university deals with students by an identification number rather than a name, which characteristic of bureaucracy is being displayed and what is its intended benefit?
   (a) division of labor . . . competency   (b) merit-based careers . . . productivity   (c) rules and procedures . . . efficiency   (d) impersonality . . . fairness

4. If an organization was performing poorly and Henri Fayol was called in as a consultant, what would he most advise as a way to improve things?
   (a) teach managers to better plan and control   (b) teach workers more efficient job methods   (c) promote to management only the most competent workers   (d) find ways to increase corporate social responsibility

5. One example of how scientific management principles are applied in organizations today would be:
   (a) a results-based compensation system   (b) a bureaucratic structure   (c) training in how to better understand worker attitudes   (d) focus on groups and teamwork rather than individual tasks

6. The Hawthorne studies are important because they raised awareness of the important influences of _____ on productivity.
   (a) structures   (b) human factors   (c) physical work conditions   (d) pay and rewards

7. Advice to study a job and carefully train workers to do that job with financial incentives tied to job performance would most likely come from _____.
   (a) scientific management   (b) contingency management   (c) Henri Fayol   (d) Abraham Maslow

8. The highest level in Maslow's hierarchy is the level of _____ needs.
   (a) safety   (b) esteem   (c) self-actualization   (d) physiological

9. Conflict between the mature adult personality and a rigid organization was a major concern of _____.
   (a) Argyris   (b) Follett   (c) Gantt   (d) Fuller

10. When people perform in a situation as they are expected to, this is sometimes called the _____ effect.
    (a) Hawthorne   (b) systems   (c) contingency   (d) open-systems

11. Resource acquisition and customer satisfaction are important when an organization is viewed as a(n) _____.
    (a) bureaucracy   (b) closed system   (c) open system   (d) pyramid

12. When your local bank or credit union is viewed as an open system, the loan-processing department would be considered a _____.
    (a) subsystem   (b) closed system   (c) resource input   (d) value center

13. When a manager notices that Sheryl has strong social needs and assigns her a job in customer relations, while also being sure to give Kwabena lots of praise because of his strong ego needs, the manager is displaying _____.
    (a) systems thinking   (b) Theory X   (c) motion study   (d) contingency thinking

14. In a learning organization, as described by Peter Senge, one would expect to find _____.

(a) priority placed on following rules and procedures (b) promotions based on seniority (c) employees who are willing to set aside old thinking and embrace new ways (d) a strict hierarchy of authority

15. The key outcomes of high-performance organizations are both consistent high performance and _____.

(a) reliance on motion studies (b) high-quality work life environments (c) effective cost controls (d) Theory X management

SHORT-RESPONSE QUESTIONS:

16. Explain how McGregor's Theory Y assumptions can create self-fulfilling prophecies consistent with the current emphasis on participation and involvement in the workplace.
17. How do the deficit and progression principles operate in Maslow's hierarchy-of-needs theory?
18. Define contingency thinking and give an example of how it might apply to management.
19. Explain why the external environment is so important in the open-systems view of organizations.

APPLICATION QUESTION:

20. Enrique Temoltzin has just been appointed the new manager of your local college bookstore. Enrique would like to make sure the store operates according to Weber's bureaucracy. Describe the characteristics of bureaucracy and answer this question: is the bureaucracy a good management approach for Enrique to follow? Discuss the possible limitations of bureaucracy and the implications for managing people as key assets of the store.

CHAPTER 3 APPLICATIONS

CASE 3

Apple Computer, Inc.: People and Design Create Apple's Future

Apple Computer paradoxically exists as both one of America's greatest successes and one of its greatest failures to achieve potential. It ignited the personal computer industry in the 1970s,[31] bringing such behemoths as IBM and Digital Equipment almost to their knees. At the same time, the history of Apple demonstrates opportunities lost. It represents a fascinating microcosm of American business as it continues to utilize its strengths while reinventing itself.

Corporate History

The history of Apple Computer is a history of passion among its founders, employees, and loyal users.[32] A pair of Stevens, who from an early age had an interest in electronics, started it. Steven Wozniak and Steven Jobs initially utilized their skills at Hewlett Packard and Atari, respectively. Wozniak constructed his first personal computer, the Apple 1, and, along with Jobs, created Apple Computer on April 1, 1976.

Early on, Apple Computer exhibited an extreme emphasis on new and innovative styling in its computer offerings. Jobs took a personal interest in the development of new products, including the Lisa and the legendary Macintosh, with its graphical interface and 3.5-inch floppy disk.

The passion that Apple is so famous for was clearly evident in the design of the Macintosh (Mac). Project teams worked around the clock to develop the machine and its graphical user interface (GUI) operating system (Mac OS), based loosely on a design developed by the Xerox Palo Alto Research Center. The use of graphical icons to create simplified user commands was an immensely popular alternative to the command-line structure of DOS.

When IBM entered the personal computer market, Jobs recognized the threat posed and realized that it was time for Apple to "grow up" and be run in a more business-like fashion. In early 1983, he persuaded John Sculley, then president of Pepsi-Cola, to join Apple as president. The two men clashed almost from the start, with Sculley eventually ousting Jobs from the company.

The launch of the Mac, with its increased speed from a Motorola chip and expandable hardware, reinvigorated Apple's sales. In tandem with the LaserWriter, the first affordable PostScript laser printer for the Mac, and Aldus's Pagemaker, one of the first desktop publishing programs, the Mac was an ideal solution for inexpensive publishing.

However, by the 1990s, IBM PCs and clones were saturating the personal computer market. In addition, Microsoft launched Windows 3.0, a greatly improved version of the Wintel operating system for use on IBM PCs and clones. While in 1991 Apple had contemplated licensing its Mac operating system to other

computer manufacturers and making it run on Intel-based machines, the idea was nixed by then chief operating officer (COO) Michael Spindler in a move that would ultimately give Windows the nod to dominate the market.

Innovative Design to the Rescue

Apple continued to rely on innovative design to remain competitive. In the 1990s, Apple introduced the very popular PowerBook notebook computer line, along with the unsuccessful Newton personal digital assistant. Sculley, having lost interest in the day-to-day operations of Apple, was eventually forced out and replaced with Michael Spindler.

Spindler oversaw a number of innovations, including the PowerMac family—the first Macs to be based on the PowerPC chip, an extremely fast processor that was co-developed with IBM and Motorola. The PowerPC processor allowed Macs to compete with, and in many cases surpass, the speed of Intel's competing processors. In addition, Apple finally licensed its operating system to a number of Mac-cloners, but never in significant numbers.

After a difficult time, Spindler was replaced with Gil Amelio, the former president of National Semiconductor. This set the stage for one of the most famous returns in corporate history.

Jobs's Return

After leaving Apple, Steven Jobs started NeXT computer, which produced an advanced personal computer with a sleek, innovative design. However, entering the market late in the game and requiring proprietary software, the device never gained a large

following. Jobs then co-founded Pixar computer-animation studios, which gained fame by co-producing a number of movies with Walt Disney Studios, including the popular *Toy Story*.[33]

In late 1996, Apple announced the purchase of NeXT and Jobs returned to Apple in an unofficial capacity as advisor to the president. However, when Gil Amelio resigned, Jobs accepted the role of "interim CEO" (iCEO) of Apple Computer and wasted no time in making his return felt.

Jobs announced an alliance with Apple's former rival, Microsoft. In exchange for $150 million in Apple stock, Microsoft and Apple would have a five-year patent cross-license for their graphical interface operating systems. He revoked licenses allowing the production of Mac clones and started offering Macs over the Web through the Apple Store.

In addition to many new product offerings, Jobs introduced the iMac, with a revolutionary see-through design that has proved popular among consumers through various incarnations. This was followed shortly by the iBook, a similarly-styled portable computer. Apple once again was viewed as an industry innovator by introducing a certifiably attractive—and powerful—line of computers at an entry-level price point.[34]

Yet Apple remains a relatively small player in the personal computer industry. While its computers are wildly popular among a dedicated set of users, it still commands only a little over 5 percent of the total computer market.

What Does the Future Hold?

Can Apple continue to offer both hardware and software solutions in a rapidly changing technology environment? Apple's early decision to keep its technology proprietary, as opposed to IBM's decision to support an open architecture system, has proved to be a costly strategy to support in the long run.

Some critics argued that Apple should reinvent itself once again, this time concentrating on software. It did just that, and then some—its operating system (OS X) and iLife software have proved immensely popular among die-hard enthusiasts and first-time users alike. And instead of trying to fight the Wintel system, Apple simply joined it: Its new line of Intel-based Macs are faster and more efficient than equivalently powered PCs, and the recent models can even run Windows XP with the help of software patches.

By doing so, Apple cleverly turned a computing axiom on its ear. When Windows licensed its operating system to multiple hardware vendors, Bill Gates stated that hardware was irrelevant, so long as you had the right OS. By introducing computers that run OS X and Windows with equal precision, Steve Jobs counters that the right hardware will run any OS.

Part of Apple's new corporate strategy, developed in the face of a massive slowdown in the technology industry, involves taking advantage of the explosion of personal electronic devices—CD players, MP3 players, digital cameras, DVD players, and so on—by initially building Mac-only applications that add value to those devices. Just as iMovie adds tremendous value to digital cameras, iDVD adds value to DVD players and iTunes adds value to CD and MP3 players. However, Apple recognizes the size of the PC market that is not being reached and has made iPod and iTunes into Windows-compatible products. In its first week, iTunes sold 1.5 million songs and captured 80 percent of the market share of legal music downloads.

It is Apple's hope that making its products the "digital hub" of the new "digital lifestyle" will revitalize Apple's sales and guarantee the company's long-term security. But can the Cupertino company retain its lead in the valuable music-player niche, especially with Microsoft's commitment to enter the market with a bang? And though Apple's designs are widely lauded by both critics and customers, will it ever earn a double-digit share of the desktop computer market? Hop online or stroll down to an Apple Store to get a taste of Apple's future.

REVIEW QUESTIONS

1. Why is Apple not a dominant provider of personal computers?
2. Was Apple's decision to use Intel processors, which allow the computers to run either Apple or Windows operating systems, a wise choice? Why or why not?
3. Where is Apple Computer company strong and weak in its operations as an open system?

TEAM PROJECT

Management in Popular Culture

Donald Trump's television show *The Apprentice* has gotten a fair amount of attention. It's not uncommon to find episodes being shown in management classrooms, with discussions focusing on leadership, group dynamics, attitudes, personalities, and more. The point is: management learning is everywhere; we just have to look for it.

Question: What management insights are available in various elements of our popular culture and reflected in our everyday living?

Research Directions:

■ Listen to music. Pick out themes that reflect important management concepts and theories. Put them together in a multimedia report that presents your music choices and describes their messages about management and working today.

■ Watch television. Look again for the management themes. In a report, describe what popular television programs have to say about management and working. Also consider TV advertisements. How do they use and present workplace themes to help communicate their messages?

■ Read the comics looking for management themes. Compare and contrast management and working in two or three popular comic strips.

■ Read a best-selling novel. Find examples of management and work themes in the novel. Report on what the author's characters and their experiences say about people at work.

■ Watch a film or video. Again, find examples of management and work themes. In a report describe the message of the movie in respect to management and work today.

PERSONAL MANAGEMENT

Learning Style

Now is a very good time for you to examine your **LEARNING STYLE**. Every person a manager deals with is unique, most problem situations are complex, and things are always changing. Success in management only comes to those who thrive on learning. Some people learn by watching; they observe others and model what they see. Others learn by doing; they act and experiment, learning as they go. There is no one best way to learn about managing—there is only the need to learn . . . all the time, from others, from formal training, and from real experiences. An organization development manager at PepsiCo once said: "I believe strongly in the notion that enhancing managers' knowledge of their strengths and particularly their weaknesses is integral to ensuring long-term, sustainable performance improvement and executive success." The problem is that many of us never dig deep enough to both get this depth of personal understanding and use it to set learning goals.

Building the Brand Called "You" Why not build a personal strengths and weaknesses scorecard? Fill out the following grid. Make a commitment to pursue a solid set of learning goals to build on strengths and elminate weaknesses. Set goals for what you can accomplish as part of your academic program.

Strengths

Where I am now	Learning goals

Weaknesses

Where I am now	Learning goals

NEXT STEPS: MANAGEMENT LEARNING WORKBOOK

Self-Assessments
- A 21st-Century Manager? (#1)
- What Are Your Managerial Assumptions? (#4)

Experiential Exercises
- What Would the Classics Say? (#4)
- The Great Management History Debate (#5)

Environment and Organizational Culture

4

Fit In or Stand Out?

Many workers today value the freedoms—such as casual dress and flex-time—offered by forward-thinking employers. But did companies of earlier generations get it right when they demanded that everyone arrive at the same time, look the same, and leave *en masse*? For some companies, that's never been a better idea.

It wasn't long ago that going to work was a strictly defined activity: Dress in a white shirt and a dark suit. Don't do anything to stand out. Laugh at your boss's jokes. Start and leave at the same time every day, Monday through Friday. Repeat ad nauseum.

Neither workers nor management thought of this as a particularly constrictive way of doing business, because few people knew of doing business in any other fashion. But fast-forward a few decades, and many companies have taken a decidedly more casual approach to establishing an identity at—or away from—work.

Dress expectations and work schedules are changing fast as new generations find their ways into the workplace. It would have been almost unheard of a few years ago, but when Chap Achen told his co-workers at Best Buy that he was heading off to a movie matinee at 2pm, no one even blinked. Such flexibility is now standard practice among corporate staffers at the firm. It's found also at many other prominent employers.[1a]

It's a delicate continuum for managers to navigate: How much does personal freedom affect creativity and innovation in the workplace? Or does it at all?

Advocates of a *loose* organization, perhaps an advertising agency, take the position that results come first, and all else follows. At Leo Burnett's home office in Chicago, creatives can come and go at all hours of the night, free to produce when inspiration strikes. The dress rules are simple: come wearing clothes. Cubicles or offices can be shrines to pop-culture icons or messier than a teenager's bedroom.

Those who succeed at managing creatives note knowingly that temperamental types are better nurtured than boxed in. A "sense of boredom with the tried and tested" is part of a person's creative assets, said Arvind Sarma, Managing Director of Leo Burnett, India.[1b]

What *They* Think

"The old way of managing and looking at work isn't going to work anymore. We want to revolutionize the way work gets done."
Cali Ressler, Human Resource Manager, Best Buy Co.

TIGHT: "Sometimes you feel lazy and you don't feel like putting some clothes on, but this is a job. We are going to have fun, but this is a job and we should look like we're going to work."
LeBron James, speaking on the NBA's dress code for players.

LOOSE: "If you want creative workers, give them enough time to play."
John Cleese, British actor.

But managers in a traditionally *tight* organization, like a financial services company, suggest a direct correlation between personal discipline and productivity.

A firm like New York Life, for instance, sets strict parameters about what few work-related materials may leave the office, if ever. Nearly all employees leave the building at the end of the clearly defined workday unless they need to be there under extenuating circumstances or have the approval of upper management. And don't even think about wearing a favorite pair of torn jeans to the office; not a chance.

Back at Best Buy, going loose with the corporate staff doesn't mean compromising on performance. In fact, the argument is that work-life balance and greater job flexibility increases it—rather dramatically. Since the new approach was started, Best Buy claims an increase of 35% in productivity and substantial decreases in voluntary turnover.

The firm focuses on measuring outputs, not inputs of its corporate workers—what time you report to work, how many meetings you attend in a day, what you wear, and even where you work from, aren't the issues. What you achieve is. Human resource manager Judy Thompson, a sponsor of the changes, says: "For years I had been focused on the wrong currency. I was always looking to see if people were here. I should have been looking at what they were getting done." Cali Ressler, another change sponsor, says: "The old way of managing and looking at work isn't going to work anymore. We want to revolutionize the way work gets done."[2]

When determining the culture of a business, managers must even consider how the imposition of language will affect the results of its employees' efforts. Procter & Gamble insists on the use of acronyms in place of technical jargon and compound names. But does the restriction of language in the workplace, in even such a simple way as the use of pre-established terminology, stifle innovation? The chemists and brand managers at P&G would say no, but what do you think?

Clearly, corporations on both sides of the aisle make it big regardless of how tight or loose their corporate cultures are. But which is right for you? Is there more benefit to playing by the rules or rewriting them?

The Numbers

Benefits of Casual Dress Code as Perceived by Employees

Improves morale	81%
I'm judged more on my performance than appearance	57%
Better camaraderie with managers and co-workers	57%
I do my best work when casually dressed	51%
My boss is more approachable	43%

Quick Facts

* Procter & Gamble has more than 2,500 acronyms in use across the corporation.[3]
* To stimulate the creativity of future animators, Walt Disney brought guests ranging from optics professors to architect Frank Lloyd Wright to his animation school.[4]
* 90% of all companies have a casual-dress day of some kind.[5]
* Google suggests that its engineers spend 10% of their working time on wild ideas that might or might not ever lead to a product.[6]
* In a recent poll, almost 40% of workers surveyed said that their workplace's dress code is more casual than it was two years ago.[7a]

What Do *You* Think?

1. Suggest a company or other organization that would benefit from a dress code and explain why this is the case. Also, suggest one where a dress code might diminish productivity.
2. Is an insistence on using proprietary terminology or "corporate speak" good or bad for organizations?

83

Environment and Organizational Culture			
Study Question 1	**Study Question 2**	**Study Question 3**	**Study Question 4**
Environment and Competitive Advantage	**Customer-Driven Organizations**	**Organizational Culture**	**Multicultural Organizations and Diversity**
■ What is competitive advantage? ■ The general environment ■ Stakeholders and the specific environment ■ Environmental uncertainty	■ What customers want ■ Customer relationship management	■ What strong cultures do ■ Levels of organizational culture ■ Value-based management ■ Symbolic leadership	■ Multicultural organizations and inclusivity ■ Organizational subcultures ■ Challenges faced by minorities and women ■ Managing diversity
Learning Check 1	**Learning Check 2**	**Learning Check 3**	**Learning Check 4**

I n his book *The Future of Success*, former U.S. Secretary of Labor Robert Reich says: "The emerging economy is offering unprecedented opportunities, an ever-expanding choice of terrific deals, fabulous products, good investments, and great jobs for people with the right talents and skills. Never before in human history have so many had access to so much so easily."[7b] In these terms, things couldn't be better for organizations and career seekers. But isn't there more to it than that?

ENVIRONMENT AND COMPETITIVE ADVANTAGE

The present-day environment is clearly filled not just with opportunities but with major challenges to be faced. When looking at things from a business vantage point, IBM's former CEO, Louis V. Gerstner Jr., described the challenge this way: "We believe very strongly that the age-old levers of competition—labor, capital, and land—are being supplemented by knowledge, and that most successful companies in the future will be those that learn how to exploit knowledge—knowledge about customer behavior, markets, economies, technology—faster than their competitors."[8]

Knowledge and speed are indispensable to success in this new economy. Even as managers strive to lead their organizations toward a high-performance edge, they cannot afford for a minute to rest on past laurels. The world is too uncertain and the competition too intense for that. "In order to survive," Reich points out, "all organizations must dramatically and continuously improve—cutting costs, adding value, creating new products."[9]

WHAT IS COMPETITIVE ADVANTAGE?

■ A **competitive advantage** allows an organization to deal with market and environmental forces better than its competitors.

What is **competitive advantage?** This term refers to a core competency that clearly sets an organization apart from its competitors and gives it an advantage over them in the marketplace.[10] It is an ability to do things better than one's competitors, ideally things others cannot replicate quickly or easily learn to do as well. An organization may achieve competitive advantage in many ways, including through its products, pricing, customer service, cost efficiency, and quality. But doing so successfully requires executives and managers who are continuously scanning the environment for opportunities and then taking effective action based on what is learned. The ability to do this begins with the answer to a basic question: what is in the external environment of organizations?

THE GENERAL ENVIRONMENT

The **general environment** consists of all conditions in the external environment that form a background context for managerial decision making. Typical external environmental issues include

■ *Economic conditions*—health of the economy in terms of inflation, income levels, gross domestic product, unemployment, and job outlook.
■ *Social-cultural conditions*—norms, customs, and social values on such matters as human rights, trends in education and related social institutions, as well as demographic patterns in society.
■ *Legal-political conditions*—prevailing philosophy and objectives of the political party or parties running the government, as well as laws and government regulations.
■ *Technological conditions*—development and availability of technology, including scientific advancements.
■ *Natural environment conditions*—nature and conditions of the natural environment, including levels of public concern expressed through environmentalism.

> ▨ The **general environment** is comprised of cultural, economic, legal-political, and educational conditions.

If we take the natural environment as an example, Japanese automakers seem to be finding the potential for competitive advantage. Both Honda and Toyota have received awards from the Sierra Club for excellence in environmental engineering. The two firms are on the leading edge of new markets for hybrid cars that combine gas and electric power. While America's automakers were betting that customers would stay loyal to large, gas-fueled and often gas-hungry vehicles, their Japanese competitors saw the potential for competitive advantage. Now they have experience and a reputation gained from being first to market the more environmentally friendly vehicles.

In respect to the sociocultural environment, population demographics are a key feature. Managers who understand demographic profiles and trends can anticipate shifts in the customer base and labor markets that affect their organizations.[11] These and other differences in general environment factors are especially noticeable internationally. External conditions vary significantly from one country and culture to the next, and managers must understand these differences. Like many large firms, the pharmaceutical giant Merck derives a substantial portion of its business from overseas operations. Its executives recognize the need to be well informed about, and responsive to, differing local conditions. In Europe, for example, they have entered into cooperative agreements with local companies, conducted research with local partners, and worked with local governments on legal matters.

STAKEHOLDERS AND THE SPECIFIC ENVIRONMENT

The **specific environment** consists of the actual organizations, groups, and persons with whom an organization interacts and conducts business. Members of the specific environment are often described as

> ▨ The **specific environment** includes the people and groups with whom an organization interacts.

INSIGHTS

Core Values Drive a Performance Environment

At Herman Miller, the innovative and award-winning manufacturer of designer furniture, the idea of the corporation goes well beyond its existence as a legal entity. Core values build an internal environment of high performance as the firm embraces a full set of stakeholders, including employees, suppliers, customers, and the community.

Values at Herman Miller drive a unique and high-performance system built on a fundamental belief in "participation."

> *Core values in the "Herman Miller way"*
> - *Making a meaningful contribution to our customers*
> - *Cultivating community, participation, and people development*
> - *Creating economic value for shareholders and employee-owners*
> - *Responding to change through design and innovation*
> - *Living with integrity and respecting the environment*

The Web site describes it this way: "For 50 years participation has been central to Herman Miller. It still is. We believe in participation because we value and benefit from the richness of ideas and opinions of thousands of people. Participation enables employee-owners to contribute their unique gifts and abilities to the corporate community."

Herman Miller calls itself "a high-performance, values-driven community of people tied together by a common purpose." And, yes, it is a different kind of company, a model of excellence in the new world of work. It is a values-driven company that finds high performance through everyday respect for people. And it works! The firm has been ranked among the 400 best-performing large corporations in America by *Forbes* magazine, and ranked by *Business Ethics* among the "100 Best Corporate Citizens" in America.

Stakeholders are the persons, groups, and institutions directly affected by an organization.

stakeholders, defined in Chapter 2 as the persons, groups, and institutions that are affected in one way or another by the organization's performance. They are key constituencies that have a stake in the organization's performance, are influenced by how it operates, and can influence it in return.

Important stakeholders for most organizations include customers, suppliers, competitors, regulators, and investors/owners as well as employees. Interestingly, a study of MBA students shows how differently stakeholders may be valued. In answer to a question regarding what a business's top priorities should be, 75 percent included "maximizing shareholder value" and 71 percent included "satisfying customers." Only 25 percent included "creating value for communities," and only 5 percent noted "concern for environmentalism."[12]

Figure 4.1 shows the typical business firm as an open system, with the interests of several stakeholder groups linked with stages in the input-transformation-output process. This type of stakeholder analysis can be used to assess the current performance of organizations through the eyes of strategic constituencies. It also focuses management attention on **value creation,**

Value creation is creating value for and satisfying needs of constituencies.

the extent to which the organization is creating value for and satisfying the needs of stakeholders. In respect to product outputs, for example, busi-

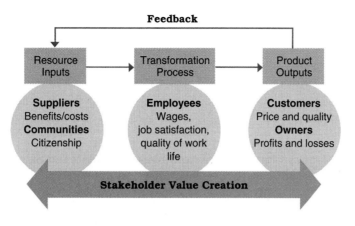

Figure 4.1 Stakeholder analysis of value creation for key constituencies of a business firm: an open-systems approach.

nesses create value for customers through product price and quality, and for owners by realized profits and losses. In respect to inputs, businesses create value for suppliers through the benefits of long-term business relationships, and for communities in such areas as the citizenship businesses display in using and contributing to public services. And in respect to throughputs, businesses create value for employees through the wages earned and satisfaction gained through their work in transforming resource inputs into product outputs.

ENVIRONMENTAL UNCERTAINTY

The fact is that there is a lot of uncertainty in the external environments of many organizations. **Environmental uncertainty** means that there is a lack of complete information regarding what exists and what developments may occur. This makes it difficult to analyze constituencies and their needs, predict future states of affairs, and understand their potential implications for the organization. Researchers describe two dimensions of environmental uncertainty: (1) complexity, or the number of different factors in the environment, and (2) the rate of change in these factors.[13]

Environmental uncertainty presents a host of management challenges. Greater uncertainty requires more concentrated attention. An uncertain environment has to be continually studied and monitored to spot emerging trends. Also, the greater the environmental uncertainty, the greater the need for flexibility and adaptability in organizational designs and work practices. Because of uncertainty, organizations must be able to respond quickly as new circumstances arise and information becomes available. Throughout this book you will find many examples of how organizations try to stay adaptable in order to best deal with the high uncertainty that so often prevails in their environments.

■ **Environmental uncertainty** is a lack of complete information about the environment.

Be sure you can ■ list key elements in the general and specific environments of organizations ■ define the terms competitive advantage, stakeholders ■ describe the stakeholders for a business in your local community ■ explain the management implications of different levels of environmental uncertainty

Learning Check 1

CUSTOMER-DRIVEN ORGANIZATIONS

Question: What's your job?

Answer: I run the cash register and sack groceries.

Question: But isn't it your job to serve the customer?

Answer: I guess, but it's not in my job description.

This conversation illustrates what often becomes the missing link in the quest for competitive advantage: customer service.[14] Contrast this conversation with the case of a customer who once called the Vermont Teddy Bear Company to complain that her new mail-order teddy bear had a problem. The company responded promptly, she said, and arranged to have the bear picked up and replaced. She wrote the firm to say "thank you for the great service and courtesy you gave me."[15]

WHAT CUSTOMERS WANT

Customers are always key stakeholders; they sit at the top when organizations are viewed as the upside-down pyramids described in Chapter 1. And without any doubt, customers put today's organizations to a very stiff test. They primarily want four things in the goods and services they buy: (1) high quality, (2) low price, (3) on-time delivery, and (4) great service. Offering them anything less is unacceptable. Organizations that can't meet customer expectations suffer the market consequences they lose competitive advantage.

A *Harvard Business Review* survey reported that American business leaders rank customer service and product quality as the first and second most important goals in the success of their organizations.[16] In a survey by the market research firm Michelson & Associates, poor service and product dissatisfaction were also ranked first and second as reasons why customers abandon a retail store.[17] Reaching the goals of providing great service and quality products isn't always easy. But when pursued relentlessly, they can be important sources of competitive advantage. Just imagine the ramifications if every customer or client contact for an organization were positive. Not only would these people return again and again as customers, but they would also tell others and expand the company's customer base.

CUSTOMER RELATIONSHIPS

■ **Customer relationship management** strategically tries to build lasting relationships with and to add value to customers.

Many organizations now use the principles of **customer relationship management** to establish and maintain high standards of customer service. Known as "CRM," this approach uses the latest information technologies to maintain intense communication with customers as well as to gather and utilize data regarding their needs and desires. At Marriott International, for example, CRM is supported by special customer management software that tracks information on customer preferences. When you check in, the likelihood is that your past requests for things like a king-size bed, no smoking room, and computer modem access are already in your record. Says Marriott's chairman: "It's a big competitive advantage."[18] Procter & Gamble, discussed in The Topic chapter opener is a master at CRM. One of the firm's latest initiatives is to improve the online experiences of its customers worldwide. Using a new technology by RightNow, P&G is able to answer customer inquiries quickly. Over 170,000 answers each month are provided on everything from make-up choices to stain removals through Web self-service, e-mails, and chats.

Just as organizations need to manage their customers on the output side, supplier relationships on the input side must be well managed, too. The concept of **supply chain management** (SCM) involves the strategic management of all operations of an organization and its suppliers. This includes the use of information technology to improve purchasing, manufacturing, transportation, and distribution.[19] The goals of SCM are straightforward: achieve efficiency in all aspects of the supply chain while ensuring on-time availability of quality resources for customer-driven operations. As retail sales are made at Wal-Mart, for example, an information system updates inventory records and sales forecasts. Suppliers access this information electronically, allowing them to adjust their operations and rapidly ship replacement products to meet the retailer's needs.

■ **Supply chain management** strategically links all operations dealing with resource supplies.

Be sure you can ■ describe how organizations operate in customer-centered ways ■ discuss the importance of customer relationship management in a competitive business environment ■ define and illustrate the practice of supply chain management

Learning Check 2

ORGANIZATIONAL CULTURE

"Culture" is a popular word in management these days. In the internal environments of organizations, **organizational culture** is the system of shared beliefs and values that shapes and guides the behavior of its members.[20] Sometimes called the *corporate culture*, it is a key aspect of any organization and work setting. Whenever someone, for example, speaks of "the way we do things here," that person is talking about the culture.

■ **Organizational culture** is the system of shared beliefs and values that guides behavior in organizations.

WHAT STRONG CULTURES DO

Strong cultures, ones that are clear, well defined, and widely shared among members, discourage dysfunctional work behaviors and encourage positive ones. They commit members to doing things for and with one another that are in the best interests of the organization.

The best organizations are likely to have strong cultures that are customer driven and performance oriented. They often emphasize teamwork, allow for risk taking, encourage innovation, and make the well-being of people a top management priority.[21] Honda is a good example. The firm's culture is tightly focused around what is known as "The Honda Way"—a set of principles emphasizing ambition, respect for ideas, open communication, work enjoyment, harmony, and hard work.

Although it is clear that culture is not the sole determinant of what happens in organizations, it is an important influence on what they accomplish . . . and how. A widely discussed study of successful businesses concluded that organizational culture has the potential to shape attitudes, reinforce beliefs, direct behavior, and establish performance expectations and the motivation to fulfill them.[22] Importantly, the cultures in high performing firms provided for a clear vision of what each organization was

KAFFEEKLATSCH

Best Jobs Going Forward

First Cup

"Do you ever read *Money* magazine? I picked it up while traveling the other day and found an interesting article rating the 'best jobs' in America. It makes you think. They started out by identifying jobs that will grow fastest in the next 10 years; then they looked at things like salaries, stress levels, work environments, scheduling flexibility and creativity."

Studying the Grounds

■ *Money* magazine lists the top ten jobs in America for college graduates: software engineer, college professor, financial advisor, human resource analyst, physician's assistant, market research analyst, computer/IT analyst, real estate appraisor, pharmacist, and psychologist.

Double Espresso

"The list is a bit surprising to me. I would have expected jobs in advertising and sales to be in the top 10, as well as health services managers and lawyers."

"Well, they're all in the top 50, just not at the top like the others. And don't forget, the magazine is projecting ahead—looking for jobs that will grow and prosper in the coming environment, not just the present one. They were identifying good jobs in 'growing' fields."

Your Turn

What job are you shooting for next? Have you looked at the trends and facts for this job category? Check projections put out by the Bureau of Labor Statistics and reports in the business press. There isn't much sense going for jobs that will be in really short supply or ones that aren't all that attractive in terms of meeting today's expectations. And by the way, just what are your job search criteria?

MANAGEMENT SMARTS 4.1

Questions for reading an organization's culture

- How tight or loose is the *structure*?
- Are decisions *change* oriented or driven by the status quo?
- What *outcomes* or results are most highly valued?
- What is the climate for *risk taking*, innovation?
- How widespread is *empowerment*, worker involvement?
- What is the competitive *style*, internal and external?

attempting to accomplish, allowing individuals to rally around the vision and work hard to support and accomplish it.[23] *Management Smarts 4.1* offers ideas for reading differences among organizational cultures.

LEVELS OF ORGANIZATIONAL CULTURE

Organizational culture is usually described from the perspective of the two levels shown in *Figure 4.2*. The outer level is the "observable" culture and the inner level is the "core" culture.[24]

The *observable culture* is visible; it is what one sees and hears when walking around an organization as a visitor, a customer, or an employee. The observable culture is apparent in the way people dress at work, how they arrange their offices, how they speak to and behave toward one another, the nature of their conversations, and how they talk about and treat their customers. It is also found in the following elements of daily organizational life:

- *Stories*—oral histories and tales, told and retold among members, about dramatic sagas and incidents in the life of the organization.
- *Heroes*—the people singled out for special attention and whose accomplishments are recognized with praise and admiration; they include founders and role models.
- *Rites and rituals*—the ceremonies and meetings, planned and spontaneous, that celebrate important occasions and performance accomplishments.

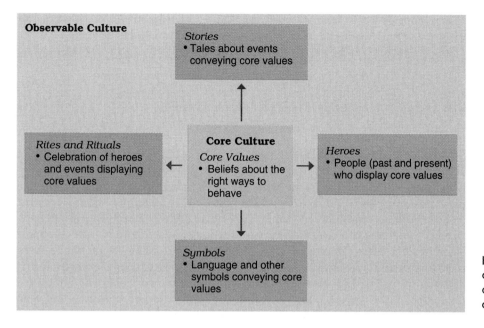

Figure 4.2 Levels of organizational culture— observable culture and core culture.

- *Symbols*—the special use of language and other nonverbal expressions to communicate important themes of organizational life.

The second and deeper level of organizational culture is the *core culture*. It consists of the **core values** or underlying assumptions and beliefs that shape and guide people's behaviors, and actually contribute to the aspects of observable culture just described. Strong-culture organizations operate with a small but enduring set of core values. At highly successful companies the core values typically emphasize the values of customer service, performance excellence, innovation, social responsibility, integrity, worker involvement, and teamwork.[25] Examples of values statements that drive the best firms include "service above all else" at Nordstrom; "science-based innovation" at Merck; "encouraging individual initiative and creativity" at SONY; and "fanatical attention to consistency and detail" at Disney.

■ **Core values** are beliefs and values shared by organization members.

VALUE-BASED MANAGEMENT

Organizations often publicize core values in corporate mission statements and on their Web sites. But, mere testimonies to values are not enough to create a strong core culture and derive its benefits. The values must be practiced. They must be real, they must be shared, and they must be modeled and reinforced by managers from top to bottom.

The term **value-based management** describes managers who actively help develop, communicate, and enact shared values within an organization. Importantly, one area where value-based management has a major impact is with respect to ethics and social responsibility. At Tom's of Maine, for example, CEO Tom Chappell didn't hesitate to recall a new all-natural deodorant when customers were dissatisfied.[26] It cost the company some $400,000, but Chappell confidently did the "right" thing. His company is founded on values that include fairness and honesty, and he lived up to them, setting a positive example for others to follow.

■ **Value-based management** actively develops, communicates, and enacts shared values.

The responsibility for value-based management extends to all managers and team leaders. Like the organization as a whole, any work team or group will have a culture. How well this culture operates to support the group and its performance objectives will depend in part on the strength of the core values and the team leader's role as a values champion. A good test of the value-based management of any work unit or team includes criteria:[27]

- *Relevance*—Core values support key performance objectives.
- *Integrity*—Core values provide clear, consistent ethical anchors.
- *Pervasiveness*—Core values are understood by all members.
- *Strength*—Core values are accepted by all members.

SYMBOLIC LEADERSHIP

■ **A symbolic leader** uses symbols to establish and maintain a desired organizational culture.

A **symbolic leader** is someone who uses symbols well to communicate values and maintain a desired organizational culture. Symbolic managers and leaders both act and talk the "language" of the organization. They are always careful to behave in ways that live up to the espoused core values; they are ever-present role models for others to emulate and follow. Symbolic leaders use spoken and written words to describe people, events, and even the competition in ways that reinforce and communicate core values. *Language metaphors*—the use of positive examples from another context—are very powerful in this regard. For example, newly hired workers at Disney World and Disneyland are counseled to always think of themselves as more than employees; they are key "members of the cast," and they work "on stage." After all, they are told, Disney isn't just any business, it is an "entertainment" business.

Good symbolic leaders highlight and even dramatize core values and the observable culture. They tell key stories over and over again, and they encourage others to tell them. They may refer to the "founding story" about the entrepreneur whose personal values set a key tone for the enterprise. They remind everyone about organizational heroes, past and present, whose performances exemplify core values. They often use rites and rituals to glorify the performance of the organization and its members. At Mary Kay Cosmetics, gala events at which top sales performers share their tales of success are legendary. So, too, are the lavish incentive awards presented at these ceremonies, especially the pink luxury cars given to the most successful salespeople.[28]

 **Learning Check 3**

Be sure you can ■ define the term organizational culture and explain the importance of strong cultures to organizations ■ distinguish between the observable and core cultures ■ explain the concept of value-based management ■ discuss how symbolic leaders build high-performance organizational cultures

MULTICULTURAL ORGANIZATIONS AND DIVERSITY

At the very time that we talk about the culture of an organization as a whole, we must also recognize diversity in its membership. As first introduced in Chapter 1, workforce diversity is a term used to describe differences among people at work. Primary dimensions of **diversity** include age, race, ethnicity, gender, physical ability, and sexual orientation. But workplace diversity also includes differences in religious beliefs, education, experience, and family status, among others.

■ The term **diversity** describes race, gender, age, and other individual differences.

In his book *Beyond Race and Gender*, consultant R. Roosevelt Thomas Jr. makes the point that "diversity includes everyone." He says: "In this expanded context, white males are as diverse as their colleagues."[29] Thomas also links diversity with organizational culture, believing that the way people are treated at work—with respect and inclusion, or with disrespect and exclusion—is a direct reflection of the organization's culture.

Thomas's message is that diversity is a potential source of competitive advantage. It offers organizations a mixture of talents and perspectives that is ready and able to deal with the complexities and uncertainty in the ever-changing environment. If you do the right things in organizational leadership, in other words, you'll gain competitive advantage through diversity. If you don't, you'll lose it. But importantly, in a study of the business case for diversity, Thomas Kochan and his colleagues at MIT found that the presence of diversity alone does not guarantee a positive performance impact.[30] Only when diversity is leveraged through training and supportive human resource practices are the advantages gained. The study offers this guidance:

> *To be successful in working with and gaining value from diversity requires a sustained, systemic approach and long-term commitment. Success is facilitated by a perspective that considers diversity to be an opportunity for everyone in an organization to learn from each other how better to accomplish their work and an occasion that requires a supportive and cooperative organizational culture as well as group leadership and process skills that can facilitate effective group functioning.*

ISSUES AND SITUATIONS

Changing Mindsets

What do you do when taking over as CEO of a very successful multinational company and doing so as a replacement for a legendary predecessor? Set out to shift mindsets and change the corporate culture; at least that's the management agenda of Jeffrey R. Immelt. The GE that Jack Welch led was a giant of efficiency, cost cutting, and deals. Immelt's GE is into creativity, innovation, and growth. It's not that he disagrees with what Welch accomplished; he just believes the future lies ahead, and that for GE to stay successful, it has to change with the new environment. Part of that change is a new managerial mindset and culture.

To bring about change, Immelt is pushing pay bonuses tied to specific targets: new ideas, customer satisfaction, and sales growth. He supports risk taking and invests heavily in new projects; leaders of major businesses have to propose at least three breakthrough projects per year for consideration. He also focuses on management development with the goal of deepening contact with GE's industries; managers stay in jobs longer and include more "outsiders" brought in to build industry expertise. And the pressure is there, too. Susan P. Peters, head of GE's executive development operation, says that the firm's employees need "to reconceptualize" and understand that "what you have been to date isn't good enough for tomorrow."

Critical Response

There's a lot more to the GE and Immelt stories than reported here. This is just a teaser. Do a little research and find out how well Immelt is doing with his cultural revolution. How do his style and strategy differ from Jack Welch's? Is he doing the right thing with pay bonuses and management expectations? Is Immelt on track to justify this prediction of a financial analyst: "If you have a revolutionary decade of growth around the world, who's going to be there to capitalize on it? GE"?

MULTICULTURAL ORGANIZATIONS AND INCLUSIVITY

■ **Multiculturalism** involves pluralism and respect for diversity.

A key issue in the culture of any organization is *inclusivity*—the degree to which the organization is open to anyone who can perform a job, regardless of race, sexual preference, gender, or other diversity attribute.[31] The term **multiculturalism** refers to inclusivity, pluralism, and respect for diversity in the workplace. The expectation today is for organizational cultures to communicate core values that respect and empower the full demographic cultural diversity is now characteristic of our workforces.

■ **A multicultural organization** is based on pluralism and operates with inclusivity and respect for diversity.

The "best" organizational cultures in this sense are inclusive, ones that value the talents, ideas, and creative potential of all members. The model is a **multicultural organization** with these characteristics:[32]

- *Pluralism*—Members of both minority cultures and majority cultures are influential in setting key values and policies.
- *Structural integration*—Minority-culture members are well represented in jobs at all levels and in all functional responsibilities.
- *Informal network integration*—Various forms of mentoring and support groups assist in the career development of minority-culture members.
- *Absence of prejudice and discrimination*—A variety of training and task-force activities address the need to eliminate culture-group biases.
- *Minimum intergroup conflict*—Diversity does not lead to destructive conflicts between members of majority and minority cultures.

ORGANIZATIONAL SUBCULTURES

■ Organizational **subcultures** exist among people with similar values and beliefs based on shared work responsibilities and personal characteristics.

■ **Ethnocentrism** is the belief that one's membership group or subculture is superior to all others.

Like society as a whole, organizations contain a mixture of **subcultures**. These are cultures common to groups of people with similar values and beliefs based on shared work responsibilities and personal characteristics. Whereas the pluralism that characterizes multicultural organizations conveys respect for different subcultures, working relations in organizations are too often hurt by the opposite tendency. Just as with life in general, **ethnocentrism**—the belief that one's membership group or subculture is superior to all others—can creep into the workplace and adversely affect the way people relate to one another.

The many possible subcultures in organizations include *occupational subcultures*.[33] Salaried professionals such as lawyers, scientists, engineers, and accountants have been described as having special needs for work autonomy and empowerment that may conflict with traditional management methods of top-down direction and control. Unless these needs are recognized and properly dealt with, salaried professionals may prove difficult to integrate into the culture of the larger organization.

There are also *functional subcultures* in organizations, and people from different functions often have difficulty understanding and working well with one another. For example, employees of a business may consider themselves "systems people" or "marketing people" or "manufacturing people" or "finance people." When such identities are overemphasized, members of the functional groups may spend most of their time with each other, develop a "jargon" or technical language that is shared among themselves, and view their role in the organization as more important than the contributions of the other functions.

Differences in *ethnic or national cultures* exist as people from various countries and regions of the world meet and work together in the global economy. And as we all know it can sometimes be hard to work well with persons whose backgrounds are very different from our own. The best understanding is most likely gained through direct contact and from being open-minded. The same advice holds true with respect to *racial subcultures*. Although one may speak in everyday conversations about "African American" or "Latino" or "Anglo" cultures, one has to wonder what we really know about them.[34] Importantly, key questions remain largely unanswered: Where can we find frameworks for understanding them? If improved cross-cultural understandings can help people work better across national boundaries, how can we create the same to help people from different racial subcultures work better together?

We live at a time when the influence of *generational subcultures* at work is of growing importance. But the issues are more subtle than young-old issues alone. It is possible to identify "generational gaps" among "baby boomers" now in their fifties and early sixties, "Generation Xers" now in their thirties and early forties, "millennials" now in their twenties, and the new "Internet generation". Members of these generations grew up in quite

REAL ETHICS

Coke's Secret Formula

This is a short, short play in one act.

Scene: *Corporate headquarters of PepsiCo. A youngish executive is gesturing excitedly, and three more obviously senior ones listen attentively. The CEO sits at her desk, swiveling occasionally in the chair while listening carefully to the conversation.*

YOUNG EXECUTIVE, *acting a bit proud to be there*
It started with a telephone call. I agreed to meet with a former employee of Coca-Cola at his request. We met and, lo and behold, he offered me the "secret formula."

ONE OF THE SENIOR EXECUTIVES, *cautiously*
Let me be sure I understand. You received a call from someone who said they used to work at Coke, and that person was requesting a face-to-face meeting. Correct?

YOUNG EXECUTIVE, *quickly and proudly*
Right!

THE SENIOR EXECUTIVE, *with a bit of challenge*
Why? Why would you meet with someone that said they just left Coke?

YOUNG EXECUTIVE, *tentative now*
Well . . . I . . . uh . . . It seemed like a great chance to get some competitive information and maybe even hire someone who really knows their strategies.

A SECOND SENIOR EXECUTIVE
So, what happened next?

YOUNG EXECUTIVE, *excited again*
Well, after just a minute or two conversing, he said that he had THE FORMULA!

SECOND SENIOR EXECUTIVE
And . . . ?

YOUNG EXECUTIVE, *uncertain all of a sudden and now speaking softly*
He said it was "for sale."

THIRD SENIOR EXECUTIVE, *with a bit of edge in her voice*
So what did you say?

YOUNG EXECUTIVE, *looking down and shuffling slightly backward*
I said that I'd take it "up the ladder." I'm supposed to call him back . . .

CEO, *breaking into the conversation*
And we're glad you did "bring it up the ladder," as you say. But now that you have, what do you propose we do about this opportunity to buy Coke's most important secret?

As CEO speaks, other senior executives move over to stand behind her. Everyone looks in the direction of the young executive.

FURTHER INQUIRY

What do you think this junior executive will recommend? His or her career might rest on the answer. Better yet, how would you respond?

In fact, after receiving a similar call Pepsi executives contacted the FBI. A sting netted three former Coke employees. Coke's CEO, Neville Isdell, thanked his Pepsi rivals for helping fight off "this attack" on its secret. Pepsi replied: "We did what any responsible company would do. Competition can be fierce, but it must also be fair and legal."

different worlds and were influenced by different values and opportunities. Their work preferences and attitudes tend to reflect these differences. Someone who is 60 years old today, a common age for senior managers, was a teenager in the 1960s. Such a person may have difficulty understanding, supervising, and working with younger managers who were teens during the 1970s, 1980s, and even the 1990s. And if you are one of the latter generations—perhaps the Millennial Generation—you'll need to ponder also how well you will do in the future when working with still younger colleagues.

Issues of relationships and discrimination based on *gender subcultures* also continue to complicate the workplace. Some research shows that when men work together, a group culture forms around a competitive atmosphere. Sports metaphors are common, and games and stories often deal with winning and losing.[35] When women work together, a rather different culture may form, with more emphasis on personal relationships and collaboration.[36]

CHALLENGES FACED BY MINORITIES AND WOMEN

The very term "diversity" basically means the presence of differences. But what does it mean when those differences are distributed unequally in the organizational power structure? What happens when one subculture is in "majority" status while others become "minorities" in respect to representation within the organization? Even though organizations are changing today, most senior executives in large organizations are older, white, and male. There is likely to be more workforce diversity at lower and middle levels of most organizations than at the top.

■ The **glass ceiling** is a hidden barrier to the advancement of women and minorities.

Take a look at the situation shown by *Figure 4.3*. It depicts the operation of the **glass ceiling,** defined in Chapter 1 as an invisible barrier that limits the advancement of women and minorities in some organizations. What are the implications for minority members, such as women or persons of color, seeking to advance and prosper in organizations traditionally dominated by a majority culture, such as white males? Consider the situation faced by Jesse Spaulding when he was a regional manager for a restaurant chain owned by Shoney's. He says that the firm used to operate on the "buddy system," which "left people of color by the wayside" when it came to promotions. Things changed with new leadership, delighting Spaulding with new opportunities. Shoney's gained ranking among *Fortune* magazine's list of America's 50 Best Companies for Minorities.[37]

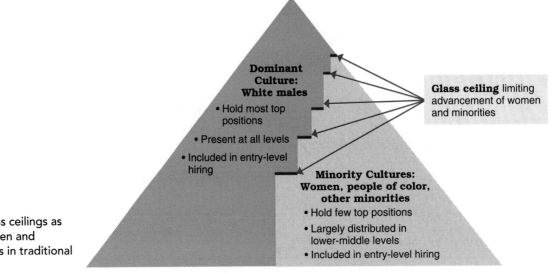

Figure 4.3 Glass ceilings as barriers to women and minority cultures in traditional organizations.

The daily work challenges faced by minorities and women can range from misunderstandings and lack of sensitivity on the one hand, to glass ceiling limitations, to even outright harassment and discrimination. *Sexual harassment* in the form of unwanted sexual advances, requests for sexual favors, and sexually laced communications is a problem female employees in particular may face. Minority workers can also be targets of cultural jokes; one survey reports some 45 percent of respondents had encountered such abuse. *Pay discrimination* is also an issue. A senior executive in the computer industry reported her surprise at finding out that the top performer in her work group, an African American male, was paid 25 percent less than anyone else. This wasn't because his pay had been cut to that level, she said. It was because his pay increases over time had always trailed those given to his white co-workers. The differences added up significantly over time, but no one noticed or stepped forward to make the appropriate adjustment.[38]

Sometimes members of minority cultures try to adapt through tendencies toward **biculturalism**. This is the display of majority culture characteristics that seem necessary to succeed in the work environment. For example, one might find gays and lesbians hiding their sexual orientation from co-workers out of fear of prejudice or discrimination. Similarly, one might find an African American carefully training herself to not use certain words or phrases at work that might be considered as subculture slang by white co-workers.

> **Biculturalism** is when minority members adopt characteristics of majority cultures in order to succeed.

MANAGING DIVERSITY

There should be no doubt today that minority workers want the same things everyone wants. They want respect for their talents and a work setting that allows them to achieve to their full potential. It takes the best in diversity leadership at all levels of organizational management to meet these expectations.[39]

R. Roosevelt Thomas describes the continuum of leadership approaches to diversity shown in *Figure 4.4*.[40] The first is *affirmative action*, in which leadership commits the organization to hiring and advancing minorities and women. The second is *valuing diversity*, in which leadership commits the organization to education and training programs designed to help people better understand and respect individual differences. The third and most comprehensive is *managing diversity*, in which leadership commits to changing the organizational culture to empower and include all people.

Thomas defines **managing diversity** as building an organizational culture that allows all members, minorities and women included, to reach their full potential. He believes that leaders committed to managing diversity create the most value in respect to competitive advantage.[41] They build organizations that are what Thomas calls "diversity mature." In these organizations there is a diversity mission as well as an organizational mission;

> **Managing diversity** is building an inclusive work environment that allows everyone to reach their full potential.

Affirmative Action	Valuing Differences	Managing Diversity
Create upward mobility for minorities and women	Build quality relationships with respect for diversity	Achieve full utilization of diverse human resources

Figure 4.4 Leadership approaches to diversity—from affirmative action to managing diversity. *Source:* Developed from R. Roosevelt Thomas Jr., *Beyond Race and Gender* (New York: AMACOM, 1991), p. 28.

RESEARCH BRIEF

Four management practices said to drive high performance

A study published in the *Harvard Business Review* identifies four practices that consistently distinguish high-performance firms: strategy, execution, culture, and structure. Scholars Nitin Nohria, William Joyce, and Bruce Roberson studied 160 companies and their use of some 200 different management practices over a 10-year period. Called the Evergreen Project, it found that firms consistently outperforming their peers emphasized four management basics.

Strategy—The better firms had well-defined strategies that were communicated in ways that led to their understanding by employees, customers, and investors. *Execution*—They were "flawless" in operations that implemented organizational strategies effectively and efficiently. *Culture*—They had inspirational cultures in which performance was val-

ued and everyone held each other accountable for living up to expectations. *Structure*—They didn't use the same structures, but they all had structures that minimized bureaucracy and made work and information sharing as easy as possible.

Standing right behind these primary performance drivers were four secondary management practices that also were widely shared. Including at least two of the following practices constituted a formula for success: focus on *talent*, great *leadership*, *innovation*, and use of *mergers and partnerships* to advantage. The researchers call this notion the 4+2 formula.

Primary Management Practices

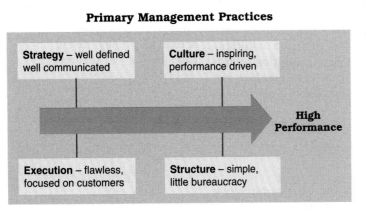

QUESTIONS & APPLICATIONS

Where do the four management functions of planning, organizing, leading, and controlling come into play with respect to the 4+2 formula? If one were to examine performance in schools, hospitals, government agencies, and nonprofit organizations, would the same 4+2 results be found?

Choose an organization—perhaps an employer or local organization familiar to you. Do a "performance audit" of the organization using the 4+2 framework. Develop a consulting plan that suggests how improvements in 4+2 practices might lead to higher performance in the future.

Reference: Nitin Nohria, William Joyce and Bruce Roberson, "What Really Works," *Harvard Business Review* (July, 2003), pp. 43–52.

diversity is viewed as a strategic imperative; the members understand diversity concepts and are themselves diversity-mature.

Perhaps the most important word in human resource management today is "inclusiveness." By valuing diversity and building multicultural organizations that include everyone, organizations of all types can be strengthened and brought into better alignment with the challenges and opportunities of today's environment. Research reported in the *Gallup Management Journal*, for example, shows that establishing a racially and ethnically inclusive workplace is good for morale.[42] In a study of 2,014 American workers, those who felt included were more likely to stay with their employers and recommend them to others. Survey questions asked such things as "Do you always trust your company to be fair to all employees?" "At work, are all employees always treated with respect?" "Does your supervisor always make the best use of employees' skills?"

Inclusivity clearly counts. It counts in terms of respect for people, and it counts in building organizational capacities for high performance. As Michael R. Losey, president of the Society for Human Resource Management (SHRM), says: "Companies must realize that the talent pool includes people of all types, including older workers; persons with disabilities; persons of various religious, cultural, and national backgrounds; persons who are not heterosexual; minorities; and women."[43]

Learning Check 4

Be sure you can ■ explain multiculturalism and the concept of a multicultural organization ■ identify typical organizational subcultures ■ discuss the common employment problems faced by minorities and women ■ explain Thomas's concept of managing diversity ■ realistically assess your diversity maturity

---

CHAPTER 4 STUDY GUIDE

STUDY QUESTIONS SUMMARY

1 What is the external environment of organizations?

- Competitive advantage is a core competency that allows an organization to outperform its competitors.
- The general environment includes background economic, sociocultural, legal-political, technological, and natural environment conditions.
- The specific or task environment consists of suppliers, customers, competitors, regulators, and other groups with which an organization interacts.
- Stakeholders are people and constituents affected by an organization's performance and for whom it creates value.
- Environmental uncertainty creates problems for organizations due to complexity and rates of change.

2 What is a customer-driven organization?

- A customer-driven organization recognizes customer service and product quality as foundations of competitive advantage.
- Customers are concerned about quality, price, delivery time, and service when they purchase goods and services.
- Customer relationship management builds and maintains strategic relationships with customers.
- Supply chain management builds and maintains strategic relationships with suppliers.

3 What is organizational culture?

- Organizational culture is an internal environment that establishes a personality for the organization and influences the behavior of members.
- The observable culture is found in the rites, rituals, stories, heroes, and symbols of the organization.
- The core culture consists of the core values and fundamental beliefs on which the organization is based.
- In organizations with strong cultures, members behave with shared understandings.
- Symbolic managers build shared values, and use stories, ceremonies, heroes, and language to reinforce these values.

4 How is diversity managed in a multicultural organization?

- Multicultural organizations operate through a culture that values pluralism and respects diversity.
- Organizations have many subcultures, including those based on occupational, functional, ethnic, racial, age, and gender differences.
- Challenges faced by organizational minorities include sexual harassment, pay discrimination, job discrimination, and the glass ceiling effect.
- Managing diversity is the process of developing an inclusive work environment that allows everyone to reach their full potential.

KEY TERMS REVIEW

Biculturalism (p. 97)
Competitive advantage (p. 84)
Core values (p. 91)
Customer relationship
   management (p. 88)
Diversity (p. 92)
Enviromental uncertainty (p. 87)

Ethnocentrism (p. 94)
General environment (p. 85)
Glass ceiling (p. 96)
Managing diversity (p. 97)
Multicultural organization (p. 94)
Multiculturalism (p. 94)
Organizational culture (p. 89)

Specific environment (p. 85)
Stakeholders (p. 86)
Subcultures (p. 94)
Supply chain management (p. 89)
Symbolic leader (p. 92)
Value-based management (p. 91)
Value creation (p. 86)

SELF-TEST 4

MULTIPLE-CHOICE QUESTIONS:

1. The general environment of an organization would include _____.
   (a) population demographics   (b) activist groups   (c) competitors   (d) customers

2. In terms of value creation for stakeholders, _____ have a major interest in a business firm's profits and losses.
   (a) employees   (b) communities   (c) owners   (d) suppliers

3. Two dimensions that determine the level of environmental uncertainty are the number of factors in the external environment and the _____ of these factors.
   (a) location   (b) rate of change   (c) importance   (d) interdependence

4. As a rule of thumb, organizations should recognize that customers today are very concerned about at least four things when they purchase goods and services—price, quality, delivery time, and _____.
   (a) style   (b) packaging   (c) labels   (d) service

5. Stories about past accomplishments and heroes such as company founders are all part of an organization's _____ culture.
   (a) observable   (b) underground   (c) functional   (d) core

6. When members of an organizational subculture view themselves as superior to those in other subcultures, they are displaying _____.
   (a) the glass ceiling effect   (b) multiculturalism   (c) ethnocentrism   (d) biculturalism

7. Planned and spontaneous ceremonies and celebrations of work achievements illustrate how _____ help build strong corporate cultures.
   (a) rewards   (b) heroes   (c) rites and rituals   (d) core values

8. When managers at Disney World use language metaphors, telling workers they are "on stage" as "members of the cast," they are engaging in _____ leadership.
   (a) symbolic   (b) competitive   (c) multicultural   (d) stakeholder

9. Pluralism and the absence of discrimination and prejudice in policies and practices are two important hallmarks of _____.
   (a) the glass ceiling effect   (b) a multicultural organization   (c) quality circles   (d) affirmative action

10. When members of minority cultures feel that they have to behave in ways similar to the majority, this is called _____.
    (a) biculturalism   (b) symbolic leadership   (c) the glass ceiling effect   (d) inclusivity

11. Wal-Mart's suppliers electronically access inventory data and sales forecasts in the stores and automatically ship replacement products. This is an example of Wal-mart's approach to _____.
    (a) supply chain management   (b) customer relationship management   (c) total quality management   (d) strategic constituencies analysis

12. Whether a structure is tight or loose and whether decisions are change oriented or driven by the status quo are indicators of an organization's _____.
    (a) inclusivity   (b) culture   (c) competitive advantage   (d) multiculturalism

13. Among the leadership approaches to diversity identified by Thomas, affirmative action is associated with _____.
    (a) building quality relationships in respect to diversity   (b) eliminating prejudice from a workforce   (c) creating upward mobility for minorities and women   (d) fully utilizing diverse resources

14. _____ means that an organization fully integrates members of minority cultures and majority cultures.
   (a) Equal employment opportunity   (b) Affirmative action   (c) Symbolic leadership   (d) Pluralism

15. The beliefs that older workers are not creative and are most interested in routine jobs are examples of stereotypes that can create bad feelings among members of different _____ subcultures in organizations.
   (a) occupational   (b) generational   (c) gender   (d) functional

SHORT-RESPONSE QUESTIONS:

16. What objectives indicate an organization seeks competitive advantage through customer service?
17. What core values might be found in high-performance organizational cultures?
18. What is value-based management?
19. Why is it important for managers to understand subcultures in organizations?

APPLICATION QUESTION:

20. Two businesswomen, former college roommates, are discussing their jobs and careers over lunch. You overhear one saying to the other: "I work for a large corporation, while you own a small retail business. In my company there is a strong corporate culture and everyone feels its influence. In fact, we are always expected to act in ways that support the culture and serve as role models for others to do so as well. This includes a commitment to diversity and multiculturalism. Because of the small size of your firm, things like corporate culture, diversity, and multiculturalism are not so important to worry about." Do you agree or disagree with this statement? Why?

CHAPTER 4 APPLICATIONS

CASE 4

Panera Bread Company: Forecasting Long-Term Trends

Panera Bread is in the business of satisfying customers with fresh baked breads, gourmet soups, and efficient service. The relatively new franchise has surpassed all expectations for success. But how did a start-up food company get so big, so fast? By watching and carefully timing market trends.

What's so great about bread and soup? For some people, it conjures up images of bland food that soothes an upset stomach. Others think of the kind of simple gruel offered to jailed prisoners in old-time movies. But for Panera Bread, a company able to successfully spot long-term trends in the food industry, artisan-style bread served with deli sandwiches and soups is a combination proven to please the hungry masses.

French Roots, American Tastes

Despite its abundance of restaurants, Panera Bread is a relatively new company, having only been known as such since 1997. Its roots go back to 1981, when Louis Kane and Ron Shaich founded Au Bon Pain Company, Inc., having merged Kane's three existing Au Bon Pain stores with Shaich's Cookie Jar store. The chain of French-style bakeries offered baguettes, coffee, and sandwiches served on either French bread or croissants. It performed quite well on the East

Coast, becoming the dominant operator in the bakery-café category, and it even expanded internationally.

As part of its expansion, Au Bon Pain purchased the Saint Louis Bread Company, a Missouri-based chain of about 20 bakery-cafes, in 1993. To experiment with a different restaurant format and menu offerings, the company renovated the Saint Louis Bread Company stores and re-imaged their identity, naming them Panera Bread. Clearly, something worked: from 1993 to 1997, the average unit volumes at these stores increased by 75%.

Executives at Au Bon Pain saw the potential for this new restaurant concept and dedicated themselves—and all of the company's financial resources—to building this brand. In 1999, the company sold all of its business units except for the Panera-concept stores. The reorganized company was, not surprisingly, christened Panera Bread.[44]

Since then, the new brand has sought to distinguish itself in the soup-and-sandwich restaurant category. Its offerings have grown to include not only a variety of soups and sandwiches, but also soufflès, salads, panini, and a variety of pastries and sweets. Most of the menu offerings somehow pay homage to the company name and heritage—bread. Panera takes great pride in noting that its loaves are hand-made and baked fresh daily. To conserve valuable real estate in the retail outlets, as well as to cut the necessary training for new employees, many bread doughs are manufactured off-site at one of the company's 17 manufacturing plants. The dough is then delivered by truck—over as many as 9.7 million miles per year—daily to the stores for shaping and baking.[45]

At this point, there are nearly 950 Panera Bread outlets in 37 states. Franchise stores outnumber company-owned outlets approximately two to one.[46]

Modern Tastes, Modern Trends

Panera's success has come partly from its ability to predict long-term trends and orient the company toward innovating to fulfill consumers. Its self-perception as a purveyor of artisan bread well predated the current national trend (having rebounded from the brief low-carb craze) for fresh bread and the explosion of artisan bakeries through metropolitan America.

Consumers' desire for organic and all-natural foods, once thought of as a marginal market force, has become a groundswell. Keenly positioning itself at the forefront of retail outlets supporting this trend, Panera recently introduced a children's menu called Panera Kids. It features kid-friendly ingredients like peanut butter, American cheese, and yogurt, and the all-natural and organic designations for the foods will please choosy parents.[47]

In addition, proactively responding to unease in the marketplace about the role of trans fats in a healthy diet, Panera voluntarily removed trans fats from its menu. "Panera recognized that trans fat was a growing concern to our customers and the medical community. Therefore we made it a priority to eliminate it from our menu," said Tom Gumpel, Director of Bakery Development for Panera Bread. Though reformulating the menu incurred unexpected costs, all Panera menu items are now free from trans fats, save for some small amounts that occur naturally in dairy and meat products, as well as some condiments.[48]

According to Ron Shaich, chairman and CEO of Panera, "Real success never comes by simply responding to the day-to-day pressures; in fact, most of that is simply noise. The key to leading an organization is understanding the long-term trends at play and getting the organization ready to respond to it."[49]

And lest it be forgotten, we are a Coffee Nation. For customers who just want to come, grab a quick cup, and get out, Panera has just the thing. In many stores, coffee customers can avoid the normal line and head straight for the cash register, where they can pick up a cup, drop a small fee into a nearby can, and go directly to the java station. Caffeine-crazed customers can avoid the maddening line during a morning rush and cut the wait for that first steaming sip.

What Makes a Customer Stay?

Panera learned from mega-competitor Starbucks that offering wireless Internet access can make customers linger after their initial purchase, thus increasing the likelihood of a secondary purchase. But the disadvantage of the Starbucks model is the cost to consumers—about $10 for daily access. And though Starbucks can afford to turn away customers, there isn't exactly a booming market for pay-per-use Wi-Fi access. Panera caught sight of the demand for free Wi-Fi early on, and now more than 700 of its stores offer customers a complimentary access. According to spokesperson Julie Somers, the decision to offer Wi-Fi began as a way to separate Panera from the competition and to exemplify the company's welcoming atmosphere.

"We are the kind of environment where all customers are welcome to hang out," Somers said. "They can get a quick bite or a cup of coffee, read the paper or use a computer, and stay as long as they like. And in the course of staying, people may have a cappuccino and a pastry or a soup." She went on to note that the chief corporate benefit to offering Wi-Fi is that wireless customers tend to help fill out the slow time between main meal segments.[50]

Executive Vice-President Neal Yanofsky concurred. "We just think it's one more reason to come visit our cafes," he said. And wireless users' tendency to linger is just fine with him. "It leads to food purchases," he concluded.[51]

Profits Rise along with the Dough

All of Panera's attention to the monitoring of trends has paid off handsomely. The company's stock has grown thirteen-fold since its founding, creating more than $1 billion in shareholder value. *Business Week* recognized Panera as one of its "100 Hot Growth Companies." Even more recently, the *Wall Street Journal* recognized the company as the top performer in the Restaurants and Bars category for one-year returns (63% return), five-year returns (42% return), and ten-year returns (32% return) to shareholders. In addition, across the 1,000 largest companies evaluated, Panera was the 28th best performer as measured by shareholder return over the last 10 years.[52]

Rising to the Top, then Staying There

Panera Bread has demonstrated that sticking to company ideals while successfully forecasting—and then leading the response to—long-term industry trends will please customers time and time again. The low-carb craze didn't faze Panera, but can it continue to navigate the changing dietary trends?

REVIEW QUESTIONS

1. Is Panera Bread company wise to limit the proportion of new stores it offers to franchisees? Why or why not?
2. Has Panera been proactive enough in responding to changing market demands for healthier, more natural food?
3. Suggest some qualities of Panera that give it a competitive advantage in its industry.

TEAM PROJECT

Organizational Culture Walk

And the end of all our exploring
Will be to arrive where we started
And know the place for the first time.

These are famous lines from T. S. Eliot's well-quoted poem *Little Gidding*. But how often do we fail to "explore" as we engage in the events of every day living and, consequently, fail to really "know" the world around us?

Question: What organizational cultures do we encounter and deal with every day, and what are their implications for employees, customers, and organizational performance?

Research Directions:

- Make two lists. *List 1* should identify the things that represent the core cultures of organizations. *List 2* should identify the things that represent the observable cultures of organizations. For each item on the two lists, identify one or more "indicators" that you might use to describe this aspect of the culture for an actual organization.

- Take an *organizational culture walk* through a major shopping area of your local community. Choose at least three business establishments. Visit each as a customer, and put your "organizational culture senses" to work. Start gathering data on your Lists 1 and 2. Keep gathering it while you are in the business and right through your departure. Make good notes and gather your thoughts together after leaving. Do this for each of the three organizations.

- Analyze and compare your data to identify the major cultural attributes of the three organizations and how they influence customers and organizational performance.

- Use the results of your walkabout for a report on the relationship between organizational cultures and performance, as well as on the relationship between organizational cultures and employee motivation and customer satisfaction.

PERSONAL MANAGEMENT

Diversity Maturity

DIVERSITY MATURITY is essential if you are to work well in today's organizations. It is a cornerstone for personal inclusivity. Consultant R. Roosevelt Thomas uses the following questions when testing diversity maturity among people in the workplace. Answer the questions. Be honest; admit where you still have work left to do. Use your answers to help set future goals to ensure that your actions, not just your words, consistently display positive diversity values.

- Do you accept responsibility for improving your performance?
- Do you understand diversity concepts?
- Do you make decisions about others based on their abilities?
- Do you understand that diversity issues are complex?
- Are you able to cope with tensions in addressing diversity?
- Are you willing to challenge the way things are?
- Are you willing to learn continuously?

Building the Brand Called "You"   Double check your diversity maturity. Keep a log for the next three days on how you approached, behaved, and emotionally reacted to situations in which you worked with or socially met persons "different" from you. Do a "similar" check for one or more of your acquaintances by observing how they react in similar situations. Try to engage them in a mutual discussion of how pluralism and inclusion is or is not part of your organizational culture. Complete the self-assessment–Diversity Awareness. Consider its insights into your diversity maturity.

NEXT STEPS: MANAGEMENT LEARNING WORKBOOK

Self-Assessments
- Diversity Awareness (#7)
- Organizational Design Preferences (#17)
- Are You Cosmopolitan? (#18)

Experiential Exercises
- Which Organization Culture Fits You? (#8)
- Case of the Contingency Workforce (#22)

Global Dimensions of Management

5

Down the Block and Around the World

More companies are realizing that in order to be competitive, they have to take sourcing, sales, and production overseas. And although the advantages are generally understood up front, sometimes hidden costs can make the decision to go global infinitely more complex.

For thousands of years, businesses of one form or another needed only worry about satisfying the needs of local consumers. But as technology has essentially cut the distance between faraway lands, many companies are so focused on worldwide ventures that they run the risk of failing to establish a brand identity unique to their home.

Such has not been the case for New Balance. Headquartered in the United States for 100 years, their shoe factory in downtown Boston—as well as four others in New England—stand as testament to the will of a competitive manufacturing company to be both a global player and maintain a domestic identity for both corporate activities and production.

New Balance has so far straddled the outsourcing dilemma: it maintains a domestic presence to create a competitive image advantage, but also outsources enough production to keep cash free for other purposes.

New Balance has gained a reputation for consistently chosing to follow a different path than their big-brand competition. As examples, consider their early emphasis on superior technology (as opposed to fashion); their reluctance to enter the many and varied markets of their competitors (for the most part, New Balance has kept to what they do best—running and walking shoes), and their

What *They* Think

The challenges of litigating in China have "nothing to do with the law as written. They have much to do with the law as applied."
Harley Lewin, intellectual property litigator

LOCAL: *"There's a tremendous number of small businesses that have been able to get tremendous economic returns because all of a sudden their market is no longer a local market."*
Eric Schmidt, CEO of Google

GLOBAL: *"The nature of the global business environment guarantees that no matter how hard we work to create a stable and healthy organization, our organization will continue to experience dramatic changes far beyond our control."*
Margaret J. Wheatley, writer and management consultant

preference to avoid sponsoring big-name sports stars (instead, billing their products as extraordinary shoes for common athletes).

With an advertising budget resembling that of a purely domestic company, New Balance has still had considerable success in the international market: Gross sales have reached $1.54 billion, with about $500 million of that coming from Europe and Japan. And to top those numbers, the company plans to target even more of Asia—mostly China, South Korea, and India—as well as South America.[1]

But international success can come at some cost. Although proud of keeping a notable amount of production in the United States, the company has been unable to resist the temptation of cheap Chinese labor. An estimated 70% of New Balance shoes are now made in China, with an additional 5% constructed in Vietnam.[2]

By doing so, the privately-held company found itself engaged in a very public battle and exposed the business world to the very real liability of foreign contractors. One Taiwanese contractor moved his factory from Taiwan to mainland China to take advantage of both the cheaper labor and burgeoning counterfeit market. The contractor sold inexpensive, unlicensed shoes throughout Asia.

The challenges of litigating in China have "nothing to do with the law as written," said Harley Lewin, an intellectual property litigator with 30 years of international experience. "They have much to do with the law as applied."[3]

Though most big brands will not admit to being victimized in this way, the practice is thought to be widespread, and New Balance earned accolades from IP professionals for bringing the issue to light.

"When a brand owner shuts down a factory," explained Jeffrey Unger, CEO of GenuOne, a brand-protection management firm, "you'll see the same factory start up two months later making counterfeit product. They know where to buy the raw materials and know how to move product."[4]

It seems for New Balance, as with so many other companies, the competitiveness of doing local business is understood by the cost-cutting dynamics of a global labor economy.

The Numbers

Most Popular Brands To Be Counterfeited

Microsoft	7.5% of all incidents
Sony	4.3%
Adobe	3%
Louis Vuitton	3%
Viagra	3%
Autodesk	2%
Christian Dior	2%
CSA	2%
Gucci	2%
Nike	2%

Quick Facts

* Judges outnumber lawyers in China 200,000 to 140,000.[5]
* Projections indicate that 3.3 million jobs will be shipped overseas by 2015.[6]
* New Balance CEO Jim Davis prizes loyalty: the members of the company's executive team have all been with the company for more than 10 years.[7]
* Intellectual property theft now accounts for 31% of global counterfeiting.[8]
* Of the 100 largest economies in the world, 52 are corporations, only 48 are countries.[9]

What Do *You* Think?

1. What advantages, if any, does New Balance gain by keeping a portion of its manufacturing within the United States?
2. To avoid issues of counterfeit manufacturing, would New Balance be better off bringing its shoe production back to the United States?

Global Dimensions of Management			
Study Question 1	**Study Question 2**	**Study Question 3**	**Study Question 4**
Management and Globalization	**Multinational Corporations**	**Culture and Global Diversity**	**Management across Cultures**
■ International management ■ Why companies go international ■ International business forms ■ International business environments	■ Types of MNCs ■ Pros and cons of MNC operations ■ Ethical issues for MNCs	■ Cultural intelligence ■ Silent languages of culture ■ Values and national cultures ■ Cultural insights from Project Globe	■ Are management theories universal? ■ Global organizational learning
Learning Check 1	**Learning Check 2**	**Learning Check 3**	**Learning Check 4**

Our global community is rich with information, opportunities, controversies, and complications. The Internet and television bring on-the-spot news from around the world into our homes; the world's newspapers can be read online. It is possible to board a plane in New York and fly nonstop to Bangkok; it is sometimes less expensive to fly from Columbus, Ohio, to Paris than to Albany, New York. Colleges and universities offer a growing variety of study-abroad programs; an international MBA is an increasingly desirable credential.

On the business side of things, IBM employs over 40,000 workers in India, where it has five software development centers. The Chrysler PT Cruiser is built in Mexico for Daimler-Chrysler of Germany; Ford owns Volvo; the "big three" Japanese automakers—Honda, Nissan, Toyota—get as much as 80 to 90 percent of their profits from sales in America. The front fuselage of Boeing's new 787 Dreamliner is made by a Japanese company. Nike is supplied by over 120 factories in China alone. Worldwide, its contractors employ over 600,000 workers outside of the United States.

The same trends and patterns are evident in other industries. Indeed, national boundaries are fast blurring as businesses of all sizes and types now travel the trade routes of the world. The growing power of global businesses affects all of us in our roles as citizens, consumers, and career-seekers.

MANAGEMENT AND GLOBALIZATION

■ In the **global economy** resources, markets, and competition are worldwide in scope.

■ **Globalization** is the process of growing interdependence among elements of the global economy.

This is the age of the **global economy** in which resource supplies, product markets, and business competition are worldwide rather than purely local or national in scope.[10] It is also a time heavily influenced by the forces of **globalization,** the process of growing interdependence among the components in the global economy.[11] Harvard scholar and consultant Rosabeth Moss Kanter describes it as "one of the most powerful and pervasive influences on nations, businesses, workplaces, communities, and lives.[12]

As businesses spread their reach around the world, large multinational businesses are increasingly adopting transnational or "global" identities, rather than being identified with a national home. The growing strength and penetration of these businesses worldwide are viewed by some as potential threats to national economies and to their local business systems, labor markets, and cultures. All this adds up to some uncertainty as executives move into new and uncharted competitive territories. America Online's cofounder Stephen M. Case once described the scene this way: "I sometimes feel like I'm behind the wheel of a race car. One of the biggest challenges is there are no road signs to help navigate. And in fact . . . no one has yet determined which side of the road we're supposed to be on."[13]

INTERNATIONAL MANAGEMENT

The term used to describe management in businesses and other organizations with interests in more than one country is **international management.** There is no denying its importance. Procter & Gamble, for example, pursues a global strategy with a presence in more than 70 countries; the majority of McDonald's sales are now coming from outside the United States, with the "Golden Arches" prominent on city streets from Moscow to Tokyo to Budapest to Rio De Janiero.

■ **International management** involves managing operations in more than one country.

As the leaders of these and other companies press forward with global initiatives, the international management challenges and opportunities of working across borders—national and cultural—must be mastered. Allen Kinzer, now retired, was the first American manager Honda hired for its Marysville, Ohio, plant. Although people were worried whether or not U.S. workers could adapt to the Japanese firm's production methods, technology, and style, it all worked out. Says Kinzer: "It wasn't easy blending the cultures; anyone who knew anything about the industry at the time would have to say it was a bold move." Bold move, indeed! Honda now produces almost 500,000 cars per year in America. It is only one among hundreds of foreign firms offering employment opportunities to U.S. workers.[14]

What about you? Are you prepared for the challenges of international management? Are you informed about the world and what is taking place amidst the forces of globalization? A new breed of manager, the **global manager,** is increasingly sought after. This is someone informed about international developments, transnational in outlook, competent in working with people from different cultures, and always aware of regional developments in a changing world.

■ A **global manager** is culturally aware and informed on international affairs.

WHY COMPANIES GO INTERNATIONAL

John Chambers, chairman of Cisco Systems Inc., says: "I will put my jobs anywhere in the world where the right infrastructure is, with the right educated workforce, with the right supportive government."[15] Cisco and other firms like it are **international businesses.** They conduct for-profit transactions of goods and services across national boundaries. International businesses are also the foundations of world trade, helping to move raw materials, finished products, and specialized services from one country to another in the global economy. The reasons why businesses go international include:

■ An **international business** conducts commercial transactions across national boundaries.

- *Profits*—Global operations offer greater profit potential.
- *Customers*—Global operations offer new markets to sell products.

- *Suppliers*—Global operations offer access to needed raw materials.
- *Capital*—Global operations offer access to financial resources.
- *Labor*—Global operations offer access to lower labor costs.

New Balance, featured in The Topic opening for this chapter, is a classic example. It started some 100 years ago in Boston, still views itself as an American firm, but sells in over 120 different countries. The firm engages the full spectrum of international business opportunities in its quest for continued business success.

FORMS OF INTERNATIONAL BUSINESS

The common forms of international business are shown in *Figure 5.1*. When a business is just getting started internationally, global sourcing, exporting/importing, and licensing and franchising are the usual ways to begin. These are *market entry strategies* that involve the sale of goods or services to foreign markets without expensive investments. Joint ventures and wholly owned subsidiaries are *direct investment strategies.* They require major capital commitments, but create rights of ownership and control over operations in the foreign country.

Market Entry Strategies

■ In **global sourcing,** materials or services are purchased around the world for local use.

A common first step into international business is **global sourcing**—the process of purchasing materials, manufacturing components, or business services from around the world. It is an international division of labor in which activities are performed in countries where they can be done well at the lowest cost. The goal is to take advantage of international wage gaps and the availability of skilled labor by contracting for goods and services in low-cost foreign locations. In auto manufacturing, global sourcing of components may mean purchasing windshields and instrument panels from Mexico and electrical components from Vietnam. In services, it may mean setting up toll-free customer support call centers in the Philippines, or contracting for computer software engineers in India.

■ In **exporting,** local products are sold abroad.

■ **Importing** is the process of acquiring products abroad and selling them in domestic markets.

A second form of international business involves **exporting**—selling locally made products in foreign markets—and/or **importing**—buying foreign-made products and selling them in domestic markets. Because the growth of export industries creates local jobs, governments often offer special advice and assistance to businesses that are trying to develop or expand their export markets. One example is an export initiative that came by chance for Franklin Jacobs, founder of the St. Louis-based Falcon Products Inc., a commercial furniture company. While on a tour through Europe, he "discovered that my products were a lot better and a lot cheaper" than those on the market there. An opportunist, Jacobs rented exposition space at the U.S. Embassy in London, shipped a container load of his furniture, and received

Figure 5.1 Common forms of international business—from market entry to direct investment strategies.

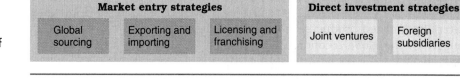

Market entry strategies			Direct investment strategies	
Global sourcing	Exporting and importing	Licensing and franchising	Joint ventures	Foreign subsidiaries

Increasing involvement in ownership and control of foreign operations

INSIGHTS

Business Thrives in a World of Opportunity

What do Victoria's Secret, Express, Bath & Body Works, The Limited, The White Barn Candle Co., Aura Science, and Henri Bendel have in common? They all trace their roots to 1963 and a small women's clothing store in Columbus, Ohio. That single store has grown to more than 4,000 now, all part of a company known globally for building a family of the best fashion names in the world—Limited Brands.

Limited Brands is one of the world's most admired fashion retailers. Founder, chairman, and CEO Leslie Wexner is a member of the retail CEOs all-star team, being cited as a "pioneer of specialty brands" and someone with special retailing "vision and focus." All this has been achieved in a competitive industry described as challenged by "logistics, merchandising, marketing, human resources, property and, in some cases, global expansion."

There is more to Limited Brands than its 4,000+ retail stores. Standing behind the displays and the fashion merchandise is a large operation that depends on vast worldwide networks of suppliers and subcontractors for its products. But its global reach must be well managed and its ethical standards must be maintained.

The firm sources its products from around the world. To ensure quality and protect its brand, its supplier and subcontractor relationships are guided by a "What We Stand For" policy designed to ensure ethical operations. The policy states: "We will not do business with individuals or suppliers that do not meet our standards. We expect our suppliers to promote an environment of dignity, respect and opportunity; provide safe and healthy working conditions; offer fair compensation through wages and other benefits; hire workers of legal age, who accept employment on a voluntary basis; and maintain reasonable working hours."

For its role in helping to expand the apparel manufacturing industry in sub-Saharan Africa to over $1 billion in sales, The Limited was recognized with a Special Recognition Award for Business Enterprise in Africa from the Africa-America Institute.

In respect to his business success, Leslie Wexner sums it up this way: "Better brands. Best brands. I don't believe bigger is better. I believe better is better. Period."

over US$ 200,000 in orders. His new export initiative resulted in job expansion at the firm.[16]

Another form of international business is the **licensing agreement,** where foreign firms pay a fee for rights to make or sell another company's products in a specified region. The license typically grants access to a unique manufacturing technology, special patent, or trademark. **Franchising** is a form of licensing in which the foreign firm buys the rights to use another's name and operating methods in its home country. As in domestic franchising agreements, firms like McDonald's, Wendy's, Subway, and others sell facility designs, equipment, product ingredients and recipes, and management systems to foreign investors, while retaining certain product and operating controls.

■ In a **licensing agreement** one firm pays a fee for rights to make or sell another company's products.

■ In **franchising** a fee is paid for rights to use another firm's name and operating methods.

Direct Investment Strategies

To establish a direct investment presence in a foreign country, many firms enter into **joint ventures.** These are co-ownership arrangements that pool resources and share risks and control for business operations. A joint

■ A **joint venture** operates in a foreign country through co-ownership with local partners.

venture may be established by equity purchases and/or direct investments by a foreign partner in an existing operation; it may also involve the creation of an entirely new business by a foreign and local partner. An international joint ventures is a type of *strategic alliance* in which partners gain things through cooperation that otherwise would be difficult to achieve independently. In return for its investment in a local operation, for example, the outside or foreign partner often gains both access to new markets and the assistance of a local partner who understands them. In return for its investment, the local partner often gains new technology as well as opportunities for its employees to learn new skills.

A foreign subsidiary is a local operation completely owned and controlled by a foreign firm. Foreign subsidiaries may be set up by direct investment in startup operations called *greenfield ventures,* or through equity purchases in existing ones. When making such investments, foreign firms are clearly taking a business risk. They must be confident that they possess the expertise needed to manage and conduct business affairs successfully in the new environment. This is where prior experience gained through joint ventures can prove very beneficial.

Although establishing a foreign subsidiary represents the highest level of involvement in international operations, it can make very good business sense. When Nissan opened a plant in Canton, Mississippi, an auto analyst for a Japanese brokerage firm said: "It's a smart strategy to shift production to North America. They're reducing their exposure through building more in their regional markets, as well as being able to meet consumers' needs more quickly."[17]

■ A **foreign subsidiary** is a local operation completely owned by a foreign firm.

INTERNATIONAL BUSINESS ENVIRONMENTS

The international business environment is complex and dynamic—and highly competitive. International managers must master the demands of operating with worldwide suppliers, distributors, customers, and competitors. Among the many challenges, two that are often center stage include the growing role of regional economic alliances around the world and differences among nations in their laws and legal structures.

Regional Economic Alliances

The **European Union** (EU) now links 27 countries that agree to support mutual economic growth by removing barriers that previously limited cross-border trade and business development.[18] Its common currency, the **Euro**, has had a major worldwide impact. The United States, Canada, and Mexico are joined in the North American Free Trade Agreement, or **NAFTA**. This alliance largely frees the flow of goods and services, workers, and investments within a region that has more potential consumers than its European rival, the EU.[19] Elsewhere in the Americas the *MERCOSUR* agreement links Bolivia, Brazil, Paraguay, Uruguay, and Argentina; the Andean Pact links Venezuela, Colombia, Equador, Peru, and Bolivia; and the Carribean Community, CARICOM, is growing as an economic linkage.

When one looks toward East and Southeast Asia, the Asia Pacific Economic Forum is growing in stature and influence. Member countries are even talking about the possibility of a regional currency along the lines of the euro.

Africa is also a continent in the business news.[20] African countries are attracting more international investments, and reports indicate that

■ The **European Union** is a political and economic alliance of European countries.

■ The **Euro** is the new common European currency.

■ **NAFTA** is the North American Free Trade Agreement linking Canada, the United States, and Mexico in an economic alliance.

the region's contextual problems are manageable.[21] The Southern Africa Development Community (SADC) links 14 countries of southern Africa in trade and economic development efforts. Its objectives include harmonizing and rationalizing strategies for sustainable development among member countries. Post-apartheid South Africa, in particular, has benefitted from political revival. A country of almost 50 million people and great natural resources, it already accounts for half the continent's purchasing power.

Laws and Legal Structures

Differences in legal environments among nations create substantial international business challenges. Organizations are expected to abide by the laws of the host country in which they are operating. In the United States, for example, executives of foreign-owned companies must worry about antitrust issues that prevent competitors from regularly talking to one another. They also must deal with a variety of special laws regarding occupational health and safety, equal employment opportunity, sexual harassment, and other matters—all constraints potentially different from those they find at home.

The more home- and host-country laws differ, the more difficult and complex it is for international businesses to adapt to local ways. In China, for example, Google, Yahoo and other firms have faced laws that restrict Internet usage for the country's citizens. They have also faced controversies elsewhere in the world when they comply with the Chinese laws.

Common legal problems in international business involve incorporation practices and business ownership; negotiating and implementing contracts with foreign parties; protecting patents, trademarks, and copyrights; and handling foreign exchange restrictions. Intellectual property rights, for example, have long been a source of dispute between Western businesses and China. Problems with software piracy and copyright violations of CDs and designer fashions are well known. But General Motors, long an investor in China, has had its own problems there. The firm's China joint venture executives noticed that a new model from a fast-growing local competitor—Chery Automobile, partially owned by GM's Chinese partner—looked very similar to one of their own cars. GM claimed in local courts that its design was copied; the competitor denied the charges and plans to export its cars to the United States.[22]

When disputes between nations relate to international trade, they can end up before the **World Trade Organization** (WTO). This is a global institution established to promote free trade and open markets around the world. Some 140+ members of the WTO agree to give one another **most favored nation status**—the most favorable treatment for imports and exports. Although members agree to ongoing negotiations and the reduction of tariffs and trade restrictions, trading relationships are often difficult. When problems arise, the WTO offers a mechanism for monitoring international trade and resolving disputes among countries.

Protectionism in the form of political calls for tariffs and favorable treatments to help protect domestic businesses from foreign competition is a common complication of international trade. Government leaders, such as the president of the United States, face internal political dilemmas involving the often-conflicting goals of seeking freer international trade while still protecting domestic industries. These dilemmas make it difficult to reach international agreement on trade matters and create controversies for the WTO.

▪ **World Trade Organization** member nations agree to negotiate and resolve disputes about tariffs and trade restrictions.

▪ **Most favored nation status** gives a trading partner most favorable treatment for imports and exports.

▪ **Protectionism** is a call for tariffs and favorable treatments to protect domestic firms from foreign competition.

MULTINATIONAL CORPORATIONS

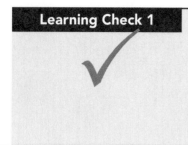

A true **multinational corporation** (MNC) is a business firm with extensive international operations in more than one foreign country. Premier MNCs found in annual listings such as *Fortune* magazine's Global 500 include such global giants as General Electric, Exxon, and Wal-Mart from the United States; Mitsubishi, Toyota, and Sony of Japan; DaimlerChrysler of Germany and Royal Dutch/Shell Group of the Netherlands and Great Britain. Also important on the world scene are *multinational organizations* whose nonprofit missions and operations span the globe. Examples include the International Federation of Red Cross and Red Crescent Societies, the United Nations, and the World Bank.

■ A **multinational corporation** is a business with extensive international operations in more than one foreign country.

TYPES OF MULTINATIONAL CORPORATIONS

A typical MNC operates in many countries but has corporate headquarters in one home or host country. Microsoft, Apple Computer, and McDonald's are among the ready examples. Although deriving substantial sales and profits from international sources, these firms and others like them typically also have strong national identifications. But as the global economy grows more competitive, many multinationals are acting more like **transnational corporations.** They try to operate worldwide without being identified with one national home.[23]

■ A **transnational corporation** is an MNC that operates worldwide on a borderless basis.

Executives of transnationals view the entire world as their domain for acquiring resources, locating production facilities, marketing goods and services, and communicating brand image. They seek total integration of global operations, try to operate across borders without home-based prejudices, make major decisions from a global perspective, distribute work among worldwide points of excellence, and employ senior executives from many different countries. Nestlé is a good example in foods; Asea Brown Boveri (ABB) is another in diversified conglomerates. When one buys a Nestlé product in Brazil or has a neighbor working for ABB in Columbus, Ohio, who would know that both are actually registered Swiss companies?

PROS AND CONS OF MULTINATIONAL CORPORATIONS

The United Nations has reported that MNCs hold one-third of the world's productive assets and control 70 percent of world trade. At recent count, 52 of the largest economies in the world are multinational corporations.

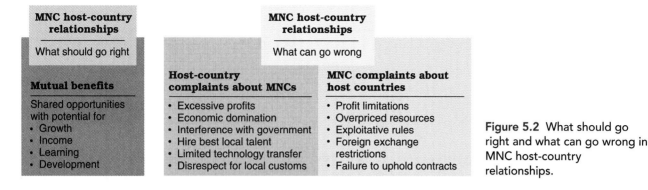

Figure 5.2 What should go right and what can go wrong in MNC host-country relationships.

Furthermore, more than 90 percent of MNCs are based in the Northern Hemisphere. While this may bring a sense of both accomplishment and future opportunity to business leaders, it can also be very threatening to small and less-developed countries and to their domestic industries.

Host-Country Issues

Ideally, global corporations and the countries that "host" their foreign operations should both benefit. But, *Figure 5.2* shows how things can and do go both right and wrong in MNC host-country relationships.

The *potential host-country benefits* of MNCs include larger tax bases, increased employment opportunities, technology transfers, the introduction of new industries, and the development of local resources. The *potential host-country costs* include complaints that MNCs extract excessive profits, dominate the local economy, interfere with the local government, do not respect local customs and laws, fail to help domestic firms develop, hire the most talented of local personnel, and do not transfer their most advanced technologies.[24]

Home-Country Issues

MNCs may also encounter difficulties in the home country where their headquarters are located. Even as many MNCs try to operate more globally, home-country governments and citizens still tend to identify them with local and national interests. When an MNC outsources, cuts back, or closes a domestic operation to shift work to lower-cost international destinations, the loss of local jobs is controversial. Corporate decision makers are likely to be engaged by government and community leaders in critical debate about a firm's domestic social responsibilities. *Home-country criticisms of MNCs* include complaints about transferring jobs out of the country, shifting capital investments abroad, and engaging in corrupt practices in foreign settings.

ETHICAL ISSUES FOR MULTINATIONAL CORPORATIONS

The ethical aspects of international business deserve special attention. **Corruption**, engaging in illegal practice to further one's business interests, is a source of continuing controversy. In the United States, the Foreign Corrupt Practices Act makes it illegal for American firms and their managers to engage in corrupt practices overseas, including giving bribes and excessive

Corruption involves illegal practices to further one's business interests.

ISSUES AND SITUATIONS

Sweatshop Hunter

Help Wanted
Sweatshop Hunter

One of the world's premier fashion merchandisers seeks an experienced executive to head staff in charge of monitoring international suppliers for ethics and social responsibility practices. The successful candidate will have a strong commitment to ethics and social responsibility in business, strong communication skills and cultural intelligence, confidence in handling conflict situations, and the capacity to work well in relationships spanning shop-floor workers to chief executives.

This ad is fabricated; the job it features is real. At Hewlett-Packard it's filled by Bonnie Nixon-Gardiner. She has a middle-management appointment, overseeing the work of some 70 auditors, and with major responsibilities for keeping track of over 200 supplier factories. Nixon-Gardiner and her staff travel the world inspecting HP suppliers with the goal of making sure that working conditions are up to HP's standards. She describes her goal this way: "My 10-year vision is for [consumers to know that] when you touch a technology product you are guaranteed it was made in a social and environmentally responsible way."

> *Traveling with a Sweatshop Hunter:*
>
> *Nixon-Gardiner arrives at Foxconn Electronics in Long Hua, China. Her hosts try to move her into a conference room, but she declines and opts to walk about the factory with its multiple buildings and 200,000 + employees. "Look," she tells her hosts when they balk, "this isn't going to work unless you're totally transparent with me."*
>
> *She found that the noise was too loud for workers on some machines; the firm agreed to purchase ear protectors. On a later visit she called for and got more changes—special enclosures for the machines and purchase of the best ear protection devices available. Her no-nonsense but polite approach has been described by a colleague as "it's like being kissed and slapped at the same time."*

Critical Response

How would you like a job like this? Should all international businesses have a similar position? What special skills and capabilities does Nixon-Gardiner need to succeed in this job? Were you surprised that she is described as a "middle manager"? With these responsibilities, should she be on the top management team?

■ **Sweatshops** employ workers at very low wages for long hours and in poor working conditions.

commissions to foreign officials in return for business favors. The law specifically bans payoffs to foreign officials to obtain or keep business, provides punishments for executives who know about or are involved in such activities, and requires detailed accounting records for international business transactions. Some critics believe this act fails to recognize the "reality" of business as practiced in many foreign nations. They complain that American companies are at a competitive disadvantage because they can't offer the same "deals" as competitors from other nations—deals that locals may regard as standard business practices. But the fact is that many nations are starting to pass similar laws.

Sweatshops, business operations that employ workers at low wages for long hours and in poor working conditions, are another concern in the global business arena. Networks of outsourcing contracts are now common as manufacturers follow the world's low-cost labor supplies—countries like the Philippines, Sri Lanka, and Vietnam are popular destinations. Yet Nike Inc. has learned that a global company will be held publicly accountable for the work standards and employment practices of its foreign subcontractors. Facing activist criticism, the company revised its labor practices after a review by the consulting firm Goodworks International. Nike now hosts a special Web site with reports and audit results on its international labor practices at more than 750 manufacturing sites and contractors in some 50 countries.[25]

Child labor, the full-time employment of children for work otherwise done by adults, is another international business ethics issue. It has been made especially visible by activist concerns regarding the manufacture of handmade carpets in countries like Pakistan. Initiatives to eliminate child labor include an effort by the Rugmark Foundation to discourage purchases of carpets that do not carry its label. The "Rugmark" label is earned by a certification process to guarantee that a carpet manufacturer does not use illegal child labor.[26]

▨ **Child labor** is the full-time employment of children for work otherwise done by adults.

Yet another ethical issue relates to global concerns for environmental protection. Industrial pollution of cities, hazardous waste, depletion of natural resources, and related concerns are now worldwide issues. The concept of **sustainable development** is a popular guideline advanced by activist groups. It is "development that meets the needs of the present without compromising the ability of future generations to meet their own needs."[27] As global corporate citizens, MNCs are increasingly expected to uphold high standards in dealing with sustainable development and protection of the natural environment—whenever and wherever they operate.

▨ **Sustainable development** meets the needs of the present without hurting future generations.

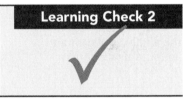

Be sure you can ▪ differentiate a multinational corporation from a transnational corporation ▪ list at least three host-country complaints and three home-country complaints about MNC operations ▪ define the terms corruption, sweatshop, and child labor ▪ illustrate how each of these practices can create ethical problems for international businesses

Learning Check 2

CULTURE AND GLOBAL DIVERSITY

Culture is the shared set of beliefs, values, and patterns of behavior common to a group of people. Anyone who has visited another country knows that cultural differences exist. **Culture shock**, the confusion and discomfort a person experiences when in an unfamiliar culture, is a reminder that many of these differences must be mastered to travel comfortably and do business around the world. And, **ethnocentrism**, the tendency to view one's culture as superior to others, is a surprisingly common tendency. Local customs vary in too many ways for most of us to become true experts in the many cultures of our diverse world. Yet there are things we can do to respect differences, avoid ethnocentrism, and minimize culture shock as suggested in *Management Smarts 5.1*.[28]

▨ **Culture** is a shared set of beliefs, values, and patterns of behavior common to a group of people.

▨ **Culture shock** is the confusion and discomfort a person experiences when in an unfamiliar culture.

▨ **Ethnocentrism** is the tendency to consider one's culture as superior to others.

CULTURAL INTELLIGENCE

A U.S. businessman once went to meet a Saudi Arabian official. He sat in the office with crossed legs and the sole of his shoe exposed, an unintentional sign of disrespect in the local culture. He passed documents to the host using his left hand, which Muslims consider unclean. He declined when coffee was offered, suggesting criticism of the Saudi's hospitality. What was the price for these cultural miscues? A $10 million contract was lost to a Korean executive better versed in Arab ways.[29]

Some might say that this American's behavior was ethnocentric, so self-centered that he ignored and showed no concern for the culture of his Arab

MANAGEMENT SMARTS 5.1

Stages in adjusting to a new culture

- *Confusion:* First contacts with the new culture leave you anxious, uncomfortable, and in need of information and advice.
- *Small victories:* Continued interactions bring some "successes," and your confidence grows in handling daily affairs.
- *The honeymoon:* A time of wonderment, cultural immersion, and even infatuation, with local ways viewed positively.
- *Irritation and anger:* A time when the "negatives" overwhelm the "positives," and the new culture becomes a target of your criticism.
- *Reality:* A time of rebalancing; you are able to enjoy the new culture while accommodating its less desirable elements.

■ **Cultural intelligence** is the ability to accept and adapt to new cultures.

host. Others might excuse him as suffering culture shock. Maybe he was so uncomfortable upon arrival in Saudi Arabia that all he could think about was offering his contract and leaving as quickly as possible. Still others might give him the benefit of the doubt. It could have been that he was well intentioned but didn't have time to learn about Saudi culture before making the trip.

Regardless of the possible reasons for the cultural miscues, however, they still worked to his disadvantage. And there is little doubt that he failed to show **cultural intelligence**—the ability to adapt and adjust to new cultures.[30] People with cultural intelligence have high cultural self-awareness, and they are flexible in dealing with cultural differences. In cross-cultural situations they are willing to learn from what is unfamiliar; they modify their behaviors to act with sensitivity to another culture's ways. In other words, someone high in cultural intelligence views cultural differences not as threats but as learning opportunities. This personal quality is probably a good indicator of someone's capacity for success both in international assignments and in relationships with persons of different cultures.[31]

SILENT LANGUAGES OF CULTURE

One of the foundations for developing cultural intelligence is the ability to recognize what Anthropologist Edward T. Hall calls the "silent" languages of culture.[32] They are found in a culture's approach to communication through context, time, and space.

■ **Low-context cultures** emphasize communication via spoken or written words.

■ **High-context cultures** rely on nonverbal and situational cues as well as on spoken or written words in communication.

If we look and listen carefully, Hall believes we should recognize how cultures differ in how their members use language in communication.[33] In **low-context cultures** most communication takes place via the written or spoken word. This is common in the United States, Canada, and Germany, for example. As the saying goes, we say (or write) what we mean, and we mean what we say. In **high-context cultures** things are different. What is actually said or written may convey only part, and sometimes a very small part, of the real message. The rest must be interpreted from nonverbal signals and the situation as a whole, including body language, physical setting, and even past relationships among the people involved. Dinner parties and social gatherings in high-context cultures allow potential business partners to get to know one another. Only after the relationships are established and a context for communication exists is it possible to make business deals.

■ In **monochronic cultures** people tend to do one thing at a time.

■ In **polychronic cultures** time is used to accomplish many different things at once.

Hall also notes that the way people approach and deal with time varies across cultures. He describes a **monochronic culture** as one in which people tend to do one thing at a time. This is typical of the United States, where most business people schedule a meeting for one person or group to focus on one issue for an allotted time.[34] And if someone is late for one of those meetings, or brings an uninvited guest, we tend not to like it. Members of a **polychronic culture** are more flexible toward time and who uses it. They often try to work on many different things at once, perhaps not in any particular order. An American visitor (monochronic culture) to an Egyptian client (polychromic culture) may be frustrated, for example, by continued interruptions as the client greets and deals with people flowing in and out of his office.

Finally, Hall points out that most Americans like and value their own space, perhaps as much space as they can get. We like big offices, big homes, big yards; we get uncomfortable in tight spaces and when others stand too close to us in lines. When someone "talks right in our face," we don't like it; the behavior may even be interpreted as an expression of anger. Members of other cultures can view all of these things quite differently. Hall describes these cultural tendencies in terms of **proxemics**, or how people use interpersonal space to communicate. If you could visit Japan you would notice the difference in proxemics very quickly. Space is precious in Japan; its use is carefully planned and it is respected. Small, tidy homes, offices, shops are the norm; gardens are tiny but immaculate; public spaces are carefully organized for most efficient use.

■ **Proxemics** is how people use space to communicate.

VALUES AND NATIONAL CULTURES

Among the research that has been accomplished on how cultural differences can influence management and organizational practices, the work of Geert Hofstede is often considered a basic starting point. He studied personnel from a U.S.-based MNC operating in 40 countries. First published in his book *Culture's Consequences: International Differences in Work-Related Values*, the research offers preliminary insights for understanding broad differences in national cultures.[35]

Figure 5.3 shows how selected countries rank on the five cultural dimensions Hofstede now uses in his model.

1. *Power distance*—the degree to which a society accepts or rejects the unequal distribution of power among people in organizations and the institutions of society.
2. *Uncertainty avoidance*—the degree to which a society is uncomfortable with risk, change, and situational uncertainty, versus having tolerance for them.

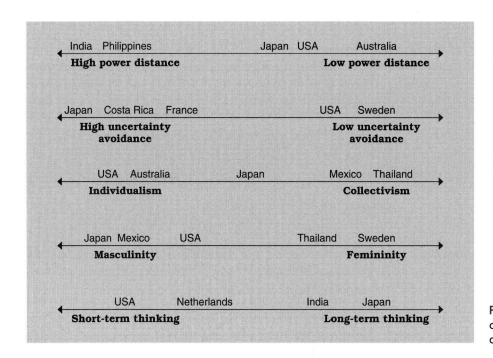

Figure 5.3 How countries compare on Hofstede's dimensions of national culture.

3. *Individualism-collectivism*—the degree to which a society emphasizes individual accomplishments and self-interests, versus collective accomplishments and the interests of groups.
4. *Masculinity-femininity*—the degree to which a society values assertiveness and material success, versus feelings and concern for relationships.[36]
5. *Time orientation*—the degree to which a society emphasizes the short-term versus greater concern for the future.[37]

Hofstede's framework helps identify managerial implications of these potential cultural differences. For example, workers from high power distance cultures such as Singapore can be expected to show great respect toward elders and those senior in authority. Persons in positions of authority, like managers, typically expect others to defer to them and may view their position as deserving of special rights and privileges. In the more uncertainty-avoidance cultures like France, employment practices that increase job security are likely to be favored. Members of high uncertainly avoidance cultures

RESEARCH BRIEF

Stable personality traits and behavioral competencies linked with expatriate effectiveness

A research collaboration brought together teams of scholars from Hong Kong and the United States to investigate the effectiveness of *expatriate workers*. The results of three empirical studies reported in the *Journal of Applied Psychology* by Margaret Shaffer and her colleagues show that individual differences have an impact on expatriate effectiveness.

When organizations send employees to work as expatriates in foreign countries, the assignments can be challenging, and the expats' performance can turn out lower than anticipated. Nevertheless, many employers fail to make fully informed decisions on expatriate assignments.

The researchers propose a model in which expatriate effectiveness is a function of *individual differences* in personalities and competencies. Specifically, they address *stable dispositions* in terms of the *"Big Five" personality traits*: conscientiousness, emotional stability, agreeableness, intellectance, and extroversion; and the *dynamic competencies* of cultural flexibility, task orientation, people orientation, and ethnocentrism.

Expatriate Effectiveness Model

Individual Differences
• Stable dispositions
• Dynamic competencies

Expatriate Effectiveness
• Adjustment
• Withdrawal cognitions
• Performance

The research model was tested in samples of expatriates working in Hong Kong and among Korean expatriates working in other nations. Results show that each of the Big Five traits except conscientiousness predicts some aspect of expatriate effectiveness. Emotional stability was the strongest predictor of withdrawal cognitions, while intellectance was the only predictor of task and contextual performance. Results were less uniform with respect to the link between dynamic competencies and performance, and the researchers believe that study design and/or the presence of unmeasured moderator variables might account for the mixed findings. One of their suggestions is that future research look at the entire model in the context of one well-designed study.

QUESTIONS & APPLICATIONS

Chances are that there are international students in your class or on campus who have worked with or as expatriates. You may also have family and friends with expatriate experience. Why not interview them to gather their views about how expatriates adapt and perform in foreign cultures? Compare the results of your investigation with the model and findings of this research study

Reference: Margaret A. Shaffer, David A. Harrison, Hal Gregersen, J. Steward Black, and Lori A. Ferzandi, "You Can Take it With You: Individual Differences and Expatriate Effectiveness," *Journal of Applied Psychology*, Vol. 91 (2006), pp. 109–125.

are likely to place great emphasis on having and following rules, and display inflexibility in behaviors.

In highly individualistic societies like the United States, workers may be expected to emphasize self-interests more than group loyalty. You will likely here a lot of references to "I" and "me" in conversations with members of individualistic cultures, while "we" and "us" will be more commonly heard in collectivist settings.

Outsiders may find that the workplace in masculine societies such as Japan displays more rigid gender stereotypes. Men and women may be typecast into differing career opportunities, and attributes like aggressiveness and assertiveness may be highly valued. Also, corporate strategies in more long-term cultures are likely to be just that—more long-term oriented. In cultures with a long-term orientation the tendencies are to value patience, persistence, and thrift in service of future goal accomplishment.

CULTURE INSIGHTS FROM PROJECT GLOBE

In an effort to integrate and extend insights on cultural influences on management, a team of international researchers led by Robert House convened to study leadership, organizational practices, and diversity among world cultures.[38] They called the effort project GLOBE, short for Global Leadership and Organizational Behavior Effectiveness.

So far the GLOBE researchers have collected data from 170,000 managers in 62 countries.[39] They discovered that these countries fall into *ten culture clusters*, with societal culture practices more similar among countries within a cluster than across them. As shown in *Figure 5.4*, the researchers use nine dimensions to explore and describe cultural differences among the country clusters.

Two of the GLOBE dimensions are direct fits with Hofstede's framework. They are *power distance*, which is higher in Confucian Asia and lower in Nordic Europe, and *uncertainty avoidance*, which is high in Germanic Europe and low in the Middle East.

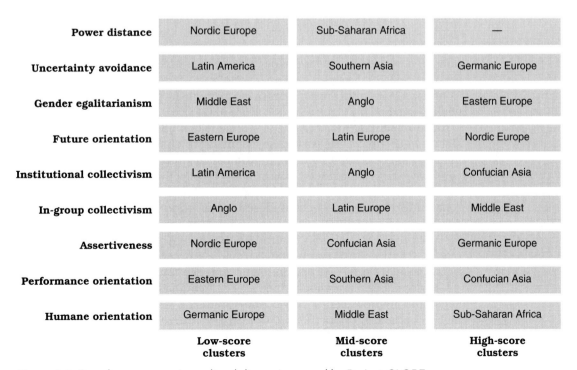

	Low-score clusters	Mid-score clusters	High-score clusters
Power distance	Nordic Europe	Sub-Saharan Africa	—
Uncertainty avoidance	Latin America	Southern Asia	Germanic Europe
Gender egalitarianism	Middle East	Anglo	Eastern Europe
Future orientation	Eastern Europe	Latin Europe	Nordic Europe
Institutional collectivism	Latin America	Anglo	Confucian Asia
In-group collectivism	Anglo	Latin Europe	Middle East
Assertiveness	Nordic Europe	Confucian Asia	Germanic Europe
Performance orientation	Eastern Europe	Southern Asia	Confucian Asia
Humane orientation	Germanic Europe	Middle East	Sub-Saharan Africa

Figure 5.4 Sample scores on nine cultural dimensions used by Project GLOBE.

REAL ETHICS

Bolivia's Nationalization of Oil and Gas Industry

Although executives from the world's oil industry couldn't say that it wasn't anticipated as a possibility, it still must have been a shocker when Bolivia's government announced that it was taking control of the country's oil and gas fields. The announcement said: "We are beginning by nationalizing oil and gas, tomorrow we will add mining, forestry and all natural resources, what our ancestors fought for."

As soon as the announcement was made, Bolivia's armed forces secured all oil and gas fields in the country. The country's newly elected president, Evo Morales, set forth new terms that gave a state-owned firm 82 percent of all revenues, leaving 18 percent for the foreign firms. He said: "Only those firms that respect these new terms will be allowed to operate in the country." The implicit threat was that any firms not willing to sign new contracts would be sent home.

While foreign governments described this nationalization as an "unfriendly move," Morales considered it patriotic.

His position is that any existing contracts with the state were in violation of the constitution, and that Bolivia's natural resources belonged to its people.

FURTHER INQUIRY

Exxon-Mobil and BP were among the firms affected by Bolivia's new law. If you were the CEO at one of these firms, how would you react to this nationalization? Do you raise the ethics of your "old" contracts with the Bolivian government? Do you try resist or comply with the new terms being offered.

Now, be what you are—an everyday citizen of the world. Consider Morales's argument that Bolivia's natural resources are a national treasure belonging to the people. Do you agree or disagree that a country has a right to protect its natural resources from exploitation by foreigners? Just what are the ethics of Morales's decision to nationalize the oil and gas industry?

Three other dimensions are quite similar with Hofstede's. *Gender egalitarianism* is the degree to which a culture minimizes gender inequalities, similar to Hofstede's masculinity/femininity. It is high in the cultures of Eastern and Nordic Europe and low in those of the Middle East. *Future orientation* is the degree to which members of a culture are willing to look ahead, delay gratifications, and make investments in the expectation of longer-term payoffs, similar to Hofstede's time orientation. Germanic and Nordic Europe are high on future orientation; Latin America and the Middle East are low. *Institutional collectivism* is the extent to which the organizations of a society emphasize and reward group action and accomplishments versus individual ones, similar to Hofstede's individualism/collectivism. Confucian Asia and Nordic Europe score high in institutional collectivism, while Germanic and Latin Europe score low.

The remaining four of GLOBE's dimensions offer additional cultural insights. *In-Group collectivism* is the extent to which people take pride in their families, small groups, and organizational memberships, acting loyally and cohesively regarding them. This form of collectivism runs high in Latin America and the Middle East but tends to be low in Anglo and Germanic Europe cultures. *Assertiveness* is described as the extent to which a culture emphasizes competition and assertiveness in social relationships, valuing behavior that is tough and confrontational as opposed to being modest and tender. Cultures in Eastern and Germanic Europe score high in assertiveness; those in Nordic Europe and Latin America score low.

Performance orientation is the degree of emphasis on performance excellence and improvements. Anglo and Confucian Asian cultures tend to be high in performance orientation. Countries in these clusters can be expected to reward performance accomplishments and invest in training to encourage future performance gains. *Humane orientation* reflects tendencies in a society for people to emphasize fairness, altruism, generosity, and caring as they deal with one another. It tends to be high in Southern Asia and Sub-Saharan Africa, and to be low in Latin and Germanic Europe.

Overall, the GLOBE research offers a timely, systematic, and empirical look at culture across a large sample of countries. Its results are being analyzed extensively for their management and leadership implications. Yet as with other cross-cultural research, the GLOBE project is insightful but not definitive. Given all of the complexity surrounding societal cultures, perhaps the best thing is to always integrate the many insights. The ideas and findings of Hall, Hofstede, the GLOBE researchers, and others are perhaps most useful if we view them each as valuable insights that can help us with a continuing quest to better understand the diversity of global cultures.[40]

Be sure you can ■ define the term culture ■ explain how ethnocentrism can create difficulties for people working across cultures ■ differentiate between low-context and high-context cultures, and between monochronic and polychronic cultures ■ define Hofstede's five dimensions of value differences among national cultures ■ illustrate each dimension by contrasting American culture with that of other countries ■ identify the major components in Project GLOBE's model of cultural differences

Learning Check 3

✓

MANAGEMENT ACROSS CULTURES

The management process—planning, organizing, leading, and controlling—is as relevant to international operations as to domestic ones. Yet as the preceding discussion of environment and culture should suggest, just how these functions are applied may vary somewhat from one country and culture to the next. **Comparative management** is the study of how management systematically differs among countries and/or cultures.

■ **Comparative management** studies how management practices differ among countries and cultures.

ARE MANAGEMENT THEORIES UNIVERSAL?

Increasingly, a significant question is being asked: "Are management theories universal?" Geert Hofstede, whose framework for understanding national cultures was introduced earlier, believes the answer is no.[41] He worries that many theories are ethnocentric and fail to take into account cultural differences.

For example, Hofstede argues that the American emphasis on participation in leadership reflects the culture's moderate stance on power distance. National cultures with lower scores, such as Sweden and Israel, are characterized by even more "democratic" leadership initiatives. By contrast, the cultures of France and some Asian countries with higher power-distance scores are comfortable with hierarchy and less concerned with participative leadership.

Hofstede also points out that the motivation theories of American scholars tend to value individual performance. This is consistent with the high individualism found in Anglo-American countries such as the United States, Canada, and the United Kingdom. Elsewhere, where values are more collectivist, the theories may be less applicable. Even a common value, such as the desire for increased humanization of work, may lead in different management directions. Until recently, practices in the United States largely emphasized redesigning jobs for individuals. Elsewhere in the world, such as in Sweden, the emphasis has been on redesigning jobs for groups of workers.

KAFFEEKLATSCH

Work Hours in Europe

First Cup

"I just read that the unions in Germany are raising heck with Volkswagen because the firm wants to increase the workweek from 28.8 hours to 35 hours. Can you believe it? They're working 28.8 hours a week over there!"

Studying the Grounds

■ Volkswagen claims that it can keep its Wolfburg, Germany, plant open if labor costs are recalculated on a 35-hour week.

■ The German trade union wants higher wages from Volkswagen if its workers are to work a longer week.

■ Volkswagen executives are looking for increased productivity in response to losses in its German and U.S. operations.

■ Volkswagen has joined other automakers in their push to open new plants outside Western Europe; one of the firm's new contracts is for a new plant near Moscow.

Double Espresso

"What are these global manufacturers to do? They have to stay competitive. Customers just aren't willing to keep paying higher prices. At some point you have to make trade-offs just to survive. The world is changing; there are new opportunities out there. You can't just continue with 'business and usual' and expect things to work out."

■ GM has already cut more than 30,000 jobs in North America; Ford is close behind.

■ GM may close a plant in Portugal that operates at a $625 "cost disadvantage" per vehicle. The European Employee Forum is threatening strikes at GM plants in Europe.

■ GM is opening a new facility in Russia, called a "growth market" by the firm's CEO.

"If I was one of those German autoworkers I'd be happy to work 35 hours a week for the same pay that I got for 28.8. What's the big difference? We work a 40-hour week here in America; to work 35 would be an outright gift. I work hard, and I support everyone that works hard. But on this one, I'm on Volkswagen's side."

Your Turn

The example is from Europe, but it could be anywhere. This might be called part of globalization's aftermath.

Should workers and unions be cooperating with business executives to find best ways to deal with globalization? Where is the management sacrifice in this example? If workers have to compromise on pay and work hours, should managers do the same?

Consider as well some of the Japanese management practices that have attracted great interest over the years.[42] Lifetime employment, gradual career advancement, and collective decision making have all been associated in one way or another with past successes in Japanese industry.[43] But as interesting as the practices may be, attempts to transfer them elsewhere must take into account the distinctive Japanese cultural traditions in which they emerged—such as long-term orientation, collectivism, and high-power distance.[44]

GLOBAL ORGANIZATIONAL LEARNING

We live at a fortunate time when managers around the world are realizing they have much to share with and learn from one another. Global organizational learning is a timely and relevant theme. This point is evident in the following words of Kenichi Ohmae, noted Japanese management consultant and author of *The Borderless World:*[45]

Companies can learn from one another, particularly from other excellent companies, both at home and abroad. The industrialized world is be-

coming increasingly homogeneous in terms of customer needs and social infrastructure, and only truly excellent companies can compete effectively in the global marketplace.

Although we do have a lot to learn from one another, it should be learned with full appreciation of the constraints and opportunities of different cultures and country environments.[46] Our approach to global organizational learning should be an alert, open, inquiring, and cautious one. As Hofstede states: "Disregard of other cultures is a luxury only the strong can afford. . . . increase in cultural awareness represents an intellectual and spiritual gain."[47]

It is important to identify great management practices found in other countries. But we must also understand how cultural differences might affect their success or failure when applied elsewhere. We should always be looking everywhere for new ideas. But we should hesitate to accept any practice, no matter how well it appears to work somewhere else, as a universal prescription for action. Indeed, the goal of comparative management studies is not to find universal principles. It is to help develop creative and critical thinking about how managers around the world do things and about whether they could be doing them better.

> *Be sure you can* ■ defend an answer to this question: "Do management theories apply universally around the world?" ■ describe the concept of global organizational learning

Learning Check 4

CHAPTER 5 STUDY GUIDE

STUDY QUESTIONS SUMMARY

1 What are the international business challenges of globalization?

- Global managers are informed about international developments, transnational in outlook, competent in working with people from different cultures, and always aware of regional developments in a changing world.

- The global economy is making the diverse countries of the world increasingly interdependent regarding resource supplies, product markets, and business competition.

- Market entry strategies of international business include global sourcing, exporting/importing, and licensing.

- Direct investment strategies of international business include joint ventures and wholly owned subsidiaries in foreign countries.

- Global operations are influenced by important environmental differences among the economic, legal-political, and educational systems of countries.

2 What are multinational corporations and what do they do?

- A multinational corporation (MNC) is a business with extensive operations in more than one foreign country.

- True MNCs are global firms with worldwide missions and strategies that earn a substantial part of their revenues abroad.

- MNCs offer potential benefits to host countries in broader tax bases, new technologies, and employment opportunities.

- MNCs can disadvantage host countries if they interfere in local government, extract excessive profits, and dominate the local economy.

- The Foreign Corrupt Practices Act prohibits American MNCs from engaging in corrupt practices abroad.

3 What is culture and how does it relate to global diversity?

- The dimensions of Hall's silent language culture include language, use of space, and time orientation.

- Hofstede's dimensions of value differences in national cultures include power distance, uncertainty avoidance, individualism-collectivism, masculinity-femininity, and time orientation.
- Project GLOBE's nine cultural dimensions describe how countries fall into ten culture/clusters.

4 How do management practices and learning transfer across cultures?

- The management process must be used appropriately and applied with sensitivity to local cultures and situations.

- The field of comparative management studies how management is practiced around the world and how management ideas are transferred from one country or culture to the next.
- Management practices are influenced by cultural values; practices that are successful in one culture may work less well in others.
- The concept of global management learning has much to offer as the "borderless" world begins to emerge and as the management practices of diverse countries and cultures become more visible.

KEY TERMS REVIEW

Child labor (p. 117)
Comparative management (p. 123)
Corruption (p. 115)
Cultural intelligence (p. 118)
Culture (p. 117)
Culture shock (p. 117)
Ethnocentrism (p. 117)
Euro (p. 112)
European Union (p. 112)
Exporting (p. 110)
Foreign subsidiary (p. 112)
Franchising (p. 111)

Global economy (p. 108)
Global manager (p. 109)
Global sourcing (p. 110)
Globalization (p. 108)
High-context cultures (p. 118)
Importing (p. 110)
International business (p. 109)
International management (p. 109)
Joint ventures (p. 111)
Licensing agreement (p. 111)
Low-context cultures (p. 118)
Monochronic cultures (p. 118)

Most favored nation status (p. 113)
Multinational corporation (p. 114)
NAFTA (p. 112)
Polychronic cultures (p. 118)
Protectionism (p. 113)
Proxemics (p. 119)
Sustainable development (p. 117)
Sweatshops (p. 116)
Transnational corporation (p. 114)
World Trade Organization (p. 113)

SELF-TEST 5

MULTIPLE-CHOICE QUESTIONS:

1. In addition to gaining new markets, the reasons why businesses go international include the search for _____.

   (a) political risk   (b) protectionism   (c) lower labor costs   (d) most favored nation status

2. When Rocky Brands decided to increase its international operations by buying 70% ownership of a manufacturing company in the Dominican Republic, Rocky was engaging in which form of international business?

   (a) import/export   (b) licensing   (c) foreign subsidiary   (d) joint venture

3. A common form of international business that falls into the category of a direct investment strategy is _____.

   (a) exporting   (b) joint venturing   (c) licensing   (d) global sourcing

4. The World Trade Organization, or WTO, would most likely become involved in disputes between countries over _____.

   (a) exchange rates   (b) ethnocentrism   (c) nationalization   (d) tariffs and protectionism

5. Business complaints about copyright protection and intellectual property rights in some countries illustrate how differences in _____ can impact international operations.

   (a) legal environments   (b) political stability   (c) sustainable development   (d) economic systems

6. In _____ cultures, members tend to do one thing at a time; in _____ cultures, members tend to do many things at once.

   (a) monochronic, polychronic   (b) polycentric, geocentric   (c) collectivist, individualist   (d) neutral, affective

7. A culture in which there is much emphasis placed on finding meaning in the written or spoken word would be described as _____ by Hall.

   (a) monochronic   (b) proxemic   (c) collectivist   (d) low context

8. It is common in Malaysian culture for people to value teamwork and to display great respect for authority. Hofsede would descibe this culture as high in both _____.

   (a) uncertain avoidance and feminism   (b) universalism and particularism   (c) collectivism and power distance   (d) long-term orientation and masculinity

9. In Hofstede's study of national cultures, America was found to be highly _____ compared with other countries in his sample.

   (a) individualistic   (b) collectivist   (c) feminine   (d) long-term oriented

10. It is _____ when a foreign visitor takes offense at a local custom such as dining with one's fingers, considering it inferior to practices of his or her own culture.

    (a) universalist   (b) prescriptive   (c) monochronic   (d) enthnocentric

11. When Limited Brands buys cotton in Egypt and has pants sewn from it in Sri Lanka according to designs made in Italy for sale in the United States by catalog orders, this form of international business is known as _____.

    (a) licensing   (b) importing   (c) joint venturing   (d) global sourcing

12. The difference between an international business and a transnational corporation is that the transnational _____.

    (a) operates without a strong national identity   (b) does business in only one or two foreign countries   (c) is led by managers with ethnocentric attitudes   (d) is ISO 14000 certified

13. The Foreign Corrupt Practices Act makes it illegal for _____.

    (a) Americans to engage in joint ventures abroad   (b) foreign businesses to pay bribes to U.S. government officials   (c) U.S. businesses to make "payoffs" abroad to gain international business contracts   (d) foreign businesses to steal intellectual property from U.S. firms operating in their countries

14. One would expect to find men and women treated equally in terms of job and carrer opportunities in a culture described as high in _____ according to Project GLOBE.

    (a) humane orientation   (b) institutional collectivism   (c) gender egalitarianism   (d) performance orientation

15. Hofstede would describe a culture in which members respect age and authority and in which workers defer to the preferences of their supervisors or team leaders as _____.

    (a) low masculinity   (b) high particularism   (c) high power distance   (d) monochronic

SHORT-RESPONSE QUESTIONS:

16. Why do host countries sometimes complain about the operations of MNCs within their borders?

17. In what ways is the "power-distance" dimension of national culture important in management?

18. What is the difference between institutional collectivism and in-group collectivism as described by Project GLOBE?

19. How do regional economic alliances impact the global economy?

APPLICATION QUESTION:

20. Kim has just returned from her first business trip to Japan. While there, she was impressed with the intense use of work teams. Now back in Iowa, she would like to totally reorganize the workflows and processes of her canoe-manufacturing company and its 75 employees around teams. There has been very little emphasis on teamwork, and she now believes this is "the way to go." Based on the discussion of culture and management in this chapter, what advice would you offer Kim?

CASE 5

Harley-Davidson: Harley Style and Strategy Have Global Reach

With a celebration of almost legendary proportions, Harley-Davidson marked a century in business with a year-long International Road Tour. The party finally culminated in hometown Milwaukee.[48] Brought back from near death, Harley-Davidson represents a true American success story. Reacting to global competition, Harley has been able to reestablish itself as the dominant maker of big bikes in the United States. However, success often breeds imitation, and Harley faces a mixture of domestic and foreign competitors encroaching on its market. Can it meet the challenge?

Harley-Davidson

When Harley-Davidson was founded in 1903, it was one of more than 100 firms producing motorcycles in the United States. The U.S. government became an important customer for the company's high-powered, reliable bikes, using them in both world wars. By the 1950s, Harley-Davidson was the only remaining American manufacturer.[49]

But British competitors were beginning to enter the market with faster, lighter-weight bikes. Honda Motor Company of Japan began marketing lightweight bikes in the United States, moving into middleweight vehicles in the 1960s. Harley initially tried to compete by manufacturing smaller bikes but had difficulty making them profitably. The company even purchased an Italian motorcycle firm, Aermacchi, but many of its dealers were reluctant to sell the small Aermacchi Harleys.[50]

American Machine and Foundry Co. (AMF) took over Harley in 1969, expanding its portfolio of recreational products. AMF increased production from 14,000 to 50,000 bikes per year. This rapid expansion led to significant problems with quality, and better-built Japanese motorcycles began to take over the market. Harley's share of its major U.S. market—heavyweight motorcycles—fell to 23 percent.[51]

In 1981 a group of 13 managers bought Harley-Davidson back from AMF and began to turn the company around with the rallying cry "The Eagle Soars Alone." As Richard Teerlink, former CEO of Harley, explained: "The solution was to get back to detail. The key was to know the business, know the customer, and pay attention to detail."[52] The key elements in this process were increasing quality and improving service to customers and dealers. Management kept the classic Harley style and focused on the company's traditional strength—heavyweight and super-heavyweight bikes.

In 1983 Harley-Davidson asked the International Trade Commission (ITC) for tariff relief on the basis that Japanese manufacturers were stockpiling inventory in the United States and providing unfair competition. The tariff relief was granted on April 1, 1983, and a tariff for five years was placed on all imported Japanese motorcycles that were 700cc or larger. In 1987 Harley petitioned the ITC to have the tariff lifted because the company felt capable and confident in its ability to compete with foreign imports. Also in 1983, the Harley Owners Group® (H.O.G.®) was formed. H.O.G. membership soared to more than 90,000 by 1989 and has ultimately exceeded 750,000 members.[53]

Once Harley's quality image had been restored, the company slowly began to expand production. The company made only 280 bikes per day in January 1992, increasing output to 345 bikes per day by the end of that year. Despite increasing demand, production was scheduled to reach only 420 per day, approximately 100,000 per year, by 1996.[54] However, in 1996 Harley recognized the demand, and the first of many grander expansion plans began with the opening of a new distribution center in Franklin, Wisconsin. In 1997 Harley began production in new facilities in Milwaukee, and Menomonee Falls, Wisconsin, and in Kansas City, Missouri. In 1998 a new assembly plant was opened in Manaus, Brazil, and Harley acquired the remaining interest in Buell motorcycles. In 2001 expansions were announced for the Milwaukee and Tomahawk, Wisconsin, and York, Pennsylvania, plants.[55]

As indicated by the expansions, the popularity of the motorcycles continued to increase throughout the 1980s. The average Harley purchaser was in his late thirties, with an average household income of over $40,000. Teerlink didn't like the description of his customers as "aging" babyboomers: "Our customers want the sense of adventure that they get on our bikes. . . . Harley-Davidson doesn't sell transportation, we sell transformation. We sell excitement, a way of life."[56] However, the average age and income of

Harley riders has continued to increase. As of late, the median age of a Harley rider was 47 and the median income was just under $80,000.[57]

Although the company had been exporting motorcycles ever since it was founded, it was not until the late 1980s that Harley-Davidson management began to think seriously about international markets. In 1987 the company acknowledged its ability to compete with foreign imports and started to consider competing more seriously in the international market. Traditionally, the company's ads had been translated word for word into foreign languages. Now, ads were developed specifically for different markets, and rallies were adapted to fit local customs.[58] The company also began to actively recruit and develop dealers in Europe and Japan. It purchased a Japanese distribution company and built a large parts warehouse in Germany to support its European operations. Harley-Davidson continued to look for ways to expand its activities. Recognizing that German motorcyclists rode at high speeds—often more than 100 mph—the company began to study ways to give Harleys a smoother ride. It also began to emphasize accessories that would give riders more protection.[59]

The company also created a line of Harley accessories available through dealers or by catalog, all adorned with the Harley-Davidson logo. These jackets, caps, T-shirts, and other items became popular with nonbikers as well. In fact, the clothing and parts had a higher profit margin than the motorcycles; nonbike products made up as much as half of sales at some dealers.

International Efforts

Harley continues to make inroads in global markets. At one time, Harley had 30 percent of the worldwide market for heavyweight motorcycles—chrome-laden cruisers, aerodynamic rocket bikes mostly produced by the Japanese, and oversize touring motorcycles. In the United States, Harley had the largest market share, 46.4 percent, followed by Honda with 20.2 percent. In Europe, Harley ranked sixth, with only 6.6 percent of the market share behind Honda, Yamaha, BMW, Suzuki, and Kawasaki. However, in the Asia/Pacific market, where it might be expected that Japanese bikes would dominate, Harley had the largest market shares for in the early part of the twenty-first century.

Harley had 21.3 percent of the market share compared to 19.2 percent of the market share for Honda.[60]

Harley motorcycles are among America's fastest-growing exports to Japan. Harley's Japanese subsidiary adapted the company's marketing approach to Japanese tastes, even producing shinier and more complete tool kits than were available in the United States. Harley bikes have long been considered symbols of prestige in Japan. Before World War II, a small company called Rikuo built them under a licensing arrangement. Consistent with their U.S. counterparts, many Japanese enthusiasts see themselves as rebels on wheels.[61]

More recently, Harley has made inroads to the previously elusive Chinese market. Hoping to enter a country on the cusp of an economic revolution, the first official Chinese Harley dealer opened its doors just outside downtown Beijing. Like other Harley stores, the Chinese outlet is stocked with bikes, parts, accessories, and branded merchandise and offers post-sales service. Despite China's growing disposable income, the new store has several hurdles ahead of it, including riding restrictions imposed by the government in urban areas and although its international sales grew 15% in recent years, the United States still represents more than 80% of Harley's sales.[62]

Another recent effort by Harley to expand its buyer base involves the development of its Blast motorcycle from its Buell division. Fifty percent of Blast sales are to women, raising the overall percentage of women buying Harleys from 2 percent in 1987 to 9 percent by 1999. That 9 percent figure has remained constant for several years in a row. With 17 consecutive years of increased production as well as record revenues and earnings, the future for Harley appears bright.[63]

REVIEW QUESTIONS

1. Did Harley-Davidson's expansion into China come at the right time? Why or why not?

2. Harley appears to have moved from selling a product to selling a way of life. How does this affect the company's domestic and international business approaches?

3. What manufacturer in a European, Asian, and African country would be a good joint venture partner for Harley?

TEAM PROJECT

In his book *The World is Flat*, Thomas L. Friedman says: ". . . the more your culture easily absorbs foreign ideas and best practices and melds those with its local traditions—the greater advantages you will have in a flat world." He's talking about a world in which the forces of globalization have ushered in a completely new world that nations, companies, and people must both understand and learn how to best deal with.

Question: "Globalization" is frequently in the news. You can easily read or listen to both advocates and opponents. What is the bottom line? Is globalization good or bad, and for whom?

Globalization—"What Are the Pros and Cons?"

Research Directions:

- What does the term "globalization" mean? Review various definitions and find the common ground.
- Read and study the scholarly arguments about globalization. Summarize what the scholars say about the forces and consequences of globalization in the past, present, and future.
- Examine current events relating to globalization. Summarize the issues and arguments. What is the positive side of globalization? What are the negatives that some might call its "dark" side?
- Consider globalization from the perspective of your local community or one of its major employers. Is globalization a threat or an opportunity, and why?
- Take a position on globalization. State what you believe to be the best course for government and business leaders to take. Justify your position.

PERSONAL MANAGEMENT

Cultural Awareness

The complications of world events are ever-present reminders that **CULTURAL AWARENESS** is one of the great challenges of the 21st century. Consultant Richard Lewis warns of "cultural spectacles" that limit our vision, causing us to see and interpret things with the biases of our own culture. You must learn to take off the spectacles and broaden your cultural horizons. Do you know, for example, that in Asian cultures Confucian values like the following are very influential?

- *Harmony*—works well in a group, doesn't disrupt group order, puts group before self-interests.
- *Hierarchy*—accepts authority and hierarchical nature of society, doesn't challenge superiors.
- *Benevolence*—acts kindly and understandingly toward others, paternalistic, willing to teach and help subordinates.
- *Loyalty*—loyal to organization and supervisor, dedicated to job, grateful for job and support of superior.
- *Learning*—eager for new knowledge, works hard to learn new job skills, strives for high performance.

Building the Brand Called "You" The college campus is a great place to start. Its rich community of international students can take you around the world every day. Make a commitment tomorrow to carefully monitor yourself as you meet, interact with, and otherwise come into contact with persons from other cultures—at school, at work, out shopping, at leisure. Jot notes on what you perceive as cultural differences. Note also your "first tendencies" in reacting to these differences. Consider the implications of the self-assessments for your skills at cultural awareness.

NEXT STEPS: MANAGEMENT LEARNING WORKBOOK

Self-Assessments
- Global Readiness Index (#8)
- Time Orientation (#9)

Experiential Exercises
- What Do You Value in Work? (#7)
- Which Organization Culture Fits You? (#8)

Entrepreneurship and Small Business Management

6

Planning Ahead

Chapter 6 Study Questions

1 What is entrepreneurship?

2 What is special about small businesses?

3 How does one start a new venture?

Make It, Manage It

Coming up with a great idea is only the first step to success. Businesses routinely find themselves beset by the numerous difficulties of getting a creative concept off the ground. As one innovative startup company shows, it's never a clear path to go from potential to profits.

"Now what do we do?"

That may be the question most often posed after an organization's creative process yields a product idea that seems both affordable to produce and competitively viable in the marketplace. It's also a question likely being posed by the management team of MooBella, a Taunton, Massachusetts, company that created an ice cream vending machine that serves frozen treats in an entirely new way.

MooBella wowed attendees at DEMO (an inventor's conference) with its self-contained technology that mixes and flash freezes dry ingredients, flavorings, and add-ins like sprinkles or chocolate chips. The result: a scoop of ice cream in one of twelve flavors, made to order in 45 seconds. That's right; it takes less than a minute to make an ice cream in a MooBella machine. But, this act of seemingly spontaneous creation was itself the product of nearly 15 years of methodical research and testing.[1]

Although the company has not put its vending machines into widespread distribution, MooBella president Bruce Ginsberg is excited about the prospect of this creative technology to open up

What *They* Think

"We could make Starbucks the largest ice cream chain overnight."
Bruce Ginsberg, President of MooBella

CREATING: "Creativity is just connecting things. When you ask creative people how they did something, they feel a little guilty because they didn't really do it, they just saw something. It seemed obvious to them after a while. That's because they were able to connect experiences they've had and synthesize new things. And the reason they were able to do that was that they've had more experiences than other people."
Steve Jobs, CEO of Apple Computers

MANAGING: "Today many American corporations spend a great deal of money and time trying to increase the originality of their employees, hoping thereby to get a competitive edge in the marketplace. But such programs make no difference unless management also learns to recognize the valuable ideas among the many novel ones, and then finds ways of implementing them."
Mihaly Csikszentmihalyi, author of Flow: The Psychology of Optimal Experience

brand new ice cream markets. Suggesting that a MooBella machine could fit into most Starbucks stores, Ginsberg wishfully hypothesizes, "We could make Starbucks the largest ice cream chain overnight."[2]

Well, yes. But then what would he do? Thus begins the crux of the flip side of the creative process, the task of *managing*.

To eliminate the human error factor, MooBella machines are managed by an onboard computer running a variant of Unix. The computer handles the mixing and dispensing processes, contacting the company via wireless Internet whenever an ingredient runs low.[3]

For this to work on a large scale, MooBella will be intensely dependent on successfully managing its engineering infrastructure, which accounts for the high number of engineers working for the company, even in its start-up phase, and explains why the engineering process spent five years in R&D.

Another dilemma for MooBella is how to manage the public image of their product and process. Because the ice cream requires no human interaction, aside from refilling the machine, the company joins the ranks of Coke, Pepsi, and other products that are vended in such a way that consumers never interact with company representatives. Instead, the vending machine and its mixing magic become MooBella's public face.

Despite having an imaginative concept, the MooBella technology and business model spent longer than average in research and development. Will this firm now be able to capture the hearts of ice cream lovers in a few pushes of a button? Try a scoop and see!

The Numbers

Vending Machine Operators by Employment Size of Enterprise

Firms with no employees	
1–4 employees	55%
5–9 employees	55%
10–19 employees	9.3%
20–99 employees	7.3%
100–499 employees	1.5%
500 employees or more	0.6%

Quick Facts

* Ninety four percent of all U.S. households buy ice cream each year.[4]
* MooBella vending machines can flash-freeze a scoop of ice cream in 10 seconds.[5]
* The average American eats 23.2 gallons of ice cream per year; the largest per city consumption of ice cream is Portland, Oregon, St. Louis, Missouri, and Seattle, Washington.[6]
* It takes about 50 licks to finish off a typical ice cream cone.[7]
* According to IBM, 80% of decision-making time is spent gathering the data, and only 20% is used to actually make decisions.[8]

What Do *You* Think?

1. What would be the best plan for distribution of MooBella's instant ice cream machines? What locations would be the most cost-effective for placement of the machines? What locations would earn MooBella the most return for its money?
2. MooBella's technology may fit well within the format of a typical vending machine, but is the company missing the mark? Could an alternate size or format for MooBella machines increase the company's chances of success?

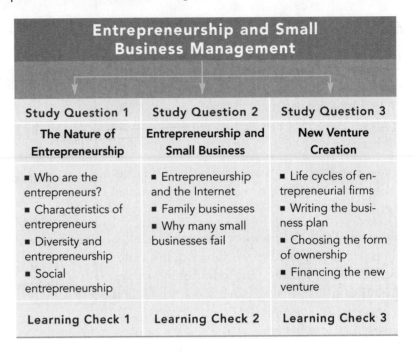

Entrepreneurship and Small Business Management		
Study Question 1	**Study Question 2**	**Study Question 3**
The Nature of Entrepreneurship	**Entrepreneurship and Small Business**	**New Venture Creation**
■ Who are the entrepreneurs? ■ Characteristics of entrepreneurs ■ Diversity and entrepreneurship ■ Social entrepreneurship	■ Entrepreneurship and the Internet ■ Family businesses ■ Why many small businesses fail	■ Life cycles of entrepreneurial firms ■ Writing the business plan ■ Choosing the form of ownership ■ Financing the new venture
Learning Check 1	**Learning Check 2**	**Learning Check 3**

Think about it. There is so much one can do with creativity and initiative in the world of work today. In fact, this is a chapter of examples. The goal is not only to inform, to better familiarize you with the nature of entrepreneurship, small business, and new venture creation. The goal is also to stimulate you to consider starting your own business, being your own boss, and making your own special contribution to society. What about it? Can we count you into the world of entrepreneurship and small business?

THE NATURE OF ENTREPRENEURSHIP

■ **Entrepreneurship** is dynamic, risk-taking, creative, growth-oriented behavior.

Success in a highly competitive business environment depends on **entrepreneurship**. This term is used to describe strategic thinking and risk-taking behavior that result in the creation of new opportunities for individuals and/or organizations. H. Wayne Huizenga, featured below and a member of the Entrepreneurs' Hall of Fame, describes it this way: "An important part of being an entrepreneur is a gut instinct that allows you to believe in your heart that something will work even though everyone else says it will not." You say, "I am going to make sure it works. I am going to go out there and make it happen."[9] These opportunities are illustrated in the success stories of business ventures that grew into large companies, such as the now-familiar Amazon, Domino's Pizza, and Federal Express. They are also represented in great products like 3M's popular Post-it® notes.

WHO ARE THE ENTREPRENEURS?

■ An **entrepreneur** is willing to pursue opportunities in situations others view as problems or threats.

An **entrepreneur** is a risk-taking individual who takes action to pursue opportunities others fail to recognize, or may even view as problems or threats. Business entrepreneurs start new ventures that bring to life new products or service ideas. Their stories are rich with ideas for all of us to consider. Although the people in the following examples are different, they share something in common. Each built a successful long-term business from good ideas and hard work.[10]

After a career in sales, Mary Kay Ash "retired" for a month. The year was 1963. When she started to write a book to help women compete in the male-dominated business world, she realized she was writing a business plan. From that plan arose Mary Kay Cosmetics. Launched on $5,000, the company now operates worldwide and has been named one of the best companies to work for in America. Mary Kay's goal from the beginning has always been "to help women everywhere reach their full potential."

Mary Kay Ash

Want to start an airline? Richard Branson did, calling it Virgin Atlantic. But he started first in his native England with a student literary magazine and small mail-order record business. Since then, he's built "Virgin" into one of the world's most recognized brand names. Today, the Virgin Group is a business conglomerate employing some 25,000 people around the globe. It holds over 200 companies, including Virgin Mobile, Virgin Records, and even Virgin Cola. It's all very creative and ambitious. But that's Branson. "I love to learn things I know little about," he says.

Richard Branson

With a vision and a $175,000 loan Earl Graves started *Black Enterprise* magazine in 1970. That success grew into the diversified business information company Earl G. Graves Ltd., including BlackEnterprise.com. Graves grew up in Brooklyn, New York, and at the age of 6 he was selling Christmas cards to neighbors. Today the business school at his college alma mater, Baltimore's Morgan State University, is named after him. Graves says: "I feel that a large part of my role as publisher of *Black Enterprise* is to be a catalyst for black economic development in this country."

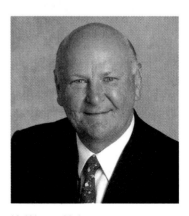

Earl Graves

What do Waste Management Inc., the Miami Dolphins football team, AutoNation Inc., and Blockbuster Video have in common? They have all at one time been owned by entrepreneur Wayne Huizenga. How did it all start? In 1962, at the age of 25, he borrowed $5,000 from his father-in-law, got a used truck, and acquired a few trash-hauling accounts. He then built the world's largest waste disposal company, Waste Management. He's been buying, building, and selling businesses ever since . . . and reaping the benefits. Huizenga says: "Success depends on seizing the moment and sometimes creating your own opportunity."

H. Wayne Huizenga

Anita Roddick

In 1973 Anita Roddick was a 33-year-old housewife looking for a way to support herself and her two children. She spotted a niche for natural-based skin and health care products, and started mixing and selling them from a small shop in Brighton, England. The Body Shop PLC has grown to some 1,500 outlets in 47 countries with 24 languages, selling a product every half-second to one of its 86 million customers. Known for her commitment to human rights, the environment, and economic development, Roddick believes in business social responsibility. She says: "If you think you're too small to have an impact, try going to bed with a mosquito."

David Thomas

Have you had your Wendy's today? A lot of people have, and there's quite a story behind it. The first Wendy's restaurant opened in Columbus, Ohio, in November 1969. It's still there; there are also about 5,000 others now operating around the world. What began as founder David Thomas's dream to own one restaurant grew into a global enterprise. He went on to become one of the world's best-known entrepreneurs: "the world's most famous hamburger cook." But there's more to Wendy's than profits and business performance alone; social responsibility counts, too. Wendy's strives to be in touch with its communities, with a special focus on helping schools and schoolchildren. In 1992 Dave founded the Dave Thomas Foundation for Adoption.

CHARACTERISTICS OF ENTREPRENEURS

Do you find any patterns in the prior examples? A common image of an entrepreneur is as the founder of a new business enterprise that achieves large-scale success, like the ones just mentioned. But entrepreneurs also operate on a smaller and less public scale. Those who take the risk of buying a local McDonald's or Subway Sandwich franchise, opening a small retail shop, or going into a self-employed service business are also entrepreneurs. Similarly, anyone who assumes responsibility for introducing a new product or change in operations within an organization is also demonstrating the qualities of entrepreneurship.

Indications are that entrepreneurs tend to share certain attitudes and personal characteristics. The general profile is of an individual who is very self-confident, determined, resilient, adaptable, and driven by excellence.[11] You should be able to identify these attributes in the prior examples. As shown in *Figure 6.1*, the typical personality traits and characteristics of entrepreneurs include the following:[12]

- *Internal locus of control:* Entrepreneurs believe that they are in control of their own destiny; they are self-directing and like autonomy.
- *High energy level:* Entrepreneurs are persistent, hard working, and willing to exert extraordinary efforts to succeed.
- *High need for achievement:* Entrepreneurs are motivated to accomplish challenging goals; they thrive on performance feedback.
- *Tolerance for ambiguity:* Entrepreneurs are risk takers; they tolerate situations with high degrees of uncertainty.
- *Self-confidence:* Entrepreneurs feel competent, believe in themselves, and are willing to make decisions.

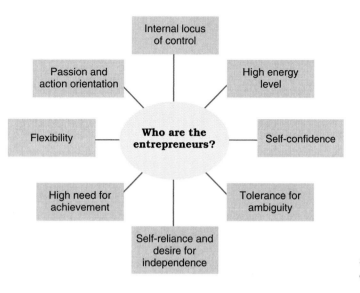

Figure 6.1 Personality traits and characteristics of entrepreneurs.

- *Passion and action orientation:* Entrepreneurs try to act ahead of problems; they want to get things done and not waste valuable time.
- *Self-reliance and desire for independence:* Entrepreneurs want independence; they are self-reliant; they want to be their own bosses, not work for others.
- *Flexibility:* Entrepreneurs are willing to admit problems and errors, and willing to change a course of action when plans aren't working.

INSIGHTS

Invest in People and Ideas

Each year people with good ideas don't get the chance to turn them into reality. A good percentage of them are women. Count-Me-In for Women's Economic Independence is out to turn the tables and give female entrepreneurs a chance to get started. Cofounded by Nell Merlino, also creator of Take Our Daughters to Work Day, and Iris Burnett, Count-Me-In uses the Internet to raise money for loans to female entrepreneurs.

When Nell Merlino and Iris Burnett got together to create Count-Me-In, they took a risk—in fact, they took more than one. They risked their own time and resources to start the firm; they risked the firm's capital on the women they helped to start new businesses. This is what entrepreneurship is all about—taking business risks to pursue one's dreams.

The firm operates a website that solicits contributions as small as $5 that are put into a revolving loan fund. The fund is then tapped to provide "microcredit" loans in amounts from $500 to $10,000 to help women start and expand small businesses. Women qualify for the loans by a unique credit scoring system that doesn't hold against them things like a divorce, time off to raise a family, or age-all things that might discourage conventional lenders.

Geneva Francais received a $1,500 loan to build storage shelves for her special cooking sauce "Geneva's Splash," brewed and bottled in her kitchen. Francais is a 65-year-old widow. She says: "A bank would not loan a woman money when she is 65 years old. It's as simple as that." With her loan she hopes to double the $400 per month Social Security income that she presently lives on. Heather McCartney is married to a high school principal in New York. She received a $5,000 loan to expand "Ethnic Edibles," her line of cookies and cookie cutters designed along traditional African motifs. The money will be used for packaging and marketing.

Merlino says: "Women own 38 percent of all businesses in this country, but still have far less access to capital than men because of today's process." Count-Me-In is out to change all that.

MANAGEMENT SMARTS 6.1

Challenging the myths about entrepreneurs

- *Entrepreneurs are born, not made.* Not true! Talent gained and enhanced by experience is a foundation for entrepreneurial success.

- *Entrepreneurs are gamblers.* Not true! Entrepreneurs are risk takers, but the risks are informed and calculated.

- *Money is the key to entrepreneurial success.* Not true! Money is no guarantee of success. There's a lot more to it than that; many entrepreneurs start with very little.

- *You have to be young to be an entrepreneur.* Not true! Age is no barrier to entrepreneurship; with age often comes experience, contacts, and other useful resources.

- *You have to have a degree in business to be an entrepreneur.* Not true! You may not need a degree at all; although a business degree is not necessary, it helps to study and understand business fundamentals.

In addition, research also suggests that entrepreneurs tend to have unique backgrounds and personal experiences.[13] *Childhood experiences and family environment* seem to make a difference. Evidence links entrepreneurs with parents who were entrepreneurial and self-employed. Similarly, entrepreneurs are often raised in families that encourage responsibility, initiative, and independence. Another issue is *career or work history.* Entrepreneurs who try one venture often go on to others. Prior work experience in the business area or industry is helpful. Entrepreneurs also tend to emerge during certain *windows of career opportunity.* Most start their businesses between the ages of 22 and 45, an age spread that seems to allow for risk taking. However, age is no barrier. When Tony DeSio was 50 he founded the Mail Boxes Etc. chain. He sold it for $300 million when he was 67 and suffering heart problems. Within a year he launched PixArts, another franchise chain based on photography and art.[14]

Finally, a report in the *Harvard Business Review* suggests that entrepreneurs may have unique and *deeply embedded life interests.* The article describes entrepreneurs as having strong interests in creative production—enjoying project initiation, working with the unknown, and finding unconventional solutions. They also have strong interests in enterprise control—finding enjoyment from running things. The combination of creative production and enterprise control is characteristic of people who want to start things and move things toward a goal.[15] *Management Smarts 6.1* helps debunk some common myths about entrepreneurship.[16]

Undoubtedly, entrepreneurs seek independence and the sense of mastery that comes with success. That seems to keep driving Tony DeSio in the example above. When asked by a reporter what he liked most about entrepreneurship, he replied: "Being able to make decisions without having to go through layers of corporate hierarchy—just being a master of your own destiny."

DIVERSITY AND ENTREPRENEURSHIP

When economists speak about entrepreneurs they differentiate between those who are driven by the quest for new opportunities and those who are driven by absolute need.[17] Those in the latter group pursue **necessity-based entrepreneurship**; they start new ventures because they have few or no employment and career options elsewhere. Sometimes these are persons, minorities and women, who have suffered the glass ceiling effect, who have found career doors closed.

■ **Necessity-based entrepreneurship** takes place because other employment options don't exist.

The National Foundation for Women Business Owners (NFWBO) reports that women own over 9 million businesses in the United States. As noted earlier, this represents about 38 percent of all U.S. businesses.[18] Entrepreneurship offers women opportunities to strike out on their own and gain economic independence, providing a pathway for career success that may be blocked otherwise.[19] The NFWBO also reports that women are starting new businesses at twice the rate of the national average. Most indicate being motivated by a new idea or by realizing that they could do for themselves what they were already doing for other employers.

Among women leaving private-sector employment to strike out on their own, 33 percent said they were not being taken seriously by their prior employer; 29 percent said they had experienced "glass ceiling" issues.[20] In *Women Business Owners of Color: Challenges and Accomplishments,* the NFWBO discusses the motivations of women of color to pursue entrepreneurship because of glass ceiling problems. These include not being recognized or valued by their prior employers, not being taken seriously, and seeing others promoted ahead of them.[21]

Career difficulties may help explain why minority entrepreneurship is one of the fastest-growing sectors of our economy. Businesses created by minority entrepreneurs employ over 4 million U.S. workers and generate over $500 billion in annual revenues. And the trend continues upward. In the last census of small businesses, those owned by African Americans had grown by 45 percent, by Hispanics 31 percent, and by Asians 24 percent. During this same time small businesses owned by women also had grown by 24 percent.[22]

SOCIAL ENTREPRENEURSHIP

Housing and job training for the homeless. Bringing technology to poor families. Improving literacy among disadvantaged youth. Making small loans to start minority-owned businesses. What do these examples have in common? They are all targets for **social entrepreneurship**, a unique form of entrepreneurship that seeks novel ways to solve pressing social problems, at home and abroad.[23] Social entrepreneurs share many characteristics with other entrepreneurs with one unique difference: a social mission drives them.[24] Their personal quests are for innovations that help solve social problems, or at least help make lives better for people who are disadvantaged.

■ **social entrepreneurship** has a mission to solve pressing social problems.

John Wood is a social entrepreneur. Once comfortably immersed in his career as a Microsoft executive, his life changed on a vacation to the Himalayas of Nepal. Wood was shocked at the lack of schools. He discovered a passion that determines what he calls the "second chapter" in his life: to provide the lifelong benefits of education to poor children. He quit his Microsoft job and started a nonprofit organization called Room to Read. So far, the organization has built over 100 schools and 1,000 libraries in Cambodia, India, Nepal, Vietnam, and Laos. Noting that one-seventh of the global population can't read or write, Wood says: "I don't see how we are going to solve the world's problems without literacy." The Room to Read model is so efficient that it can build schools for as little as $6,000. *Time* magazine has honored Wood and his team as "Asian Heroes," and *Fast Company* magazine tapped his organization for a Social Capitalist Award.[25]

Be sure you can ■ define the term entrepreneurship ■ list key personal characteristics of entrepreneurs ■ explain the influence of background and experience on entrepreneurs ■ discuss opportunities for entrepreneurship by women and minorities ■ define necessity-based entrepreneurship ■ discuss what makes social entrepreneurship unique

Learning Check 1

ENTREPRENEURSHIP AND SMALL BUSINESS

■ A **small business** has fewer than 500 employees, is independently owned and operated, and does not dominate its industry.

The U.S. Small Business Administration (SBA) defines a **small business** as one with 500 or fewer employees, with the definition varying a bit by industry. The SBA also states that a small business is one that is independently owned and operated and that does not dominate its industry.[26] Almost 99 percent of American businesses meet this definition, and some 87 percent employ fewer than 20 persons.

The small business sector is very important in most nations of the world. Among other things, small businesses offer major economic advantages. In the United States, for example, they employ some 52 percent of private workers, provide 51 percent of private-sector output, receive 35 percent of federal government contract dollars, and provide as many as 7 out of every 10 new jobs in the economy.[27] Smaller businesses are especially prevalent in the service and retailing sectors of the economy. Higher costs of entry make them less common in other industries such as manufacturing and transportation.

There are many reasons why people pursue entrepreneurship and launch their own businesses. One study reports the following motivations: #1—wanting to be your own boss and control your future; #2—going to work for a family-owned business; and #3—seeking to fulfill a dream.[28] Most likely it is the own boss and dream components that kept the ideas for MooBella, featured in The Topic chapter opener, alive. It took more than 15 years to get from concept to where the firm is today—with its innovative vending machines starting to move.

■ A **franchise** is when one business owner sells to another the right to operate the same business in another location.

Once a decision is made to go the small business route, the most common ways to get involved are (1) start one, (2) buy an existing one, or (3) buy and run a **franchise**—where a business owner sells to another the right to operate the same business in another location. A franchise runs under the original owner's business name and guidance. In return, the franchise parent receives a share of income or a flat fee from the franchisee.

ENTREPRENEURSHIP AND THE INTERNET

Have you started a "dot-com" today? The Internet has opened a whole new array of entrepreneurial possibilities. Just take a look at the action on eBay and imagine how many people are now running small trading businesses from their homes.

The SBA has predicted that some 85 percent of small firms are already conducting business over the Internet.[29] Many of these firms are existing firms that modified traditional ways to pursue new Internet-driven opportunities. For some of these, the old ways of operating from a bricks-and-mortar retail establishment have given way to entirely online business activities. That's what happened to Rod Spencer and his S&S Sportscards store in Worthington, Ohio. He closed his store not because business was bad; it was really good. But the nature of the business was shifting into cyberspace. When sales over the Internet became much greater than in-store sales, Spencer decided to follow the world of e-commerce. He now works from his own home with a computer and high-speed Internet connection. This saves the cost of renting retail space and hiring store employees. "I can do less business overall," he says, "to make a higher profit."[30]

REAL ETHICS

Social Entrepreneurship in Action

Anthony Essaye—helped found the International Senior Lawyers Project, a nonprofit matchmaker bringing experienced U.S. attorneys together with projects in developing nations. Project lawyers have assisted public defenders in Bulgaria, supported domestic violence litigation in India, and taught black attorneys in South Africa. Essaye says: "The needs to be filled have been much more than we contemplated."

Jack McConnell—recruited retired doctors to open a health clinic on Hilton Head Island, South Carolina. He lobbied successfully to change a state law requiring doctors from other states to be retested in South Carolina. He believes some 90,000 retired doctors would work free of charge around the U.S., saying: "The retirees could provide much, if not most, of the care for the uninsured in America if they were properly organized."

Paul Newman—used his name and financial gains from a movie career to start Newman's Own Inc., a self-sustaining social enterprise. Profits of some $175 million have been given to various charities.

FURTHER INQUIRY

Newman's Own is a for-profit business, but the profits go to charity. Is this a good way to fund social development needs in our nation and its communities? What do you think about "volunteer networks" like those set up by Essaye and McConnell? Can similar arrangements tackle other social problems and assist development elsewhere in the world? And, are we giving up a vast pool of talent by not taking better advantage of the senior citizens in our local communities?

FAMILY BUSINESSES

Family businesses, ones owned and financially controlled by family members, represent the largest percentage of businesses operating worldwide. The Family Firm Institute reports that family businesses account for 78 percent of new jobs created in the United States and provide 60 percent of the nation's employment.[31]

> A **family business** is owned and controlled by members of a family.

Family businesses must solve the same problems of other small or large businesses—meeting the challenges of strategy, competitive advantage, and operational excellence. When everything goes right, the family firm is almost an ideal situation—everyone working together, sharing values and a common goal, and knowing that what they do benefits the family. But it doesn't always work out this way or stay this way as a business changes hands over successive generations. Indeed, family businesses often face quite unique problems.

"Okay, Dad, so he's your brother. But does that mean we have to put up with inferior work and an erratic schedule that we would never tolerate from anyone else in the business?"[32] This conversation introduces a problem that can all too often set the stage for failure in a family business—the *family business feud*. Simply put, members of the controlling family get into disagreements about work responsibilities, business strategy, operating approaches, finances, or other matters. The example is indicative of an intergenerational problem, but the feud can be between spouses, among siblings, or between parents and children. It really doesn't matter. Unless disagreements are resolved satisfactorily among family members and to the benefit of the business itself, the firm will have difficulty surviving in a highly competitive environment.

Another significant problem faced by family businesses is the **succession problem**—transferring leadership from one generation to the next. A survey of small and midsized family businesses indicated that 66 percent planned on keeping the business within the family.[33] The management question is

> The **succession problem** is the issue of who will run the business when the current head leaves.

■ A **succession plan** describes how the leadership transition and related financial matters will be handled.

this: how will the assets be distributed and who will run the business when the current head leaves? Although this problem is not specific to the small firm, it is especially significant in the family business context. The data on succession are eye-opening. About 30 percent of family firms survive to the second generation; only 12 percent survive to the third; only 3 percent are expected to survive beyond that.[34]

A family business that has been in operation for some time is a source of both business momentum and financial wealth. Both must be maintained in the succession process. Business advisors recommend a **succession plan**—a formal statement that describes how the leadership transition and related financial matters will be handled when the time for changeover arrives. A succession plan should include at least procedures for choosing or designating the firm's new leadership, legal aspects of any ownership transfer, and financial and estate plans relating to the transfer. The foundations for effective implementation of a succession plan are set up well ahead of the need to use it. The plan should be shared and understood among all affected by it. The chosen successor should be prepared through experience and training to perform the new role when needed.

WHY MANY SMALL BUSINESSES FAIL

Small businesses have a high failure rate—one high enough to be scary. The SBA reports that as many as 60 to 80 percent of new businesses fail in their first five years of operation.[35] Part of this is a "counting" issue—the government counts as a "failure" any business that closes, whether it is because of the death or retirement of an owner, sale to someone else, or the inability to earn a profit.[36] Nevertheless, the fact remains: a lot of small business start-ups don't make it. And as shown in *Figure 6.2*, most of the failures are the result of bad judgment and management mistakes of the following types.[37]

- *Lack of experience*—not having sufficient know-how to run a business in the chosen market or area.
- *Lack of expertise*—not having expertise in the essentials of business operations, including finance, purchasing, selling, and production.
- *Lack of strategy and strategic leadership*—not taking the time to craft a vision and mission, as well as formulate and properly implement a strategy.
- *Poor financial control*—not keeping track of the numbers and failure to control business finances.

Figure 6.2 Eight reasons why many small businesses fail.

- *Growing too fast*—not taking the time to consolidate a position, fine-tune the organization, and systematically meet the challenges of growth.
- *Insufficient commitment*—not devoting enough time to the requirements of running a competitive business.
- *Ethical failure*—falling prey to the temptations of fraud, deception, and embezzlement.

Be sure you can ▪ give the SBA definition of small business ▪ illustrate opportunities for entrepreneurship on the Internet ▪ discuss the succession problem in family-owned businesses and possible ways to deal with it ▪ list several reasons why many small businesses fail

Learning Check 2

✓

NEW VENTURE CREATION

Whether your interest is low-tech or high-tech, online or offline, opportunities for new ventures are always there for the true entrepreneur. To pursue entrepreneurship and start a new venture, you need good ideas and the courage to give them a chance. But you must also be prepared to meet and master the test of strategy and competitive advantage. Can you identify a *market niche* that is being missed by other established firms? Can you identify a *new market* that has not yet been discovered by existing firms? Can you generate **first-mover advantage** by exploiting a niche or entering a market before competitors? These are among the questions that entrepreneurs must ask and answer in the process of beginning a new venture.

▨ A **first-mover advantage** comes from being first to exploit a niche or enter a market.

LIFE CYCLES OF ENTREPRENEURIAL FIRMS

Figure 6.3 describes the stages common to the life cycles of entrepreneurial companies. It shows the relatively predictable progression of the small business. The firm begins with the *birth stage*—where the entrepreneur struggles to get the new venture established and survive long enough to test the viability of the underlying business model in the marketplace. The firm then passes into the *breakthrough stage*—where the business model begins to work well, growth is experienced, and the complexity of managing the business operation expands significantly. Next comes the *maturity stage*—where the entrepreneur experiences the advantages of market success and financial stability, while also facing continuing management challenges of remaining competitive in a changing environment.

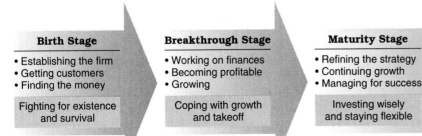

Birth Stage
- Establishing the firm
- Getting customers
- Finding the money

Fighting for existence and survival

Breakthrough Stage
- Working on finances
- Becoming profitable
- Growing

Coping with growth and takeoff

Maturity Stage
- Refining the strategy
- Continuing growth
- Managing for success

Investing wisely and staying flexible

Figure 6.3 Stages in the life cycle of an entrepreneurial firm.

ISSUES AND SITUATIONS

Pizzas with Passion

Brooklyn, New York

In a small shop and at the post-retirement age of 69, Dominick DeMarco pursues his quest of making the perfect pizza. The shop, DiFara's, isn't much to look at, and it's a clear model of inefficiency. Yes, that's right. Inefficiency. Dominick doesn't even start a pizza until he has an order. That's when all the dough stretching, sauce and ingredient spreading and all else takes place. And he takes his time doing it. But the customers don't seem to mind; in fact, they line up to wait and wait for their turn at a DiFara's pizza. Even after it comes out of the oven, they have to wait just a moment more—Dominick grinds fresh Parmegiano Reggiano (flown in from Dominick's native village in Italy) for an added taste delight.

A newspaper reporter and thoroughly satisfied customer describes a DiFara's pizza as "a masterpiece, challenging my expectations every moment . . . I sighed, wondering how pizza could be so good." Then he answers his own question, with a focus on Dominick: "He flies in his cheese because he loves it. He stretches dough only after it's ordered because he loves it. He does not run a restaurant—he makes pizza because he loves it."

Critical Response

Think of this story the next time you purchase a not-so-special meal from a server with a blank stare, a rude demeanor, a could-care-less attitude. Why is it that so many service workers today seem to be unconcerned about their work and customers? Is it because they aren't the entrepreneurs and thus don't really connect with what the business is all about? Is the only way to get a great pizza or any other product in our society today to go out and find the Dominick DeMarco's who do things for themselves, and do them exceptionally well . . . because they love to do it?

Entrepreneurs often face control and management dilemmas when their firms experience growth, including possible diversification or global expansion. They encounter a variation of the succession problem described earlier for family businesses. This time the problem is succession from entrepreneurial leadership to professional strategic leadership. The former brings the venture into being and sees it through the early stages of life; the latter manages and leads the venture into maturity as an ever-evolving and perhaps still-growing corporate enterprise. If the entrepreneur is incapable of meeting or unwilling to meet the firm's leadership needs in later life-cycle stages, continued business survival and success may well depend on the business being sold or management control being passed to professionals.

WRITING THE BUSINESS PLAN

■ A **business plan** describes the direction for a new business and the financing needed to operate it.

When people start new businesses, or even start new units within existing ones, they can greatly benefit from a good **business plan.** This is a plan that describes the details needed to obtain startup financing and operate a new business.[38] Banks and other financiers want to see a business plan before they loan money or invest in a new venture; senior managers want to see a business plan before they allocate scarce organizational resources to support a new entrepreneurial project. Importantly, the detailed thinking required to prepare a business plan can contribute to the success of the new initiative. Says Ed Federkeil, who founded a small business called California Custom Sport Trucks: "It gives you direction instead of haphazardly sticking your key in the door every day and saying—'What are we going to do?'"[39]

MANAGEMENT SMARTS 6.2

What to include in a business plan

- *Executive summary*—overview of business purpose and highlight of key elements of the plan.
- *Industry analysis*—nature of the industry, including economic trends, important legal or regulatory issues, and potential risks.
- *Company description*—mission, owners, and legal form.
- *Products and services description*—major goods or services, with competitive uniqueness.
- *Market description*—size of market, competitor strengths and weaknesses, five-year sales goals.
- *Marketing strategy*—product characteristics, distribution, promotion, pricing, and market research.
- *Operations description*—manufacturing or service methods, supplies and suppliers, and control procedures.
- *Staffing description*—management and staffing skills needed and available, compensation, human resource systems.
- *Financial projection*—cash flow projections for one to five years, break-even points, and phased investment capital.
- *Capital needs*—amount of funds needed to run the business, amount available, amount requested from new sources.
- *Milestones*—a timetable of dates showing when key stages of new venture will be completed.

Although there is no single template for a successful business plan, there is general agreement on the framework presented in *Management Smarts 6.2*. Any business plan should have an executive summary, cover certain business fundamentals, be well organized with headings, be easy to read, and be no more than about 20 pages in length. One of the great advantages of a business plan, of course, is it forces the entrepreneur to think through important issues and challenges before starting out. In addition to advice you find in books and magazines, there are many online resources available to assist in the development of a business plan.[40]

CHOOSING THE FORM OF OWNERSHIP

One of the important planning choices that must be made in starting a new venture is the legal form of ownership. There are a number of alternatives, and the choice among them involves careful consideration of their respective advantages and disadvantages. Briefly, the ownership forms include the following:

A **sole proprietorship** is simply an individual or a married couple pursuing business for a profit. This does not involve incorporation. One does business, for example, under a personal name—such as "Tiaña Lopez Designs." A sole proprietorship is simple to start, run, and terminate. However, the business owner is personally liable for business debts and claims. This is the most common form of small business ownership in the United States.

A **partnership** is formed when two or more people agree to contribute resources to start and operate a business together. Most typically it is backed by a legal and written partnership agreement. Business partners

■ A **sole proprietorship** is an individual pursuing business for a profit.

■ A **partnership** is when two or more people agree to contribute resources to start and operate a business together.

RESEARCH BRIEF

Do founders take less compensation from the ventures that they start than other senior managers in their firms?

"Yes, but," says Noam Wasserman in an article published in the *Academy of Management Journal*. Wasserman examines two theories that might explain the founders' approaches to compensation. Stewardship theory argues that founders are likely to act as "stewards" of the firms they create. They are likely to derive psychic rewards from their roles in the enterprise, and, thus, take less monetary compensation. Agency theory argues that non-founders are "agents" hired by founders to work on their behalf. Agency costs are incurred because the interests of the founders and agents may diverge. Incentive compensation is one way of reducing those agency costs.

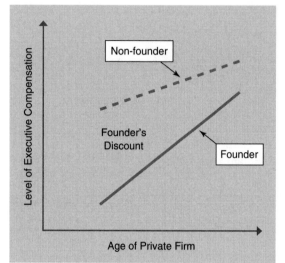

Wasserman hypothesized that founders will act more like stewards and non-founder executives more like agents. He used data from 1,238 executives in 528 private companies to test his ideas. Of the executives, 41 percent were company founders. His results confirmed the stewardship and agency predictions. Founders and executives holding higher amounts of equity in private firms earned less monetary compensation, often less than other executives reporting to them. He describes this as a "founder's discount" where they essentially "pay to be founders" and take more soft compensation in the form of psychic rewards. But Wasserman also found that as private firms grow in size, compensation for all executives increases. And as it does, the "founder's discount" becomes smaller.

QUESTIONS & APPLICATIONS

There seems to be a logic to the founder's discount. They own most of the assets and will thus profit more in the long run, especially if the company is sold. They should also be highly motivated to work hard and make these financial gains and firm success possible.

Most of us, as employees, act as "agents" for those who own the firms or organizations for which we work. Look at your job or job opportunities. What difference would it make to you if you were made a part owner and thus had feelings of stewardship? Would you work harder and help the employer perform better? Could this logic be applied to more organizations and their members?

Reference: Noam Wasserman, "Stewards, Agents and the Founder Discount: Executive Compensation in New Ventures," *Academy of Management Journal*, Vol. 49 (2006), pp. 960–976.

---

agree on the contribution of resources and skills to the new venture and on the sharing of profits and losses. In a *general partnership*, the simplest and most common form, they also share management responsibilities. A *limited partnership* consists of a general partner and one or more "limited" partners who do not participate in day-to-day business management. They share in profits, but their losses are limited to the amount of their investment. *A limited liability partnership*, common among professionals such as accountants and attorneys, limits the liability of one partner for the negligence of another.

A **corporation**, commonly identified by the "Inc." designation in a name, is a legal entity that is chartered by the state and exists separately from its owners. The corporation can be for-profit, such as Microsoft Inc., or non-profit, such as Count-Me-In Inc.—a firm helping women entrepreneurs get started with small loans. The corporate form offers two major advantages: (1) it grants the organization certain legal rights (e.g., to engage in contracts),

■ A **corporation** is a legal entity that exists separately from its owners.

and (2) the corporation becomes responsible for its own liabilities. This separates the owners from personal liability and gives the firm a life of its own that can extend beyond that of its owners. The disadvantage of incorporation rests largely with the cost of incorporating and the complexity of the documentation required to operate an incorporated business.

Recently, the **limited liability corporation (LLC)** has gained popularity. A limited liability corporation combines the advantages of the other forms—sole proprietorship, partnership, and corporation. For liability purposes, it functions like a corporation, protecting the assets of owners against claims made against the company. For tax purposes, it functions as a partnership in the case of multiple owners and as a sole proprietorship in the case of a single owner.

> A **limited liability corporation (LLC)** is a hybrid business form combining advantages of the sole proprietorship, partnership, and corporation.

FINANCING THE NEW VENTURE

Starting a new venture takes money, and that money often must be raised. The cost of startup will most likely exceed the amount available from personal sources.

There are two major ways the entrepreneur can obtain outside financing for a new venture. **Debt financing** involves going into debt by borrowing money from another person, a bank, or a financial institution. This

> **Debt financing** involves borrowing money that must be repaid over time with interest.

KAFFEEKLATSCH

Gates+Buffett=Good Works?

First Cup

"So one of America's wealthiest entrepreneurs Warren Buffett is giving away his billions—31 of them to be exact! And do you believe he's giving it to the another rich entrepreneur—Bill Gates?"

Studying the Grounds

■ Warren Buffett, founder and Chairman of Berkshire Hathaway, and the second richest person in the world, announced that $1.5 billion per year of his personal wealth would flow to the Bill & Melinda Gates Foundation each year, to the tune of $31 billion total.

■ The Gates Foundation, already funded by Bill Gates with $28 billion in assets earned from Microsoft, has a well-regarded track record in promoting education, especially in U.S. inner cities, and global health, including the fight against HIV/AIDS and other diseases.

■ Some say Buffett (age 77) chose Gates (age 52) because he wants a "living donor" to oversee the funds and spend them each year with an impact that he can see.

Double Espresso

"A lot of rich people want to create a financial legacy for their children and for generations to come. They want to keep most of the money in the family. But did you read what Buffett says about this?"

■ "I don't believe in inheriting your position in society."

■ "I would argue that when your kids have all the advantages anyway, in terms of how they grow up and the opportunities they have for education, including what they learn at home—I would say it's neither right nor rational to be flooding them with money."

Your Turn

The Buffett philanthropy stands in contrast to many of the stories we all hear about corporate and executive greed. And his generosity is a nice story no doubt. But if you were Buffett would you be confident that your gift monies will be well spent? Is there anything you would want to do by way of controls over the Gates Foundation to try and protect your objectives?

And by the way, what about the rest of us? We scrimp and save for every dollar. We'll probably never become as wealthy as Buffett or a Gates. But can we still make a difference in the world through personal philanthropy?"

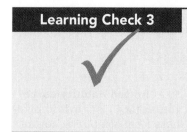

Learning Check 3

Be sure you can ■ explain the concept of first-mover advantage in new venture creation ■ illustrate new venture life-cycle stages from birth to breakthrough to maturity ■ identify the major elements in a business plan ■ differentiate between common forms of small business ownership—sole proprietorship, partnership, and corporation ■ differentiate between debt financing and equity financing ■ explain the roles of venture capitalists and angel investors in new venture financing

---

■ **Equity financing** involves exchanging ownership shares for outside investment monies.

■ **Venture capitalists** make large investments in new ventures in return for an equity stake in the business.

■ An **initial public offering (IPO)** is an initial selling of shares of stock to the public at large.

■ An **angel investor** is a wealthy individual willing to invest in return for equity in a new venture.

loan must be paid back over time with interest. A loan also requires collateral that pledges business assets or personal assets, such as a home, to secure the loan in case of default. **Equity financing** involves giving ownership shares in the business to outsiders in return for outside investment monies. This money does not need to be paid back. It is an investment, and the investor assumes the risk for potential gains and losses. In return for taking that risk, the equity investor gains some proportionate ownership control.

Equity financing is usually obtained from **venture capitalists**, companies that pool capital and make investments in new ventures in return for an equity stake in the business. Typically, venture capitalists finance only a very small proportion of new ventures. They tend to focus on relatively large investments, such as $1 million or more, and they usually take a management role in order to grow the business and add value as soon as possible. Sometimes that value is returned when a fast-growing firm gains a solid market base and becomes a candidate for an **initial public offering**, or **IPO**. This is when shares of stock in the business are first sold to the public and then begin trading on a major stock exchange. When an IPO is successful and the share prices are bid up by the market, the original investments of the venture capitalist and entrepreneur rise in value. The anticipation of such return on investment is a large part of the venture capitalist's motivation; indeed, it is the nature of the venture capital business.

When venture capital isn't available to the entrepreneur, another important financing option is the **angel investor**. This is a wealthy individual who is willing to make an investment in return for equity in a new venture. Angel investors are especially common and helpful in the very early startup stage. Their presence can help raise investor confidence and attract additional venture funding that would otherwise not be available. For example, when Liz Cobb wanted to start her sales compensation firm, Incentive Systems, she contacted 15 to 20 venture capital firms. She was interviewed by 10 and turned down by all of them. After she located $250,000 from two angel investors, the venture capital firms got interested again. She was able to obtain her first $2 million in financing and has since built the firm into a 70-plus employee business.[41]

CHAPTER 6 STUDY GUIDE

STUDY QUESTIONS SUMMARY

1 What is entrepreneurship?

- Entrepreneurship is risk-taking behavior that results in the creation of new opportunities for individuals and/or organizations.
- An entrepreneur is someone who takes risks to pursue opportunities in situations others may view as problems or threats.
- Entrepreneurs tend to be creative people who are self-confident, determined, resilient, adaptable, and driven to excel; they like to be masters of their own destinies.
- Women and minorities are well represented among entrepreneurs, with some being driven by necessity or the lack of alternative career options.
- Social entrepreneurs apply their energies to create innovations that help to solve important problems in society.

2 What is special about small businesses?

- Entrepreneurship results in the founding of many small businesses that offer job creation and other benefits to economies.
- The Internet has opened a whole new array of entrepreneurial possibilities for small businesses.
- Family businesses, ones owned and financially controlled by family members, represent the largest percentage of businesses operating worldwide; they sometimes suffer from the succession problem.

- Small businesses have a high failure rate, with as many as 60 to 80 percent of new businesses failing in their first five years of operation; many failures are the result of poor management decisions.

3 How does one start a new venture?

- Entrepreneurial firms tend to follow the life-cycle stages of birth, breakthrough, and maturity, with each stage offering different management challenges.
- A new startup should be guided by a good business plan that describes the intended nature of the business, how it will operate, and how financing will be obtained.
- An important choice is the form of business ownership, with the proprietorship, corporate, and limited liability forms offering different advantages and disadvantages.
- Two basic ways of financing a new venture are through debt financing, by taking loans, and equity financing, which exchanges ownership shares in return for outside investment.
- Venture capitalists pool capital and make investments in new ventures in return for an equity stake in the business; an angel investor is a wealthy individual who is willing to invest money in return for equity in a new venture.

KEY TERMS REVIEW

Angel investor (p. 147)

Business plan (p. 144)

Corporation (p. 146)

Debt financing (p. 147)

Entrepreneur (p. 134)

Entrepreneurship (p. 134)

Equity financing (p. 147)

Family business (p. 141)

First-mover advantage (p. 143)

Franchise (p. 140)

Initial Public Offering (IPO) (p. 147)

Limited Liability Corporation (p. 147)

Necessity-based entrepreneurship (p 138)

Partnership (p. 145)

Small business (p. 140)

Social entrepreneurship (p. 139)

Sole proprietorship (p. 145)

Succession plan (p. 142)

Succession problem (p. 141)

Venture capitalists (p. 147)

SELF-TEST 6

MULTIPLE-CHOICE QUESTIONS:

1. _____ is among the personality characteristics commonly found among entrepreneurs.
   (a) External locus of control   (b) Inflexibility   (c) Self-confidence   (d) Low self reliance

2. When an entrepreneur is comfortable with uncertainty and willing to take risks, these are indicators of someone with a(n) _____.
   (a) high tolerance for ambiguity   (b) internal locus of control   (c) need for achievement   (d) action orientation

3. Almost _____ percent of American businesses meet the definition of "small business" used by the Small Business Administration.

   (a) 40   (b) 99   (c) 75   (d) 81

4. When a business owner sells to another person the right to operate that business in another location, this is a _____.

   (a) conglomerate   (b) franchise   (c) joint venture   (d) limited partnership

5. A small business owner who is concerned about passing the business on to heirs after retirement or death should prepare a formal _____ plan.

   (a) retirement   (b) succession   (c) franchising   (d) liquidation

6. Among the most common reasons that new small business startups often fail is _____.

   (a) lack of business expertise   (b) strict financial controls   (c) slow growth   (d) high ethical standards

7. When a new business is quick to capture a market niche before competitors, this is called _____.

   (a) intrapreneurship   (b) an initial public offering   (c) succession planning   (d) first-mover advantage

8. When a small business is just starting, the business owner is typically struggling to _____.

   (a) gain acceptance in the marketplace   (b) find partners for expansion   (c) prepare an initial public offering   (d) bring professional skills into the management team

9. A venture capitalist who receives an ownership share in return for investing in a new business is providing _____ financing.

   (a) debt   (b) equity   (c) corporate   (d) partnership

10. In _____ financing, the business owner borrows money as a loan that must eventually be paid along with agreed-upon interest to the lender.

    (a) debt   (b) equity   (c) partnership   (d) limited

11. _____ take ownership shares in a new venture in return for providing the entrepreneur with critical startup funds.

    (a) Business incubators   (b) Angel investors   (c) SBDCS   (d) Intrapreneurs

12. Among the forms of small business ownership, a _____ protects the owners from any personal liabilities for business losses.

    (a) sole proprietorship   (b) franchise   (c) limited partnership   (d) corporation

13. The first component of a good business plan is usually _____.

    (a) an industry analysis   (b) a marketing strategy   (c) an executive summary   (d) a set of milestones

14. Current trends in small business ownership in the United States would most likely show that _____.

    (a) the numbers of women- and minority-owned businesses are declining   (b) the majority of small businesses conduct some business by Internet   (c) large businesses create more jobs than small businesses   (d) very few small business engage in international import/export activities

15. The unique feature distinguishing social entrepreneurship is _____.

    (a) lack of other career options   (b) focus on international markets   (c) refusal to finance by loans   (d) commitment to solving social problems

SHORT-RESPONSE QUESTIONS:

16. What is the relationship between diversity and entrepreneurship?

17. What are the major stages in the life cycle of an entrepreneurial firm, and what are the management challenges at each stage?

18. What are the advantages of a limited partnership form of small business ownership?

19. What is the difference, if any, between a venture capitalist and an angel investor?

APPLICATION QUESTION:

20. Assume for the moment that you have a great idea for a potential Internet-based startup business. In discussing the idea with a friend, she advises you to be very careful to tie your business idea to potential customers and then describe it well in a business plan. "After all," she says, "you won't succeed without customers, and you'll never get a chance to succeed if you can't attract financial backers through a good business plan." With these words to the wise, you proceed. What questions will you ask and answer to ensure that you are customer-focused in this business? What are the major areas that you would address in writing your initial business plan?

Domino's Pizza: Great Ideas Bring Domino's to Your Door

Domino's Pizza had more than 7,900 company-owned and franchised stores in the United States and more than 50 other countries. Pizza Today recently named it "Chain of the Year." With sales of more than 400 million pizzas and revenues of nearly $4 billion, it represents an impressive success story. Starting in 1960 with one store in Ypsilanti, Michigan, Tom Monaghan redefined the pizza industry and, in so doing, built a corporate powerhouse. It entered the international market in 1983 with its first store outside the United States, which was in Winnipeg, Canada. As of late, more than 2,500 of the stores were international and revenues generated in those stores exceeded $1 billion.[42] Could you be another Tom, given the chance?

The Domino Story

Tom Monaghan and his brother, James, borrowed $500 in 1960 to purchase "DomiNick's," a pizza store, in Ypsilanti, Michigan. The following year Tom bought out his brother's half interest for a used Volkswagen Beetle. In 1965, Tom changed the name of the establishment to "Domino's Pizza." Two years later, he opened the first franchise location in Ypsilanti.[43]

Growing up in orphanages, Tom dreamed of succeeding in a big way. In his first 13 years in the business, he worked 100-hour weeks, seven days a week. He only had one vacation, and that was for six days when he got married to his wife, Margie.[44] The following quote exhibits his high need to be the best at whatever he does:

I was distracted by some of the rewards of success, which was hurting my business. I put all of those distractions aside, and focused solely on Domino's Pizza. I decided to take a "millionaire's vow of poverty." I am focusing on God, family and Domino's Pizza.[45]

The pizza industry is highly fragmented, with nearly 70,000 pizzerias and $35 billion in sales per year. More than 3 billion pizzas are sold each year in America, representing annual consumption of over 23 pounds of pizza per capita.[46] The issue for any pizzeria is how to create an advantage and differentiate its product.

Monaghan decided to concentrate only on pizzas and developed the strategy of delivering a hot pie in 30 minutes or less. He chose to locate his early franchises in college towns and near military bases, whose populations are both high consumers of pizzas. This strategy proved to be very successful, and Domino's passed 200 locations in the late 1970s.[47]

Monaghan is credited with developing many of the pizza practices now taken for granted within the industry, including dough trays, the corrugated pizza box, insulated bags to transport pizzas, and a unique system of internal franchising. "Tom Monaghan made pizza delivery what it is today," says Eric Marcus, a 46-unit Domino's franchisee based in Dayton, Ohio. "The one thing about Tom is that he knew what he wanted, and he knew how to stay focused on what he wanted. He had a vision that pizza should be delivered in 30 minutes or less."[48]

The 1980s proved to be a huge time for Domino's growth, as it closed out the decade with more than 5,000 locations and $2 billion in sales.[49] During that time, Monaghan purchased the Detroit Tigers baseball team and developed significant philanthropic activities in various Domino's communities.

However, the road to success was not entirely smooth, and Domino's did have to face hurdles and challenges along the way. In 1968, the firm's commissary and company headquarters were destroyed by fire. In 1976, Amstar Corp., maker of Domino Sugar, filed a trademark infringement lawsuit against the firm that was settled in Domino's favor in 1980. In 1993, responding to concerns for drivers' safety, the firm discontinued the "30-minute guarantee" and replaced it with the total satisfaction guarantee: "If for any reason you are dissatisfied with your Domino's Pizza dining experience, we will remake you pizza or refund your money."[50]

In 1998, Monaghan sold "a significant" portion of his ownership in Domino's to Bain Capital Inc., a Massachusetts investment firm. While he remained on the board of directors, he was no longer engaged in the day-to-day activities of the firm. Instead, he wanted to devote his time to religious pursuits, including the development of a planned Catholic community—Ave Maria, Florida—and a Catholic university by the same name.[51]

David Brandon, formerly of Procter & Gamble and Valassis Communications, was hired as president. In his first full year as president, Domino's achieved a 4.4 percent growth in sales. Now chairman and CEO, Brandon has been recognized as the visionary who led Domino's to win the coveted "Chain of the Year" award given by *Pizza Today*. Jeremy White, editor-in-chief of the monthly trade publication, observed: "Domino's had an impressive year. Between solid product introductions, savvy advertising and a 'People First' mentality that has trickled down from Chairman and CEO Dave Brandon to store employees, the chain managed to post positive financial results in a time of economic instability."[52]

Domino's Future

With a history of innovations in the pizza industry, Domino's constantly looks for new ways to enhance customer value. *Pizza Today* honored the company for outstanding sales, strong leadership, innovation, brand image, and customer satisfaction.[53]

In Domino's early years, Tom Monaghan set the stage for the company's later successes with his innovations and brand development strategies. He even recognized how important it was to adapt to local culture in order to achieve success overseas. "Culture comes first. Some early attempts to open Domino's stores internationally faltered because the company tried to establish in markets that had cultures unaccustomed to pizza or the convenience of home delivery. Understanding cultures and adapting to them was the first step in the process of global expansion."[54] For example, CEO Brandon notes that although delivery service has proven very popular in Japan and Taiwan, customers in China seem to want to leave their home to enjoy it. Consequently, the company is experimenting with enlarged stores featuring sit-down areas.

Monaghan displayed the drive and determination representative of many entrepreneurs in today's dynamic market. He had what it took to succeed.

REVIEW QUESTIONS

1. What allowed Tom Monaghan to develop Domino's from a one-store pizza shop into a worldwide enterprise?

2. How do Tom Monaghan and David Brandon differ? How are they similar? Why was each the right person for the company at the time?

3. If Tom Monaghan decided to develop the Domino's franchise in the present day, what advantages might he have as an entrepreneur in today's environment? What disadvantages might he face?

TEAM PROJECT

Community Entrepreneurs

Michael Gerber, author and entrepreneur, says: "The entrepreneur in us sees opportunities everywhere we look, but many people see only problems everywhere they look." The entrepreneurs he describes are everywhere, some might live next door and one might be you; many own and operate the small businesses of your community.

Question: Who are the entrepreneurs in your community and what are they accomplishing?

Research Directions:

■ Read the local news, talk to your friends and locals, consider where you shop. Make a list of the businesses and other organizations that have an entrepreneurial character. Be as complete as possible—look at both businesses and nonprofits.

■ For each of the organizations, do further research to identify the persons who are the entrepreneurs responsible for them.

■ Contact as many of the entrepreneurs as possible and interview them. Try to learn how they got started, why, what they encountered as obstacles or problems, what they learned about entrepreneurship that could be passed along to others. Add to these questions a list of your own—what do you want to know about entrepreneurship?

■ Analyze your results for class presentation and discussion. Look for patterns and differences in terms of entrepreneurs as persons, the entrepreneurial experience, and potential insights into business versus social entrepreneurship.

■ Consider writing short cases that summarize the "founding stories" of the entrepreneurs you find especially interesting.

Not everyone is comfortable with **RISK-TAKING**. The uncertainty of risky situations is unsettling, and the anxieties are threatening for some of us. But risks, small and large, are a part of everyday living. In school and around campus there are many opportunities to explore your openness to risk and entrepreneurial tendencies. The Irish entrepreneur Bill Lynch offers this observation: "The entrepreneurs I have met are not geniuses, but people who have ideas . . . and act on them. Many people have ideas, talk about them, and then do nothing." What will it take for you to start your own business or propose a new venture to your employer? Two former managers of Footlocker stores took the risk, and it paid off handsomely. After noticing that customers kept asking for sports caps unavailable in stores, Glenn Campbell and Scott Molander decided to start a store of their own—Hat World. "People thought we were crazy," Campbell says. But Hat World took off, selling over 6,000 caps in two months. The entrepreneurs opened four more stores within a year. At last check, Campbell and Molander's risk had turned into a firm with annual sales of $150 million. Could this story be yours someday?

Building The Brand Called "You"   Be realistic. Are you an idea person? Are you someone who acts on ideas? Or, are you someone who talks about ideas but rarely does anything about them? Write an inventory of the "best" ideas you've had recently, or even over the years. Next to each, describe what you did with it. Complete the recommended self-assessments Write a short paragraph that assesses your risk-taking tendencies.

Risk-taking

NEXT STEPS: MANAGEMENT LEARNING WORKBOOK

Self-Assessments
- Entrepreneurship Orientation (#10)
- Turbulence Tolerance Test (#16)
- Internal/External Control (#26)

Exercises in Teamwork
- Strategic Scenarios (#12)
- Work vs. Family (#17)
- Why Do We Work? (#21)

Information and Decision Making

7

Planning Ahead

Succeeding with a Plan and a Hunch

Imagine two modes of thought: One—systematic—is methodical; it gets things done according to a fixed system or plan. The other—intuitive—is all about instinct; it operates on what it thinks to be true without any conscious reasoning. Now imagine these two ways of doing things nestled comfortably under the roof of one of the information age's most successful businesses.

It may seem like a pairing of odd-couple-like proportions—the union of systematic and intuitive thinking. But according to Google, it's a winning combination. The Silicon Valley giant's successful merging of the seemingly divergent modes of thought has brought it fame and fortune, and even earned it a spot in our cultural lexicography.

As a company, Google is devoutly preoccupied with searching the great depths of the Web, and making doing so as easy as possible. Its inventions seek to apply systematic technologies to intuitive thought processes to generate relevant, concrete results. Humans don't so much want to learn new technologies as much as they want to apply their intuitive thought processes to achieve their goals with a minimum of effort.

What *They* Think

"I want to be looked back on as being very innovative, very trusted and ethical and ultimately making a big difference in the world."
Sergey Brin, Google co-founder

SYSTEMATIC: *"It is best to do things systematically, because we are only human, and disorder is our worst enemy."*
Hesiod, early Greek poet

INTUITIVE: *"During [these] periods of relaxation after concentrated intellectual activity, the intuitive mind seems to take over and can produce the sudden clarifying insights which give so much joy and delight."*
Fritjof Capra, physicist

Enter Google. Co-founder Sergey Brin says: "Obviously everyone wants to ba a successful, but I want to be looked back on as being very innovative, very trusted and ethical and ultimately making a big difference in the world."

The company's success has been built on the strength of its search engine technology, which goes beyond simply scanning and analyzing the content of pages. Google's PageRank algorithm systematically reviews the links that connect Web pages. The more often a page is linked to by other pages, the more likely it is to have authority on its particular topic, and it is thus ranked higher in search results.[1]

But trying to make the systematic fit the intuitive doesn't always work. Google made a big to-do about the release of its Google Spreadsheet software, which allows users to edit and save spreadsheets online, but the response from critics and information technology professionals has been lukewarm at best. No one is really sure, aside from front-end costs, whether Web-based office applications will be worth the security headaches and access issues. Will users' data be safe all the time? Will it be accessible all the time? Google can't yet say, so decision makers can't yet move. Nor has Google offered much in the way of customer service, directing questions to e-mail support.

The Google search engine's unique ability to seem to intuitively grasp what pages users are searching for (even if the users don't yet know which pages those are) has made its name an iconic representation for searching on the Web, regardless of the technology used. People may say, "I'll google XYZ," whether they use search engines from Yahoo!, Amazon, or MSN. This subtle infusion into the vernacular intuitively links the name "Google" with aspirations to find information quickly, easily, and efficiently.

And that's just the way Google likes it.

The Numbers

American Market Share for Internet Search Engines

Google	43%
Google + AOL*	50%
Yahoo!	28%
MSN (Microsoft)	13%
Ask.com	6%

Quick facts

* In an average month, Google processes 2.7 billion Internet searches.[2]
* Google began as a research project by Larry Page and Sergey Brin, when students at Stanford University.[3]
* To parallel the 2GB of storage offered by Google's Gmail, Microsoft plans to switch all 230 million Hotmail users to Windows Live Mail accounts.[4]
* Google will spend more than $14 billion on basic physical necessities—buildings, computer equipment, utilities—in a year.[5]
* Google's employees are known as googlers; they work at a headquarters called googleplex; the ratio of male to female employees is approximately 70 to 30.[6]

What Do *You* Think?

1. Is Google's ability to provide easy online access to systematic and intuitive decision-making support its main competitive advantage?
2. Behind all of Google's creative accomplishments, is it really good old-fashioned business analysis that allows the firm to so successfully take on its rivals?

Information and Decision Making			
Study Question 1	**Study Question 2**	**Study Question 3**	**Study Question 4**
Information and Management	Information and Managerial Decisions	The Decision-Making Process	Issues in Managerial Decision Making
■ How information technology changes organizations ■ Roles of managers as information processors	■ Types of managerial decisions ■ Decision environments ■ Problem-solving styles	■ Identify problem ■ Examine alternatives ■ Make a decision ■ Implement decision ■ Evaluate results	■ Decision errors and traps ■ Individual and group decisions ■ Ethical decisions ■ Knowledge management and organizational learning
Learning Check 1	**Learning Check 2**	**Learning Check 3**	**Learning Check 4**

Whenever one talks about decision making it's hard not to think about how people and organizations dealt with Hurricane Katrina. New Orleans was devastated; people lost homes, fortunes, and lives; organizations lost reputations for failures in their response capabilities. And in retrospect, it is clear that a lot of things could have been done differently and better. But when things are happening "real time" it's not easy to do all the right things; information gets missed or lost or poorly used, mistakes get made, well-intended decisions go wrong or prove inadequate to the task.

Anyone who practices management knows that decision making is part of the job. They also know that not all decisions are going to be easy ones and that some will have to be made under tough conditions. All of those case studies, experiential exercises, class discussions, and even exam questions in college courses are intended to help students gain familiarity with the nature of decision making, the potential problems and pitfalls, and even the pressures of crisis situations. From that point on, however, only you can determine whether you step forward and make the best decisions even in very difficult circumstances, or collapse under pressure.

In regards to the challenges ahead, dealing with information and decision making, we may do well to remember this famous quote.[7]

The significant problems we face cannot be solved at the same level of thinking we were at when we created them. Albert Einstein

INFORMATION TECHNOLOGY AND MANAGEMENT

Society today is different. It is without any doubt information-driven, digital, networked, and continuously evolving. An important key to managerial performance in this new world is information technology, or IT, and the way it is utilized. We live and work at a time when computers make more information about more things available to more people more quickly than ever before. The question is: how well do we take advantage of it?

The late management scholar and consultant Peter Drucker said that in our IT-driven economy "the productivity of knowledge and knowledge workers" is the decisive competitive factor.[8] It's a setting where knowledge and intellectual capital are irreplaceable organizational resources.[9] Both grow from information that, today, increasingly moves at high speed through electronic networks that link each of us to the world at large with an access and intensity never before possible. Thus, what Drucker called "the productivity of knowledge and knowledge workers" depends on two "must have" competencies: (1) *computer competency*—the ability to understand computers and to use them to their best advantage; and (2) *information competency*—the ability to utilize technology to locate, retrieve, evaluate, organize, and analyze information for decision making.

HOW INFORMATION TECHNOLOGY CHANGES ORGANIZATIONS

Organizations are changing as continuing developments in information technology exert their influence. Information departments or centers are now mainstream on organization charts. The number and variety of information career fields is rapidly expanding. Managers are increasingly expected to excel in their information processing roles. All of this, and more, is characteristic of the great opportunities of an information age.

Information technology is changing organizations by breaking down barriers.[10] As shown in *Figure 7.1*, within organizations this means that people working in different departments, levels, and physical locations can more easily communicate and share information. It also means that the organization can operate with fewer middle managers, whose jobs otherwise would be to facilitate these information flows; computers now do the job. IT-intensive organizations are "flatter" and operate with fewer levels than their more traditional organizational counterparts. This creates opportunities for competitive advantage through faster decision making, better use of timely information, and better coordination of decisions and actions.

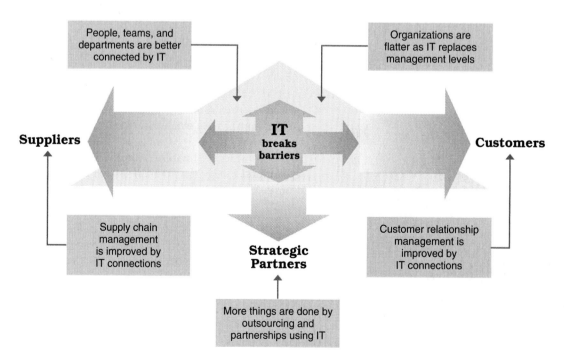

Figure 7.1 Information technology is breaking barriers and changing organizations.

IT also breaks barriers between organizations and key elements in the external environment. It plays an important role in *customer relationship management* by quickly and accurately providing information for decision makers regarding customer needs, preferences, and satisfactions. It helps manage and control costs in all aspects of *supply chain management,* from initiation of purchase, to logistics and transportation, to point of delivery and ultimate use. IT also allows outsourcing and other business contracts to be continuously and efficiently monitored.

In order to perform well, people in any work setting, large or small, must have available to them the right information at the right time and in the right place. **Information systems** use the latest in information technology to collect, organize, and distribute data in such a way that they become meaningful as information.

Management information systems, or MIS, meet the specific information needs of managers as they make a variety of day-to-day decisions. And today's developments make possible performance levels that are truly extraordinary. C.R. England Inc., a long-haul refrigerated trucking company, for example, uses a computerized MIS to monitor more than 500 aspects of organizational performance. The system tracks everything from billing accuracy to arrival times to driver satisfaction with company maintenance on their vehicles. Says CEO Dan England: "Our view was, if we could measure it, we could manage it."[11]

■ **Information systems** use IT to collect, organize, and distribute data for use in decision making.

■ **Management information systems** meet the information needs of managers in making daily decisions.

ROLES OF MANAGERS AS INFORMATION PROCESSORS

■ **Data** are raw facts and observations.

■ **Information** is data made useful for decision making.

Data are raw facts and observations. **Information** is data made useful and meaningful for decision making. The management process of planning, organizing, leading, and controlling is ultimately driven by information, not by data alone. Managers need good information, and they need it all the time. Information that is truly useful meets the test of these five criteria:

1. *Timely*—the information is available when needed; it meets deadlines for decision making and action.
2. *High quality*—the information is accurate, and it is reliable; it can be used with confidence.
3. *Complete*—the information is complete and sufficient for the task at hand; it is as current and up-to-date as possible.
4. *Relevant*—the information is appropriate for the task at hand; it is free from extraneous or irrelevant materials.
5. *Understandable*—the information is clear and easily understood by the user; it is free from unnecessary detail.

The manager's job as shown in *Figure 7.2* is a nerve center of information flows, with information being continually gathered, given, and received from many sources. All of the managerial roles identified by Henry Mintzberg and discussed in Chapter 1—interpersonal, decisional, and informational—involve communication and information processing.[12] So, too, do all aspects of the management process—planning, organizing, leading, and controlling. Success in management is increasingly tied to the opportunities of IT.

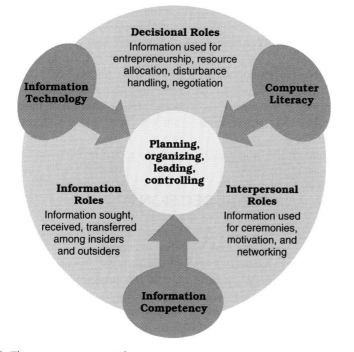

Figure 7.2 The manager as an information-processing nerve center.

- *Planning advantages*—better and more timely access to useful information, involving more people in the planning process.
- *Organizing advantages*—more ongoing and informed communication among all parts, improving coordination and integration.
- *Leading advantages*—more frequent and better communication with staff and diverse stakeholders, keeping objectives clear.
- *Controlling advantages*—more immediate measures of performance results, allowing real-time solutions to problems.

Be sure you can ■ define and discuss how IT is breaking barriers within organizations and between organizations and their environments ■ describe the role of information systems in organizations ■ differentiate data and information ■ list the criteria of useful information ■ describe how IT influences the four functions of management

Learning Check 1

INFORMATION AND MANAGERIAL DECISIONS

As managers use information to solve a continuous stream of daily problems, the most obvious problem situation is a *performance deficiency*. This is when actual performance is less than desired. For example, a manager faces a possible problem when turnover or absenteeism suddenly increases in the work unit, when a subordinate's daily output decreases, or when a higher executive complains about something that has been said or done. Another important problem situation emerges as a *performance opportunity*. This is when an actual situation either turns out better than anticipated or offers the potential to do so.

■ **Problem solving** involves identifying and taking action to resolve problems.

The challenge in dealing with any performance deficiency or performance opportunity is to proceed with effective **problem solving**—the process of identifying a discrepancy between an actual and desired state of affairs and then taking action to resolve the deficiency or take advantage of the opportunity. Success in problem solving is dependent on the right information being available to the right people at the right times so that they can make good problem-solving decisions. A **decision**, to be precise, is a choice among alternative possible courses of action. In today's IT-enriched organizations, information systems assist managers in gathering data, turning data into useful information, and utilizing that information individually and collaboratively to make problem-solving decisions.

■ A **decision** is a choice among possible alternative courses of action.

TYPES OF MANAGERIAL DECISIONS

■ A **programmed decision** applies a solution from past experience to a routine problem.

■ **Structured problems** are straightforward and clear in information needs.

Managers make different types of decisions in their day-to-day work. **Programmed decisions** use solutions already available from past experience to solve **structured problems**—ones that are familiar, straightforward, and clear with respect to information needs. These problems are routine; although perhaps not predictable, they can at least be anticipated. This means that decisions can be planned or programmed in advance to be implemented as needed. In human resource management, for example, problems are common whenever decisions are made on pay raises and promotions, vacation requests, committee assignments, and the like. Knowing this, forward-looking managers plan ahead on how to handle complaints and conflicts when and if they should arise.

ISSUES AND SITUATIONS

Lego's Wrong Turn

Surely you've played with Legos, probably even given them as gifts. The world of children has been enriched by the multicolored blocks and the many different forms, figures, and shapes into which they can be crafted at individual initiative. But how about the company that makes them—do its bits and pieces always fit together in ways that make good business sense?

It wasn't too long ago that the strategy at the firm seemed to shift. We saw advertisements for Legoland theme parks, and we could buy Lego branded clothing and computer games for children. The company saw huge losses. Chief Executive Jorgen Vig Knudstorp says: "It was the wrong strategy." But it took 7 years before the firm regained its focus with a "back-to-the-core" strategy based on plastic building blocks. Says Soren Torp Laursen, president of Lego Americas: "What I have learned the hard way is that Lego is not a lifestyle brand."

Look for Lego's new strategy in a range of new and trendy products. The firm is placing bets now on "Mindstorms," self-designed and programmable robots controlled by Lego brains—Spike, AlphaRex, and RobotArm, to name three. Even though these robots constitute just 7 percent of sales, Knudstorp considers their software and electronic capabilities a doorway to the future. He's hoping this "right" turn will go a long way to correcting the firm's "wrong" turns of the past.

Critical Response

A business that runs 7 years with the wrong strategy! Why do you think it took so long to break away from it? Are we talking about executive egos that were on the line, with no one wanting to admit a mistake? Or are we looking at the sheer difficulty of disengaging from a strategy that was already being implemented at very high costs?

When top management makes decisions that set organizations in hard-to-reverse, long-term directions, there's obviously a lot at stake. So, should they be left alone to risk and decide, and then be rewarded or penalized for how well the decisions turn out? Or should there be checks and balances in management decision making that minimize the chances for such errors?

Managers must also deal with new or unusual situations that present **unstructured problems**, full of ambiguities and information deficiencies. These problems require **nonprogrammed decisions** that craft novel solutions to meet the demands of the unique situation at hand. Most problems faced by higher-level managers are of this type, often involving the choice of strategies and objectives in situations of some uncertainty.

An extreme type of nonprogrammed decision must be made in times of **crisis**—the occurrence of an unexpected problem that can lead to disaster if not resolved quickly and appropriately. Terrorism in a post–9/11 world, outbreaks of workplace violence, man-made environmental catastrophes, ethical scandals, and IT failures are examples.

The ability to handle crises (see *Management Smarts 7.1*) may be the ultimate test of a manager's problem-solving capabilities.[13] Unfortunately, research indicates that managers may react to crises by doing the wrong things. They isolate themselves and try to solve the problem alone or in a small "closed" group.[14] This denies them access to crucial information and assistance at the very time they are most needed. The crisis can even be accentuated when more problems are created because critical decisions are made with poor or inadequate information and from a limited perspective. The organizational consequences of alienated customers, lost profits, damaged reputations, and increased costs can be very severe.

For these and other reasons, many organizations are developing formal **crisis management** programs. They are designed to help managers and others prepare for unexpected high-impact events that threaten an organization's health and well-being. Anticipation is one aspect of crisis management; preparation is another. People can be assigned ahead of time to *crisis management teams*, and *crisis management plans* can be developed to deal with various contingencies. Just as police departments and community groups plan ahead and train to best handle civil and natural disasters, so, too, can managers and work teams plan ahead and train to best deal with organizational crises.

■ **Unstructured problems** have ambiguities and information deficiencies.

■ A **nonprogrammed decision** applies a specific solution crafted for a unique problem.

■ A **crisis** is an unexpected problem that can lead to disaster if not resolved quickly and appropriately.

■ **Crisis management** is preparation for the management of crises that threaten an organization's health and well-being.

■ A **certain environment** offers complete information on possible action alternatives and their consequences

DECISION ENVIRONMENTS

Figure 7.3 shows three different decision environments—certainty, risk, and uncertainty. Although managers make decisions in each, the conditions of risk and uncertainty are common at higher management levels where problems are more complex and unstructured. Former Coca-Cola CEO Roberto Goizueta, for example, was known as a risk taker. Among his risky moves were introducing Diet Coke to the market, changing the formula of Coca-Cola to create New Coke, and then reversing direction after New Coke flopped.[15]

The decision to market any new products is made in conditions quite different from the relative predictability of a **certain environment**. This is an ideal decision situation where factual information is available about the possible alternative courses of action and their outcomes. The decision maker's task is simply to study the alternatives and choose the best solution. But very few managerial problems are like this.

MANAGEMENT SMARTS 7.1

Six rules for crisis management

1. *Figure out what is going on*—Take the time to understand what's happening and the conditions under which the crisis must be resolved.
2. *Remember that speed matters*—Attack the crisis as quickly as possible, trying to catch it when it is as small as possible.
3. *Remember that slow counts, too*—Know when to back off and wait for a better opportunity to make progress with the crisis.
4. *Respect the danger of the unfamiliar*—Understand the danger of all-new territory where you and others have never been before.
5. *Value the skeptic*—Don't look for and get too comfortable with agreement; appreciate skeptics and let them help you see things differently.
6. *Be ready to "fight fire with fire"*—When things are going wrong and no one seems to care, you may have to start a crisis to get their attention.

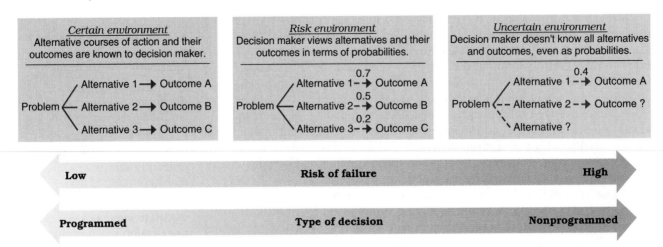

Certain environment	Risk environment	Uncertain environment
Alternative courses of action and their outcomes are known to decision maker.	Decision maker views alternatives and their outcomes in terms of probabilities.	Decision maker doesn't know all alternatives and outcomes, even as probabilities.

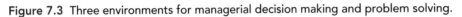

Low — Risk of failure — High

Programmed — Type of decision — Nonprogrammed

Figure 7.3 Three environments for managerial decision making and problem solving.

It is more common to face a **risk environment** where facts and information on action alternatives and their consequences are incomplete, but some estimates of "probabilities" can be made. A *probability* is the degree of likelihood (e.g., 4 chances out of 10) that an event will occur. Risk is typical for entrepreneurs and organizations that depend on ideas and continued innovation for their success. Steps can be taken to reduce risk in many situations. In the case of a new cola product, for example, the firm can make the go-ahead decision only after receiving favorable reports from special focus groups testing it.

When facts are few and information is so poor that managers are unable even to assign probabilities to the likely outcomes of alternatives, an **uncertain environment** exists. This is the most difficult decision condition.[16] The high level of uncertainty forces managers to rely heavily on creativity in solving problems. Because uncertainty requires unique, novel, and often totally innovative alternatives, groups are often useful for problem solving. But, the responses to uncertainty depend greatly on intuition, judgment, informed guessing, and hunches—all of which leave considerable room for error.

PROBLEM-SOLVING STYLES

Managers tend to display alternative approaches or "styles" in the way they process information and deal with problems. Some are *problem avoiders* who ignore information that would otherwise signal the presence of an opportunity or performance deficiency. They are passive in information gathering, not wanting to make decisions and deal with problems. *Problem solvers*, by contrast, are willing to make decisions and try to solve problems, but only when forced to by the situation. They are reactive in gathering information and responding to problems after they occur. They may deal reasonably well with performance deficiencies, but they miss many performance opportunities. *Problem seekers* actively process information and constantly look for problems to solve or opportunities to explore. True problem seekers are proactive and forward thinking. They anticipate problems and opportunities, and they take appropriate action to gain the advantage. Success at problem seeking is one of the ways exceptional managers distinguish themselves from the merely good ones.

■ A **risk environment** lacks complete information but offers "probabilities" of the likely outcomes for possible action alternatives.

■ An **uncertain environment** lacks so much information that it is difficult to assign probabilities to the likely outcomes of alternatives.

Managers also differ in tendencies toward "systematic" and "intuitive" thinking. In **systematic thinking** a person approaches problems in a rational, step-by-step, and analytical fashion. This type of thinking involves breaking a complex problem into smaller components and then addressing them in a logical and integrated fashion. Managers who are systematic can be expected to make a plan before taking action and then to search for information to facilitate problem solving in a step-by-step fashion.

Someone using **intuitive thinking**, by contrast, is more flexible and spontaneous and also may be quite creative.[17] This type of thinking allows a person to respond imaginatively to a problem based on a quick and broad evaluation of the situation and the possible alternative courses of action. Managers who are intuitive can be expected to deal with many aspects of a problem at once, jump quickly from one issue to another, and consider "hunches" based on experience or spontaneous ideas. This approach tends to work best in situations where facts are limited and few decision precedents exist.

Senior managers, in particular, must deal with portfolios of problems and opportunities that consist of multiple and interrelated issues. This requires *multidimensional thinking*, or the ability to view many problems at once, in relationship to one another and across both long and short time horizons.[18] The best managers are able to "map" multiple problems into a network that can be actively managed over time as priorities, events, and demands continuously change. And importantly, they are able to make decisions and take actions in the short run that benefit longer-run objectives; they avoid being sidetracked while sorting through a shifting mix of daily problems. Harvard scholar Daniel

■ **Systematic thinking** approaches problems in a rational and analytical fashion.

■ **Intuitive thinking** approaches problems in a flexible and spontaneous fashion.

INSIGHTS

Stay Tuned in to the Environment

Stay tuned in to the environment? Berry Gordy, founder of Motown Records sure did. His Motown trip had one decision after another . . . good ones at that. And the songs he produced from the "Motor City" help tell the story. Turn on your PC to the Motown jukebox and punch in the 1950s. Let the music steer your way back to the 1960s—Lionel Ritchie, Mary Welles, Martha and the

Vandellas . . . to the 1970s—Marvin Gaye, Gladys Knight and the Pips, Stevie Wonder, Diana Ross. And still, the beat goes on. Grab the award-winning DVD *Standing in the Shadows of Motown* and learn the story of the Funk Brothers, Uriel Junes, Joe Hunter, and the other musicians, who shaped the Motown sound at "Hitsville U.S.A."

Berry Gordy made many decisions while creating the Motown sound and forging a successful career in music and entertainment. At each step of the way he combined talent and business insight with risk and environmental awareness. He was a master at gathering information and turning it into plans that met market needs and kept his business well positioned for continued success.

An entrepreneur by nature, Gordy started Motown Records in 1957. He had been writing songs with his friend Smokey Robinson while working on the assembly line at a Detroit Ford plant. Encouraged by Robinson, he took the risk and started his own studio, using local talent with a distinctive sound. His strategy was to make a total package of background musicians and singers available to new artists from the Detroit neighborhoods. He had an ear for the marketplace and great business sense. By 1973 Motown was hailed by the *Detroit Free Press* as the "nation's largest black-owned entertainment conglomerate."

Berry Gordy sold Motown in 1988 and was inducted into the Rock and Roll Hall of Fame. Motown today is part of Universal Music Studios, living on, into the 21st century.

■ **Strategic opportunism** focuses on long-term objectives while being flexible in dealing with short-term problems.

Isenberg calls this skill **strategic opportunism**—the ability to remain focused on long-term objectives while being flexible enough to resolve short-term problems and opportunities in a timely manner.[19]

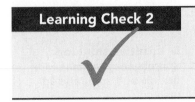

| **Learning Check 2** | *Be sure you can* ■ define the terms problem solving and decision ■ differentiate among programmed and nonprogrammed decisions ■ describe the challenges of crisis decision making ■ explain decision making in certain, risk, and uncertain environments ■ discuss the differences between systematic and intuitive thinking in problem solving |

THE DECISION-MAKING PROCESS

■ The **decision-making process** begins with identification of a problem and ends with evaluation of implemented solutions.

The **decision-making process** involves a set of activities that begins with identification of a problem, includes making a decision, and ends with the evaluation of results.[20] As shown in *Figure 7.4*, the steps in managerial decision making are (1) identify and define the problem, (2) generate and evaluate alternative solutions, (3) choose a preferred course of action and conduct the "ethics double check," (4) implement the decision, and (5) evaluate results. All five steps can be understood in the context of the following short-but-true case.

> *The Ajax Case.* On December 31, the Ajax Company decided to close down its Murphysboro plant. Market conditions were forcing layoffs, and the company could not find a buyer for the plant. Of the 172 employees, some had been with the company as long as 18 years, others as little as 6 months. All were to be terminated. Under company policy, they would be given severance pay equal to one week's pay per year of service. Top management faced a difficult problem: how to minimize the negative impact of the plant closing on employees, their families, and the small town of Murphysboro.

This case reflects how competition, changing times, and the forces of globalization can take their toll on organizations, the people that work for them, and the communities in which they operate. Think about how you would feel as one of the affected employees. Think about how you would feel as the mayor of this small town. Think about how you would feel as a corporate executive having to make the business decisions.

STEP 1–IDENTIFY AND DEFINE THE PROBLEM

The first step in decision making is to find and define the problem. This is a stage of information gathering, information processing, and deliberation.[21] It is important to clarify goals by identifying exactly what a decision should

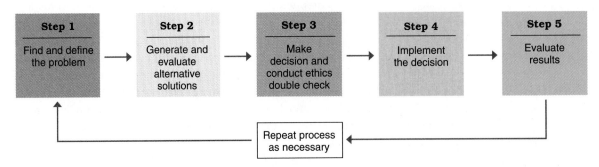

Figure 7.4 Steps in managerial decision making and problem solving.

accomplish. The more specific the goals, the easier it is to evaluate results after the decision is actually implemented. The way a problem is defined can have a major impact on how it is resolved.

Three common mistakes occur in this critical first step in decision making. *Mistake number 1* is defining the problem too broadly or too narrowly. To take a classic example, the problem stated as "build a better mousetrap" might be better defined as "get rid of the mice." That is, managers should define problems in ways that give them the best possible range of problem-solving options. *Mistake number 2* is focusing on symptoms instead of causes. Symptoms are indicators that problems may exist, but they shouldn't be mistaken for the problems themselves. Although managers should be alert to spot problem symptoms (e.g., a drop in performance), they must also dig deeper to address root causes (such as discovering the worker's need for training in the use of a complex new computer system). *Mistake number 3* is choosing the wrong problem to deal with. It's important to set priorities and deal with the most important problems first, and give priority to problems that are truly solvable.

> *Back to the Ajax Case.* Closing the Ajax plant will put a substantial number of people from the small community of Murphysboro out of work. The unemployment created will have a negative impact on individuals, their families, and the community as a whole. The loss of the Ajax tax base will further hurt the community. The local financial implications of the plant closure will be great. The problem for Ajax management is how to minimize the adverse impact of the plant closing on the employees, their families, and the community.

STEP 2–GENERATE AND EVALUATE ALTERNATIVE COURSES OF ACTION

Once the problem is defined, it is time to assemble the facts and information that will be helpful for problem solving. It is important here to clarify exactly what is known and what needs to be known. Extensive information gathering should identify alternative courses of action, as well as their anticipated consequences.

The process of evaluating alternatives often benefits from a *stakeholder analysis*. Key stakeholders in the problem should be identified, and the effects of possible courses of action on each of them should be considered. Another useful approach for the evaluation of alternatives is a **cost-benefit analysis**, the comparison of what an alternative will cost in relation to the expected benefits. At a minimum, the benefits of an alternative should be greater than its costs. Typical criteria for evaluating alternatives include the following:

■ *Benefits:* What are the "benefits" of using the alternative to solve a performance deficiency or take advantage of an opportunity?
■ *Costs:* What are the "costs" of implementing the alternative, including resource investments as well as potential negative side effects?
■ *Timeliness:* How fast will the benefits occur and a positive impact be achieved?
■ *Acceptability:* To what extent will the alternative be accepted and supported by those who must work with it?
■ *Ethical soundness:* How well does the alternative meet acceptable ethical criteria in the eyes of the various stakeholders?

The end result of this decision-making step can only be as good as the quality of the options considered; the better the pool of alternatives, the more likely that a good solution will be achieved. A common error is abandoning

■ **Cost-benefit analysis** involves comparing the costs and benefits of each potential course of action.

the search for alternatives too quickly. This often happens under pressures of time and other circumstances. Just because an alternative is convenient doesn't make it the best. It could have damaging side effects, or it could be less good than others that might be discovered with extra effort. One way to minimize this error is through participation and involvement. Bringing more people into the process brings more information and perspectives to bear on the problem.

Back to the Ajax Case. The Ajax plant is going to be closed. Among the possible alternatives that can be considered are (1) close the plant on schedule and be done with it; (2) delay the plant closing until all efforts have been made to sell it to another firm; (3) offer to sell the plant to the employees and/or local interests; (4) close the plant and offer transfers to other Ajax plant locations; or (5) close the plant, offer transfers, and help the employees find new jobs in and around Murphysboro.

STEP 3–DECIDE ON A PREFERRED COURSE OF ACTION

This is the point of choice, where an actual decision is made to select a preferred course of action. Just how this is done and by whom must be successfully resolved in each problem situation. Management theory recognizes differences between the classical and behavioral models of decision making as shown in *Figure 7.5*.

■ The **classical decision model** describes decision making with complete information.

The **classical decision model** views the manager as acting rationally in a certain world. Here, the manager faces a clearly defined problem and knows all possible action alternatives as well as their consequences. As a result, he or she makes an **optimizing decision** that gives the absolute best solution to the problem. The classical approach is a rational model that assumes perfect information is available for decision making.

■ An **optimizing decision** chooses the alternative giving the absolute best solution to a problem.

Behavioral scientists question these assumptions. Perhaps best represented by the work of Herbert Simon, they recognize limits to our human information-processing capabilities.[22] These *cognitive limitations* make it hard for managers to become fully informed and make perfectly rational decisions. They create a *bounded rationality* such that managerial decisions are rational only within the boundaries defined by the available information.

■ The **behavioral decision model** describes decision making with limited information and bounded rationality.

The **behavioral decision model,** accordingly, assumes that people act only in terms of what they perceive about a given situation. Because such perceptions are frequently imperfect, the decision maker has only partial knowledge about the available action alternatives and their consequences. Consequently, the first alternative that appears to give a satisfactory resolution of the problem is likely to be chosen. Simon, who won a Nobel Prize for his work, calls this the tendency toward **satisficing decisions**—choosing

■ A **satisficing decision** chooses the first satisfactory alternative that comes to one's attention.

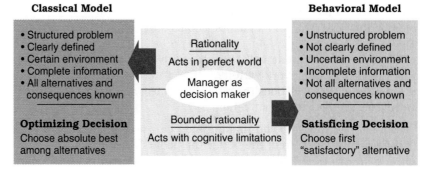

Figure 7.5 Differences in the classifical and behavioral models of managerial decision making.

Classical Model
- Structured problem
- Clearly defined
- Certain environment
- Complete information
- All alternatives and consequences known

Rationality
Acts in perfect world

Manager as decision maker

Optimizing Decision
Choose absolute best among alternatives

Bounded rationality
Acts with cognitive limitations

Behavioral Model
- Unstructured problem
- Not clearly defined
- Uncertain environment
- Incomplete information
- Not all alternatives and consequences known

Satisficing Decision
Choose first "satisfactory" alternative

the first satisfactory alternative that comes to your attention. This model seems especially accurate in describing how people make decisions about ambiguous problems in risky and uncertain conditions.

Back to the Ajax Case. Management at Ajax decided to close the plant, offer transfers to company plants in another state, and offer to help displaced employees find new jobs in and around Murphysboro.

STEP 4–IMPLEMENT THE DECISION

Once a preferred solution is chosen, actions must be taken to fully implement it. Nothing new can or will happen unless action is taken to actually solve the problem. Managers not only need the determination and creativity to arrive at a decision, they also need the ability and willingness to implement it.

The "ways" in which decision making steps 1, 2, 3 are accomplished can have a powerful impact on how well decisions get implemented. Difficulties encountered at the point of implementation often trace to the *lack-of-participation error.* This is a failure to adequately involve in the process those persons whose support is necessary to implement the decision. Managers who use participation wisely get the right people involved in problem solving from the beginning. When they do, implementation typically

KAFFEEKLATSCH

Special Circumstances

First Cup

"I read that one of the world's great flutists once said: 'Some nights I go out and play a piece perfectly. The next night . . . I play it better.'"

"Wouldn't you like to have everyone on your team saying this about his or her job performance? But I'll tell you what—we're not playing the flute here. We're getting customers served and problems solved. It isn't a very creative process and there isn't a lot of room for people to make up solutions to problems. Yet still, I wonder: 'Can we do better?'"

Studying the Grounds

■ Blockbuster's COO, Mike Roemer, told a reporter about one of the firm's managers who "reeks of leadership" and "really energizes a room."

■ This manager was Shane Evangelist. When interviewed about his style, he gave an example. He once decided that Blockbuster needed to get DVD online orders packed and shipped in less than a minute. He took the proposal to his team. Instead of telling them how to do it, he said: "I'm wondering if there is some way to get the transaction down to, say, 50 seconds." Their response was: "We can do it in 40 seconds."

Double Espresso

"We talk a lot about people being the 'human capital' of organizations. I've even heard that the best managers make sure everyone that works for and with them 'bring their brains to work everyday, and don't check them at the door.'"

"I suppose that's the lesson in the Blockbuster story. But you know what, I don't think my team would respond that same way Shane's did. If I go back to the office and just 'toss out an idea' rather than 'stating' it as a formal goal, they're likely to reject it, laugh at it or just avoid it. Then where would I be?"

Your Turn

Don't check your brains at the door . . . Get involved . . . Tell us what you would do . . . Give me your suggestions . . . Let us have your input . . . Tell me what we're doing wrong.

These are all phrases that we're often advised to say as part of good management. They and others like them are designed to create involvement by allowing others to participate in and influence decisions about their work and workplace. But what are the risks? Can we really manage by always turning decisions over to the group? Are there times when a group decision may not be the best decision?

follows quickly, smoothly, and to everyone's satisfaction. Participation in decision making makes everyone better informed and builds the commitments needed for implementation.

Back to the Ajax Case. Ajax ran ads in the local and regional newspapers. The ad called attention to an "Ajax skill bank" composed of "qualified, dedicated, and well-motivated employees with a variety of skills and experiences." Interested employers were urged to contact Ajax for further information.

STEP 5–EVALUATE RESULTS

The decision-making process is not complete until results are evaluated. If the desired results are not achieved and/or if undesired side effects occur, corrective action should be taken. Such evaluation is a form of managerial control. It involves gathering data to measure performance results against goals, and consider both the positive and negative outcomes. If the original choice appears inadequate, it is time to reassess and return to earlier steps. In this way, problem solving becomes a dynamic and ongoing activity within the management process. And, the evaluation is always easier when clear goals, measurable targets, and timetables were established to begin with.

Back to the Ajax Case. The advertisement ran for some 15 days. The plant's industrial relations manager commented, "I've been very pleased with the results." That's all we know. How well did Ajax management do in dealing with this very difficult problem? You can look back on the case and problem-solving process just described and judge for yourself. Perhaps you would have approached the situation and the five steps in decision making somewhat differently.

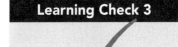

Learning Check 3

Be sure you can ■ list the steps in the decision-making process ■ apply these steps to a sample decision-making situation ■ explain the roles of stakeholder analysis and cost-benefit analysis in decision making ■ define the terms optimizing and satisficing ■ discuss differences between the classical and behavioral decision models

ISSUES IN MANAGERIAL DECISION MAKING

Most management situations are rich in decision-making challenges. By way of preparation, it helps to be aware of the common decision-making errors and traps, the advantages and disadvantages of individual and group decision making, the imperative of ethical decision making, and the growing importance of knowledge management and organizational learning.

DECISION-MAKING ERRORS AND TRAPS

■ **Heuristics** are strategies for simplifying decision making.

Faced with limited information, time, and even energy, people often use simplifying strategies for decision making. These strategies, known as **heuristics**, can cause decision-making errors.[23]

The *availability heuristic* occurs when people use information "readily available" from memory as a basis for assessing a current event or situation.

An example is deciding not to invest in a new product based on your recollection of a recent product failure. The potential bias is that the readily available information may be fallible and irrelevant. For example, the product that recently failed may have been a good idea that was released to market at the wrong time of year.

The *representativeness heuristic* occurs when people assess the likelihood of something occurring based on its similarity to a stereotyped set of occurrences. An example is deciding to hire someone for a job vacancy simply because he or she graduated from the same school attended by your last and most successful new hire. The potential bias is that the representative stereotype may mask the truly important factors relevant to the decision. For instance, the abilities and career expectations of the person receiving the offer may not fit the job requirements.

The *anchoring and adjustment heuristic* involves making decisions based on adjustments to a previously existing value or starting point. An example is setting a new salary level for an employee by simply raising the prior year's salary a reasonable percentage. This biases the decision toward only incremental movement from the starting point. But the individual's market value may be substantially higher than the existing salary. An incremental adjustment may not keep this person from looking for another job.

Sometimes managers suffer from **framing error** when making decisions. Framing occurs when a problem is evaluated and resolved in the context in which it is perceived—either positively or negatively. An example from the world of marketing is a product that data show has a 40 percent market share. A negative frame views the product as being deficient because it is missing 60 percent of the market. The likely discussion and problem solving in this frame would focus on this question: "What are we doing wrong?"

> ■ **Framing error** is solving a problem in the context perceived.

REAL ETHICS

Left to Die

Setting:
Some 40 climbers are winding their ways to the top of Mt. Everest. About 1,000 feet below the summit sits a British mountain climber, in trouble, collapsed in a shallow snow cave. Most of those on the way up look while continuing their climbs; none stop to assist, abandoning their quest. Sherpas from one passing team pause to give him oxygen before moving on. Within hours David Sharp, 34, is dead, on the mountain, of oxygen deficiency.

Justification from a climber who passed by:
"At 28,000 feet it's hard to stay alive yourself . . . he was in very poor condition . . , it was a very hard decision . . . he wasn't a member of our team."

Comment of a past successful climber:
"If you're going to go to Everest . . . I think you have to accept responsibility that you may end up doing something that's not ethically nice . . . you have to realize that you're in a different world."

Reaction from Sir Edmund Hillary who reached the top in 1953:
"Human life is far more important than just getting to the top of a mountain."

FURTHER INQUIRY

It's decision time. Who's right and who's wrong?

In our personal affairs, daily lives, and careers we are all, in our own ways, climbing Mt. Everest. What are the ethics of our climbs? How often do we notice others in trouble, struggling along the way, and, like the mountain climbers heading to the summit of Everest, pass them by to continue our own journeys?

As you read and listen to the events of our days, can you identify other examples – business, school, career, sports, etc., that pose similar ethical dilemmas as people face decision trade-offs between self-interests and the interests of others?

MANAGEMENT SMARTS 7.2

How to avoid the escalation trap in decision making

- Set advance limits on your involvement and commitment to a particular course of action; stick with these limits.
- Make your own decisions; don't follow the leads of others, since they are also prone to escalation.
- Carefully assess why you are continuing a course of action; if there are no good reasons to continue, don't.
- Remind yourself of what a course of action is costing; consider saving these costs as a reason to discontinue.
- Watch for escalation tendencies in your behaviors and that of others.

■ **Escalating commitment** is the continuation of a course of action even though it is not working.

Alternatively, the frame could be a positive one, looking at the 40 percent share as a good accomplishment. In this case the discussion is more likely to proceed with this question: "How do we do things better?" Sometimes people use framing as a tactic for presenting information in a way that gets other people to think inside the desired frame. In politics this is often referred to as "spinning" the data.

Good managers are also aware of another decision-making trap known as **escalating commitment**. This is a decision to increase effort and perhaps apply more resources to pursue a course of action that is not working.[24] In such cases, managers let the momentum of the situation overwhelm them. They are unable to decide to "call it quits," even when experience otherwise indicates that this is the best thing to do. *Management Smarts 7.2* offers advice on avoiding tendencies toward escalating commitments to previously chosen courses of action.

INDIVIDUAL AND GROUP DECISION MAKING

One of the important issues in decision making is the choice of whether to make the decision individually or with the participation of a group. The best managers and team leaders don't limit themselves to just one way. Instead, they switch back and forth among individual and group decisions to fit the problems at hand.

The "right" decision method is one that provides for a timely and quality decision, and one to which people involved in the implementation will be highly committed. To best meet these criteria it helps to recognize both assets and liabilities for group decision making.[25]

The potential *advantages of group decision making* are highly significant, and they are well worth pursuing whenever time and other circumstances permit. Team decisions make greater amounts of information, knowledge, and expertise available to solve problems. They expand the number of action alternatives that are examined; they help to avoid tunnel vision and consideration of only limited options. Team decisions also increase the understanding and acceptance of outcomes by members. And importantly, team decisions increase the commitments of members to work hard to implement final plans.

The *potential disadvantages of group decision making* trace largely to the difficulties that can be experienced in a group process. In a team decision there may be social pressure to conform. Some individuals may feel intimidated or compelled to go along with the apparent wishes of others. There may be minority domination, where some members feel forced or "railroaded" to accept a decision advocated by one vocal individual or small coalition. Also, there is no doubt that the time required to make team decisions can sometimes be a disadvantage. As more people are involved in the dialogue and discussion, decision making takes longer. This added time may be costly, even prohibitively so, in certain circumstances.

ETHICAL DECISION MAKING

Our decisions should always meet the test of the "ethics double check." This involves asking and answering two straightforward but powerful *spotlight questions:* "How would I feel if my family found out about this decision?"

"How would I feel if this decision were published in the local newspaper?" The Josephson Institute model for ethical decision making suggests a third question to further strengthen the ethics double check: "Think of the person you know or know of (in real life or fiction) who has the strongest character and best ethical judgment. Then ask yourself—what would that person do in your situation?"[26]

Although it adds time to decision making, the ethics double check helps ensure that the ethical aspects of a problem are properly considered in all situations. It is also consistent with the demanding moral standards of modern society. A willingness to pause to examine the ethics of a proposed decision may well result in both a better decision and the prevention of costly litigation. Ethicist Gerald Cavanaugh and his associates suggest that managers can proceed with the most confidence when the following criteria are met:[27]

1. *Utility*—Does the decision satisfy all constituents or stakeholders?
2. *Rights*—Does the decision respect the rights and duties of everyone?
3. *Justice*—Is the decision consistent with the canons of justice?
4. *Caring*—Is the decision consistent with my responsibilities to care?

RESEARCH BRIEF

Escalation increases risk of unethical decisions

That's the conclusion reached in an empirical study by Marc and Vera L. Street. They review research confirming that escalating commitments to previously chosen courses of action can explain many poor decisions and undesirable outcomes in organizations. But they also point out that little has been done to investigate whether or not escalation tendencies lead to unethical behaviors.

To address this void in our understanding of decision making, the researchers conducted an experiment with 155 undergraduate students working on a computerized investment task. They found that exposure to escalation situations increases tendencies toward unethical acts, and that the tendencies further increase with the magnitude of the escalation. Street and Street explain this link between escalation and poor ethics as driven by desires

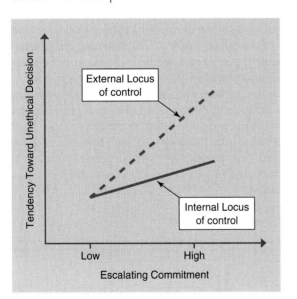

to get out of and avoid the increasing stress of painful situations.

Additional findings from the study showed that students with an external locus of control had a higher propensity to choose an unethical decision alternative than their counterparts with an internal locus of control. This confirmed prior research findings reporting a link between locus of control and ethical behavior.

QUESTIONS & APPLICATIONS

This study was done in the college classroom and under simulated decision conditions. How well would these results stand up in the real world? How would you design a study that tests the same hypotheses with persons at work?

The "Spotlight Questions" are ways to double-check the ethics of one's decisions. Is it possible to design a training program that would use these questions and other techniques to help people better deal with unethical decision options in escalation situations?

Reference: Marc Street and Vera L. Street, "The Effects of Escalating Commitment on Ethical Decision Making," *Journal of Business Ethics*, Vol. 64 (2006), pp. 343–356.

KNOWLEDGE MANAGEMENT AND ORGANIZATIONAL LEARNING

A technology-driven world is both rich with information and demanding in the pace and uncertainty of change. Although this is the setting in which knowledge workers excel, Peter Drucker has warned that "knowledge constantly makes itself obsolete."[28] His message must be taken to heart. People and organizations cannot rest on past laurels; future success will be earned only by those who continually learn through experience.

■ **Knowledge management** is the process of using intellectual capital for competitive advantage.

The term **knowledge management** describes the processes through which organizations develop, organize, and share knowledge to achieve competitive advantage.[29] The significance of knowledge management as a strategic and integrating force in organizations is represented by the emergence of a new executive job title—*chief knowledge officer* (CKO). The CKO is responsible for energizing learning processes and making sure that an organization's portfolio of intellectual assets is well managed and continually enhanced. These assets include such things as patents, intellectual property rights, trade secrets, and special processes and methods, as well as the accumulated knowledge and understanding of the entire workforce.

Knowledge management requires the creation of an organizational culture that truly values learning, and Google, featured in The Topic opener, is a true knowledge management company. It operates with an information-rich culture driven by creativity and knowledge, keeping competitors and the business world at large always guessing what its next steps might be. Google's CEO Eric Schmidt and his colleague Hal Varian describe these principles for creating competitive advantage through people. *Hire by committee* – let great people hire other great people; *cater to every need* – make sure nothing gets in anyone's way; *make coordination easy* – put people in close proximity to one another, physically and electronically; *encourage creativity* – let people spend some time on projects they choose; *seek consensus* – get inputs before decisions are made; *use data* – make informed decisions based on solid quantitative analysis; *don't be evil* – create a climate of respect, tolerance, and ethical behavior.[30]

■ A **learning organization** continuously changes and improves using the lessons of experience.

The more you study the Google case the more clear it becomes that this is a firm moving toward what Peter Senge calls a real **learning organization**. This is an organizations that "by virtue of people, values, and systems is able to continuously change and improve its performance based upon the lessons of experience."[31] Organizations can learn from many sources. They can learn from their own experience. They can learn from the experiences of their contractors, suppliers, partners, and customers. And they can learn from firms in unrelated businesses. All of this, of course, depends on creating an organizational culture in which people are enthusiastic about learning opportunities and in which information sharing is an expected and valued work behavior.

Learning Check 4

Be sure you can ■ explain the availability, representativeness, anchoring, and adjustment heuristics ■ illustrate framing error and escalating commitment in decision making ■ list questions that can be asked to double check the ethics of a decision ■ discuss the importance of knowledge management and organizational learning

CHAPTER 7 STUDY GUIDE

STUDY QUESTIONS SUMMARY

1 What is the role of information in the management process?

- Information technology is breaking barriers within and between organizations to speed work flows and cut costs.
- Management information systems collect, organize, store, and distribute data to meet the information needs of managers.
- Data are raw facts and figures; information is data made useful for decision making.
- Managers serve as information nerve centers in the process of planning, organizing, leading, and controlling activities in organizations.

2 How do managers use information to make decisions?

- A problem is a discrepancy between an actual and a desired state of affairs.
- The most threatening type of problem is the crisis, which occurs unexpectedly and can lead to disaster if not handled quickly and properly.
- Managers face structured and unstructured problems in environments of certainty, risk, and uncertainty.
- Managers approach problems and make decisions using both systematic and intuitive thinking.

3 What are the steps in the decision-making process?

- The steps in the decision-making process are 1) find and define the problem, 2) generate and evaluate alternatives, 3) decide on the preferred course of action, 4) implement the decision, and 5) evaluate the results.
- An optimizing decision, following the classical model, chooses the absolute best solution from a known set of alternatives.
- A satisficing decision, following the behavioral model, chooses the first satisfactory alternative to come to attention.

4 What are the current issues in managerial decision making?

- Judgmental heuristics, framing errors, and escalating commitment can bias decision making.
- Group decisions offer the potential advantages of greater information and expanded commitment, but they are often slower than individual decisions.
- Use of the spotlight questions for an ethics double-check is a good way for managers to ensure ethical decision making.
- Knowledge management captures information, and develops and uses knowledge for competitive advantage.
- A learning organization is committed to continuous learning, always changing and making improvements based on the lessons of experience.

KEY TERMS REVIEW

Behavioral decision model (p. 168)
Certain environment (p. 163)
Classical decision model (p. 168)
Cost-benefit analysis (p. 167)
Crisis (p. 163)
Crisis management (p. 163)
Data (p. 160)
Decision (p. 162)
Decision-making process (p. 166)
Escalating commitment (p. 172)

Framing error (p. 171)
Heuristics (p. 170)
Information (p. 160)
Information system (p. 160)
Intuitive thinking (p. 165)
Knowledge management (p. 174)
Learning organization (p. 174)
Management information systems (p. 160)
Nonprogrammed decision (p. 163)

Optimizing decision (p. 168)
Problem solving (p. 162)
Programmed decision (p. 162)
Risk environment (p. 164)
Satisficing decision (p. 168)
Strategic opportunism (p. 165)
Structured problems (p. 162)
Systematic thinking (p. 165)
Uncertain environment (p. 164)
Unstructured problems (p. 163)

SELF-TEST 7

MULTIPLE-CHOICE QUESTIONS:

1. Among the ways IT is changing organizations today, _____ is one of its most noteworthy characteristics.

    (a) eliminating the need for top managers (b) reducing the amount of information available for decision making (c) breaking down barriers internally and externally (d) decreasing the need for environmental awareness

2. The information made available by IT assists with the function of organizing because it _____.

(a) gives more timely access to information   (b) allows more immediate measures of performance results   (c) allows for better coordination among individuals and groups   (d) makes it easier to communicate with diverse stakeholders

3. A manager who is reactive and works hard to address problems after they occur is known as a _____.

(a) problem seeker   (b) problem avoider   (c) problem solver   (d) problem manager

4. A(n) _____ thinker approaches problems in a rational and analytic fashion.

(a) systematic   (b) intuitive   (c) internal   (d) external

5. The use of probabilities for action alternatives and their consequences indicates the presence of _____ in the decision environment.

(a) certainty   (b) optimizing   (c) risk   (d) satisficing

6. The first step in the decision-making process is to _____.

(a) identify alternatives   (b) evaluate results   (c) find and define the problem   (d) choose a solution

7. Being asked to develop a plan to increase international sales of a product is an example of the types of _____ problems that managers must be prepared to deal with.

(a) routine   (b) unstructured   (c) crisis   (d) structured

8. Costs, timeliness, and _____ are among the recommended criteria for evaluating alternative courses of action.

(a) ethical soundness   (b) competitiveness   (c) availability   (d) simplicity

9. A common mistake made by managers facing crisis situations is that they _____.

(a) try to get too much information before responding   (b) rely too much on group decision making   (c) isolate themselves to make the decision alone   (d) forget to use their crisis management plan

10. The _____ decision model views managers as making optimizing decisions, whereas the _____ decision model views them as making satisficing decisions.

(a) behavioral, human relations   (b) classical, behavioral   (c) heuristic, humanistic   (d) quantitative, behavioral

11. When a manager makes a decision about someone's annual pay raise only after looking at their current salary, the risk is that the decision will be biased because of _____.

(a) a framing error   (b) escalating commitment   (c) anchoring and adjustment   (d) strategic opportunism

12. When a problem is addressed according to the positive or negative context in which it is presented, this is an example of _____.

(a) framing error   (b) escalating commitment   (c) availability and adjustment   (d) strategic opportunism

13. When people are not enthused about implementing a decision, one possible cause is known as _____.

(a) lack of participation error   (b) strategic opportunism   (c) escalating commitment   (d) the representative heuristic

14. A manager who asks whether or not the decision will satisfy all stakeholders is using the criterion of _____ to check the ethical soundness of the intended course of action.

(a) justice   (b) rights   (c) cost vs. benefit   (d) utility

15. Among the environments for managerial decision making, certainty is the most favorable, and it can be addressed through _____ decisions.

(a) programmed   (b) risk   (c) satisficing   (d) intuitive

SHORT-RESPONSE QUESTIONS:

16. What is the difference between an optimizing decision and a satisficing decision?
17. How can a manager double-check the ethics of a decision?
18. How would a manager use systematic thinking and intuitive thinking in problem solving?
19. How can the members of an organization be trained in crisis management?

APPLICATION QUESTION:

20. As a participant in a new mentoring program between your university and a local high school, you have volunteered to give a presentation to a class of sophomores on the challenges in the new "electronic office." The goal is to sensitize them to developments in IT and motivate them to take the best advantage of their high school academics so as to prepare themselves for the workplace of the future. What will you say to them?

CHAPTER 7 APPLICATIONS

Amazon: One E-Store to Rule Them All

Amazon.com has soared ahead of other e-retailers to become the leading online merchant of just about everything. What Amazon can't carry in its 21 worldwide warehouses, affiliated retailers distribute for it. Not content to rest on his laurels, CEO Jeff Bezos has introduced a number of new services to keep customers glued to the Amazon site. But will the investments pay off?

Like a bottle rocket loaded with jet fuel, Internet commerce has soared off the launch pad in the last decade. No matter what products may set a shopper's heart aflutter, some up-and-coming marketer has likely already set up a specialty e-store to take care of just that. But one online vendor has grander aspirations: why stop at selling a single line of products, or 2, or 20, when you could instead offer customers the equivalent of an online Mall of America?

From a modest beginning in Jeff Bezos's garage in 1995, Amazon.com has quickly sprouted into the most megalithic of online retailers. Once it became clear that Amazon could outgrow simply being a book retailer (albeit an immense book retailer), Bezos began to pursue other media, logically adding CDs and DVDs. Now it seems that almost anything for sale outside of esoteric specialty stores can be had on Amazon.com.

And that only takes into account Amazon's U.S. presence. At latest count, customers in six other countries, including China, Japan, and France, can access Amazon sister-sites built especially for them.[32] And its 21 "fulfillment centers" around the world enclose more than 9 million square feet of operating space.[33]

So what's to be done at this point? Grow. As of late, Bezos has pursued a two-pronged strategy to perpetuate Amazon's growth and continue to increase its value for shareholders.

The first part of the plan has been to diversify Amazon's product offerings and broaden the brand by partnering with existing retailers to add new product lines. It's a win-win proposition for more than 100 companies—including Target, Toys "R" Us, and Wine.com—that already make their wares available on Amazon, or are planning to. The companies profit from the additional exposure and sales (which don't affect or undercut their existing business), and the Amazon brand thrives from the opportunity to keep customers who might otherwise have shopped elsewhere.

Traditional Content, Accessed Nontraditionally

Not forgetting its roots, Amazon has recently enhanced its media offerings with several key acquisitions. Its purchase of on-demand book self-publisher BookSurge does triple duty to reinforce Amazon's literary heritage: customers publishing their memoirs or first books of poetry have the option (for a small fee, of course) to have their work listed and made available for sale over Amazon's Web site.[34] Considering how many pairs of eyeballs visit the site in the average week, this can make a very compelling offer for a writer who may be considering other on-demand services. Readers appreciate the expanded range of literary offerings, and Amazon wins because it simply has more products to sell, which it made a profit on by stocking them in the first place.

Bezos is optimistic about the value his purchase of BookSurge might offer his customers. "I think there'll be more happening on the Internet over the next 10 years than in the last 10," he said. "Over the next decade, the raw materials—technology, computers, disc space, bandwidth—will get cheaper and more powerful at a very rapid rate. Our job is to figure out how to layer invention on top of those raw materials to make things that actually matter to people."[35]

And although many customers have purchased DVDs from Amazon, not as many may think of the online superstore as the next great media hub. But if Bezos has his way, it will become the download destination for movies, TV shows, or other exclusive content. The first chance to test this theory comes with *Amazon Fishbowl with Bill Maher*, a variety show hosted by the television pundit and satirist, which airs weekly on the Amazon Web site. Says Kathy Savitt, Amazon's vice president for strategic communications: "The Internet gives us the ability of having a show that fits the constraints of the content as opposed to the constraints of a programming schedule."[36]

Layer upon Layer of Value

Besides simply finding more and more products to sell on Amazon.com, Bezos realized that to prevent his brand from becoming stagnant, he would have to innovate and find new levels of service to provide customers that would complement existing products.

"We have to say, 'What kind of innovation can we layer on top of that, that will be meaningful for our customers?' " Bezos said.[37]

To this point, much of this innovation has come from the depth of free content available to Amazon customers. Far from being a loss leader, Amazon's free content helps spur sales and reinforce customers' perception of Amazon's commitment to customer service.

As David Meerman Scott put it in *eContent*, "Here is the flip side of free in action—a smart content company figuring out how to get people to contribute compelling content for free and then building a for-profit business model around it. Amazon.com has built a huge content site by having all of the content provided to it for no cost. Of course, Amazon.com makes money by selling products based on the contributed content on the site—another example of the flip side of free."[38]

Amazon's legendary customer reviews—some more helpful than others—reinforce the Amazon brand and keep customers returning to the site. A number of new services give Amazon customers more access to and information about their prospective paged purchases than ever before, truly making shopping on Amazon much closer to a traditional bookstore experience.

More than 50 percent of all books listed on Amazon's U.S. Web site offer the Browse option, whereby curious readers can sneak peeks at the Table of Contents, front and back covers, copyright information, index, and even a portion of a sample chapter. According to the company, sales of books offering the Browse feature increase by nine percent in just five days.[39]

Still curious? A feature called Search Inside the Book lets you browse for often-used phrases in a book and even find other books in which that phrase appears frequently.[40] To soothe concerns from authors or publishers, Bezos said that only books in the public domain or whose copyright holders have granted permission are included in the program.[41] In this way, he hopes to avoid the copyright brouhaha Google raised with its Print Library project.

Not good enough yet? It gets better. Maybe you'd rather only nab a few chapters from a particular cookbook. Or perhaps your life would be much improved if you could access your new book about Photoshop from your computer. Either way, Amazon will soon have you covered.

The Amazon Pages service allows customers to buy portions of a book to be read online. And Amazon Upgrade offers full electronic access when buyers pick up a traditional text. The value for customers lies not only in the access, but also in the price: Bezos speculates that Amazon Pages will probably cost buyers a few cents per page, and one Amazon Upgrade example he gave would cost about 10 percent of the retail price of its book. "There is no one-type-fits-all model," he said.[42]

Entering Busy Markets

Amazon also offers another entrant to the already crowded playing field of Web-based search engines. Bezos touts its A9 engine as being just a little smarter than its competitors. "It's a websearch engine with a memory," he said. "It will greet you by name and remember all the searches you've done, and any annotations you've made about the searches you've done."[43]

Not only that, but Amazon is integrating digital images into its virtual Yellow Pages to offer users a previously unknown advantage. "We've got cameras mounted to trucks, integrated with GPS [global positioning system] units, that drove around the 15 largest cities in the United States and took more than 20 million photographs of businesses. Those photographs are all on A9.com, so when you do a search for a local business, you can actually see what the business looks like."[44]

Noting that one in ten digital music players are purchased on Amazon, Bezos and Company are expected to enter the music market and tap into their customer base of 55 million to rival Apple's hegemony. Amazon is taking on Apple in movie downloads, with the two firms announcing their services within a week of each other. Amazon music downloads should be available by the time you're reading this, likely using an Amazon-branded MP3 player—already dubbed "aPod" by tech talkers. The leveraging of Amazon's huge database of existing customers could finally put some serious heat on Apple, which owns 80 percent of the music downloading market.[45]

"I imagine Apple and Amazon will be having some heart-to-heart negotiations," said one Wall Street analyst, "and there will be some friction between them, particularly if Amazon is undercutting the iPod. Ultimately, I think Amazon can be confident Apple will decide Amazon remains a strong distribution channel for them."[46]

Despite Amazon's successful growth into so many markets other than its initial specialty of books, some critics have challenged whether Amazon.com, let alone the Internet, is really the optimum place to make high-involvement purchases. Once again, Bezos is upbeat.

"We sell a lot of high-ticket items," he countered. "We sell diamonds that cost thousands of dollars and $8,000 plasma TVs. There doesn't seem to be any resistance, and in fact those high-priced items are growing very rapidly as a percentage of our sales."[47]

In fact, it seems hard to catch Bezos *not* being upbeat. Although Amazon stock values may have dipped a bit, he still believes that customer service, not the stock ticker, defines the Amazon experience.

"I think one of the things people don't understand is we can build more shareholder value by lowering product prices than we can by trying to raise margins," he said. "It's a more patient approach, but we think it leads to a stronger, healthier company. It also serves customers much, much better."[48]

Looking Ahead

In just over a decade, Amazon.com has grown from a one-man operation into a global giant in Internet commerce. By forging alliances to ensure that he has what customers want, Jeff Bezos has ensured that Amazon is the go-to brand for online shopping. But with its significant investments in new media and services, does the company risk spreading itself too thin? Or will customers fall in love all over again, as they have with past Amazon offerings?

REVIEW QUESTIONS

1. Apple sells lots of iPods through Amazon. But it is certain to have mixed feelings about Amazon.com competing in music and movie downloads. As an Amazon executive, what reasoning could you use to mitigate Apple's concern and justify Amazon's decision on the new products?

2. To this point, shoppers seem to be satisfied by Amazon's "superstore" approach. But is it wise to continue down this path? Can you describe a scenario in which Amazon's holdings have become so diversified that the brand becomes diluted and customers rethink their allegiance?

3. Do you think that Amazon.com came into existence through systematic or intuitive thinking? Explain your answer. How about the ongoing efforts to expand its holdings? What style of thinking drives those decisions?

TEAM PROJECT

Crisis Decision Making

Reports are that manufacturing flaws behind the well publicized problem of Sony-made laptop batteries catching fire in Dell notebook computers was known some ten months before a product recall was issued. While declining comment, a Dell spokesperson said: "Now our focus is erring on the side of caution to ensure no more incidents occur."

Question: What types of crises do business leaders face and how do they deal with them?

Research Directions:

- Identify three crisis events from the recent local, national, and international business news.

- Read at least three different news reports on each crisis, trying to learn as much as possible about its specifics, how it was dealt with, what the results were, and what was the aftermath.

- Use a balance sheet approach to create a list for each crisis—sources or causes of the conflict and management responses to it. Analyze the lists to see if there are any differences based on the nature of the crisis faced in each situation. Look also for any patterns in the responses by the business executives to these crises.

- Score each crisis (from 1 = low to 5 = high) in terms of how successfully it was handled. Be sure to identify the criteria you use to determine the level of "success" in handling a crisis situation. Using your three examples, make a master list of "Done Rights" and "Done Wrongs" in crisis management.

- Summarize the results of your study into a report on "Realities of Crisis Management."

PERSONAL MANAGEMENT

Self-Confidence

Managers must have the **SELF-CONFIDENCE** not only to make decisions but also to implement them. Too many of us find all sorts of excuses for doing everything but that—we have difficulty deciding, and we have difficulty acting. Opportunities to improve and develop your self-confidence abound, especially through involvement in the many student organizations on your campus. Carole Clay Winters was the first member of her family to go to college. With the encouragement of an economics professor, she joined Students in Free Enterprise (SIFE) and ended up on a team teaching business concepts to elementary school children in the local community. Her team was chosen to participate in a national competition. They didn't win, but Carole did. "I felt my life had changed," she said. "I realized that if I could answer all the questions being posed by some of the country's most powerful executives, I had what I needed to become an executive myself." Carole went on to become a manager in the Washington, D.C., office of KPMG.

Building the Brand Called "You"   What about you? Do you have the self-confidence to make decisions relating to your career goals and future success? Are you taking full advantage of opportunities, on campus and off, to experience the responsibilities of leadership and gain confidence in your decision-making capabilities? What do the recommended self-assessments suggest for further personal development?

NEXT STEPS: MANAGEMENT LEARNING WORKBOOK

Self-Assessments
■ Your Intuitive Ability (#11)
■ Facts and Inferences (#14)
■ Cognitive Style (#25)

Experiential Exercises
■ Decision-Making Biases (#11)
■ Dots and Squares Puzzle (#15)
■ Lost at Sea (#26)

Planning—Processes and Techniques

8

Planning Ahead

Thinking Now for the Future

Decisions made by management don't just affect what happens at a company today or tomorrow. Although no one can see into the future, a lack of long-term planning can lead to short-term decision-making that can adversely affect a company's subsequent prosperity.

Why would anyone buy a car he or she didn't really want?

If you're a General Motors executive, the bet may still be that cash incentives will motivate consumers to purchase otherwise less-than-desirable vehicles.[1] But will tempting would-be customers with cash rather than nifty vehicles loaded with must-have features really meet the problems of the moment? Will the practice do anything to improve things in the future? Or, will this short-term fix just worsen the company's current predicament-renevue shortfalls and declining credit rating?[2]

Even some of the firm's parts suppliers are balking at working further with GM. As its profit margins shrink, GM demands from them lower prices as a way of cutting its short-term expenses.

What's going on here? Perhaps it's an example of GM's ongoing conflict between *short-term* and *long-term thinking*. The gap has been magnified by GM's financial hardships and the challenging efforts undertaken to try to turn the company around.

All firms rely on both long and short-term forecasts to develop operating strategies. But the pressures of GM's financial troubles have been compounded by decisions that, while intended to remedy short-term issues, not only exacerbated the immediate problems but make it even more difficult to achieve long-term market viability.

"We're still hemorrhaging," said GM vice chairman and CFO Frederick A. Henderson. "Job One is to reduce our cash burn."[3]

GM and its Big Three brethren—Ford and Daimler-Chrysler—have traditionally held volatile, one-sided relationships with their parts suppliers. Detroit automakers tend to push potential suppliers vigorously to compete for each carmaker's business.

What *They* Think

"*Alan has a deep experience in customer satisfaction, manufacturing, supplier relations and labor relations, all of which have applications to the challenges of Ford*".
Douglas Del Grosso, Executive Chairman of Ford Motor Company

LONG TERM: "*In a scheme of policy which is devised for a nation, we should not limit our views to its operation during a single year, or even for a short term of years. We should look at its operation for a considerable time, and in war as well as in peace.*"
Henry Clay, American congressman and senator

SHORT TERM: "*Goals help you overcome short-term problems.*"
Hannah More, English writer

And once selected, the suppliers must contend with ever-fluctuating parts orders, which make it challenging for them to successfully set and keep their own long-term operational goals.

Contrast this with the model pioneered by Toyota, in which single-source suppliers receive an order for a set number of parts in advance of the coming model year. It's easy to see why Big Three suppliers might prefer to take their business elsewhere, especially as Japanese automakers continue to break ground on American assembly plants.

"All the [automakers] are recognizing long term that there has to be some level of stability in the supply base," Lear [a parts suppliers to Ford] president Douglas DelGrosso said. "There is some positive movement there."[4]

Like GM, Ford has also been challenged by an apparent lack of long-term thinking. In order to both rectify a sizeable cash shortfall and not overproduce vehicles, Ford is cutting the production schedule and the payroll. Finding stiffer than anticipated competition in the truck market, which Ford dominated for decades, it is reducing its truck production as compared to previous annual targets. This is especially hard news for workers at Ford's Michigan truck factory, which was one of the world's most profitable production facilities.[5]

Facing up to the challenges, Bill Ford, Executive Chairman of the Ford Motor Company, announced the firm's hiring of a new president, Alan Mulally. He said: "Alan has deep experience in customer satisfaction, manufacturing, supplier relations and labor relations, all of which have applications to the challenges of Ford. He also has the personality and team-building skills that will help guide our Company in the right direction".[6]

Mulally's job will be a substantial one. But, as Bill Ford suggests, his multi-faceted skills are hopefully up to task—acting quickly in ways that will move the firm forward into a profitable future.

Especially in troubled times, it can be a challenge to set long-term goals for a company, and even harder to keep them. But for organizations that are stuck in short-term thinking, the benefits are certainly worth the costs.

The Numbers

Suppliers Indifferent About Business With Automakers

GM	60%
Ford	34%
Chrysler	20%
Nissan	13%
Honda	3%
Toyota	2%

Quick Facts

* Gm has 565.61 million shares outstanding; 91% are held by institutions and mutual funds.
* GM has 335,000 employees.
* Facing the high cost of layoff settlements, GM estimates it could end up paying $1.7 billion to workers who aren't working.
* 34,000 of GM's 120,000 union workers accepted buyouts during 2006.
* Over half of Ford's hourly production workers, some 38,000, accepted buyouts or early retirement offers in late 2006[7].
* Alan Mulally had a 37 year career at Boeing before taking the top position at Ford.
* Toyota has moved past Ford to become the #2 car seller in the U.S.

What Do You Think?

1. One of the challenges of long-term thinking is that it often gets overwhelmed by short-term problems. What long-term objectives could create short-term benefits for General Motors?
2. What signals do production and staff cuts by GM and Ford send to shareholders? Employees? Competition?

Planning—Processes and Techniques			
Study Question 1	**Study Question 2**	**Study Question 3**	**Study Question 4**
Why and How Managers Plan	**Types of Plans Used by Managers**	**Planning Tools and Techniques**	**Management by Objectives**
■ Importance of planning ■ The planning process ■ Benefits of planning	■ Short-range and long-range plans ■ Strategic and operational plans ■ Policies and procedures ■ Budgets and projects	■ Forecasting ■ Contingency planning ■ Scenario planning ■ Benchmarking ■ Staff planners ■ Participation and involvement	■ Performance objectives in MBO ■ MBO pros and cons
Learning Check 1	**Learning Check 2**	**Learning Check 3**	**Learning Check 4**

Managers need the ability to look ahead, make good plans, and help others meet the challenges of the future. With the future full of uncertainty, however, the likelihood is that even the best of plans will have to be changed at some point. Thus, managers also need the insight and courage to be flexible in response to new circumstances and the discipline to stay focused even as situations become hectic and the performance pressures stay unrelenting. In the ever-changing technology industry, for example, CEO T. J. Rodgers of Cypress Semiconductor Corp. is known for valuing both performance goals and accountability. Cypress employees work with clear and quantified work goals, which they help set. Rodgers believes the system helps find problems before they interfere with performance. He says: "Managers monitor the goals, look for problems, and expect people who fall behind to ask for help before they lose control of or damage a major project."[8]

WHY AND HOW MANAGERS PLAN

■ **Planning** is the process of setting objectives and determining how to accomplish them.

In Chapter 1 the management process was described as planning, organizing, leading, and controlling the use of resources to achieve performance objectives. The first of these functions, **planning**, sets the stage for the others by providing a sense of direction. It is a process of setting objectives and determining how best to accomplish them. Said a bit differently, planning involves deciding exactly what you want to accomplish and how best to go about it.

IMPORTANCE OF PLANNING

When planning is done well, it creates a solid platform for the other management functions: *organizing*—allocating and arranging resources to accomplish tasks; *leading*—guiding the efforts of human resources to ensure high levels of task accomplishment; and *controlling*—monitoring task accomplishments and taking necessary corrective action.

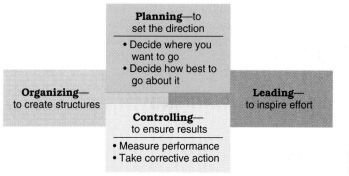

Figure 8.1 The roles of planning and controlling in the management process.

The centrality of planning in management, as shown in *Figure 8.1*, is important to understand. In today's demanding organizational and career environments it is essential to stay one step ahead of the competition. This involves always striving to become better at what you are doing and to be action oriented. An Eaton Corporation annual report, for example, once stated: "Planning at Eaton means taking the hard decisions before events force them upon you, and anticipating the future needs of the market before the demand asserts itself."[9]

THE PLANNING PROCESS

In the planning process, **objectives** identify the specific results or desired outcomes that one intends to achieve. The **plan** is a statement of action steps to be taken in order to accomplish the objectives. Fives steps in the planning process are:

1. *Define your objectives:* Identify desired outcomes or results in very specific ways. Know where you want to go; be specific enough that you will know you have arrived when you get there, or know how far off the mark you are at various points along the way.
2. *Determine where you stand vis-à-vis objectives:* Evaluate current accomplishments relative to the desired results. Know where you stand in reaching the objectives; know what strengths work in your favor and what weaknesses may hold you back.
3. *Develop premises regarding future conditions:* Anticipate future events. Generate alternative "scenarios" for what may happen; identify for each scenario things that may help or hinder progress toward your objectives.
4. *Analyze and choose among action alternatives:* List and carefully evaluate possible actions. Choose the alternative(s) most likely to accomplish your objectives; describe step-by-step what must be done to follow the chosen course of action.
5. *Implement the plan and evaluate results:* Take action and carefully measure your progress toward objectives. Do what the plan requires, evaluate results, take corrective action, and revise plans as needed.

Planning as just described is an application of the decision-making process presented in Chapter 7. It is a systematic way to approach two important tasks: setting performance objectives, and deciding how best to achieve them. But remember, planning is not something managers do while working alone in quiet rooms, free from distractions, and at scheduled times. It is an ongoing process, often continuously being done even while dealing with an otherwise busy and demanding work setting.[10] And

■ **Objectives** are specific results that one wishes to achieve.

■ A **plan** is a statement of intended means for accomplishing objectives.

like other decision making, the best planning is done with the active participation of those people whose work efforts will eventually determine whether or not the plans are well implemented and the objectives are accomplished.

BENEFITS OF PLANNING

Organizations in today's dynamic times are facing pressures from many sources. Externally, these include ethical expectations, government regulations, uncertainties of a global economy, changing technologies, and the sheer cost of investments in labor, capital, and other supporting resources. Internally, they include the quest for operating efficiencies, new structures and technologies, alternative work arrangements, greater diversity in the workplace, and related managerial challenges. As you would expect, planning in such conditions offers a number of benefits.

Planning Improves Focus and Flexibility

Good planning improves focus and flexibility, both of which are important for performance success. An *organization with focus* knows what it does best, knows the needs of its customers, and knows how to serve them well. An *individual with focus* knows where he or she wants to go in a career or

INSIGHTS

Know What You Want to Accomplish

The next time you visit a Kinko's, look around and consider the operation. Make your visit a trip into both the past and the future. It all started in 1970 when Paul Orfalea, newly graduated from college, decided to put a photocopier, film-processing equipment, and a small selection of stationery supplies in a shop near the University of Califomia at Santa Barbara. He called his business "Kinko's"—the nickname given to him by friends.

In business, timing means a lot, and Orfalea's timing was perfect. Copying was in; he was so busy at times that the photocopier had to be moved out into the street, where customers served themselves. Location counts, too, and there was no better place than next door to a university. What began as a single small shop is now self-proclaimed to be "the world's leading provider of document solutions and business services." Kinko's, recently purchased by Federal Express, employs more than 20,000 "team members" worldwide and operates in more than 1100 locations and nine countries.

The story is that Paul Orfalea got the idea for Kinko's when he saw so many students lining up to use the photocopy machine in his university's library. That's insight—spotting opportunity in one's environment. It's also a good example of planning that helps turn insight and opportunity into real performance accomplishments.

Orfalea began with a good idea. His continuing business success was due to an ability to spot business opportunities, decide how to best deal with them, and then do it. These are planning skills we all need, managers included. But needing them is one thing; having them is another. While General Motors was closing nine plants in North America and laying off 30,000 workers, Toyota was opening them; while GM kept emphasizing large SUVs and pick-up trucks, Toyota was focusing on smaller, gas friendly vehicles; while GM was losing money, Toyota was making money.

Maybe GM should have hired Paul Orfela years ago as a planning consultant. Do you think he would have missed the market trends?

situation, and in life overall. An *organization with flexibility* is willing and able to change and adapt to shifting circumstances, and operates with an orientation toward the future rather than the past. An *individual with flexibility* adjusts career plans to fit new and developing opportunities.

Planning Improves Action Orientation

Planning is a way for people and organizations to stay ahead of the competition and become better at what they are doing. It helps avoid the *complacency trap* simply being carried along by the flow of events. It keeps the future visible as a performance target and reminds us that the best decisions are often those made before events force problems upon us.

Management consultant Stephen R. Covey talks about the importance of priorities. He points out that the most successful executives "zero in on what they do that 'adds value' to an organization."[11] Instead of working on too many things, they work on the things that really count. Covey says that good planning makes us more (1) *results oriented*—creating a performance-oriented sense of direction; (2) *priority oriented*—making sure the most important things get first attention; (3) *advantage oriented*—ensuring that all resources are used to best advantage; and (4) *change oriented*—anticipating problems and opportunities so they can be best dealt with.

Planning Improves Coordination

Planning improves coordination.[12] The different individuals, groups, and subsystems in organizations are each doing many different things at the same time. But even as they pursue their specific tasks and objectives, their accomplishments must add up to meaningful contributions to the organization as a whole. Good planning throughout an organization creates a *means-ends chain* or **hierarchy of objectives** in which lower-level objectives lead to the accomplishment of higher-level ones. Higher-level objectives as *ends* are directly tied to lower-level objectives as the *means* for their accomplishment. *Figure 8.2* uses the example of quality management to show how a means-ends chain helps guide and integrate quality efforts within a large manufacturing firm.

■ In a **hierarchy of objectives**, lower-level objectives are means to accomplishing higher level ones.

Planning Improves Time Management

One of the side benefits that planning offers is better time management. Lewis Platt, former chairman of Hewlett-Packard, says: "Basically, the whole day is a series of choices."[13] These choices have to be made in ways that allocate your time to the most important priorities. Platt says that he was

Shift supervisor quality objectives	Plant quality objectives	Manufacturing division quality objectives	Corporate quality objectives
Assess capabilities of machine operators and provide/arrange appropriate training.	Increase percent accepted by 16% to meet customers' delivery requirements.	Become a preferred supplier by achieving 100% on-time delivery of all products.	Deliver error-free products that meet customer requirements 100% of the time.

Figure 8.2 A sample hierarchy of objectives for total quality management.

MANAGEMENT SMARTS 8.1

Personal Time Management Tips

- *Do* say no to requests that divert you from what you really should be doing
- *Don't* get bogged down in details that you can address later or leave for others
- *Do* have a system for screening telephone calls, e-mails, and requests for meetings
- *Don't* let "drop-in" visitors or instant messages use too much of your time
- *Do* prioritize what you will work on in terms of importance and urgency
- *Don't* become "calendar bound" by letting others control your schedule
- *Do* follow priorities; work on the most important and urgent tasks first

"ruthless about priorities" and that you "have to continually work to optimize your time."

Most of us have experienced the difficulties of balancing available time with the many commitments and opportunities we would like to fulfill. It is easy to lose track of time and fall prey to what consultants identify as "time wasters." Too many of us allow our time to be dominated by other people and/or by nonessential activities.[14] "To do" lists can help, but they have to contain the right things. In daily living and in management, it is important to distinguish between things that you *must do* (top priority), *should do* (high priority), would be *nice to do* (low priority), and really *don't need to do* (no priority). See *Management Smarts 8.1* for further time management tips.

Planning Improves Control

When planning is done well, it facilitates control, making it easier to measure performance results and take action to improve things as necessary. Planning helps make this possible by defining the objectives along with the specific actions through which they are to be pursued. If results are less than expected, either the objectives or the actions being taken, or both, can be evaluated and adjusted. In this way planning and controlling work closely together in the management process. Without planning, control lacks objectives and standards for measuring how well things are going and what could be done to make them go better. Without control, planning lacks the follow-through needed to ensure that things work out as planned.

Learning Check 1

Be sure you can ■ define planning as a management function ■ list the steps in the formal planning process ■ describe the benefits of planning for a business or organization that is familiar to you ■ illustrate how good planning assists with personal career development

---

TYPES OF PLANS USED BY MANAGERS

Managers face many different planning challenges in the flow and pace of activities in organizations. In some cases the planning environment is stable and quite predictable; in others it is more dynamic and uncertain. A variety of plans are used to meet these different needs.

SHORT-RANGE AND LONG-RANGE PLANS

A rule of thumb is that *short-range plans* cover 1 year or less, *intermediate-range plans* cover 1 to 2 years, and *long-range plans* look 3 or more years into the future. Top management is most likely to be involved in setting long-range plans and directions for the organization as a whole, while lower management levels focus more on short-run plans that help achieve long-term objectives.

Unless everyone understands an organization's long-term plans, there is always risk that the pressures of daily events will create confusion and divert attention from important tasks. In other words, without a sense of long-term direction, people can end up working hard but without achieving significant results. General Motors and Ford executives know this only too well. Featured in The Topic chapter opener, these firms are operating today in what used to be the far-off "future," and they have arrived here only to be in lots of trouble. Was it the inability to think long term that got them here, or was it an inability to recognize and adjust to changing events that let to their downfalls?

Management researcher Elliot Jaques suggests that people vary in their capability to think about, organize, and work through events with different time horizons.[15] In fact, he believes that most people work comfortably with only 3-month time spans; a smaller group works well with a one-year span; and only about one person in several million can handle a 20-year time frame. These are provocative ideas. Although a team leader's planning challenges may rest mainly in the weekly or monthly range, a chief executive is expected to have a vision extending several years into the future. Career progress to higher management levels requires the conceptual skills to work well with longer-range time frames.[16]

Complexities and uncertainties in today's environments put pressure on these planning horizons. In an increasingly global economy, planning opportunities and challenges are often worldwide in scope, not just local. And, of course, the information age is ever present in its planning implications. We now talk about planning in *Internet time*, where businesses are continually changing and updating plans. Even top managers now face the reality that Internet time keeps making the "long" range of planning shorter and shorter.

STRATEGIC AND OPERATIONAL PLANS

Plans differ not only in time horizons but also in scope. **Strategic plans** set broad, comprehensive, and longer-term action directions. Strategic planning by top management involves determining objectives for the entire organization, describing what and where it wants to be in the future. There was a time, for example, when many large businesses strategically sought to diversify into unrelated areas. A successful oil firm might have acquired an office products company or a successful cereal manufacturer might have acquired an apparel company. In the next chapter on strategic management we will examine the process through which such strategic choices are made and how they can be analyzed. For now, suffice it to say that diversification strategies haven't always proved successful.

Operational plans define what needs to be done in specific functions or work units to implement strategic plans. Typical operational plans for a business firm include *production plans*—dealing with the methods and technology needed by people in their work; *financial plans*—dealing with money required to support various operations; *facilities plans*—dealing with facilities and work layouts; *marketing plans*—dealing with the requirements of selling and distributing goods or services; and *human resource plans*—dealing with the recruitment, selection, and placement of people into various jobs.

■ A **strategic plan** identifies long-term directions for the organization.

■ An **operational plan** identifies activities to implement strategic plans.

POLICIES AND PROCEDURES

Among the many plans in organizations, *standing plans* in the form of organizational policies and procedures are designed for use over and over again. A **policy** communicates broad guidelines for making decisions and taking action in specific circumstances. For example, typical human resource policies address such matters as employee hiring, termination, performance appraisals, pay increases, promotions, and discipline. Another policy area of special organizational

■ A **policy** is a standing plan that communicates broad guidelines for decisions and action.

consequence is sexual harassment. When Judith Nitsch started her own engineering consulting business, for example, she defined a sexual harassment policy, took a hard line on its enforcement, and appointed both a male and a female employee for others to talk with about sexual harassment concerns.[17]

■ A procedure or rule precisely describes actions that are to be taken in specific situations.

Rules or **procedures** describe exactly what actions are to be taken in specific situations. They are often found stated in employee handbooks or manuals as "SOPs"—standard operating procedures. Whereas a policy sets a broad guideline for action, procedures define precise actions to be taken. In the prior example, Judith Nitsch should put in place procedures that ensure everyone receives fair, equal, and nondiscriminatory treatment under the sexual harassment policy. Everyone should know how to file a sexual harassment complaint and how that complaint will be handled.

BUDGETS AND PROJECTS

■ A budget is a plan that commits resources to projects or activities.

In contrast to standing plans, *single-use plans* are used once, serving the needs and objectives of well-defined situations in a timely manner. **Budgets** are single-use plans that commit resources to activities, projects, or programs. They are powerful tools that allocate scarce resources among multiple and often competing uses. Most managers bargain for adequate budgets to support the needs of their work units or teams. They are also expected to achieve performance objectives while keeping within the allocated budget.

A *fixed budget* allocates a fixed amount of resources for a specific purpose. For example, a manager may have a $50,000 budget for equipment purchases in a given year. A *flexible budget* allows the allocation of resources to vary in pro-

ISSUES AND SITUATIONS

Camp Samsung

Call it planning with a difference. Better yet, call it market-driven planning. And even better, call it creativity-based planning for high value product innovations. That's what Camp Samsung is all about. Samsung Electronics Corp. is one of South Korea's giant multinational corporations. Its CEO, Yun Jong Yong, wants to double its present sales to $170 billion by 2010. To meet this ambitious goal, however, Yong admits that the firm has a long way to go. It's "a good company," he says, while adding that "we still have a lot of things to do before we're a great company." As an example he points out the firm brought out an MP3 player two years ahead of Apple, but that Apple's iPod took the market by storm. His plan for the future includes making Samsung a hotbed of market-driven product innovations; Camp Samsung is one of its launching pads.

Camp Samsung is really the Value Innovation Program Center. It's a place where teams come together to work on new product ideas. For example, product planners, designers, programmers, and engineers working on a new flat-screen TV do so with the guidance of a "value innovation specialist." Driven by a tight timetable, separated from other work pressures and responsibilities, kept together until the project is completed, guided and supported by all sorts of technical and team-oriented staff members, and nurtured by communal leisure activities, the innovation teams do it.

In one year alone, Samsung sent 2,000 employees through the VIP center, and they created 90 new products. Look for a Samsung notebook computer that doubles as a mobile TV, or a color laser printer selling at the same price as "old" black-and-whites. With CEO Yong focusing on stretch goals and supporting them with investments like Camp Samsung, where else might this company go in the future?

Critical Response

Goals and objectives are one thing; making plans to achieve them is another; implementing the plans successfully is still another. Can you spot examples in your personal and work experiences of goals that aren't well supported by plans, and of plans that aren't well implemented? What makes the difference between planning with success and just planning? Is this one of the great differentiators between the great managers and the also-rans?

portion with various levels of activity. For example, a manager may have flexibility to hire extra temporary workers if work load exceeds a certain level.

A common problem with budgets is that resource allocations get "rolled over" from one budgeting period to the next, often without a rigorous performance review. A **zero-based budget** deals with this problem by approaching each new budget period as it if were brand new. There is no guarantee that any past funding will be renewed; all proposals compete anew for available funds at the start of each new budget cycle. In a major division of Campbell Soups, for example, managers using zero-based budgeting once discovered that 10 percent of the marketing budget was going to sales promotions no longer relevant to current product lines.

A lot of work in organizations takes the form of **projects,** one-time activities that have clear beginning and end points. Examples are the completion of a new student activities building on a campus, the development of a new computer software program, or the implementation of a new advertising campaign for a sports team. **Project management** involves making sure that the activities required to complete a project are completed on time, within budget, and in ways that otherwise meet objectives. Managers of projects make extensive use of *project schedules* that define specific task objectives, link activities to be accomplished with due dates, and identify the amounts and time of resource requirements. These responsibilities are further discussed in Chapter 19 on Operations Management and Services.

■ A **zero-based budget** allocates resources as if each budget was brand new.

■ **Projects** are one-time activities that have clear beginning and end points.

■ **Project management** makes sure that activities required to complete a project are accomplished on time and correctly.

Be sure you can ■ differentiate between short-range and long-range plans ■ differentiate between strategic and operational plans and explain their relationships to one another ■ define the terms "policy" and "procedure" and give an example of each in the university setting ■ explain the unique operation of a zero-based budget

Learning Check 2

✓

PLANNING TOOLS AND TECHNIQUES

The benefits of planning are best realized when the foundations are strong. Among the useful tools and techniques of managerial planning are forecasting, contingency planning, scenarios, benchmarking, participative planning, and the use of staff planners.

FORECASTING

Forecasting is the process of predicting what will happen in the future.[18] All plans involve forecasts of some sort. Periodicals such as *Business Week, Fortune,* and the *Economist* regularly report forecasts of economic conditions, interest rates, unemployment, and trade deficits, among other issues. Some are based on *qualitative forecasting,* which uses expert opinions to predict the future. Others involve *quantitative forecasting,* which uses mathematical models and statistical analyses of historical data and surveys to predict future events.

■ **Forecasting** attempts to predict the future.

Although useful, all forecasts should be treated cautiously. They are planning aids, not substitutes. It is said that a music agent once told Elvis Presley: "You ought to go back to driving a truck because you ain't going nowhere." He was obviously mistaken. That's the problem with forecasts. They always rely on human judgment. And, they can be wrong.

CONTINGENCY PLANNING

■ **Contingency planning**
identifies alternative courses
of action to take when things
go wrong.

Planning, by definition, involves thinking ahead. But the more uncertain the planning environment, the more likely that one's original assumptions, forecasts, and intentions may prove inadequate or wrong. **Contingency planning** identifies alternative courses of action that can be implemented to meet the needs of changing circumstances.

Although one can't always predict when things will go wrong, it can be anticipated that they will. It is highly unlikely that any plan will ever be perfect; changes in the environment will sooner or later occur, as will crises and emergencies. And when they do, the best managers and organizations have contingency plans ready to be implemented. Contingency plans contain "trigger points" that indicate when preselected alternative plans should be activated.

Coke and Pepsi spend hundreds of millions of dollars on advertising as they engage one another in the ongoing "Cola War." It may seem that they have nothing to worry about save each other and a few discounters. But more than 50 percent of their revenues come internationally. And, the world at large is a dynamic place with new developments continually taking center stage. Contingency planning would help executives at both firms prepare for things like the appearance of Mecca Cola and Qibla Cola. These new colas entered European markets riding a wave of resentment of U.S. brands and multinationals. The founder of Qibla says: "By choosing to boycott major brands, consumers are sending an important signal: that the exploitation of Muslims cannot continue unchecked."[19]

SCENARIO PLANNING

■ **Scenario planning**
identifies alternative future
scenarios and makes plans to
deal with each.

A long-term version of contingency planning, called **scenario planning,** involves identifying several alternative future scenarios or states of affairs that may occur. Plans are then made to deal with each should it actually happen.[20] At Royal Dutch/Shell, scenario planning began years ago when top managers asked themselves a perplexing question: "What would Shell do after its oil supplies ran out?" Identifying different possible scenarios ahead of time helps organizations like Shell plan ahead to make major adjustments in strategies and operations. Although recognizing that scenario planning can never be inclusive of all future possibilities, a Shell executive once said that it helps "condition the organization to think" and better prepare for "future shocks." Today, in fact, many question just how well Shell, BP, Exxon and other major petroleum firms planned for unfolding scenarios rich with challenges of climate change, human rights, environmental degradation, biodiversity, sustainable development, and more.

BENCHMARKING

All too often planners become too comfortable with the ways things are going and overconfident that the past is a good indicator of the future. It is often better to keep challenging the status quo and not simply accept things as they are. One way to do this is through **benchmarking,** the use of external comparisons to better evaluate one's current performance and identify possible actions for the future.[21]

The purpose of benchmarking is to find out what other people and organizations are doing very well, and then plan how to incorporate these ideas into one's own operations. One benchmarking technique is to search for **best practices,** thing people and organizations do that help them achieve superior performance. Well-run organizations emphasize internal benchmarking that encourages all members and work units to learn and improve by sharing one another's best practices. They also use external benchmarking to learn from competitors and non competitors alike. In the fast moving apparel industry, for example, the Spanish retailer Zara has exploded on the world scene. It's growth has attracted attention and it has become a benchmark for both worried competitors and others outside the industry.[22] Zara is praised for excellence in "fast-fashion." The firm's design and manufacturing systems allow it to get new fashions from design to stores in two weeks; competitors may take months with the process. Zara produces only in small batches that sell

■ **Benchmarking** uses external comparisons to gain insights for planning.

■ **Best practices** are things that lead to superior performance.

REAL ETHICS

Fighting Poverty

Facts: Developing countries send $100+ billion in aid to poor countries; private foundations and charities spend $70+ billion more fighting poverty and its effects around the world.

Question: Are these monies being well spent?

Answer: Not all of them, that's for sure. And that's a problem being tackled by the Poverty Action Lab at the Massachusetts Institute of Technology. It director, Abhijit Banerjee, a development economist, says: "We aren't really interested in the more-aid-less-aid debate. We're interested in seeing what works and what doesn't."

Ruth Levine, director of programs for the Center for Global Development, says: "You don't see many reports of projects that fail. But it's very hard to learn what works if you are only exposed to a nonrandom subset of things that work." The Poverty Action Lab pans "feel good" evaluations and pushes rigorous evaluations of poverty-fighting programs using scientific methods. Here's an example.

The Indian anti-poverty group Sev Mandir was concerned about teacher absenteeism and low performance by rural school children. Its original plan was to pay extra tutors to assist teachers in 120 rural schools. The Poverty Lab Plan suggested paying extra tutors in 60 schools, making no changes in the other 60, and then comparing outcomes to see if the plan worked. An evaluation of results showed no difference in children's performance even with the higher costs of extra tutors.

A new plan was made to buy cameras for 60 teachers, have them take time/date-stamped photos with children at the start and end of each school day, and have the photos analyzed each month. Teachers would receive bonuses or fines based on teacher absenteeism and student performance. Again, no changes were made in the other 60 schools. After 2 years, the evaluation revealed that teacher absenteeism was 20 percent lower and student performance was significantly higher in the camera schools. With the Poverty Lab's help, Sevi Mandir concluded that investing in closely monitored pay incentives would positively influence teacher attendance in rural schools.

FURTHER INQUIRY

Look around your organization and at cases reported in the news. How often do we draw conclusions that "plans are working" based on feel-good evaluations rather than solid scientific evaluations? What are the consequences in our personal lives, at work and in society at large when plans are implemented at great cost but without way defensible systems of evaluation?

out and create impressions of scarcity. Shoppers at Zara know they have to buy now because an item will not be replaced; at its competitors they can often wait for sales and inventory clearance bargains. And if something doesn't sell at Zara, it's not a big problem since there wasn't a large stock of the item to begin with.

STAFF PLANNERS

As organizations grow, there is a corresponding need to increase the sophistication of the planning system itself. In some cases, staff planners are employed to help coordinate planning for the organization as a whole or for one of its major components. These planning specialists are skilled in all steps of the planning process, as well as with planning tools and techniques. They can help bring focus and energy to accomplish important, often strategic, planning tasks. But one risk is a tendency for a communication "gap" to develop between staff planners and line managers. Unless everyone works closely together, the resulting plans may be inadequate, and people may lack commitment to implement the plans no matter how good they are.

PARTICIPATION AND INVOLVEMENT

■ **Participatory planning** includes the persons who will be affected by plans and/or who will implement them.

"Participation" is a key word in the planning process. **Participatory planning** includes in all planning steps the people who will be affected by the plans and/or who will be asked to help implement them. This process, as shown in *Figure 8.3*, offers many benefits. Participation can increase the creativity and information available for planning. It can also increase the understanding and acceptance of plans, as well as commitment to their success. And even though participatory planning takes more time, it can improve results by improving implementation.

An example of the benefits of a participatory approach to planning is found at Boeing. Former CEO Alan Mulally faced indecision in the firm's management

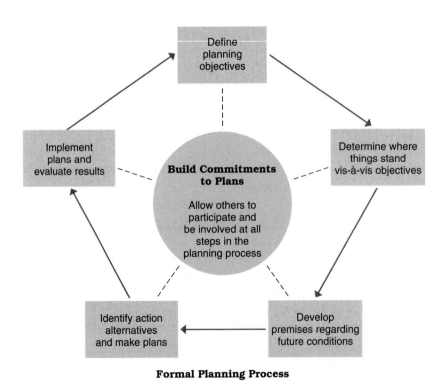

Figure 8.3 How participation and involvement help build commitments to plans.

Formal Planning Process

KAFFEEKLATSCH

Management Ethnographers

First Cup

"I hear that the anthropologists are now helping business planners. They say that *ethnography*, the science of observing people, is the new key to product development, planning and market success."

Studying the Grounds

▪ Sirius' S50 portable satellite radio player was developed after an ethnographic team studied 45 people for four weeks, learning how they listened to music, watched TV and read magazines.

▪ The OXO Hammer was developed after ethnographers visited contractors and home renovators, learning about desires for less vibration and a rubber bumper to reduce marks when nails were pulled.

▪ Consulting ethnographers helped Procter & Gamble design its Magic Reach Tool after watching service personnel at Marriott hotels struggle to clean hard-to-reach spots in bathrooms.

Double Espresso

"Well it only makes sense. Products should be developed with the needs of the people who will use them clearly in mind. Now, I say it's time to turn consumer ethnographers into real 'management ethnographers.' Don't you think that organizations should make plans based on a real understanding of the needs of the people like you and me that do the everyday work. As it is, 'they' plan inside their offices and then 'tell' us what we need to change in order to do 'our' jobs better. If Sirius had done that its customers would be toting around radios the size of lunchboxes, and refrigerators would look just like the ones our parents used."

Your Turn

The idea of "management ethnographers" seems interesting. But, isn't this what managers are supposed to do anyway? Shouldn't all managers be ethnographers who spend time with the people they supervise, get to know their needs and the work they do really well, and then make sure that information is used to make good plans for the future?

---

ranks after 9/11 left the airline industry in turmoil and new plane orders plummeted. To regain momentum he instituted a new planning approach that started with strategy sessions on Thursdays with 30 top executives. His message was to look ahead to the time when the "slump" in airplane orders would be over, and plan for a new generation of planes. He added 60 new managers from lower levels to the process every second Thursday. And, he credits this approach with bringing to market the 787 "Dreamliner," the fastest selling plane in the firm's history. About the benefits of engaging so many managers in the planning process he says: "They gave us a wider perspective and could tell us if what we were planning actually worked and made sense." [23]

Be sure you can ▪ define the terms forecasting, contingency planning, scenario planning, and benchmarking ▪ explain the values of contingency planning and scenario planning ▪ describe a possible risk of relying on staff planners ▪ explain the concept of participatory planning and defend its importance in organizations today

Learning Check 3

MANAGEMENT BY OBJECTIVES

A useful planning technique that also helps integrate planning with the control process is **management by objectives (MBO)**. This is a structured process of regular communication in which a supervisor or team leader and subordinates or team members jointly set performance objectives and review

▪ **MBO** is a process of joint objective setting between a superior and subordinate.

results accomplished.[24] As shown in *Figure 8.4*, MBO creates an agreement between the two parties regarding (1) performance objectives for a given time period, (2) plans through which they will be accomplished, (3) standards for measuring whether they have been accomplished, and (4) procedures for reviewing performance results. Both parties in my MBO agreement are supposed to work closely together to fulfill the terms of the agreement.

PERFORMANCE OBJECTIVES IN MBO

The way objectives are described and how they are established can influence the success of MBO. Three types of objectives may be specified in an MBO contract. *Improvement objectives* document intentions for improving performance in a specific way. An example is "to reduce quality rejects by 10 percent." *Personal development objectives* pertain to personal growth activities, often those resulting in expanded job knowledge or skills. An example is "to learn the latest version of a computer spreadsheet package." Some MBO contracts also include *maintenance objectives* that formally express intentions to maintain performance at an existing level. Each of these objectives should meet the following criteria.

1. *Specific*—targets a key result to be accomplished.
2. *Time defined*—identifies a date for achieving results.
3. *Challenging*—offers a realistic and attainable challenge.
4. *Measurable*—is as specific and quantitative as possible.

One of the more difficult aspects of MBO relates to the last criterion—the need to make performance objectives measureable. Ideally this involves agreement on a *measurable end product*, for example "to reduce housekeeping supply costs by 5 percent by the end of the fiscal year." But performance in some jobs, particularly managerial ones, is hard to quantify. Rather than abandon MBO in such cases, it is often possible to agree on performance objectives that are stated as *verifiable work activities*. The accomplishment of the activities serves as an indicator of progress under the performance objective. An example is "to improve communications with my subordinates in the next 3 months by holding weekly group meetings." Whereas it can be difficult to measure "improved communications," it is easy to document whether the "weekly group meetings" have been held.

MBO PROS AND CONS

MBO is one of the most talked about and debated management concepts.[25] As a result, good advice is available. Things to avoid include tying MBO to pay, focusing too much attention on easy objectives, requiring excessive paperwork, and having supervisors simply *tell* subordinates their objectives.

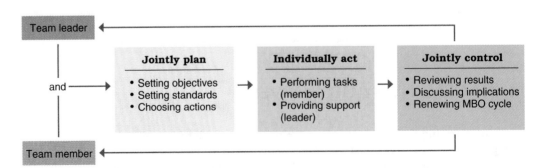

Figure 8.4 Management by objectives as an integrated planning and control framework.

RESEARCH BRIEF

You've got to move beyond planning by the calendar

Organizations today need executives that can make faster and better decisions, and that means strategic planning must be done more continuously. Michael C. Mankins and Richard Steele, writing in the *Harvard Business Review*, express their concerns that planning is too often viewed as an annual activity focused more on documenting plans for the record than on action. Little wonder, they suggest, that only 11% of executives in a survey 156 firms with sales of $1+ billion were highly satisfied that strategic planning is worthwhile.

The research, conducted in collaboration with Marakon Associates and the *Economist Intelligence Unit*, inquired as to how long range strategic planning was conducted and how effective these planning activities were. Results showed that executives perceived a substantial disconnect between the way many firms approached strategic planning and the way they approached strategic decisions. Some 66% of the time executives said that strategic planning at their firms was conducted only at set times, and very often was accomplished by a formal and structured process. Survey respondents also indicated that planning was often considered as only a "periodic event" and not something to be continuously engaged. Mankins and Steele call such planning "calendar driven" and question its effectiveness.

In calendar driven planning the researchers found that firms averaged only 2.5 major strategic decisions per year, with "major" meaning a decision that could move profits by 10+%. They also point out that when planning is decoupled from the calendar companies make higher quality and more strategic decisions. The researchers call this alternative planning approach "continuous review" and argue it is more consistent with the way executives actually make decisions and business realities.

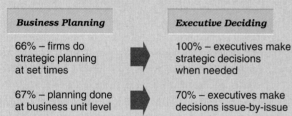

QUESTIONS & APPLICATIONS

Why is it that structuring the planning process around a certain calendar date may be dysfunctional for a business? On the other hand, how can we plan almost continuously? Choose two or three organizations in your community for some field research. Arrange interviews at each with a senior executive. Find out if they plan on a set schedule, if so what that schedule might be, and overall how effective they consider planning in their organization to be.

Reference: Michael C. Mankins and Richard Steele, "Stop Making Plans; Start Making Decisions," *Harvard Business Review* (January, 2006), reprint R0601F.

The advantages are also clear. MBO focuses workers on the most important tasks and objectives. And it focuses the supervisor on areas of support that can truly help subordinates meet the agreed-upon objectives. Because the process involves direct face-to-face communication, MBO also contributes to relationship building. By giving people the opportunity to participate in decisions that affect their work, MBO encourages self-management.[26]

One of the things that research is most clear about is that participation in setting objectives creates motivation to work hard and accomplish them.[27] In this sense, management by objectives is another example of the power of participation and involvement as a planning technique.

Be sure you can ■ define the term management by objectives ■ list the criteria of a good performance objective and give an example satisfying each ■ illustrate how MBO might operate in the relationships between a team leader and team members

Learning Check 4

CHAPTER 8 STUDY GUIDE

STUDY QUESTIONS SUMMARY

1 Why and how do managers plan?

■ Planning is the process of setting performance objectives and determining what should be done to accomplish them.

■ A plan is a set of intended actions for accomplishing important objectives.

■ Planning sets the stage for the other management functions—organizing, leading, and controlling.

■ Five steps in the planning process are: (1) define your objectives, (2) determine where you stand vis-à-vis objectives, (3) develop your premises regarding future conditions, (4) identify and choose among alternative ways of accomplishing objectives, and (5) implement action plans and evaluate results.

■ The benefits of planning include better focus and flexibility, action orientation, coordination, control, and time management.

2 What types of plans do managers use?

■ Short-range plans tend to cover a year or less, while long-range plans extend up to 3 years or more.

■ Strategic plans set critical long-range directions; operational plans are designed to implement strategic plans.

■ Policies, such as a sexual harassment policy, are plans that set guidelines for the behavior of organizational members.

■ Procedures and rules are plans that describe actions to be taken in specific situations, such as the steps to be taken when persons believe they have been subjected to sexual harassment.

■ Budgets are plans that allocate resources to activities or projects.

3 What are the useful planning tools and techniques?

■ Forecasting, which attempts to predict what might happen in the future, is a planning aid but not a planning substitute.

■ Contingency planning identifies alternative courses of action that can be implemented if and when circumstances change.

■ Scenario planning analyzes the implications of alternative versions of the future.

■ Planning through benchmarking utilizes external and internal comparisons to identify best practices for possible adoption.

■ Participation and involvement open the planning process to valuable inputs from people whose efforts are essential to the effective implementation of plans.

4 What is management by objectives?

■ Management by objectives is a process through which supervisors work with subordinates to "jointly" set performance objectives and review performance results.

■ Good performance objectives are stated in ways that are specific, measureable, and time defined.

■ The MBO process is highly participatory, both clarifying performance objectives for an individual and identifying helpful support that can be provided by the manager.

KEY TERMS REVIEW

Benchmarking (p. 193)

Best practices (p. 193)

Budget (p. 190)

Contingency planning (p. 192)

Forecasting (p. 191)

Hierarchy of objectives (p. 187)

Management by objectives (MBO)
 (p. 195)

Objectives (p. 185)

Operational plan (p. 189)

Participatory planning (p. 194)

Plan (p. 185)

Planning (p. 184)

Policy (p. 189)

Procedures (p. 190)

Project (p. 191)

Project management (p. 191)

Scenario planning (p. 192)

Strategic plan (p. 189)

Zero-based budget (p. 191)

SELF-TEST 8

MULTIPLE-CHOICE QUESTIONS:

1. Planning is the process of _____ and _____.
   (a) developing premises about the future, evaluating them   (b) measuring results, taking corrective action   (c) measuring past performance, targeting future performance   (d) setting objectives, deciding how to accomplish them

2. The benefits of planning include _____.

   (a) improved focus   (b) lower labor costs   (c) more accurate forecasts   (d) guaranteed profits

3. In order to help implement its strategy, a business firm would likely develop a(n) _____ plan for the marketing function.

   (a) benchmarking IT   (b) operational   (c) productivity   (d) zero-based

4. _____ planning identifies alternative courses of action that can be taken if and when certain situations arise.

   (a) Benchmark   (b) Participative   (c) Strategic   (d) Contingency

5. The first step in the control process is to _____.

   (a) measure actual performance   (b) establish objectives and standards   (c) compare results with objectives
   (d) take corrective action

6. A "No Smoking" rule and a sexual harassment policy are examples of _____ plans used by organizations.

   (a) long-range   (b) single-use   (c) standing-use   (d) operational

7. When a manager is asked to justify a new budget proposal on the basis of projected activities rather than past practices, this is an example of _____ budgeting.

   (a) zero-based   (b) variable   (c) fixed   (d) contingency

8. One of the benefits of participatory planning is _____.

   (a) reduced time for planning   (b) less need for forecasting   (c) greater attention to contingencies   (d) more commitment to implementation

9. In a hierarchy of objectives, the ideal situation is that plans set at lower levels become the _____ for accomplishing higher-level plans.

   (a) means   (b) ends   (c) scenarios   (d) benchmarks

10. When managers use the benchmarking approach to planning they _____.

    (a) use flexible budgets   (b) identify best practices used by others   (c) are seeking the most accurate forecasts that are available   (d) focus more on the short term than long term

11. One of the problems in relying too much on staff planners to make plans is _____.

    (a) a communication gap between planners and implementers   (b) lack of expertise in the planning process
    (c) short-term rather than long-term focus   (d) neglect of budgets as links between resources and activities

12. The planning process isn't complete until _____.

    (a) future conditions have been identified   (b) stretch goals have been set   (c) plans are implemented and results evaluated   (d) budgets commit resources to plans

13. Review of an individual's performance accomplishments in an MBO system is done by _____.

    (a) the person   (b) the person's supervisor   (c) the person and the supervisor   (d) the person, the supervisor, and a lawyer

14. A good performance objective is written in such a way that it _____.

    (a) has no precise timetable   (b) is general and not too specific   (c) is almost impossible to accomplish   (d) can be easily measured

15. A manager is failing to live up to the concept of MBO when he or she _____.

    (a) sets performance objectives for subordinates   (b) actively supports subordinates in their work   (c) jointly reviews performance results with subordinates   (d) keeps a written record of subordinates' performance objectives

SHORT-RESPONSE QUESTIONS:

16. List five steps in the planning process and give examples of each.
17. How might planning through benchmarking be used by the owner of a local bookstore?
18. How does planning help to improve focus?
19. Why does participatory planning facilitate implementation?

APPLICATION QUESTION:

20. Put yourself in the position of a management trainer. You have been asked to make a short presentation to the local Small Business Enterprise Association at its biweekly luncheon. The topic you are to speak on is "How Each of You Can Use Management by Objectives for Better Planning and Control." What will you tell them and why?

CHAPTER 8 APPLICATIONS

CASE 8

Wal-Mart: Planning for Superstore Competition

Wal-Mart, first opened in 1962 by Sam Walton in Rogers, Arkansas, has become the largest retailer in the world, with more than 6,500 store locations and approximately 1.8 million associates worldwide.[28] Despite Walton's death in 1992, Wal-Mart continues to be successful, reaching record annual sales of $312.4 billion and earnings of $11.2 billion.[29] Maintaining this phenomenal growth presents an important challenge to the firm's current leadership.

Carrying on Sam Walton's Legacy

In his 1990 letter to Wal-Mart stockholders, then-CEO David Glass laid out the company's philosophy: "We approach this new exciting decade of the '90s much as we did in the '80s—focused on only two main objectives, (a) providing the customers what they want, when they want it, all at a value, and (b) treating each other as we would hope to be treated, acknowledging our total dependency on our associate-partners to sustain our success."[30] Following in Sam Walton's footsteps, Glass believed that the traditional format of organization, employee commitment, cost control, carefully planned locations for new stores, and attention to customer needs and desires would enable Wal-Mart to enjoy continued success.

Wal-Mart grew by paying careful attention to its market niche of customers who were looking for quality at a bargain price. Customers did not have to wait for a sale to realize savings. Many of its stores were located in smaller towns, primarily throughout the South and Midwest. As Glass looked ahead, he recognized the opportunities and threats that confronted Wal-Mart. While the traditional geographical markets served by Wal-Mart were not saturated, growth in these areas was limited. Any strategy to achieve continuing growth would have to include expansion into additional geographical regions. Glass recognized that

continued growth might also have to include new product lines and higher-priced products to allow existing stores to achieve year-to-year sales growth.

He also began considering international expansion. In March 1994, the company bought 122 Canadian Woolco stores, formerly owned by Woolworth Corp., the largest single purchase Wal-Mart had made. Wal-Mart's international division is now the second largest with respect to sales and earnings. The almost 2,600 international locations have reported $62.7 billion in sales and an operating profit of $3.3 billion.[31]

Wal-Mart is now made up of five retail divisions and five specialty divisions. The retail divisions include Wal-Mart Stores, SAM's Clubs (membership warehouse clubs), Neighborhood Markets (selling groceries, pharmaceuticals, and general merchandise), International Division, and Walmart.com (an online version of the neighborhood Wal-Mart store). Three of the specialty divisions—Tire & Lube Express, Wal-Mart Optical, and Wal-Mart Pharmacy—are commonly operated in conjunction with the Wal-Mart Stores, Supercenters, and SAM'S Club outlets.[32]

Wal-Mart subscribes to the corporate policy "buy American whenever possible." Nonetheless, it has a global procurement system that enables it to effectively coordinate its entire worldwide supply chain and to share its buying power and merchandise network with all its operations throughout the world.[33] The company has set up an extensive inventory control procedure based on a satellite communication system that links all stores with the Bentonville, Arkansas, headquarters. The satellite system is also used to transmit messages from headquarters, training materials, and communications among stores, and can even be used to track the company's delivery trucks. In addition, Wal-Mart has an online system that links the company's computer systems with its suppliers. Because of its use of innovative technology, Wal-Mart has gained a competitive advantage in the speed with which it delivers goods to its customers.

While each new Wal-Mart brings in new jobs, it can also bring detrimental effects to the community as well. A 1991 *Wall Street Journal* article noted that many small retailers are forced to close after Wal-Mart opens nearby.[34] In one Wisconsin town, even J. C. Penney lost 50 percent of its Christmas sales and closed down when Wal-Mart opened up. In an Iowa town, four clothing and shoe stores, a hardware store, a drug store, and a dime store all went out of business. Wal-Mart has had to give up plans to build in Bath, Maine; Simi Valley, California; and two towns in Pennsylvania; Vermont has successfully resisted all Wal-Mart plans thus far to locate in that state.

After facing considerable cultural resistance for its low-paying part-time jobs and the proportionately few number of its employees who qualify for full-time benefits like insurance, Wal-Mart is making an inexpensive "value plan" form of insurance available to some employees. The plan offers high-deductible catastrophic coverage with low copays for a limited number of office visits.[35]

Even Wal-Mart's "Bring it home to the USA" buying program produced controversy when an NBC news program found clothing that had been made abroad hanging on racks under a "Made in the USA" sign in 11 Wal-Mart stores. In addition, the program showed a tape of children sewing at a Wal-Mart supplier's factory in Bangladesh. Wal-Mart insisted that its supplier was obeying local labor laws, which allowed 14-year-olds to work, and that company official had also paid a surprise visit to the factory and had not found any problems. Then-CEO David Glass stated: "I can't tell you today that illegal child labor hasn't happened someplace, somewhere. All we can do is try our best to prevent it." [36]

Sam's Cultural Legacy

Wal-Mart's success is built upon its culture. Rob Walton, the company's current chairman of the board, says: "Although Wal-Mart has grown large, we still focus daily on the culture and values established by my father, Sam Walton."[37] Sam Walton founded and built Wal-Mart around three basic beliefs: *respect for the individual, service to our customers*, and *striving for excellence*. Wal-Mart's slogan that "our people make the difference" reflects the company's respect for and commitment to its associates (employees). Diversity is also highly valued. Wal-Mart's philosophy of customer service emphasizes the lowest possible prices along with the best possible service to each and every customer. Lee Scott, Wal-Mart Stores' current president and CEO, observes: "Sam was never satisfied that prices were as low as they needed to be or that our product's quality was as high as they deserved—he

believed in the concept of striving for excellence before it became a fashionable concept."[38]

Three critical elements in Wal-Mart's approach to customer service are the *sundown rule*, the *ten-foot rule*, and *every day low prices*. The *sundown rule* means Wal-Mart sets a standard of accomplishing tasks on the same day that the need arises—in short, responding to requests by sundown on the day it receives them. The *ten-foot rule* promises that if an employee comes within ten feet of a customer, the employee must look the customer in the eye and ask if the person would like to be helped. *Every day low prices* is another important operating philosophy. Wal-Mart believes that by lowering markup, it will earn more because of increased volume, thereby bringing consumers added value for the dollar every day.[39]

Although Wal-Mart has enjoyed phenomenal success, there is no guarantee that it will continue to do so in the future. As the company's annual report points out, preserving and advancing the *every day low prices* concept and helping thousands of new associates to embrace the customer-centered Wal-Mart culture are essential for the company to continue growing.[40] But given the ever-increasing pressures of business, as well as a growing tide of resistance to Wal-Mart's competitive practices, how long can the company stay on top? What's its plan for the future?

REVIEW QUESTIONS

1. How have Wal-Mart's managerial philosophies and principles supported pursuit of the firm's key objectives?

2. How do planning and controlling seem to be linked at Wal-Mart?

3. As a planning consultant what alternative future scenarios would you identify for Wal-Mart's executives to consider as they plan for the future in today's dynamic times?

TEAM PROJECT

Dateline Detroit: Ford Motor Co. announces plans to trim $5 billion in costs; 10,000 white-collar jobs to be cut and buyouts offered to 75,000 unionized employees.

Saving Legacy Companies

Question: Are the great legacy companies of the past dying? And if so, can anything be done about it?

Research Directions:

▪ Read and gather information about the competitive problems of General Motors and Ford.

▪ Read and gather information about the bankruptcy experiences of Northwest Airlines, Delta Airlines, and USAir.

▪ Find out what each of these companies has done and are presently doing in attempting to overcome performance problems and reestablish themselves as successful businesses with a chance for sustainable competitive advantage.

▪ Check what the financial analysts are saying about future prospects for these companies.

▪ Compile the results of your investigation and prepare a report that answers the project question.

PERSONAL MANAGEMENT

Time Management

Time is one of our most precious resources, and **TIME MANAGEMENT** is an essential skill in today's high-pressure and fast-paced world of work. Some 77 percent of managers in one survey said the new digital age has increased the number of decisions they have to make; 43 percent complained there was less time available to make them. Others say that 20 percent of their telephone time is wasted. Of course, you have to be careful in defining "waste." It isn't a waste of time to occasionally relax, take a breather from work, and find humor and pleasure in social interaction. Such breaks help us gather energies to do well in our work. But it is a waste to let friends dominate your time so that you don't work on a term paper until it is too late to write a really good one, or delay a decision to apply for an internship until the deadline is passed. Perhaps you are one of those who plans to do so many things in a day that you never get to the most important ones. Perhaps you don't plan, letting events take you where they may, and on many days don't accomplish much at all. Learning to manage your time better will serve you very well in the future, both at work and in your personal life.

Building the Brand Called "You"   Complete the self-assessment, Time Management Profile. Consider your time management skills. One of the best things anyone can do is to keep for a day or two a daily time log – carefully listing what we do and how long it takes. This log can then be analyzed to determine where we are wasting time and where we are using it well. Combining the insights of the log with available tips on time management can go a long way toward helping us make better use of our time everyday.

NEXT STEPS: MANAGEMENT LEARNING WORKBOOK

Strategic Management

9

Planning Ahead

Chapter 9 Study Questions

1 What are the foundations of strategic competitiveness?

2 What is the strategic management process?

3 What types of strategies are used by organizations?

4 How are strategies formulated?

5 What are current issues in strategy implementation?

Working Together to Get Ahead

Common sense dictates that cooperation and competition are mutually exclusive. But do they have to be? As one successful Silicon Valley company demonstrates, synergy could be key to success.

What if a car company had the insight—or the guts—to tell consumers "our designers know a lot, but they don't know everything. We're out to design the best car ever driven, and we want your input. During the build process, we'll make test vehicles freely available for anyone to drive. Tell us honestly what you think. Or even better, tinker with the car as you please, and then return it to us. If your idea improves the car, we'll use it."

That's the concept behind open-source software, and it explains a good deal about the recent meteoric success of the Firefox Web browser and parent company Mozilla. Although fighting in the browser wars is an inherently *competitive* endeavor, Mozilla has found success and innovation through its inherent spirit of *cooperation*.

Firefox has a niche among Web geeks and casual surfers alike. Its popularity came about in part

What *They* Think

"We're not out to get Microsoft. Our goal is to offer people a better experience so the Web remains open and people actually have a choice."
Mitchell Baker, Chair of Mozilla Foundation

"I have always loved the competitive forces in this business. You know I certainly have meetings where I spur people on by saying, Hey, we can do better than this. How come we are not out ahead on that?"
Bill Gates, Founder of Microsoft

COOPERATION: *"Competition has been shown to be useful up to a certain point and no further, but cooperation, which is the thing we must strive for today, begins where competition leaves off."*
Franklin D. Roosevelt, Former U.S. President

because it's light on resources, blocks pop-ups, doesn't have Internet Explorer's reputation for security breaches, and can be easily customized by scores of add-on utilities that increase functionality and personalize the Web experience.

On top of all that, it's totally free.

"The browser matters—it's the piece [of the Internet] that touches human beings," says Mitchell Baker, president of the Mozilla Foundation. "This area shouldn't be stagnant; it should be exciting."[1]

She should know. Baker is also self-described "chief lizard wrangler" of the foundation,[2] whose Web site defines it as a "non-profit organization whose mission is to promote choice and innovation on the Internet." Like a concerned parent, the foundation provides logistical, financial, and legal support to the Firefox open-source project and to its originator, the Mozilla Corporation.[3]

Sprung from the ashes of Netscape, where Baker was a lawyer working in software licensing, the Mozilla Corporation coalesced around the idea that dedicated volunteers could cooperate to create a new open-source browser by capitalizing on Netscape's code.[4]

After the initial release, a rabid campaign by thousands of volunteers began to spread the Firefox gospel by word of mouth, an evangelizing blog, and heaps of inter-industry buzz. And true to its culture, the cooperative marketing efforts for Firefox are nearly as open-source as the browser itself: Anyone can participate in the nearly all-volunteer effort.

For once, too many cooks have not spoiled the broth. Firefox has captured significant market share from Internet Explorer; the little browser that could has already entered the zone of double-digit market share 11+% and counting.[5] And with close to 50 million downloads and 12 million users,[6] it's clear that this fox isn't afraid of the big dogs.

"We're not out to get Microsoft," says Baker. "Our goal is to offer people a better experience so the Web remains open and people actually have a choice."[7] Her organization also proudly proclaims on its web site Mozilla.org, that "We can't achieve these goals by ourselves, so we partner with for-profit and non-profit organizations that share our vision."

The Numbers

Top Ten Web Brands[8]

Rank for Audience Size	Growth 7/05–7/06
1 My Space	183%
2 Google	23%
3 eBay	13%
4 MapQuest	11%
5 Yahoo!	8%
6 MSN/Live	5%
7 Amazon	5%
8 Real	3%
9 AOL	1%
10 Microsoft	−5%

Quick facts

* Well exceeding the American market share, close to 30 percent of all computers in Poland run Firefox.[9]
* Comparing visitors to the Firefox website, men outnumber women nearly three to one.[10]
* Over 800 code contributors keep Mozilla products up to date.[11]
* Mozilla partners with IBM, Sun Microsystems, Hewlett-Packard, Red Hat, and Inspire.[12]
* Mozilla's mission is: "To preserve choice and innovation on the Internet."[13]

Discussion Questions

1. Could the Firefox browser have succeeded if Mozilla's management hadn't made it an open-source program?
2. Suppose Microsoft shifted gears; would the computing public accept an open-source version of Internet Explorer?

Strategic Management				
Study Question 1	**Study Question 2**	**Study Question 3**	**Study Question 4**	**Study Question 5**
Strategic Competitiveness	**The Strategic Management Process**	**Strategies Used by Organizations**	**Strategy Formulation**	**Strategy Implementation**
■ What is strategy? ■ What is strategic management?	■ Analysis of mission, values, and objectives ■ Analysis of resources and capabilities ■ Analysis of industry and environment	■ Levels of strategy ■ Growth and diversification ■ Restructuring and divestiture ■ Global strategies ■ Cooperation ■ E-business	■ Porter's competitive strategies ■ Portfolio planning ■ Incrementalism and emergent strategy	■ Management practices and systems ■ Corporate governance ■ Strategic leadership
Learning Check 1	**Learning Check 2**	**Learning Check 3**	**Learning Check 4**	**Learning Check 5**

Wal-Mart, amid all its controversies, is still America's largest retailer, and its master plan is elegant in its simplicity: to deliver consistently low prices and high-quality customer service.[14] This plan is pursued with use of the latest technology and sophisticated logistics. Inventories are monitored around the clock, and a world-class distribution system ensures that stores are rarely out of the items customers are seeking. All systems and people are rallied to deliver on the objectives—low prices, quality service. While the firm's competitors are asking, "How can we keep up?" executives at Wal-Mart are asking "How can we stay ahead?"

But even Wal-Mart can't rest on past laurels, as current debates on the company's future attest. It's been challenged on everything from its wage levels to employee benefits to its impact on competition in local communities. As you follow the Wal-Mart story, though, it's clear that the firm's management has learned that success today is no guarantee of success tomorrow. Changes and adjustments are taking place all the time even while the firm sticks to its master plan. When announcing a new initiative to cut prices of generic drugs sold through its pharmacies, CEO H. Lee Scott, Jr., said Wal-Mart was ". . . excited to take the lead in doing what we do best—driving costs out of the system—and passing those savings on to our customers and associates."[15]

We will surely see many changes in competitive retailing in the years ahead; we're already seeing many today. Similar forces and challenges confront managers in all organizations and industries. Today's environment places a great premium on effective "strategy" and "strategic management" as prerequisites for organizational success. "If you want to make a difference as a leader," says *Fast Company* magazine, "you've got to make time for strategy."[16]

STRATEGIC COMPETITIVENESS

One of Wal-Mart's major strengths is its abilities to cut costs, or "drive them out of the system" as its CEO says. To do this the retailer makes aggressive use of the latest computer technologies to gain efficiencies in its supply chains, track sales, and quickly adjust orders and inventories to match buying trends. This is all part of Wal-Mart's quest for **competitive advantage**, operating with a combination of attributes that allow it to outperform rivals.

Organizations pursue competitive advantage in different ways. In other industries, Dell Computer eliminates wholesale supplier markups by marketing directly to consumers; Toyota's manufacturing systems reduce shorter cycle times and allow it to carry smaller amounts of work-in-process inventory; Mozilla's open source networks allow for continual problem solving and ongoing innovations that keep improving its Firefox Web browser. But even as each of these organizations does such things very well, rivals keep the pressure on by trying to duplicate and copy the success stories. Thus, the goal becomes creating a *sustainable competitive advantage*, one that is difficult for competitors to imitate.

> ■ A **competitive advantage** comes from operating in successful ways that are difficult to imitate.

WHAT IS STRATEGY?

If sustainable competitive advantage is the goal, "strategy" is the means for its achievement.[17] **Strategy** is a comprehensive action plan that identifies the long-term direction for an organization and guides resource utilization to achieve sustainable competitive advantage. A strategy focuses attention on the competitive environment and represents a "best guess" about what must be done to ensure future success in the face of rivalry and changing conditions.

Importantly, a strategy provides the plan for allocating and using resources with consistent **strategic intent**—that is, with all organizational energies directed toward a unifying and compelling target or goal.[18] At Coca-Cola, for example, strategic intent has been described as "to put a Coke within 'arm's reach' of every consumer in the world." Given the focus provided by this strategic intent, we would not expect Coca-Cola to be diversifying by investing in snack and convenience foods, as does its archrival PepsiCo. But those investments are consistent with Pepsi's strategic intent, stated as: "to be the world's premier consumer products company focused on convenient foods and beverages."[19]

In our fast-paced world of globalization and changing technologies, the "long-term" aspect of strategy is becoming ever shorter. As it does so, the challenges to the strategist become even greater. It used to be that companies could count on traditional "build-and-sell" business models that put them in control. In the early days of the automobile industry, for example, Henry Ford once said: "The customer can have any color he wants as long as it's black." His firm, quite literally, was in the driver's seat. Today things have changed, and strategy is increasingly driven by customers and flexibility. The lessons were evidenced in the staff reductions and plant closings at Ford, GM, and Chrysler, as unsold vehicles failed to attract buyers increasingly concerned about fuel efficiency. Stephen Haeckel, director of strategic studies at IBM's Advanced Business Institute, has described the shift this way: "It's a difference between a bus, which follows a set route, and a taxi, which goes where customers tell it to go."[20]

> ■ A **strategy** is a comprehensive plan guiding resource allocation to achieve long-term organization goals.

> ■ **Strategic intent** focuses and applies organizational energies on a unifying and compelling goal.

WHAT IS STRATEGIC MANAGEMENT?

Crafting strategy for a business may seem a deceptively simple task: find out what customers want, then provide it for them at the best prices and service. In practice, this task is made complex and risky by the forces and uncertainties of competitive environments.[21] At the same time one is trying to create competitive advantage for an organization, competitors are always trying to do the same. This gives rise to demands for strategies that are "bold," "aggressive," "fast-moving," and "innovative." But call them what you will, good strategies don't just happen. They must be created. And good strategies alone don't guarantee success; they must also be well implemented. These are the challenges of **strategic management**, the process of formulating and implementing strategies to accomplish long-term goals and sustain competitive advantage.

■ **Strategic management** is the process of formulating and implementing strategies.

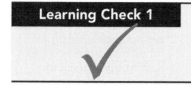

Learning Check 1

Be sure you can ■ define the terms competitive advantage, strategy, and strategic management ■ explain the concept of sustainable competitive advantage

INSIGHTS

Get and Stay Ahead with Strategy

Coffee just might be the most popular drink in the world. And the well-known Starbucks may hold claim to the most valuable brand name in the industry. The strategic question is, How long can Starbucks keep brewing a better cup of coffee?

"Forever," might answer Howard Schultz, chairman and chief global strategist of the company. When he joined Starbucks in 1982 as director of retail operations, the firm was a small coffee retailer in Seattle. But Schultz had the idea to build a coffee bar culture with

Most likely you're not very far away from a cup of Starbucks coffee. With more than 6,000 locations around the world, the firm is a growth business in more ways than one. The firm's continuing evolution of branded products still shows a commitment to aggressive growth. But behind Starbucks' strategy is also execution—even the best strategies deliver high-performance results only when they are well implemented.

Starbucks at its center. The rest is Starbucks' history.

Schultz's vision was of Starbucks becoming a national chain of stores offering the finest coffee drinks and "educating consumers everywhere about fine coffee." Not only has Starbucks fulfilled this vision on the national scene, it has stuck to core values. Employees are recognized in guiding principles: (1) "Provide a great work environment and treat each other with respect and dignity. (2) Embrace diversity as an essential component in the way we do business." You'll also find a strong commitment to the natural environment, the community, and coffee origin countries.

Today Starbucks is more than just another coffee bar retailer. Visit a store or go online, and you'll find it now selling tea, chocolates, a variety of gift items, and even music. It's all part of a global strategy for growth. Schultz says: "Moving forward, we will continue to pursue opportunities that increase long-term value for our shareholders and our partners, provide unique experiences for our customers, and bring us ever closer to our goal of becoming the most recognized and respected brand of coffee in the world."

THE STRATEGIC MANAGEMENT PROCESS

The first responsibility in the strategic management process, as shown in *Figure 9.1*, is **strategy formulation**. This involves creating a new strategy by first assessing existing strategies, the organization, and its environment. Peter Drucker identified this process with a set of five strategic questions: (1) *What is our business mission?* (2) *Who are our customers?* (3) *What do our customers value?* (4) *What have been our results?* (5) *What is our plan?*[22]

The second strategic management responsibility is **strategy implementation**, the process of allocating resources and putting strategies into action. Once strategies are created, they must be successfully acted upon to achieve the desired results. Every organizational and management system must be mobilized to support and reinforce the accomplishment of strategies. As Drucker says, "The future will not just happen if one wishes hard enough. It requires decision—now. It imposes risk—now. It requires action—now. It demands allocation of resources, and above all, of human resources—now. It requires work—now."[23]

■ **Strategy formulation** is the process of creating strategies.

■ **Strategy implementation** is the process of putting strategies into action.

ANALYSIS OF MISSION, VALUES, AND OBJECTIVES

The strategic management process begins with a careful review and clarification of organizational mission, values, and objectives. This sets the stage for critically assessing the organization's resources and capabilities as well as competitive opportunities and threats in the external environment.

Mission

As first discussed in Chapter 1, the **mission** or purpose of an organization may be described as its reason for existence in society.[24] Strategy consultant Michael Hammer believes that a mission should represent what the strategy or underlying business model is trying to accomplish. He suggests asking: "What are we moving to?" "What is our dream?" "What kind of a difference do we want to make in the world?" "What do we want to be known for?"[25]

When the mission is clear and compelling, it is easier for an organization to rally resources and systems to pursue its strategic intent. At Patagonia, the outdoor clothing and equipment retailer, the mission is clear and straightforward: "To produce the highest-quality products while doing the least possible harm to the environment."[26] In this mission one finds not only

■ The **mission** is the organization's reason for existence in society.

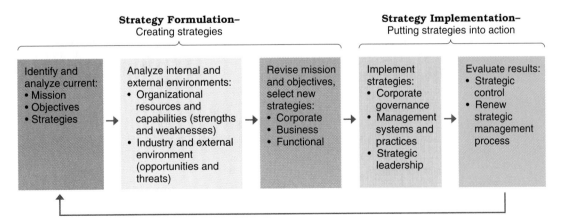

Figure 9.1 Strategy formulation and implementation in the strategic management process.

a business direction but also a distinctive value commitment. Together, they establish a clear identity for Patagonia as it competes with much larger rivals in its industry.

The best organizations have a clear sense of mission, and they utilize resources with strategic intent in respect to its fulfillment. At Mary Kay, Inc., for example, the firm's mission is defined as "To enrich women's lives." Starbucks's mission is to be "the premier purveyor of the finest coffee in the world while maintaining our uncompromising principles as we grow." The mission of the American Red Cross is to "provide relief to victims of disasters and help people prevent, prepare for, and respond to emergencies."

■ **Stakeholders** are individuals and groups directly affected by an organization and its accomplishments.

A mission statement should identify the purpose and philosophy of the organization in a way that inspires employees and generates respect among external **stakeholders**. You should recall that these are individuals and groups—including customers, shareholders, suppliers, creditors, community groups, and others who are directly affected by the organization and its strategic accomplishments. In the strategic management process, the stakeholder test can be done as a *strategic constituencies analysis*. Here, the specific interests of each stakeholder are assessed along with the organization's record in responding to them. *Figure 9.2* gives an example of how stakeholder interests can be reflected in the mission of a business firm.

Core Values

Behavior in and by organizations will always be affected in part by *values*, which are broad beliefs about what is or is not appropriate. Using Patagonia as an example again, Founder and Chairman Yvon Chouinard says "Most people want to do good things but don't. At Patagonia it's an essential part of your life." [27] His company recognizes pollution as a by-product of business activity and declares its values: "So we work steadily to reduce those harms. We use recycled polyester in many of our clothes and only organic, rather than pesticide-intensive, cotton." [28]

■ **Organizational culture** is the predominant value system for the organization as a whole.

Core values are reflected in and shaped by **organizational culture**, first defined in Chapter 4 as the predominant value system of the organization as a whole. [29] In strategic management, the presence of strong core values for an organization helps build institutional identity. It gives character to an organization in the eyes of its employees and external stakeholders, and it backs up the mission statement. Shared values help guide the behavior of organization members in meaningful and consistent ways. For those browsing Patagonia's Website for job openings, the message

Figure 9.2 External stakeholders as strategic constituencies in organization's mission statement.

about the corporate culture is clear: "We're especially interested in people who share our love of the outdoors, our passion for quality and our desire to make a difference."[30]

Objectives

Whereas a mission statement sets forth an official purpose for the organization and the core values describe appropriate standards of behavior for its accomplishment, **operating objectives** direct activities toward key and specific performance results. These objectives are shorter-term targets against which actual performance results can be measured as indicators of progress and continuous improvement. According to Peter Drucker, the *operating objectives of a business* might include the following:[31]

■ *Profitability*—producing at a net profit in business.
■ *Market share*—gaining and holding a specific market share.
■ *Human talent*—recruiting and maintaining a high-quality workforce.
■ *Financial health*—acquiring capital; earning positive returns.
■ *Cost efficiency*—using resources well to operate at low cost.
■ *Product quality*—producing high-quality goods or services.
■ *Innovation*—developing new products and/or processes.
■ *Social responsibility*—making a positive contribution to society.

■ **Operating objectives** are specific results that organizations try to accomplish.

In the case of Patagonia, the operating objectives are framed by the mission and values of the firm; everything fits together as a coherent whole. Chairman Chouinard says that he wants to run Patagonia "so that it's here 100 years from now and always makes the best-quality stuff." [32] For him this means that the firm's objective is growth, but that it is also modest, not extreme or uncontrolled, growth. Patagonia presently is growing about 5% per year.

REAL ETHICS

Bankruptcy by Design

The news from Detroit might not have looked unusual given the times. CEO Robert S. Miller of the large auto parts supplier Delphi announced that it would like workers to take 40 percent pay cuts so that the firm could emerge from bankruptcy and be competitive in world markets. Also, it probably wasn't surprising that the United Auto Workers union resisted the move.

Let's look at the facts. U.S. law allows firms to file for Chapter 11 bankruptcy protection while they regroup and make changes to restore profitability. But Miller seemed to be using bankruptcy protection as a way of shifting Delphi's production overseas. He was already drastically cutting the firm's U.S. operations, presently accounting for two-thirds of the firm's activities, and wanted to do more. The goal appeared to be to move as much work as possible to Delphi's low-wage, nonunion foreign factories, which were excluded from the bankruptcy filing. In a nutshell, the strategy appeared to be retrenchment through downsizing in the United States, where labor costs are high, while upsizing internationally where labor costs are low.

Delphi's actions prompted Senators Bayh (Indiana) and Conyers (Michigan) to file legislation to tighten bankruptcy laws in an age of globalization. At the time they said: "Some international corporations that are struggling domestically use their losses at home to justify breaking contracts with American workers while their overall company is still thriving."

FURTHER INQUIRY

What Delphi is doing seems perfectly legal. But is it ethical? Check the current status of this case. Check also to find out what has happened with the Bayh/Conyers proposal in the Senate. Analyze Chapter 11 bankruptcies that have been recently reported in the business press. Look behind the headlines to check the strategy: Is bankruptcy being used to facilitate job shifting to overseas locations?

ANALYSIS OF ORGANIZATIONAL RESOURCES AND CAPABILITIES

■ A **SWOT analysis** examines organizational strengths and weaknesses and environmental opportunities and threats.

■ A **core competency** is a special strength that gives an organization a competitive advantage.

Given an understanding of mission, values, and objectives, the strategic management process next analyzes organization resources and capabilities. This is helped by a technique known as **SWOT analysis:** the internal analysis of organizational Strengths and Weaknesses as well as the external analysis of environmental Opportunities and Threats.

As shown in *Figure 9.3*, a SWOT analysis begins with a systematic evaluation of the organization's resources and capabilities. A major goal is to identify **core competencies** in the form of special strengths that the organization has or does exceptionally well in comparison with competitors. They are capabilities that by virtue of being rare, costly to imitate, and nonsubstitutable, become viable sources of competitive advantage.[33] Core competencies may be found in special knowledge or expertise, superior technologies, efficient manufacturing technologies, or unique product distribution systems, among many other possibilities.

Organizational weaknesses, of course, are the other side of the picture. They must also be identified to gain a realistic perspective on the formulation of strategies. The goal in strategy formulation is to create strategies that build upon organizational strengths and minimize the impact of weaknesses.

ANALYSIS OF INDUSTRY AND ENVIRONMENT

A SWOT analysis is not complete until opportunities and threats in the external environment are also analyzed. They can be found among *macroenvironmental* factors such as technology, government, social structures, population demographics, the global economy, and the natural environment. They can also include developments in the *industry environment* of resource suppliers, competitors, and customers.

As shown in *Figure 9.3*, opportunities may exist as possible new markets, a strong economy, weaknesses in competitors, and emerging technologies.

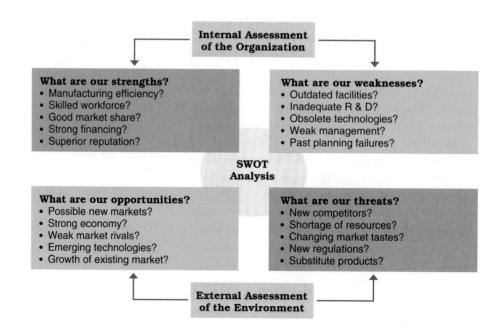

Figure 9.3 SWOT analysis of strengths, weaknesses, opportunities, and threats.

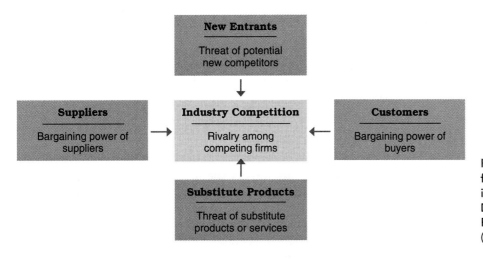

Figure 9.4 Porter's model of five strategic forces affecting industry competition. *Source:* Developed from Michael E. Porter, *Competitive Strategy* (New York: Free Press, 1980).

Weaknesses may be identified in such things as the emergence of new competitors, resource scarcities, changing customer tastes, and new government regulations, among other possibilities.

Scholar and consultant Michael Porter believes that the critical issue in the external environment is the nature of rivalry and competition within the industry. He offers the five forces model shown in *Figure 9.4* as a framework for competitive industry analysis.[34] The five strategic forces are:

1. *Competitors*—intensity of rivalry among firms in the industry.
2. *New entrants*—threats of new competitors entering the market.
3. *Suppliers*—bargaining power of suppliers.
4. *Customers*—bargaining power of buyers.
5. *Substitutes*—threats of substitute products or services.

From Porter's perspective, these competitive forces constitute the "industry structure." The strategic management challenge is to position an organization strategically within its industry, taking into account the implications of forces that make it more or less attractive.

In general, an *unattractive industry* is one in which rivalry among competitors is intense, substantial threats exist in the form of possible new entrants and substitute products, and suppliers and buyers are very powerful in bargaining over such things as prices and quality. An *attractive industry*, by contrast, has less existing competition, few threats from new entrants or substitutes, and low bargaining power among suppliers and buyers. By systematically analyzing industry attractiveness in respect to the five forces, Porter believes that strategies can be chosen to give the organization a competitive advantage relative to its rivals.

Be sure you can ■ differentiate between strategy formulation from strategy implementation ■ list the major components in the strategic management process ■ explain what a mission statement is and illustrate how a good mission statement helps organizations ■ list several operating objectives of organizations ■ define the term core competency ■ explain SWOT analysis ■ explain how Porter's five forces model can be used to assess the attractiveness of an industry

Learning Check 2

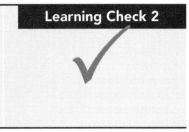

STRATEGIES USED BY ORGANIZATIONS

The strategic management process encompasses the three levels of strategy shown in *Figure 9.5*. Strategies are formulated and implemented at the organizational or corporate level, business level, and functional level.

LEVELS OF STRATEGY

▨ A **corporate strategy** sets long-term direction for the total enterprise.

The level of **corporate strategy** directs the organization as a whole toward sustainable competitive advantage. For a business it describes the scope of operations by answering the following *strategic question:* "In what industries and markets should we compete?" The purpose of corporate strategy is to set direction and guide resource allocations for the entire enterprise.

In large, complex organizations, corporate strategy identifies how the company intends to compete across multiple industries and markets. At General Electric, for example, the firm pursues global business interests in a wide variety of areas, including aircraft engines, appliances, capital services, lighting, medical systems, broadcasting, and power systems, among others. Typical strategic decisions at the corporate level relate to the allocation of resources for acquisitions, new business development, divestitures, and the like across this business portfolio.

▨ A **business strategy** identifies how a division or strategic business unit will compete in its product or service domain.

Business strategy is the strategy for a single business unit or product line. It describes strategic intent to compete within a specific industry or market. Large *conglomerates* like General Electric are composed of many businesses, with many differences among them in product lines and even industries. The term **strategic business unit (SBU)** is often used to describe a single business firm or a component that operates with a major business line within a larger enterprise. The selection of strategy at the business level involves answering this *strategic question:* "How are we going to compete for customers in this industry and market?" Typical business strategy decisions include choices about product/service mix, facilities locations, new technologies, and the like. In single-business enterprises, business strategy is the corporate strategy.

▨ A **functional strategy** guides activities within one specific area of operations.

Functional strategy guides the use of organizational resources to implement business strategy. This level of strategy focuses on activities within a specific functional area, such as marketing, manufacturing, finance, or human resources. The *strategic question* to be answered in selecting functional strategies is "How can we best utilize resources within a function to implement our business strategy?" Answers to this question typically

Figure 9.5 Three levels of strategy in organizations—corporate, business, and functional strategies.

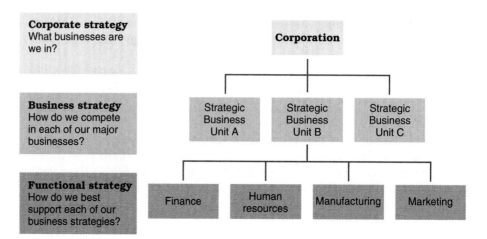

involve the choice of management practices within each function that improve operating efficiency, product or service quality, customer service, or innovativeness.

GROWTH AND DIVERSIFICATION STRATEGIES

One of the most common and popular of the grand or master strategies followed by organizations is growth.[35] **Growth strategies** pursue an increase in size and the expansion of current operations. They are popular in part because growth is viewed as necessary for long-run survival in some industries.

One approach to growth is through **concentration**, where expansion is within the same business area. McDonald's, Wal-Mart, Starbucks, and others are pursuing aggressive growth strategies while still concentrating on their primary business areas. And because of limits to growth in domestic markets, they are expanding globally into markets and countries around the world.

Growth can also be pursued through **diversification**, where expansion takes place through the acquisition of or investment in new and different business areas. A strategy of *related diversification* involves growth by acquiring new businesses or entering business areas that are related to what one already does. An example is the acquisition of Tropicana by PepsiCo. Although Tropicana specializes in fruit juices, the business is related to PepsiCo's expertise in the beverages industry. A strategy of *unrelated diversification* involves growth by acquiring businesses or entering business areas that are different from what one already does.

Diversification can also take the form of **vertical integration**, where a business acquires suppliers (*backward vertical integration*) or distributors (*forward vertical integration*). Backward vertical integration has been common in the automobile industry, as firms purchased suppliers to ensure quality and control over the availability of key parts. In beverages, both Coca-Cola and PepsiCo have pursued forward vertical integration by purchasing some of their major bottlers.

There is a tendency to equate growth with effectiveness, but that is not necessarily true. Any growth strategy, whether by concentration or some form of diversification, must be well planned and well managed to achieve the desired results. Increased size of operation in any form adds challenge to the management process. Diversification, in particular, brings the difficulties of complexity and the needs to manage and integrate dissimilar operations. Research indicates that business performance may decline with too much unrelated diversification.[36]

RESTRUCTURING AND DIVESTITURE STRATEGIES

When organizations are in trouble, perhaps experiencing problems brought about by difficulties managing growth, some sort of readjustment must be made. Among the master strategies used by organizations, a **retrenchment strategy** seeks to correct weaknesses by making changes to current ways of operating. The goal is most often to reverse or change an approach that isn't working and to reorganize to compete better in the future.

The most extreme form of retrenchment is *liquidation*, where business ceases and assets are sold to pay creditors. Less extreme and more common is **restructuring** of some sort. This involves making major changes to reduce the scale and/or mix of operations, with the twin goals of consolidating to gain short-term efficiencies and taking time to craft new strategies to improve future success.

■ A **growth strategy** involves expansion of the organization's current operations.

■ Growth through **concentration** is within the same business area.

■ Growth through **diversification** is by acquisition of or investment in new and different business areas.

■ Growth through **vertical integration** is by acquiring suppliers or distributors.

■ A **retrenchment strategy** changes operations to correct weaknesses.

■ **Restructuring** reduces the scale and/or mix of operations.

■ **Downsizing** decreases the size of operations.

Restructuring is sometimes accomplished by **downsizing** which decreases the size of operations.[37] The expected benefits are reduced costs and improved operating efficiency. A common way to downsize is to cut the size of the workforce. Research has shown that this is most successful when the workforce is reduced strategically or in a way that improves focus on key performance objectives.[38] Downsizing with a strategic focus is sometimes referred to as *rightsizing*. This contrasts with the less-well-regarded approach of simply cutting staff "across the board."

■ **Divestiture** sells off parts of the organization to refocus attention on core business areas.

Restructuring by **divestiture** involves selling off parts of the organization to refocus on core competencies, cut costs, and improve operating efficiency. This is a common strategy for organizations that find they have become overdiversified and are encountering problems managing too much complexity. It is also a way for organizations to take advantage of the value of internal assets by selling them off as independent business.

GLOBAL STRATEGIES

Very few businesses operate today without some exposure to and direct involvement in international operations. A key aspect of strategy, therefore, becomes how the firm approaches the global economy and its mix of business risks and opportunities. Very often, a grand or master strategy of growth is pursued with the support of an accompanying global strategy.[39]

An easy way to spot differences in global strategies is to notice how products are developed and advertised around the world. A firm pursuing a **globalization strategy** tends to view the world as one large market, trying as much as possible to standardize products and their advertising for use everywhere. Authority for major management decisions will largely reside with corporate headquarters. The latest Gillette razors, for example, are typically sold and advertised similarly around the world. This reflects a somewhat *ethnocentric view* that assumes that everyone everywhere wants the same thing that one has developed and sold successfully at home.

■ A **globalization strategy** adopts standardized products and advertising for use worldwide.

■ A **multidomestic strategy** customizes products and advertising to best fit local needs.

Firms using a **multidomestic strategy** try to customize products and their advertising as much as possible to fit the local needs of different countries or regions. They distribute authority for major decisions to local and area managers to provide this differentiation. This is a popular strategy for many consumer goods companies—Bristol Myers, Procter & Gamble, Unilever—that vary their products according to consumer preferences in different countries and cultures. This reflects a more *polycentric view*, one showing respect for both market diversity and the capabilities of locals to best interpret their strategic implications.

■ A **transnational strategy** seeks efficiencies of global operations with attention to local markets.

A third approach to international business is the **transnational strategy** that seeks balance among efficiencies in global operations and responsiveness to local markets. The *transnational firm*, first described in Chapter 5, tries to operate without a strong national identity and to blend with the global economy to fully tap its business potential. Material resources and human capital are acquired worldwide; manufacturing and other business functions are performed wherever in the world they can be done best at lowest cost. Ford, for example, draws upon design, manufacturing, and distribution expertise all over the world to build car "platforms" that can then be efficiently modified to meet regional tastes. Such a transnational strategy reflects a *geocentric view* that respects diversity and values talents around the world. Transnational firms typically operate in a highly networked way, with information and learning continually flowing between headquarters and subsidiaries, and among the subsidiaries themselves.

COOPERATIVE STRATEGIES

One of the trends today is toward more cooperation among organizations, such as the *joint ventures* that are a common form of international business. They are one among many forms of **strategic alliances** in which two or more organizations join together in partnership to pursue an area of mutual interest. One way to cooperate strategically is through *outsourcing alliances*, contracting to purchase important services from another organization. Many organizations today, for example, are outsourcing their IT function to firms like EDS, Infosys, and IBM in the belief that these services are better provided by a firm that specializes and maintains its expertise in this area. Cooperation in the supply chain also takes the form of *supplier alliances*, in which preferred supplier relationships guarantee a smooth and timely flow of quality supplies among alliance partners. Another common approach today is cooperation in *distribution alliances*, in which firms join together to accomplish product or services sales and distribution.

In a **strategic alliance** organizations join together in partnership to pursue an area of mutual interest.

The term often used to describe cooperation strategies that involve strategic alliances with competitors is **co-opetition**. Consistent with ideas raised in The Topic chapter opener, it applies to situations in which competitors work cooperatively with rivals on projects that can benefit both parties. It reflects what scholars M. Brandenburger and Barry J. Nalebuff call a "revolution mindset." The focus shifts from business only as competition to business as a playing field of both competitors and potential cooperating partners.[40] It is a shift of vision from business as a win–lose game with a fixed pie of possible returns, to a new one of collaboration to find ways of making the pie bigger for

Co-opetition is the strategy of working with rivals on projects of mutual benefit.

KAFFEEKLATSCH

Strategy Drivers

First Cup

"You can't win with strategy if you can't implement. It's just like sports—tennis, golf, soccer, or whatever. You need talented people who can execute the requirements of a strategy. People are the real strategy drivers. In fact, I'd argue that this firm could be a great success with just a 'good' strategy if it would only focus more on developing and promoting high-potential employees."

Studying the Grounds

■ A survey by the Corporate Leadership Council found that only 29 percent of all high-performing employees are high potentials, that is—ready to perform equally well at the next higher level.

■ High performers may not be high potential because they lack requisite abilities, are not highly engaged with the organization, and/or lack the aspiration for greater responsibilities.

Double Espresso

"This is really interesting. My guess is that our management doesn't differentiate between 'high performance'

with 'high potential.' We've got too many people not performing well in their jobs, and I'll bet it's because a lot of them were promoted out of their areas of competency. And you're also right on target with the point that you have to have talented people in place and performing on all cylinders if the firm is to fully succeed with any strategy."

Your Turn

Quite a few years ago Laurence J. Peter received a lot of publicity for a book called *the Peter Principle*. It stated that people rise in organizations until they reach their levels of incompetency; they are promoted beyond the point where they perform with any degree of excellence.

Maybe Peter had a valid point. Perhaps many organizations have people in positions of major responsibility not because they can do those jobs exceptionally well, but just because they did their prior jobs well. If that's the case, what does that say about their capacities for strategy implementation and high performance?

MANAGEMENT SMARTS 9.1

Web-based business models

- *Brokerage*—bringing buyers and sellers together to make transactions (e.g., CarsDirect.com).

- *Advertising*—providing information or services while generating revenue from advertising (e.g., Yahoo!).

- *Merchant model*—selling products wholesale and retail through the Web, e-tailing (e.g., Bluelight.com).

- *Subscription model*—selling access to a Web site through subscription (e.g., *Wall Street Journal* Interactive).

- *Infomediary model*—collecting information on users and selling it to other businesses (ePinions.com).

- *Community model*—supporting sites by donations from community of users (e.g., National Public Radio Online).

■ An **e-business strategy** strategically uses the Internet to gain competitive advantage.

■ A **B2B business strategy** uses IT and Web portals to link organizations vertically in supply chains.

■ A **B2C business strategy** uses IT and Web portals to link businesses with customers.

everyone. For example, Red Hat sells Linux software and so does IBM, but the two firms cooperate on aspects of Linux development. The idea is that better software creates a larger market for Linux that will benefit both firms.[41]

E-BUSINESS STRATEGIES

Without a doubt, one of the most frequently asked questions these days for the business executive is "What is your **e-business strategy**?" This is the strategic use of the Internet to gain competitive advantage (see *Management Smarts 9.1*).[42] Popular e-business strategies involve B2B (business-to-business) and B2C (business-to-customer) applications.

B2B business strategies use IT and Web portals to vertically link organizations with members of their supply chains. When Dell Computer sets up special Web site services that allow its major corporate customers to manage their accounts online, when Wal-Mart suppliers are linked to the firm's information systems and manage inventories for their own products electronically, and even when a business uses an online auction site to bid for supplies at the cheapest prices, they are utilizing B2B in various forms. B2B is the largest e-business component in the economy, and its benefits apply to large and small organizations alike.

Most of us probably are more aware of **B2C business strategies** that use IT and Web portals to link organizations with their customers. A common B2C strategy has already been illustrated several times in this book—*e-tailing*, or the sale of goods directly to customers via the Internet. But, importantly, there is more to success with B2C than simply having a Web site that advertises products for customer purchase. The B2C strategy must be fully integrated with supporting functional strategies and operations. Among the e-tailers, for example, Dell has set a benchmarking standard. Its easy-to-use Dell Web site allows customization of an individual's computer order, in effect offering a design-your-own-product capability. Then a highly efficient and streamlined manufacturing and distribution system takes over to build and quickly ship the computer.

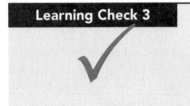

Learning Check 3

Be sure you can ■ differentiate the three levels of strategy—corporate, business, and functional ■ list and explain the major types of growth and diversification strategies, and restructuring and divestiture strategies ■ list and give examples of major global strategies ■ define the term strategic alliance and explain how cooperation is used as a business strategy ■ explain B2B and B2C as forms of e-business strategy

STRATEGY FORMULATION

Michael Porter says: "The company without a strategy is willing to try anything."[43] With a good strategy in place, by contrast, he believes the resources of the entire organization can be focused on achieving superior profitability or above-average returns. Whether one is talking about building e-business strategies for the new economy or crafting strategies for more traditional operations, Porter points attention toward these *opportunities for competitive advantage* in the strategy formulation process:

- *Cost and quality*—where strategy drives an emphasis on operating efficiency and/or product or service quality.
- *Knowledge and speed*—where strategy drives an emphasis on innovation and speed of delivery to market for new ideas.
- *Barriers to entry*—where strategy drives an emphasis on creating a market stronghold that is protected from entry by others.
- *Financial resources*—where strategy drives an emphasis on investments and/or loss sustainment that competitors can't match.

PORTER'S COMPETITIVE STRATEGIES

Within an industry, the strategic challenge becomes positioning one's firm and products relative to competitors. The strategy formulation question is "how can we best compete for customers in this industry?" Porter advises managers to answer this question by using the competitive strategies framework shown in *Figure 9.6.*[44]

According to Porter, business-level strategic decisions are driven by two basic factors: (1) *market scope*—ask: "How broad or narrow is your market or target market?" (2) *source of competitive advantage*—ask: "Will you compete for competitive advantage by lower price or product uniqueness?" As shown in the figure, these factors combine to create the following four strategies that organizations can pursue. The examples are of competitive positions within the soft-drink industry.

1. **Differentiation**—where the organization's resources and attention are directed toward making its products appear different from those of the competition (*example:* Coke, Pepsi).
2. **Cost leadership**—where the organization's resources and attention are directed toward minimizing costs to operate more efficiently than the competition (*example:* Big K Kola, discounter cola brands).
3. **Focused differentiation**—where the organization concentrates on one special market segment and tries to offer customers in that segment a unique product (*example:* A&W Root Beer, YooHoo).
4. **Focused cost leadership**—where the organization concentrates on one special market segment and tries in that segment to be the provider with lowest costs (*example:* Red Cherry Pop).

▨ A **focused differentiation** strategy offers a unique product to a special market segment.

▨ A **focused cost leadership** strategy seeks the lowest costs of operations within a special market segment.

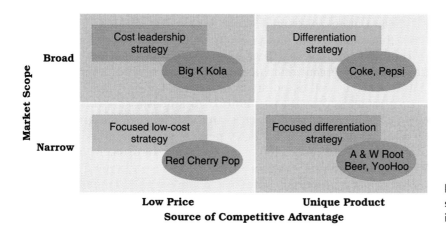

Figure 9.6 Porter's competitive strategies framework: soft-drink industry examples.

ISSUES AND SITUATIONS

Video Game Contrarian

You may be seeing less sex and gore in video games these days. The industry is broadening markets and responding to criticisms of its traditional product lines. It's moving from the violence of "Mortal Kombat" and sexual situations embedded in "Grand Theft Auto's" secret room into a new world of gaming options. And standing in the middle of the new direction is video game contrarian Will Wright. He was the originator of "Sim City", and co-creator of "The Sims," which has become a best seller. His latest is "Spore," in which players create their own whimsical creatures. To fully explore the possibilities, he says it would take "79 years if you never slept."

When Wright was a kid, his mother said he used to love to take things apart to see how they worked, including her sewing machine. As a game creator, however, he hasn't always had an easy time. After years of successes with follow-ups to "Sim City," he wanted to work on a new version based on people. An analyst said that executives of Electronic Arts, which by then owned Wright's original firm, "had a hard time communicating with Will." But Wright persevered even against internal opposition from the sales and marketing departments. At one point they forecast that "The Sims" would sell 400,000 units lifetime; 2 million shipped within 2 months of its publication.

Critical Response

Why has the video game industry been slow to move in new directions? Why would Will Wright experience such internal resistance to his idea for "The Sims"? Is it because customers already spend $7 billion per year buying traditional games, and this creates very little "edge" for the industry to change?

Now the facts are undeniable: younger people are shifting away from TV time to gaming time, more women are becoming regular gamers, and the average age of gamers is now up to 33. In an environment like this, no wonder the executives are shifting their strategies. But do we pay CEOs to be "followers," reaping the benefits of existing markets? Or do we pay them to be "strategic leaders" that move businesses toward new and profitable markets of the future?

■ A **differentiation strategy** offers products that are unique and different from the competition.

Organizations pursuing a **differentiation strategy** seek competitive advantage through uniqueness. They try to develop goods and services that are clearly different from the competition. The objective is to attract customers who become loyal to the organization's products and lose interest in those of competitors. This strategy requires organizational strengths in marketing, research and development, and creativity. Its success depends on continuing customer perceptions of product quality and uniqueness. An example in the apparel industry is Polo Ralph Lauren, retailer of upscale classic fashions and accessories. In Ralph Lauren's words, "Polo redefined how American style and quality is perceived. Polo has always been about selling quality products by creating worlds and inviting our customers to be part of our dream."[45]

■ A **cost leadership strategy** seeks to operate with lower costs than competitors.

Organizations pursuing a **cost leadership strategy** try to have lower costs than competitors and therefore achieve higher profits. The objective is to continuously improve the operating efficiencies of production, distribution, and other organizational systems. This requires tight cost and managerial controls as well as products that are easy to manufacture and distribute. In retailing, Wal-Mart aims to keep its costs so low that it can always offer customers the lowest prices and still make a reasonable profit. Most discounters operate with 18 to 20 percent gross margins. Wal-Mart can accept less and still make the same or higher returns. In financial services, Vanguard Group has succeeded with a strategy of keeping its costs low and therefore offering mutual funds to customers with minimum fees. Its Web site proudly proclaims that Vanguard is the industry leader in having the lowest average expense ratios.

Organizations pursuing focus strategies concentrate on a special market segment with the objective of serving its needs better than anyone else. The strategies focus organizational resources and expertise on a particular customer group, geographical region, or product or service line. They seek competitive advantage in that market segment through product differentiation or cost leadership. Low-fare airlines, for example, offer heavily discounted fares and "no frills" service. They focus on serving customers who want to travel point-to-point for the lowest prices. They profit by lowering their costs—for example, by flying to regional airports and limiting traditional free on-board services such as meals and drinks.

PORTFOLIO PLANNING

In a single-product or single-business firm, the strategic context is one industry. Corporate strategy and business strategy are the same, and resources are allocated on that basis. But when firms operate in multiple industries with many products or services, they become internally more complex and often larger in size. This makes resource allocation a more challenging strategic management task, since the mix of businesses must be well managed. The strategy problem is similar to that faced by an individual with limited money who must choose among alternative stocks, bonds, and real estate in a personal investment portfolio. In multibusiness situations, strategy formulation makes use of **portfolio planning** to help allocate scarce resources among competing uses.[46]

■ A **portfolio planning** approach seeks the best mix of investments among alternative business opportunities.

BCG Matrix

Figure 9.7 summarizes an approach to business portfolio planning developed by the Boston Consulting Group and known as the **BCG matrix**. This framework analyzes business opportunities according to industry or market growth rate and market share.[47] As shown in the figure, this comparison results in four possible business conditions, with each being associated with a strategic implication: (1) *stars*—high-market-share/high-growth businesses; (2) *cash cows*—high-market-share/low-growth businesses; (3) *question marks*—low-market-share/high-growth businesses; and (4) *dogs*—low-market-share/ low-growth businesses.

■ The **BCG matrix** analyzes business opportunities according to market growth rate and market share.

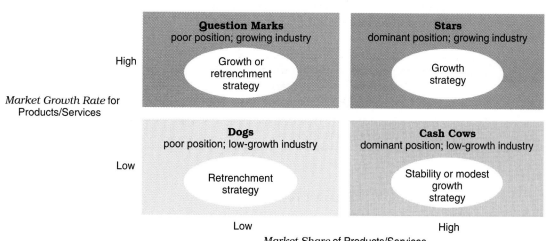

Figure 9.7 The BCG matrix approach to corporate strategy formulation.

Stars are high-market-share businesses in high-growth markets. They produce large profits through substantial penetration of expanding markets. The preferred strategy for stars is growth, and further resource investments in them are recommended.

Question marks are low-market-share businesses in high-growth markets. They do not produce much profit but compete in rapidly growing markets. They are the source of difficult strategic decisions. The preferred strategy is growth, but the risk exists that further investments will not result in improved market share. Only the most promising question marks should be targeted for growth; others are candidates for retrenchment by restructuring or divesititure.

Cash cows are high-market-share businesses in low-growth markets. They produce large profits and a strong cash flow. Because the markets offer little growth opportunity, the preferred strategy is stability or modest growth. "Cows" should be "milked" to generate cash that can be used to support investments in stars and question marks.

Dogs are low-market-share businesses in low-growth markets. They do not produce much profit, and they show little potential for future improvement. The preferred strategy for dogs is retrenchment by divestiture.

INCREMENTALISM AND EMERGENT STRATEGY

Not all strategies are created in systematic and deliberate fashion and then implemented step-by-step. Instead, strategies sometimes take shape, change, and develop over time as modest adjustments to past patterns. James Brian Quinn calls this a process of *incrementalism*, whereby modest and incremental changes in strategy occur as managers learn from experience and make adjustments.[48]

This approach has much in common with Henry Mintzberg's and John Kotter's descriptions of managerial behavior, as described in Chapter 1.[49] They view managers as planning and acting in complex interpersonal networks and in hectic, fast-paced work settings. Given these challenges, effective managers must have the capacity to stay focused on long-term objectives while still remaining flexible enough to master short-run problems and opportunities as they occur.

■ An **emergent strategy** develops over time as managers learn from and respond to experience.

Such reasoning has led Mintzberg to identify what he calls **emergent strategies**.[50] These are strategies that develop progressively over time as "streams" of decisions made by managers as they learn from and respond to work situations. There is an important element of "craftsmanship" here that Mintzberg worries may be overlooked by managers who choose and discard strategies in rapid succession while using the formal planning models. He also believes that incremental or emergent strategic planning allows managers and organizations to become really good at implementing strategies, not just at formulating them.

Learning Check 4

Be sure you can ■ explain the four competitive strategies in Porter's model ■ illustrate how these strategies apply to products in a market familiar to you ■ describe the BCG matrix for portfolio planning and use it to analyze strategic opportunities for a business ■ explain the concepts of incrementalism and emergent strategy

STRATEGY IMPLEMENTATION

No strategy, no matter how well formulated, can achieve long-term success if it is not properly implemented. This includes the willingness to exercise control and make modifications to meet the needs of changing conditions.

Current issues in strategy implementation include excellence in all management systems and practices, the responsibilities of corporate governance, and the importance of strategic leadership.

MANAGEMENT PRACTICES AND SYSTEMS

The rest of *Management 9/e* is really all about strategy implementation. In order to successfully put strategies into action, the entire organization and all of its resources must be mobilized in support of them. This, in effect, involves the complete management process from planning and controlling through organizing and leading.

No matter how well or elegantly selected, a strategy requires supporting structures, a good allocation of tasks and workflow designs, and the right people to staff all aspects of operations. The strategy needs to be enthusiastically

---

RESEARCH BRIEF

Female directors on corporate boards linked with positive management practices

A growing body of research is linking the composition of boards of directors with both the financial performance of the firms and their social responsibility behaviors. Building on prior studies, Richard Bernard, Susan Bosco, and Katie Vassill examined the gender diversity of board membership as an indicator of corporate social responsibility.

The research question guiding their article in *Business and Society* was: "Do firms listed in *Fortune's* '100 Best Companies to Work For' have a higher percentage of female directors than do *Fortune* 500 companies?" The researchers chose the "100 Best" listing because it includes firms whose employees consider them to have positive organizational cultures and supportive work practices. The evaluations were measured on a 225-item Great Place to Work Trust Index, sent to a random sample of employees in each company. Documentation of female board representatives was obtained by examining company annual reports.

Results confirmed expectations: the percentage of female directors was higher for firms on the "100 Best" list than for those in the *Fortune* 500 overall. In discussing the finding, the researchers suggest that gender diversity on boards of directors may bring about positive organizational changes that make firms better places to work. They also cite the growing presence of women on corporate boards as evidence that firms are changing board memberships to be "more representative of its employee and customer pools."

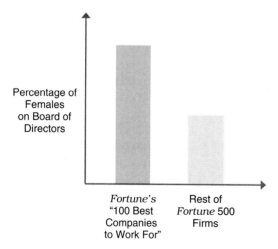

QUESTIONS & APPLICATIONS

Why would the presence of more female directors on a board of directors be causally linked to better corporate social performance? Does board diversity, including minorities and women, lead to different agendas, deliberations, concerns, and strategies? Does it lead to better strategy implementation through greater employee involvement and loyalty?

This study looked at gender diversity at the highest level of corporate leadership—membership on boards of directors. Look at organizations with which you are familiar. Can you see where greater membership diversity in general, not just at the top, makes a difference in the way an organization performs?

Reference: Richard A. Vernardi, Susan M. Bosco, and Katie M. Vassill, "Does Female Representation on Boards of Directors Associate with *Fortune's* '100 Best Companies to Work For' List? *Business and Society*, vol. 45 (June 2006), pp. 235–248.

supported by leaders who are capable of motivating everyone, building individual performance commitments, and utilizing teams and teamwork to their best advantage. And the strategy needs to be well and continually communicated to all relevant persons and parties. Only with such total system support for implementation can strategies succeed in today's challenging and highly competitive environments.

Two types of failures often hinder strategy implementation. *Failures of substance* reflect inadequate attention to the major strategic planning elements—analysis of mission and purpose, core values and corporate culture, organizational strengths and weaknesses, and environmental opportunities and threats. *Failures of process* reflect poor handling of the ways in which the various aspects of strategic planning were accomplished.

An important process failure is the *lack of participation error*. This is failure to include key persons in the strategic planning effort.[51] As a result, they lack commitment to all-important action and follow-through. Process failure also occurs with too much centralization of planning in top management, or too much delegation to staff planners or separate planning departments. Another process failure is the tendency to get so bogged down in details that the planning process becomes an end in itself, instead of a means to an end. This is sometimes called "goal displacement."

CORPORATE GOVERNANCE

■ **Corporate governance** is the system of control and performance monitoring of top management.

As was discussed in Chapter 2 on ethics and social responsibility, organizations today are experiencing new pressures at the level of **corporate governance.** This is the system of control and monitoring of top management performance that is exercised by boards of directors and other major stakeholder representatives.

In businesses, members of a board of directors are expected to make sure that an organization operates in the best interests of its owners and that the strategic management of the enterprise is successful.[52] But boards may sometimes be too compliant in endorsing or confirming the strategic initiatives of top management. Governance controversies sometimes arise over the role of *inside directors*, who are chosen from the senior management of the organization, and *outside directors*, who are chosen from other organizations and positions external to the organization. In some cases insiders may have too much control; in others the outsiders may be selected because they are friends of top management or at least sympathetic to them.

The current trend is toward greater emphasis on the responsibilities of corporate governance. Top managers probably feel more performance accountability today than ever before to boards of directors and other stakeholder interest groups. At General Electric, for example, CEO Jeffrey Immelt makes it a practice to absent himself at times from director's meetings.[53] His predecessor, Jack Welch, always wanted to be present when directors met, but Immelt believes differently. His practice helps ensure that the governance responsibilities of the board, including oversight of the CEO's decisions and actions, are independently exercised.

STRATEGIC LEADERSHIP

■ **Strategic leadership** inspires people to continuously change, refine, and improve strategies and their implementation.

Effective strategy implementation depends on the full commitment of all managers to support and lead strategic initiatives within their areas of supervisory responsibility. In our dynamic and often-uncertain environment, the premium is on **strategic leadership**—the capability to inspire people to successfully engage in a process of continuous change, performance en-hancement, and implementation of organizational strategies.[54]

Porter argues that the CEO of a business has to be the chief strategist, someone who provides strategic leadership.[55] He describes the task in the following ways.

A strategic leader has to be the *guardian of trade-offs*. It is the leader's job to make sure that the organization's resources are allocated in ways con-sistent with the strategy. This requires the discipline to sort through many competing ideas and alternatives to stay on course and not get sidetracked. A strategic leader also needs to *create a sense of urgency*, not allowing the organization and its members to grow slow and complacent. Even when do-ing well, the leader keeps the focus on getting better and being alert to con-ditions that require adjustments to the strategy.

A strategic leader needs to *make sure that everyone understands the strategy*. Unless strategies are understood, the daily tasks and contributions of people lose context and purpose. Everyone might work very hard, but without alignment to strategy the impact is dispersed and fails to advance common goals. Importantly, a strategic leader must *be a teacher*. It is the leader's job to teach the strategy and make it a "cause," says Porter. In order for strategy to work, it must become an ever-present commitment through-out the organization. This means that a strategic leader must *be a great communicator*. Everyone must under-stand the strategy and how it makes their organization different from others.

To Porter's list, Michael Dell, founder and chairman of Dell Computer, might add a final point: A strategic leader must *be a team player*. He began the firm in 1984 with $1,000, selling computers out of his dormi-tory room in college. It now has billions in world-wide sales and over 75,000 employees. He was the youngest CEO to lead a Fortune 500 company, and is also on record as an advocate of top management teams. He also believes that Dell's team is up to the challenge. "We bounce ideas off one another," he says, "and at the end of the day if we say 'who did this?' the only right answer is that we all did. Three heads are better than one."[56]

Be sure you can ■ explain how the management process supports strategy implementation ■ define the term corporate governance ■ explain why boards of directors sometimes fail in their governance responsibilities ■ define the term strategic leadership ■ list the responsibilities of a strategic leader in today's organizations

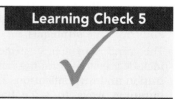

Learning Check 5

CHAPTER 9 STUDY GUIDE

STUDY QUESTIONS SUMMARY

1 What are the foundations of strategic competitiveness?

- Competitive advantage is achieved by operating in ways that allow an organization to outperform its rivals; a competitive advantage is sustainable when it is difficult for competitors to imitate.
- A strategy is a comprehensive plan that sets long-term direction and guides resource allocation for sustainable competitive advantage.
- Strategic intent directs organizational resources and energies toward a compelling goal.

2 What is the strategic management process?

- Strategic management is the process of formulating and implementing strategies that achieve goals in a competitive environment.
- The strategic management process begins with analysis of mission, clarification of core values, and identification of objectives.
- A SWOT analysis systematically assesses organizational resources and capabilities and environmental opportunities and threats.
- Porter's five forces model analyzes industry attractiveness in terms of competititors, new entrants, substitute products, and the bargaining powers of suppliers and buyers.

3 What types of strategies are used by organizations?

- Corporate strategy sets direction for an entire organization; business strategy sets direction for a business division or product/service line; functional strategy sets direction for the operational support of business and corporate strategies.
- The grand or master strategies used by organizations include growth—pursuing expansion through concentration and diversification, and also retrenchment—pursuing ways to scale back operations through restructuring and divestiture.

- Global strategies take advantage of international business opportunities; cooperative strategies use strategic alliances and co-opetition as pathways to performance gains.
- E-business strategies use information technology and the Internet to pursue competitive advantage in business to business and business-to-customer transactions.

4 How are strategies formulated?

- Porter's model of competitive strategy includes: differentiation—distinguishing one's products from the competition; cost leadership—minimizing costs relative to the competition; and focus—concentrating on a special market segment.
- The BCG matrix is a portfolio planning approach that classifies businesses or product lines as "stars," "cash cows," "question marks," or "dogs."
- The incremental or emergent model recognizes that many strategies are formulated and implemented incrementally over time.

5 What are current issues in strategy implementation?

- Management practices and systems—including the functions of planning, organizing, leading, and controlling—must be mobilized to support strategy implementation.
- Pitfalls that inhibit strategy implementation include failures of substance—such as poor analysis of the environment, and failures of process—such as lack of participation in the planning process.
- Boards of directors play important roles in corporate governance, including monitoring top management and how well it fulfills strategic management responsibilities.
- Strategic leadership inspires the process of continuous evaluation and improvement of strategies and their implementation.

KEY TERMS REVIEW

SELF-TEST 9

MULTIPLE-CHOICE QUESTIONS:

1. The most appropriate first question to ask in strategic planning is _____.

   (a) "Where do we want to be in the future?" (b) "How well are we currently doing?" (c) "How can we get where we want to be?" (d) "Why aren't we doing better?"

2. The ability of a firm to consistently outperform its rivals is called _____.

   (a) vertical integration (b) competitive advantage (c) incrementalism (d) strategic intent

3. In a complex conglomerate business such as General Electric, a(n) _____ -level strategy sets strategic direction for a strategic business unit or product division.

   (a) institutional (b) corporate (c) business (d) functional

4. An organization that is downsizing to reduce costs is implementing a grand strategy of _____.

   (a) growth (b) cost differentiation (c) retrenchment (d) stability

5. The _____ is a predominant value system for an organization as a whole.

   (a) strategy (b) core competency (c) mission (d) corporate culture

6. A _____ in the BCG matrix would have a high market share in a low-growth market.

   (a) dog (b) cash cow (c) question mark (d) star

7. In Porter's five forces framework, which of the following increases industry attractiveness?

   (a) many rivals (b) many substitute products (c) low bargaining power of suppliers (d) few barriers to entry

8. When PepsiCo acquired Tropicana, a maker of orange juice, the firm's strategy was one of _____.

   (a) related diversification (b) concentration (c) vertical integration (d) cooperation

9. Cost efficiency and product quality are two examples of _____ objectives of organizations.

   (a) official (b) operating (c) informal (d) institutional

10. Restructuring by downsizing operations and reducing staff is a form of _____ strategy.

    (a) retrenchment (b) growth (c) concentration (d) incremental

11. Among the global strategies that might be pursued by international businesses, the _____ strategy is the most targeted on local needs, local management, and local products.

    (a) ethnocentric (b) transnational (c) geocentric (d) multidomestic

12. According to Porter's model of competitive strategies, a firm that wants to compete with its rivals in a broad market by selling a very low-priced product would need to succesfully implement a _____ strategy.

    (a) retrenchment (b) differentiation (c) cost leadership (d) diversification

13. When Coke and Pepsi spend millions on ads trying to convince customer that their products are unique, they are pursuing a/an _____ strategy.

    (a) transnational   (b) concentrate   (c) diversification   (d) differentiation

14. The role of the board of directors as an oversight body that holds top executives accountable for the success of business strategies is called _____.

    (a) strategic leadership (b) corporate governance (c) logical incrementalism (d) strategic opportunism

15. An example of a process failure in strategic planning is _____.

    (a) lack of participation (b) poorly worded mission (c) incorrect core values (d) insufficient financial resources

SHORT-RESPONSE QUESTIONS:

16. What is the difference between corporate strategy and functional strategy?

17. What would a manager look at in a SWOT analysis?

18. Explain the differences between B2B and B2C as e-business strategies.

19. What is strategic leadership?

APPLICATION QUESTION:

20. Kim Harris owns and operates a small retail store selling the outdoor clothing of an American manufacturer to a predominately college-student market. Lately, a large department store outside of town has started selling similar but lower-priced clothing manufactured in China, Thailand, and Bangladesh. Kim believes he is starting to lose business to this store. Assume you are part of a student team assigned to do a management class project for Kim. His question for the team is "How can I best deal with my strategic management challenges in this situation?" How will you reply?

CHAPTER 9 APPLICATIONS

CASE 9

Dunkin' Donuts: Westward Pioneers

Once a niche company operating in the northeast, Dunkin' Donuts is on a hearty wave of expansion, opening hundreds of stores and entering new markets. At the same time, the java giant is broadly expanding both its food and coffee menus to catch the momentum of fresh trends and appeal to a new generation of customers. But is the rest of America ready for Dunkin' Donuts? And can the company keep up with its own rapid growth?

Serving the caffeinated masses nets more than change in the tip jar. Some 400 billion cups of coffee are consumed every year, making it the most popular beverage worldwide. Closer to home, estimates indicate that more than 100 million Americans drink a total of 350 million cups of coffee a day.[56a]

Blame it on Starbucks. In the 1990s, the "green giant" aggressively brought the promise of upscale coffee to the marketplace. These days some customers may wonder whether any coffee vendors remember the days when drip coffee came in only two varieties—regular and decaf.

Dunkin' Donuts does. And it's betting dollars to doughnuts that consumers nationwide will embrace its reputation for value, simplicity, and a superior Boston Kreme Donut.

Winning New Customers

Most of America has had an occasional relationship with the Dunkin' Donuts brand. The company currently has more than 4,000 domestic outlets, with the densest cluster in the Northeast and sporadic presence in the rest of the country.[57] Yet the brand has managed to carve out an international niche (in some markets you might expect—Canada and Brazil—and in some you might not—Qatar, South Korea, Pakistan, and the Philippines, among others).[58]

If the company has its way, you probably won't have to go very far to pick up a box of doughnuts. The retailer wants to establish a large-scale presence outside the Northeast to gain national competitive advantage. It is expanding rapidly into New York and Ohio and down the East Coast.

"We're [currently] only represented large-scale in the Northeastern market," said Jayne Fitzpatrick, strategy officer for Dunkin' Brands, adding that Dunkin' Donuts plans to expand "as aggressively" as possible. "We're able to do that because we're a franchise system, so access to operators and capital is easier," she said.[59]

How aggressively? According to John Fassak, vice president of business development for Dunkin' Donuts, the company plans to expand to have 15,000 outlets by 2020. Current targets include: 150 new stores in Washington, D.C. and Baltimore, and 60 new units in Charlotte, North Carolina.[60]

What Would Consumers Think?

None of Dunkin' Donuts' strategies make much of a difference unless consumers buy into the notion that the company has the culinary imperative to sell more than its name suggests. If its plans prove successful, more customers than ever may flock to indulge in the company's breakfast-to-go menu.

On the other hand, the only thing potentially worse for Dunkin' Donuts than diluted coffee is a diluted brand image. At more than 50 years old, the company has a reputation for doing two things simply and successfully—coffee and donuts. As consumers see the line of products expand into what was once solely the realm of Dunkin' Donuts' competitors, they may be unsure whether Dunkin' Donuts is *the* shop to go to for breakfast.

For most of its existence, Dunkin' Donuts' main product focus has been implicit in its name: donuts and coffee in which to dip them. Acquainted with this simple reputation, first-time customers were often overwhelmed by the wide varieties of doughnuts stacked end-to-end in neat, mouthwatering rows. Playing catch-up to the rest of the morning market, Dunkin' Donuts got into the breakfast sandwich game in 1997.[61]

According to spokesperson Andrew Mastroangelo, Dunkin' Donuts sells approximately one billion cups of coffee a year, accounting for 62 percent of the company's annual store revenue.[62] Considering that coffee is the most profitable product on the menu, it's a good bet that those margins give the company room to experiment with its food offerings.

Changing Course to Follow Demand

Faced with the challenge of maintaining a relevant brand image in spite of fierce and innovative competition, Dunkin' Donuts pursued a time-honored business tradition—it followed the leader. The company now offers a competitive variety of espresso-based drinks in a number of flavors, such as Caramel, Vanilla, and Mocha Swirl.[63]

Given the ever-increasing competition in the morning meal market, an update to Dunkin' Donuts' food selection was inevitable. Like its competitors, it offers several permutations of eggs, cheese, and choices of meat. The company distinguishes itself by offering a wider choice of bread products upon which to build its sandwiches: biscuits, croissants, English muffins, and bagels.

On Every Corner, and on Every Other Corner

Starbucks is known for its aggressive dominance of the coffee marketplace. When a competitor opens a new store in town, Starbucks doesn't worry. It just opens a new store across the street. This pattern of vigorous one-upmanship simultaneously conquers new ground and deters competitors. But many who have gone up against Starbucks did so with limited resources or with only a few franchises.

Not so with Dunkin' Donuts, whose parent company, the food and beverage giant Allied Domecq (recently acquired by Pernod Ricard), also owns Baskin-Robbins and Togo's Sandwiches. This David might just have the muscle power and strategy necessary to take on the "Green Goliath."

Cooperative Partnerships

Although much of Dunkin' Donuts' growth is planned to occupy new, freestanding retail spaces, the brand clearly recognizes the strategic value of partnerships. It has secured mutually beneficial relationships with a number of host stores, such as Stop & Shop and Wal-Mart. In such situations, Dunkin' Donuts sets up a small full-service outlet within a larger retailer's space. This synergy cuts costs and enhances traffic for both companies.

Simple Food for Simple People

With a history of offering simple and straightforward morning snacks, Dunkin' Donuts has the competitive advantage of distinguishing itself as *the* anti-Starbucks: earnest and without pretense. Like Craftsman tools and Levi's jeans, the company serves the everyman with a comforting, Yankee sensibility that appeals to simple, modest, and frugal customers alike.

It's also distinctive for a company to limit itself to serving breakfast. When you consider that Dunkin' Donuts doesn't limit its morning fare to the wee early hours—its breakfast sandwiches are available throughout the day—it becomes apparent that if you're looking for lunch or dinner, Dunkin' Donuts would be perfectly happy to point you elsewhere . . . such as to Togo's.

The Sweet Spot Has a Jelly Center

In adopting these strategies, Dunkin' Donuts is trying to grow in all directions—to reach more customers in more places with more products. According to Fassak, achieving proper retail placement can be a delicate balance. For instance, Dunkin' Donuts won't put an outlet into just any grocery store. "We want to be situated in supermarkets that provide a superior overall customer experience," he said.

Fassak added, "Of course, we also want to ensure that the supermarket is large enough to allow us to provide the full expression of our brand, . . . which includes hot and iced coffee, our line of high-quality espresso beverages, doughnuts, bagels, muffins, and even our breakfast sandwiches."

Furthermore, the outlet's location within the supermarket is critical for a successful relationship. "We want to be accessible and visible to customers because we feel that gives us the best chance to increase incremental traffic and help the supermarket to enhance their overall performance," Fassak said.

The company is banking on these mutually beneficial partnerships with supermarkets and noncompeting food merchants to help them achieve widespread prominence in the marketplace. Despite its concentration in the Northeast, Dunkin' Donuts is a nationally known brand with a long reputation for quality, and so the company has had the benefit of not having to work as hard to earn many customers' trust.

If Dunkin' Donuts could find that sweet spot of being within most consumers' reach while falling just short of becoming Big Brother—in a word, omnipresence—the company's strategy of westward expansion could very well reward it handsomely.

This strategy is not without its risks. In its quest to appeal to new customers, offering too many original products could dilute the essential brand appeal and alienate long-time customers who respected the company's simplicity and authenticity. Conversely, new customers previously unexposed to Dunkin' Donuts might see it as "yesterday's brand."

If Dunkin' Donuts' executives are too focused on rolling out new stores, they might not be aware of developing issues in existing or recently established stores. Some older franchises are long overdue for a makeover, especially when compared with the Starbucks down the block.

For the time being, however, Dunkin' Donuts seems happy to progress with its methodical quest for continental domination of the coffee and breakfast market. To keep up with the latest health concerns, it has reformulated its cookies and muffins to avoid trans fats. The company has even begun shifting its donut production from the individual stores into centralized production facilities, intended to serve up to 100 stores each. But Starbucks will not be the kind of company to take such a challenge lying down. Will Dunkin' Donuts have the right mix of products and placement to mount a formidable challenge in both the breakfast and coffee markets? There's only one way to be sure: have a Boston Kreme and see for yourself!

REVIEW QUESTIONS

1. Is Dunkin' Donuts' "follow the leader" approach the best way to succeed when a firm faces a dominating competitor like Starbucks?

2. By widening the scope of its coffee and breakfast offerings, is Dunkin' Donuts straying too far from its longstanding brand image?

3. Dunkin' Donuts is pursuing strategic alliances with retailers like Wal-Mart and grocers like Stop & Shop. Can you think of other strategic alliances that might benefit Dunkin' Donuts's growth strategy?

TEAM PROJECT

Contrasting Strategies

Starbucks is the dominant name among coffee kiosks; how does Dunkin Donuts compete? Google has become the world's search engine of choice, can Yahoo ever catch up? Does it make a difference to you whether you shop at a Borders or Barnes & Noble bookstore, or buy gasoline from BP, Shell, or the local convenience store?

Question: How do organizations in the same industry fare when they pursue somewhat or very different strategies?

Research Directions:

■ Look up recent news reports and analyst summaries for each of the following organizations:

■ Coach and Kate Spade

■ Southwest Airlines and Delta Airlines

- *New York Times* and *USA Today*
- Electronic Arts and Take 2 Interactive
- National Public Radio and Sirius
- Coca-Cola and PepsiCo

■ Use this information to write a short description of the strategies that each seem to be following in the quest for performance success.

■ Compare the strategies for each organizational pair, with the goal of identifying whether or not one organization has a strategic advantage in the industry.

■ Try to identify other pairs of organizations and do similar strategic comparisons for them.

■ Prepare a summary report highlighting (1) the strategy comparisons and (2) those organizations whose strategies seem best positioned for competitive advantage.

PERSONAL MANAGEMENT

Critical Thinking

CRITICAL THINKING is essential for executive leadership success. It is an analytical skill that involves the ability to gather and interpret information for decision making in a problem context. A good way to develop critical thinking skills is through case studies and problem-solving projects in your courses. But beware, one of the risks of our information-rich environment is over-reliance on what we hear or read—especially when it comes from the Web. A lot of what circulates is anecdotal, superficial, irrelevant, and even just plain inaccurate. You must be disciplined, cautious, and discerning in interpreting the credibility and usefulness of any information you retrieve. Whether you are talking about searching the Web, talking with others, listening to presentations, or browsing reports and other information sources, critical thinking demands more than the ability to read and hear. Accessing information is one thing; sorting through it to identify what is solid and what is weak or pure nonsense is another; determining what information is useful in a specific problem context is another; analyzing and integrating useful information for solid problem solving is yet another. Once you understand this and are willing to invest the time for critical thinking, the Web offers a world of opportunities.

Building the brand called "You"   Consider your personal career strategy: how well prepared are you to succeed in the *future* job market, not just the present one? At the *U.S. Bureau of Labor Statistics* Web site you can find the latest data on unemployment, productivity, and the economies of states, regions, and major metropolitan areas. The site also offers an up-to-date *Career Guide to Industries*. Take a look and practice information gathering for critical thinking about your career.

NEXT STEPS: MANAGEMENT LEARNING WORKBOOK

Self-Assessments
- A 21st-century Manager? (#1)
- Facts and Inferences (#14)
- Empowering Others (#15)
- Turbulence Tolerance Test (#16)

Experiential Exercises
- Personal Career Planning (#10)
- Decision-Making Bases (#11)
- Strategic Scenarios (#14)
- The Future Workplace (#15)

Organizing Structures and Designs

10

Not Too Small, Not Too Big

It used to be that having a large company was a sign of corporate accomplishment. But lately, it's gone the other way—having a lean, pared-down workforce is a sign of efficiency and effective planning. Why is bigger no longer better?

Q: What do effective management and baking the perfect cake have in common?

A: They're both about having the right number of layers.

It's a banal joke, plucked from the note cards of a forgettable speech by a corny executive. But before you dismiss this trite morsel, consider the bite of wisdom that might lie within.

One of the greatest challenges faced by management establishing a new company, or taking a hard look at an existing one, is determining the optimum number of management levels. Too few, and the company won't have enough discrete levels of supervision to adequately divide the workload. Too many, and the costs of inefficiency will tip the company's balance sheet.

One company that has successfully achieved such a balance of management is Nucor. This North Carolina-based steel producer has an unusual management hierarchy for the manufacturing industry, in that it's extremely compact.

What *They* Think

"An overly centralized company is slow, bureaucratic, out of touch with their local markets, and overly hierarchical. An overly decentralized organization is chaotic, lacking any consistency, exceptionally inefficient, and prone to silo-thinking and fragmentation."
Peter Topping, EmeryLeadership.org.

STREAMLINED: *"We want as few management layers as possible, so that executives are very close to the operations."*
Carlos Slim Helu, Mexican businessman and third-richest man in the world.

SUPERSIZED: *"When the size of an executive's pay is determined by how big the business is—instead of how well it is performing economically or meeting customer needs—unwise expansion is seldom far behind."*
Bob Tomasko, management consultant and author of Bigger Isn't Always Better.

At Nucor, hourly employees are separated from CEO Dan DiMicco by just a few layers of management. So if an employee has a suggestion or grievance, they do not have to pursue appeals with multiple levels of management in order for their concern to be heard. And because workers do not have to wade through the bureaucracy required at other businesses, they find that their needs are addressed much faster, which makes for a happier, more productive workforce.[1]

Nucor managers, too, benefit from the reduced hierarchy. Because the company is highly decentralized, individual managers have the freedom to make decisions about issues that directly affect their workers without seeking approval from several layers of management. In fact, one of Nucor's four principles of employee relations states that, "Management is obligated to manage Nucor in such a way that employees will have the opportunity to earn according to their productivity."

Employee productivity and satisfaction is so important to Nucor that its managers have been given the mandate to make the decisions necessary to keep productivity high. In this sprit, general managers (who report to the president) have the autonomy to run their facilities as independent businesses.[2]

There's no simple balance, according to Peter Topping of EmoryLeadership.org. "An overly centralized company is slow, bureaucratic, out to touch with their local markets, and overly hierarchical," Topping wrote. "An overly decentralized organization is chaotic, lacking any consistency, exceptionally inefficient, and prone to silo-thinking and fragmentation."[3]

Compare Nucor's experience with that of other, more successful corporations. After relying for years on original sales or marketing offices, both State Farm and Procter & Gamble reorganized their management structures to bring the majority of their employees closer to their world headquarters (Bloomington, Illinois, and Cincinnati, Ohio, respectively). Both companies believed that a centralized, hands-on approach to internal management would benefit the organization while cutting costs. Given the continued success of each company, it's hard to disagree with their decisions.

Just as with athletes, it seems, the healthiest companies are also the leanest. And in today's competitive business environment, you can bet that this trend for "fitness" is one craze that won't go away.

The Numbers

America's Top Employers

Company	Employees
1. Wal-Mart	1,800,000
2. McDonald's	447,000
3. United Parcel Service	407,000
4. Sears Holdings	355,000
5. Home Depot	345,000
6. Target	337,000
7. IBM	329,373
8. General Motors	327,000
9. General Electric	316,000
10. Citigroup	303,000

Quick Facts

* 85 percent of manufacturing companies surveyed indicate they are implementing, have implemented, or plan to implement lean manufacturing.[4]
* Taiichi Ohno, pioneer of the ultra-efficient Toyota Production System, credits Henry Ford as his inspiration.[5]
* Nucor CEO Dan DiMicco says one of the biggest worries is China subsidizing its steel industry.[6]
* China produces almost 1/3 of the world's steel; Japan and the United States rank 2 and 3, respectively.[7]
* Over 66% of global steel production relies on coal.[8a]
* Steel is 100% recyclable.[8b]

What Do *You* Think?

1. Consider the organization of your college or university. Is it is more streamlined or supersized?

2. Are there any potential downsides to Nucor's "simple, streamlined organizational structure?"

Organizing Structures and Designs			
Study Question 1	**Study Question 2**	**Study Question 3**	**Study Question 4**
Organizing as a Management Function	**Traditional Organization Structures**	**Newer Organization Structures**	**Organizational Designs**
■ What is organization structure? ■ Formal structures ■ Informal structures	■ Functional structures ■ Divisional structures ■ Matrix structures	■ Team structures ■ Network structures ■ Boundaryless organizations	■ Mechanistic and organic designs ■ Subsystems design and integration ■ Trends toward horizontal organizations
Learning Check 1	**Learning Check 2**	**Learning Check 3**	**Learning Check 4**

M anagement scholar and consultant Henry Mintzberg points out that as organizations change fast in today's world, people within them are struggling to find their places.[9] One of his points is that people need to understand how their organizations work if they are to work well within them. Mintzberg notes some common questions: "What parts connect to one another?" "How should processes and people come together?" "Whose ideas have to flow where?" These and related questions raise critical issues about organization structures and how well they meet an organization's performance needs.

ORGANIZING AS A MANAGEMENT FUNCTION

■ **Organizing** arranges people and resources to work toward a goal.

Organizing is the process of arranging people and other resources to work together to accomplish a goal. As one of the basic functions of management, it involves both creating a division of labor for tasks to be performed and then coordinating results to achieve a common purpose.

Figure 10.1 shows the central role that organizing plays in the management process. Once plans are created, the manager's task is to see to

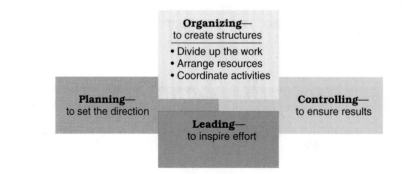

Figure 10.1 Organizing viewed in relationship with the other management functions.

it they are carried out. Given a clear mission, core values, objectives, and strategy, *organizing* begins the process of implementation by clarifying jobs and working relationships. It identifies who is to do what, who is in charge of whom, and how different people and parts of the organization relate to and work with one another. All of this, of course, can be done in different ways. The strategic leadership challenge is to choose the best organizational form to fit the strategy and other situational demands.

WHAT IS ORGANIZATION STRUCTURE?

The way in which the various parts of an organization are formally arranged is usually referred to as the **organization structure**. It is the system of tasks, workflows, reporting relationships, and communication channels that link together the work of diverse individuals and groups. Any structure should both allocate tasks through a division of labor and provide for the coordination of performance results. A structure that does both of these things well is an important asset, helping to implement an organization's strategy.[10] Unfortunately, it is easier to talk about good structures than it is to actually create them. This is why you often read and hear about organizations changing their structures in an attempt to improve performance.

■ **Organization structure** is a system of tasks, reporting relationships, and communication linkages.

FORMAL STRUCTURES

You may know the concept of structure best in the form of an **organization chart**. This is a diagram that shows reporting relationships and the formal arrangement of work positions within an organization.[11] A typical organization chart identifies various positions and job titles as well as the lines of authority and communication between them. It shows the **formal structure**, or the structure of the organization in its official state. This is how the organization is intended to function. By reading an organization chart, you can learn the basics of an organization's formal structure, including

■ An **organization chart** describes the arrangement of work positions within an organization.

■ **Formal structure** is the official structure of the organization.

- *Division of work:* Positions and titles show work responsibilities.
- *Supervisory relationships:* Lines show who reports to whom.
- *Communication channels:* Lines show formal communication flows.
- *Major subunits:* Positions reporting to a common manager are shown.
- *Levels of management:* Vertical layers of management are shown.

INFORMAL STRUCTURES

Behind every formal structure typically lies an **informal structure**. This is a "shadow" organization made up of the unofficial, but often critical, working relationships between organizational members. If the informal structure could be drawn, it would show who talks to and interacts regularly with whom regardless of their formal titles and relationships. The lines of the informal structure would cut across levels and move from side to side. They would show people meeting for coffee, in exercise groups, and in frendship cliques, among other possibilities. Importantly, no organization can be fully understood without gaining insight into the informal structure as well as the formal one.[12]

■ **Informal structure** is the set of unofficial relationships among an organization's members.

Informal structures can be very helpful in getting work accomplished. Indeed, they may be essential in many ways to organizational success. This is especially true during times of change, when out-of-date formal structures may fail to provide the support people need to deal with new or unusual situations. Because it takes time to change or modify formal structures, the informal structure helps fill the void.

People benefit from the emergent and spontaneous relationships of informal structures. The emergent and spontaneous relationships of informal structures. They make contacts with others who can help them get things done when necessary. They gain the advantages of *informal learning* that takes place while working and interacting together throughout the workday. Informal structures are also helpful in giving people access to emotional support and friendship that satisfy important social needs.

Of course, informal structures also have potential disadvantages. Because they exist outside the formal authority system, informal structures can sometimes work against the best interests of the organization as a whole. They can be susceptible to rumor, carry inaccurate information, breed resistance to change, and even divert work efforts from important objectives. Also, "outsiders" or people who are left out of informal groupings may feel less a part of daily activities and become dissatisfied. Some American managers of Japanese firms, for example, have complained about being excluded from what they call the "shadow cabinet"—an informal group of Japanese executives who hold the real power to get things done and sometimes act to the exclusion of others."[13]

Learning Check 1

Be sure you can ■ define organizing as a management function ■ explain the difference between formal and informal structures ■ discuss the potential advantages and disadvantages of informal structures in organizations

---

TRADITIONAL ORGANIZATION STRUCTURES

■ **Departmentalization** is the process of grouping together people and jobs into work units.

A traditional principle of organizing is that performance improves when people are allowed to specialize and become expert in specific jobs or tasks. Given this division of labor, however, decisions must be made regarding **departmentalization**, how to group work positions into formal teams or departments that are linked together in a coordinated way. These decisions have traditionally resulted in three major types of organizational structures—the functional, divisional, and matrix structures.[14]

FUNCTIONAL STRUCTURES

■ A **functional structure** groups together people with similar skills who perform similar tasks.

In **functional structures**, people with similar skills and performing similar tasks are grouped together into formal work units. Members of functional departments share technical expertise, interests, and responsibilities. The first example in *Figure 10.2* shows a functional structure common in business firms, with top management arranged by the functions of marketing, finance, production, and human resources. In this functional structure, manufacturing problems are the responsibility of the production vice president, marketing problems are the province of the marketing vice president, and so on. The key point is that members of a function work within their areas of expertise. If each function does its work properly, the expectation is that the business will operate successfully.

Functional structures are not limited to businesses. The figure also shows how they are used in other types of organizations, such as banks and hospitals. Functional structures typically work well for small organizations that produce only one or a few products or services. They also tend to work best in relatively stable environments where problems are predictable and the demands for change and innovation are limited. The major *advantages of a functional structure* include the following:

■ Economies of scale with efficient use of resources.
■ Task assignments consistent with expertise and training.
■ High-quality technical problem solving.
■ In-depth training and skill development within functions.
■ Clear career paths within functions.

There are also potential *disadvantages of functional structures*. Common problems include difficulties in pinpointing responsibilities for things like cost containment, product or service quality, and innovation. A significant concern is with the **functional chimneys problem**—lack of communication, coordination, and problem solving across functions. Because the functions become formalized not only on an organization chart but also in the mindsets of people, the sense of cooperation and common purpose can break down. The total system perspective is lost to self-centered and narrow viewpoints. When problems occur between functions, they are too often referred

The **functional chimneys problem** is a lack of communication and coordination across functions.

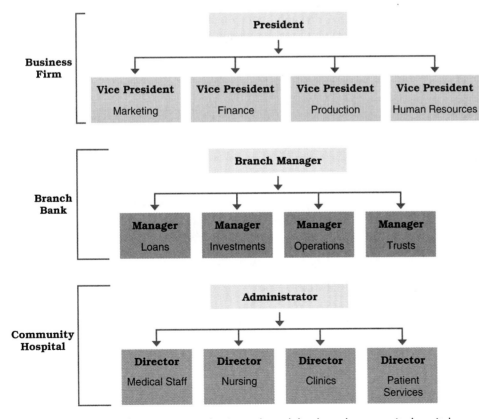

Figure 10.2 Functional structures in a business, branch bank, and community hospital.

up to higher levels for resolution rather than being addressed by people at the same level. This slows decision making and can harm organizational performance. For example, when Ford took over as the new owner of Jaguar, it had to resolve many quality problems. The quality turnaround took longer than anticipated, in part because of what Jaguar's chairman called "excessive compartmentalization." In building cars, the different departments did very little talking and working with one another. Ford's response was to push for more interdepartmental coordination and consensus decision making.[15]

DIVISIONAL STRUCTURES

■ A **divisional structure** groups together people working on the same product, in the same area, with similar customers, or on the same processes.

A second organizational alternative is the **divisional structure**. It groups together people who work on the same product or process, serve similar customers, and/or are located in the same area or geographical region. As illustrated in *Figure 10.3*, divisional structures are common in complex organizations with diverse operations that extend across many products, territories, customers, and work processes.[16]

Organizations use divisional structures for a variety of reasons, including opportunities to avoid problems common to functional structures. The potential *advantages of divisional structures* include

■ More flexibility in responding to environmental changes.
■ Improved coordination across functional departments.
■ Clear points of responsibility for product or service delivery.
■ Expertise focused on specific customers, products, and regions.
■ Greater ease in changing size by adding or deleting divisions.

As with other alternatives, there are potential *disadvantages of divisional structures*. They can reduce economies of scale and increase costs through the duplication of resources and efforts across divisions. They can also create unhealthy rivalries as divisions compete for resources and top mangement attention, and as they emphasize division needs to the detriment of the goals of the organization as a whole.

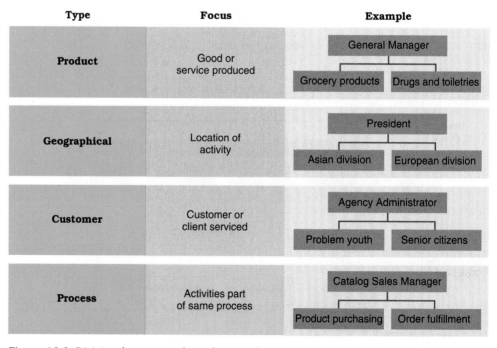

Type	Focus	Example
Product	Good or service produced	General Manager → Grocery products, Drugs and toiletries
Geographical	Location of activity	President → Asian division, European division
Customer	Customer or client serviced	Agency Administrator → Problem youth, Senior citizens
Process	Activities part of same process	Catalog Sales Manager → Product purchasing, Order fulfillment

Figure 10.3 Divisional structures based on product, geography, customer, and process.

Product Structures

Product structures, sometimes called *market structures*, group together jobs and activities focused on a single product or service. They clearly identify costs, profits, problems, and successes in a market area with a central point of accountability. Consequently, managers are encouraged to be responsive to changing market demands and customer tastes. Common in large organizations, product structures may even extend into global operations. When taking over as H. J. Heinz's CEO, William R. Johnson became concerned about the company's international performance. He decided a change in structure could help improve performance. The existing structure that emphasized countries and regions was changed to global product divisions. The choice was based on Johnson's belief that a product structure would bring the best brand management to all countries and increase cooperation around the world within product lines.

▪ A **product structure** groups together people and jobs focused on a single product or service.

Geographical Structures

Geographical structures, sometimes called *area structures*, group together jobs and activities being performed in the same location or geographical region. They are typically used when there is a need to differentiate products or services in various locations, such as in different regions of a country. They are also quite common in international operations, where they help to focus attention on the unique cultures and requirements of particular regions. As United Parcel Service (UPS) operations expanded worldwide, for example, the company announced a change from a product to a geographical organizational structure. Two geographical divisions were created—the Americas and Europe/Asia. Each area was given responsibility for its own logistics, sales, and other business functions.

▪ A **geographical structure** groups together people and jobs performed in the same location.

INSIGHTS

Brands with Values Are Really Sweet

At least that's the idea one gets from digging into one of Dancing Deer Baking's Cherry Almond Ginger Chew cookies. The company sells about $8 million of them and other confectionary concoctions. All are made with all natural ingredients, packaged in recycled materials, and produced in inner city Boston. Along with her 65 employees, CEO Patricia Karter is determined to stick with her principles and market a brand with values.

All of Dancing Deer's employees get stock options and free lunches; 35% of profits from the firm's Sweet Home cakes are donated to help the homeless find accommodations and jobs.

Even with success and expansion (the company needs to double its current space) Karter has no intention of moving from Dancing Deer's low-income Roxbury home territory. When offered a chance to make a large cookie sale to Williams-Sonoma, she declined; the contract would have required use of preservatives. But Williams-Sonoma was so impressed with her products and principles that it contracted for sale of her bakery mixes. Starting with a $20,000 investment in 1994, Karter's goal is to hit $50 million in sales. At that point she says the firm will be "big enough to make an impact, to be a social economic force." But even as she faces the challenges of growth *Business Week* reports she "has no intention of letting her company, or her ideals, get lost."

Customer Structures

▨ A **customer structure** groups together people and jobs that serve the same customers or clients.

Customer structures, sometimes called *market structures*, group together jobs and activities that are serving the same customers or clients. The major appeal is the ability to best serve the special needs of the different customer groups. This is a common form of structure for complex businesses in the consumer products industries. 3M corporation structures itself to focus attention around the world on such diverse markets as consumer and office, speciality materials, industrial, health care, electronics and communications, transportation, graphics, and safety. Customer structures are also useful in services, for example, where banks use them to give separate attention to consumer and commercial customers for loans. The example used in *Figure 10.3* also shows a government agency serving different client populations.

Process Structures

▨ A **process structure** groups jobs and activities that are part of the same processes.

A *work process* is a group of tasks related to one another that collectively creates something of value to a customer.[17] An example is order fulfillment, as when you telephone a catalog retailer and request a particular item. The process of order fulfillment takes the order from point of initiation by the customer to point of fulfillment by a delivered product. A **process structure** groups together jobs and activities that are part of the same processes. In the example in *Figure 10.4*, this might take the form of product-purchasing teams, order-fulfillment teams, and systems-support teams for the mail-order catalog business.

MATRIX STRUCTURES

▨ A **matrix structure** combines functional and divisional approaches to emphasize project or program teams.

The **matrix structure**, often called the *matrix organization*, combines the functional and divisional structures just described. In effect, it is an attempt to gain the advantages and minimize the disadvantages of each. This is accomplished in the matrix by using permanent cross-functional teams to support specific products, projects, or programs.[18] As shown in *Figure 10.4*, workers in

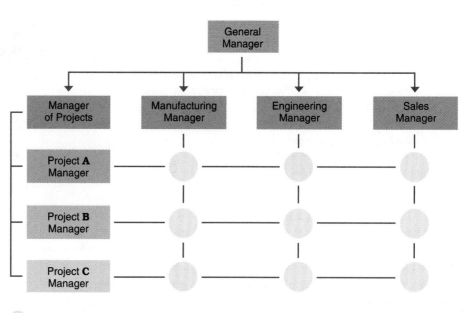

Figure 10.4 Matrix structure in a small multiproject business firm.

⬤ Persons assigned to both projects and functional departments a matrix structure belong to at least two formal groups at the same time—a functional group and a product, program, or project team. They also report to two bosses—one within the function and the other within the team.

The matrix organization has gained a strong foothold in the workplace, with applications in such diverse settings as manufacturing (e.g., aerospace, electronics, pharmaceuticals), service industries (e.g., banking, brokerage, retailing), professional fields (e.g., accounting, advertising, law), and the nonprofit sector (e.g., city, state, and federal agencies, hospitals, universities). Matrix structures are also found in multinational corporations, where they offer the flexibility to deal with regional differences as well as multiple product, program, or project needs.

The main contribution of matrix structures to organizational performance lies with the cross-functional teams whose members work closely together to share expertise and information in a timely manner to solve problems. The potential *advantages of matrix structures* include the following:

- Better cooperation across functions.
- Improved decision making as problem solving takes place at the team level, where the best information is available.
- Increased flexibility in adding, removing, and/or changing operations to meet changing demands.
- Better customer service, since there is always a program, product, or project manager informed and available to answer questions.
- Better performance accountability through the program, product, or project managers.
- Improved strategic management, since top managers are freed from unnecessary problem solving to focus time on strategic issues.

Predictably, there are also potential *disadvantages of matrix structures.* The two-boss system is susceptible to power struggles, as functional supervisors and team leaders vie with one another to exercise authority. The two-boss system can be frustrating if it creates task confusion and conflicting work priorities. Team meetings in the matrix are also time consuming. Teams may develop "groupitis," or strong team loyalties that cause a loss of focus on larger organizational goals. And the requirements of adding the team leaders to a matrix structure can result in increased costs.[19]

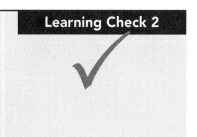

Learning Check 2

Be sure you can ■ explain the differences between functional, divisional, and matrix structures ■ list advantages and disadvantages of a functional structure, and draw a chart to show its use in an organization familiar to you ■ list advantages and disadvantages of a divisional structure, and draw a chart to show use of each divisional type in an organization familiar to you ■ list advantages and disadvantages of a matrix structure, and draw a chart to show its use in an organization familiar to you

NEWER ORGANIZATION STRUCTURES

The matrix structure is a first step toward improving flexibility and problem solving through better cross-functional integration. But, it is just one part of a broader movement toward more horizontal structures that decrease hierarchy, increase empowerment, and better mobilize technology and human talents.[20]

TEAM STRUCTURES

■ A **team structure** uses permanent and temporary cross-functional teams to improve lateral relations.

■ A **cross-functional team** brings together members from different functional departments.

■ **Project teams** are convened for a particular task or project and disband once it is completed.

As traditional vertical structures give way to more horizontal ones, teams are serving as the basic building blocks.[21] Organizations with **team structures** extensively use both permanent and temporary teams to solve problems, complete special projects, and accomplish day-to-day tasks.[22] As illustrated in *Figure 10.5*, these are often **cross-functional teams** composed of members from different areas of work responsibility.[23] The intention is to break down the functional chimneys or barriers inside the organization and create more effective lateral relations for problem solving and work performance. They are also often **project teams** that are convened for a particular task or "project" and that disband once it is completed. The intention here is to quickly convene people with the needed talents and focus their efforts intensely to solve a problem or take advantage of a special opportunity.

There are many potential *advantages of team structures*. They help eliminate difficulties with communication and decision making resulting from the functional chimneys problem described earlier. Team assignments help to break down barriers between departments as people from different parts of an organization get to know one another. They can also boost morale. People working in teams often experience a greater sense of involvement and identification, increasing their enthusiasm for the job. Because teams focus shared knowledge and expertise on specific problems, they can also improve the speed and quality of decisions in many situations. After a research team at Polaroid Corporation developed a new medical imaging system in one-half the predicted time, a senior executive said, "Our researchers are not any smarter, but by working together they get the value of each other's intelligence almost instantaneously."[24]

The complexities of teams and teamwork contribute to the potential *disadvantages of team structures*. These include conflicting loyalties for persons with both team and functional assignments. They also include issues of time management and group process. By their very nature, teams spend a lot of time in meetings. Not all of this time is productive. How well team members spend their time together often depends on the quality of interpersonal relations, group dynamics, and team management. All of these concerns are manageable, as will be described in Chapter 16 on teams and teamwork.

NETWORK STRUCTURES

■ A **network structure** uses IT to link with networks of outside suppliers and service contractors.

Organizations using a **network structure** operate with a central core that is linked through "networks" of relationships with outside contractors and suppliers of essential services.[25] The old model was for organizations to own

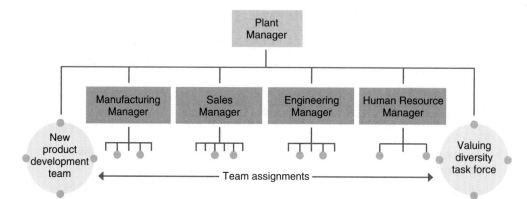

Figure 10.5 How a team structure uses cross-functional teams for improved lateral relations.

everything. The new model is to own only the most essential or "core" components of the business, and to engage in strategic alliances and outsourcing to provide the rest.

Figure 10.6 illustrates a network structure as it might work for a mail-order company selling lawn and deck furniture through a catalog. The firm itself is very small, consisting of a relatively few full-time core employees working from a central headquarters. Beyond that, it is structured as a network of outsourcing and partner relationships, maintained operationally using the latest in information technology. Merchandise is designed on contract with a furniture design firm—which responds quickly as designs are shared and customized via computer networking. It is manufactured and packaged by subcontractors located around the world—wherever materials, quality, and cost are found at best advantage. Stock is maintained and shipped from a contract warehouse—ensuring quality storage and on-time expert shipping. All of the accounting and financial details are managed on contract with an outside firm—providing better technical expertise than the firm could afford to employ on a full-time basis. And, the quarterly catalog is designed, printed, and mailed cooperatively as a strategic alliance with two other firms that sell different home furnishings with a related price appeal. All of this, of course, is supported by a company Web site also maintained by an outside contractor.

The creative use of information technology adds to the potential *advantages of network structures*. With the technological edge, the mail-order company in this example can operate with fewer full-time employees and less-complex internal systems. Network structures are lean and streamlined. They help organizations stay cost competitive through reduced overhead and increased operating efficiency. Network concepts allow organizations to employ outsourcing strategies and contract out specialized business functions rather than maintain full-time staff to do them. Information technology makes it easy to manage these contracts and business alliances, even across great distances. Within the operating core of a network structure, furthermore, a variety of interesting jobs are created for those who must coordinate the entire system of relationships.

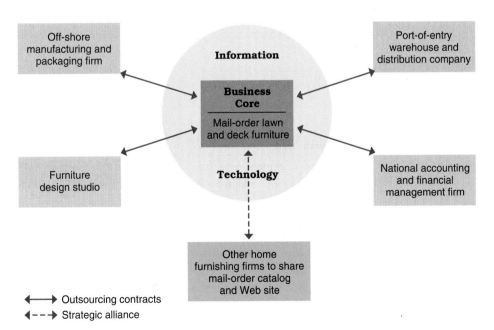

Figure 10.6 A network structure for a Web-based retail business.

The potential *disadvantages of network structures* largely lie with the demands of new management responsibilities. The more complex the business or mission of the organization, the more complicated the network of contracts and alliances that must be maintained. It may be difficult to control and coordinate among them. If one part of the network breaks down or fails to deliver, the entire system suffers. Also, there is the potential for loss of control over activities contracted out and for a lack of loyalty to develop among contractors who are used infrequently rather than on a long-term basis. Some worry that outsourcing can become so aggressive as to be dangerous to the firm, especially when ever-more-critical activities such as finance, logistics, and human resources management are outsourced.[26]

BOUNDARYLESS ORGANIZATIONS

■ A **boundaryless organization** eliminates internal boundaries among subsystems and external boundaries with the external environment.

It is popular today to speak about creating a **boundaryless organization** that eliminates internal boundaries among subsystems and external boundaries with the external environment.[27] The boundaryless organization can be viewed as a combination of the team and network structures just described, with the addition of "temporariness." Within the organization, teamwork and communication—spontaneous, as needed, and intense—replace formal lines of authority. There is an absence of boundaries that separate organizational members from one another. In the external context, organizational needs are met by a shifting mix of outsourcing contracts and operating alliances that

KAFFEEKLATSCH

Social Network Analysis

First Cup

"You know what this organization needs? It needs an X-ray. What they have on the organization chart is meaningless; you need to peer inside the system to find out who talks to whom and how work really gets done. Why don't you draw your 'informal map' of the place, and I'll draw mine, and then we'll compare?"

Studying the Grounds

■ Sociologists are bringing into the corporate arena a technique known as social network analysis.

■ A social network analysis typically asks people to identify others whom they turn to for help most often, whom they communicate regularly, and who energizes and de-energizes them.

■ When results are analyzed, often by computer programs, social networks are drawn with lines running from person to person according to frequency and type of relationship maintained.

■ Social network analysis helps identify how work really gets done in organizations, in contrast to the formal arrangements usually depicted on organization charts.

Double Espresso

"I get a lot done through the people I know, not necessarily with the ones that are in my formal reporting relationships. But don't you think that the formal structure is important when it comes to things like management communications, new policy directives, and the like? I'm thinking that organizations need two structures—the formal and the informal. However, I think what you're saying is that the informal structure, or the social network structure, should be legitimized and given credit for the role it plays in helping organizations perform."

Your Turn

More and more organizations are turning to experts to help map the informal networks. These maps are useful in identifying key players in merger and acquisition situations, in highlighting persons with lots of respect who can help move organizational change initiatives forward in their peer groups, and even in spotting the high-talent people who should be fast tracked and supported for organizational advancement. But, suppose the informal map is drawn in your workplace and you're an isolate; the social network analysis shows that very few people are connected to you. What happens then?

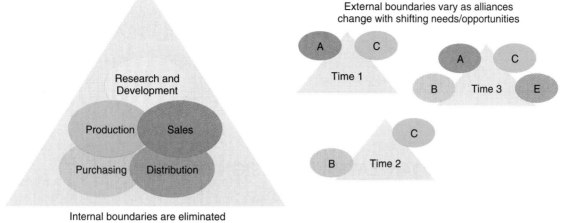

Figure 10.7 The boundaryless organization eliminates internal and external barriers.

form and disband with changing circumstances. A "photograph" that documents an organization's configuration of external relationships today will look different from one taken tomorrow, as the form naturally adjusts to new pressures and circumstances. *Figure 10.7* shows how the absence of internal and external barriers helps people work in ways that bring speed and flexibility to the boundaryless firm.

Key requirements of boundaryless organizations are the absence of hierarchy, empowerment of team members, technology utilization, and acceptance of impermanence. Knowledge sharing is both a goal and an essential component. One way to think of this is in the context of a very small organization, perhaps a startup. In the small firm everyone pitches in to help out as needed and when appropriate to get things done. There are no formal assignments, and there are no job titles or job descriptions standing in the way. People with talent work together as needed to get the job done. The boundaryless organization, in its pure form, is just like that. Even in the larger organizational context, meetings and spontaneous sharing are happening continuously; perhaps thousands of people working together in hundreds of teams form and disband as needed.

At consulting giant PricewaterhouseCoopers, for example, knowledge sharing brings together 160,000 partners spread across 150 countries in a vast virtual learning and problem-solving network. Partners collaborate electronically through online databases where information is stored, problems posted, and questions asked and answered in real time by those with experience and knowledge relevant to the problem at hand. Technology makes collaboration instantaneously and always possible, breaking down boundaries that might otherwise slow or impede the firm's performance.[28]

Boundaryless operations emerge in a special form sometimes called the **virtual organization**.[29] This is an organization that operates in a shifting network of external alliances that are engaged as needed using IT and the Internet. The boundaries that traditionally separate a firm from its suppliers, customers, and even competitors are largely eliminated, temporarily and in respect to a given transaction or business purpose. Virtual organizations come into being "as needed" when alliances are called into action to meet specific operating needs and objectives. When the work is complete, the alliance rests until next called into action. The virtual organization operates in this manner with the mix of mobilized alliances, continuously shifting and with an expansive pool of potential alliances always ready to be called upon as needed.

▪ A **virtual organization** uses IT and the Internet to engage a shifting network of strategic alliances.

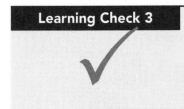

Learning Check 3

Be sure you can ■ describe how organizations can include cross-functional teams and project teams in their structures ■ define the term network structure ■ illustrate how a new venture, such as a Web-based retailer, might use a network structure to organize its various operations ■ discuss the potential advantages and disadvantages of following a network approach ■ explain the concept of the boundaryless organization

ORGANIZATIONAL DESIGN DIRECTIONS

■ **Organizational design** is the process of creating structures that accomplish mission and objectives.

Organizational design is the process of choosing and implementing structures that best arrange resources to accomplish the organization's mission and objectives.[30] Because every organization faces its own set of unique problems and opportunities, the best design at any moment is the one that achieves a good match between structure and situation.[31] The process of organizational design is thus a problem-solving activity; no one design applies in all circumstances. The goal is to achieve a best fit among structure and the unique situation faced by each organization. In management and organization theory, the choices among design alternatives are broadly framed in the distinction between mechanistic or bureaucratic designs at one extreme and organic or adaptive designs at the other.

ISSUES AND SITUATIONS

Microsoft's Bureaucracy

So, there's a new music player available. Microsoft is taking on Apple, and doing so one-on-one. Previously known as a company that focused on alliances and partnerships, the firm sidestepped its cooperation with iRiver to bring out its own MP3 player. The word is that at Microsoft they call it an "Apple killer."

But in many ways, Microsoft seems to be trying to kill an "apple" by throwing a different type of "apple" at it. Is this real product innovation, or is it an advanced and expensive form of copycatting? Has Microsoft lost its real creative edge?

At least some analysts seem worried. *Business Week* reported that the software giant is suffering from "bureaucratic red tape" and endless meetings that bog down employees and limit their abilities to be creative and on top of market demands. The *Wall Street Journal* takes the case even further, suggesting that Microsoft should be broken into three pieces to free the firm from "bureaucracy that's stifling entrepreneurial spirits." What is recommended? One part would focus on operating systems, another on Office software, and the third—suggested name "Blue Sky"—would focus on Xbox and new products.

Critical Response

What do you think? Might Microsoft perform better with a different configuration? Perhaps breaking the firm up would let new and smaller components operate with more organic designs—stimulating creativity and innovation—pleasing customers and shareholders alike. Research the firm's current structure. Propose an alternative configuration that would help ensure that the firm remains both profitable and innovative in meeting customer needs.

MECHANISTIC AND ORGANIC DESIGNS

As first introduced in the discussion on historical foundations of management in Chapter 3, a **bureaucracy** is a form of organization based on logic, order, and the legitimate use of formal authority. Its distinguishing features include a clear-cut division of labor, strict hierarchy of authority, formal rules and procedures, and promotion based on competency.

> ■ A **bureaucracy** emphasizes formal authority, order, fairness, and efficiency.

According to sociologist Max Weber, bureaucracies were supposed to be orderly, fair, and highly efficient.[32] In short, they were a model form of organization. Yet, instead of operating efficiency, the bureaucracies that we know are often associated with "red tape." And, instead of being orderly and fair, they are often seen as cumbersome and impersonal to the point of insensitivity to customer or client needs.[33] But rather than view all bureaucratic structures as inevitably flawed, management theory asks the contingency questions: (1) When is a bureaucratic form a good choice for an organization? (2) What alternatives exist when it is not a good choice?

Pioneering research conducted in England during the early 1960s by Tom Burns and George Stalker helps answer these questions.[34] After investigating 20 manufacturing firms, they concluded that two quite different organizational forms could be successful, depending on the nature of a firm's external environment. A more bureaucratic form, which Burns and Stalker called *mechanistic*, thrived when the environment was stable. But it experienced difficulty when the environment was rapidly changing and uncertain. In these dynamic situations, a much less bureaucratic form, called *organic*, performed best. *Figure 10.8* portrays these two approaches as opposite extremes on a continuum of organizational design alternatives.

Mechanistic Designs

Organizations with more **mechanistic designs** are highly bureaucratic in nature. As shown in the figure, they are vertical structures that typically operate with more centralized authority, many rules and procedures, a precise division of labor, narrow spans of control, and formal means of coordination. Mechanistic designs are described as "tight" structures of the traditional vertical or pyramid form.[35]

> ■ A **mechanistic design** is centralized, with many rules and procedures, a clear-cut division of labor, narrow spans of control, and formal coordination.

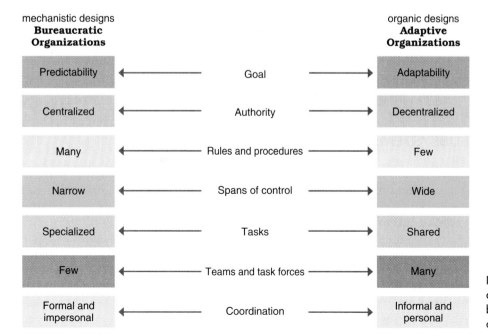

Figure 10.8 Organizational design alternatives: from bureaucratic to adaptive organizations.

For a good example, visit your local fast-food restaurant. As a relatively small operation, each store operates quite like others in the franchise chain and according to rules established by the corporate management. Service personnel work in orderly and disciplined ways, guided by training, rules and procedures, and close supervision by crew leaders who work alongside them. Even their appearances are carefully regulated, with everyone working in a standardized uniform. These restaurants perform well as they repetitively deliver items that are part of their standard menus. You quickly encounter the limits, however, if you try to order something not on the menu. The chains also encounter difficulty when consumer tastes change or take on regional preferences that are different from what the corporate menu provides. Adjustments to these mechanistic systems take a long time.

Organic Designs

The limits of mechanistic designs and their tight vertical structures are especially apparent in organizations that operate in dynamic, often uncertain, environments. It is hard, for example, to find a technology company, consumer products firm, financial services business, or dot.com retailer that isn't making continual adjustments in operations and organizational design. Their effectiveness depends on being able to change with the times.

The ability to respond quickly to shifting environmental challenges is characteristic of organizations with more **organic designs**.[36] As portrayed in *Figure 10.8*, they operate with decentralized authority, fewer rules and procedures, less precise division of labor, wider spans of control, and more personal means of coordination. These features create **adaptive organizations** with horizontal structures and cultures that encourage worker empowerment and teamwork. They are described as relatively loose systems in which a lot of work gets done through informal structures and networks of interpersonal contacts.[37]

Organic designs work well for organizations facing dynamic environments that demand flexibility in dealing with changing conditions. They are built upon a foundation of trust that people will do the right things on their own initiative. Moving toward the adaptive form means letting workers take over production scheduling and problem solving; it means letting workers set up their own control systems; it means letting workers use their ideas to improve customer service. In the ultimately adaptive organizations, it means that members are given the freedom to do what they can do best—get the job done. This helps create what has been described in earlier chapters as a *learning organization*, one designed for continuous adaptation through problem solving, innovation, and learning.[38]

SUBSYSTEMS DESIGN AND INTEGRATION

Organizations are composed of **subsystems** that operate as smaller parts of a larger and total organizational system. A major challenge of organizational design is to create subsystems and coordinate relationships so that the entire organization's interests are best met.

Important research in this area was reported in 1967 by Paul Lawrence and Jay Lorsch of Harvard University.[39] They studied 10 firms in three different industries—plastics, consumer goods, and containers. The firms were chosen because they differed in performance. The industries were chosen because they faced different levels of environmental uncertainty. The plastics industry was uncertain; the containers industry was more certain; the

■ An **organic design** is decentralized with fewer rules and procedures, open divisions of labor, wide spans of control, and more personal coordination.

■ An **adaptive organization** operates with a minimum of bureaucratic features and encourages worker empowerment and teamwork.

■ A **subsystem** is a work unit or smaller component within a larger organization.

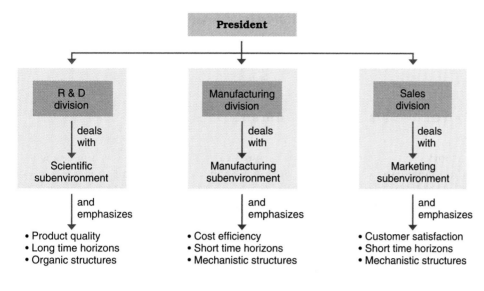

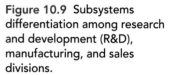

Figure 10.9 Subsystems differentiation among research and development (R&D), manufacturing, and sales divisions.

consumer goods industry was moderately uncertain. The results of the Lawrence and Lorsch study can be summarized as follows.

First, successful plastics firms in uncertain environments had more organic designs; successful container firms in certain environments had more mechanistic designs. This result was consistent with the research by Burns and Stalker, as already discussed.[40] Second, Lawrence and Lorsch found that subsystems in the successful firms used different structures to accommodate the special problems and opportunities of their subenvironments. Third, the researchers found that subsystems in the successful firms worked well with one another, even though they were also very different from one another.

Figure 10.9 shows how research and development, manufacturing, and sales subunits may operate in response to unique needs. This illustrates **differentiation**—the degree of difference that exists between the internal components of the organization, and suggests the need for **integration**, the level of coordination achieved among an organization's internal components. The creation of both differentiated subsystems and appropriate integrating mechanisms is a particularly challenging managerial task. Increased differentiation creates the need for greater integration. However, integration becomes harder to achieve as differentiation increases.

Management Smarts 10.1 identifies several mechanisms for achieving subsystem integration.[41] Integrating mechanisms that rely on vertical coordination and the use of authority relationships work best when differentiation is low. They include use of rules and procedures, hierarchical referral, and planning. Integrating mechanisms that emphasize horizontal coordination and improved lateral relations work better when differentiation is high.[42] They include the use of direct contact between managers, liaison roles, task forces, teams, and matrix structures.

▪ **Differentiation** is the degree of difference between subsystems in an organization.

▪ **Integration** is the level of coordination achieved between subsystems in an organization.

MANAGEMENT SMARTS 10.1

How to improve subsystems integration

- *Rules and procedures:* Clearly specify required activities.
- *Hierarchical referral:* Refer problems upward to a common superior.
- *Planning:* Set targets that keep everyone headed in the same direction.
- *Direct contact:* Have subunit managers coordinate directly.
- *Liaison roles:* Assign formal coordinators to link subunits together.
- *Task forces:* Form temporary task forces to coordinate activities and solve problems on a timetable.
- *Teams:* Form permanent teams with the authority to coordinate and solve problems over time.
- *Matrix organizations:* Create a matrix structure to improve coordination on specific programs.

TRENDS IN ORGANIZATIONAL DESIGNS

There is little doubt that more and more organizations are adopting horizontal structures and organic designs. As they do so, a number of trends are evident.

Fewer Levels of Management

■ The **chain of command** links all persons with successively higher levels of authority.

A typical organization chart shows the **chain of command**, or, the line of authority that vertically links each position with successively higher levels of management. When organizations grow in size, they tend to get taller as more and more levels of management are added to the chain of command. Yet, high performing firms like Nucor, discussed in The Topic chapter opener, show preferences for fewer management levels. Nucor's structure is described as "simple" and "streamlined," with the goal "to allow employees to innovate and make quick decisions." The three management levels in a typical division are General Manager, Department Manager, and Supervisor/ Professional.[44]

■ **Span of control** is the number of subordinates directly reporting to a manager.

One of the influences on management levels is **span of control**—the number of persons directly reporting to a manager. *Flat structures* have wider spans of control and fewer levels of management; *tall structures* have narrow spans of control and many levels of management. Because tall organizations have more managers, they are more costly. They are

also generally viewed as less efficient, less flexible, and less customer sensitive. Flat organizations with wider spans of control, by contrast, have lower overhead costs. Their workers also benefit from more empowerment and independence.[43] These are all reasons why the current trend is toward fewer levels of management.

Trend. Many organizations are cutting unnecessary levels of management and shifting to wider spans of control; managers are taking responsibility for larger numbers of subordinates who operate with less direct supervision.

More Delegation and Empowerment

■ **Delegation** is the process of distributing and entrusting work to other persons.

All managers must decide what work they should do themselves and what should be left for others. At issue here is **delegation**—the process of entrusting work to others by giving them the right to make decisions and take action.

In *step 1 of delegation, the manager assigns responsibility* by carefully explaining the work or duties someone else is expected to do. This responsibility is an expectation for the other person to perform assigned tasks. In *step 2, the manager grants authority to act.* Along with the assigned task, the right to take necessary actions (for example, to spend money, direct the work of others, use resources) is given to the other person. Authority is a right to act in ways needed to carry out the assigned tasks. In *step 3, the manager creates accountability.* By accepting an assignment, the person takes on a direct obligation to the manager to complete the job as agreed upon.

A classical principle of organization warns managers not to delegate without giving the other person sufficient authority to perform. Without authority, it is very hard for someone to live up to performance expectations. The *authority-and-responsibility principle* states that authority should equal responsibility when work is delegated from a supervisor to a subordinate.

A common management failure is unwillingness to delegate. Whether resulting from a lack of trust in others or to a manager's inflexibility in the way things get done, failure to delegate can be damaging. It overloads the manager with work that could be done by others; it also denies others many opportunities to fully utilize their talents on the job. When well done, by contrast, delegation leads to empowerment, by allowing people freedom to contribute ideas and do their jobs in the best possible ways. This involvement can increase job satisfaction for the individual and frequently results in better job performance.

Trend. Managers are delegating more; they are finding more ways to empower people at all levels to make more decisions affecting themselves and their work.

Decentralization with Centralization

A question frequently asked is "Should most decisions be made at the top levels of an organization, or should they be dispersed by extensive delegation throughout all levels of management?" The former approach is referred to as **centralization;** the latter is called **decentralization.** But the issue doesn't have to be framed as an either/or choice. Today's organizations can use information technology, operate with greater decentralization without giving up centralized control.[40]

With computer networks and advanced information systems, managers at higher levels can more easily stay informed about a wide range of day-to-day performance matters. Because they have information on results readily

■ **Centralization** is the concentration of authority for most decisions at the top level of an organization.

■ **Decentralization** is the dispersion of authority to make decisions throughout all organization levels.

REAL ETHICS

Downsized into Exhaustion

Dear Stress Doctor:

My manager is consistently asking me to work overtime, including almost every weekend. I have less and less time available for my family.

As my organization "downsizes" and cuts back staff, it is putting a greater burden on those of us that remain. We work the overtime, we get exhausted, and our families get short changed and even angry. I can't tell you how many nights I take my laptop home and work until midnight or later just to catch up.

I even feel guilty now taking time to watch my daughter play soccer on Saturday mornings. Sure, there's some decent pay involved, but that doesn't make up for the heavy price I'm paying with the family.

But you know what? My boss doesn't get it. I never hear her ask: "Henry, are you working too much, don't you think it's time to get back on a reasonable schedule?" No! What I often hear instead is "Look at Andy; he's a real go-getter; Andy hasn't been out of here one night this week before 8 P.M. And Sally, wow, I bet she's worked every weekend for the past month."

What am I to do, just keep it up until everything falls apart one day?

Sincerely,
Overworked in Cincinnati

FURTHER INQUIRY

Is it ethical to expect people to work consistently over and above their agreed-upon schedules? Is it ethical for an employer to reduce staff and then expect those who remain to work longer and harder? Why is it that some employers recognize that overwork can reduce productivity and harm motivation, while others just don't seem to care? Sometimes people need help to sort out their tasks and daily work demands so that they work on the important things and don't get bogged down by the others. Isn't this part of what a manager is supposed to do—helping people understand their jobs, set priorities and do them well while still maintaining reasonable work-life balance?

available, they can allow more decentralization in decision making. If something goes wrong, presumably the information systems will sound an alarm and allow corrective action to be taken quickly.

Trend. Whereas delegation, empowerment, and horizontal structures are contributing to more decentralization in organizations, advances in information technology allow for adequate centralized control.

Reduced Use of Staff

When it comes to coordination and control in organizations, the issue of line-staff relationships is important. Chapter 1 described staff roles as providing expert advice and guidance to line personnel. Persons appointed in **staff positions** perform a technical service or provide special problem-solving expertise for other parts of the organization. This could be a single person, such as a corporate safety director, or a complete unit, such as a corporate safety department.

■ **Staff positions** provide technical expertise for other parts of the organization.

RESEARCH BRIEF

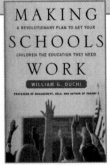

Making schools work better is the focus of management researcher

Scholar and consultant William Ouchi believes that our public schools can be improved through organizational design. In his book *Making Schools Work: A Revolutionary Plan to Get Your Children the Education They Need*, Ouchi points out that as organizations grow in size, they tend to "bulk up" with staff personnel and higher-level managers that are distant from customers and operating workers. He finds many less successful schools following this pattern.

Ouchi's study of 223 school districts suggests that adding administrative weight and cost at the top does little to improve organizational performance and can actually harm it. Even though most school districts are highly centralized, he finds decentralization a characteristic of the more successful ones. The better districts in his study had fewer central office staff personnel per student and allowed maximum autonomy to school principals. Ouchi advocates redesigning schools so that decision making is more decentralized. He believes in allowing principals more autonomy to control school budgets and work with their staffs, and in allowing teachers more freedom to solve their own problems.

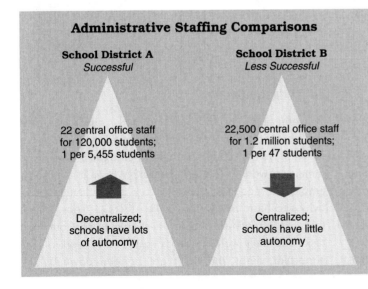

Administrative Staffing Comparisons

School District A
Successful

22 central office staff for 120,000 students; 1 per 5,455 students

Decentralized; schools have lots of autonomy

School District B
Less Successful

22,500 central office staff for 1.2 million students; 1 per 47 students

Centralized; schools have little autonomy

QUESTIONS & APPLICATIONS

Does Ouchi offer us a general organizational design principle—systems perform best with streamlined designs and greater decentralization? Or, can you come up with examples of organizations that function best with large staffs and lots of centralization? What follow-up research questions do you think Ouchi and others should consider pursuing in the future?

Don't you wonder how School District B justifies the size of its administrative staff and a centralized approach when School District A, with a far different configuration, has a reputation for success? What are the ratios of administrative to instructional staff at your college or university? Is it possible that "performance" could be improved along lines suggested by Ouchi?

Reference: William Ouchi, *Making Schools Work: A Revolutionary Plan to Get Your Children the Education They Need* (New York: Simon & Schuster, 2003); and, Richard Riordan, Linda Lingle and Lyman Porter, "Making Public Schools Work: Management Reform as the Key," *Academy of Management Journal*, vol. 48, No. 6 (2005), pp. 929–940.

Many organizations rely on staff specialists to maintain coordination and control over a variety of matters. In a large retail chain, line managers in each store typically make daily operating decisions regarding direct sales of merchandise. But staff specialists at the corporate or regional levels provide direction and support so that all the stores operate with the same credit, purchasing, employment, and advertising procedures.

Problems in line-staff distinctions can and do arise, and organizations sometimes find that staff size grows to the point where it costs more in administrative overhead than it is worth. This is why staff cutbacks are common in downsizing and other turnaround efforts. There is no one best solution to the problem of how to divide work between line and staff responsibilities. What is best for any organization will be a cost-effective staff component that satisfies, but doesn't overreact to, needs for specialized technical assistance to line operations.

Trend. Organizations are reducing the size of staff; they are seeking lower costs and increased operating efficiency by employing fewer staff personnel and using smaller staff units.

Learning Check 4

Be sure you can ▪ define the term organizational design ▪ explain the characteristics of mechanistic and organic designs ▪ illustrate situations in which the mechanistic design and the organic design work best ▪ explain the difference between a system and a subsystem ▪ define the terms differentiation and integration ▪ discuss the implications of the Lawrence and Lorsch study for subsystem design ▪ list several ways to improve subsystem integration in organizations ▪ describe organizational trends on levels of management, delegation and empowerment, decentralization and centralization, and use of staff

CHAPTER 10 STUDY GUIDE

STUDY QUESTIONS SUMMARY

1 What is organizing as a management function?

- Organizing is the process of arranging people and resources to work toward a common goal.
- Organizing decisions divide up the work that needs to be done, allocate people and resources to do it, and coordinate results to achieve productivity.
- Structure is the system of tasks, reporting relationships, and communication that links people and positions within an organization.
- The formal structure, such as shown on an organization chart, describes how an organization is supposed to work.
- The informal structure of an organization consists of the unofficial relationships that develop among members.

2 What are the traditional organization structures?

- In functional structures, people with similar skills who perform similar activities are grouped together under a common manager.
- In divisional structures, people who work on a similar product, work in the same geographical region, serve the same customers, or participate in the same work process are grouped together under common managers.
- A matrix structure combines the functional and divisional approaches to create permanent cross-functional project teams.

3 What are the newer types of organization structures?

- Team structures use cross-functional teams and task forces to improve lateral relations and problem solving at all levels.
- Network structures use contracted services and strategic alliances to support a core business or organizational center.
- Boundaryless organizations combine team and network structures with the advantages of technology to accomplish tasks and projects.
- Virtual organizations utilize information technology to mobilize a shifting mix of strategic alliances to accomplish tasks and projects.

4 How are directions in organizational design changing the workplace?

- Mechanistic designs are bureaucratic and vertical, performing best for routine and predictable tasks; organic designs are adaptive and horizontal, performing best in conditions requiring change and flexibility.
- Differentiation is the degree of difference that exists between various subsystems; integration is the level of coordination achieved among them.
- Organizations with little internal differentiation can be integrated vertically through authority relationships; greater differentiation requires more intense horizontal integration emphasizing cross-functional teams and lateral relations.
- Key organizing trends include fewer levels of management, more delegation and empowerment, decentralization with centralization, and fewer staff positions.

KEY TERMS REVIEW

Adaptive organization (p. 250)
Boundaryless organization (p. 246)
Bureaucracy (p. 249)
Centralization (p. 253)
Chain of command (p. 252)
Cross-functional teams (p. 244)
Customer structure (p. 242)
Decentralization (p. 253)
Delegation (p. 252)
Departmentalization (p. 238)
Differentiation (p. 251)
Divisional structure (p. 240)

Formal structure (p. 237)
Functional chimneys problem (p. 239)
Functional structure (p. 238)
Geographical structure (p. 241)
Informal structure (p. 237)
Integration (p. 251)
Matrix structure (p. 242)
Mechanistic design (p. 249)
Network structure (p. 244)
Organic design (p. 250)
Organization chart (p. 237)
Organization structure (p. 237)

Organizing (p. 236)
Organizational design (p. 248)
Process structure (p. 242)
Product structure (p. 241)
Project teams (p. 244)
Span of control (p. 252)
Staff positions (p. 254)
Subsystem (p. 250)
Team structure (p. 244)
Virtual organization (p. 247)

MULTIPLE-CHOICE QUESTIONS:

1. The main purpose of organizing as a management function is to _____.

   (a) make sure that results match plans   (b) arrange people and resources to accomplish work   (c) create enthusiasm for the work to be done   (d) match strategies with operational plans

2. _____ is the system of tasks, reporting relationships, and communication that links together the various parts of an organization.

   (a) Structure   (b) Staff   (c) Decentralization   (d) Differentiation

3. Transmission of rumors and resistance to change are potential disadvantages often associated with _____.

   (a) virtual organizations   (b) informal structures   (c) delegation   (d) specialized staff

4. An organization chart showing vice presidents of marketing, finance, manufacturing, and purchasing all reporting to the president is depicting a _____ structure.

   (a) functional   (b) matrix   (c) network   (d) product

5. The "two-boss" system of reporting relationships is found in the _____ structure.

   (a) functional   (b) matrix   (c) network   (d) product

6. A manufacturing business with a functional structure has recently developed two new product lines. The president of the company might consider shifting to a/an _____ structure to gain a stronger focus on each product.

   (a) virtual   (b) informal   (c) divisional   (d) network

7. Better lower-level teamwork and more top-level strategic management are among the expected advantages of a _____ structure.

   (a) divisional   (b) matrix   (c) geographical   (d) product

8. "Tall" organizations tend to have long chains of command and _____ spans of control.

   (a) wide   (b) narrow   (c) informal   (d) centralized

9. The functional chimneys problem occurs when people in different functions _____.

   (a) fail to communicate with one another   (b) try to help each other work with customers   (c) spend too much time coordinating decisions   (d) focus on products rather than functions

10. A _____ structure tries to combine the best elements of the functional and divisional forms.

    (a) matrix   (b) boundaryless   (c) team   (d) virtual

11. A student volunteers to gather information on a company for a group case analysis project. The other members of the group agree and tell her that she can choose the information sources. In terms of delegation, this group is giving the student _____ to fulfill the agreed-upon task.

    (a) responsibility   (b) accountability   (c) authority   (d) decentralization

12. The current trend in the use of staff in organizations is to _____.

    (a) give staff personnel more authority over operations   (b) reduce the number of staff personnel (c) remove all staff from the organization   (d) combine all staff functions in one department

13. The bureaucratic organization described by Max Weber is similar to the _____ organization described by Burns and Stalker.

    (a) adaptive   (b) mechanistic   (c) organic   (d) adhocracy

14. A basic paradox in subsystem design is that as differentiation increases, the need for _____ also increases but this becomes harder to accomplish.

    (a) cost efficiency   (b) innovation   (c) integration   (d) transformation

15. When the members of a marketing department pursue sales volume objectives and those in manufacturing pursue cost efficiency objectives, this is an example of _____.

    (a) simultaneous systems   (b) subsystems differentiation   (c) long-linked technology   (d) small-batch production

SHORT-RESPONSE QUESTIONS:

16. What symptoms might indicate a functional structure is causing problems for the organization?

17. Explain by example the concept of a network organization structure.

18. Explain the practical significance of this statement: "Organizational design should always be addressed in contingency fashion."

19. Describe differentiation and integration as issues in subsystem design.

APPLICATION QUESTION:

20. Faisal Sham supervises a group of 7 project engineers. His unit is experiencing a heavy workload as the demand for different versions of one of his firm's computer components is growing. Faisal finds that he doesn't have time to follow up on all design details for each version. Up until now he has tried to do this all by himself. Two of the engineers have shown interest in helping him coordinate work on the various designs. As a consultant, what would you advise Faisal in terms of delegating work to them?

CHAPTER 10 APPLICATIONS

CASE 10

Nike: Spreading Out to Stay Together

Nike is, indisputably, a giant in the athletics industry. Yet the Portland, Oregon, company has grown so large precisely because it knows how to stay small. By focusing on its core competencies—and outsourcing the rest—Nike has managed to become a sharply-focused industry leader. But can it keep the lead?

What do you call a company of thinkers?

It's not a joke or a Buddhist riddle. Rather, it's a conundrum about one of the most successful companies in the United States. It's known worldwide for its products, none of which it actually makes. This begs two questions: If you don't make anything, what do you actually do? If you outsource everything, what's left?

A whole lot of brand recognition, for starters. Nike, denoted by its trademark Swoosh, is still among the most recognized brands in the world and an industry leader in the $57 billion U.S. sports footwear

and apparel market. And with 33 percent market share, it dominates the global athletic shoe market.[45]

Since captivating the shoe-buying public in the early 1980s with indomitable spokesperson Michael Jordan, Nike continues to outpace the athletic shoe competition while branding an ever-widening universe of sports equipment, apparel, and paraphernalia. The omnipresent Swoosh graces everything from bumper stickers to sunglasses to high school sports uniforms.

Not long after the introduction of Air Jordans, the first strains of the "Just Do It" ad campaign sealed Nike's reputation as a megabrand. Nike made the strategic image shift from simply pushing products to embodying love of sport, discipline, ambition, practice, and all other desirable traits of athleticism. It was also among the first in a long line of brands to latch on to the strategy of representing the freedom of self-expression.

Advertising has played no small part in Nike's continued success. In the United States alone, Nike recently spent $85 million annually on advertising,[46] with a recent combined total of $213 million in measured media, according to TNS Media Intelligence.[47] (In comparison, Adidas spent $47 million and Reebok spent $26 million.)[48]

Portland ad agency Wieden + Kennedy has been instrumental in creating and perpetuating Nike's image, so much so that the agency has a large division in-house at Nike headquarters. This intimate relationship allows creatives to focus solely on Nike work, and it gives them unparalleled access to executives, researchers, and anyone else who might provide the next inspiration for marketing greatness.

Although Nike has cleverly kept its ad agency nestled close to home, it has relied on outsourcing many of its non-executive responsibilities in order to reduce overhead. It could be argued that Nike, recognizing that its core competency lies in the design—and not the manufacturing—of shoes, was wise to transfer production overseas.

What's Left, Then?

Yet Nike took outsourcing to a new level, barely producing any of its products in its own factories. All of its shoes, for instance, are made by subcontractors. Although this allocation of production hasn't hurt the quality of the shoes at all, it has challenged Nike's reputation among fair-trade critics.

After initial allegations of sweatshop labor surfaced at Nike-sponsored factories, the company tried to reach out and reason with its more moderate critics. But this approach failed, and Nike found itself in the unenviable position of trying to defend its outsourcing practices while defending the location of its favored production shops from the competition.

So in a bold move designed to make converts of critics, Nike recently posted information on its Web site about all of the approximately 750 factories it uses to make shoes, apparel, and other sporting goods. It released the data alongside a comprehensive new corporate responsibility report summarizing the environmental and labor situations of its contract factories.[49] "This is a significant step that will blow away the myth that companies can't release their factory names because it's proprietary information," said Charles Kernaghan, executive director of the National Labor Committee, a New York-based anti-sweatshop group that has been no friend to Nike over the years. "If Nike can do it, so can Wal-Mart and all the rest."[50]

Jordan Isn't Forever

Knowing that shoe sales alone wouldn't be enough to sustain continued growth, Nike made the lateral move to learn more about its customers' involvement in sports and what needs it might be able to fill. Banking on the star power of the Swoosh, Nike has successfully branded apparel, sporting goods, sunglasses, and even an MP3 player made by Philips. Like many large companies who have found themselves at odds with the possible limitations of their brands, Nike realized that it would have to master the one-two punch of identifying new needs and supplying creative and desirable solutions.

To this end, Nike has branched into previously unexplored merchandising arenas. Assuming the company's original name from longtime CEO Phil Knight, it quietly launched the Blue Ribbon Sports line of urban-themed apparel. Sold only at high-end shops like Fred Segal and Barney's, the line seeks to fill a niche only recently discovered by the Adidas/Stella McCartney collaboration.[51]

In fitting with the times, Nike's head design honcho, John R. Hoke III, is encouraging his designers to develop environmentally sustainable designs. This may come as a surprise to anyone who's ever thought about how much foam and plastic goes into the average Nike sneaker, but a corporate-wide mission called "Considered" has designers rethinking the toxic materials used to put the spring in millions of steps.

"I'm very passionate about this idea," Hoke said. "We are going to challenge ourselves to think a little bit differently about the way we create products."[52]

Nipping at Nike's Heels

But despite its success and market retention, it hasn't been all roses for Nike recently. Feeling the need to step down, Phil Knight handed the reins to Bill Perez, former CEO of S.C. Johnson and Sons, who became the first outsider recruited for the executive tier since Nike's founding in 1968. But after barely a year on the job, Knight, who stayed close as chairman of the board, decided Perez couldn't "get his arms around the company." Citing numerous other conflicts, Knight accepted Perez's resignation and promoted Mark Parker, a 27-year veteran who was co-president of the Nike brand, as a replacement.[53]

Pressures are mounting from outside its Beaverton, Oregon, headquarters as well. German rival Adidas drew a few strides closer to Nike when it purchased Reebok for approximately $3.8 billion.[54] Joining forces will collectively help the brands negotiate shelf space and other sales issues in American stores, as well as aid in price discussion with Asian manufacturers. With recent combined global sales of $12 billion, the new supergroup of shoes isn't far from Nike's $14 billion.[55]

According to Jon Hickey, senior vice president of sports and entertainment marketing for the ad agency Mullen, Nike has its "first real, legitimate threat since the '80s. There's no way either one would even approach Nike, much less overtake them, on their own," he said. But now, "Nike has to respond. This new, combined entity has a chance to make a run. Now, it's game on."[56]

But when faced with a challenge, Nike simply knocks its bat against its cleats and steps up to the plate. "Our focus is on growing our own business," said Nike spokesman Alan Marks. "Of course we're in a competitive business, but we win by staying focused on our strategies and our consumers. And from that perspective nothing has changed."[57]

Putting It All Together

Nike has balanced its immense size and tremendous pressures for success by leaving individual business centers—such as research, production, and marketing—free to focus on their core competencies without worrying about the effects of corporate bloat. Along these lines, Nike has found continued success in the marketplace by moving away from being simply a sneaker company, instead positioning itself as a brand fulfilling the evolving needs of athletes. Will Nike continue to profit as it grows, or will it spread itself so thin that the competition will overtake it?

REVIEW QUESTIONS

1. Does Nike's structure adequately support the firm's strategy?
2. Has Nikely done an acceptable job in addressing the criticisms of its outsourcing and the practices of some of its suppliers?
3. If you were charged today with the task of creating an athletic apparel company comparable to Nike and were given the budget to do so, would you adopt the same networked structure as Nike? Why or why not?

TEAM PROJECT

Downsizing or Rightsizing?   If you're one of those losing a job, the process may be called "downsizing." Among managers making the decisions, you might hear it called "rightsizing." But it's all about restructuring through workforce reductions, and you'll find it common in business news reports.

Question: When organizations restructure and reduce the size of their workforces, is this best described as "downsizing" or "rightsizing"?

Research Directions:
- Find case studies and/or news reports that give actual examples of restructurings that involve workforce reductions.
- Identify the "goals" of the restructuring, that is, the purpose and objectives sought by management. What is it that management hopes to accomplish by restructuring?
- Identify the consequences of the restructuring for people, the workers who are displaced and those who remain. Who benefits; who suffers? What do they gain; what do they lose?
- Use the cases and your analysis to report whether or not the restructurings in these cases are best described as "downsizings" or "rightsizings." In your report take a critical position on each restructuring you have investigated: was it the correct thing to do or not, and why?

PERSONAL MANAGEMENT

Empowerment   It takes a lot of trust to be comfortable with **EMPOWERMENT**. But if you aren't willing and able to empower others, you'll not only compromise your own performance but also add to the stress of daily work. Empowerment involves allowing and helping others to do things, even things that you might be very good at doing yourself. The beauty of organizations is synergy—bringing together the contributions of many people to achieve something that is much greater than what any individual can accomplish alone. Empowerment gives synergy a chance. But many people, perhaps even you, suffer from control anxiety. They don't empower others because they fear losing control over a task or situation. In groups, they want or try to do everything by themselves; they are afraid to trust other team members with important tasks. Being "unwilling to let go," they try to do too much, with the risk of missed deadlines and even poor performance. They deny others opportunities to contribute, losing the benefits of their talents and often alienating them in the process.

Building the Brand Called "You"   Does the prior description apply to you? Are you someone who easily and comfortably empowers others? Or, do you suffer from control anxiety and an unwillingness to delegate? In group work, be a self-observer and test your present answers to these questions. Use the recommended self-assessments for more insights.

NEXT STEPS: MANAGEMENT LEARNING WORKBOOK

Self-Assessments
- What Are Your Managerial Assumptions? (#4)
- Empowering Others (#15)
- Organizational Design Preference (#17)

Experiential Exercises
- Leading through Participation (#16)
- The Future Workplace (#14)
- Organizational Design Preferences (#17)
- Which Organization Culture Fits You? (#8)

Human Resource Management

Planning Ahead

Chapter 11 Study Questions

1. What is human resource management?

2. How do organizations attract a quality workforce?

3. How do organizations develop a quality workforce?

4. How do organizations maintain a quality workforce?

How Do You *Really* Stack Up?

Most of us like to think we've got the talent to make it big. But odds are, in any organization there are only a handful of top performers and a far greater number of Average Joes. So how should an organization compensate? By hiring more superstars? Could that potentially be more trouble than its worth?

It can be a humbling day when a salesperson learns how he or she really stacks up against the 80/20 rule.

This time-honored truism of the retail industry holds that approximately 80 percent of sales are produced by approximately 20 percent of the sales staff.[1] What about organizations in general? Could it be that their core sales or performance objectives are accomplished mainly by a handful of *superstars?*

What *They* Think

"There are differences between someone who's amazingly productive and someone who's an amazing employee."
Brent Newhall, Fog Street Software contributor

SUPERSTARS: *"Superstars think like superstars long before the fans or the press anoint them."*
John Eliot, author of Overachievement: The New Model for Exceptional Performance.

REST OF US: *"I have this theory of life that there are four popular people in high school and then there are the rest of us. I write movies for the rest of us who never peaked in high school. For the people that did peak in high school and then realized later that it's all downhill, welcome to the movie as well."*
Nia Vardalos, actress and screenwriter—My Big Fat Greek Wedding.

Superstars are easy to identify in any industry. Whether they score an average of 35 points per NBA game or close nearly every deal that comes their way, they seem to have that magic touch that leaves *the rest of us* wondering how they do it.

Most managers with team performance goals to enforce would love to have at least one superstar in their stable. And most managers like to believe that when given the responsibility to bring on new personnel, that they innately "hire talent."

But what does this mean? How do managers decide what balance to strike in their workforce between high achievers and Average Joes? And what makes a "superstar," anyway? "There are differences between someone who's amazingly productive and someone who's an amazing employee," notes Brent Newhall, a contributor to the Fog Creek Software web site. "Productivity is part of it, but a person's personality has a huge impact on how well they work in an organization."[2]

In professional sports, a team doesn't have set performance goals—say, to score *X* number of points each game. Rather, sports teams succeed when they maximize their potential and score as many points as possible.

In such an instance, a high ratio of superstars to average players is preferable; not only will the superstars improve the team's potential for high scoring, but their talent will also elevate the performance of other players.

Contrast this with a Honda assembly plant. Here, a plant manager who looks for superstars to place on the shop floor would be wasting time. No matter how fast a worker can attach a door to a vehicle body, for instance, the body can't move along any faster than the rest of the line; the worker's speed, or degree of accomplishment, is relative to the rest of the crew's speed.

Because of this, a Honda plant manager might be better off hiring a crew of consistently performing autoworkers while seeking hot talent in the form of a creative floor manager who could innovate ways to cut costs or shorten the total product assembly time.

Then there are companies, like Hewlett-Packard, that specialize in innovation. To succeed amongst fierce competition, HP needs no shortage of superstars, because success in the marketplace depends on beating the competition in every category, from product conception to development to production to marketing.

So, have you thought about which you'd prefer—a team of superstars or a blend of talents? It's a competitive world out there, so get choosing!

The Numbers

"Stars and Scrubs" Major League Baseball Pitchers

Scrub	ERA >5.50
Fringe	ERA 5.00–5.50
Regular	ERA 4.00–5.00
Star	ERA 3.25–4.00
Superstar	ERA <3.25

Quick Facts

* Kobe Bryant's nine-game scoring streak of at least 40 points per game in 2003 matched one of equal length by Michael Jordan in the 1986–1987 NBA season.[3]
* The top 10 corporate chief information officers (CIOs) collectively earned $50 million last year.[4]
* Since 1989, poker superstar Phil Hellmuth has won more tournaments than anyone else.[5]
* Superstars are losing their hold on the Billboard music charts: the number of different artists appearing on the Top 200 chart grew by 31.5% in 10 years.[6]
* When *Harry Potter* author J. K. Rowling revealed the title of her latest book on the Web, the site received a peak of 600 hits per second, with 16 million in a 12-hour period.[7]

What Do *You* Think?

1. Can you think of any other industries besides sports where the advantages of having a "team" of superstars would be worth the cost?
2. What does it take to hire both superstars and strong supporting staff, and then keep each happy enough to keep working well together?

Human Resource Management			
Study Question 1	**Study Question 2**	**Study Question 3**	**Study Question 4**
Human Resource Management	**Attracting a Quality Workforce**	**Developing a Quality Workforce**	**Maintaining a Quality Workforce**
■ Human resource management process ■ Human capital and diversity ■ Laws against employment discrimination ■ Legal issues in HRM	■ Human resource planning ■ The recruiting process ■ Selection decisions	■ Employee orientation ■ Training and development ■ Performance management systems	■ Career development ■ Work-life balance ■ Compensation and benefits ■ Retention and turnover ■ Labor–management relations
Learning Check 1	**Learning Check 2**	**Learning Check 3**	**Learning Check 4**

I n his book *The Future of Success*, Robert Reich describes a shift away from a system in which people work loyally as traditional "employees" for "employers" who provide them career-long job and employment security.[8] In the emerging system we become sellers of our services (talents) to buyers (employers) who are willing to pay for them. Those employers who do "buy" are looking for the very best people, ones whose capabilities and motivations match the demands of high-performance situations.

■ The **social contract** reflects expectations in the employee–employer relationship.

Reich is talking about changes to the **social contract,** or expectations of the employee– employer relationship. As today's organizations reconfigure around networks, teams, and projects in the quest for flexibility, speed, and efficiency, the social contract is changing. For the individual, this means an emphasis on skills, responsibility, continuous learning, and mobility. For the organization, it means providing career development opportunities, challenging work assignments, the best support, high involvement, and incentive compensation.[9]

All of this, of course, affects your future career. "Create a brand called 'You,'" "Build a portfolio of skills," "Protect your mobility," "Take charge of your destiny," "Add value to your organization" advise the career gurus.[10] The advice is on target, but the really tough career readiness questions are these: Who am I? What do I want? What have I done? What do I know? What can I do? Why should someone hire me?

HUMAN RESOURCE MANAGEMENT

A marketing manager at Ideo, a Palo Alto–based industrial design firm, once said: "If you hire the right people . . . if you've got the right fit . . . then everything will take care of itself."[11] It really isn't quite that simple, but one fact of management remains very clear: if an organization doesn't have the right people available to do the required work, it has very little chance of long-term success.

HUMAN RESOURCE MANAGEMENT PROCESS

The process of **human resource management,** or HRM, involves attracting, developing, and maintaining a talented and energetic workforce. In an *Academy of Management Executive* article entitled "Putting People First for Organizational Success," scholars Jeffrey Pfeffer and John F. Veiga state: "There is a substantial and rapidly expanding body of evidence . . . that speaks to the strong connection between how firms manage their people and the economic results achieved."[12] They forcefully argue that organizations perform better when they treat their members better. This is what human resource management is all about.

The basic goal of human resource management is to build organizational performance capacity through people, to ensure that highly capable and enthusiastic people are always available. The three major responsibilities of human resource management are typically described as:

1. *Attracting a quality workforce*—human resource planning, employee recruitment, and employee selection.
2. *Developing a quality workforce*—employee orientation, training and development, and performance appraisal.
3. *Maintaining a quality workforce*—career development, work-life balance, compensation and benefits, retention and turnover, and labor– management relations.

There are many career opportunities in the human resource management profession. HRM departments are common in most organizations. HRM specialists are increasingly important in an environment complicated by legal issues, labor shortages, economic turmoil, changing corporate strategies, changing personal values, and more. As outsourcing of professional services becomes more popular, a growing number of firms provide specialized HRM services such as recruiting, compensation, outplacement, and the like. The Society for Human Resource Management, or SHRM, is a professional organization dedicated to keeping its membership up to date in all aspects of HRM and its complex legal environment.

Today, the human resources function is considered an integral component of strategic management. The concept of **strategic human resource management** refers to mobilizing human capital through the HRM process to best implement organizational strategies.[13] One indicator that the HRM process is truly strategic to an organization is when it is headed by a senior executive reporting directly to the chief executive officer. When Robert Nardelli took over as new CEO of Home Depot, for example, the first senior manager he hired was Denis Donovan, who became the firm's executive vice president for human resources. Donovan says: "CEOs and boards of directors are learning that human resources can be one of your biggest game-changers in terms of competitive advantage."[14] The strategic importance of HRM has been further accentuated by the spate of corporate ethics scandals. "It was a failure of people and that isn't lost on those in the executive suite," says Susan Meisinger, president of the Society for Human Resource Development.[15]

HUMAN CAPITAL AND DIVERSITY

A strong foundation of **human capital**—the economic value of people with job-relevant abilities, knowledge, experience, ideas, energies, and commitments—is essential to any organization's long-term performance success. Consider the management implications of these comments made by Jeffrey Pfeffer in his book, *The Human Equation: Building Profits by Putting People First.*[16]

■ **Human resource management** is the process of attracting, developing, and maintaining a high-quality workforce.

■ **Strategic human resource management** mobilizes human capital to implement organizational strategies.

■ **Human capital** is the economic value of people with job-relevant abilities, knowledge, ideas, energies, and commitments.

The key to managing people in ways that lead to profit, productivity, innovation, and real organizational learning ultimately lies in how you think about your organization and its people. . . . When you look at your people, do you see costs to be reduced? . . . Or, when you look at your people do you see intelligent, motivated, trustworthy individuals— the most critical and valuable strategic assets your organization can have?

The best employers know that to succeed in today's challenging times they must place a primacy on people. Author and consultant Lawrence Otis Graham suggests that managers committed to building high-performance work environments should take a simple test.[17] The first question is: "Which of the following qualities would you look for in anyone who works for you—work ethic, ambition and energy, knowledge, creativity, motivation, sincerity, outlook, collegiality and collaborativeness, curiosity, judgment and maturity, and integrity?" In answering, you most likely selected all of these qualities, or at least you should have. The next test question is: "Where can you find people with these workplace qualities?" The correct answer is "everywhere."

Graham is highlighting the importance of valuing diversity in human resources and being fully inclusive of all people with the talent and desire to do good work. Going back to The Topic chapter opener, the diversity found on sports teams is well representative of this human resource management principle. Job-relevant talent is not restricted because of anyone's race, gender, religion, marital or parental status, sexual orientation, ethnicity, or other diversity characteristics. And any time these characteristics interfere with finding, hiring, and utilizing the best employees, the loss in human capital will be someone else's gain.[18]

LAWS AGAINST EMPLOYMENT DISCRIMINATION

■ **Discrimination** occurs when someone is denied a job or job assignment for reasons not job relevant.

Discrimination in employment occurs when someone is denied a job or a job assignment for reasons that are not job relevant. A sample of major U.S. laws prohibiting job discrimination is provided in *Figure 11.1*. An important cornerstone of this legal protection is *Title VII of the Civil Rights Act of 1964*, as amended by the *Equal Employment Opportunity Act of 1972* and the *Civil Rights Act (EEOA) of 1991*.

■ **Equal employment opportunity** is the right to employment and advancement without regard to race, sex, religion, color, or national origin.

These acts provide for **equal employment opportunity** (EEO)—the right to employment without regard to race, color, national origin, religion, gender, age, or physical and mental ability. The intent is to ensure all citizens the right to gain and keep employment based only on ability to do the job, and performance once on the job. EEO is federally enforced by the Equal Employment Opportunity Commission (EEOC), which has the power to file civil lawsuits against organizations that do not provide timely resolution of any discrimination charges lodged against them. These laws generally apply to all public and private organizations employing 15 or more people.

■ **Affirmative action** is an effort to give preference in employment to women and minority group members.

Under Title VII, organizations are expected to show **affirmative action** in setting goals and having plans to ensure equal employment opportunity for members of *protected groups*, those historically underrepresented in the workforce. The purpose of *affirmative action plans* is to ensure that women and minorities are represented in the workforce in proportion to their labor market availability.[19] The pros and cons of affirmative action are debated at both the federal and state levels. Criticisms tend to focus on the use of group membership (e.g., female or minority status) as a criterion in employment decisions.[20] The issues raised include claims of *reverse discrimination*

Equal Pay Act of 1963	Requires equal pay for men and women performing equal work in an organization.
Title VII of the Civil Rights Act of 1964 (as amended)	Prohibits discrimination in employment based on race, color, religion, sex, or national origin.
Age Discrimination in Employment Act of 1967	Prohibits discrimination against persons over 40; restricts mandatory retirement.
Occupational Health and Safety Act of 1970	Establishes mandatory health and safety standards in workplaces.
Pregnancy Discrimination Act of 1978	Prohibits employment discrimination against pregnant workers.
Americans with Disabilities Act of 1990	Prohibits discrimination against a qualified individual on the basis of disability.
Civil Rights Act of 1991	Reaffirms Title VII of the 1964 Civil Rights Act; reinstates burden of proof by employer, and allows for punitive and compensatory damages.
Family and Medical Leave Act of 1993	Allows employees up to 12 weeks of unpaid leave with job guarantees for childbirth, adoption, or family illness.

Figure 11.1 Sample of U.S. laws against employment discrimination.

by members of majority populations. White males, for example, may claim that preferential treatment given to minorities in a particular situation interferes with their individual rights.

As a general rule EEO legal protections do not restrict an employer's right to establish **bona fide occupational qualifications.** These are criteria for employment that can be clearly justified as being related to a person's capacity to perform a job. The use of bona fide occupational qualifications based on race and color is not allowed under any circumstances; those based on sex, religion, and age are very difficult to support.[21]

Legal protection against employment discrimination is extensive. Listed below are four examples and brief summaries of their supporting laws.

▪ *Disabilities:* The *Americans with Disabilities Act of 1990* prevents discrimination against people with disabilities. The law forces employers to focus on abilities and what a person can do.

▪ *Age:* The *Age Discrimination in Employment Act of 1967 as amended in 1978 and 1986* protects workers against mandatory retirement ages. Age discrimination occurs when a qualified individual is adversely affected by a job action that replaces him or her with a younger worker.

▪ *Pregnancy:* The *Pregnancy Discrimination Act of 1978* protects female workers from discrimination because of pregnancy. A pregnant employee is protected against termination or adverse job action because of the pregnancy and is entitled to reasonable time off work.

▪ *Family matters:* The *Family and Medical Leave Act of 1993* protects workers who take unpaid leaves for family matters from losing their jobs or employment status. Workers are allowed up to 12 weeks leave for childbirth, adoption, personal illness, or illness of a family member.

▪ **Bona fide occupational qualifications** are employment criteria justified by capacity to perform a job.

LEGAL ISSUES IN HUMAN RESOURCE MANAGEMENT

All aspects of human resource management should be accomplished within our legal frameworks. Failure to do so is not only unjustified in a free society, but it can also be a very expensive mistake resulting in fines and penalties. Of course, the American legal and regulatory environment is constantly changing, and both managers and human resource professionals should always stay informed on the following and other issues of legal and ethical consequence.[22]

■ **Sexual harassment** is behavior of a sexual nature that affects a person's employment situation.

Sexual harassment occurs when a person experiences conduct or language of a sexual nature that affects their employment situation. According to the EEOC, sexual harassment is behavior that creates a hostile work environment, interferes with a person's ability to do a job, or interferes with a person's promotion potential. Organizations should have clear sexual harassment policies in place, along with fair and equitable procedures for implementing them.

The *Equal Pay Act of 1963* provides that men and women in the same organization should be paid equally for doing equal work in terms of skills, responsibilities, and working conditions. But a lingering issue with gender disparities in pay involves **comparable worth,** the notion that persons performing jobs of similar importance should be paid at comparable levels. Why should a long-distance truck driver, for example, be paid more than an elementary teacher in a public school? Does it make any difference that the former is a traditionally male occupation and the latter a traditionally female occupation? Advocates of comparable worth argue that such historical disparities result from gender bias. They would like to have the issue legally resolved.

■ **Comparable worth** holds that persons performing jobs of similar importance should be paid at comparable levels.

ISSUES AND SITUATIONS

Sexual Harassment Laws Are Strict

"If I had known you were getting married, I wouldn't have bothered you."

That statement, allegedly made by former CEO of Toyota's North American operations, Hideaki Otaka, is part of a $190 million lawsuit filed by his former personal assistant, Sayaka Kobayashi. She claimed that Otaka sexually harassed her with unwelcome romantic overtures, physical contact, and personal gifts. When she reported the problem to one of the firm's human resource executives, she was advised to meet one-on-one with Otaka to discuss the matter. Within a month the firm's general counsel suggested she might want to consider leaving the firm.

Kobayashi believes that Otaka's behaviors reflected patterns of "sexual discrimination" in Japanese culture. But whether culturally linked or not, sexual harassment laws are strict in the United States, and employers are expected to protect workers from "hostile work environments."

Toyota responded to the lawsuit by placing Otaka on leave (he later stepped down), and reiterated corporate policy: "zero tolerance toward sexual harassment or discrimination of any kind."

Legal experts say that any sexual harassment charge needs to be fully and fairly investigated, even when the accused is the chief executive. Because this might place a human resources director in a difficult position, the recommendation is that such complaints be reviewed by neutral outside experts or taken directly to the board of directors. In respect to the suggestion that Kobayashi meet alone with Otaka to discuss her claims, one says: "Having those two individuals meet alone is probably the worst way to bring about a resolution."

Critical Response

Should foreign employers in the United States be forgiven, or at least face relaxed penalties, when they run afoul of American employment laws that are very different from those of their home countries? Does this example prompt you to think about personal situations or cases where sexual harassment is an issue? Suppose you learn from another student or co-worker that she or he is the target of romantic overtures from an instructor or boss? What do you recommend or do, if anything?

The legal status and employee entitlements of *part-time workers* and **independent contractors** are also being debated. In today's era of downsizing and outsourcing projects, more and more persons are hired as temporary workers who work under contract to an organization and do not become part of its permanent workforce. They work only "as needed." But a problem occurs when they are engaged regularly by the same organization and become what many now call *permatemps*. They must often work without benefits such as health insurance and pension eligibilities. A number of legal cases are now before the courts seeking to make such independent contractors eligible for benefits.

Workplace privacy is the right of individuals to privacy on the job.[23] It is quite acceptable for employers to monitor the work performance and behavior of their employees. But employer practices can become invasive and cross legal and ethical lines, especially with the capabilities of information technology. Computers can easily monitor e-mails and Internet searches to track personal and unauthorized usage; they can identify who is called by telephone and how long conversations last; they can document work performance moment to moment; and they can easily do more. All of this information, furthermore, can be stored in vast databases that make it available to others, even without the individual's permission. The legal status of such electronic surveillance is being debated. Until things are cleared up, one consultant recommends the best approach for everyone is to "assume you have no privacy at work."[24]

▪ **Independent contractors** are hired as needed and are not part of the organization's permanent workforce.

▪ **Workplace privacy** is the right to privacy while at work.

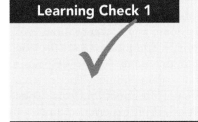

Learning Check 1

Be sure you can ▪ explain the human resource management process ▪ define the terms discrimination, equal employment opportunity, affirmative action, and bona fide occupational qualification ▪ define the terms social contract and human capital ▪ discuss how and why workforce diversity can be a source of performance advantage ▪ identify major laws that protect against discrimination in employment ▪ discuss legal issues of sexual harassment, comparable worth, and independent contractors

ATTRACTING A QUALITY WORKFORCE

The first responsibility of human resource management is to attract to the organization a high-quality workforce. An advertisement once run by the Motorola Corporation clearly identifies the goal: "Productivity is learning how to hire the person who is right for the job." To attract the right people to its workforce, an organization must first know exactly what it is looking for; it must have a clear understanding of the jobs to be done and the talents required to do them well. Then it must have the systems in place to excel at employee recruitment and selection.

HUMAN RESOURCE PLANNING

Human resource planning is the process of analyzing an organization's human resource needs and determining how to best fill them. The goal is to make sure that the best people are always in place when needed by the organization. The major elements in this process are shown in *Figure 11.2.*

Strategic human resource planning begins with a review of organizational mission, objectives, and strategies. This establishes a frame of reference for forecasting human resource needs and labor supplies. Ultimately, the planning process should help managers identify staffing requirements,

▪ **Human resource planning** analyzes staffing needs and identifies actions to fill those needs.

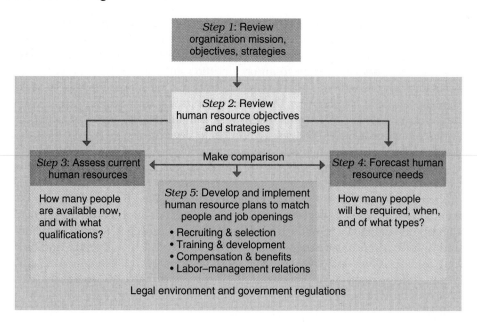

Figure 11.2 Steps in strategic human resource planning.

━━━

▨ A **job analysis** studies exactly what is done in a job, and why.

▨ A **job description** details the duties and responsibilities of a job holder.

▨ **Job specifications** list the qualifications required of a job holder.

▨ **Recruitment** is a set of activities designed to attract a qualified pool of job applicants.

━━━

assess the existing workforce, and determine what additions and/or replacements are required to meet future needs.

The foundations for human resource planning include **job analysis**—the orderly study of job facts to determine what is done, when, where, how, why, and by whom, in existing or potential new jobs.[25] The job analysis provides information that can then be used to write and/or update **job descriptions.** These are written statements of job duties and responsibilities. The information in a job analysis can also be used to create **job specifications.** These are lists of the qualifications—such as education, prior experience, and skill requirements—needed by someone hired for a given job.

THE RECRUITING PROCESS

Recruitment is a set of activities designed to attract a *qualified* pool of job applicants to an organization. Emphasis on the word "qualified" is important; recruiting should bring employment opportunities to the attention of people whose abilities and skills meet job specifications. The three steps in a typical recruitment process are (1) advertisement of a job vacancy, (2) preliminary contact with potential job candidates, and (3) initial screening to create a pool of qualified applicants.

External and Internal Recruitment

The recruiting taking place on college campuses in one example of *external recruitment*, in which job candidates are sought from outside the hiring organization. Web sites like HotJobs.com and Monster.com, newspapers, employment agencies, colleges, technical training centers, personal contacts, walk-ins, employee referrals, and even persons in competing organizations are all sources of external recruits. And, labor markets and recruiting are increasingly global in the new economy. When Nokia, the Finnish mobile phone maker, needed high-tech talent, it posted all job openings on a Web site and received thousands of résumés from all over the world. The head of Nokia's recruiting strategy said: "There are no geographical boundaries anymore."[26]

Internal recruitment seeks applicants from inside the organization. Most organizations have a procedure for announcing vacancies through newsletters, electronic bulletin boards, and the like. They also rely on managers to recommend subordinates as candidates for advancement. Internal recruitment creates opportunities for long-term career paths. Consider the story of Robert Goizueta. As CEO of Coca-Cola when he died, Goizueta owned over $1 billion of the company's stock. He made his way to the top over a 43-year career in the firm, an example of how loyalty and hard work can pay off.[27]

Both recruitment strategies offer potential advantages and disadvantages. External recruiting brings in outsiders with fresh perspectives, expertise and work experience. Internal recruitment is usually less expensive, and it deals with persons whose performance records are well known. A history of serious internal recruitment also builds employee loyalty and motivation, showing that one can advance by working hard and doing well when given responsibility.

Realistic Job Previews

In what may be called *traditional recruitment*, the emphasis is selling the organization to job applicants. The focus is on communicating the most positive features, perhaps to the point where these are exaggerated while negative features are avoided or concealed. This form of recruitment may create unrealistic expectations that cause costly turnover when new hires become disillusioned and quit. The individual suffers a career disruption; the employer suffers lost productivity and the added costs of having to recruit again.

The alternative is to provide **realistic job previews** that give the candidate all pertinent information about the job and organization without distortion and before the job is accepted.[28] Instead of "selling" only positive features, this approach tries to be open and balanced in describing the job and

▪ **Realistic job previews** provide job candidates with all pertinent information about a job and organization.

REAL ETHICS

Help Wanted–Saleswoman

Are you successful working in sales at mall fashion clothing and retail shops?

If so, a new and higher-paying option may be right for you. A local car dealership selling luxury vehicles wants outgoing, helpful women for client sales positions. Applicants should be honest and money motivated, with high initiative and excellent communication skills. Pay based on wages, commissions, and bonuses can reach $80,000 per year. Watch for our recruiters at your mall this weekend.

This add isn't real; you're unlikely to see anything like it in your local paper. But it is reflective of a trend in automobile sales—trying to hire more women and trying to recruit them in nontraditional settings.

Marketing surveys show that women influence some 80 percent of car purchases, and that many men prefer dealing with a female salesperson. One New York dealer

wants to move his sales force from 11 percent to 50 percent female. At a St. Louis dealership, the female owner claims that women are better organized and better at building a client base than are men; she wants to hire more.

A law professor at Washington University in St. Louis says that it's okay to try to hire more women if the dealers aren't getting enough applicants.

FURTHER INQUIRY

Suppose you're a qualified man, working in sales at a mall fashion store; you're honest, self-starting, a good communicator, turned on by money, and in love with cars. Where does this ad leave you? Is it ethical for the car dealer to interview only women for this position?

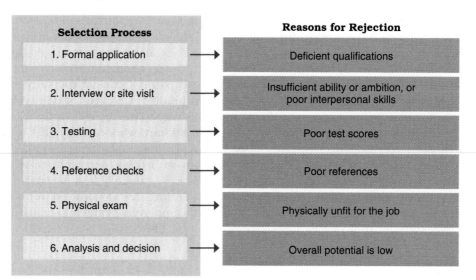

Selection Process	Reasons for Rejection
1. Formal application	Deficient qualifications
2. Interview or site visit	Insufficient ability or ambition, or poor interpersonal skills
3. Testing	Poor test scores
4. Reference checks	Poor references
5. Physical exam	Physically unfit for the job
6. Analysis and decision	Overall potential is low

Figure 11.3 Steps in the selection process: the case of a rejected job applicant.

■ **Selection** is choosing individuals to hire from a pool of qualified job applicants.

organization. Both favorable and unfavorable aspects are covered. The interviewer in a realistic job preview might use phrases such as "Of course, there are some downsides. . . ." "Things don't always go the way we hope. . . ." "Something that you will want to be prepared for is. . . .""We have found that some new hires had difficulty with. . . ." This type of conversation helps the candidate establish realistic job expectations and better prepare for the inevitable "ups and downs" of a new job. Higher levels of early job satisfaction and less inclination to quit prematurely are among the expected benefits.

HOW TO MAKE SELECTION DECISIONS

The process of **selection** involves choosing from a pool of applicants the person or persons who offer the greatest performance potential. Steps in a typical selection process are shown in *Figure 11.3*. They are (1) completion of a formal application, (2) interviewing, (3) testing, (4) reference checks, (5) physical examination, and (6) final analysis and decision to hire or reject. The goal in selection decisions is to get the best fit between the new hire and the organization.

Applications

The application declares the individual as a formal candidate for a job. It documents the applicant's personal history and qualifications. The personal résumé is often included with the job application. This important document should accurately summarize a person's special background and accomplishments. As a job applicant, you should exercise great care in preparing your résumé for job searches. As a recruiter, you should also learn how to screen applications and résumés for insights that can help you make good selection decisions.

Interviews

Interviews are times in the selection process when both the job applicant and potential employer can learn a lot about one another. However, they can be difficult for both parties. Sometimes interviewers ask the wrong things, sometimes they talk too much, sometimes the wrong people do the interviewing, sometimes their personal biases prevent an applicant's capabilities from being fully considered. Interviewees fail, too. They may be unprepared; they may be poor communicators; they may lack interpersonal skills. An increasingly common and challenging interview setting for job applicants is highlighted in *Management Smarts 11.1*—the telephone interview.

Employment Tests

Testing is often used in the screening of job applicants. Some of the common employment tests are designed to identify intelligence, aptitudes, personality, and interests. Whenever tests are used, the goal should be to gather information that will help predict the applicant's eventual performance success. Like any selection device, tests should meet the criteria of reliability and validity. **Reliability** means that the device is consistent in measurement; it returns the same results time after time. **Validity** means that there is a demonstrable relationship between a person's score or rating on a selection device and his or her eventual job performance. In simple terms, validity means that a good test score really does predict good performance.

New developments in testing extend into actual demonstrations of job-relevant skills and personal characteristics. An **assessment center** evaluates a person's potential by observing his or her performance in experiential activities designed to simulate daily work. A related approach is **work sampling,** which asks applicants to work on actual job tasks while being graded by observers on their performance. When Mercedes opened its new plant in Alabama, for example, it set up job-specific exercises to determine who had the best of the required skills and attitudes.[29] One was a tire-changing test, with color-coded bolts and a set of instructions. As Charlene Paige took the test, she went slowly and carefully followed directions; two men with her changed the tires really fast. Charlene got the job and soon worked into a team leader position.

Reference and Background Checks

Reference checks are inquiries to previous employers, academic advisors, co-workers, and/or acquaintances regarding the qualifications, experience, and past work records of a job applicant. Although they may be biased if friends are prearranged "to say the right things if called," reference checks are important. The Society for Human Resources Management estimates that 25 percent of job applications and résumés contain errors.[30] Reference checks can better inform the potential employer. They can also add credibility to the candidate if they back up what is said in an application.

Physical Examinations

Many organizations ask job applicants to take a physical examination. This health check helps ensure that the person is physically capable of fulfilling job requirements. It may also be used as a basis for enrolling the applicant

---

MANAGEMENT SMARTS 11.1

How to succeed in a telephone interview

- *Prepare ahead of time*—study the organization; carefully list your strengths and capabilities.
- *Take the call in private*—make sure you are in a quiet room, with privacy and without the possibility of interruptions.
- *Dress professionally*—don't be casual; dressing right increases confidence and sets a tone for your side of the conversation.
- *Practice your interview "voice"*—your impression will be made quickly; how you sound counts; it even helps to stand up while you talk.
- *Have reference materials handy*—your résumé and other supporting documents should be within easy reach.
- *Have a list of questions ready*—don't be caught hesitating; intersperse your best questions during the interview.
- *Ask what happens next*—find out how to follow up by telephone or e-mail; ask what other information you can provide.

■ **Reliability** means a selection device gives consistent results over repeated measures.

■ **Validity** means scores on a selection device have demonstrated links with future job performance.

■ An **assessment center** examines how job candidates handle simulated work situations.

■ In **work sampling,** applicants are evaluated while performing actual work tasks.

in health-related fringe benefits such as life, health, and disability insurance programs. A controversial development is drug testing, used for pre-employment health screening and even as a basis for continued employment in some organizations.

Final Decisions to Hire or Reject

The best selection decisions are most likely to be those involving extensive consultation among an applicant, future manager or team leader, and new co-workers, as well as the human resource staff. Importantly, the emphasis in selection should be comprehensive and should focus on the person's capacity to perform well. Just as a "good fit" can produce long-term advantage, a "bad fit" can be the source of many long-term problems.

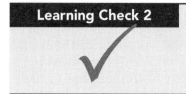

Learning Check 2

Be sure you can ■ explain the difference between internal recruitment and external recruitment ■ discuss the value of realistic job previews to employers and job candidates ■ differentiate reliability and validity as two criteria of selection devices ■ illustrate the operation of an assessment center ■ discuss the importance of conducting background and reference checks

DEVELOPING A QUALITY WORKFORCE

When people join an organization, they must "learn the ropes" and become familiar with "the way things are done." It is important to help newcomers fit into the work environment in a way that furthers their development and performance potential. **Socialization** is the process of influencing the expectations, behavior, and attitudes of a new employee in a desirable way.[31]

■ **Socialization** systematically influences the expectations, behavior, and attitudes of new employees.

EMPLOYEE ORIENTATION

Socialization of newcomers begins with **orientation**—a set of activities designed to familiarize new employees with their jobs, coworkers, and key aspects of the organization as a whole. This includes clarifying mission and culture, explaining operating objectives and job expectations, and communicating policies and procedures. At the Disney World Resort in Buena Vista, Florida, each employee is carefully selected and trained to provide high-quality customer service as a "cast member." During orientation, newly hired employees are taught the corporate culture. They learn that everyone employed by the company, regardless of her or his specific job—be it entertainer, ticket seller, or groundskeeper—is there "to make the customer happy." The company's interviewers say that they place a premium on personality. "We can train for skills," says an HRM specialist. "We want people who are enthusiastic, who have pride in their work, who can take charge of a situation without supervision."[32]

■ **Orientation** familiarizes new employees with jobs, co-workers, and organizational policies and services.

The first six months of employment are often crucial in determining how well someone is going to fit in and perform over the long run. It is a time when the original expectations are tested and patterns are set for future relationships between an individual and employer. Unfortunately, orientation is sometimes neglected and newcomers are often left to fend for themselves. They may learn job and organizational routines on their own or through casual interactions with co-workers, and they may acquire job attitudes the same way.[33] The result is that otherwise well-intentioned and capable persons may learn the wrong things and pick up bad attitudes and habits. A good orientation, like Disney's, can set the stage for high performance, job satisfaction, and work enthusiasm.

TRAINING AND DEVELOPMENT

Training is a set of activities that helps people acquire and improve job-related skills. This applies both to initial training of an employee and to upgrading or improving skills to meet changing job requirements. Organizations committed to their employees invest in extensive training and development programs to ensure that everyone always has the capabilities needed to perform well.

■ **Training** provides learning opportunities to acquire and improve job-related skills.

RESEARCH BRIEF

Racial bias may exist in supervisor ratings of workers

That is a conclusion of a research study by Joseph M. Stauffer and M. Ronald Buckley and reported in the *Journal of Applied Psychology*. The authors point out that it is important to have performance criteria and supervisory ratings that are free of bias. They cite a meta-analysis by Kraiger and Ford (1985) that showed White raters tending to rate White employees more favorably than Black employees, while Black raters rated Blacks more favorably than did Whites. They also cite a later study by Dackett and DuBois (1991) that disputed the finding that raters tended to favor members of their own racial groups.

In their study, Stauffer and Buckley re-analyzed the Dackett and DuBois data for possible interactions between rater and ratee race. The data included samples of military and civilian workers each of whom was rated by Black and White supervisors. Their findings are that in both samples White supervisors gave significantly higher ratings to White workers than they did Black workers, while Black supervisors also tended to favor White workers in their ratings.

Stauffer and Buckley advise caution in concluding that the rating differences are the result of racial prejudice, saying the data aren't sufficient to address this issue. They call for future studies to examine both the existence of bias in supervisory ratings and the causes of such bias. In terms of present implications, however, the authors say: "If you are a White ratee, then it doesn't matter if your supervisor is Black or White. If you are a Black ratee, then it is important whether your supervisor is Black or White."

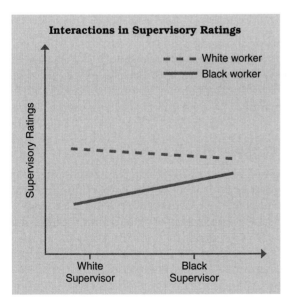

QUESTIONS & APPLICATIONS

Why would White supervisors rate Black workers lower than White workers in this study if it weren't based on racial prejudice? Why would Black supervisors consistently favor White workers over Black workers in their ratings? As you ponder this study, what research questions come to mind that you would like to see definitively answered through rigorous scientific studies in the future?

Is it possible that such findings could be replicated in respect to teacher ratings of student performance in our primary and secondary schools, as well as in college? Suggest a study design that would examine this possibility. Are you aware of any controversies involving the possibility of racial or any other type of bias in how workers are rated in other organizations?

References: Joseph M. Stauffer and M. Ronald Buckley, *"The Existence and Nature of Racial Bias in Supervisory Raitings,"* *Journal of Applied Psychology*, vol. 90 (2005), pp. 586–591. Also cited: K. Kraiger and J. K. Ford, "A Meta-analysis of Ratee Race Effects in Performance Ratings," *Journal of Applied Psychology*, vol. 70 (1985), pp. 56–65; and, P. R. Sackett and C. L. Z. DuBuois, "Rater-Ratee Race Effects on Performance Evaluations: Challenging Meta-Analytic Conclusion," *Journal of Applied Psychology*, vol. 76 (1991), pp. 873–877.

On-the-Job Training

On-the-job training takes place in the work setting while someone is doing a job. A common approach is job rotation that allows people to spend time working in different jobs and thus expand the range of their job capabilities. Another is **coaching,** in which an experienced person provides performance advice to someone else. **Mentoring** is a form of coaching in which early-career employees are formally assigned as protégés to senior persons. The mentoring relationship gives them regular access to advice on developing skills and getting better informed about the organization. **Modeling** is another type of coaching where someone demonstrates through their behavior that which is expected of others. A good example is how the behaviors of senior managers help set the ethical culture and standards for other employees.

■ **Coaching** occurs as an experienced person offers performance advice to a less-experienced person.

■ **Mentoring** assigns early career employees as protégés to more senior ones.

■ **Modeling** uses personal behavior to demonstrate performance expected of others.

Off-the-Job Training

Off-the-job training is accomplished outside the work setting. An important form is **management development,** training designed to improve a person's knowledge and skill in the fundamentals of management. For example, *beginning managers* often benefit from training that emphasizes team leadership and communication; *middle managers* may benefit from training to better understand multifunctional viewpoints; *top managers* may benefit from advanced management training to sharpen their decision-making and negotiating skills, and to expand their awareness of corporate strategy and direction. At the Center for Creative Leadership, managers learn by participating in the Looking Glass simulation that models the pressures of daily work. The simulation is followed by extensive debriefings and discussions in which participants give feedback to one another. One participant commented, "You can look in the mirror but you don't see yourself. People have to say how you look."[34]

■ **Management development** is training to improve knowledge and skills in the management process.

PERFORMANCE MANAGEMENT SYSTEMS

An important part of human resource management is design and implementation of a successful **performance management system.** This is a system that ensures that performance standards and objectives are set, that performance is regularly assessed for accomplishments, and that actions are taken to improve future performance.

■ A **performance management system** sets standards, assesses results, and plans for performance improvements.

Purpose of Performance Appraisal

The process of formally assessing someone's work accomplishments and providing feedback is **performance appraisal.** It serves both evaluation and development purposes. The *evaluation purpose* is intended to let people know where they stand relative to performance objectives and standards. The *development purpose* is intended to assist in their training and continued personal development.[35]

The evaluation purpose of performance appraisal focuses on past performance and measures results against standards. Performance is documented for the record and to establish a basis for allocating rewards. Here the manager acts in a *judgmental role*, in which he or she gives a direct evaluation of another person's accomplishments.

The development purpose of performance appraisal, by contrast, focuses on future performance and the clarification of success standards. It is a way of

■ **Performance appraisal** is the process of formally evaluating performance and providing feedback to a job holder.

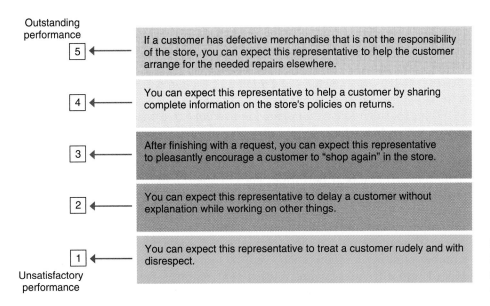

Outstanding performance

5 ← If a customer has defective merchandise that is not the responsibility of the store, you can expect this representative to help the customer arrange for the needed repairs elsewhere.

4 ← You can expect this representative to help a customer by sharing complete information on the store's policies on returns.

3 ← After finishing with a request, you can expect this representative to pleasantly encourage a customer to "shop again" in the store.

2 ← You can expect this representative to delay a customer without explanation while working on other things.

1 ← You can expect this representative to treat a customer rudely and with disrespect.

Unsatisfactory performance

Figure 11.4 Sample behaviorally anchored rating scale for performance appraisal.

discovering performance obstacles and identifying training and development opportunities. Here the manager acts in a *counseling role*, focusing on the other person's developmental needs.

Like employment tests, any performance appraisal method should meet the criteria of *reliability* and *validity*. To be reliable, the method should consistently yield the same result over time and/or for different raters. To be valid, it should be unbiased and measure only factors directly relevant to job performance. Both criteria are especially important in today's complex legal environment. At a minimum, written documentation of rigorous performance appraisals and a record of consistent past actions will be required to back up any contested evaluations.

Performance Appraisal Methods

Organizations use a variety of performance appraisal methods.[36] One of the simplest is a **graphic rating scale** in which appraisers complete checklists of traits or performance characteristics, such as quality of work and punctuality. A manager rates the individual on each item using a numerical score. Athough this approach is quick and easy to complete, its reliability and validity are questionable.

A more advanced approach is the **behaviorally anchored rating scale** (BARS), which describes actual behaviors for various levels of performance achievement in a job. Look at the case of a customer service representative illustrated in *Figure 11.4.* "Extremely poor" performance is clearly defined as rude or disrespectful treatment of a customer. Because performance assessments are anchored to specific descriptions of work behavior, a BARS is more reliable and valid than the graphic rating scale. The behavioral anchors can also be helpful in training people to master job skills. The city of Irving, Texas, used a BARS approach in redesigning its performance appraisal system. Many examples of different levels of job performance were written so that appraisers could pick the ones most representative of city workers' job performance.[37]

The **critical-incident technique** involves keeping a running log or inventory of effective and ineffective job behaviors. This written record documents success or failure patterns that can be specifically discussed with the

▪ A **graphic rating scale** uses a checklist of traits or characteristics to evaluate performance.

▪ A **behaviorally anchored rating scale** uses specific descriptions of actual behaviors to rate various levels of performance.

▪ The **critical-incident technique** keeps a log of someone's effective and ineffective job behaviors.

▪ A **multiperson comparison** compares one person's performance with that of others.

individual. Using the case of the customer service representative again, a critical-incidents log might contain the following types of entries: *Positive example* —"Took extraordinary care of a customer who had purchased a defective item from a company store in another city"; *negative example* — "Acted rudely in dismissing the complaint of a customer who felt that a sale item was erroneously advertised."

Some performance management systems use **multiperson comparisons,** which formally compare one person's performance with that of one or more others. Such comparisons can be done in different ways. In *rank ordering*, all persons being rated are arranged in order of performance achievement. The best performer goes at the top of the list, the worst performer at the bottom; no ties are allowed. In *paired comparisons*, each person is formally compared with every other person and rated as either the superior or the weaker member of the pair. After all paired comparisons are made, each person is assigned a summary ranking based on the number of superior scores achieved. In *forced distribution*, each person is placed into a frequency distribution that requires that a certain percentage fall into specific performance classifications, such as top 10 percent, next 40 percent, next 40 percent, and bottom 10 percent.

▪ **360° feedback** includes in the appraisal process superiors, subordinates, peers, and even customers.

Not all performance appraisals are completed only by one's immediate boss. It is increasingly popular to include more of a job's stakeholders in the appraisal process. The new workplace often involves use of *peer appraisal* that includes in the process others who work regularly and directly with a job holder, and *upward appraisal* that includes subordinates reporting to the job holder. An even broader stakeholder approach is known as **360° feedback,** where superiors, subordinates, peers, and even internal and external customers are involved in the appraisal of a job holder's performance.[38]

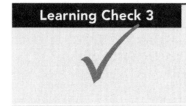

Learning Check 3

Be sure you can ▪ define the term socialization and describe its importance to organizations ▪ explain coaching, mentoring, and modeling as on-the-job training approaches ▪ discuss strengths and weaknesses of performance appraisal methods—graphic rating scales, behaviorally anchored rating scales, critical-incident technique, and multiperson comparisons ▪ explain the process of 360° feedback

MAINTAINING A QUALITY WORKFORCE

It is not enough to hire and train workers to meet an organization's immediate needs. They must be successfully retained, nurtured, and managed for long-term effectiveness. If talented workers leave to pursue other opportunities, the resulting costs for the employer can be staggering. Employers surveyed by the Society for Human Resource Management reported that the most effective tools for maintaining a quality workforce were good benefits—especially health care—competitive salaries, flexible work schedules and personal time off, and opportunities for training and development.[39]

CAREER DEVELOPMENT

In his book *The Age of Unreason*, British scholar and consultant Charles Handy discusses dramatic new developments in the world of work and careers. Specifically, Handy says: "The times are changing and we must change with them."[40]

A **career** is a sequence of jobs and work pursuits that constitutes what a person does for a living. For many of us, a career begins on an anticipatory basis with our formal education. From there it progresses into an initial job choice and any number of subsequent choices that may involve changes in task assignments, employing organizations, and even occupations.

A *career path* is a sequence of jobs held over time during a career. Career paths vary between those that are pursued internally with the same employer and those pursued externally among various employers. Although many organizations place great emphasis on making long-term career opportunities available to their employees, Handy believes that external career paths will be increasingly important in the future. The difference can be described as the "lifetime loyalty model" versus the "self-directed career model."[41]

Career planning is the process of systematically matching career goals and individual capabilities with opportunities for their fulfillment. It involves answering such questions as "Who am I?" "Where do I want to go?" and "How do I get there?" While some suggest that a career should be allowed to progress in a somewhat random but always opportunistic way, others view a career as something to be rationally planned and pursued in a logical step-by-step fashion. In fact, a well-managed career will probably

■ A **career** is a sequence of jobs that constitutes what a person does for a living.

■ **Career planning** is the process of matching career goals and individual capabilities with opportunities for their fulfillment.

INSIGHTS

People are Valuable Assets, not Costs

Working Mother magazine's annual listing of the "100 Best Companies for Working Mothers" has become an important management benchmark—both for employers that want to be able to say that they are among the best, and for potential employees who only want to work for the best. The magazine has achieved prominence as a major supporter of mothers with work careers. Monthly topics cover the full gamut from kids to health to personal motivation and more. Self-described as helping women "integrate their professional lives, their family lives and their inner lives," *Working Mother* mainstreams coverage of work–life balance issues and needs for women. Its focus has garnered a monthly readership of over 3 million.

Pick up any copy of Working Mother *magazine or browse the online version. It should remind you of the complexities of work-life balance in our complex environment and the resulting challenges faced by people and their employers, including the challenges and opportunities faced by women at work, and of blending motherhood with a career.*

Working Mother magazine is part of Working Mother Media, a conglomerate headed by CEO Carol Evans and including the National Association for Female Executives (NAFE)—the country's largest women's professional organization. NAFE focuses on "education, networking, and public advocacy, to empower its members to achieve career success and financial security." Working Mother Media also operates Business Advisory Services for women business owners and a conference division.

One issue of *Working Mother* reported on moms who "pushed for more family-friendly benefits and got them." The article described how Kristina Marsh worked to get lactation support for nursing mothers as a formal benefit at Dow Corning, and how Beth Schiavo started a Working Moms Network in Ernst & Young's Atlanta offices and then got it approved as a nationwide corporate program. As soon as a woman announces that she is pregnant, a network forms to support and assist her. Schiavo says: "The goal is to make sure these women understand that, yes, it can be an intimidating time, but all the aspects of a career at Ernst & Young are still there for you."

include elements of each. The carefully thought-out plan can point you in a general career direction; an eye for opportunity can fill in the details along the way.

When you think about adult life stages or transitions, you should recognize that sooner or later most people's careers level off. A **career plateau** is a position from which someone is unlikely to move to a higher level of work responsibility.[42] Three common reasons for career plateaus are personal choice, limited abilities, and lack of opportunity. For some, the plateau may occur at a point in life when it suits their individual needs. For others, plateaus can be very frustrating. For employers the challenge is to find ways to engage plateaued employees with new opportunities such as lateral moves, mentoring assignments, and even overseas jobs.

> ▨ A **career plateau** is a position from which someone is unlikely to move to a higher level of work responsibility.

WORK-LIFE BALANCE

"Hiring good people is tough," starts an article in the *Harvard Business Review.* The sentence finishes with "keeping them can be even tougher."[43] A very important retention issue given today's fast-paced and complicated lifestyles is **work-life balance**—how people balance the demands of careers with their personal and family needs. "Family" in this context includes not just children but also elderly parents and other relatives in need of care.

> ▨ **Work-life balance** involves balancing career demands with personal and family needs.

Included among work-life balance concerns are the unique needs of *single parents*, who must balance parenting responsibilities with a job, and *dual-career couples*, who must balance the career needs and opportunities of each partner. The special situations of both working mothers and working fathers are also being recognized.[44] Not surprisingly, the "family-friendliness" of an employer is now frequently and justifiably used as a screening criterion by job candidates. *Business Week, Working Mother*, and *Fortune* are among the magazines annually ranking employers on this criterion.

COMPENSATION AND BENEFITS

Good compensation and benefit systems attract qualified people to the organization and help retain them. **Base compensation** in the form of salary or hourly wages can help get the right people into jobs to begin with and keep them there by making outside opportunities less attractive. Unless an organization's prevailing wage and salary structure is competitive in the relevant labor markets, it will be difficult to attract and retain a staff of highly competent workers.

> ▨ **Base compensation** is a salary or hourly wage paid to an individual.

Also important are **fringe benefits,** the additional nonwage or nonsalary forms of compensation. Benefit packages can constitute some 30 percent or more of a typical worker's earnings. They usually include various options for disability protection, health and life insurance, and retirement plans.

The ever-rising cost of fringe benefits, particularly employee medical benefits, is a major worry for employers. Many are attempting to gain control over health care costs by becoming more active in their employees' choices

> ▨ **Fringe benefits** are nonmonetary forms of compensation such as health insurance and retirement plans.

of health care providers and by encouraging healthy lifestyles. An increasingly common approach is **flexible benefits,** sometimes known as *cafeteria benefits*, which lets the employee choose a set of benefits within a certain dollar amount.

The growing significance of work-life balance in the new social contract is reflected in a trend toward more **family-friendly benefits** that help employees better balance work and non-work responsibilities. These include child care, elder care, flexible schedules, parental leave, and part-time employment options, among others. Increasingly common also are **employee assistance programs** that help employees deal with troublesome personal problems. EAP programs may include assistance in dealing with stress, counseling on alcohol and substance abuse problems, referrals for domestic violence and sexual abuse, family and marital counseling, and advice on community resources.

■ **Flexible benefits** programs allow employees to choose from a range of benefit options.

■ **Family-friendly benefits** help employees achieve better work-life balance.

■ **Employee assistance programs** help employees cope with personal stresses and problems.

RETENTION AND TURNOVER

The several steps in the human resource management process both conclude and recycle with *replacement* decisions. These involve the management of promotions, transfers, terminations, layoffs, and retirements. Any replacement situation is an opportunity to review human resource plans, update job analyses, rewrite job descriptions and job specifications, and ensure that the best people are selected to perform the required tasks.

Some replacement decisions shift people between positions within the organization. *Promotion* is movement to a higher-level position; *transfer* is movement to a different job at a similar level of responsibility. Another set of replacement decisions relates to *retirement*, something most people look forward to . . . until it is close at hand. Then the prospect of being retired often raises fears and apprehensions. Many organizations offer special counseling and other forms of support for retiring employees, including advice on company benefits, money management, estate planning, and use of leisure time.

The most extreme replacement decisions involve *termination*, the involuntary and permanent dismissal of an employee. In some cases the termination is based on performance problems. The person involved is not meeting the requirements of the job or has violated key organizational policy. In other cases the termination may be the result of the employer's financial conditions, such as those requiring downsizing or restructuring. The persons involved may be performing well but are being terminated as part of a workforce reduction.

It is common that a person being dismissed finds it hard to accept the decision. Where possible, organizations should provide outplacement services to help terminated employees find other jobs. In any and all cases, terminations should be handled fairly according to organizational policies and in full legal compliance.

LABOR-MANAGEMENT RELATIONS

A final aspect of human resource management involves the role of organized labor. **Labor unions** are organizations to which workers belong that deal with employers on the workers' behalf.[45] Although they used to be associated primarily with industrial and business occupations, labor unions increasingly represent such public-sector employees as teachers, college professors, police officers, and government workers. They are important forces in the modern workplace both in the United States and around the world.

■ A **labor union** is an organization that deals with employers on the workers' collective behalf.

■ A **labor contract** is a formal agreement between a union and employer about the terms of work for union members.

■ **Collective bargaining** is the process of negotiating, administering, and interpreting a labor contract.

About 12.5 percent of American workers belong to a union; the figures are over 30 percent for Canada and some 25 percent for Great Britain.[46]

Labor unions act as a collective "voice" for members in dealing with employers. They serve as bargaining agents that negotiate legal contracts affecting many aspects of the employment relationship. These **labor contracts** typically specify the rights and obligations of employees and management with respect to wages, work hours, work rules, seniority, hiring, grievances, and other conditions of employment. All of this has implications for management.

The foundation of any labor and management relationship is **collective bargaining,** which is the process of negotiating, administering, and interpreting labor contracts. Labor contracts and the collective bargaining process—from negotiating a new contract to resolving disputes under an existing one—are major influences on human resource management in unionized work settings. They are also governed closely in the United States by a strict legal framework with three important foundations. The *National Labor Relations Act of 1935* (known as the *Wagner Act*) protects employees by recognizing their right to join unions and engage in union activities. It is

KAFFEEKLATSCH

Work Sabbaticals

First Cup

"You know this coffee tastes so good it makes me wonder. Suppose we had a 'coffee break' that was a couple of months long—say every five years. Wouldn't that refresh you and rejuvenate the system, bringing you back to work full of energy, ideas, and enthusiasm? I know that universities give their faculty members sabbaticals every six or seven years. Why don't other employers do the same?"

Studying the Grounds

■ Charles Schwab gives 4 weeks off after 5 years' employment, with supervisor's approval; Intel offers 8 weeks after 7 years; McDonald's gives salaried employees 8 weeks off after 10 years' employment.

■ Studies suggest that vacations aren't sufficient for workers to "rest and reflect"; also, the fact is that many workers don't use their full vacation time each year.

■ Most companies reward longevity with modesty; Hewitt Associates reports that 75 percent in one survey gave gifts up to $50, while 67 percent added a party.

Double Espresso

"That may be a dream for us. Sure, I'd take a 'sabbatical' if it was offered and be very thankful in return. But let me push you further. Suppose the company just allowed us re-

lief from all this extra workload on occasion—mini-sabbaticals so to speak, even the occasional 'long weekend'. I don't feel like I'm ever caught up. I take that notebook computer home all the time, and between it and my Blackberry, it's like having the office with you 24 hours a day."

■ Cummins (Columbus, Indiana) and Alcan (Montreal) are among firms finding decreased employee satisfaction with increasing workloads. Both started programs designed to help employees "push back" and work smarter to reduce workloads.

■ Consulting advice for employers on how to cut back work overloads includes: holding fewer and shorter meetings, requiring fewer internal reports, eliminating unnecessary tasks, discouraging overtime work, and counseling employees on the importance of personal and vacation time.

Your Turn

Time management is a popular theme; but what about workload management? Is this something we have to do for ourselves, or do employers have responsibilities also? Are firms like Cummins and Alcan moving in the right direction when they train managers and revise systems in order to help reduce work overloads? Is it a small price to pay to "overstaff" a bit so that people can take personal time, use their vacations, and even go on the occasional "sabbatical"?

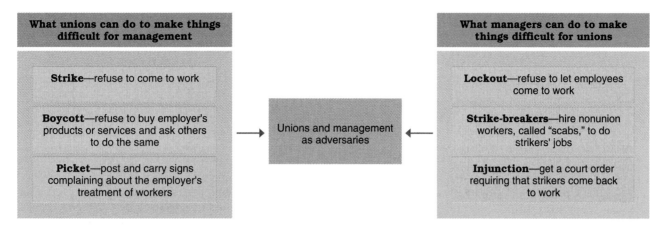

Figure 11.5 Traditional adversarial view of labor–management relations.

enforced by the National Labor Relations Board (NLRB). The *Taft-Hartley Act of 1947* protects employers from unfair labor practices by unions and allows workers to decertify unions. And, the *Civil Service Reform Act Title VII of 1978* clarifies the right of government employees to join and be represented by labor unions.

The collective bargaining process typically occurs in face-to-face meetings between labor and management representatives. During this time, a variety of demands, proposals, and counterproposals are exchanged. Several rounds of bargaining may be required before a contract is reached or a dispute over a contract issue is resolved. And, as you might expect, the process can lead to problems. In *Figure 11.5*, labor and management are viewed as "win-lose" adversaries destined to be in opposition and possessed of certain weapons with which to fight one another. If labor–management relations take this form, a lot of energy on both sides can be expended in prolonged conflict.

The adversarial approach is, to some extent, giving way as each side seems more willing to understand the need for cooperation in new and challenging times. An example is the way the United Auto Workers union responded to Ford's plans to reduce its workforce by 30,000 and close several plants, as it faced stiff competition from Japanese automakers and declining sales of its products. The union's approach was to try and work with Ford's management to help reduce operating costs, gain efficiency, and improve profits. Ford, in turn, offered displaced workers buyouts and early retirement packages, as well as tuition assistance for training in alternative careers. Tim Levandusky, president of a UAW local, described the situation this way: "We all have a lot to lose in this. We understand the importance of working together."[47]

Be sure you can ■ define the terms career plateau and work-life balance ■ discuss the significance of each term for the human resource management process ■ explain why compensation and benefits are important elements in human resource management ■ define the terms labor union, labor contract, and collective bargaining ■ compare the adversarial and cooperative approaches to labor–management relations

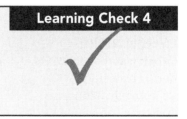

Learning Check 4

CHAPTER 11 STUDY GUIDE

STUDY QUESTIONS SUMMARY

1 What is human resource management?

- The human resource management process involves attracting, developing, and maintaining a quality workforce.
- Human resource management becomes strategic when it is integrated into the organization's top management structure.
- Employees have legal protections against employment discrimination; equal employment opportunity guarantees people the right to employment and advancement without discrimination.
- Legal issues in human resource management include sexual harassment, comparable worth, rights of independent contractors, and employee privacy.

2 How do organizations attract a quality workforce?

- Human resource planning analyzes staffing needs and identifies actions to meet these needs over time.
- Recruitment is the process of attracting qualified job candidates to fill vacant positions.
- Realistic job previews provide candidates with accurate information on the job and organization.
- Interviews, employment tests, and reference checks help managers make selection decisions.
- The use of assessment centers and work sampling is becoming more common in the selection process.

3 How do organizations develop a quality workforce?

- Orientation is the process of formally introducing new employees to their jobs, performance expectations, and the organization.
- On-the-job training includes coaching, apprenticeship, modeling, and mentoring; off-the-job training includes formal job training and management development courses.
- Performance management systems establish work standards and the means for assessing performance results.
- Common performance appraisal methods are graphic rating scales, narratives, behaviorally anchored rating scales, and multiperson comparisons.

4 How do organizations maintain a quality workforce?

- Career planning systematically matches individual career goals and capabilities with opportunities for their fulfillment.
- Complex demands of job and family responsibilities have made work-life balance programs increasingly important in human resource management.
- Compensation and benefits packages must be attractive so that an organization stays competitive in labor markets.
- Replacement decisions in human resource management involve promotions, transfers, retirements, and/or terminations.
- The collective bargaining process and labor–management relations are carefully governed by law.

KEY TERMS REVIEW

Affirmative action (p. 266)
Assessment center (p. 273)
Base compensation (p. 280)
Behaviorally anchored rating scale (p. 277)
Bona fide occupational qualifications (p. 267)
Career (p. 279)
Career planning (p. 279)
Career plateau (p. 280)
Coaching (p. 276)
Collective bargaining (p. 282)
Comparable worth (p. 268)

Critical-incident technique (p. 277)
Discrimination (p. 266)
Employee assistance programs (p. 281)
Equal employment opportunity (p. 266)
Family-friendly benefits (p. 281)
Flexible benefits (p. 281)
Fringe benefits (p. 280)
Graphic rating scale (p. 277)
Human capital (p. 265)
Human resource management (p. 265)

Human resource planning (p. 269)
Independent contractors (p. 269)
Job analysis (p. 270)
Job description (p. 270)
Job specification (p. 270)
Labor contract (p. 282)
Labor union (p. 281)
Management development (p. 276)
Mentoring (p. 276)
Modeling (p. 276)
Multiperson comparison (p. 278)
Orientation (p. 274)
Performance appraisal (p. 276)

Performance management system
   (p. 276)
Realistic job preview (p. 271)
Recruitment (p. 270)
Reliability (p. 273)
Selection (p. 272)

Sexual harassment (p. 268)
Social contract (p. 264)
Socialization (p. 274)
Strategic human resource
   management (p. 265)
360° feedback (p. 278)

Training (p. 275)
Validity (p. 273)
Work sampling (p. 273)
Work-life balance (p. 280)
Workplace privacy (p. 269)

SELF-TEST 11

MULTIPLE-CHOICE QUESTIONS:

1. Human resource management is the process of _____, developing, and maintaining a high-quality workforce.

   (a) attracting　(b) compensating　(c) appraising　(d) selecting

2. A _____ is a criterion that can be legally justified for use in screening candidates for employment.

   (a) job description　(b) bona fide occupational qualification　(c) job specification　(d) BARS

3. _____ programs are designed to ensure equal employment opportunities for persons historically under-represented in the workforce.

   (a) Realistic recruiting　(b) External recruiting　(c) Affirmative action　(d) Employee assistance

4. If an employment test yields different results over time when taken by the same person, it lacks _____.

   (a) validity　(b) specificity　(c) realism　(d) reliability

5. The assessment center approach to employee selection relies heavily on _____.

   (a) pencil-and-paper tests　(b) simulations and experiential exercises　(c) 360° feedback　(d) formal one-on-one interviews

6. _____ is a form of on-the-job training wherein an individual learns by observing others who demonstrate desirable job behaviors.

   (a) Case study　(b) Work sampling　(c) Modeling　(d) Simulation

7. The first step in strategic human resource planning is to _____.

   (a) forecast human resource needs　(b) forecast labor supplies　(c) assess the existing workforce　(d) review organizational mission, objectives, and strategies

8. In the United States, the _____ Act of 1947 protects employers from unfair labor practices by unions.

   (a) Wagner　(b) Taft-Hartley　(c) Labor Union　(d) Hawley-Smoot

9. Socialization of newcomers occurs during the _____ step of the staffing process.

   (a) recruiting　(b) orientation　(c) selecting　(d) training

10. In human resource planning, a/an _____ is used to determine exactly what is done in an existing job.

    (a) critical-incident technique　(b) assessment center　(c) job analysis　(d) multiperson comparison

11. In what is called the new "social contract" between employers and employees, the implications for the individual include accepting more personal responsibility for _____.

    (a) learning and career mobility　(b) salary negotiation　(c) labor–management relations　(d) socialization

12. The _____ purpose of performance appraisal is being addressed when a manager describes training options that might help an employee improve future performance.

    (a) development　(b) evaluation　(c) judgmental　(d) legal

13. When a team leader is required to rate 10 percent of team members as "superior," 80 percent as "good," and 10 percent as "unacceptable" for their performance on a project, this is an example of the _____ approach to performance appraisal.

    (a) graphic　(b) forced distribution　(c) behaviorally anchored rating scale　(d) realistic

14. An employee with family problems that are starting to interfere with work would be pleased to learn that his employer had a(n) _____ plan to help on such matters.

    (a) employee assistance　(b) cafeteria benefits　(c) comparable worth　(d) collective bargaining

15. A manager who _____ is displaying a commitment to valuing human capital.

    (a) believes payroll costs should be reduced wherever possible　(b) is always looking for new ways to replace people with machines　(c) protects workers from stress by withholding information from them about the organization's performance　(d) views people as assets to be nurtured and developed over time

SHORT-RESPONSE QUESTIONS:

16. How do internal recruitment and external recruitment compare in terms of advantages and disadvantages for the employer?
17. Why is orientation an important part of the staffing process?
18. What is the difference between the graphic rating scale and the BARS as performance appraisal methods?
19. How does mentoring work as a form of on-the-job training?

APPLICATION QUESTION:

20. Sy Smith is not doing well in his job. The problems began to appear shortly after Sy's job was changed from a manual to a computer-based operation. He has tried hard but is just not doing well in learning to use the computer, and as a result is having difficulty meeting performance expectations. As a 55-year-old employee with over 30 years with the company, Sy is both popular and influential among his work peers. Along with his performance problems, you have also noticed the appearance of some negative attitudes, including a tendency for Sy to sometimes "badmouth" the firm. As Sy's manager, what options would you consider in terms of dealing with the issue of his retention in the job and in the company? What would you do and why?

CHAPTER 11 APPLICATIONS

CASE 11

Hewlett-Packard: Leading the Pack

Had Thomas Edison, one of America's most prolific and storied inventors, lived long enough to observe any portion of Hewlett-Packard's long history of innovation, he might well have applied for a job there. The Palo Alto, California, company's heritage is steeped in technological breakthroughs, and their innovations have shaped the efficiency and progress of nearly every scientific and technical discipline. How did they go from being a two-man shop in a backyard garage to one of the world's most successful tech companies?

From Humble Roots

Though Hewlett-Packard is currently best known as a manufacturer of digital computing devices, the company's roots extend deep into the development of precomputing technology. The company was founded by Bill Hewlett and Dave Packard in 1939, starting life as a manufacturer of test and measurement instruments. Both Hewlett and Packard graduated from Stanford in 1934, and they started the company on a $538 investment. (According to legend, the order of their last names in the company name was determined by a coin toss.)[48]

The first product produced by HP was a precision audio oscillator, the Model 200A, which innovated on prior oscillators by its inventive use of a night-light bulb as a resistor in a crucial area of the circuit. This breakthrough allowed the fledgling company to sell its new creation at about a quarter of the price that competitors were asking for less stable oscillators. According to Dave Packard, the Model 200A was named as such "because we thought the name would make us look like we'd been around for awhile." Walt Disney Productions relied on eight of the succeeding models of oscillators to test their innovative Fantasound stereophonic sound system during the production of *Fantasia.*[49]

Over the years, HP continued to produce oscilloscopes, logic analyzers, and other measurement instruments that won a reputation among scientists as being durable and well-conceived; the emphasis on products that held up to scientific rigor was summarized in the design philosophy "design for the guy at the next bench."[50] In 1999, HP spun off the measurement product line to form Agilent Technologies, which specializes in manufacturing scientific instruments, optical networking devices, and semiconductors, among other products.[51]

Coming in First in Innovation

Hewlett-Packard has made a name for itself by pioneering new electronics products and technological innovations. Though claims abound as to who produced the first personal computer, the credit widely goes to HP for its 1968 model 9100A.

Curiously, its makers decided not to label it as the very thing it was. "If we had called it a computer, it would have been rejected by our customers' computer gurus because it didn't look like an IBM," said Bill Hewlett, looking back on the 9100A's debut. "We therefore decided to call it a calculator, and all such nonsense disappeared."[52] HP would go on to debut many more firsts in the scientific and engineering communities, especially with its development of specialty calculators.[53]

Expanding in All Directions

As the demand for personal computers grew to reach home consumers in the mid-1980s—fueled by innovations from IBM and Apple—Hewlett-Packard continued to expand into new markets. In 1984, HP introduced both laser and inkjet printers for desktop computers.[54] These printers, combined with HP's successful line of scanners, eventually formed the basis for its successful line of multifunction products, such as the stand-alone printer/scanner/copier/fax machines. Currently, HP is globally #1 in this market, as well as in the laser printer, large-format printing, scanner, and print server markets.[55]

Like many companies, HP looked to a combination of overseas plants and third-party companies to outsource its manufacturing needs. Though servers and workstations are still assembled in the United States, HP's desktop computers are assembled at an HP plant in Guadalajara, Mexico; its notebooks are assembled in China by third-party vendors.[56]

A number of acquisitions continually expanded the HP portfolio. But perhaps the most important was its 2002 merger with Compaq, creating an $87 billion company serving more than one billion customers in 162 countries. The consolidation gave HP access to Compaq's share of the desktop computing market, along with the technology that got it there, and it made the new HP the world's largest manufacturer of personal computers.[57] Moving beyond its traditional role of manufacturing, HP now bills itself as a consulting company offering a broad latitude of resources to design, implement, and ultimately support modern IT infrastructure.[58]

Bypassing Hurdles along the Way

As Hewlett-Packard continues to evolve and grow, it is seeking to leave behind a few public issues that drew negative publicity to a largely successful company. Carleton "Carly" Fiorina was a veteran of AT&T and Lucent Technologies who had been named "The Most Powerful Woman in Business" for six years running by *Fortune* magazine. HP named her president and CEO in July 1999, when then-CEO Lew Platt retired. The following September, she was named chair of the board of directors. Though she successfully navigated the merger with Compaq, she flew in the face of HP tradition when she accelerated layoffs to increase corporate profits. Other measures, like replacing the HP lobby portraits of company founders Hewlett and Packard with her own likeness, left a bitter taste among employees and investors alike. In February 2005, the board of directors ousted Fiorina and replaced her with former NCR Corporation

CEO Mark Hurd; HP stock jumped 7% at that news, and it has continued to rise since 2006, HP posted a record profit of $1.5 billion in just one quarter.[59]

Things looked bright for Hurd and HP until a major corporate spy scandal broke over the firm's secretive accessing of board members' private telephone records and setting up e-mail stings in an attempt to identify the source of confidential leaks.[60] In testimony before a Congressional House panel, Hurd called the snooping and "rouge investigation" and said: "If Bill Hewlett and Dave Packard were alive today they would be appalled." The former Board Chair, who had resigned over the scandal, said: "I do not accept personal responsibility for what happened." An employee wrote to the committee, "I think we need to re-focus our strategy and proceed on the high ground course."

Amidst all the furor and losses to corporate credibility, speculation existed over whether or not Hurd could withstand the scandal.

In the current era of ecological awareness, HP has been criticized by leading environmental groups, which have accused the company of poor practice regarding the reduction of hazardous substances from its products. In addition, Greenpeace claims that HP has not done enough to recycle discarded computers and other technology equipment.[61] To demonstrate its commitment to environmental stewardship, the company has begun to assist customers with the liquidation of old HP products through trade-ins or recycling. By its own count, last year HP refurbished and resold more than 2.5 million computers and recycled 140 million pounds of electronic equipment.[62] To foster public relations in an alternate venue, HP sponsored a Photo Restoration Event in St. Bernard, Louisiana, to assist victims of Hurricane Katrina with the restoration and reproduction of treasured photos damaged by the storm.[63]

Innovating for the Long Haul

Hewlett-Packard's ability to attract fresh talent has helped it perpetuate a history of innovation in product development. Even after a challenging merger with Compaq, it continues to lead in sales of many key digital technologies. And on the day following House hearings over its Board scandal, H-P announced that it was acquiring Voodoo Computers, Inc., as part of its push into pc gaming. Will HP be able to continue setting the pace of innovation by luring and keeping the brilliant talent it needs? Can it maintain its lead in the ever-competitive desktop computer market?

REVIEW QUESTIONS

1. For years, the "HP Way" essentially involved a no-layoff policy. Such a position might seem untenable in today's economy. But what might have been the human relations benefits of such a policy?

2. Though many analysts decried Hewlett-Packard's merger with Compaq, was there a bright side?

3. How does a large and successful firm with great traditions get dragged into scandal? Is the issue structure, staffing, or something else?

TEAM PROJECT

Fringe Benefits Management

On a luncheon trip to a fast-food restaurant my server was bubbling over with excitement. "I'm saying goodbye today," she said. "I just took a job with company X. I'm so happy, now I'll be getting benefits!"

Question: Employers complain that the rising cost of "fringe benefits" is a major problem. Is this concern legitimate? If so, how can fringe benefits be best managed?

Research Directions:

■ Find out exactly what constitutes "fringe benefits" as part of a typical compensation package. Look in the literature and also talk to local employers. Find out what percentage of a typical salary is represented in fringe benefits.

■ Find and interview 2 or 3 human resource managers in your community. Ask them to describe their fringe benefits programs and how they manage fringe benefits costs. What do they see happening in the future? What do they recommend? Talk to 2 or 3 workers from different employers in your community. Find out how things look to them and what they recommend.

■ Pick a specific benefit such as health insurance. What are the facts? How are employers trying to manage the rising cost of health insurance? What are the implications for workers?

■ Examine union positions on fringe benefits. How is this issue reflected in major labor negotiations? What are the results of major recent negotiations?

■ Look at fringe benefits from the perspective of temporary, part-time, or contingent workers. What do they get? What do they want? How are they affected by rising costs?

PERSONAL MANAGEMENT

Professionalism

PROFESSIONALISM! What does this term mean? The code of ethics of the Society for Human Resource Management offers a framework for consideration.[64] SHRM defines "Professional Responsibility" as

■ adding value to your organization
■ contributing to its ethical success
■ serving as a leadership role model for ethical conduct
■ accepting personal responsibility for one's decisions and actions
■ promoting fairness and justice in the workplace
■ being truthful in communications
■ protecting the rights of individuals
■ striving to meet high standards of competence
■ strengthening one's competencies continually

Building the Brand Called "You" These guidelines are a good starting point for anyone who wants to meet high standards of professionalism at work. What about you? How well do you rate? Would you add anything to make this list more meaningful to your career? What do your self-assessments scores suggest?

NEXT STEPS: MANAGEMENT LEARNING WORKBOOK

Self-Assessments
■ Diversity Awareness (#7)
■ Are You Cosmopolitan? (#18)
■ Performance Appraisal Assumptions (#19)

Experiential Exercises
■ Work vs. Family (#17)
■ Compensation and Benefits (#18)
■ Contingency Workforce (#22)
■ Upward Appraisal (#24)

Innovation and Organizational Change

12

Planning Ahead

Business . . . at What Speed

Judging by the actions of many companies today, faster is better. Businesses strive to shorten production times and development cycles, all in the name of capitalizing on the latest tastes and trends. But, like the hare against the tortoise, are there still advantages to moving slow and steady?

For business leaders today, how fast is fast?

Not fast enough, it seems, judging by a recent survey of 1,000 senior executives that *Business-Week* and Boston Consulting Group (BCG) conducted while compiling their list of the World's Top 25 Most Innovative Companies.

According to this survey, 72 percent of senior executives named innovation as one of their top three priorities. No surprise there. Yet nearly one-third acknowledged being discontented with the rate of innovation in their companies. The chief

What *They* Think

"A good idea for a new business tends not to occur in isolation, and often the window of opportunity is very small. So speed is of the essence."
Sir Richard Branson, founder of Virgin Group Ltd.

FAST: *"It's like having a popular nightclub: You have to keep opening new ones. To stay cool, you have to speed up."*
Michael Greeson, CEO and director of research, The Diffusion Group.

SLOW: *"While markets are competitive, competition works more slowly than we sometimes assume, i.e., customers can be slow to shift allegiance. This, however, is less a result of positive loyalty than of sheer inertia, which means that customers put up with unsatisfactory products and services to a remarkable degree."*
Patrick Barwise, professor of marketing and management at London Business School.

obstacle to innovation, they felt, was slow new-product development cycle times.[1]

You've heard the clichés: living in an Internet economy; business at the speed of sound. But for companies in many industries, their success is determined by the speed with which they can respond to changes in the marketplace. And new ideas are the sustenance of a fast-moving company.

"A good idea for a new business tends not to occur in isolation, and often the window of opportunity is very small," noted Sir Richard Branson, founder of Virgin Group Ltd. "So speed is of the essence."[2]

Take the mobile phone industry, for instance. *BusinessWeek* reports that companies like Motorola and Nokia have shortened the cycle time it takes to develop new mobile phones from an average of 12 to 18 months to just under nine months. Considering that the tech tastes of consumers have the attention span of a hyperactive teenager, that's still incredibly responsive.[3]

Tastes don't change as rapidly in the auto industry, yet turnaround time is imperative to maintain a competitive advantage in consumers' minds. Nissan has addressed this perceived demand by shortening their development time for new cars from 21 to 10.5 months.[4]

But do all businesses want to move as quickly as Nissan or Motorola? Should they?

In certain industries, consistency is prized over responsiveness. In certain industries where the business model is cyclical—be it on a daily, weekly, or quarterly basis—innovation is less desirable than efficiency.

Newspaper giant Knight-Ridder has been following a well-defined business model for decades. And at a business like a newspaper, where business is done the same way day after day, method is extremely important, as is succeeding efficiently within designated parameters of operation.

For years, newspapers operated on the strategy of converting a monopoly on printed news in a town into ownership of that town's classified ads—which worked well until the Internet came along and shook things up. Between Craigslist, eBay, and the multitude of other online classified listings, Knight-Ridder was forced to re-evaluate its hold on local advertising, and its place in the market as a whole.

Is faster always better? Is there any room for deliberation in today's economy? Don't take too long to answer, or you may get left behind!

The Numbers

AT&T Per-Minute New York to Chicago

1902	$5.45
1919	$4.65
1950	$1.50
1960	$1.45
1970	$1.05
2006	$0.20

Quick Facts

* Virgin Group Ltd. purchased and began developing Virgin Comics LLC before executives could even scout out the site of the existing comics-distribution business they partnered with.[5]
* Procter & Gamble has launched more than 100 products in the last two years.[6]
* 72 percent of senior executives named innovation as one of their top three priorities.[7]
* Nearly one-third of senior executives are discontented with the rate of innovation in their companies.[8]
* Swedish clothing company H&M allocates new designs among more than 700 manufacturers worldwide; it can get a design into production in hours or days.[9]

What Do *You* Think?

1. Suppose that you inherited your local newspaper. As the new CEO, what are some ways in which you could get the business to move faster?
2. Even with product development times down to less than nine months, are mobile phone companies moving fast enough to stay on top of trends and fashions?

Innovation and Organizational Change			
Study Question 1	**Study Question 2**	**Study Question 3**	**Study Question 4**
Innovation in Organizations	**Organizational Change**	**Managing Planned Change**	**Organization Development**
■ Creativity and innovation ■ The innovation process ■ Characteristics of innovative organizations	■ Change leaders ■ Models of change leadership ■ Transformational and incremental change ■ Forces and targets for change	■ Phases of planned change ■ Change strategies ■ Resistance to change ■ Challenges of technological change	■ Organization development goals ■ How organization development works ■ Organization development interventions
Learning Check 1	**Learning Check 2**	**Learning Check 3**	**Learning Check 4**

Novel answers to perplexing problems move people, organizations, and societies continuously ahead in our dynamic and challenging world. We are living and working at a time when intellectual capital, knowledge management, and learning organizations are taking center stage. And rightfully so. Harvard scholars Michael Beer and Nitin Nohria observe: "The new economy has ushered in great business opportunities and great turmoil. Not since the Industrial Revolution have the stakes of dealing with change been so high. Most traditional organizations have accepted, in theory at least, that they must either change or die."[10] Speaking from the vantage point of a corporate leader always looking toward the future, John Chambers, CEO of Cisco Systems, would no doubt agree. "Companies that are successful will have cultures that thrive on change," he says, "even though change makes most people uncomfortable."[11]

Unfortunately, even though the watchwords of today continue to be *change, change*, and *change*, many organizations and too many leaders are slow or unsuccessful in responding to the challenge. Creating positive change in organizations is not easy. Change involves risk, complexity, uncertainty, anxiety, and stress. Leading organizations on the pathways of change is essential, but takes great understanding, discipline, and commitment to creativity and human ingenuity. In his book *The Circle of Innovation*, consultant Tom Peters warns that we must refocus the attention of managers and leaders away from past accomplishments and toward the role of innovation as the primary source of competitive advantage. Doing well in the past, simply put, is no guarantee of future success.[12]

INNOVATION IN ORGANIZATIONS

When futurists get together to think about the changing nature of organizations in the new economy, there are some that go so far as to say that the corporation as we have traditionally known it is dead, or at least dying. For sure the traditional forms, practices, and systems of the past are being replaced by dramatic new developments.

In Chapter 9, **strategic leadership** was defined as the "ability to antici-pate, envision, maintain flexibility, think strategically, and work with others to initiate changes that will create a viable future for the organization."[13] Strategic leaders are change leaders who build learning organizations and keep them competitive even in difficult and uncertain times. The goal is to make a core competency out of the ability to innovate and continuously change.[14]

▒ **Strategic leadership** cre-ates the capacity for ongoing strategic change.

CREATIVITY AND INNOVATION

Creativity is the generation of a novel idea or unique approach to solving problems or crafting opportunities.[15] It is one of the great assets of human capital. People have ideas; people possess ingenuity; people have the capacity to invent. Creativity is what allows us to turn technologies and other resources into unique processes and products that differentiate the accomplishments of any one organization from those of the next. And let's not forget, the same issues hold when we are talking about the world's social problems – poverty, famine, literacy, diseases, and the general condi-tions for economic and social development. Consider these examples of where one person's creativity has made a world of difference for many others.[16]

▒ **Creativity** is the genera-tion of a novel idea or unique approach that solves a prob-lem or crafts an opportunity.

What happens when the digital age meets the developing world? Progress, at least if you are part of the Grammeen Bank network in Bangladesh. Most of the country's 68,000 villages have no phone service; the average annual income is about $200. That is changing due to Muhmmad Yunus's efforts to rally ingenuity to help fight poverty through microfinance. His innovative program, the Grammeen Bank, makes loans to women entrepreneurs to allow them to buy

INSIGHTS

Motorola: from RAZR to SLVR to ???

It may have seemed unremarkable when a group of Motorola engineers, designers, and marketers met in a Chicago office. But that office, now known as the innovation lab Moto City, was to become their new home, away from corporate headquarters and its bureaucracy. Their task was simple but challenging: come up with a better cell phone. What they created together

was new and different: the Motorola Razr. The firm sold 12.5 million Razr's in their first year on the market, very

It wasn't an easy ride creating the Razr. Motorola engineer Roger Jellicoe says: "Anytime you've got something radically different, there will be people who feel that we should be putting our resources on other stuff. It was kind of a lock-the-door-and-put-a-key-beneath-it approach to product development."

close to the number of units sold by another famous product innovation—the iPod.

That was all in process when Edward J. Zander took over as CEO. But ac-cording to *Business Week*, he made it "the key to inspiring a cultural renais-sance at the company." For Zander, the Razr wasn't just a success, it was a launching pad to the future. To keep the momentum going, he pushed ever more teamwork and customer service. Moto City was turned into an in-house icon for creativity and innovation. He tried to make Motorola, as an employer, a place to be proud of once again—the firm was on top of and not just following the market anymore.

and operate cellular telephones, each typically serving an entire village. The bank's goal is twofold: to receive an economic return on its investment and to contribute to economic development. The model is now spreading to serve the rural poor in other nations. Yunus received the Nobel Peace Prize for his efforts. The award committee said that "Yunus and Grameen Bank have shown that even the poorest of the poor can work to bring about their own development."

What do you do when chronic hunger is the leading cause of death among African children? Sympathy wasn't enough for Andrew Youn. After returning from a Northwestern University internship in South Africa he attacked the problem with an innovative program—the One Acre Fund. It provides small loans to Kenya's poor families, enabling them to work their land with new seed, fertilizer, equipment, and training. The goal is to increase crop yields and avoid the devastation of Kenya's three month "hunger season." The One Acre Fund won the SC Johnson Award for Socially Responsible Entrepreneurship. Says Youn: "The mothers are absolutely inspiring. The things they do out of necessity are heroic."

■ **Innovation** is the process of taking a new idea and putting it into practice.

Creativity exerts its influence in organizations through **innovation,** the process of creating new ideas and putting them into practice.[17] Management consultant Peter Drucker calls innovation "an effort to create purposeful, focused change in an enterprise's economic or social potential."[18] Said a bit differently, it is the act of converting new ideas into usable applications with positive economic or social consequences.

Innovation in and by organizations occurs in three broad forms: (1) **process innovations,** which result in better ways of doing things; (2) **product innovations,** which result in the creation of new or improved goods and services; and (3) **business model innovations**, which result in new ways of making money for the firm.[19] Consider these examples from *Business Week*'s listing of "The World's Most Innovative Companies."[20]

■ **Process innovations** result in better ways of doing things.

■ **Product innovations** result in new or improved goods or services.

■ **Business model innovations** result in ways for firms to make money.

- *Process Innovation*—Southwest Airlines continues to improve operations underpinning its low-cost business strategy; IKEA transformed retail shopping for furniture and fixtures; Amazon.com keeps improving the online shopping experience; Proctor & Gamble reorganized to bring design executives into the top management circle.
- *Product Innovation*—Apple introduced us to the "iPod world;" Toyota, has been the market mover in new hybrid vehicles; Research in Motion, its Blackberry ushered in a new era of hand-held mobile devices; 3M gives talented staff free time to experiment and create new products and applications.
- *Business Model Innovation*—Virgin Group Ltd. uses "hip lifestyle" branding to infuse traditional industries; Starbucks continues to turn its coffee machine into a global branding business; eBay created the world's largest online marketplace; Google thrives on advertising revenues driven by ever-expanding and great Web technology.

THE INNOVATION PROCESS

The management of creativity and innovation requires encouragement and support for both *invention*—the act of discovery—and for *application*—the act of use. Managers need to invest in and build work environments that stimulate creativity and an ongoing stream of new ideas. They must also make sure that good ideas for new or modified processes and products are actually implemented.

One way to describe the full set of responsibilities for the innovation process is in these five steps, constituting what consultant Gary Hamel calls the *wheel of innovation*.[21]

1. *Imagining*—thinking about new possibilities; making discoveries by ingenuity or communicating with others; extending existing ways.
2. *Designing*—testing ideas in concept; discussing them with peers, customers, clients, or technical experts; building initial models, prototypes, or samples.
3. *Experimenting*—examining practicality and financial value through experiments and feasibility studies.
4. *Assessing*—identifying strengths and weaknesses, potential costs and benefits, and potential markets or applications; making constructive changes.
5. *Scaling*—gearing up and implementing new processes; putting to work what has been learned; commercializing new products or services.

One of the major requirements of successful innovation is that the entire process meets real needs of the organization and its marketplace. New ideas alone do not guarantee success; they must be relevant, and they must be well implemented. In business, **commercializing innovation** is the process of turning new ideas into products or processes that can increase profits through greater sales or reduced costs.[22] For example, 3M Corporation generates as much as one-third or more of its revenues from products that didn't exist four years ago. The firm, where product innovation is a way of life, owes its success to the imagination of employees like Art Fry. He's the person whose creativity turned an adhesive that "wasn't sticky enough" into the blockbuster product known worldwide today as Post-It Notes™. *Figure 12.1* shows how new products like this move through the typical steps of commercializing innovation.

▪ **Commercializing innovation** turns ideas into economic value added.

CHARACTERISTICS OF INNOVATIVE ORGANIZATIONS

Innovative organizations like 3M, eBay, and Apple Computer are great at supporting creativity and entrepreneurship. As with the examples of Virgin, Nokia, and Nissan in The Topic chapter opener, they show the capacity to move fast with new product developments. But let's not forget, even though 72% of executives considered innovation a top priority at their firms, about one-third are not happy with how fast companies innovate.[23]

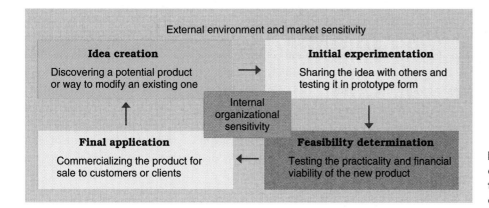

Figure 12.1 Process of commercializing innovation: the case of new product development.

What does it take to create a highly innovative organization?

Insights from the literature tell us that in highly innovative organizations, the *corporate strategy and culture support innovation*. The strategies of the organization, the visions and values of senior management, and the framework of policies and expectations all emphasize an entrepreneurial spirit. Innovation is expected, failure is accepted, and the organization is willing to take risks. Johnson & Johnson's former CEO James Burke once said: "I try to give people the feeling that it's okay to fail, that it's important to fail."[24] His point is that managers should eliminate risk-averse climates and replace them with organizational cultures in which innovation is a norm.

In highly innovative organizations, *organization structures support innovation*. More and more large organizations are trying to capture the structural flexibility of smaller ones. They are striving for organic operations that emphasize lateral communications and extensively use teams and task forces. As Peter Drucker points out, "Successful innovations . . . are now being turned out by cross-functional teams with people from marketing, manufacturing, and finance participating in research work from the very beginning."[25]

In highly innovative organizations, *top management supports innovation*. In the case of 3M, for example, many top managers have been the innovators and product champions in the company's past. They understand the in-

ISSUES AND SITUATIONS

Innovators-In-Chief

IBM's CEO Samuel J. Palmisano says: "The way you will thrive in this environment is by innovating—innovating in technologies, innovating in strategies, innovating in business models." His words probably speak volumes for business leaders today. Innovation is a top theme in most executive suites, and the CEO is increasingly expected to be the "innovator-in-chief."

But top CEOs know that innovation doesn't come easily. It has to be nurtured constantly, and the innovation killers have to be dealt with: lengthy development times, poor coordination, risk-averse cultures, little customer insight, and more. Lots needs to be done to keep the innovation pipeline flowing. BMW relocates engineers and designers to a central location for face-to-face product development; GE measures and tracks innovation records; 3M expects its "old timers" to pass along stories and values associated with the firm's long-standing commitments to innovation; Research In Motion CEO Mike Lazaridis holds weekly "vision sessions" to get everyone excited; Procter & Gamble created a new vice president position for innovation and knowledge.

Innovators-in-chief CEOs seem to recognize that you can't innovate if key players aren't talking with and working closely with one another. You can't innovate consistently if the "we believe in innovation" message isn't consistently delivered from the top.

At IBM, Palmisano says: "CEOs realize they have to get these new types of innovation done through their own leadership." He further believes that collaboration is critical to his firm's innovation future. He pushes internal collaboration among employees across some 173 countries, and he pushes external collaboration with other firms, governments, and educational institutions. His message seems to be: You can't always innovate alone. Whether you are an individual or a multinational corporation, good partners can often help greatly.

Critical Response

It doesn't seem hard to agree that innovation needs to be spearheaded and championed by top management. But shouldn't every manager view himself or herself as "innovator-in-chief?" Shouldn't "demonstrated excellence in fostering innovation" be a part of any manager's individual performance scorecard?

novation process, are tolerant of criticisms and differences of opinion, and take all possible steps to keep the goals clear and the pressure on. The key, once again, is to allow the creative potential of people to operate fully.

In highly innovative organizations, *the organization's staffing supports innovation.* Organizations need different kinds of people working in different roles to support the innovation process. The critical innovation roles to be filled include:[26]

- *Idea generators*—people who create new insights from internal discovery or external awareness, or both.
- *Information gatekeepers*—people who serve as links between people and groups within the organization and with external sources.
- *Product champions*—people who advocate and push for change and innovation, and for the adoption of specific product or process ideas.
- *Project managers*—people who perform technical functions needed to keep an innovative project on track with necessary resource support.
- *Innovation leaders*—people who encourage, sponsor, and coach others to keep the innovation values, goals, and energies in place.

Learning Check 1

Be sure you can ■ define the terms creativity and innovation ■ discuss the differences between process, product, and business model innovations ■ list the five steps in Hamel's wheel of innovation ■ define the term commercializing innovation ■ list and explain the characteristics of innovative organizations ■ identify the critical innovation roles in organizations

---

ORGANIZATIONAL CHANGE

Because innovation in our society is so positively valued, the tendency may be to make change sound almost a matter of routine, something readily accepted by everyone involved. But what are the realities of trying to change organizations and the behaviors of people within them?

When Angel Martinez became CEO of Rockport Company, for example, he sought to move the firm from traditional ways that were not aligned with future competition. Rather than embrace the changes he sponsored, employees resisted. Martinez said they "gave lip service to my ideas and hoped I'd go away."[27] And after Bank of America announced a large quarterly operating loss, the new CEO at the time, Samuel Armacost, complained about the lack of "agents of change" among his top managers. Claiming that managers seemed more interested in taking orders than initiating change, he said: "I came away quite distressed from my first couple of management meetings. Not only couldn't I get conflict, I couldn't even get comment. They were all waiting to see which way the wind blew."[28]

CHANGE LEADERS

A **change leader** is a *change agent* who takes leadership responsibility for changing the existing pattern of behavior of another person or social system. Change leaders make things happen. They are alert to situations or to people needing change, open to good ideas and opportunities, and ready and able to support the implementation of new ideas in actual practice.

■ A **change leader** is a *change agent* who tries to change the behavior of another person or social system.

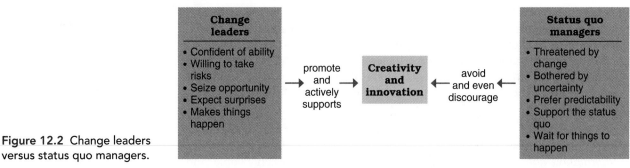

Figure 12.2 Change leaders versus status quo managers.

Figure 12.2 contrasts a true "change leader" with a "status quo manager." The former is forward looking, proactive, and supportive of new ideas; the latter is backward looking, reactive, and comfortable with habit. Obviously, the new workplace demands change leadership at all levels of management.

MODELS OF CHANGE LEADERSHIP

In Chapter 16 on teams and teamwork, the concept of distributed leadership in teams is discussed. The point is that every team member has the potential to lead by serving group needs for task and maintenance activities. The same notion applies when it comes to change leadership. The responsibilities for change leadership are ideally distributed and shared by all managers top to bottom in any organization.

Top-Down Change

■ In **top-down change**, the change initiatives come from senior management.

In **top-down change,** senior managers initiate changes with the goal of improving organizational performance. This is the domain of strategic leadership as discussed earlier in the chapter. Importantly, however, reports indicate that some 70 percent or more of large-scale change efforts actually fail.[29] The most common reason is poor implementation.

The success of top-down change is usually determined by the willingness of middle-level and lower-level workers to actively support top-management initiatives. Change programs have little chance of success without the support of those who must implement them. Any change that is driven from the top and perceived as insensitive to the needs of lower-level personnel can easily fail. Successful top-down change is led in ways that earn the support of others throughout the organization.

Bottom-Up Change

■ In **bottom-up change**, change initiatives come from all levels in the organization.

In **bottom-up change,** the initiatives for change come from any and all parts of the organization, not just from top management. Such change is made possible by management commitments to empowerment, involvement, and participation.

Bottom-up change is essential to organizational innovation and very useful in adapting operations and technologies to the changing requirements of work. For example, at Johnson Controls Inc., Jason Moncer was given the nickname "Mr. Kaizen"

by his co-workers.[30] The nickname refers to a Japanese practice of continuous improvement. Moncer earned it by offering many ideas for changes in his work area. At his plant, workers contributed over 200 suggestions that were implemented in just one year alone. The company is committed to the belief that workers should be encouraged to use their job knowledge and common sense to improve things. In other words, when the workers talk at Johnson Controls, managers listen.

Integrated Change Leadership

The most successful and enduring change leadership harnesses the advantages of both top-down and bottom-up change. Top-down initiatives may be needed to break traditional patterns or make difficult economic adjustments; bottom-up initiatives are necessary to build institutional capability for sustainable change and organizational learning. When first taking over as CEO of General Electric, Jack Welch, for example, began an aggressive top-down restructuring that led to major workforce cuts and a trimmer organization structure. Once underway, however, this evolved into bottom-up change focusing on employee involvement. He started a widely benchmarked program called Work-Out to invigorate a process of continuous reassessment and planned change.[31] In Work-Out sessions employees confront their managers in a "town meeting" format, with the manager in front listening to suggestions for removing performance obstacles and improving operations. The managers are expected to respond immediately to the suggestions and support positive change initiatives raised during the session.

TRANSFORMATIONAL AND INCREMENTAL CHANGE

Some changes occur spontaneously in organizations, largely in response to unanticipated events. Managers deal with them by **reactive change,** hopefully doing a good job of responding to events as or after they occur. But the really great managers are not satisfied with being reactive. They are forward thinking and always alert **performance gaps,** or discrepancies between desired and actual states of affairs that indicate problems to be resolved or opportunities to be explored. They activate **planned change**—taking steps to best align the organization with future challenges.[32]

There are two major types of planned organizational change. The first is radical or frame-breaking **transformational change** that results in a major and comprehensive redirection of the organization.[33] Transformational change creates fundamental shifts in strategies, culture, structures, and even the underlying sense of purpose or mission. It is led from the top and designed to change the basic character of the organization. Consider the situation at the Federal Emergency Management Agency (FEMA), the U.S. government agency soundly criticized for its handling of the Hurricane Katrina disaster. In announcing that the agency was going to get a major overhaul, Homeland Security Secretary Michael Chertoff

■ **Reactive change** responds to events as or after they occur.

■ A **performance gap** is a discrepancy between a desired and actual state of affairs.

■ **Planned change** aligns the organization with anticipated future challenges.

■ **Transformational change** results in a major and comprehensive redirection of the organization.

MANAGEMENT SMARTS 12.1

How to lead transformational change

• Establish a sense of urgency for change.

• Form a powerful coalition to lead the change.

• Create and communicate a change vision.

• Empower others to move change forward.

• Celebrate short-term "wins" and recognize those who help.

• Build on success; align people and systems with new ways.

• Stay with it; keep the message consistent; champion the vision.

said: "We will retool FEMA, maybe even radically, to increase our ability to deal with catastrophic events."[34]

Management Smarts 12.1 offers several lessons learned from studies of large-scale transformational change in business.[35] As you might expect, transformational change is intense, highly stressful, and very complex to achieve. Only time will tell if FEMA achieves Chertoff's change goals.

■ **Incremental change**
bends and adjusts existing
ways to improve performance.

There is another more modest, frame-bending, version of planned organizational change—**incremental change.** This is change that bends and nudges existing systems and practices to better align them with emerging problems and opportunities. The intent isn't to break and remake the system, but to move it forward through continuous improvements. Common incremental changes in organizations involve evolutions in products, processes, technologies, and work systems.

One shouldn't get the idea, by the way, that incremental change is somehow inferior to transformational change. Both are important. Incremental changes keep things tuned up (like the engine on a car) in between transformations (when the old car is replaced with a new one).

FORCES AND TARGETS FOR CHANGE

The impetus for organizational change, transformational or incremental, can arise from a variety of external forces.[36] These include globalization, market competition, local economic conditions, government laws and regulations, technological developments, market trends, and social forces and values, among others. As an organization's general and specific environments develop and change over time, the organization has to adapt or suffer the consequences.

Internal forces for change are important, too. Indeed, any change in one part of the complex systems of an organization—perhaps a change initiated in response to one or more of the external forces just identified—can often create the need for change in another part of the system. The common internal *organizational targets for change*—tasks, people, culture, technology, and structure—are highly interrelated:[37]

- *Tasks*—the nature of work as represented by organizational mission, objectives, and strategy, and the job designs for individuals and groups.
- *People*—the attitudes and competencies of the employees and the human resource systems that support them.
- *Culture*—the value system for the organization as a whole, and the norms guiding individual and group behavior.
- *Technology*—the operations and information technology used to support job designs, arrange workflows, and integrate people and machines in systems.
- *Structure*—the configuration of the organization as a complex system, including its design features and lines of authority and communications.

Learning Check 2

Be sure you can ■ define the term change agent ■ discuss the pros and cons of top-down change and bottom-up change ■ differentiate planned and unplanned change ■ differentiate transformational and incremental change ■ list common organizational targets for change

MANAGING PLANNED CHANGE

The many complications of planned change in organizations begin with human nature. People tend to act habitually and in stable ways over time. They may not want to change even when circumstances require it. Any manager needs to recognize and deal with such tendencies in order to successfully lead planned change.

PHASES OF PLANNED CHANGE

The noted psychologist Kurt Lewin recommends that any planned change be viewed as a process with the three phases shown in *Figure 12.3*: (1) *unfreezing*—preparing a system for change; (2) *changing*—making actual changes in the system; and, (3) *refreezing*—stabilizing the system after change.[38]

Unfreezing

Change has a better chance for success when people are ready for it and open to doing things differently. **Unfreezing** is the stage in which a situation is prepared for change and felt needs for change are developed. It can be facilitated in several ways: through environmental pressures for change, declining performance, the recognition that problems or opportunities exist, and the observation of behavioral models or benchmarks. When

> ■ **Unfreezing** is the phase during which a situation is prepared for change.

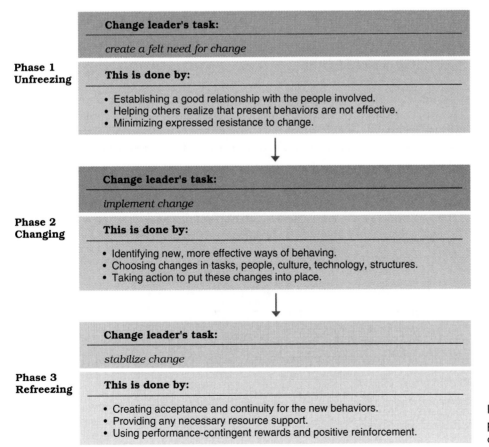

Phase 1 Unfreezing

Change leader's task:

create a felt need for change

This is done by:

- Establishing a good relationship with the people involved.
- Helping others realize that present behaviors are not effective.
- Minimizing expressed resistance to change.

Phase 2 Changing

Change leader's task:

implement change

This is done by:

- Identifying new, more effective ways of behaving.
- Choosing changes in tasks, people, culture, technology, structures.
- Taking action to put these changes into place.

Phase 3 Refreezing

Change leader's task:

stabilize change

This is done by:

- Creating acceptance and continuity for the new behaviors.
- Providing any necessary resource support.
- Using performance-contingent rewards and positive reinforcement.

Figure 12.3 Lewin's three phases of planned organizational change.

handled well, conflict can be an important unfreezing force in organizations. It often helps people break old habits and recognize alternative ways of thinking about or doing things.

Changing

■ **Changing** is the phase where a planned change actually takes place.

In the **changing** phase, something new takes place in a system, and change is actually implemented. This is the point at which managers initiate changes in such organizational targets as tasks, people, culture, technology, and structure. This phase is ideally reached after unfreezing, and with a good diagnosis of a problem and a careful examination of alternatives. However, Lewin believes that many change agents enter the changing phase prematurely, are too quick to change things, and therefore end up creating harmful resistance. When managers implement change before people feel a need for it, there is an increased likelihood of failure.

Refreezing

■ **Refreezing** is the phase at which change is stabilized.

The final stage in the planned change process is **refreezing.** Here, the manager is concerned about stabilizing the change and creating the conditions for its long-term continuity. Refreezing is accomplished by linking change with appropriate rewards, positive reinforcement, and resource support. It is also important in this phase to evaluate results carefully, provide feedback to the people involved, and make any required modifications in the original change. When refreezing is done poorly, changes are too easily forgotten or abandoned with the passage of time. When it is done well, change should be more long lasting.

Of course, in today's dynamic environments there may not be a lot of time for refreezing before things are ready to change again. In other words, we are often preparing for more changes even while trying to take full advantage of the present one.

CHANGE STRATEGIES

The act of actually changing or moving people to do things differently can be pursued in different ways. *Figure 12.4* summarizes three common change strategies known as force-coercion, rational persuasion, and shared power.[39] Managers, as change agents, should understand each strategy and its likely results.

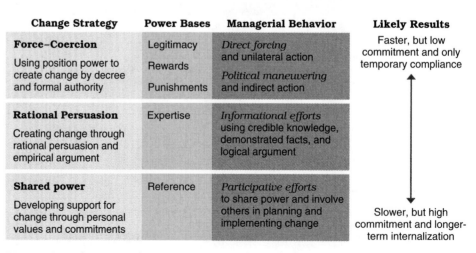

Change Strategy	Power Bases	Managerial Behavior	Likely Results
Force–Coercion Using position power to create change by decree and formal authority	Legitimacy Rewards Punishments	*Direct forcing* and unilateral action *Political maneuvering* and indirect action	Faster, but low commitment and only temporary compliance
Rational Persuasion Creating change through rational persuasion and empirical argument	Expertise	*Informational efforts* using credible knowledge, demonstrated facts, and logical argument	
Shared power Developing support for change through personal values and commitments	Reference	*Participative efforts* to share power and involve others in planning and implementing change	Slower, but high commitment and longer-term internalization

Figure 12.4 Alternative change strategies and their leadership implications.

Force-Coercion Strategies

A **force-coercion strategy** uses the power bases of legitimacy, rewards, and punishments as the primary inducements to change. A change agent that seeks to create change through force-coercion believes that people are basically motivated by self-interest and by what the situation offers in terms of potential personal gains or losses.[40] This change agent believes that people change only in response to such motives, tries to find out where their vested interests lie, and then puts the pressure on. Once a weakness is found, it is exploited.

In a *direct forcing* strategy, the change agent takes direct and unilateral action to "command" that change take place. This involves the exercise of formal authority or legitimate power, offering special rewards and/or threatening punishment. In *political maneuvering*, the change agent works indirectly to gain special advantage over other persons and thereby make them change. This involves bargaining, obtaining control of important resources, forming alliances, or granting small favors.

Any force-coercion strategy usually produces limited results. Although it can be quickly tried, most people respond to force-coercion out of fear of punishment or hope for a reward. The likely result is temporary compliance with the change agent's desires; the new behavior continues only so long as the rewards and punishments are present. For this reason, force-coercion may be most useful for unfreezing, helping people break old patterns and gain impetus to try new ones. The earlier example of General Electric's Work-Out program applies here.[41] Jack Welch started Work-Out to create a forum for active employee empowerment of continuous change. But he didn't make the program optional; participation in Work-Out was mandatory from the start. Part of his commitment to change leadership was a willingness to use authority to unfreeze situations and get new things started. Once the program was under way, he was confident it would survive and prosper on its own—and it did.

■ A **force-coercion strategy** pursues change through formal authority and/or the use of rewards or punishments.

REAL ETHICS

Corporate Greens and Global Warming

Get ready—you'll be reading and hearing a lot more about "corporate greens." No, we're not talking about a new political party; we are talking about a growing voice from the business community that it really does care about global warming . . . and is going to do its share in trying to best deal with it. There's emerging consensus not only that global warming is harming our planet even faster than expected, but that business innovation is needed to deal with it.

HSBC was the first large bank to declare that it was going "carbon neutral," committing to cut its carbon output as much as possible and then offsetting the remainder by paying to reduce emissions elsewhere. As concerns for global warming build, so, too, do pressures for change in traditional business ways. More business leaders seem to be taking the challenge seriously. The monitoring organization, Climate Group, reports that four firms—Bayer, British Telecom, DuPont, and Norske Canada—alone have saved $4

billion by cutting greenhouse-gas emissions. "Carbon down, profits up," they say. Indications are that giving global warming a top business priority can make good financial sense.

FURTHER INQUIRY

Is it ethical for a business to pursue anything but "carbon neutrality" in today's day and age? What differentiates executives that resist and those that seem willing to make changes in behalf of the global warming challenges? And, while you are thinking about the issues, is it ethical to claim social responsibility for pursuing environmentally friendly practices only to avoid government regulation or adverse publicity? In other words, does it make a difference in a firm does "good things" for selfish reasons?

Rational Persuasion Strategies

■ A **rational persuasion strategy** pursues change through empirical data and rational argument.

Change agents using a **rational persuasion strategy** attempt to bring about change through persuasion backed by special knowledge, empirical data, and rational argument. A change agent following this strategy believes that people are inherently rational and are guided by reason in their actions and decision making. Once a specific course of action is demonstrated to be in a person's self-interest, the change agent assumes that reason and rationality will cause the person to adopt it. Thus, he or she uses information and facts to communicate the essential desirability of change.

The likely outcome of rational persuasion is eventual compliance with reasonable commitment. When successful, a rational persuasion strategy helps both unfreeze and refreeze a change situation. Although slower than force-coercion, it can result in longer-lasting and more internalized change.

To succeed at rational persuasion a manager must convince others that the cost-benefit value of a planned change is high, and that it will leave them better off than before. This power can come directly from the change agent if she or he has personal credibility as an "expert." It can also be borrowed in the form of consultants and other outside experts, or gained from credible demonstration projects and benchmarks. Many firms, for example, use Disney as a benchmark to demonstrate to their own employees how changes in customer orientation can improve operations. A Ford vice president says: "Disney's track record is one of the best in the country as far as dealing with customers."[42] In this sense the power of rational persuasion is straightforward: If it works for Disney, why can't it work for us?

Shared Power Strategies

■ A **shared power strategy** pursues change by participation in assessing change needs, values, and goals.

A **shared power strategy** engages people in a collaborative process of identifying values, assumptions, and goals from which support for change will naturally emerge. The process is slow, but it is likely to yield high commitment. Sometimes called a *normative reeducative strategy*, this approach is based on empowerment and is highly participative in nature. It relies on involving others in examining personal needs and values, group norms, and operating goals as they relate to the issues at hand. Power is shared by the change agent and other persons as they work together to develop a new consensus to support needed change. Because it entails a high level of involvement, this strategy is often quite time consuming. But importantly, power sharing is likely to result in longer-lasting and internalized change.

Managers using the shared power strategy of planned change need referent power, meaning that others positively identify with them. They must have skills to work effectively in groups. And, they must be comfortable allowing others to participate in making decisions that affect the change planning and implementation.

A change agent who shares power begins by recognizing that people have varied needs and complex motivations. He or she believes people behave as they do because of sociocultural norms and commitments to the expectations of others. Changes in organizations are understood to inevitably involve changes in attitudes, values, skills, and significant relationships, not just changes in knowledge, information, or intellectual rationales for action and practice. Thus, when seeking to change others, this change agent is sensitive to the way group pressures can support or inhibit change. In working with people, every attempt is made to gather their opinions, identify their feelings and expectations, and incorporate them fully into the change process.

The great "power" of sharing power in the change process lies with unlocking the creativity and experience of people within the system. Unfortunately, many managers are hesitant to engage this process for fear of losing control or of having to compromise on important organizational goals. Harvard scholar Teresa M. Amabile, however, points out that managers and change leaders should have the confidence to share power regarding means and processes, but not overall goals. "People will be more creative," she says, "if you give them freedom to decide how to climb particular mountains. You needn't let them choose which mountains to climb."[43]

RESISTANCE TO CHANGE

Change typically brings with it resistance. When people resist change, furthermore, they are most often defending something important that appears threatened. A change of work schedules for workers in ON Semiconductor's Rhode Island plant, for example, may not have seemed like much to top management. But to the workers it was significant enough to bring about an organizing attempt by the Teamsters' union. When management delved into the issues, they found that workers viewed changes in weekend work schedules as threatening to their personal lives. With input from the workers, the problem was resolved satisfactorily.[44]

There are any number of reasons why people in organizations may resist planned change. Some of the more common ones are shown in *Management Smarts 12.2*. Change agents and managers often view such resistance as something that must be "overcome" in order for change to be successful. But, resistance is better viewed as feedback. When resistance appears, it usually means that something can be done to achieve a better "fit" among the planned change, the situation, and the people involved. Consider the implications of this conversation reported by a management consultant *Manager*—"Come on, Jim, there must be one schedule that's the right schedule for this industry." *Jim*—"Yes, it's the one the people in the plant pick."[45]

Once resistance to change is recognized and understood, it can be dealt with in various ways.[46] Among the alternatives for effectively managing resistance, *education and communication* uses discussions, presentations, and demonstrations to educate people beforehand about a change. *Participation and involvement* allows others to contribute ideas and help design and implement the change. The *facilitation and support* approach involves providing encouragement and training, actively listening to problems and complaints, and helping to overcome performance pressures. *Negotiation and agreement* provides incentives that appeal to those who are actively resisting or ready to resist. It also makes trade-offs in exchange for assurances that change will not be blocked.

Manipulation and co-optation tries to covertly influence others by selectively providing information and structuring events in favor of the desired change. *Explicit and implicit coercion* forces people to accept change by threatening resistors

---

MANAGEMENT SMARTS 12.2

Why people may resist change

- *Fear of the unknown*—not understanding what is happening or what comes next.
- *Disrupted habits*—feeling upset to see the end of the old ways of doing things.
- *Loss of confidence*—feeling incapable of performing well under the new ways of doing things.
- *Loss of control*—feeling that things are being done "to" you rather than "by" or "with" you.
- *Poor timing*—feeling overwhelmed by the situation or that things are moving too fast.
- *Work overload*—not having the physical or psychic energy to commit to the change.
- *Loss of face*—feeling inadequate or humiliated because the "old" ways weren't "good" ways.
- *Lack of purpose*—not seeing a reason for the change and/or not understanding its benefits.

with undesirable consequences if they do not do what is being asked. Obviously, the last two approaches are risky in terms of potential negative side effects.

CHALLENGES OF TECHNOLOGICAL CHANGE

Ongoing technological change is a way of life in today's organizations, but it also brings special challenges to change leaders. For the full advantages of new technologies to be realized, a good fit must be achieved with work needs, practices, and people. And, this is where sensitivity to resistance and continual gathering of information can make a great difference.

The demands of managing technological change have been described using the analogy of contrasting styles between navigators from the Micronesian island of Truk and their European counterparts.[47]

The European navigator works from a plan, relates all moves during a voyage to the plan, and tries to always stay "on course." When something unexpected happens, the plan is revised systematically, and the new plan is followed again until the navigator finds the ship to be off course.

The Trukese navigator starts with an objective and moves off in its general direction. Always alert to information from waves, clouds, winds, etc., the navigator senses subtle changes in conditions and steers and alters the ship's course continually to reach the ultimate objective.

KAFFEEKLATSCH

Change Fast or Change Slow

First Cup

"Another new CEO! What do you think, will this one go fast, or go slow? There are days when I think we need a total overhaul to stay competitive. That argues for 'the faster we change things the better.' And a new person has the advantage: change things fast while everyone is on edge and susceptible to initiatives from a new authority. What about you? Should she make fast and dramatic changes? Or should she take her time, get to know the place and its people, and then move ahead with more cautious changes?"

Studying the Grounds

■ Research with American firms suggests that 70 percent of large-scale change efforts fail.

■ Surveys of European firms show only 20 percent reporting "substantial success" with change; another 63 percent claim only temporary success.

Double Espresso

"Well if she's going to change things fast, I'd say she needs to bring in a number of new people at the top.

If not, she's going to get a lot of push back. There are too many people here who are going to feel threatened. They'll take fast change as a criticism of their past work. They'll resist and make it hard on her, even though they may voice their support in public."

Your Turn

The "go slow/go fast" dilemma for a new leader is perplexing. Maybe it's easier to "go fast" if you're coming in from the outside and aren't all caught up in existing relationships, politics, and emotions. But, if you are to move fast, don't you need good advice from a "number 2" who is from the inside and knows the systems, people, and traditions? And if you are an insider taking over, does that make "going slow" your only option since you are already identified with "the way things are?" Or does this inside vantage point give you a "once only" chance to use your new power to create change in ways that you believe best, based on personal experience?

Like the navigators of Truk, technological change may best be approached as an ongoing process that will inevitably require improvisation as things are being implemented. New technologies are often designed external to the organization in which they are to be used. The implications for local applications may be difficult to anticipate and plan for ahead of time. A technology that is attractive in concept may appear complicated to the new users; the full extent of its benefits and/or inadequacies may not become known until it is tried. All this means that the change leader should be alert to resistance, continually gather and process information relating to the change, and be willing to customize the new technology to best meet the needs of the local situation.[48]

Be sure you can ■ identify Lewin's phases of planned change ■ discuss a change leader's action responsibilities for each phase ■ explain the force-coercion, rational persuasion, and shared power change strategies ■ discuss the pros and cons of each change strategy ■ list several reasons why people resist change ■ identify strategies for dealing with resistance to change ■ discuss the challenges of leading technological change

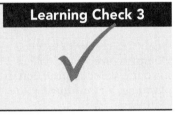

Learning Check 3

ORGANIZATION DEVELOPMENT

There will always be times when the members of organizations should sit together and systematically reflect on strengths and weaknesses, performance accomplishments and failures, and the future. One way to ensure that this happens in a participative and action-oriented environment is through **organization development.** This is a comprehensive approach to planned organizational change that involves the application of behavioral science in a systematic and long-range effort to improve organizational effectiveness.[49] Although "OD" often involves the assistance of a consultant with special training, all managers can and should utilize it in their change leadership agendas.

■ **Organization development** is a comprehensive effort to improve an organization's ability to solve problems and improve performance.

ORGANIZATION DEVELOPMENT GOALS

Two goals are pursued simultaneously in organization development. The *outcome goals of OD* focus on task accomplishments, while the *process goals of OD* focus on the ways people work together. This second goal strongly differentiates OD from more general attempts at planned change in organizations. You may think of OD as a form of "planned change plus," with the "plus" meaning that change is accomplished in such a way that organization members develop a capacity for continued self-renewal. That is, OD tries to achieve change in ways that help organization members become more active and self-reliant in their ability to continue changing in the future. What also makes OD unique is its commitment to strong humanistic values and established principles of behavioral science. OD is committed to improving organizations through freedom of choice, shared power, and self-reliance, and by taking the best advantage of what we know about human behavior in organizations.

HOW ORGANIZATION DEVELOPMENT WORKS

Figure 12.5 presents a general model of OD and shows its relationship to Lewin's three phases of planned change. The first step in the OD process is for the consultant or facilitator to *establish a working relationship* with members of the client system. The next step is *diagnosis*—gathering and analyzing data to assess the situation and set appropriate change objectives. This helps with unfreezing and also clarifies possible action directions. Diagnosis leads to active *intervention*, wherein change objectives are pursued through a variety of structural interventions, a number of which will be discussed shortly. The next step is *evaluation* to determine whether things are proceeding as desired and whether further action is needed. Eventually, the OD consultant or facilitator should *achieve a terminal relationship* that leaves the client able to function on its own.

■ **Action research** is a collaborative process of collecting data, using it for action planning, and evaluating the results.

The success or failure of any OD program lies in part with the strength of its methodological foundations in **action research**. This is a process of systematically collecting data on an organization, feeding it back to the members for action planning, and evaluating results by collecting more data and repeating the process as necessary. The data gathering can be done in several ways. Interviews are a common means. Formal written surveys of employee attitudes and needs are also popular. Many such "climate," "attitude," or "morale" questionnaires have been tested for reliability and validity. Some have norms that allow one organization to compare its results with those from a broad sample of counterparts.

ORGANIZATION DEVELOPMENT INTERVENTIONS

■ An **OD intervention** is a structured activity that helps create change for organization development.

In many ways, organization development is employee involvement in action. The process uses a variety of **OD interventions** to activate participation in self-directed change efforts. Importantly, these interventions reflect concepts and ideas discussed throughout in this book and that are well represented in the practices and approaches of the new workplace.[50]

Individual Interventions

Organization development practitioners accept the premise that most people are capable of assuming responsibility for their own actions and of making positive contributions to organizational performance. Based on these princi-

Figure 12.5 Organization development and the planned change process.

ples, some of the more popular OD interventions designed to help improve individual effectiveness include:

- *Sensitivity training*—unstructured sessions where participants learn interpersonal skills and increased sensitivity to other people.
- *Management training*—structured educational opportunities for developing important managerial skills and competencies.
- *Role negotiation*—structured interactions to clarify and negotiate role expectations among people who work together.
- *Job redesign*—realigning task components to better fit the needs and capabilities of individuals.
- *Career planning*—structured advice and discussion sessions to help individuals plan career paths and personal development programs.

RESEARCH BRIEF

Top management must get and stay committed for organization development to work in tandem with top-down change

Harry Sminia and Antonie Van Nistelrooij's case study of a public sector organization in the Netherlands sheds light on what happens when top-down change and bottom-up organization development are used simultaneously.

Writing in the *Journal of Change Management*, they describe how top management initiated a strategic change involving organization design, procedures, work standards and systems. Called the "project strand," this change was well structured with deadlines and a management hierarchy. Simultaneously, a "change strand" was initiated with organization development interventions to develop information and create foundations helpful to the success of the project strand. The change strand involved conferences, workshops, and meetings. The goal was for both strands to operate in parallel and eventually converge in joint implementation.

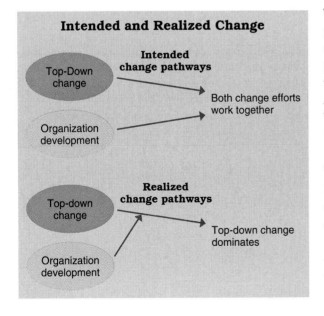

Intended and Realized Change

Intended change pathways
Top-Down change
Organization development
Both change efforts work together

Realized change pathways
Top-down change
Organization development
Top-down change dominates

What the researchers found was that top management favored the project strand and resisted challenges to its decision making prerogatives that came from the change strand. Eventually the OD aspects of the change initiative pretty much disappeared and activities centered around completing the project changes as scheduled. Although the workforce "embraced" the OD methods, Sminia and Van Nistelrooij conclude that their success was hampered by "management refusal to share power with the employees . . ."

QUESTIONS & APPLICATIONS

It seems that the goal in this case was to utilize organization development to develop input and involvement that would assist in the accomplishment of top management strategic goals. But, is it realistic to expect that top-down and bottom-up changes can operate simultaneously? Can any organization development activity be successful without continuing support and legitimacy from top management?

Reference: Harry Sminia and Anonie Van Nistelrooij, "Strategic Management and Organizational Development: Planned Change in a Public Sector Organization," *Journal of Change Management*, Vol. 6 (March, 2006), pp. 99–113.

Team Interventions

The team plays a very important role in organization development. OD practitioners recognize two principles in this respect. First, teams are viewed as important vehicles for helping people satisfy important needs. Second, it is believed that improved collaboration within and among teams can improve organizational performance. Selected OD interventions designed to improve team effectiveness include:

- *Team building*—structured experiences to help team members set goals, improve interpersonal relations, and become a better-functioning team.
- *Process consultation*—third-party observation and advice on critical team processes (e.g., communication, conflict, and decision making).
- *Intergroup team building*—structured experiences to help two or more teams set shared goals, reduce conflict, improve intergroup relations, and become better coordinated.

Organization-Wide Interventions

At the level of the total organization, OD practitioners operate on the premise that any changes in one part of the system will also affect other parts. The organization's culture is considered to have an important impact on member attitudes and morale. And it is believed that structures and jobs can be designed to bring together people, technology, and systems in highly productive and satisfying working combinations. Some of the OD interventions with an emphasis on overall organizational effectiveness include:

- *Survey feedback*—comprehensive and systematic data collection to identify attitudes and needs, analyze results, and plan for constructive action.
- *Confrontation meeting*—one-day intensive, structured meetings to gather data on workplace problems and plan for constructive actions.
- *Structural redesign*—realigning the organization structure to meet the needs of environmental and contextual forces.
- *Management by objectives*—Formalizing MBO throughout the organization to link individual, group, and organizational objectives.

Learning Check 4

✓

Be sure you can ■ define the term organization development ■ differentiate outcome and process goals of OD ■ explain the steps in the OD process ■ explain the role of action research in OD ■ list OD interventions focusing on individuals and on teams ■ list organization-wide OD interventions

CHAPTER 12 STUDY GUIDE

1 How do organizations accomplish innovation?

■ Organizations need strategic leaders who initiate and successfully implement changes that help them perform well in changing environments.

■ Organizations benefit from process innovations, product innovations, and business model innovations.

■ Highly innovative organizations tend to have supportive cultures, strategies, structures, staffing, and top management.

2 What is the nature of organizational change?

■ Change leaders are change agents who take responsibility for helping to change the behavior of people and organizational systems.

■ Organizational change can proceed with a top-down emphasis, with a bottom-up emphasis, or a combination of both.

■ Transformational change is led from the top and makes radical changes in organizational directions. Incremental change is led from all levels and makes continuing adjustments to existing ways and practices.

■ The many possible targets for change include organizational tasks, people, cultures, technologies, and structures.

3 How can planned organizational change be managed?

■ Lewin's three phases of planned change are unfreezing—preparing a system for change; changing—

making a change; and refreezing—stabilizing the system with a new change in place.

■ Change agents should understand the nature of force-coercion, rational persuasion, and shared power change strategies.

■ People resist change for a variety of reasons, including fear of the unknown and force of habit.

■ Good change agents deal with resistance positively and in a variety of ways, including education, participation, support and facilitation.

■ Success with technological change requires an openness to resistance and willingness to improvise as implementation proceeds.

4 What is organization development?

■ Organization development (OD) is a comprehensive approach to planned organization change that uses principles of behavioral science to improve organizational effectiveness over the long term.

■ Outcome goals of OD focus on improved task accomplishment; process goals of OD focus on improvements in the way people work together to accomplish important tasks.

■ The OD process involves action research wherein people work together to collect and analyze data on system performance and decide what actions to take to improve things.

■ OD interventions are structured activities that help people work together to accomplish change; they may be implemented at the individual, group, and/or organizational levels.

Action research (p. 308)
Bottom-up change (p. 298)
Business model innovation (p. 294)
Change leader (p. 297)
Changing (p. 302)
Commercializing innovation (p. 295)
Creativity (p. 293)
Force-coercion strategy (p. 303)

Incremental change (p. 300)
Innovation (p. 294)
OD interventions (p. 308)
Organization development (p. 307)
Performance gap (p. 299)
Planned change (p. 299)
Process innovations (p. 294)
Product innovations (p. 294)

Rational persuasion strategy (p. 304)
Reactive change (p. 299)
Refreezing (p. 302)
Shared power strategy (p. 304)
Strategic leadership (p. 293)
Top-down change (p. 298)
Transformational change (p. 299)
Unfreezing (p. 301)

SELF-TEST 12

MULTIPLE-CHOICE QUESTIONS:

1. In organizations, product innovation (creating new goods or services) and _____ innovation (creating new ways of doing things) are both important.

   (a) content   (b) process   (c) quality   (d) task

2. The first step in Hamel's wheel of innovation is _____.

   (a) imagining   (b) assessing   (c) experimenting   (d) scaling

3. An executive pursuing transformational change would give highest priority to which one of these change targets?

   (a) an out-of-date policy   (b) the organizational culture   (c) a new MIS   (d) job designs in a customer service department

4. A manager using a force-coercion strategy will rely on the power of _____ to bring about change.

   (a) expertise   (b) reference   (c) rewards, punishments, or authority   (d) information

5. The most participative of the planned change strategies is _____.

   (a) force-coercion   (b) rational persuasion   (c) shared power   (d) command and control

6. Trying to covertly influence others, offering only selective information, and/or structuring events in favor of the desired change are ways of dealing with resistance by _____.

   (a) participation   (b) manipulation and co-optation   (c) force-coercion   (d) facilitation

7. In organization development both _____ and _____ goals are important.

   (a) task, maintenance   (b) management, labor   (c) outcome, process   (d) profit, market share

8. Sensitivity training and role negotiation are examples of organization development interventions targeted at the _____ level.

   (a) individual   (b) group   (c) system-wide   (d) organization

9. The concept of empowerment is most often associated with the _____ strategy of planned change.

   (a) market-driven   (b) rational persuasion   (c) direct forcing   (d) normative-reeducative

10. Unfreezing occurs during the _____ step of organizational development.

    (a) diagnosis   (b) intervention   (c) evaluation   (d) termination

11. The quality concept of continuous improvement is most consistent with the notion of _____.

    (a) incremental change   (b) transformational change   (c) radical change   (d) reactive change

12. True internalization and commitment to a planned change is most likely to occur when a manager uses a(n) _____ change strategy.

    (a) education and communication   (b) rational persuasion   (c) manipulation and co-optation   (d) shared power

13. When a manager listens to users, makes adaptations, and continuously tweeks and changes a new MIS as it is being implemented, the approach to technological change can be described as _____

    (a) top-down   (b) improvisational   (c) organization development   (d) frame breaking

14. In the change management literature the recommendation is to view resistance to change as _____

    (a) feedback of potential value   (b) an indicator of political maneuvering   (c) a sign that change is moving too slow   (d) a warning that force-coercion may be needed

15. When the organization development process utilizes role negotiation and job redesign as approaches to improve effectiveness, the interventions are targeted at the _____ level.

    (a) individual   (b) group   (c) organization   (d) organization-environment

SHORT-RESPONSE QUESTIONS:

16. How do product, process, and business model innovations differ from one another?

17. What are the three phases of change described by Lewin, and what are their implications for change leadership?

18. What are the major differences in potential outcomes of force-coercion, rational persuasion, and shared power strategies of planned change?

19. What does the statement "OD equals planned change plus" mean?

APPLICATION QUESTION:

20. As a newly appointed manager in any work setting, you are likely to spot many things that "could be done better" and to have many "new ideas" that you would like to implement. Based on the ideas presented in this chapter, how should you go about effecting successful planned change in such situations?

CHAPTER 12 APPLICATIONS

CASE 12

Skype: Making the Case for Free Calls

Look out all you traditional telephone companies: There's a new kid on the block who's aiming to take a bite out of your customer base. In its brief time in business, Skype has amassed more than 75 million customers around the world, from savvy teens to Internet moguls to businesses of all sizes.[51] Skype's peer-to-peer phone service allows users to make crystal clear computer-to-computer calls anywhere around the world for free. And Skype users pay long-distance and international rates comparable to traditional phone plans, but without the overhead of a land line or regulatory fees. Why are customers in such a rush to sign up with Skype? And what's next for the burgeoning Luxembourg startup?

A History of Bringing People Together

Skype founders Niklas Zennstrom and Janus Friis are familiar to the business of connecting computer users worldwide, having previously created KaZaA—the well-known file-sharing network. Before its sale to Sharman Networks, KaZaA was one of the most popular peer-to-peer networking programs. Creating a network consisting entirely of users' computers, KaZaA allowed people to share video and music to their hearts content, and much to the ire of the entertainment industry.[52]

Taking the peer-to-peer knowledge they acquired from KaZaA, Zennstrom and Friis turned their energies toward making a dent in the burgeoning VoIP (voice over Internet Protocol) movement. (VoIP is a technology that encodes voice signals into data packets which can be sent along high-speed Internet lines.) In 2003, they launched Skype, which at that time could only connect users to the computers of other Skype members. Twenty-seven languages and four supported operating systems later, Skype users can now have text and video chats, as well as make outgoing calls to landline and mobile phones around the world. Windows to Mac, Mac to Linux, Linux to Windows Mobile—Skype users are not bound by the inter-operating system limitations that characterize other voice chat systems. And like other messaging services, Skype can let other users know if you're free to take a call, busy "on the other line," or entirely away from your computer.[53]

Cashing In on Your Calls

A bare-bones Skype setup only requires a computer, a high-speed Internet connection, and a combination headset/microphone to join the fun. But as with any tech trend, many retailers have created add-on products to enhance the VoIP experience. A number of companies make feather-weight headsets for callers who plan to spend hours upon hours on the "phone." Users whose Internet devices support Bluetooth—such as most modern laptops and Blackberry-style organizers—can mate one of the many wireless Bluetooth headsets for a truly "mobile" experience. And to get their pieces of the pie, gear vendors like Netgear and Belkin offer a new take on the traditional mobile phone: a phone that, without the aid of a computer, can place Skype calls from any open Wi-Fi source.[54]

Leaving Behind Dinosaurs of the Internet Age

With more customers than ever turning to computer-based telephony as an alternative or complement to traditional phone service, it should come as no surprise that the biggest names of the Web are scrambling to offer similar services and preserve brand allegiance. Yahoo!, Google, and MSN all have competing VoIP services, though none are currently as fully functioned as Skype. Yahoo! Messenger only supports PC-PC calls. GoogleTalk is about the same: a proprietary messenger service that also connects via voice. Like so many of Google's other services, it's still in beta mode. However recent SEC filings indicate that Google will use VoIP, Inc.'s VoiceOne Communications to get into the VoIP business. VoiceOne will handle peering services for Google VoIP. And Microsoft jump-started the tech rumor mill when it purchased Teleo, a provider of PC-PC calling services. Much like the rest of the competition, the giant from Redmond plans to integrate voice services into its Messenger and mail services.[55]

Can It Turn a Profit?

KaZaA's rampant adware became the bane of many PC users' existence, clogging the systems of its most devout enthusiasts. So this time around Zennstrom and Friis seem determined to keep Skype's reputation squeaky clean at all costs. They plan to build Skype's profits through its SkypeOut service, which lets users make worldwide calls for very reasonable rates, and by offering value-added services to businesses. Knowing how much of Skype's awareness is driven through viral means at this point, Zennstrom concedes that "if we had adware in Skype, it would kind of be counterproductive to our business model." He acknowledges that for a virally-marketed product to succeed, "you need to gain trust of end users. . . . If there is a bunch of adware in the software, you probably don't recommend it to friends and family."[56]

In Business for Business

With the advent of feasible VoIP providers like Skype, many businesses are thinking twice about their outdated PBX phone systems. New businesses see the cost and maintenance advantage of only laying one cable network. And while larger businesses can currently make calls within the same building or across a campus for free, VoIP service brings that same cost savings to calls to off-site employees or contractors.[57] This would bring freelancers or work-at-home parents even closer to the office. And since broadband tends to be a fixed expense per month, businesses would no longer have to worry about the length or frequency of the thousands of calls they make.

None of this is lost on Skype, which has made special marketing efforts to attract businesses to its service. Businesses using Skype can conference with up to five callers at a time, whether all or just one of them are Skype users. Companies with toll-free numbers can be sure that Skype users can call them for free because Skype supports toll-free calling.[58] And to soothe the concerns of any reasonable company, Skype has specific security protocol in place to protect both the callers and their content.[59]

eBay's Turn to Place a Bid

Like so many Internet innovators before them, the founders of Skype eventually received an offer they couldn't refuse. The startup was acquired in 2005 by eBay for $2.6 billion in cash and stock, with the offer of an additional $1.5 billion in bonuses.[60] And the online bidding giant wasted no time integrating Skype's services into its business plan. Sellers can now add the option to be contacted by text chat of voice by Skype users, assuming they are Skype users, too. This gives unsure buyers the opportunity to engage with sellers of expensive or complex items; sellers can build trust with prospective clients by making themselves available for reference.[61]

Watch Out, YouTube

While Skype shows no signs of slowing down, founders Zennstrom and Friis have another venture up their sleeves. Working under the code name "The Venice Project," they've assembled top programmers in a handful of cities around the world to develop software for distributing TV shows and other video files over the Web. They've entered negotiations with TV networks, and though no plans have been finalized, it's safe to say that they won't stray far from Skype or the $1.5 billion in additional eBay payments.[62]

More Than Just Hype

Rising from the ashes of a peer-to-peer phenomena, Skype has charmed millions of users around the world by providing free, high-quality voice and video conversations. And by making it easy and affordable for Skype users to interact with more traditional phone users, the company has ensured that its ranks will be filled with more than just tech geeks and long-distance sweethearts. Whether actively soliciting businesses or opening its technology to third-party gear vendors, Skype is staying quick and mobile, reaching out in all directions to make new friends and customers.

But is there really the demand for video chatting that Skype predicts? And could the competing Internet portal brands harness the sheer size of its user bases to mount a formidable challenge? Stay tuned and see!

REVIEW QUESTIONS

1. Is this a case of innovation by acquisition? What are the advantages for Skype of its acquisition by eBay? What are some possible disadvantages?

2. Project Skype forward. How can it innovate from within the eBay corporate structure?

3. Does Skype's growth and success fit with the characteristics of an adaptive organization?

TEAM PROJECT

Innovation Audit

Did you know: Apple had a computer named "Lisa," Coca-Cola once launched "New Coke" with a formula thought sure to reenergize the brand, SONY invested heavily in a video recording technology "Betamax" as an alternative to VHS? All were failures, but the firms are considered innovative nonetheless.

Question: How do highly innovative organizations do it?

Research Directions:

■ Make a list of organizations—businesses, non-profits, government agencies—that you believe are highly innovative.

■ Choose 1 and preferably 2 of them to investigate further.

■ Use Web sites, news reports, and other possible information sources to gather data on how each organization supports, encourages, and accomplishes significant innovation in products, processes, and/or business models.

■ Where possible, identify an employee or two of the organization and contact them for an interview by telephone, e-mail, or face-to-face. Use the interview to gain additional insight on the organization's innovation practices.

■ Create a descriptive profile that identifies how each organization achieves success as an innovator; compare the profiles to identify major similiarities and differences. Put this together in a final research report or presentation.

PERSONAL MANAGEMENT

Tolerance for Ambiguity

In the new world of work, change is common as unstructured problems require us to make decisions with incomplete information under uncertain conditions. But, change also evokes anxiety as it breaks us from past habits and conditions. Depending on your **TOLERANCE FOR AMBIGUITY**, you may be comfortable or uncomfortable dealing with these change realities. It takes personal flexibility and lots of confidence to cope well with unpredictability. Some people have a hard time dealing with the unfamiliar. They prefer to work with directions that minimize ambiguity and provide clear decision-making rules; they like the structure of mechanistic organizations with bureaucratic features; they like the way things are and are afraid of anything "new." Other people are willing and able to perform in less structured settings that give them lots of flexibility in responding to changing situations. They like the freedom of organic organizations designed for adaptation; they are excited by the prospects of change and new opportunities.

Building the Brand Called "You"   You must find a good fit between your personal preferences and the nature of the organizations in which you choose to work. To achieve this fit, you have to understand how you react in change situations. Take one or more of the recommended self-assessments. Consider your scores and relate them back to your tolerance for ambiguity. The best time to explore tendencies in change situations is now, before you take your first or next job.

NEXT STEPS: MANAGEMENT LEARNING WORKBOOK

Self-Assessments
- Empowering Others (#15)
- T-t Leadership Style (#21)
- Turbulence Tolerance Test (#16)

Experiential Exercises
- The Future Workplace (#14)
- Creative Solutions (#29)
- Force-Field Analysis (#30)

Leading and Leadership Development

13

Lead by the Numbers? Or from the Gut?

Many managers are taught to lead their employees on the basis of analytics—the science of logical analysis. But a new breed of managers is leading their workers to success on the basis of their personal style. For these leaders, it's more important to lead in a way that's honest to their core approach to business. Is one tactic better?

If you played for a professional basketball team, would you rather have a coach who, after conferring with assistant coaches, deliberately selected a last-minute play from a predefined playbook; or a coach who called plays from her gut?

Transfer that question into the business world, and you've set up a contrast between two key leadership styles—analytical and inspirational. Many CEOs see the value in both approaches, but lean toward one or the other in their own tendencies.

Heads of large manufacturing or production companies frequently tend toward *analytical* ways—a sense of responding to facts and measurables with logic and assessment. Procter & Gamble has relied on a set means of assessing future business plans and measuring the potential of an opportunity against its costs. In such a business model, decisions are not made by personality or emotion, but rather by consensus as facts stack up against a set methodology that is known and trusted.

What *They* Think

"You can only run a company of our size and scope with the right information."
Jeff Immelt, GE Chairman and CEO.

ANALYTICS: "Science is analytical, descriptive, informative. Man does not live by bread alone, but by science he attempts to do so. Hence the deadliness of all that is purely scientific."
Eric Gill, British sculptor, typographer, and engraver.

INSPIRATION: "Just dont't give up on trying to do what you really want to do. Where there is love and inspiration, I don't think you can go wrong."
Ella Fitzgerald, noted American jazz singer.

General Electric Chairman and CEO Jeff Immelt, like predecessor Jack Welch, believes that understanding the metrics of a business is crucial to its success. "You can only run a company of our size and scope with the right information," Immelt said. "At GE, bad news travels up very quickly. We have to know."[1]

Leaning in the opposite direction are leaders whose *inspirational* style plays to the emotions and attitude of the company.

The behavior of such charismatic figures often sets an example for the values necessary to sustain their brands. This can be valuable when the persona of a leader adds value to the brand by helping employees—and ultimately their customers—feel distinguished from the competition.

Consider such personalities as Southwest Airlines' Herb Kelleher or Virgin's Richard Branson. Both leaders were visionaries, building brands with values that became impressed upon customers. And, according to Kelleher: "It's more than just providing the customer with value," he said. "It's giving them an experience, giving people something they're seeking psychically."[2]

Branson concurs. "Branding demands commitment, and striking chords in people to stir their emotions," he said. "It's easy to be cynical about such things, much harder to be successful."[3]

Neither approach is relevant, of course, unless a manager is able to control costs and steer his or her organization toward continuous improvement. But there are numerous contemporary examples of successful leaders from both camps.

How do you plan to lead? Will you go for analytics, inspiration, or a blending of both?

The Numbers

Global CEO Turnover

Largest 2500 firms	15.3%
Japan	19.8%
North America	16.2%
Europe	15.3%
Asia/Pacific	10.5%

Quick Facts

* One-third of global CEO turnover involved forced resignations over poor performance.[4]
* 85 percent of all operational failures are the fault of fallible managers, not failing workers.[5]
* After taking Virgin public, Richard Branson found that he didn't want to share profits and work with outside directors. So Branson and his management team executed a management buyout to take the company private again.[6]
* Southwest Airlines' continuous posting of profits for 29 years is attributed largely to former CEO Herb Kelleher's "unorthodox personality and engaging management style."[7]
* According to a case study on management and leadership, improving a company's style of management can increase its operating effectiveness by 20–30 percent.[8]

What Do *You* Think?

1. Select a corporate leader whose leadership style was recently either beneficial or detrimental to a company's performance. How and why did the style influence performance?

2. Are there potential negative outcomes to leading by analytics? ... or by inspiration?

Leading and leadership development			
Study Question 1	**Study Question 2**	**Study Question 3**	**Study Question 4**
The Nature of Leadership	**Leadership Traits and Behaviors**	**Contingency Approaches to Leadership**	**Issues in Leadership Development**
■ Leadership and position power ■ Leadership and personal power ■ Leadership and vision ■ Servant leadership	■ Leadership traits ■ Leadership behaviors ■ Classic leadership styles	■ Fiedler's contingency model ■ Hersey-Blanchard situational model ■ House's path-goal theory ■ Vroom-Jago leader-participation model	■ Transformational leadership ■ Emotional intelligence and leadership ■ Gender and leadership ■ Drucker's "old-fashioned" leadership ■ Moral leadership
Learning Check 1	**Learning Check 2**	**Learning Check 3**	**Learning Check 4**

At Herman Miller Inc., the innovative Michigan-based maker of office furniture, Max DePree, the firm's former chairperson and the son of its founder, tells the story of a millwright who worked for his father.[9] When the man died, DePree's father, wishing to express his sympathy to the family, went to their home. There he listened as the widow read some beautiful poems, which, he was surprised to learn, had been written by the millwright. To this day, DePree says, he and his father still wonder, "Was the man a poet who did millwright's work, or a millwright who wrote poetry?"

DePree summarizes the leadership lesson of his story this way: "It is fundamental that leaders endorse a concept of persons. This begins with an understanding of the diversity of people's gifts, talents, and skills." His point is well taken. When we recognize the unique qualities of others, we become less inclined to believe that we alone know what is best. By valuing and respecting people, we learn how to provide them with meaningful work and opportunities. This leadership insight extends to all types and sizes of organizations.

Great leaders bring out the best in people. Consultant and author Tom Peters says that the leader is "rarely—possibly never?—the best performer."[10] Leaders don't have to be; they thrive through and by the successes of others.

THE NATURE OF LEADERSHIP

Leadership is the process of inspiring others to work hard to accomplish important tasks.

A glance at the shelves in your local bookstore will quickly confirm that **leadership**—the process of inspiring others to work hard to accomplish important tasks—is one of the most popular management topics.[11] As shown in *Figure 13.1*, it is also one of the four functions that constitute the management process. Planning sets the direction and objectives; organizing brings together resources to turn plans into action; *leading* builds the commitments and enthusiasm for people to apply their talents to help accomplish plans; controlling makes sure things turn out right.

The late Grace Hopper, management expert and the first female admiral in the U.S. Navy, once said: "You manage things; you lead people."[12] Managers

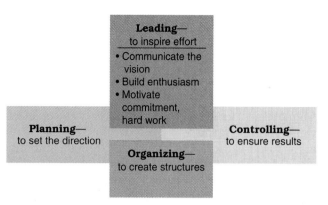

Figure 13.1 Leading viewed in relationship to the other management functions.

today must lead under new and difficult conditions. The time frames for getting things accomplished are becoming shorter; leaders are expected to get things right the first time, with second chances sometimes few and far between. The problems to be resolved through leadership are complex, ambiguous, and multidimensional; leaders are expected to stay focused an long-term goals even while dealing with problems and pressures in the short term.[13] Anyone aspiring to career success in leadership must rise to these challenges, and more, becoming good at communication, interpersonal relations, motivation, teamwork, and change—all topics in this part of *Management 9/e*.

LEADERSHIP AND POSITION POWER

Power is the ability to get someone else to do something you want done. It is the ability to make things happen the way you want them to.[14] Leadership begins with the ways a manager uses power to influence the behavior of other people. Although a need for power is essential to executive success, it is not a desire to control for the sake of personal satisfaction. It is a desire to influence and control others for the good of the group or organization as a whole.[15] This "positive" face of power is the foundation of effective leadership.

Figure 13.2 shows that leaders gain power both from the positions they hold and from their personal qualities.[16] Anyone holding a managerial position theoretically has power, but how well it is used will vary from one person to the next. The three bases of *position power* are reward power, coercive power, and legitimate power.

Reward power is the ability to influence through rewards. It is the capability to offer something of value—a positive outcome—as a means of influencing another person's behavior. This involves use of things like pay raises, bonuses, promotions, special assignments, and verbal or written

■ **Power** is the ability to get someone else to do something you want done or to make things happen the way you want.

■ **Reward power** is the capacity to offer something of value as a means of influencing other people.

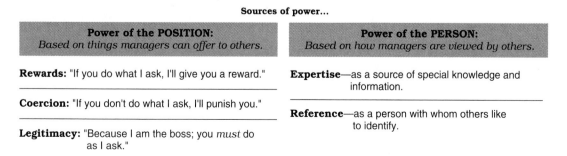

Figure 13.2 Sources of position power and personal power used by leaders.

compliments. To mobilize reward power, a manager says, in effect, "If you do what I ask, I'll give you a reward."

■ **Coercive power** is the capacity to punish or withhold positive outcomes as a means of influencing other people.

Coercive power is the ability to influence through punishment. It is the capacity to punish or withhold positive outcomes as a way to influence the behavior of other people. A manager may attempt to coerce someone by threatening him or her with verbal reprimands, pay penalties, and even termination. To mobilize coercive power, a manager says, in effect, "If you don't do what I want, I'll punish you."

■ **Legitimate power** is the capacity to influence other people by virtue of formal authority, or the rights of office.

Legitimate power is the ability to influence through authority—the right by virtue of one's organizational position or status to exercise control over persons in subordinate positions. It is the capacity to influence the behavior of other people by virtue of the rights of office. To mobilize legitimate power, a manager says, in effect, "I am the boss; therefore, you are supposed to do as I ask."

LEADERSHIP AND PERSONAL POWER

The unique personal qualities of a manager are further sources of power. In fact, a truly successful leader is very good at building and using two bases of *personal power*—expert power and referent power.

■ **Expert power** is the capacity to influence other people because of specialized knowledge.

Expert power is the ability to influence through special expertise. It is the capacity to influence the behavior of other people because of one's knowledge and skills. Expertise derives from the possession of technical understanding or special information. It is developed by acquiring relevant skills or competencies and by gaining a central position in relevant information networks. It is maintained by protecting one's credibility and not overstepping the boundaries of true expertise. When a manager uses expert power, the implied message is "You should do what I want because of my special expertise or information."

INSIGHTS

Employees are a Firm's Most Important Customers

When most people think of Southwest Airlines, they think first of reasonable prices, second of success in a turbulent industry and a service spirit, and third of its well-known founder and retired CEO, Herb Kelleher. Indeed, all points are on target. You can learn more about Kelleher and his leadership style by reading the Southwest Airlines case in this chapter. Before doing that, however, consider Colleen Barrett, Southwest's president.

> *Leadership development at Southwest is supported from the top, with everyone expected to be great at "TLC"—tender loving care for employees and customers. Barrett describes herself as a mentor, willing to work with "anyone who seems to have a passion for what he or she does, or who has a desire to learn."*

In an interview with *BizEd* magazine, Barrett indicates that the airline's success begins with its high-priority commitment to all employees. She says the firm has three types of customers: employees, passengers, and shareholders. Whereas many would consider it strange and perhaps even wrong to define employees as an organization's most important customers, Barrett says it has a purpose: "If senior leaders regularly communicate with employees, if we're truthful and factual, if we show them that we care, and we do our best to respond to their needs, they'll feel good about their work environment and they'll be better at serving the passenger." Satisfied passengers, of course, are essential for business reputation and profits.

At Southwest, a strong and unique sense of mission helps leaders at all levels rally themselves and others to everyday performance excellence. "We tell job applicants we're in the customer service business," says Barrett. "We just happen to provide airline transportation." That is a unique spin in an industry known for customer complaints and dissatisfaction.

Referent power is the ability to influence through identification. It is the capacity to influence the behavior of other people because they admire you and want to identify positively with you. Reference is a power derived from charisma or interpersonal attractiveness. It is developed and maintained through good interpersonal relations that encourage the admiration and respect of others. When a manager uses referent power, the implied message is "You should do what I want in order to maintain a positive, self-defined relationship with me."

LEADERSHIP AND VISION

"Great leaders," it is said, "get extraordinary things done in organizations by inspiring and motivating others toward a common purpose."[17] In other words, they use their power exceptionally well. And frequently today, successful leadership is associated with **vision**—a future that one hopes to create or achieve in order to improve upon the present state of affairs.

The term **visionary leadership** describes a leader who brings to the situation a clear and compelling sense of the future, as well as an understanding of the actions needed to get there successfully.[18] But simply having the vision of a desirable future is not enough. Truly great leaders are extraordinarily good at turning their visions into accomplishments. This means having a clear vision, communicating the vision, and getting people motivated and inspired to pursue the vision in their daily work. Think of it this way: visionary leadership brings meaning to people's work, making what they do seem worthy and valuable.

A visionary leader may combine the elements of analytics and style raised in The Topic chapter opener. At her Leadership Institute in New York City, for example, founder Lorraine Monroe brings visionary leadership to life in the analytics of the "Monroe Doctrine"—"We can reform society only if every place we live—every school, workplace, church, and family—becomes a site of reform." Her style emphasizes principles, starting with what she calls the "heart of the matter": "Leadership is about making a vision happen. . . . The job of a good leader is to articulate a vision that others are inspired to follow. . . . That leader makes everybody in an organization understand how to make the vision active."[19]

■ **Referent power** is the capacity to influence other people because of their desire to identify personally with you.

■ A **vision** is a clear sense of the future.

■ **Visionary leadership** brings to the situation a clear sense of the future and an understanding of how to get there.

SERVANT LEADERSHIP

When thinking about leadership, power, and vision, the concept of **servant leadership** deserves attention. This is leadership based on a commitment to serving others, to helping people use their talents to full potential while working together for organizations that benefit society.[20] You might think of servant leadership with this question in mind: who is most important in leadership, the leader or the followers? For those who believe in servant leadership, there is no doubt about the correct answer: the followers. Servant leadership is "other-centered" and not "self-centered."

If one shifts the focus away from the self and toward others, what does that generate in terms of leadership directions and opportunities? **Empowerment** for one thing. This is the process through which managers enable and help others gain power and achieve influence within the organization. Servant leaders empower others by providing them with the information, responsibility, authority, and trust to make decisions and act independently. They expect that when people feel empowered to act, they will follow through with commitment and high-quality work. They also realize

■ **Servant leadership** is follower-centered and committed to helping others in their work.

■ **Empowerment** enables others to gain and use decision-making power.

that power in organizations is not a "zero-sum" quantity, rejecting the idea that in order for one person to gain power, someone else needs to give it up.[21] In this way servant leadership becomes empowering for everyone, making the whole organization more powerful in serving its cause or mission.

Consider how servant leadership is described by others. Max DePree of Herman Miller praises leaders who "permit others to share ownership of problems—to take possession of the situation."[22] Lorraine Monroe of the School Leadership Academy says: "The real leader is a servant of the people she leads . . . a really great boss is not afraid to hire smart people. You want people who are smart about things you are not smart about."[23] Robert Greenleaf, who is credited with coining the term servant leadership, says: "Institutions function better when the idea, the dream, is to the fore, and the person, the leader, is seen as servant to the dream." [24]

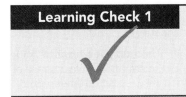

Learning Check 1

Be sure you can ■ define the term power ■ illustrate three types of position power and discuss how managers use each ■ illustrate two types of personal power and discuss how managers use each ■ define the term vision ■ explain the concept of visionary leadership ■ define the term empowerment ■ explain the notion of servant leadership

LEADERSHIP TRAITS AND BEHAVIORS

For centuries people have recognized that some persons perform very well as leaders, whereas others do not. The question still debated is why. Historically, the issue of leadership success has been studied from the perspective of the trait, behavioral, and contingency approaches. Each offers a slightly different explanation of leadership effectiveness and the pathways to leadership development.

LEADERSHIP TRAITS

An early direction in leadership research involved the search for universal traits or distinguishing personal characteristics that would separate effective and ineffective leaders.[25] Sometimes called the *great person theory,* the results of many years of research in this direction can be summarized as follows.

Physical characteristics such as a person's height, weight, and physique make no difference in determining leadership success. On the other hand, certain personal traits do seem common among the best leaders. A study of over 3,400 managers, for example, found that followers rather consistently admired leaders who were honest, competent, forward looking, inspiring, and credible.[26] A comprehensive review by Shelley Kirkpatrick and Edwin Locke further identifies these personal traits of many successful leaders.[27]

- *Drive:* Successful leaders have high energy, display initiative, and are tenacious.
- *Self-confidence:* Successful leaders trust themselves and have confidence in their abilities.
- *Creativity:* Successful leaders are creative and original in their thinking.
- *Cognitive ability:* Successful leaders have the intelligence to integrate and interpret information.

- *Business knowledge:* Successful leaders know their industry and its technical foundations.
- *Motivation:* Successful leaders enjoy influencing others to achieve shared goals.
- *Flexibility:* Successful leaders adapt to fit the needs of followers and the demands of situations.
- *Honesty and integrity:* Successful leaders are trustworthy; they are honest, predictable, and dependable.

LEADERSHIP BEHAVIORS

As the early trait studies proved inconclusive, researchers turned their attention toward how leaders behave when working with followers. Work in this tradition investigated **leadership styles**—the recurring patterns of behaviors exhibited by leaders.[28] If the best style could be identified, the implications were straightforward and practical: train leaders to become skilled at using it.

A stream of research that began in the 1940s, spearheaded by studies at Ohio State University and the University of Michigan, focused attention on two dimensions of leadership style: (1) concern for the task to be accomplished, and (2) concern for the people doing the work. The Ohio State studies used the terms *initiating structure* and *consideration* for the respective dimensions; the University of Michigan studies called them *production-centered* and *employee-centered.*[29]

But regardless of the terminology used, the behaviors characteristic of each leadership dimension were quite clear. A *leader high in concern for task* plans and defines work to be done, assigns task responsibilities, sets clear work standards, urges task completion, and monitors performance results. By contrast, a *leader high in concern for people* acts warm and supportive toward followers, maintains good social relations with them, respects their feelings, is sensitive to their needs, and shows trust in them.

The results of leader behavior research at first suggested that followers of people-oriented leaders would be more productive and satisfied than those working for more task-oriented leaders.[30] However, researchers eventually moved toward the position that truly effective leaders were high in both concerns for people and concerns for task.

Figure 13.3 describes one of the popular versions of this conclusion—the Leadership Grid™ of Robert Blake and Jane Mouton.[31] This grid describes leaders with respect to their respective tendencies toward people and production concerns. The preferred combination of "high-high" leadership is

> **Leadership style** is the recurring pattern of behaviors exhibited by a leader.

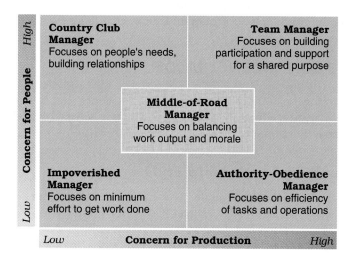

Figure 13.3 Managerial styles in Blake and Mouton's Leadership Grid.

called the *team manager*. This is a leader who shares decisions with team members, empowers them and encourages participation, and supports the teamwork needed for high levels of task accomplishment.

CLASSIC LEADERSHIP STYLES

▨ A leader with an **autocratic style** acts in a unilateral, command-and-control fashion.

▨ A leader with a **human relations style** emphasizes people over task.

▨ A leader with a **laissez-faire style** displays a "do the best you can and don't bother me" attitude.

▨ A leader with a **democratic style** encourages participation with an emphasis on both task accomplishment and development of people.

Even today, when people talk about the leaders with whom they work, their vocabulary often describes classic styles of leadership relating back to the behavioral leadership theories.[32] A leader identified with an **autocratic style** emphasizes task over people, keeps authority and information to himself or herself, and acts in a unilateral, command-and-control fashion. A leader with a **human relations style** does just the opposite, emphasizing people over task. A leader with a **laissez-faire style** shows little concern for task, letting the group make decisions and acting with a "do the best you can and don't bother me" attitude. A leader with a **democratic style** is committed to both task and people, trying to get things done while sharing information, encouraging participation in decision making, and otherwise helping others develop their skills and capabilities.

Speaking of styles, this is a good point to ask: "What type of leader are you?" "How would the people with whom you work and study describe your style—autocratic, human relations, laissez-faire, or democratic?"

Learning Check 2

Be sure you can ▪ contrast the trait and leader-behavior approaches to leadership research ▪ identify five personal traits of successful leaders ▪ illustrate leader behaviors consistent with a high concern for task ▪ illustrate leader behaviors consistent with a high concern for people ▪ explain the leadership development implications of Blake and Mouton's Leadership Grid ▪ describe four classic leadership styles

CONTINGENCY APPROACHES TO LEADERSHIP

As leadership research continued, scholars next recognized the need to probe beyond leader behaviors and examine yet another question: when and under what circumstances is a particular leadership style preferable to others? They developed the following *contingency approaches*, which share the goal of understanding the conditions for leadership success in different situations.

FIEDLER'S CONTINGENCY MODEL

An early contingency leadership model was developed by Fred Fiedler. He proposed that good leadership depends on a match between leadership style and situational demands.[33]

Understanding Leadership style

Leadership style in Fiedler's model is measured on the *least-preferred co-worker scale*, known as the LPC scale. It describes tendencies to behave either as a task-motivated (low LPC score) or relationship-motivated (high LPC score) leader. This "either/or" concept is important. Fiedler believes that leadership style is part of one's personality; therefore, it is relatively endur-ing and difficult to change. He doesn't place much hope in trying to train a task-motivated leader to behave in a relationship-motivated manner, or vice versa. Rather, Fiedler believes that the key to leadership success is putting our existing styles to work in situations for which they are the best "fit."

Understanding Leadership Situations

In Fiedler's model, the amount of control a situation allows the leader is a critical issue in determining the correct style-situation fit. Three contingency variables are used to diagnose situational control. The *quality of leader-member relations* (good or poor) measures the degree to which the group sup-ports the leader. The *degree of task structure* (high or low) measures the ex-tent to which task goals, procedures, and guidelines are clearly spelled out. The *amount of position power* (strong or weak) measures the degree to which the position gives the leader power to reward and punish subordinates.

Figure 13.4 shows eight leadership situations that result from different combinations of these variables. They range from the most favorable situa-tion of high control (good leader-member relations, high task structure, strong position power) to the least favorable situation of low control (poor leader-member relations, low task structure, weak position power).

Matching Leadership Style and Situation

Figure 13.4 also summarizes Fiedler's extensive research on the contingency relationships between situation control, leadership style, and leader effec-tiveness. Note that neither the task-oriented nor the relationship-oriented leadership style is effective all the time. Instead, each style seems to work best when used in the right situation.

Fiedler's findings can be stated as two propositions. *Proposition 1*—a task-oriented leader will be most successful in either very favorable (high-control) or very unfavorable (low-control) situations. *Proposition 2*—a relation-ship-oriented leader will be most successful in situations of moderate control.

Assume, for example, that you are the leader of a team of bank tellers. The tellers seem highly supportive of you, and their job is clearly defined re-garding what needs to be done. You have the authority to evaluate their per-formance and to make pay and promotion recommendations. This is a high-control situation consisting of good leader-member relations, high task structure, and high position power. *Figure 13.4* shows that a task-motivated leader would be most effective in this situation.

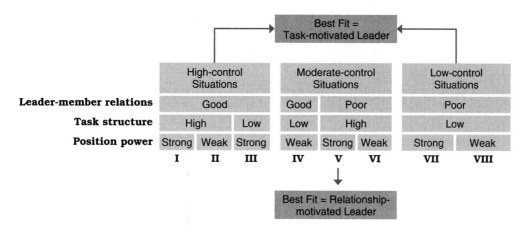

Figure 13.4 Predictions from Fiedler's contingency leadership model.

ISSUES AND SITUATIONS

Managing the Boss

To: Megan Dove
From: Glenn Pool
Subject: Performance Review

Hi Megan:

My To-Do List indicates that it's time for us to meet and discuss your six-month performance. I know we haven't spoken for quite awhile, but we need to get this scheduled. Just access my online calendar and choose at least a one-hour block of time during the third week of the month when I am free. We'll meet in my office. Bring a list of your major accomplishments and also be prepared to discuss any problems that you have been having. We should also set some concrete goals for your next performance period, so be thinking of those as well.

See you in a couple of weeks.

Glenn

Focus on Glenn –

How is he doing as a manager? How should he deal with Megan?

1. Point out the troublesome aspects of his memo to Mary.
2. Recommend a set of goals for Glenn to accomplish in this meeting.
3. Prepare an agenda and script to help Glenn when he speaks with Megan.

Focus on Megan –

Does she have a "managing the boss" problem? How should she handle this e-mail?

1. Recommend a set of goals for Megan to accomplish in the meeting with Glenn.
2. Prepare an agenda and script that she can use to achieve her goals in the meeting.
3. Advise Megan on how to get "Glenn" to understand her side of the employee-boss relationship.

Now, suppose that you are chairperson of a committee asked to improve labor-management relations in a manufacturing plant. Although the goal is clear, no one can say for sure how to accomplish it. Task structure is low. Because committee members are free to quit any time they want, the chairperson has little position power. Because not all members believe the committee is necessary, poor leader-member relations are apparent. According to the figure, this low-control situation also calls for a task-motivated leader.

Finally, assume that you are the new head of a fashion section in a large department store. Because you were selected over one of the popular sales clerks you now supervise, leader-member relations are poor. Task structure is high since the clerk's job is well defined. Your position power is low because the clerks work under a seniority system and fixed wage schedule. The figure shows that this moderate-control situation requires a relationship-motivated leader.

HERSEY-BLANCHARD SITUATIONAL LEADERSHIP MODEL

In contrast to Fiedler's notion that leadership style is hard to change, the Hersey-Blanchard situational leadership model suggests that successful leaders do adjust their styles. They do so contingently and based on the *maturity* of followers, as indicated by their readiness to perform in a given situation.[34] "Readiness," in this sense, is based on how able and willing or confident followers are to perform required tasks. As shown in *Figure 13.5*, the possible combinations of task-oriented and relationship-oriented behaviors result in four leadership styles.

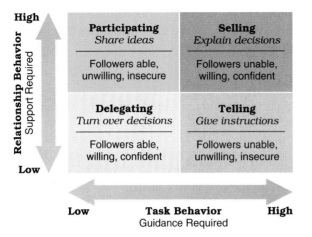

High

Low

Relationship Behavior
Support Required

Participating
Share ideas

Followers able,
unwilling, insecure

Selling
Explain decisions

Followers unable,
willing, confident

Delegating
Turn over decisions

Followers able,
willing, confident

Telling
Give instructions

Followers unable,
unwilling, insecure

Low   **Task Behavior**   High
Guidance Required

Figure 13.5 Leadership implications of the Hersey-Blanchard situational leadership model.

- *Delegating*—allowing the group to take responsibility for task decisions; a low-task, low-relationship style.
- *Participating*—emphasizing shared ideas and participative decisions on task directions; a low-task, high-relationship style.
- *Selling*—explaining task directions in a supportive and persuasive way; a high-task, high-relationship style.
- *Telling*—giving specific task directions and closely supervising work; a high-task, low-relationship style.

The *delegating style* works best in high-readiness situations with able and willing or confident followers. The *telling style* works best at the other extreme of low readiness, where followers are unable and unwilling or insecure. The *participating style* is recommended for low-to-moderate readiness (followers able but unwilling or insecure) and the *selling style* for moderate-to-high readiness (followers unable but willing or confident).

Hersey and Blanchard further believe that leadership styles should be adjusted as followers change over time. The model also implies that if the correct styles are used in lower-readiness situations, followers will "mature" and grow in ability, willingness, and confidence. This allows the leader to become less directive as followers mature. Although the Hersey-Blanchard model is intuitively appealing, limited research has been accomplished on it to date.[35]

HOUSE'S PATH-GOAL LEADERSHIP THEORY

A third contingency leadership approach is the *path-goal theory* advanced by Robert House.[36] This theory suggests that an effective leader is one who clarifies paths by which followers can achieve both task-related and personal goals. The best leaders raise motivation and help followers move along these paths. They remove any barriers that stand in the way and provide appropriate rewards for task accomplishment.

Path-goal theorists believe leaders should be flexible and move back and forth among four leadership styles to create positive path-goal linkages.

- *Directive leadership*—letting subordinates know what is expected; giving directions on what to do and how; scheduling work to be done; maintaining definite standards of performance; clarifying the leader's role in the group.
- *Supportive leadership*—doing things to make work more pleasant; treating group members as equals; being friendly and approachable; showing concern for the well-being of subordinates.
- *Achievement-oriented leadership*—setting challenging goals; expecting the highest levels of performance; emphasizing continuous improvement in performance; displaying confidence in meeting high standards.

- *Participative leadership*—involving subordinates in decision making; consulting with subordinates; asking for suggestions from subordinates; using these suggestions when making a decision.

Path-Goal Contingencies

The path-goal theory, summarized in *Figure 13.6*, advises managers to use leadership styles that fit situational needs. This allows the leader to add value by contributing things that are missing from the situation or that need strengthening, and by avoiding redundant behaviors. For example, when team members are expert and competent at their tasks it is unnecessary and even dysfunctional for the leader to tell them how to do things.

The important contingencies for making good path-goal leadership choices include follower characteristics (ability, experience, and locus of control) and work environment characteristics (task structure, authority system, and work group). For example, the match of leader behaviors and situation might take the following forms.[37] When *job assignments* are unclear, directive leadership is appropriate to clarify task objectives and expected rewards. When *worker self-confidence* is low, supportive leadership is appropriate to increase confidence by emphasizing individual abilities and offering needed assistance. When *performance incentives* are poor, participative leadership is appropriate to clarify individual needs and identify appropriate rewards. When *task challenge* is insufficient in a job, achievement-oriented leadership is appropriate to set goals and raise performance aspirations.

REAL ETHICS

Would you volunteer?

Boss: "I've been blessed with the opportunity to work in my spare time with Better World. It's a fine organization, and they do great things for our community and internationally—providing temporary housing for the homeless and giving them hot evening meals at the town hall. They have just completed a sponsored walkathon that earned $5,000 to be sent to assist with a reconstruction project in East Timor."

You: "Interesting. I'll bet you get a lot of satisfaction from that."

Boss: "Yes, and that's part of my point. I'd like you to volunteer also. It would be good for you, and you'd be helping create a good image for our firm in the community."

You: "Oh . . ."

Boss: "I mostly work with Better World on Wednesday and Thursday evenings. It takes away a bit from my family, but I'll tell you it's really worth it. You could go with me tomorrow right after work and get started. How about it?"

You: "Um . . ."

Boss: "Oh my, it almost sounds like I'm being pushy. Don't misinterpret things. I just want to bring a great opportunity for community service to your attention. I know this is short notice. If you can't make it this week, we'll just start next week. Do we have a plan?"

FURTHER INQUIRY

Managers, as bosses, have authority over the persons who report directly to them. That's part of the employment contract. But how far does this authority extend? Does it include requests for others to "volunteer" for various boss-sponsored or employer-sponsored charitable activities? When a manager makes requests like this, are they really "orders" veiled in the form of a "request." Just what are the ethics of this situation and of the broader set of possibilities that it describes? How should we respond when higher-ups ask us to "volunteer" to do things?

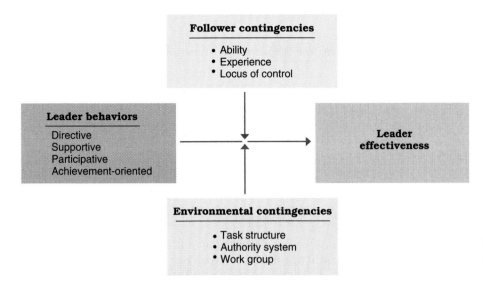

Figure 13.6 Contingency relationships in House's path-goal leadership theory.

Substitutes for Leadership

Path-goal theory has contributed to the recognition of what are called **substitutes for leadership**.[38] These are aspects of the work setting and the people involved that can reduce the need for a leader's personal involvement. In effect, they make leadership from the "outside" unnecessary because leadership is already provided from within the situation.

Possible substitutes for leadership include *subordinate characteristics* such as ability, experience, and independence; *task characteristics* such as routineness and availability of feedback; and *organizational characteristics* such as clarity of plans and formalization of rules and procedures. When these substitutes are present, managers are advised to avoid duplicating them. Instead, they should concentrate on doing other and more important things.

■ **Substitutes for leadership** are factors in the work setting that direct work efforts without the involvement of a leader.

VROOM-JAGO LEADER-PARTICIPATION MODEL

The Vroom-Jago leader-participation model is designed to help a leader choose the decision-making method that best fits the problem being faced.[39] In its current version, the model views a manager as using the five options shown in *Management Smarts 13.1*. And in true contingency fashion, no one option is universally superior. Each of the five decision methods is appropriate in certain situations, and each has its advantages and disadvantages.[40]

Leadership success results when the decision type correctly matches the characteristics of the problem to be solved. The key rules guiding the choice relate to (1) *decision quality*—based on who has the information needed for problem solving; (2) *decision acceptance*—based on the importance of follower acceptance of the decision to its eventual implementation; and (3) *decision time*—based on the time available to make and implement the decision.

MANAGEMENT SMARTS 13.1

Five ways for managers to make decisions

1. *Decide alone*—This is an authority decision; the manager decides how to solve the problem and communicates the decision to the group.
2. *Consult individually*—The manager makes the decision after sharing the problem and consulting individually with group members to get their suggestions.
3. *Consult with group*—The manager makes the decision after convening the group, sharing the problem, and consulting with everyone to get their suggestions.
4. *Facilitate*—The manager convenes the group, shares the problem, and then facilitates group discussion to make a decision.
5. *Delegate*—The manager convenes the group and delegates to group members the authority to define the problem and make a decision.

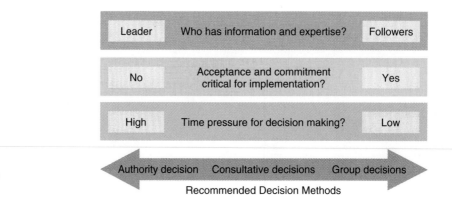

Figure 13.7 Leadership implications of Vroom-Jago leader-participation model.

■ An **authority decision** is made by the leader and then communicated to the group.

■ A **consultative decision** is made by a leader after receiving information, advice, or opinions from group members.

■ A **group decision** is made by group members themselves.

Figure 13.7 frames the leader's choices among **authority**, **consultative**, or **group decisions**.[41] Authority decisions work best when leaders personally have the expertise needed to solve the problem, they are confident and capable of acting alone, others are likely to accept and implement the decision they make, and little or no time is available for discussion. By contrast, consultative and group decisions are recommended when:

- The leader lacks sufficient expertise and information to solve this problem alone.
- The problem is unclear and help is needed to clarify the situation.
- Acceptance of the decision and commitment by others are necessary for implementation.
- Adequate time is available to allow for true participation.

Using consultative and group decisions offers important leadership benefits.[42] Participation helps improve decision quality by bringing more information to bear on the problem. It helps improve decision acceptance as participants gain understanding and become committed to the process. It also contributes to leadership development by allowing others to gain experience in the problem-solving process. However, a potential cost of participation is lost efficiency. Participation often adds to the time required for decision making, and leaders don't always have extra time available. When problems must be resolved immediately, the authority decision may be the only option.[43]

Learning Check 3

Be sure you can ■ contrast the leader-behavior and contingency approaches to leadership research ■ explain the link between leadership style and personality according to Fiedler ■ explain Fiedler's contingency thinking on matching leadership style and situation ■ identify the four leadership styles in the Hersey-Blanchard situational model ■ explain House's path-goal theory ■ illustrate the behaviors of directive, supportive, achievement-oriented, and participative leadership styles ■ define the term substitutes for leadership ■ contrast the authority, consultative, and group decisions in the Vroom-Jago model ■ explain when more group-oriented decisions work best

ISSUES IN LEADERSHIP DEVELOPMENT

■ A **charismatic leader** develops special leader-follower relationships and inspires followers in extraordinary ways.

There is a great deal of interest today in "superleaders," persons whose visions and strong personalities have an extraordinary impact on others. They are often called **charismatic leaders** because of their special powers to inspire others in exceptional ways. Although charisma was traditionally thought of as being limited to a few lucky persons who were born with it, it is now considered part of a broader set of special personal leadership qualities that can be developed with foresight and practice.[44]

TRANSFORMATIONAL LEADERSHIP

Leadership scholars James MacGregor Burns and Bernard Bass suggest that the research and models we have discussed so far tend toward **transactional leadership**.[45] The impression is that if you learn the frameworks, you can then apply them systematically to keep others moving forward to implement plans and achieve performance goals. This is more of the analytical approach as discussed in The Topic chapter opener. Managers using transactional leadership change styles, adjust tasks, and allocate rewards to achieve positive influence.

> ■ **Transactional leadership** directs the efforts of others through tasks, rewards, and structures.

Notably absent from this last description is any evidence of "enthusiasm" and "emotion," more inspirational qualities characteristic of superleaders with charismatic appeal. Importantly, these are the very qualities that Burns and Bass associate with **transformational leadership**. This describes someone who is truly inspiring as a leader, who is personally excited about what she or he is doing, and who arouses others to seek extraordinary performance accomplishments. A transformational leader raises aspirations and shifts people and organizational systems into new, high-performance patterns. The presence of transformational leadership is reflected in followers who are enthusiastic about the leader and his or her ideas, who work very hard to support them, who remain loyal and devoted, and who strive for superior performance accomplishments.

> ■ **Transformational leadership** is inspirational and arouses extraordinary effort and performance.

The goal of excellence in transformational leadership is a challenge with important personal development implications. It is not enough to possess leadership traits, know the leadership behaviors, and understand leadership contingencies. One must also be prepared to lead in an inspirational way and with a compelling personality. The transformational leader brings a strong sense of vision and a contagious enthusiasm that substantially raises the confidence, aspirations, and performance commitments of followers. These special transformational qualities include:[46]

- *Vision*—having ideas and a clear sense of direction; communicating these to others; developing excitement about accomplishing shared "dreams."
- *Charisma*—using the power of personal reference and emotion to arouse others' enthusiasm, faith, loyalty, pride, and trust in themselves.
- *Symbolism*—identifying "heroes" and holding spontaneous and planned ceremonies to celebrate excellence and high achievement.
- *Empowerment*—helping others develop by removing performance obstacles, sharing responsibilities, and delegating truly challenging work.
- *Intellectual stimulation*—gaining the involvement of others by creating awareness of problems and stirring their imaginations.
- *Integrity*—being honest and credible, acting consistently out of personal conviction, and following through on commitments.

EMOTIONAL INTELLIGENCE AND LEADERSHIP

An area of leadership development that has become popular is **emotional intelligence**, first discussed in Chapter 1 as part of the essential human skills of managers. In the work of Daniel Goleman, "EI" is defined as "the ability to manage ourselves and our relationships effectively."[47] According to his research, emotional intelligence is an important influence on leadership effectiveness, especially in more senior management positions. In Goleman's words, "the higher the rank of the person considered to be a star performer, the more emotional intelligence capabilities showed up as the reason for his

> ■ **Emotional intelligence** is the ability to manage our emotions in social relationships.

or her effectiveness."[48] This is a strong endorsement for considering whether or not EI is one of your leadership assets.

Goleman believes that emotional intelligence skills can be learned. And for purposes of leadership development, he breaks emotional intelligence down into five personal competencies.[49]

1. *Self-awareness*—ability to understand our own moods and emotions, and to understand their impact on our work and on others.
2. *Self-management (self-regulation)*—ability to think before we act and to control otherwise disruptive impulses.
3. *Motivation*—ability to work hard with persistence and for reasons other than money and status.
4. *Social awareness (empathy)*—ability to understand the emotions of others and to use this understanding to better relate to them.
5. *Relationship management (social awareness)*—ability to establish rapport with others and to build good relationships and networks.

RESEARCH BRIEF

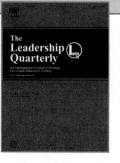

Charismatic leaders display positive emotions that followers find contagious

When leaders show positive emotions, the effect on followers is positive, creating positive moods and also creating tendencies toward positive leader ratings and feelings of attraction to the leader. These are the major conclusions from four research studies conducted by Joyce E. Bono and Remus Ilies, and reported in *Leadership Quarterly*.

Noting the growing interest in the role of emotions in leadership and recognizing the emotional aspects of transformational leadership, Bono and Ilies set out to examine how charismatic leaders "use emotion to influence followers." They advanced hypotheses as indicated in the figure, expecting to find that: charismatic leaders display positive emotions, positive leader emotions create positive follower moods, and positive follower moods generate both positive ratings of the leader and attraction toward the leader. These hypotheses were examined in a series of four empirical studies.

Leader Charisma and Emotional Contagion

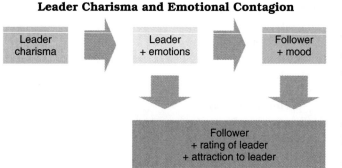

The researchers conclude that positive emotions are an important aspect of charismatic leadership. They found that leaders rated high in charisma use more positive emotions in word choices for vision statements and speeches. They also found that the positive emotions of leaders were transferred into positive moods among followers; that is, the positive leader moods were contagious. They also found that followers with positive moods had more positive perceptions of leader effectiveness.

One of the limitations of these studies, as pointed out by Bono and Ilies, is that they only focused on positive leader emotions. This leaves open the questions of how leaders use negative emotions and how these emotions affect followers. Also, the researchers suggest the need to examine the impact of leader moods on follower performance and creativity.

QUESTIONS & APPLICATIONS

This research suggests how leaders, through their emotions, have an impact on the emotions and moods of their followers. While agreeing with the logic of emotional contagion, should we conclude that a leader can never have a "bad" day and can never communicate, verbally or nonverbally, anything other than positive emotional messages? Is it realistic for managers to live up to these expectations every day?

Reference: Joyce E. Bono and Remus Ilies, "Charisma, Positive Emotions and Mood Contagion," *Leadership Quarterly*, Vol. 17(2006), pp. 317–334.

GENDER AND LEADERSHIP

Sara Levinson, President of NFL Properties Inc. of New York, for example, once asked the all-male members of her management team this question: "Is my leadership style different from a man's?" "Yes," they replied, suggesting that the very fact that she was asking the question was evidence of the difference. They also indicated that her leadership style emphasized communication as well as gathering ideas and opinions from others. When Levinson probed further by asking, "Is this a distinctly 'female' trait?" they said that they thought it was.[50]

This example poses an interesting question: Are there gender differences in leadership? In pondering the question, two background points deserve highlighting. First, social science research largely supports the *gender similarities hypothesis*; that is, males and females are very similar to one another in terms of psychological properties.[51] Second, research leaves no doubt that both women and men can be equally effective as leaders.[52]

But, having acknowledged these points, we must also admit that Sara Levinson's experience isn't an anomaly. It's real, at least in respect to our perceptions. What research on gender in leadership does show is that men and women are sometimes perceived as using somewhat different styles, and that they may arrive at leadership success from different angles.[53]

Victor Vroom and his colleagues have investigated gender differences in respect to the leader-participation model discussed earlier.[54] They find women managers to be significantly more participative in style than their male counterparts. Other studies have reported male leaders being viewed as directive and assertive, and using position power to get things done in traditional command-and-control ways.[55] By contrast, female leaders are described as being more participative and strong on motivating others, fostering communication, listening to others, mentoring, and supporting high-quality work.[56]

The pattern of behaviors described for female leaders has been called *interactive leadership*.[57] Leaders with this style typically act democratic and participative—showing respect for others, caring for others, and sharing power and information with others. They focus on building consensus and good interpersonal relations through communication and involvement.

The interactive style has qualities in common with the transformational leadership just discussed.[58] An interactive leader tends to use personal power, gaining influence over others through support and interpersonal relationships. This contrasts with the more transactional approaches that may rely on directive and assertive behaviors, and on using position power in traditional command-and-control ways.

If interactive leadership is a tendency associated with female leaders, these comments by Rosabeth Moss Kanter are worth thinking about: "Women get high ratings on exactly those skills required to succeed in the Global Information Age, where teamwork and partnering are so important."[59] But one of the risks in this discussion is falling prey to stereotypes that place men and women into leadership boxes in which they don't necessarily belong.[60] Perhaps we should set gender issues aside for the moment, accept the gender similarities hypothesis, and focus instead on the notion of the interactive leadership style itself. The likelihood is that interactive leadership is a very good fit with the needs of today's organizations and workers. And furthermore, there seems every reason to believe that both men and women can do it equally well. All indications are that one's future leadership success will require the capacity to lead through openness, positive relationships, support, and empowerment.

KAFFEEKLATSCH

Leadership Stereotypes

First Cup

"Okay, here's the question: Do women lead differently from men? I'm looking at a *Wall Street Journal* column discussing this. But before I tell you the results, you tell me—in your experience, do women lead differently from men?"

"Well, I've found women and men to be effective as managers, and equally ineffective. I don't think that managerial success runs with gender; I believe it's a matter of skills and capabilities. When you're good, you're good, and it doesn't make any difference if you are a man or a woman. And when you're bad, the same holds."

Studying the Grounds

■ A Catalyst research study compared ratings of female and male leaders. Men said that both genders were about equal on team building, mentoring, consulting, and networking, but that women were better at supporting and rewarding. The men also said that they were better at problem solving, delegating, inspiring, and influencing upward.

■ Women in the same study said that they were better at supporting and rewarding; agreed that men were better at networking, influencing upward, and delegating; and felt men and women were otherwise equal.

Double Espresso

"The *WSJ* reporter says that both the women and men are stereotyping women as being better at so-called caretaker behaviors—supporting and rewarding. In fact, it goes on to say that if women don't display these behaviors, they get negative ratings, but that when men don't display them, no one really seems to care."

Your Turn

The *WSJ* article discussed here seems to be saying that even if there is no real difference in male and female leadership behaviors, most of us expect women to lead differently; in fact, we may penalize them when they don't fit our expectations. Is this fair? Shouldn't the leadership issues be behavior and performance, not perceptions and stereotypes?

DRUCKER'S "OLD-FASHIONED" LEADERSHIP

The late management consultant Peter Drucker took a time-tested and very pragmatic view of leadership. It is based on what he refers to as a "good old-fashioned" look at the plain hard work it takes to be a successful leader. Consider, for example, his description of a telephone conversation with a potential consulting client: "We'd want you to run a seminar for us on how one acquires charisma," she said. Drucker's response was not what she expected. He advised her that there was more to leadership than the popular emphasis on personal "dash" or charisma. In fact, he said that "leadership . . . is work."[61]

Drucker's observations remind us that leadership effectiveness must have strong foundations. First, he believes that the basic building block of effective leadership is *defining and establishing a sense of mission*. A good leader sets the goals, priorities, and standards. A good leader keeps them all clear and visible, and maintains them. In Drucker's words, "The leader's first task is to be the trumpet that sounds a clear sound." Second, he believes in *accepting leadership as a responsibility rather than a rank*. Good leaders surround themselves with talented people. They are not afraid to develop strong and capable subordinates. And they do not blame others when things go wrong. As Drucker says: "The buck stops here" is still a good adage to remember. Third, he stresses the importance of *earning and keeping the trust of others*. The key here is the leader's personal integrity. The followers of good leaders trust them. This means that they believe the leader means what he or she says, and that his or her actions will be consistent with what is said. In Drucker's words again, "effective leadership . . . is not based on being clever; it is based primarily on being consistent."[62]

MORAL LEADERSHIP

As discussed in Chapter 2, society today is unforgiving in its demands that organizations be run with **moral leadership**—that is, leadership by ethical standards that clearly meet the test of being "good" and "correct."[63] The expectation is that anyone in a leadership position will practice high ethical standards of behavior, help to build and maintain an ethical organizational culture, and both help and require others to behave ethically in their work.

Moral leadership begins with personal integrity, a concept fundamental to the notions of both transformational and good old-fashioned leadership. A leader with **integrity** is honest, credible, and consistent in putting values into action. When a leader has integrity, he or she earns the *trust* of followers. And when followers believe leaders are trustworthy, they try to behave in ways that live up to the leader's expectations. For managers in our high-pressure and competitive work environments, nothing can substitute for leadership strongly anchored in personal integrity. When viewed through the lens of what is truly the right thing to do, even the most difficult decisions become easier.

In his book *Transforming Leadership: A New Pursuit of Happiness*, James MacGregor Burns explains that transformational leadership creates significant, even revolutionary, change in social systems. But he disassociates certain historical figures from this definition: Napoleon is out—too much order-and-obey in his style; Hitler is out—no moral foundations; Mao is out, too—no true empowerment of followers. Among Burns's positive role models from history are Gandhi, George Washington, and Eleanor Roosevelt. He firmly believes that great leaders follow agendas true to the wishes of followers. He gives the example of Franklin Delano Roosevelt who said: "If we do not have the courage to lead the American people where they want to go, someone else will." Burns also says that wherever in the world great leadership is found, it will always have a moral anchor point.[64]

The concept of *servant leadership* discussed earlier is consistent with this thinking. So, too, is the notion of **authentic leadership** advanced by Fred Luthans and Bruce Avolio.[65] An authentic leader has a high level of self-awareness, understanding his or her personal values. This leader also acts consistent with those values, being honest and avoiding self-deceptions. The result is that the authentic leader is perceived as genuine, gaining the respect of followers and developing a capacity to serve as role model that positively influences their behaviors. Luthans and his colleagues believe authentic leadership is activated by the positive psychological states of confidence, hope, optimism, and resilience. This results in positive self-regulation that helps authentic leaders clearly frame moral dilemmas, transparently respond to them, and consistently serve as ethical role models.[66]

▪ **Moral leadership** is always "good" and "right" by ethical standards.

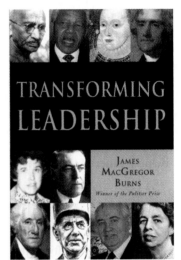

▪ **Integrity** in leadership is honesty, credibility, and consistency in putting values into action.

▪ **Authentic leadership** activates positive psychological states to achieve self-awareness and positive self-regulation.

Be sure you can ▪ differentiate transformational leadership and transactional leadership ▪ explain how emotional intelligence contributes to leadership success ▪ discuss research insights on the relationship between gender and leadership ▪ list Drucker's three essentials of good old-fashioned leadership ▪ define integrity and discuss it as a foundation for moral leadership

Learning Check 4

✓

CHAPTER 13 STUDY GUIDE

STUDY QUESTIONS SUMMARY

1 What is the nature of leadership?

- Leadership is the process of inspiring others to work hard to accomplish important tasks.

- The ability to communicate a vision, a clear sense of the future, is increasingly considered essential for effective leadership.

- Power is the ability to get others to do what you want them to do through leadership.

- Sources of position power include rewards, coercion, and legitimacy or formal authority; sources of personal power include expertise and reference.

- Effective leaders empower others, allowing them to make job-related decisions on their own.

- Servant leadership is follower-centered, focusing on helping others fully utilize their talents.

2 What are the important leadership traits and behaviors?

- Traits that seem to have a positive impact on leadership include drive, integrity, and self-confidence.

- Research on leader behaviors focused on alternative leadership styles based on concerns for task and concerns for people.

- One suggestion of leader-behavior researchers is that effective leaders will be good at team-based or participative leadership that is high in both task and people concerns.

3 What are the contingency theories of leadership?

- Contingency leadership approaches point out that no one leadership style always works best; the best style

is one that properly matches the demands of each unique situation.

- Fiedler's contingency model describes how situational differences in task structure, position power, and leader-member relations may influence which leadership style works best.

- The Hersey-Blanchard situational model recommends using task-oriented and people-oriented behaviors, depending on the "maturity" levels of followers.

- House's path-goal theory points out that leaders should add value to situations by responding with supportive, directive, achievement-oriented, and/or participative styles as needed.

- The Vroom-Jago leader-participation theory advises leaders to choose decision-making methods—individual, consultative, group—that best fit the problems they are trying to solve.

4 What are current issues in leadership development?

- Transformational leaders use charisma and emotion to inspire others toward extraordinary efforts in support of change and performance excellence.

- Emotional intelligence, the ability to manage our relationships and ourselves effectively, is an important leadership capability.

- The interactive leadership style emphasizes communication, involvement, and interpersonal respect, all consistent with the demands of the new workplace.

- Managers today are expected to be moral leaders who communicate high ethical standards and show personal integrity in all dealings with other people.

KEY TERMS REVIEW

Authentic leadership (p. 337)

Authority decision (p. 332)

Autocratic style (p. 326)

Charismatic leader (p. 332)

Coercive power (p. 322)

Consultative decision (p. 332)

Democratic style (p. 326)

Emotional intelligence (p. 333)

Empowerment (p. 323)

Expert power (p. 322)

Group decision (p. 332)

Human relations style (p. 326)

Integrity (p. 337)

Laissez-faire style (p. 326)

Leadership (p. 320)

Leadership style (p. 325)

Legitimate power (p. 322)

Moral leadership (p. 337)

Power (p. 321)

Referent power (p. 323)

Reward power (p. 321)

Servant leadership (p. 323)

Substitutes for leadership (p. 331)

Transactional leadership (p. 333)

Transformational leadership (p. 333)

Vision (p. 323)

Visionary leadership (p. 323)

MULTIPLE-CHOICE QUESTIONS:

1. Someone with a clear sense of the future and the actions needed to get there is considered a _____ leader.
   (a) task-oriented   (b) people-oriented   (c) transactional   (d) visionary
2. Leader power= _____ power× _____ power.
   (a) reward, punishment   (b) reward, expert   (c) legitimate, position   (d) position, personal
3. A manager who says "because I am the boss, you must do what I ask" is relying on _____ power.
   (a) reward   (b) legitimate   (c) expert   (d) referent
4. The personal traits now considered important for managerial success include _____.
   (a) self-confidence   (b) gender   (c) age   (d) personality
5. According to the Blake and Mouton model of leader behaviors, the most successful leader is one who acts with _____.
   (a) high initiating structure   (b) high consideration   (c) high concern for task and high concern for people
   (d) low job stress and high task goals
6. In Fiedler's contingency model, both highly favorable and highly unfavorable leadership situations are best dealt with by a _____ leader.
   (a) task-oriented   (b) laissez-faire   (c) participative   (d) relationship-oriented
7. Directive leadership and achievement-oriented leadership are among the options in House's _____ theory of leadership.
   (a) trait   (b) path-goal   (c) transformational   (d) life-cycle
8. Vision, charisma, integrity, and symbolism are all on the list of attributes typically associated with _____ leaders.
   (a) contingency   (b) informal   (c) transformational   (d) transactional
9. _____ leadership theory suggests that leadership success is achieved by correctly matching leadership style with situations.
   (a) Trait   (b) Fiedler's   (c) Transformational   (d) Blake and Mouton's
10. In the leader-behavior approaches to leadership, someone who does a very good job of planning work, setting standards, and monitoring results would be considered a(n) _____ leader.
    (a) task-oriented   (b) control-oriented   (c) achievement-oriented   (d) employee-centered
11. When a leader assumes that others will do as she asks because they want to positively identify with her, she is relying on _____ power to influence their behavior.
    (a) expert   (b) reference   (c) legitimate   (d) reward
12. The interactive leadership style, sometimes associated with women, is characterized by _____.
    (a) inclusion and information sharing   (b) use of rewards and punishments   (c) command and control   (d) emphasis on position power
13. A leader whose actions indicate an attitude of "do as you want and don't bother me" would be described as having a(n) _____ leadership style.
    (a) autocratic   (b) country club   (c) democratic   (d) laissez-faire
14. The critical contingency variable in the Hersey-Blanchard situational model of leadership is _____.
    (a) followers' maturity   (b) LPC   (c) task structure   (d) emotional intelligence
15. A leader who _____ would be described as achievement oriented in the path-goal theory.
    (a) works hard to achieve high performance   (b) sets challenging goals for others   (c) gives directions and monitors results   (d) builds commitment through participation

SHORT-RESPONSE QUESTIONS:

16. Why does a person need both position power and personal power to achieve long-term managerial effectiveness?
17. What is the major insight of the Vroom-Jago leader-participation model?
18. What are the three variables that Fiedler's contingency model uses to diagnose the favorability of leadership situations, and what does each mean?
19. How does Peter Drucker's view of "good old-fashioned leadership" differ from the popular concept of transformational leadership?

APPLICATION QUESTION:

20. When Marcel Henry took over as leader of a new product development team, he was both excited and apprehensive. "I wonder," he said to himself on the first day in his new assignment, "if I can meet the challenges of leadership." Later that day, Marcel shared this concern with you during a coffee break. Based on the insights of this chapter, how would you describe to him the implications for his personal leadership development of current thinking on transformational leadership and moral leadership?

CHAPTER 13 APPLICATIONS

CASE 13

Southwest Airlines: How Herb Kelleher Led the Way

The U.S. airline industry has experienced many problems, with some of the largest airlines losing millions of dollars. Through all the turmoil, Southwest Airlines has remained profitable. Herb Kelleher, co-founder of South-west in 1971 and until recently its CEO, pointed out that "we didn't make much for a while there. It was like being the tallest guy in a tribe of dwarfs."[67] Nevertheless, Southwest Airlines has grown to the point of having recent operating revenues of $7.6 billion. This is particularly noteworthy since Southwest flies to only 62 cities in 32 states, and its average flight length is 537 miles.[68] How did a little airline get to be so big? Its success is due to its core values, developed by Kelleher and carried out daily by the company's 32,000 employees. These core values are humor, altruism, and "luv" (the company's stock ticker symbol).[69]

Southwest Airlines' Unique Character and Success

One of the things that make Southwest Airlines so unique is its short-haul focus. The airline does not assign seats or sell tickets through the reservation systems used by travel agents. The only foods served are peanuts, pretzels, and similar snacks, but passengers don't seem to mind. In fact, serving Customers (at Southwest, always written with a capital *C*) is the focus of the company's employees. When Colleen Barrett, currently Southwest's president, was the executive vice president for customers, she said, "We will never jump on employees for leaning too far toward the customer, but we come down on them hard for not using common sense."[70] Southwest's core values produce employees who are highly motivated and who care about the customers and about one another.

One way in which Southwest carries out this philosophy is by treating employees and their ideas with respect. As executive vice president, Colleen Barrett formed a "culture committee," made up of employees from different functional areas and levels. The committee continues and meets quarterly to come up with ideas for maintaining Southwest's corporate spirit and image. All managers, officers, and directors are expected to "get out in the field," meet and talk to employees, and understand their jobs. Employees are encouraged to use their creativity and sense of humor to make their jobs and the customers' experiences more enjoyable. Gate agents, for example, are given a book of games to play with waiting passengers when a flight is delayed. Flight agents might do an imitation of Elvis or Mr. Rogers while making announcements. Others have jumped out of the overhead luggage bins to surprise boarding passengers.[71]

Kelleher, currently chairman of the board and chairman of the executive committee, knows that not everyone would be happy as a Southwest employee: "What we are looking for, first and foremost, is a sense of humor. Then we are looking for people who have to excel to satisfy themselves and who work well in a collegial environment." He feels that the company can teach specific skills but that a compatible attitude is most important. When asked to prove that she had a sense of humor, Mary Ann Adams, hired as a finance executive, recounted a practical joke in which she turned an unflattering picture of her boss into a screen saver for her department.[72]

To encourage employees to treat one another as well as they treat their customers, departments examine linkages within Southwest to see what their "internal customers" need. The provisioning department, for example, whose responsibility is to provide the snacks and drinks for each flight, selects a flight attendant as "customer of the month." The provisioning department's own board of directors makes the selection decision, as well as other departmental managerial decisions. Other departments have sent pizza and ice cream to their "internal customers." Employees write letters commending the work of other employees or departments, and these letters are valued as much as those from "external customers." When problems do occur between departments, the employees work out solutions in supervised meetings.

Employees exhibit the same attitude of altruism and "luv" (also Southwest's term for its relationship with its customers) toward other groups as well. A significant portion of Southwest employees volunteer their time at Ronald McDonald Houses throughout Southwest's service territory. When the company purchased a small regional airline, employees personally sent cards and company T-shirts to their new colleagues to welcome them to the Southwest family. They demonstrate similar caring toward the company itself.

Acting in the company's best interests is also directly in the interest of the employees. Southwest has a profit-sharing plan for all eligible employees; and unlike many of its competitors, Southwest consistently has profits to share. Employees can also purchase Southwest stock at 90 percent of market value; at least 13 percent of Southwest's employees own company stock. Although approximately 81 percent of employees are unionized, the company has a history of good labor relations.[73]

Southwest Airlines is an award winner. It has won the monthly "Triple Crown" distinction of airline service—Best On-Time Record, Best Baggage Handling, and Fewest Customer Complaints—more than 30 times.[74] Southwest Airlines is also a low-cost operator. According to Harvard University professor John Kotter, setting the standard for low costs in the airline industry does not mean Southwest is *cheap*. "Cheap is trying to get your prices down by nibbling costs off everything . . . [firms like Southwest Airlines] are thinking 'efficient,' which is very different. . . . They recognize that you don't necessarily have to take a few pennies off of everything. Sometimes you might even spend more."[75]

By buying one type of plane—the Boeing 737—Southwest saves on both pilot training and maintenance costs. The *cheap* paradigm would favor used planes; Southwest's choice results in the youngest fleet of airplanes in the industry because the model favors high productivity over lower capital expenditures.[76]

By using each plane an average of 12 hours per day, Southwest is able to make more trips with fewer planes than any other airline.

Southwest's Ongoing Challenges

Despite its impressive record of success, Southwest Airlines has pressing concerns. Management worries about the effects on morale of limited opportunities for promotion. The company has created "job families" with different grade levels so that employees can work

their way up within their job category. However, after five or six years employees begin to hit the maximum compensation level for their job category.

Another issue is how to maintain the culture of caring and fun while expanding into new markets. Southwest's success has been built with the enthusiasm and hard work of its employees; as Kelleher said, "The people who work here don't think of Southwest as a business. They think of it as a crusade."[77] Cultivating that crusading atmosphere is a continuing priority for the company.

As Herb Kelleher was preparing to relinquish his role as Southwest's CEO, a major concern for investors was whether the company's success could be maintained because so much of Southwest's success was attributable to Kelleher's unique management and leadership style. Recent events, however, seem to demonstrate that Kelleher's successors were well prepared to handle the challenges of maintaining Southwest's culture and success. As Barrett wrote in the company's *Spirit Magazine*: "Air travel changed forever two years ago, but our steadfast determination remains unbroken to provide the high-spirited Customer Service, low fares, and frequent nonstop flights that Americans want and need."[78]

Not even terrorist attacks can derail the company that Herb Kelleher led to success. Southwest Airlines continues to be recognized by *Fortune* magazine as America's most admired airline as well as one of the most admired companies in America. When *Air Transport World* magazine selected Southwest as the "Airline for the Year," it cited 30 consecutive years of profitability while providing affordable fares for millions of passengers. Other recognitions of Southwest culture and success continue to pile up.

Sometimes the Voyage Is Better than the Destination

From its roots as a regional carrier in Texas, Southwest Airlines grew to become one of the most profitable—and arguably the most beloved—airline in American history. The company has managed perpetual employee satisfaction by focusing on its internal "Customers" above all else, who, in turn, are positively motivated to show that same degree of concern to external customers. And Southwest's perpetual profitability stems not from miserliness, but attention to value and rational cost-savings.

But as fuel prices continue to climb and airlines consolidate for security, can Southwest hang on as that rare breed of an independent, domestic airline? How clear are the skies ahead?

REVIEW QUESTIONS

1. What role has leadership played in the success of Southwest Airlines?
2. What is the key to Southwest's continued success under leaders like Colleen Barrett who have followed Herb Kelleher?
3. In what ways has Herb Kelleher exemplified Peter Drucker's notion of "old-fashioned" leadership?

TEAM PROJECT

Leadership Believe It-or-Not You would think leaders would spend lots of time talking with the people who make products and deliver services, trying to understand problems and asking for advice. But *Business Week* reports a survey that shows quite the opposite. Persons with high school educations or less are asked for advice by only 24% of their bosses; for those with a college degree the number jumps to 54%.

Question: What stories do your friends, acquaintances, family members and you tell about their bosses that are truly hard to believe?

Research Directions:

■ Listen to others and ask others to talk about the leaders they have had or presently do have. What strange-but-true stories are they telling?

■ Create a journal that can be shared with class members that summarizes, role plays, or otherwise communicates the real life experiences of people whose bosses sometimes behave in ways that are hard to believe.

■ For each of the situations in your report try to explain the boss's behaviors.

■ Also for each of the situations, assume that you observed or heard about it as the boss's supervisor. Describe how you would "coach" or "counsel" the boss in order to turn the situation into a "learning moment" for positive leadership development.

PERSONAL MANAGEMENT

Integrity Whether you call it ethical leadership or moral leadership, the personal implications are the same: respect flows toward those who behave with **INTEGRITY**. You should recall that integrity is defined as being honest, credible, and consistent in all that we do. Here are some of the things that cause people to say someone lacks it.

■ Giving special treatment to favored people
■ Willing to lie
■ Blaming others for personal mistakes
■ Letting others take blame for personal mistakes
■ Wanting others to fail
■ Falsifying reports, records
■ Instigating conflict and disharmony
■ Taking credit for others' ideas
■ Stealing

How often have you worked for someone that meets one of more of these criteria? How did you feel about it, and what did you do?

Building the Brand Called "You" Have there ever been occasions when others might say that "You" fit one or some of these descriptions? Consider also what the recommended self-assessments may have to say. Write a set of notes on your behavior in situations – work, study groups, sports, shopping, friendship gatherings, or whatever – in which your leadership integrity could be questioned. What are the lessons for the future?

NEXT STEPS: MANAGEMENT LEARNING WORKBOOK

Self-Assessments
■ Emotional Intelligence (#2)
■ "T-P" Leadership Questionnaire (#20)
■ "T-t" Leadership Style (#21)
■ Least-Preferred Co-worker Scale (#22)

Experiential Exercises
■ My Best Manager (#1)
■ The Future Workplace (#14)
■ Leading through Participation (#16)
■ Sources and Uses of Power (#19)

Motivation— Theory and Practice

14

Age or Experience?

Once upon a time, getting that big promotion was just a matter of waiting around for your boss to get promoted and then stepping into her or his shoes.

But many workers at organizations big and small are learning that promotions are earned on the basis of performance.

Imagine that as a manager, you have a position to fill and have the choice between two potential candidates for the job. Of course, there are many possible factors that would play into a real-life decision. But here are some facts to experiment with.

The first candidate is a veteran of your company who has been a loyal employee for a number of years.

The second contender has not been with your company for nearly as long but has implemented a number of profitable ideas in that short time.

Who do you choose?

What *They* Think

"My main job was nourishing talent. I was a gardener providing water and other nourishment to our top 750 people. Of course, I had to pull out some weeds too."
Jack Welch, former GE Chairman and CEO

MERIT: "The market system requires that people be committed and willing to work hard. Inherent with that is what I call a merit system, which I think gives people the greatest opportunity."
Lee R. Raymond, former CEO and chairman of ExxonMobil.

SENIORITY: "Dues-paying has lost its relevance, which means that over time, people are going to think less about whether you've been here long enough to be promoted. It'll be simply about looking at your skills and maturity."
Robert W. Mendover, managing director of the Center for Generational Studies.

For some corporations promotions based on *merit* are part of the corporate culture; in others *seniority* rules. While some employers may be outspoken about their preferences and others not, new hires often know right away whether they will be promoted on the basis of performance or obedience.

Organizations that promote by merit often look for a person who will shape or define the open position. By asking a candidate to take a leadership role in defining their jobs, the employer asks, "What will you bring to the table?"

Merit-oriented businesses seek employees who will work to distinguish themselves, regardless of their position, often through effort or innovation. Jack Welch, former CEO of General Electric, got right down to the analytics of merit.

Welch was known in and out of GE for his yearly ranking of all employees. By firing the lowest-ranking 10% and rewarding the top 20% with bonuses and stock options, he established a high-performance corporate culture that visibly encouraged initiative and innovation.[1]

"My main job was nourishing talent," Welch said. "I was a gardener providing water and other nourishment to our top 750 people. Of course, I had to pull out some weeds too."[2]

In contrast, managers who value seniority often seek candidates who they feel embody existing ways and traditions. Corporations that have very set ways of doing business often don't want to take a risk on a maverick employee who might attempt to remake well-established processes or disrupt employee relationships. Their tendencies are to fill openings with internal candidates who have been around long enough that their tendencies and instincts have been well observed.

Seniority is often an issue with unions and in collective bargaining. Labor contracts typically contain seniority provisions that require more junior workers to be relased first in case of layoffs, and some may require that more senior workers be given preferences for promotions and job assignments.

Regardless of which promoting method organizations adopt, they still need highly motivated people whose hard work can help bring success in a world where business has never been more competitive.

The Numbers

"Go-Getter" Profiles

91%	Have gone into office on weekends
40%	Have checked e-mail at least once a day on their vacations
38%	Have missed start dates of vacations
35%	Have missed important events in child's life
33%	Have missed birthday or anniversary dinners with spouse

Quick Facts

* Jack Welch was #4 in *Business Week's* list of the world's most competitive businesspeople; Donald Trump was #1, Bill Gates #2, and Warren Buffet #3.[3]

* According to a Supreme Court decision, a company's seniority system can take precedence over accommodating the needs of disabled employees.[4]

* In a recent year, the federal government only denied merit-based pay increases to 0.09 percent of its employees.[5]

* Merit-based hiring for civil-service jobs is guaranteed by California's state constitution.[6]

* A study on seniority hiring practices determined that color-blind seniority systems tend to protect white workers against layoffs because in most companies, senior employees are usually white.[7]

What Do *You* Think?

1. In a business culture where more and more companies are choosing to promote by merit, is their any good argument for promotion by seniority?

2. What might be potential disadvantages to promoting by merit?

345

Motivation—theory and practice			
Study Question 1	**Study Question 2**	**Study Question 3**	**Study Question 4**
Individual Needs and Motivation	**Process Theories of Motivation**	**Reinforcement Theory of Motivation**	**Motivation and Job Design**
■ Hierarchy of needs ■ ERG theory ■ Two-factor theory ■ Acquired needs theory	■ Equity theory ■ Expectancy theory ■ Goal-setting theory	■ Reinforcement strategies ■ Positive reinforcement ■ Punishment	■ Scientific management ■ Job rotation and enlargement ■ Job enrichment ■ Alternative work schedules
Learning Check 1	**Learning Check 2**	**Learning Check 3**	**Learning Check 4**

Why do some people work enthusiastically, often doing more than required to turn out an extraordinary performance? Why do others hold back and do the minimum needed to avoid reprimand or termination? What can be done to ensure that the best possible performance is achieved by every person in every job on every work day? These questions are, or should be, asked by managers in all work settings. Good answers begin with a true respect for people, with all of their talents and diversity, as the human capital of organizations. They show an awareness that "productivity through people" is an irreplaceable foundation for long-term success.[8]

INDIVIDUAL NEEDS AND MOTIVATION

■ **Motivation** accounts for the level, direction, and persistence of effort expended at work.

The term **motivation** is used in management theory to describe forces within the individual that account for the level, direction, and persistence of effort expended at work. Simply put, a highly motivated person works hard at a job; an unmotivated person does not. A manager who leads through motivation does so by creating conditions under which other people feel consistently inspired to work hard.

■ A **need** is an unfulfilled physiological or psychological desire.

Most discussions of motivation begin with the concept of individual **needs**—the unfulfilled physiological or psychological desires of an individual. Although each of the following theories discusses a slightly different set of needs, all agree that needs cause tensions that influence attitudes and behavior. Their advice to managers is to help people satisfy important needs through their work, and try to eliminate work obstacles that interfere with the satisfaction of important needs.

■ **Lower-order needs** are physiological, safety, and social needs in Maslow's hierarchy.

HIERARCHY OF NEEDS THEORY

■ **Higher-order needs** are esteem and self-actualization needs in Maslow's hierarchy.

The theory of human needs developed by Abraham Maslow was introduced in Chapter 3 as an important foundation of the history of management thought. According to his hierarchy of human needs, **lower-order needs** include physiological, safety, and social concerns, and **higher-order needs** include esteem and self-actualization concerns.[9] Whereas lower-order needs are desires for social and physical well-being, the higher-order needs are desires for psychological development and growth.

Maslow uses two principles to describe how these needs affect human behavior. The *deficit principle* states that a satisfied need is not a motivator of behavior. People are expected to act in ways that satisfy deprived needs— that is, needs for which a "deficit" exists. The *progression principle* states that a need at one level does not become activated until the next-lower-level need is already satisfied. People are expected to advance step-by-step up the hierarchy in their search for need satisfactions. At the level of self-actualization, the more these needs are satisfied, the stronger they are supposed to grow. According to Maslow, a person should continue to be motivated by opportunities for self-fulfillment as long as the other needs remain satisfied.

Although research has not verified the strict deficit and progression principles, Maslow's ideas are very helpful for understanding the needs of people at work and for considering what can be done to satisfy them. His theory advises managers to recognize that deprived needs may result in negative attitudes and behaviors. By the same token, opportunities for need satisfaction may have positive motivational consequences.

Figure 14.1 illustrates how managers can use Maslow's ideas to better meet the needs of the people with whom they work. Notice that the higher-order self-actualization needs are served by things like creative and challenging work, and job autonomy; esteem needs are served by responsibility, praise, and recognition. The satisfactions of lower-order social, safety, and physiological needs deal more with conditions of the work environment. Employee benefits are one example. A Harris interactive survey of American workers showed that the top two most valued benefits are health insurance and employer-matched 401(K) investments[10] In the same survey, 78% of respondents said that better benefits would increase their work motivation.

ERG THEORY

One of the most promising efforts to build on Maslow's work is the ERG theory proposed by Clayton Alderfer.[11] This theory collapses Maslow's five needs categories into three. *Existence needs* are desires for physiological and material well-being. *Relatedness needs* are desires for satisfying interpersonal

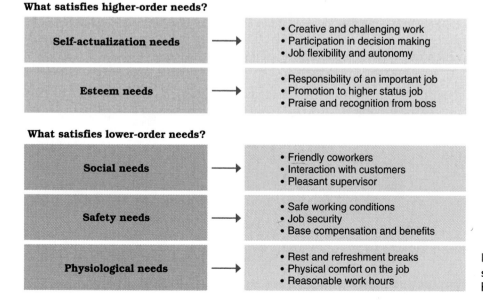

What satisfies higher-order needs?

Self-actualization needs	→	• Creative and challenging work • Participation in decision making • Job flexibility and autonomy
Esteem needs	→	• Responsibility of an important job • Promotion to higher status job • Praise and recognition from boss

What satisfies lower-order needs?

Social needs	→	• Friendly coworkers • Interaction with customers • Pleasant supervisor
Safety needs	→	• Safe working conditions • Job security • Base compensation and benefits
Physiological needs	→	• Rest and refreshment breaks • Physical comfort on the job • Reasonable work hours

Figure 14.1 Opportunities for satisfaction in Maslow's hierarchy of human needs.

relationships. *Growth needs* are desires for continued psychological growth and development.

The dynamics among needs in ERG theory also differ from Maslow's thinking. ERG does not assume that lower-level needs must be satisfied before higher-level needs become activated; any or all types of needs can influence individual behavior at a given time. Further, Alderfer does not believe that satisfied needs lose their motivational impact. His ERG theory contains a *frustration-regression principle*, according to which an already-satisfied lower-level need can become reactivated and influence behavior when a higher-level need cannot be satisfied.

TWO-FACTOR THEORY

The two-factor theory of Frederick Herzberg was developed from a pattern identified in the responses of almost 4,000 people to questions about their work.[12] When questioned about what "turned them on," they tended to identify things relating to the nature of the job itself. Herzberg calls these **satisfier factors.** When questioned about what "turned them off," they tended to identify things relating more to the work setting. Herzberg calls these **hygiene factors.**

As shown in *Figure 14.2,* the two-factor theory associates hygiene factors with job *dissatisfaction.* The hygiene factors are found in the job context and include such things as working conditions, interpersonal relations, organizational policies and administration, technical quality of supervision, and base wage or salary. These factors contribute to more or less job dissatisfaction. Herzberg argues that improving hygiene factors, such as by adding piped-in music or implementing a no-smoking policy, can make people less dissatisfied at work. But it will not increase job satisfaction and motivation.

To improve motivation Herzberg advises managers to act on the satisfier factors by making improvements in *job content.* The important satisfier factors include such things as a sense of achievement, feelings of recognition, a sense of responsibility, the opportunity for advancement, and feelings of personal growth.

Scholars have criticized Herzberg's theory as being method-bound and difficult to replicate.[13] For his part, Herzberg reports confirming studies in countries located in Europe, Africa, the Middle East, and Asia.[14] At the very least, the two-factor theory remains a useful reminder that there are two important aspects of all jobs: *job content,* what people do in terms of job tasks; and *job context,* the work setting in which they do it. Herzberg's advice to managers is still timely: (1) always correct poor context to eliminate actual or potential sources of job dissatisfaction; and (2) be sure to build satisfier factors into job content to maximize opportunities for job satisfaction.

■ A **satisfier factor** is found in job content, such as a sense of achievement, recognition, responsibility, advancement, or personal growth.

■ A **hygiene factor** is found in the job context, such as working conditions, interpersonal relations, organizational policies, and salary.

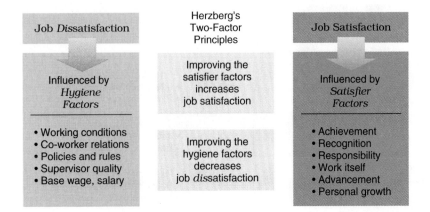

Figure 14.2 Elements in Herzberg's two-factor theory.

The two-factor theory cautions managers not to expect too much by way of motivational improvements from investments in things like special office fixtures, attractive lounges for breaks, and even high base salaries. Instead, it focuses attention on the nature of the job itself, and on such things as responsibility and personal growth as opportunities for higher-order need satisfaction.

ACQUIRED NEEDS THEORY

In the late 1940s, David McClelland and his colleagues began experimenting with the Thematic Apperception Test (TAT) as a way of examining human needs. The TAT asks people to view pictures and write stories about what they see. The stories are then content analyzed for themes that display the strengths of three needs.[15] **Need for Achievement** is the desire to do something better or more efficiently, to solve problems, or to master complex tasks. **Need for Power** is the desire to control other people, to influence their behavior, or to be responsible for them. **Need for Affiliation** is the desire to establish and maintain friendly and warm relations with other people.

According to McClelland, people acquire or develop these needs over time as a result of individual life experiences. Because each need can be linked with a distinct set of work preferences, he encourages managers to understand these needs in themselves and others and try to create work environments responsive to them.

People high in the need for achievement like to put their competencies to work; they take moderate risks in competitive situations, and they are willing to work alone. As a result, the work preferences of high-need achievers include (1) individual responsibility for results, (2) achievable but challenging goals, and (3) feedback on performance.

People high in the need for affiliation seek companionship, social approval, and satisfying interpersonal relationships. They take a special interest in work

■ **Need for Achievement** is the desire to do something better, to solve problems, or to master complex tasks.

■ **Need for Power** is the desire to control, influence, or be responsible for other people.

■ **Need for Affiliation** is the desire to establish and maintain good relations with people.

INSIGHTS

Make People Your Top Priority

The Butcher Company, a maker of floor-care products, made headlines when its founder Charlie Butcher, at age 83, sold the firm to family-owned S. C. Johnson Company. It was a good deal for Charlie and family, but the story is deeper than that. After Charlie sold the company, he shared $18 million of the proceeds with the firm's 325 employees, an

average of $55,000 per person. Each received about $1.50 for every hour they had worked for the firm over the years.

This is a unique example of management commitment to employees—considering each and every one an owner. There is no doubt that Charlie Butcher's style paid off over the years; his company achieved success because of the motivation and accomplishments of the workers

The day after the sale, Charlie was at the plant handing out checks. The firm's president, Paul P. McClaughlin, said the employees "just filled up with tears. They would just throw their arms around Charlie and give him a hug." But this wasn't anything new; Charlie had always been a believer in people. This was just another chance to confirm the theory that he'd been practicing for years—a belief that treating talented people well will create business success. "When people are happy in their jobs, they are at least twice as productive," Charlie says.

that involves interpersonal relationships, work that provides for companionship, and work that brings social approval.

People high in the need for power are motivated to behave in ways that have a clear impact on other people and events. They enjoy being in control of a situation and being recognized for this responsibility. A person with a high need for power prefers work that involves control over other persons, has an impact on people and events, and brings public recognition and attention.

Importantly, McClelland distinguishes between two forms of the power need. *The need for "personal" power* is exploitative and involves manipulation for the pure sake of personal gratification. This type of power need is not successful in management. By contrast, the *need for "social" power* is the positive face of power. It involves the use of power in a socially responsible way, one that is directed toward group or organizational objectives rather than personal ones. This need for social power is essential to managerial leadership.

McClelland believes that people very high in the need for affiliation alone may not make the best managers; their desires for social approval and friendship may complicate decision making. There are times when managers and leaders must decide and act in ways that other persons may disagree with. To the extent that the need for affiliation interferes with someone's ability to make these decisions, managerial effectiveness will be sacrificed. Thus, the successful executive, in McClelland's view, is likely to possess a high need for social power that is greater than an otherwise strong need for affiliation.

Learning Check 1	*Be sure you can* ■ define the terms motivation and needs ■ describe work practices that satisfy higher-order and lower-order needs in Maslow's hierarchy ■ contrast Maslow's hierarchy with ERG theory ■ describe work practices that influence hygiene factors and satisfier factors in Herzberg's two-factor theory ■ define McClelland's needs for achievement, affiliation, and power ■ describe work conditions that satisfy a person with a high need for achievement

PROCESS THEORIES OF MOTIVATION

Although the details vary, each of the needs theories can help managers better understand individual differences and deal positively with them. Another set of motivation theories, the process theories, add further to this understanding. The equity, expectancy, and goal-setting theories offer advice and insight on how people actually make choices to work hard or not, based on their individual preferences, the available rewards, and possible work outcomes.

EQUITY THEORY

The equity theory of motivation is best known in management through the work of J. Stacy Adams.[16] It is based on the logic of social comparisons and the notion that perceived inequity is a motivating state. That is, when people believe that they have been unfairly treated in comparison to others, they will be motivated to eliminate the discomfort and restore a sense of perceived equity: to the situation. The classic example is pay, and the equity question is: "In comparison with others, how fairly am I being compensated for the work that I do?"

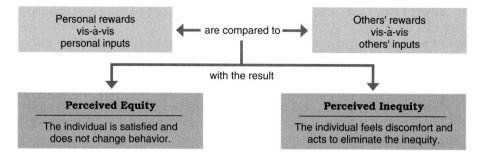

Figure 14.3 Equity theory and the role of social comparison.

Figure 14.3 shows how the equity dynamic works in the form of input-to-outcome comparisons. These equity comparisons are especially common whenever managers allocate things like pay raises, vacation schedules, preferred job assignments, work privileges, and office space. The equity comparisons may be with co-workers in the group, workers elsewhere in the organization, and even persons employed by other organizations.

Perceived inequities occur whenever people feel that the rewards received for their work efforts are unfair given the rewards others appear to be getting. According to equity theory, an individual who perceives that she or he is being treated unfairly in comparison to others will be motivated to act in ways that reduce the perceived inequity. And when perceived negative inequity exists, Adams predicts that people will try to deal with it by:

■ Changing their work inputs by putting less effort into their jobs.
■ Changing the rewards received by asking for better treatment.
■ Changing the comparison points to make things seem better.
■ Changing the situation by leaving the job.

REAL ETHICS

Information Goldmine

This really happened.

A worker opens the top of the office photocopier and finds a document someone had left behind. It's a list of performance evaluations, pay, and bonuses for 80 co-workers. She reads the document. Lo and behold, someone considered a "nonstarter" is getting paid more than others regarded as "super workers." New hires are being brought in at substantially higher pay and bonuses than are paid to existing staff. And to make matters worse, she's in the middle of the list and not near the top, where she would have expected to be. She makes a lot less money than some others are getting.

Looking at the data, she begins to wonder why she is spending extra hours working on her laptop evenings and weekends at home, trying to do a really great job for the firm.

Should I pass this information around anonymously so that everyone knows what's going on, she wonders? Or, should I quit and find another employer who fully values me for my talents and hard work?

FURTHER INQUIRY

What would you do in this circumstance? Obviously, you are going to be concerned and perhaps upset at what you have just learned. Suppose you were to just hit "print," make about 80 copies, and put them in everyone's mailboxes—or even just leave them stacked in a couple of convenient locations? That would get the information out and right into the gossip chains pretty quickly. But then again, maybe this wouldn't be ethical.

In the real case, our worker decided to quit, saying: "I just couldn't stand the inequity." She also decided not to distribute the information to others in the office. "I couldn't give it to people who were still working there because it would make them depressed, like it made me depressed," she said.

A key point in the equity theory is that people behave according to their perceptions. What influences individual behavior is not the reward's absolute value or the manager's intentions; the recipient's perceptions determine the motivational outcomes. Rewards perceived as equitable should have a positive result on satisfaction and performance; those perceived as inequitable may create dissatisfaction and cause performance problems.

Research on equity theory has largely been accomplished in the laboratory. It is most conclusive with respect to perceived negative inequity. People who feel underpaid, for example, may try to restore perceived equity by pursuing one or more of the actions described in the prior list, such as reducing current work efforts to compensate for the missing rewards, or even quitting the job.[17] There is also evidence that the equity dynamic occurs among people who feel overpaid. This time the perceived inequity is associated with a sense of guilt. The attempt to restore perceived equity may involve, for example, increasing the quantity or quality of work, taking on more difficult assignments, or working overtime.

Managers should probably anticipate perceived negative inequities whenever especially visible rewards such as pay or promotions are allocated. Then, instead of letting equity dynamics get out of hand, they can try to manage perceptions. This might involve carefully communicating the intended value of rewards being given, clarifying the performance appraisals upon which they are based, and suggesting appropriate comparison points. This advice may be especially relevant in organizations using merit-based instead of seniority-based reward systems, as discussed in The Topic chapter opener. Just what constitutes "meritorious" performance can be a source of considerable debate. And, any disagreements over performance ratings, makes problems due to negative equity dynamics more likely.

Another area where pay equity raises questions is in respect to the disparities between top executive pay and that received by hourly-wage workers. When Wal-Mart's CEO made just over $17 million in 2004 (about $8,000 per hour), the average Wal-Mart employee was earning $9.68 per hour.[18] And in the oil and gas industries, a report showed the gap between CEO pay and worker pay rose from 107 to 1 in 1990 to 441 to 1 by 2004.[19]

ISSUES AND SITUATIONS

Executive Compensation

- In 1965 average CEO pay was 24 times the average worker's; in 2005 it was 262 times.
- In 2005 the average CEO took home about $11 million; the average worker $42,000.
- CEOs in America outearn their counterparts in other advanced countries by 13 times.

Are corporate CEOs and senior executives paid too much? If you follow the news you'll find a fair amount of "bad press" about the heights of executive pay. But researchers at Wharton and Stanford report that the bad press hasn't had much effect on pay packages. They also indicate that "cosmetic" changes sometimes make the paychecks look smaller while total compensation remains high or higher. For example: *Analog Devices* CEO Jerald Fishman was paid $2.35 million in "salary, bonus and 'other' compensation," says *Business Week*, but his total pay package was worth about $12.75 million. Extra compensation came from interest payments on deferred salary ($1 + million); stock option awards ($4+ million); and retirement savings match ($65,000+). *Occidental Petroleum*—CEO Ray Irani received this package: base salary $1.3 million, bonus $3.6 million, free shares $30.9 million, stock options $16.4 million, long-term incentive payout $10.6 million, and miscellaneous $2.6 million.

Critical Response

When Analog Devices reported Fishman's pay, was it done in an ethical way? And regardless of the reporting, is it right for business executives to receive these high levels of compensation when the situation faced by the average worker is very different? Is corporate America doing the right things when it comes to executive pay?

In respect to pay, two other equity situations mentioned earlier in the book are worth remembering. First is *gender equity*. It is well established that women on the average earn less than men. This difference is most evident in occupations traditionally dominated by men, such as the legal professions, but it also includes ones where females have traditionally held most jobs, such as teaching. Second is *comparable worth*. This is the concept that people doing jobs of similar value based on required education, training, and skills (such as nursing and accounting) should receive similar pay. Advocates of comparable worth claim that it corrects historical pay inequities and is a natural extension of the "equal-pay-for-equal-work" concept. Critics claim that "similar value" is too difficult to define, and that the dramatic restructuring of wage scales would have a negative economic impact on society.

EXPECTANCY THEORY

Victor Vroom's expectancy theory of motivation asks the question: What determines the willingness of an individual to work hard at tasks important to the organization?[20] In response, the theory indicates that "people will do what they can do when they want to do it." More specifically, Vroom suggests that the motivation to work depends on the relationships between the *three expectancy factors*, depicted in *Figure 14.4* and described here:

- **Expectancy**—a person's belief that working hard will result in a desired level of task performance being achieved (this is sometimes called effort-performance expectancy).
- **Instrumentality**—a person's belief that successful performance will be followed by rewards and other potential outcomes (this is sometimes called performance-outcome expectancy).
- **Valence**—the value a person assigns to the possible rewards and other work-related outcomes.

In the expectancy theory, motivation *(M)*, expectancy *(E)*, instrumentality *(I)*, and valence *(V)* are related to one another in a multiplicative fashion: $M = E \times I \times V$. In other words, motivation is determined by expectancy times instrumentality times valence. Mathematically speaking, a zero at any location on the right side of the equation (that is, for *E, I,* or *V*) will result in zero motivation. This multiplier effect has important managerial implications. The advice is to: (1) maximize expectancy—people must believe that if they try, they can perform; (2) maximize instrumentality—people must perceive that high performance will be followed by certain outcomes; and (3) maximize valence—people must value the outcomes.

Suppose, for example, that a manager is wondering whether or not the prospect of earning a promotion will be motivational to a subordinate.

▪ **Expectancy** is a person's belief that working hard will result in high task performance.

▪ **Instrumentality** is a person's belief that various outcomes will occur as a result of task performance.

▪ **Valence** is the value a person assigns to work-related outcomes.

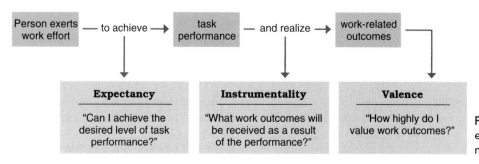

Person exerts work effort — to achieve → task performance — and realize → work-related outcomes

Expectancy	**Instrumentality**	**Valence**
"Can I achieve the desired level of task performance?"	"What work outcomes will be received as a result of the performance?"	"How highly do I value work outcomes?"

Figure 14.4 Elements in the expectancy theory of motivation.

MANAGEMENT SMARTS 14.1

How to make goal setting work for you

- *Set specific goals:* they lead to higher performance than do more generally stated ones such as "do your best."
- *Set challenging goals:* when viewed as realistic and attainable, more difficult goals lead to higher performance than do easy goals.
- *Build goal acceptance and commitment:* People work harder for goals they accept and believe in; they resist goals forced on them.
- *Clarify goal priorities:* Make sure that expectations are clear as to which goals should be accomplished first and why.
- *Provide feedback on goal accomplishment:* Make sure that people know how well they are doing in respect to goal accomplishment.
- *Reward goal accomplishment:* Don't let positive accomplishments pass unnoticed; reward people for doing what they set out to do.

Expectancy theory predicts that a person's motivation to work hard for a promotion will be low if any one or more of the following three conditions apply. First, *if expectancy is low, motivation will suffer.* The person may believe that he or she cannot achieve the performance level necessary to get promoted. So why try? Second, *if instrumentality is low, motivation will suffer.* The person may lack confidence that a high level of task performance will result in being promoted. So why try? Third, *if valence is low, motivation will suffer.* The person may place little value on receiving a promotion. It simply isn't much of a reward. So, once again, why try?

Expectancy theory reminds managers that different people answer the question "Why should I work hard today?" in different ways. The implication is that every person must be respected as an individual with unique needs, preferences, and concerns. Knowing this, a manager can try to customize work environments to best fit individual needs and preferences, always maximizing expectancies, instrumentalities, and valences.

GOAL-SETTING THEORY

The goal-setting theory described by Edwin Locke focuses on the motivational properties of task goals.[21] The basic premise is that task goals can be highly motivating *if* they are properly set and *if* they are well managed. Goals give direction to people in their work. Goals clarify the performance expectations in supervisory relationships, between co-workers, and across subunits in an organization. Goals establish a frame of reference for task feedback. Goals also provide a foundation for behavioral self-management.[22] In these and related ways, Locke believes goal setting can enhance individual work performance and job satisfaction.

To achieve the motivational benefits of goal setting, research by Locke and his associates indicates that managers and team leaders must work with others to set the right goals in the right ways. Things like *goal specificity, goal difficulty, goal acceptance*, and *goal commitment* are among the goal-setting recommendations provided in *Management Smarts 14.1.*

Participation is often a key to unlocking the motivational value of task goals. The concept of MBO, described in Chapter 8 on planning, is a good example. When done well, MBO brings supervisors and subordinates together in a participative process of goal setting and performance review. A positive impact in MBO is most likely to occur when participation (1) allows for increased understanding of specific and difficult goals, and (2) provides for greater acceptance and commitment to them. Along with participation, the opportunity to receive feedback on goal accomplishment is also essential to motivation.

Managers should be aware of the participation options in goal setting. It may not always be possible to allow participation when selecting exactly which goals need to be pursued. But, it may be possible to allow participation in the decisions about how to best pursue them. Also, the constraints of time and other factors operating in some situations may not allow for participation. But, Locke's research suggests that workers will respond positively to externally imposed goals if supervisors assigning them are trusted and if workers believe they will be adequately supported in their attempts to achieve them.

REINFORCEMENT THEORY OF MOTIVATION

The motivation theories discussed so far are concerned with explaining "why" people do things in terms of satisfying needs, resolving felt inequities, and/or pursuing positive expectancies and task goals. Reinforcement theory, by contrast, views human behavior as determined by its environmental consequences. Instead of looking within the individual to explain motivation, it focuses on the external environment and the consequences it holds for the individual. The basic premises of reinforcement theory are based on what E. L. Thorndike called the **law of effect**: behavior that results in a pleasant outcome is likely to be repeated; behavior that results in an unpleasant outcome is not likely to be repeated.[23]

> The **law of effect** states that behavior followed by pleasant consequences is likely to be repeated; behavior followed by unpleasant consequences is not.

REINFORCEMENT STRATEGIES

Psychologist B. F. Skinner popularized the concept of **operant conditioning** as the process of applying the law of effect to control behavior by manipulating its consequences.[24] You may think of operant conditioning as learning by reinforcement. In management the goal is to use reinforcement principles to systematically reinforce desirable work behavior and discourage undesirable work behavior.[25]

Four strategies of reinforcement are used in operant conditioning. **Positive reinforcement** strengthens or increases the frequency of desirable behavior by making a pleasant consequence contingent on its occurrence. *Example:* A manager nods to express approval to someone who makes a useful comment during a staff meeting. **Negative reinforcement** increases the frequency of or strengthens desirable behavior by making the avoidance of an unpleasant consequence contingent on its occurrence. *Example:* A manager who has been nagging a worker every day about tardiness does not nag when the worker comes to work on time.

Punishment decreases the frequency of or eliminates an undesirable behavior by making an unpleasant consequence contingent on its occurrence. *Example:* A manager issues a written reprimand to an employee whose careless work creates quality problems. **Extinction** decreases the frequency of or eliminates an undesirable behavior by making the removal of a pleasant consequence contingent on its occurrence. *Example:* A manager observes that a disruptive employee is receiving social approval from co-workers; the manager counsels co-workers to stop giving this approval.

> **Operant conditioning** is the control of behavior by manipulating its consequences.

> **Positive reinforcement** strengthens a behavior by making a desirable consequence contingent on its occurrence.

> **Negative reinforcement** strengthens a behavior by making the avoidance of an undesirable consequence contingent on its occurrence.

> **Punishment** discourages a behavior by making an unpleasant consequence contingent on its occurrence.

> **Extinction** discourages a behavior by making the removal of a desirable consequence contingent on its occurrence.

MANAGEMENT SMARTS 14.2

Guidelines for positive reinforcement ... and punishment

Positive Reinforcement:

- Clearly identify desired work behaviors.
- Maintain a diverse inventory of rewards.
- Inform everyone what must be done to get rewards.
- Recognize individual differences when allocating rewards.
- Follow the laws of immediate and contingent reinforcement.

Punishment:

- Tell the person what is being done wrong.
- Tell the person what is being done right.
- Make sure the punishment matches the behavior.
- Administer the punishment in private.
- Follow the laws of immediate and contingent reinforcement.

■ **Shaping** is positive reinforcement of successive approximations to the desired behavior.

Figure 14.5 shows how these four reinforcement strategies can be applied in management. The supervisor's goal in the example is to improve work quality as part of a TQM program. Notice how the supervisor can use each of the strategies to influence continuous improvement practices among employees. Note, too, that both positive and negative reinforcement strategies strengthen desirable behavior when it occurs. The punishment and extinction strategies weaken or eliminate undesirable behaviors.

POSITIVE REINFORCEMENT

Among the reinforcement strategies, positive reinforcement deserves special attention. It is governed by two important laws. First, the *law of contingent reinforcement* states that for a reward to have maximum reinforcing value, it must be delivered only if the desired behavior is exhibited. Second, the *law of immediate reinforcement* states that the more immediate the delivery of a reward after the occurrence of a desirable behavior, the greater the reinforcing value of the reward. Additional guidelines for using positive reinforcement are presented in *Management Smarts 14.2.*

The power of positive reinforcement can be mobilized through a process known as **shaping.** This is the creation of a new behavior by the positive reinforcement of successive approximations to it. The timing of positive reinforcement can also make a difference in its impact. A *continuous reinforcement schedule* administers a reward each time a desired behavior occurs. An *intermittent reinforcement schedule* rewards behavior only periodically. In general, a manager can expect that continuous reinforcement will elicit a desired behavior more quickly than will intermittent reinforcement. Also, behavior acquired under an intermittent schedule will be more permanent than will behavior acquired under a continuous schedule. One way to succeed with a shaping strategy, for example, is to give reinforcement on a continuous basis until the desired behavior is achieved. Then an intermittent schedule can be used to maintain the behavior at the new level.

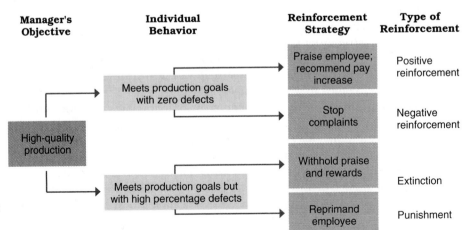

Figure 14.5 Four reinforcement strategies: case of total quality management.

One of the best examples of using positive reinforcement in business is the classic story of Mary Kay Cosmetics. Among Mary Kay's sales force, the legendary pink Cadillac has been a sought-after prize by top performers for many years. More recently and to keep pace with changing times, the firm has added sport vehicles and other cars to the list of prizes. Of course, all are awarded with great ceremony at gala celebrations.[26]

PUNISHMENT

As a reinforcement strategy, punishment attempts to eliminate undesirable behavior by making an unpleasant consequence contingent upon its occurence. To punish an employee, for example, a manager may deny a valued reward, such as praise or merit pay, or administer an unpleasant outcome, such as a verbal reprimand or pay reduction. Like positive reinforcement, punishment can be done poorly or it can be done well. All too often, it is probably done poorly. If you look again at *Management Smarts 14.2*, it offers guidance on how to best handle punishment as a reinforcement strategy.

Be sure you can ■ explain the law of effect and operant conditioning ■ illustrate how positive reinforcement, negative reinforcement, punishment, and extinction influence work behavior ■ explain the reinforcement technique of shaping ■ describe how managers can use the laws of immediate and contingent reinforcement when allocating rewards

Learning Check 3

✓

MOTIVATION AND JOB DESIGN

One area of practice in which the various ideas on motivation come into play is **job design**, the process of arranging work tasks for individuals and groups. Job design applies the insights of motivation theories to achieve high levels of both job satisfaction and job performance. Building jobs so that satisfaction and performance go hand in hand is in many ways an exercise in "fit" between the individual and task requirements. *Figure 14.6* shows the basic job design alternatives of job simplification, job enlargement and rotation, and job enrichment.

▨ **Job design** is arranging work tasks for individuals and groups.

SCIENTIFIC MANAGEMENT

Job simplification involves standardizing work procedures and employing people in well-defined and highly specialized tasks. This is an extension of the scientific management approach discussed in Chapter 3. Simplified jobs are narrow in *job scope*—that is, the number and variety of different tasks a person performs. Many employees around the world earn their livings working at highly simplified tasks, often on assembly lines. The most extreme form of job simplification is **automation,** or the total mechanization of a job.

The logic of job simplification is straightforward. Because the jobs don't require complex skills, workers should be easier and quicker to train, less difficult to supervise, and easy to replace if they leave. Furthermore, because tasks are well defined, workers should become good at them while performing the same work over and over again. Consider the case of Cindy Vang, on an assembly line for Medtronics Inc. She works in a dust-free room making a specialized medical component. She is certified on 5 of 14 job skills in her department. At any given

▨ **Job simplification** employs people in clearly defined and very specialized tasks.

▨ **Automation** is the total mechanization of a job.

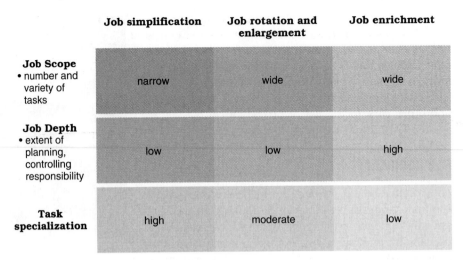

	Job simplification	Job rotation and enlargement	Job enrichment
Job Scope • number and variety of tasks	narrow	wide	wide
Job Depth • extent of planning, controlling responsibility	low	low	high
Task specialization	high	moderate	low

Figure 14.6 Basic job design alternatives.

time, however, she performs one of them, for example, feeding small devices by tweezers into special containers. It is tedious work without much challenge. But Vang says: "I like it." Importantly, she notes that the job doesn't interfere with her home life with a husband and 3 sons. Her economic needs are met in a low-stress job and comfortable work environment.[27]

Situations don't always work out this well in highly simplified jobs. Productivity can suffer when unhappy workers drive up costs through absenteeism and turnover, and through poor performance caused by boredom and alienation. Although simplified jobs appeal to some people, disadvantages can develop with the structured and repetitive tasks.

JOB ROTATION AND JOB ENLARGEMENT

■ **Job rotation** increases task variety by periodically shifting workers between different jobs.

■ **Job enlargement** increases task variety by combining into one job two or more tasks previously assigned to separate workers.

A step beyond simplification in job design, **job rotation,** increases task variety by periodically shifting workers between jobs involving different task assignments. Job rotation can be done on a regular schedule; it can also be done periodically or occasionally. The latter is often used as a training approach, helping people learn about jobs performed by others. Another alternative is **job enlargement,** increasing task variety by combining two or more tasks that were previously assigned to separate workers. Often these are tasks done immediately before or after the work performed in the original job. This is sometimes called *horizontal loading*—pulling prework and/or later work stages into the job.

JOB ENRICHMENT

■ **Job enrichment** increases job depth by adding work planning and evaluating duties normally performed by the supervisor.

Frederick Herzberg, whose two-factor theory of motivation was discussed earlier, questions the motivational value of horizontally loading jobs through enlargement and rotation. "Why," he asks, "should a worker become motivated when one or more meaningless tasks are added to previously existing ones or when work assignments are rotated among equally meaningless tasks?" By contrast, he says, "If you want people to do a good job, give them a good job to do."[28] He argues that this is best done through **job enrichment,** the practice of expanding job content to create more opportunities for satisfaction.

In contrast to job enlargement and rotation, job enrichment focuses on *job depth*—that is, the extent to which task planning and evaluating duties are performed by the individual worker rather than the supervisor. Changes designed to increase job depth are sometimes referred to as *vertical loading.*

Modern management theory adopts a contingency perspective that takes job enrichment a step beyond the suggestions of Frederick Herzberg. Most importantly, it recognizes that job enrichment may not be best for everyone. This thinking is reflected in the core characteristics model developed by J. Richard Hackman and his associates. It offers the diagnostic approach to job enrichment described in *Figure 14.7*, and is based on *5 core job characteristics.*[29]

1. *Skill variety*—the degree to which a job requires a variety of different activities to carry out the work, and involves the use of a number of different skills and talents of the individual.
2. *Task identity*—the degree to which the job requires completion of a "whole" and identifiable piece of work, one that involves doing a job from beginning to end with a visible outcome.
3. *Task significance*—the degree to which the job has a substantial impact on the lives or work of other people elsewhere in the organization or in the external environment.
4. *Autonomy*—the degree to which the job gives the individual freedom, independence, and discretion in scheduling work and in choosing procedures for carrying it out.
5. *Feedback from the job itself*—the degree to which work activities required by the job result in the individual obtaining direct and clear information on his or her performance.

According to this model, job satisfaction and performance are influenced by 3 critical psychological states: (1) experienced meaningfulness of the work; (2) experienced responsibility for the outcomes of the work; and (3) knowledge of actual results of work activities. These, in turn, are influenced by the presence or absence of the five core job characteristics. A job that is high in the five core characteristics is considered enriched; the lower a job scores on these characteristics, the less enriched it is. In true contingency fashion, however, the core characteristics will not affect all people in the same way.

Generally speaking, people who respond most favorably to enriched jobs will have strong higher-order needs, appropriate job knowledge and skills, and be otherwise satisfied with job context. They will also have strong growth-needs (see Alderfer's ERG theory). The expectation is that people that seek psychological growth in their work will respond most positively to enriched jobs.

For those situations when job enrichment is a good choice, Hackman and his colleagues recommend 5 ways to improve the core characteristics. First, you can *form natural units of work.* Make sure that the tasks people perform are logically related to one another and provide a clear and meaningful task identity.

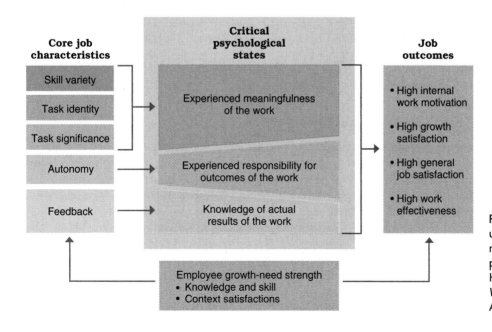

Figure 14.7 Designing jobs using the core characteristics model. *Source:* Reprinted by permission from J. Richard Hackman and Greg R. Oldham, *Work Redesign* (Reading, MA: Addison-Wesley, 1980), p. 90.

KAFFEEKLATSCH

Job Disengagement

First Cup

"Did you ever wonder what's going on inside Vinnie's office? Does he really do any work in there? I'll tell you this—he's the last one off the elevator in the morning, and the first one on it at night. And don't ever ask him to help you out; he doesn't have time!"

Studying the Grounds

■ Gallup Surveys report that only 33% of American workers are "passionate" about their jobs; self-reported job disengagement ranges from 19 to 22 percent in any given year.

■ A Towers Perrin survey found 24 percent disengagement, with only 14 percent of American workers "willing to go the extra mile for their employers"; 40 percent of Mexican workers surveyed were highly engaged.

■ Worker engagement tends to be higher in nonprofit organizations than in businesses.

Double Espresso

"It's like an automobile running on only 6 of 8 cylinders. How can the company expect to perform well when 20 percent or more of the workforce isn't working up to capacity? Just how many 'Vinnies' do you think we have here anyway? Are we better or worse than the results reported in those surveys?"

Your Turn

Think of your organization or one that's important to you. Draw a circle about 1 inch in diameter. The circle represents the organization. Then color in that part of the circle you believe represents the percentage of members who are not fully engaged in their jobs. That shaded area of the circle represents lost productivity, lost performance opportunity, and lost organizational potential. Now assume that you are the head of this organization. What can be done about this "job disengagement" problem?

Second, try to *combine tasks.* Expand job responsibilities by pulling together into one larger job a number of smaller tasks previously done by others. Third, *establish client relationships.* Put people in contact with others who, as clients inside and/or outside the organization, use the results of their work. Fourth, *open feedback channels.* Provide opportunities for people to receive performance feedback as they work and to learn how performance changes over time. Fifth, *practice vertical loading.* Give people more control over their work by increasing their authority to perform the planning and controlling previously done by supervisors.

ALTERNATIVE WORK SCHEDULES

Not only is the content of jobs important, the context is too. Among the more significant developments is the emergence of a number of alternative ways for people to schedule their work time.[30] And "flexibility" is the key word. Many employers are finding that providing alternative work schedules can help attract and retain the best workers.

The Compressed Work Week

■ A **compressed work week** allows a full-time job to be completed in less than five days.

A **compressed work week** is any work schedule that allows a full-time job to be completed in less than the standard 5 days of 8-hour shifts.[31] Its most common form is the "4–40," that is, accomplishing 40 hours of work in four 10-hour days. One advantage of the 4–40 schedule is that the employee receives 3 consecutive days off from work each week. This benefits the individual through more leisure time and lower commuting costs. The organization should also benefit through lower absenteeism and any improved performance that may result. Potential disadvantages include increased fatigue and family adjustment problems for the individual, as well as increased scheduling problems, possible customer complaints, and union objections on behalf of the organization. At USAA, a diversified financial services company that has been listed among the

100 best companies to work for in America, many employees are on a 4-day schedule, with some working Monday through Thursday and others working Tuesday through Friday. Reported benefits include improved employee morale, lower overtime costs, less absenteeism, and less sick leave.[32]

Flexible Working Hours

The term **flexible working hours,** also called *flexitime* or *flextime*, describes any work schedule that gives employees some choice in the pattern of their daily work hours. Flexible schedules with choices of starting and ending times give employees greater autonomy while still meeting their work responsibilities. Some

may choose to come in earlier and leave earlier, while still completing an 8-hour day; others may choose to start later in the morning and leave later. In between these extremes are opportunities to attend to personal affairs, such as dental appointments, home emergencies, visits to children's schools, and so on. All top 100 companies in *Working Mother* magazine's list of best employers for working moms offer flexible scheduling. Reports indicate that flexibility in dealing with non-work obligations reduces stress and unwanted job turnover.[33]

▪ **Flexible working hours** give employees some choice in daily work hours.

Job Sharing

Another work scheduling alternative is **job sharing,** where 1 full-time job is split between 2 or more persons. This often involves each person working one-half day, but it can also be done on weekly or monthly sharing arrangements. Organizations benefit by employing talented people who would otherwise be unable to work. The qualified specialist who is also a parent may be unable to stay away from home for a full workday, but may be able to work a half day. Job sharing allows two such persons to be employed as one, often to great benefit.[34]

▪ **Job sharing** splits one job between two people.

Telecommuting

It is increasingly popular for people to work away from a fixed office location. **Telecommuting** is a work arrangement that allows at least a portion of scheduled work hours to be completed outside the office. It is often facilitated by computers and information technology that allow electronic links with customers and a central office. New terms are even becoming associated with telecommuting practices. We speak of *hoteling* when telecommuters come to the central office and use temporary office facilities; we also refer to *virtual offices* that include everything from an office at home to a mobile workspace in an automobile. When asked what they like, telecommuters tend to report increased productivity, fewer distractions, the freedom to be your own boss, and the benefit of having more time for themselves. On the negative side, they cite working too much, having less time to themselves, difficulty separating work and personal life, and having less time for family.[35] One telecommuter's advice to others is this: "You have to have self-discipline and pride in what you do, but you also have to have a boss that trusts you enough to get out of the way."[36]

▪ **Telecommuting** involves using IT to work at home or outside the office.

Part-Time Work

The growing use of temporary workers is another striking employment trend, and it has a controversial side. **Part-time work** is done on any schedule less than the standard 40-hour work week and that does not qualify the individual as a full-time employee. Many employers rely on **contingency workers**—part-timers or *permatemps* who supplement the full-time workforce, often on a long-term

▪ **Part-time work** is temporary employment for less than the standard 40-hour work week.

▪ **Contingency workers** are employed on a part-time and temporary basis to supplement a permanent workforce.

basis. Such workers now constitute some 30 percent of the American workforce; over 90 percent of firms surveyed by the American Management Association use them.[37] No longer limited to the traditional areas of clerical services, sales personnel, and unskilled labor, these workers serve an increasingly broad range of employer needs. It is now possible to hire on a part-time basis everything from executive support, such as a chief financial officer, to such special expertise as engineering, computer programming, and market research.

Because part-time or contingency workers can be easily hired, contracted with, and/or terminated in response to changing needs, many employers like the flexibility they offer in controlling labor costs and dealing with cyclical demand. On the other hand, some worry that temporaries lack the commitment of permanent workers and often lower productivity. Perhaps the most controversial issue of the part-time work trend relates to the different treatment part-timers often receive from employers. They may be paid less than their full-time counterparts, and many do not receive important benefits, such as health care, life insurance, pension plans, and paid vacations.

| **Learning Check 4** | *Be sure you can* ■ illustrate a job designed by job simplification rotation and enlargement ■ list and describe the 5 core job characteristics ■ explain how a person's growth needs, skills, and context satisfaction can affect his or her responses to these characteristics ■ describe the compressed work week, flexible work hours, job sharing, and telecommuting as alternative work schedules ■ discuss the significance of part-time contingency workers in the economy |

RESEARCH BRIEF

Positive psychological capital important influence on performance and satisfaction

A concept known as PsyCap, or psychological capital, is defined by Fred Luthans and his colleagues as "an individual's positive psychological state of development." This positive state is composed of (1) high personal confidence and self-efficacy in working on a task, (2) optimism about present and future success, (3) hope and perseverance in pursuing goals and adjusting them as needed, and (4) resiliency in responding to setbacks and problems.

A briefings report from the Gallup Leadership Institute summarizes studies that address the measurement of PsyCap, developing PsyCap as an individual state, and the impact of PsyCap on work attitudes and performance. In samples of management students and managers, the researchers report success with a training intervention designed to raise the level of Psy-Cap for participants. When performance measures were taken among the manager samples, increases in performance were associated with the PsyCap gains. In comparing the costs of the training intervention with the performance gains, the researchers calculated the return on investment as 270%.

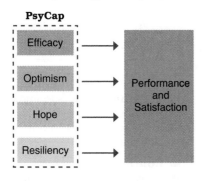

Psychological Capital

Overall conclusions for this stream of research so far are that the measurement of PsyCap is reliable and valid, and that PsyCap is positively related to individual performance and satisfaction. They further point out that psychological capital deals with "who you are" and "who you are becoming." They contrast this with human capital—"what you know" and social capital—"who you know."

RESEARCH & APPLICATIONS

Does this concept of psychological capital make sense to you? Do a self-assessment—rate yourself on hope, optimism, efficacy/confidence, and resiliency. Observe others with whom you work or study; rate them too. Is it reasonable to think that persons with high PsyCap will be more motivated and productive, whether we are talking about their work, academic performance, or approach to life overall?

Reference: "Psychological Capital (PsyCap) Measurement, Development, and Performance Impact," Briefings Report 2006-01 (Gallup Leadership Institute); and, Fred Luthans, James B. Avey, Bruce J. Avoilio, Steven M. Norman and Gwendolyn M. Combs, "Psychological Capital Development: Toward a Micro-Intervention," *Journal of Organizational Behavior*, Vol. 27 (2006), pp. 387-393.

CHAPTER 14 STUDY GUIDE

STUDY QUESTIONS SUMMARY

1 How do individual needs influence motivation?

- Motivation involves the level, direction, and persistence of effort expended at work; simply put, a highly motivated person works hard.
- Maslow's hierarchy of human needs suggests a progression from lower-order physiological, safety, and social needs to higher-order ego and self-actualization needs.
- Alderfer's ERG theory identifies existence, relatedness, and growth needs.
- Herzberg's two-factor theory points out the importance of both job content and job context to motivation and performance.
- McClelland's acquired needs theory identifies the needs for achievement, affiliation, and power, all of which may influence what a person desires from work.

2 What are the process theories of motivation?

- Adams's equity theory recognizes that social comparisons take place when rewards are distributed in the workplace.
- People who feel inequitably treated are motivated to act in ways that reduce the sense of inequity; perceived negative inequity may result in someone working less hard in the future.
- Vroom's expectancy theory states that Motivation = Expectancy × Instrumentality × Valence.
- Expectancy theory encourages managers to make sure that any rewards offered for motivational purposes are achievable, predictable, and individually valued.
- Locke's goal-setting theory emphasizes the motivational power of goals; task goals should be specific rather than ambiguous, difficult but achievable, and set through participatory means.

3 What role does reinforcement play in motivation?

- Reinforcement theory recognizes that human behavior is influenced by its environmental consequences.
- The law of effect states that behavior followed by a pleasant consequence is likely to be repeated; behavior followed by an unpleasant consequence is unlikely to be repeated.
- Reinforcement strategies used by managers include positive reinforcement, negative reinforcement, punishment, and extinction.
- Positive reinforcement works best when applied according to the laws of contingent and immediate reinforcement.

4 What are alternative approaches to job design?

- Job design is the process of creating or defining jobs by assigning specific work tasks to individuals and groups.
- Job simplification creates narrow and repetitive jobs consisting of well-defined tasks with many routine operations, such as the typical assembly-line job.
- Job enlargement allows individuals to perform a broader range of simplified tasks; job rotation allows individuals to shift among different jobs of similar skill levels.
- The diagnostic approach to job enrichment involves analyzing jobs according to 5 core characteristics: skill variety, task identity, task significance, autonomy, and feedback.
- Alternative work schedules make work hours less inconvenient and enable organizations to better respect worker's needs and personal responsibilities; options include the compressed work week, flexible working hours, job sharing, telecommuting, and part-time work.

KEY TERMS REVIEW

Automation (p. 357)

Compressed work week (p. 360)

Contingency workers (p. 361)

Expectancy (p. 353)

Extinction (p. 353)

Flexible working hours (p. 361)

Higher-order needs (p. 346)

Hygiene factor (p. 348)

Instrumentality (p. 353)

Job design (p. 357)

Job enlargement (p. 358)

Job enrichment (p. 358)

Job rotation (p. 358)

Job sharing (p. 361)

Job simplification (p. 357)

Law of effect (p. 355)

Lower-order needs (p. 346)

Motivation (p. 346)

Need (p. 346)

Need for Achievement (p. 349)

Need for Affiliation (p. 349)

Need for Power (p. 349)

Negative reinforcement (p. 355)

Operant conditioning (p. 355)

Part-time work (p. 361)

Positive reinforcement (p. 355)

Punishment (p. 355)

Satisfier factors (p. 348)

Shaping (p. 356)

Telecommuting (p. 361)

Valence (p. 353)

SELF-TEST 14

MULTIPLE-CHOICE QUESTIONS:

1. Lower-order needs in Maslow's hierarchy correspond to _____ needs in ERG theory.

   (a) growth   (b) affiliation   (c) existence   (d) achievement

2. A worker high in need for _____ power in McClelland's theory tries to use power for the good of the organization.

   (a) position   (b) expert   (c) personal   (d) social

3. In the _____ theory of motivation, an individual who feels underrewarded relative to a co-worker might be expected to reduce his or her performance in the future.

   (a) ERG   (b) acquired needs   (c) two-factor   (d) equity

4. Which of the following is a correct match? _____

   (a) McClelland—ERG theory   (b) Skinner—reinforcement theory   (c) Vroom—equity theory   (d) Locke—expectancy theory

5. The expectancy theory of motivation says that motivation=expectancy×_____×_____.

   (a) rewards, valence   (b) instrumentality, valence   (c) equity, instrumentality   (d) rewards, valence

6. The law of _____ states that behavior followed by a positive consequence is likely to be repeated, whereas behavior followed by an undesirable consequence is not likely to be repeated.

   (a) reinforcement   (b) contingency   (c) goal setting   (d) effect

7. _____ is a positive reinforcement strategy that rewards successive approximations to a desirable behavior.

   (a) Extinction   (b) Negative reinforcement   (c) Shaping   (d) Merit pay

8. In Herzberg's two-factor theory, base pay is considered a(n) _____ factor.

   (a) valence   (b) satisfier   (c) equity   (d) hygiene

9. When someone has a high and positive "expectancy" in the expectancy theory of motivation, this means that the person _____.

   (a) believes he or she can meet performance expectations   (b) highly values the rewards being offered   (c) sees a relationship between high performance and the available rewards   (d) believes that rewards are equitable

10. In goal-setting theory, the goal of "becoming more productive in my work" would not be considered a source of motivation since it fails the criterion of goal _____.

    (a) acceptance   (b) specificity   (c) challenge   (d) commitment

11. B. F. Skinner would argue that "getting a paycheck on Friday" reinforces a person for coming to work on Friday but would not reinforce the person for doing an extraordinary job on Tuesday. This is because the Friday paycheck fails the law of _____ reinforcement.

    (a) negative   (b) continuous   (c) immediate   (d) intermittent

12. The addition of more planning and evaluating responsibilities to a job is an example of the _____ job design strategy.

    (a) job enrichment   (b) job enlargement   (c) job rotation   (d) job sharing

13. Workers in a compressed work week typically work 40 hours in _____ days.

    (a) 3   (b) 4   (c) 5   (d) a flexible number of

14. Another term used to describe part-time workers is _____.

    (a) contingency workers   (b) virtual workers   (c) flexible workers   (d) secondary workers

15. Hoteling is a development associated with the growing importance of _____ in the new workplace.

    (a) personal wellness   (b) telecommuting   (c) compressed work weeks   (d) Type A personalities

SHORT-RESPONSE QUESTIONS:

16. What preferences does a person high in the need for achievement bring to the workplace?

17. Why is participation important to goal-setting theory?

18. What is the common ground in Maslow's, Alderfer's, and McClelland's views of human needs?

19. Why might an employer not want to offer employees the option of working on a compressed work week schedule?

APPLICATION QUESTION:

20. How can a manager combine the powers of goal setting and positive reinforcement to create a highly motivational work environment for a group of workers with high needs for achievement?

CHAPTER 14 APPLICATIONS

CASE 14

Nucor: A Case for Less Management

Unlike many industry competitors, North Carolina-based Nucor has achieved both financial success and a satisfied, productive workforce. As its mission statement affirms, Nucor is "the safest, highest quality, lowest cost, most productive and most profitable steel and steel products company in the world."[38] For much of this, Nucor credits the quality of its employees, who enjoy some of the most immediate access to upper management in the business world. But can superior employee relations really build a $12.7 billion company?[39]

A History of Heavy Metal

Nucor's roots lie with auto entrepreneur Ransom E. Olds, who founded the venerable Oldsmobile brand and later Reo Motor Cars. As technology evolved and ownership changed hands, the name of the company ultimately became the Nuclear Corporation of America, which did business in the nuclear instrument and electronics sectors through the middle of the twentieth century.[40]

After facing several lean years, and a close call with bankruptcy in 1964, newly installed president F. Kenneth Iverson and vice-president of finance Samuel Siegel led the company through a major restructuring. They logically chose to reorganize the company around its primary profit centers—a steel joist business name Vulcraft, based out of South Carolina and Nebraska. The reshaped company pulled up its Arizonan roots and transplanted to Charlotte, North Carolina, just two years later, expanding its joist business into Alabama and Texas.[41]

Just four years after remaking the company, management made another pivotal decision: to integrate backward through the supply chain by building a steel mill—their first—in South Carolina. In another four years, the company changed its name again, to the Nucor Corporation. It spent the remainder of the 1970s supplementing its Vulcraft facilities with additional joist plants and steel bar mills.[42]

The 1980s saw Nucor pioneering within the field of steel production. At its Crawfordsville, Indiana, plant Nucor developed a process called thin slab casting, which dramatically reduced the investment and oper-

ating costs necessary to produce sheet steel. Through this process, Nucor could expand its business into growing markets, like the domestic auto assembly industry, achieving record profits while keeping expenditures to a minimum. Clients and critics were equally impressed, and *Forbes* magazine described Nucor's achievement as "the most substantial, technological, industrial innovation in the past 50 years."[43]

Since the 1990s, Nucor has continued a series of record-setting strategic expansions: through a partnership with Yamato Kogyo, a Japanese steelmaker, Nucor added two mills to a site in Arkansas which has grown to be the largest structural beam facility in the Western Hemisphere. Adding two mills to a site in Berkeley County, South Carolina, created the largest mini-mill in the world, which produces more than three million tons of steel a year.[44]

These days, Nucor is the largest steel producer in the United States. Having recycled approximately 17 million tons of scrap steel (five million of those tons being made of scrap automobiles) in a recent year, Nucor is also the nation's largest recycler. The company seeks growth by a four-part expansion strategy, the first part of which is to optimize existing operations. The second part is to pursue strategic acquisitions.[45] Third, Nucor seeks to commercialize new technologies Fourth, it intends to grow internationally through joint ventures.[46]

Keeping Equal Company

Worldwide, there are approximately 11,500 Nucor employees, most of whom would rather work nowhere else. And Nucor management has worked hard to make it so. The company is divided into operational divisions, each of which sports an extremely streamlined management structure which keeps them light, nimble, and able to adjust quickly to market fluctuations. A typical Nucor division has only three levels of management between hourly employees and the company president.[47]

Like the Japanese manufacturing giants before it, Nucor empowers its workers to make decisions as necessary to keep operations running smoothly. As long as Nucor's goals and measurables are understood by everyone, there exist firm guidelines by which employees may judge their responses.

Much of this is owed to the egalitarian philosophies of former president Ken Iverson, who espoused equality among all his employees and firmly believed that associates of every level could make creative and beneficial contributions if given the opportunity. Typical of his style was his decision to do away with colored hardhats in the plants, which had become status symbols that kept distance between functional areas. Not everyone saw the benefits right away. "I got all kinds of flack from our foremen," Iverson recalled in an interview. "They said, 'You can't do that!' So we held training programs to explain that their authority didn't come from the color of the hat that they wore."[48] True to his own philosophies, Iverson was later convinced to revise his idea when it was discovered that maintenance personnel couldn't be located quickly enough in an emergency, so they eventually donned yellow hardhats.

And in an American business culture fraught with executive perks, Nucor's rather modest appointments offer a refreshing alternative to CEOs gone wild. Not only do executives *not* enjoy top perks like better va-

cation schedules or insurance programs, but Nucor officers also aren't eligible for certain benefits like profit sharing or the employee stock purchase plan. All executives fly coach, and they eat in the same dining halls as line workers when working on-site. No company cars or executive parking places, either.[49]

All Nucor employees are eligible for bonus earnings based on the company's performance. And for upper executives, performance goal rewards may account for up to 80 percent of their total compensation. Employees at all levels understand that the company's success—and thus their earnings—are tied to their collective performance.[50]

Making Steel, Making Profits

Once teetering on the brink of bankruptcy, Nucor became a manufacturing success story through a reorganization that emphasized the business's core talents and the innovative potential of its employees. By valuing individual contributions and creating an atmosphere in which employees are inclined to take ownership, Nucor has persuaded its associates to take a big-picture view of their roles in the company, which has led to substantial year-on-year profits and growth. But in an era of continued consolidation in the steel industry and rising material prices, can Nucor continue to innovate and lead the pack? Where could this manufacturing leader go next?

REVIEW QUESTIONS

1. Why do you think that Nucor has deliberately adopted a streamlined management structure?
2. By setting performance goal rewards for upper executives at up to 80 percent of their total compensation, how do you think that Nucor motivates its top management?
3. How does Nucor's method of employee compensation satisfy both workers' lower-order needs and their higher-order needs?

TEAM PROJECT

CEO PAY

In 2005, Barry Diller of InterActiveCorp, was the highest paid corporate CEO. He earned $4,770,153 in salary and bonus, plus $295,136,421 in stock options, restricted stock, and long-term incentives. His total was just over $295.1 million.

Question: What is happening in the area of executive compensation and what do you think about it?

Research Directions:

■ Check the latest reports on CEO pay. Get the facts and prepare a briefing report as if you were writing a short, informative article for *Fortune* magazine. The title of your article should be "Status Report: Where We Stand Today on CEO Pay."

- Address the equity issue: are CEOs paid too much, especially relative to the pay of average workers?
- Address the pay-for-performance issue: Do corporate CEOs get paid for performance or for something else? What do the researchers say? What do the business periodicals say? Find some examples to explain and defend your answers to these questions.
- Take a position: Should a limit be set on CEO pay? If not, why not? If yes, what type of limit should be set? Who, if anyone, should set these limits—government, company boards of directors, or someone else?

PERSONAL MANAGEMENT

It is very difficult to say that someone completely lacks **INITIATIVE**. Each of us has to display a certain amount of initiative just to survive each day. But the initiative of people at work varies greatly, just as it does among students. The issue for you becomes whether you have the self-initiative to work hard and apply your talents to achieve high performance in school, in a job, on an assigned task. Don't hide from the answer. The way you work now in school or on a job is a good predictor of the future. Part of the key to initiative lies in a good person–job fit, finding the right job in the right career field. A person with high initiative is:

Initiative

- Willing to look for problems and fix them.
- Willing to do more than required, to work beyond expectations.
- Willing to help others when they are stuck or overwhelmed.
- Willing to try to do things better; not being comfortable with the status quo.
- Willing to think ahead, to craft ideas and make plans for the future.

Building the Brand Called "You" Only you can decide that you want to work really hard. Look at the prior criteria for someone high in self-initiative. Consider how you behave as a student or on a job. Can you honestly say that each statement accurately describes you?

NEXT STEPS: MANAGEMENT LEARNING WORKBOOK

Self-Assessments
- Organizational Design Preference (#17)
- Student Engagement Survey (#23)
- Job Design Choices (#24)

Experiential Exercises
- What Do You Value in Work? (#7)
- Work vs. Family (#17)
- Compensation and Benefits (#18)
- Why Do We Work? (#21)

Individual Behavior

15

Planning Ahead

Chapter 15 Study Questions

1 How do perceptions influence individual behavior?

2 What should we know about personalities in the workplace?

3 How do attitudes influence individual behavior?

4 What are the dynamics of emotions, moods, and stress?

Does One Drive the Other?

The relationship between attitudes and behaviors is complex and difficult to discern. How do the two interact? | Is one more dominant than the other? And how do the two influence consumers' actions in the marketplace?

Of all the "chicken or egg" dilemmas for business leaders, one continually confounds those who might try to decipher it. Marketers, strategists, and managers alike have all struggled in attempting to determine whether attitudes determine behaviors, or the other way around.

Perhaps no company knows this better than MySpace.com. For the young social networking site, attitudes and behaviors are its *raisons d'être*—the company exists to catalog the actions, emotions, dreams, and desires of its customers.

As with most upstart companies, the initial identity of MySpace grew out of the passions of its founders, Tom Anderson and Chris DeWolfe, who conceived of a social networking site unhampered by the proprietary restrictions of existing models. "We're not deciding what's cool. Our users are," DeWolfe said. "MySpace is all about letting people be what they want to be."[1]

What *They* Think

"We're not deciding what's cool. MySpace is all about letting people be what they want to be."
Chris DeWolfe, MySpace co-founder

BEHAVIORS: *"The key to MySpace is that it's controlled by the user. Friendster is a much more controlled environment."*
Joel Bartlett, organizer for People for the Ethical Treatment of Animals (PETA)

ATTITUDES: *"A lot of it makes me think, what kind of judgment does this person have? Why are you allowing this to be viewed publicly, effectively, or semipublicly?"*
Brad Karsh, president of a Chicago-based consulting company.

The effect of their "users rule" attitude was that their customers took the opportunity to post just about anything that came to mind, regardless of how explicit. It didn't take long for many users' pages to get plastered with descriptions of tell-all dating exploits, illicit activities, and revealing pho-

MySpace.com founders Tom Anderson and Chris DeWolfe.

tos. And it wasn't much longer before concerned parents, school administrators, and youth advocates worried that the lustful Id of the MySpace demographic had mortally infected the site.

To adapt, MySpace adopted a vigorous self-policing policy, ruthlessly excising material that might be viewed as objectionable by a variety of audiences. DeWolfe and Anderson quickly learned that corporate attitudes which inspire freedom in customers' behaviors may earn them popularity, but it also increases a company's responsibility and liability. And in the meantime, the censoring won the temporary approval of concerned parties. According to Shawn Gold, senior vice-president of MySpace, the site kicks some 5,000 underage users off per day.[2]

The consequences of the attitudes/behavior mix can extend well beyond the traditional consumer-producer relationship. The broad perception of some MySpace users that posting anything and everything lacks any real ramifications has prompted behavior modification on the part of both employers and college career centers. Employers now use sites like MySpace to check up on job applicants, rejecting those whose cavalier postings demonstrate what employers see as a lack of discretion. To keep up, career counselors are advising that young job seekers temper their online presence before applying for that first big job.

"It's a growing phenomenon," said Michael Sciola, director of Wesleyan University's career resource center. "There are lots of employers that Google. Now they've taken the next step."[3]

Advertisers seeking to mine the awesome customer base of MySpace users had to revise both their attitudes and behaviors in order to reach this immense audience. Because the MySpace founders felt strongly that they didn't want traditional Web ads cluttering up users' already-busy pages, marketers took a back-door approach, personifying the attributes of their products or brands in online profiles similar to those of MySpace users.

MySpace founders Tom Anderson and Chris DeWolfe have spent an immense amount of time exploring the complex relationship between their users' attitudes and behaviors. How do you think the two are related?

The Numbers

Registered Users of Social Networking Web Sites, in millions

MySpace	100
Yahoo Photos	30
Photobucket	15
LiveJournal	11
Facebook	7.5
Flickr	3

Quick facts

* MySpace averages more than 48 million unique visitors a month.[4]
* Eighty-seven percent of 12- to 17-year-olds use the Internet vs. 66 percent of adults, according to the Pew Internet & American Life Project.[5]
* Fifteen-to 18-year-olds average nearly 6.5 hours a day watching TV, playing video games, and surfing the Net, according to a Kaiser Family Foundation survey.[6]
* Ads on MySpace account for 10 percent of all ads viewed online.[7]
* The teen consumer spending market is estimated at $175 billion.[8]

What Do *You* Think?

1. Has the leadership of MySpace done enough to curb inappropriate use and users?
2. To what extent have the attitudes of the MySpace founders become reflected in the site's content?

Individual Behavior			
Study Question 1	**Study Question 2**	**Study Question 3**	**Study Question 4**
Perception	**Personality**	**Attitudes**	**Emotions, Moods, and Stress**
■ Psychological contracts ■ Perception and attribution ■ Perceptual tendencies and distortions ■ Impression management	■ Big five model ■ Additional personality factors	■ What is an attitude? ■ Important work attitudes ■ Job satisfaction and its outcomes	■ Emotions and moods ■ Stress ■ Stress consequences ■ Stress management
Learning Check 1	**Learning Check 2**	**Learning Check 3**	**Learning Check 4**

All too often, observe scholars Jeffrey Pfeffer and Charles O'Reilly, too many organizations underperform because they operate with great untapped "hidden value" in human resources. It's not that they lack talent; they fail to take full advantage of the talent they already have available. Pfeffer and O'Reilly criticize organizations "with smart, motivated, hardworking, decent people who nevertheless don't perform very well because the company doesn't let them shine and doesn't really capitalize on their talent and motivation."[9]

What do you think about when you see or hear the word "work"? Is it a "turn-on" or a "turn-off"? When Dolly Parton sang "Working 9 to 5; what a way to make a living," she reminded us of an unfortunate reality—that work is not a positive experience for everyone. But isn't this a shame? Some years ago, Karen Nussbaum founded an organization called 9 to 5, devoted to improving women's salaries and promotion opportunities in the workplace. She started the business after leaving her job as a secretary at Harvard University. Describing what she calls "the incident that put her over the edge," Nussbaum says: "One day . . . I was sitting at my desk at lunchtime, when most of the professors were out. A student walked into the office and looked me dead in the eye and said, 'Isn't *anyone* here?'"[10] Nussbaum founded 9 to 5 to support her personal commitment to "remake the system so that it does not produce these individuals."

Although expressed in different ways and through different media, Parton and Nussbaum direct our attention toward an unfortunate fact of life in the modern workplace—some people, too many people, work under conditions that fail to provide them with motivation, self-respect, and satisfaction. Center stage in this situation are issues of individual behavior and its consequences—including perception, personality, attitudes, and work stress.

PERCEPTION

■ **Perception** is the process through which people receive, organize, and interpret information from the environment.

Perception is the process through which people receive and interpret information from the environment. It is the way we form impressions about ourselves, other people, and daily life experiences. And it is the way we process information to make the decisions that ultimately guide our actions.[11] Perception acts as a screen or filter through which information passes before it has an impact on communication, decision making, and behavior. Because perceptions are influenced by such things as cultural background, values, and other personal and situational circumstances, people can and do perceive the same things or situations differently. And importantly, people behave according to their perceptions.

PSYCHOLOGICAL CONTRACTS

Our interest in perception begins with the notion of the **psychological contract,** or set of expectations held by the individual about what will be given and received in the employment relationship.[12] The ideal work situation is one in which the exchange of values in the psychological contract is perceived as fair. Morale problems are more likely when the psychological contract is perceived as unfair, unbalanced, or broken.

Figure 15.1 shows that a healthy psychological contract offers a balance between individual contributions made to the organization and inducements received in return. *Contributions* are work activities, such as effort, time, creativity, and loyalty, that make the individual a valuable human resource. *Inducements* are things the organization gives to the individual in exchange for these contributions. Typical inducements include pay, fringe benefits, training, opportunities for personal growth and advancement, and job security. Such inducements should be valued by employees and should make it worthwhile for them to work hard for the organization.

A **psychological contract** is the set of individual expectations about the employment relationship.

PERCEPTION AND ATTRIBUTION

Another of the ways in which perception exerts its influence on individual behavior is through **attribution**, the process of developing explanations for events. It is natural for people to try to explain what they observe and the things that happen to them. The fact that people can perceive the same things quite differently has an important influence on attributions and their ultimate influence on behavior.

In social psychology, attribution theory describes how people try to explain the behavior of themselves and other people.[13] One of its significant applications is in the context of people's performance at work. Fundamental **attribution error** occurs when observers blame another person's performance failures more on internal factors relating to the individual than on

Attribution is a process of explaining events.

Fundamental **attribution error** overestimates internal factors and underestimates external factors as influences on someone's behavior.

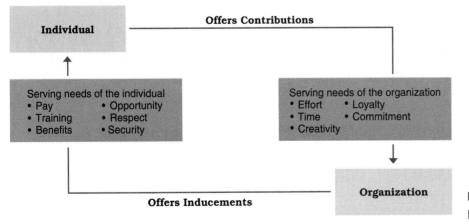

Figure 15.1 Components in the psychological contract.

external factors relating to the environment. In the case of someone who is producing poor-quality work, for example, a team leader might blame a lack of job skills or laziness—an unwillingness to work hard enough. In response, the leader is likely to try to resolve the problem through training, motivation, or even replacement. The attribution error leads to the neglect of possible external explanations for the poor-quality work, such as unrealistic time pressures or substandard technology. Opportunities to improve upon these factors through managerial action will probably be missed.

Another confounding aspect of perception and attribution occurs as a **self-serving bias.** This happens when individuals blame their personal failures or problems on external causes and attribute their successes to internal causes. You might think of this tendency the next time you "blame" your instructor for a poor course grade. The self-serving bias is harmful when it causes us to give insufficient attention to the need for personal change and development. While readily taking credit for successes, we are often too quick to focus on the environment to explain away our failures.

■ **Self-serving bias** explains personal success by internal causes and personal failures by external causes.

PERCEPTUAL TENDENCIES AND DISTORTIONS

In addition to the attribution errors just discussed, a variety of perceptual tendencies and distortions can also influence how people behave and communicate with one another. Of particular interest are the use of stereotypes, halo effects, selective perception, and projection.

Stereotypes

■ A **stereotype** is when attributes commonly associated with a group are assigned to an individual.

A **stereotype** occurs when someone is identified with a group or category, and then oversimplified attributes associated with the group or category are used to describe the individual. We all use stereotypes, and they are not always negative or ill intended. But those based on such factors as gender, age, and race can, and unfortunately still do, bias the perceptions of people in some work settings.

INSIGHTS

Whole Foods, Whole People, Whole Planet

That's how Whole Foods Market, the nation's largest retailer of natural and organic foods, describes its motto on the Web. The corporate Web site goes on to proclaim that Whole Foods is devoted to maintaining excellence in all aspects of the company's operations. Along with its founder and CEO John Mackey, Whole Foods has developed a reputation for social responsibility. Shoppers, for example, can be assured that the Halibut they purchase comes from Pacific fisheries that are certified as sustainable and well-managed.

Business Week reports that 78% of teenagers today believe that money is less important than personal fulfillment. They want to work for employers with a broad social purpose.

Among the values promoted by the firm is a commitment to employees, called "team members," whose fulfillment ranks with wages and benefits as basic rights of employment. One of the unique programs is a salary cap; no team member earns more in any year than 14 times the company-wide annual average. This is one of the reasons why *Fortune* magazine ranked Whole Foods #15 on its list of 100 Best Companies to Work For.

The *glass ceiling*, mentioned in Chapter 1 as an invisible barrier to career advancement, still exists and stereotypes may place a role in its perpetuation. Legitimate questions can be asked about *racial and ethnic stereotypes* and about the slow progress of minority managers into America's corporate mainstream.[14]

In the world of international business, only about 13 percent of American managers sent abroad on work assignments by their employers are women. Why? A Catalyst study of opportunities for women in global business points to *gender stereotypes* that place women at a disadvantage compared to men for these types of opportunities. The tendency is to assume women lack the ability and/or willingness to work abroad.[15] Although employment barriers caused by gender stereotypes are falling, women may still suffer from false impressions and biases imposed on them. Even everyday behavior may be misconstrued. Consider this example: "*He's* talking with co-workers." (*Interpretation:* He's discussing a new deal); " *She's* talking with co-workers." (*Interpretation:* She's gossiping).[16]

Ability stereotypes and *age stereotypes* also exist in the workplace. A physically or mentally challenged candidate may be overlooked by a recruiter even though her skills are perfect for the job. A talented older worker may not be promoted because a manager assumes older workers are cautious and tend to avoid risk. For those employers who break through the stereotypes, however, the rewards are there. A Conference Board survey of workers 50 and older, for example, found that 72 percent felt they could take on additional responsibilities, and two-thirds were interested in further training and development.[17]

Halo Effects

A **halo effect** occurs when one attribute is used to develop an overall impression of a person or situation. When meeting someone new, for example, the halo effect may cause one trait, such as a pleasant smile, to result in a positive first impression. By contrast, a particular hairstyle or manner of dressing may create a negative reaction. Halo effects cause the same problem for managers as do stereotypes; that is, individual differences become obscured. This is especially significant in performance evaluations. One factor, such as a person's punctuality, may become the "halo" for a positive overall performance assessment. Even though the general conclusion seems to make sense, it may or may not be true.

■ A **halo effect** occurs when one attribute is used to develop an overall impression of a person or situation.

Selective Perception

Selective perception is the tendency to single out for attention those aspects of a situation or person that reinforce or appear consistent with one's existing beliefs, values, or needs.[18] Information that makes us uncomfortable is screened out. What this often means in an organization is that people from different departments or functions—such as marketing and manufacturing—tend to see things from their own points of view and fail to recognize other points of view. Like the other perceptual distortions, selective perception can bias a manager's view of situations and individuals. One way to reduce its impact is to be sure to gather additional opinions from other people.

■ **Selective perception** is the tendency to define problems from one's own point of view.

Projection

Projection is a perceptual error that involves the assignment of personal attributes to other individuals. A classic projection error is to assume that other persons share our needs, desires, and values. Suppose, for example,

■ **Projection** is the assignment of personal attributes to other individuals.

that you enjoy a lot of responsibility and challenge in your work. Suppose, too, that you are the newly appointed manager for people whose jobs you consider dull and routine. You might move quickly to start a program of job enrichment to help them experience more responsibility and challenge. But, this may not be a good decision. Instead of designing jobs to best fit their needs, you have designed their jobs to fit *your needs*. In fact, your subordinates may be quite satisfied and productive doing jobs that, to you, seem routine. Projection errors can be controlled through self-awareness and a willingness to communicate and empathize with other persons, to try to see things through their eyes.

Impression Management

Richard Branson, CEO of the Virgin Group, may be one of the richest and most famous executives in the world. One of his early business accomplishments was the successful startup of Virgin Airlines, now a major competitor of British Airways (BA). In a memoir, the former head of BA, Lord King, said: "If Richard Branson had worn a shirt and tie instead of a goatee and jumper, I would not have underestimated him."[19] This is an example of how much our impressions count—both positive and negative. Knowing this, scholars today emphasize the importance of **impression management**, the systematic attempt to influence how others perceive us.[20]

■ **Impression management** is the systematic attempt to influence how others perceive us.

You might notice that we often practice impression management as a matter of routine in everyday life. We dress, talk, act, and surround ourselves with things that reinforce a desireable self-image and help to convey that same image to other persons. When well done, impression management can help us to advance in jobs and careers, form relationships with people we admire, and even create pathways to group memberships.

Some basic tactics of impression management are worth remembering: Dress in ways that convey positive appeal in certain circumstances—for example, knowing when to "dress up" and when to "dress down." Use words to flatter other people in ways that generate positive feelings toward you. Make eye contact and smile when engaged in conversations to create a personal bond. Display a high level of energy suggestive of work commitment and initiative.[21]

Learning Check 1

✓

Be sure you can ■ define the term perception ■ define and illustrate the concept of a psychological contract ■ explain the benefits of a healthy psychological contract ■ explain the concepts of attribution error and self-serving bias ■ define the terms stereotype, halo effect, selective perception, and projection ■ illustrate how each of these perceptual tendencies can adversely affect work behavior ■ explain impression management

---

PERSONALITY

"Of course he's a bad fit for the job; with a personality like that, he doesn't work well with others." "Put Laila on the project; her personality is perfect for the intensity that we expect from the team." These are examples of everyday conversations about people at work, with the key word being **personality**—the combination or overall profile of characteristics that makes one person unique from every other. The ways behaviors are shaped and influenced by individual personalities and variations among them are important managerial considerations in any work setting.

■ **Personality** is the profile of characteristics making a person unique from others.

BIG FIVE MODEL

One of the most popular ways to look at personalities is with a model of what psychologists call the *Big Five personality traits*.[22] The "Big Five" traits are:

- **Extraversion**—The degree to which someone is outgoing, sociable, and assertive. An extravert is comfortable and confident in interpersonal relationships; an introvert is more withdrawn and reserved.
- **Agreeableness**—The degree to which someone is good-natured, cooperative, and trusting. An agreeable person gets along well with others; a disagreeable person is a source of conflict and discomfort for others.
- **Conscientiousness**—The degree to which someone is responsible, dependable, and careful. A conscientious person focuses on what can be accomplished and meets commitments; a person who lacks conscientiousness is careless, often trying to do too much and failing, or doing little.
- **Emotional stability**—The degree to which someone is relaxed, secure, and unworried. A person who is emotionally stable is calm and confident; a person lacking in emotional stability is anxious, nervous, and tense.
- **Openness to experience**—The degree to which someone is curious, open to new ideas, and imaginative. An open person is broad-minded, receptive to new things, open to change; a person who lacks openness is narrow-minded, has few interests, and is resistant to change.

You can easily spot these personality traits in people with whom you work, study, and socialize. But don't forget that they also apply to you; others have impressions of your personality on these very same dimensions. In the social context of the workplace, managers must be able to understand and respond to these personality differences when making job assignments, building teams, and otherwise engaging in the daily give-and-take of work. Psychologists also use the Big Five to steer people in the direction of career choices that provide the best fit between personality and job or career.

ADDITIONAL PERSONALITY FACTORS

Figure 15.2 displays the Big Five along with five other personality dimensions that can also make a difference in individual behavior and how well people work together in organizations.[23]

Scholars have a strong interest in **locus of control,** recognizing that some people believe they are in control of their destinies, while others believe that what happens to them is beyond their control.[24] "Internals" are more self-confident and accept responsibility for their own actions, while "externals" are more prone to blame others and outside forces for what happens to

■ **Extraversion** is being outgoing, sociable, and assertive.

■ **Agreeableness** is being good-natured, cooperative, and trusting.

■ **Conscientiousness** is being responsible, dependable, and careful.

■ **Emotional stability** is being relaxed, secure, and unworried.

■ **Openness to experience** is being curious, receptive to new ideas, and imaginative.

■ **Locus of control** is the extent to which one believes that what happens is within one's control.

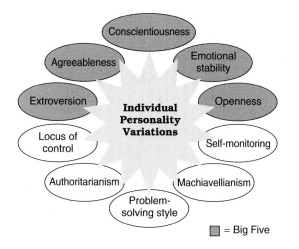

Figure 15.2 The Big Five and five more personality dimensions that influence human behavior at work.

them. Interestingly, research suggests that internals tend to be more satisfied and less alienated from their work.

■ **Authoritarianism** is the degree to which a person tends to defer to authority.

Authoritarianism is the degree to which a person defers to authority and accepts status differences.[25] Someone with an authoritarian personality would tend to act rigidly and be control-oriented when in a leadership capacity; this same person would be subservient and follow the rules when in a follower capacity. The tendency of people with authoritarian personalities to obey orders can be problematic if they follow higher-level directives to the point of acting unethically—or even illegally.

■ **Machiavellianism** describes the extent to which someone is emotionally detached and manipulative.

In his 16th-century book *The Prince*, Niccolo Machiavelli gained lasting fame for giving advice on how to use power to achieve personal goals.[26] **Machiavellianism** describes the extent to which someone is emotionally detached and manipulative in using power.[27] A person with a "high-Mach" personality is usually viewed as exploitative and unconcerned about others, with the guiding rule being that the end justifies the means. A person with a "low-Mach" personality, by contrast, would be deferential in allowing others to exert power over them.

■ **Problem-solving style** is the way people gather and evaluate information.

The psychologist Carl Jung pointed out that people display significant differences in **problem-solving styles,** or the way they gather and evaluate information for decision making.[28] Information is gathered by *sensation* (emphasizing details, facts, and routine) or by *intuition* (looking for the "big picture" and being willing to deal with various possibilities). Information is evaluated by *thinking* (using reason and analysis) or by *feeling* (responding to the feelings and desires of others). Because these differences are so extreme, it is not surprising that people approach their jobs in different ways and at times have difficulty working with one another.

Many organizations use the Myers-Briggs Type Indicator, a 100-question survey instrument, to measure personality variations in problem-solving styles. Employees are then trained to both understand their own styles and to learn how to work more productively with people having different styles. There

REAL ETHICS

Personality Testing

Dear . . . *your name goes here:*

I am very pleased to invite you to a second round of screening interviews with XYZ Corporation. Your on-campus session with our representative went very well, and we would like to consider you further for a full-time position.

Please telephone me (555-457-0748) to arrange a visit date. We will need a full day. The schedule will include several meetings with executives and your potential team members, as well as a round of personality tests.

Thank you again for your interest in XYZ Corp. I look forward to meeting you during the next step in our recruiting process.

Sincerely,

. . . signed . . .

Human Resource Director

Getting a letter like this is great news: a nice confirmation of your hard work and performance in college. You obviously made a good first impression. But have you thought about this "personality test" thing? What do

you know about them and how they are used for employment screening?

The U.S. Equal Employment Opportunity Commission says that personality tests can't have adverse impact on members of protected groups. A report in the *Wall Street Journal* advises that lawsuits can result when employers use personality tests that weren't specifically designed for hiring decisions. Some people might even consider their use an invasion of privacy.

Further Inquiry

So, will you take the tests at XWZ? Will you ask any questions about the specific tests used at XWZ when you telephone the human resource director? Is the fact that XYZ uses personality tests a positive or negative in terms of your likely fit with the firm?

are 16 alternative MBTI personality types that result from combinations of these four basic dimensions:[29]

Extraverted vs. introverted—whether a person tends toward being outgoing and sociable or shy and quiet.

Sensing vs. intuitive—whether a person tends to focus on details or the big picture in dealing with problems.

Thinking vs. feeling—whether a person tends to rely on logical or emotions in dealing with problems.

Judging vs. perceiving—whether a person prefers order and control or acts flexible and spontaneous.

Finally, **self-monitoring** reflects the degree to which someone is able to adjust and modify behavior in response to the situation and external factors.[30] A person high in self-monitoring tends to be a learner, comfortable with feedback, and both willing and able to change. Because high self-monitors are flexible in changing behavior from one situation to the next, it may be hard to get a clear reading on where they stand. A person low in self-monitoring, by contrast, is predictable, tending to act consistently regardless of circumstances.

■ **Self-monitoring** is the degree to which someone is able to adjust behavior in response to external factors.

Learning Check 2
Be sure you can ■ list the Big Five personality traits and give work-related examples of each ■ list five additional personality traits and give work-related examples for each

ATTITUDES

At one time Challis M. Lowe was one of only two African American women among the five highest-paid executives in over 400 U.S. companies surveyed by the woman's advocacy and research organization Catalyst.[31] She became executive vice president at Ryder System after a 25-year career that included several changes of employers and lots of stressors—working-mother guilt, a failed marriage, gender bias on the job, and an MBA degree earned part-time. Through it all she says: "I've never let being scared stop me from doing something. Just because you haven't done it before doesn't mean you shouldn't try." That, simply put, is what we would call a can-do attitude!

WHAT IS AN ATTITUDE?

An **attitude** is a predisposition to act in a certain way toward people and things in one's environment.[32] Challis Lowe, for example, was predisposed to take risks and embrace challenges. This "positive" attitude influenced her behavior when dealing with the inevitable problems, choices, and opportunities of work and career.

To fully understand attitudes, positive or negative, you must recognize their three components. First, the *cognitive component* reflects a belief or opinion. You might believe, for example, that your management course is very interesting. Second, the *affective or emotional component* of an attitude reflects a specific feeling. For example, you might feel very good about being a management major. Third, the *behavioral component* of an attitude reflects an intention to behave consistently with the belief and feeling. Using the same example again, you might say to yourself: "I am going to work hard and try to get an A in all my management courses."

■ An **attitude** is a predisposition to act in a certain way.

Importantly, the intentions reflected in an attitude may or may not be confirmed in one's actual behavior. Despite having a positive attitude and all good intentions, for example, the demands of family, friends, or leisure activities might use up the time you would otherwise need to devote to studying hard enough to get an A in your management courses. Thus, you might fail to live up to your own expectations.

■ **Cognitive dissonance** is discomfort felt when attitude and behavior are inconsistent.

The psychological concept of **cognitive dissonance** describes the discomfort felt when one's attitude and behavior are inconsistent.[33] For most people, dissonance is very uncomfortable and results in changing the attitude to fit the behavior ("Oh, I really don't like management that much anyway"), changing future behavior to fit the attitude (dropping out of intramural sports to get extra study time), or rationalizing to force the two to be compatible ("Management is an okay major, but being a manager also requires the experience I'm gaining in my extracurricular activities").

IMPORTANT WORK ATTITUDES

■ **Job satisfaction** is the degree to which an individual feels positive or negative about a job.

People hold attitudes about many things in the workplace—bosses, each other, tasks, policies, goals, and more. A comprehensive work attitude is **job satisfaction,** the degree to which an individual feels positive or negative about various aspects of work.[34] The evaluative points of reference in job satisfaction are such things as pay, co-workers, supervisor, work setting, advancement opportunities, and workload. In a poll of American workers, the *Wall Street Journal* asked this question: How satisfied are you with your current job? Interestingly, a majority were at least to some extent satisfied with their jobs. The responses were 37 percent completely satisfied, 47 percent somewhat satisfied, 10 percent somewhat dissatisfied, 4 percent completely dissatisfied, and 2 percent not sure.[35]

ISSUES & SITUATIONS

CEO Likability

Does someone have to be "likable" to succeed as a CEO?

These days the answer to this question seems to be yes more often than no. A *Business Week* article proclaims that "harsh is out, caring is in." It seems that CEOs are even hiring "executive coaches" to help them adopt more personable and friendly styles. If a CEO goes to a meeting and gets described as "cheerful," "charming," "humorous," "friendly," and "candid," she or he may be viewed as on the upswing. But if the CEO comes away perceived as "prickly," "impatient," "remote," "tough," "acrimonious," or even "ruthless," she or he may be seen as on the downhill slope.

Kim Cameron runs the Center for Positive Organizational Scholarship at the University of Michigan. He says that being positive as a CEO is good for one's career and for the organization's bottom line. He also says it's all about creating and unlocking positive energy in oneself and in others. He advises the interested executive to be an optimist and a team player, and not to be a pessimist. Further, Cameron advises executives to spend more time with others who have positive energy, helping unlock their performance and spreading their energy to others. An executive should avoid spending most of his or her time with low-energy problem workers.

Critical Response

This message about CEO likability and positiveness seems appealing: be likable and positive, and good things will follow. But is it too simple? Isn't there more to top executive and general managerial success than this? Does one have to be "charmer" to succeed in executive leadership? Do the introverts of the world have a chance at managerial success? The *Wall Street Journal* suggests there are many counter examples out there—Bill Gates, Warren Buffett, Charles Schwab, and Steven Spielberg among them. Brenda Barnes, CEO of Sarah Lee, is another. She says: "I've always been shy. People wouldn't call me that, but I am."

Closely related to job satisfaction are three other concepts. **Job involvement** is defined as the extent to which an individual is dedicated to a job. Someone with high job involvement psychologically identifies with her or his job, and, for example, would be expected to work beyond expectations to complete a special project. Such efforts that go "above and beyond the call of duty" represent **organizational citizenship behaviors**, extra things that people do that improve their job performance and otherwise help to better accomplish the work of the organization.[36] **Organizational commitment** is defined as the loyalty of an individual to the organization.

Individuals with a high organizational commitment identify strongly with the organization and take pride in considering themselves a member. A survey of 55,000 American workers by the Gallup Organization found evidence that worker attitudes reflecting job involvement and commitment correlated with higher profits for their employers. The four attitudes that counted most were believing one has the opportunity to do one's best every day, believing one's opinions count, believing fellow workers are committed to quality, and believing there is a direct connection between one's work and the company's mission.[37]

Job involvement is the extent to which an individual is dedicated to a job.

Organizational citizenship behaviors are things people do above and beyond basic job requirements.

Organizational commitment is the loyalty of an individual to the organization.

JOB SATISFACTION AND ITS OUTCOMES

Job satisfaction is known to influence *absenteeism*. Workers who are more satisfied with their jobs are absent less often than those who are dissatisfied. There is also a relationship between job satisfaction and *turnover*. Satisfied workers are more likely to remain with an organization and dissatisfied workers are more likely to quit their jobs.[38] Both of these findings are important. Absenteeism and turnover are costly in terms of the recruitment and training needed to replace workers, as well as in the productivity lost while new workers are learning how to perform up to expectations. For example, one study reports that changing retention rates up or down results in magnified changes to corporate earnings. The author warns about the adverse impact on corporate performance of declining employee loyalty and "revolving door" defections.[39]

When it comes to the job satisfaction and *job performance* relationship, things are more complicated.[40] Recent conclusions are that there is probably a modest link between job satisfaction and performance.[41] But we need to be careful before rushing off to conclude that making people happy on the job is a sure-fire way to improve their job performance. The reality is that some people will like their jobs, be very satisfied, and still not perform very well. That's just part of the complexity regarding individual differences. When you think of this, remember a sign that once hung in a tavern near a Ford plant in Michigan: "I spend 40 hours a week here, am I supposed to work too?"

There is also evidence that performance influences satisfaction; high performing workers are likely to feel satisfied. Once again, however, a realistic interpretation is probably best. Some people may get their work done and meet performance expectations while still not feeling good about it. In fact, given that job satisfaction is a good predictor of absenteeism and turnover, managers might be well advised to worry about losing highly productive but unhappy workers unless changes are made to increase their job satisfactions.

Finally, it is highly likely that job satisfaction and job performance influence one another. One of the more popular positions is that job performance followed by rewards that are valued and perceived as fair will likely create job satisfaction. This, in turn, will likely increase ones motivation to work harder to achieve high performance in the future.

KAFFEEKLATSCH

Typecasting

First Cup

"Don't you get a little tired of the old timers who think just because we're new hires that we don't know anything? I even heard one of them refer to us as the 'kids' the other day, and that really ticked me off. I think we should be taken for what we are worth; the issues should be talent, initiative, and job performance, and that's it. Our age has nothing to do with our work performance."

"Well, that's only part of it. You're talking about stereotypes. And by the way, you seem to be doing it, too, by calling them 'old timers.' But there's a related issue that worries me even more—being 'pigeonholed.' I helped expedite a service request for one of Sarah's clients the other day. Since then, everyone's calling me the 'expediter' and calling on me, help take care of their clients as well. Heck, I want my own clients to work with and don't be want to be viewed as just a back-up man. I've been 'typecast.' "

Studying the Grounds

■ Typecasting is a form of stereotyping. It puts people in work boxes and uses shortcut labels to describe them.

■ You can get typecast as someone who does a particular job well or poorly; you can get typecast for a helpful or disagreeable personality; you can get typecast as ethical or unethical, and much more.

■ Once typecast, it can be hard to break out; as soon as the label hits the office grapevines, it tends to stick and to travel.

Double Espresso

"Okay, I accept the hit on my choice of words. And I really think you're on to something with this pigeonhole phenomenon. It almost seems that once you get typecast, the chances are that your career will be pretty much narrowed from that point forward. Of course it might be a comfortable fit; no problem then. But suppose it isn't, or that you want more options. What can a person do?"

Your Turn

Experts say the first step in breaking free of typecasting is to recognize that you're in a pigeonhole to begin with. This means listening to comments made about you by friends; being sure to identify the labels used to describe you in office conversations; and making sure you understand what the boss really means when saying "you are really great at . . .". This may mean that you are not considered good at anything else.

Once you recognize the pigeonholing, it may well be time for impression management. Are you acting in ways that confirm the typecasting? What can you do differently to negate or broaden it?

Learning Check 3	*Be sure you can* ■ define the terms attitude, job satisfaction, job involvement, and organizational commitment ■ list the three components of an attitude ■ explain cognitive dissonance ■ explain the potential consequences of high and low job satisfaction ■ list and explain research findings on the satisfaction-performance relationship

---

EMOTIONS, MOODS, AND STRESS

One of the biggest corporate scandals of recent note involved a spy operation conducted at Hewlett-Packard to uncover what were considered to be confidential leaks by members of its Board of Directors. When trying to explain to the press the situation and resignation of Board Chair Patricia C. Dunn, CEO Mark V. Hurd called the actions "very disturbing" and said that "I could have and I should have" read in internal report on the matter that he had been given. *The Wall Street Journal* described him as speaking with "his voice shaking."[42]

Looking back on this situation, one might say that Hurd was emotional and angry that the incident was causing public humiliation for him and the company, that he was in a bad mood because of it, and that the whole episode was very stressful for him. For present purposes we have all wrapped up in one example a set of facets in individual psychology that are of growing interest to management scholars–emotions, moods, and stress.

EMOTIONS AND MOODS

We have already discussed *emotional intelligence* as both an important human skill for managers (Chapter 1) and an important consideration in one's personal leadership development (Chapter 13). Danield Goleman defines "EI" as the "ability to manage ourselves and our relationships effectively,"[43] But what is an emotion and how does it influence our behavior, positively and negatively?

An **emotion** is a strong feeling directed toward someone or something. For example, you might feel positive emotion or elation when an instructor congratulates you on a fine class presentation; you might feel negative emotion or anger when an instructor criticizes you in front of the class. In both cases the object of your emotion is the instructor, but in each case the impact of the instructor's behavior on your feelings is quite different. And your behavior in response to the aroused emotions is likely to differ as well—perhaps breaking into a wide smile with the compliment, or making a nasty comment in response to the criticism. Goleman's point with EI is that we perform better in such situations when we are good at recognizing and dealing with emotions in ourselves and others. In other words, EI allows us to avoid having emotions "get the better of us."

> ■ **Emotions** are strong feelings directed toward someone or something.

Whereas emotions tend to be short-term and clearly targeted, **moods** are different but equally significant. They are more generalized positive and negative feelings or states of mind that may persist for some time. Everyone seems to have occasional moods, and we each know the full range of possibilities they represent. How often do you wake up in the morning and feel excited, refreshed and just happy, or feel low, depressed and generally unhappy? And what are the consequences of these different moods for your behavior with friends and family, and at work or school? Researchers are increasingly interested in the influence of emotions and moods on workplace behaviors.[44] For example, the Research Brief in Chapter 13 highlighted how positive emotions of leaders can be "contagious," causing followers to display more positive moods and both be more attracted to the leaders and rate the leaders more highly.[45]

> ■ **Moods** are generalized positive and negative feelings or states on mind.

STRESS

Closely aligned with a person's emotions and moods is **stress,** a state of tension experienced by individuals facing extraordinary demands, constraints, or opportunities.[46] Any look toward your future work career would be incomplete without considering stress as a challenge that you are sure to encounter along the way—and a challenge you must be prepared to help others learn to deal with. In his book *The Future of Success*, for example, Robert Reich says that even though the new economy gives us much to celebrate, its "rewards are coming at the price of lives that are more frenzied, less secure, more economically divergent, more socially stratified."[47] Consider also this statement by a psychologist who worked with top-level managers having alcohol abuse problems: "All executives deal with stress. They wouldn't be executives if they didn't. Some handle it well, others handle it poorly."[48]

> ■ **Stress** is a state of tension experienced by individuals facing extraordinary demands, constraints, or opportunities.

Stressors are things that cause stress. Whether they originate directly from a change environment, other aspects of the work setting, or in personal and nonwork situations, stressors can influence our attitudes, emotions and moods, behavior, job performance, and even health.

> ■ A **stressor** is anything that causes stress.

Work factors have an obvious potential to create job stress. In fact, some 34 percent of workers in one survey said that their jobs were so stressful they were thinking of quitting.[49] We often experience such stress from long hours of work, excessive e-mails, unrealistic work deadlines, difficult bosses or co-workers, unwelcome or unfamiliar work, and unrelenting change. It is also associated with excessively high or low task demands, role conflicts or ambiguities, poor interpersonal relations, or career progress that is too slow or too fast. Two of the common work-related stress syndromes are (1) *set up to fail*—where the performance expectations are impossible or the support is totally inadequate to the task; and (2) *mistaken identity*—where the individual ends up in a job that doesn't at all match talents or that he or she simply doesn't like.[50]

■ A **Type A personality** is a person oriented toward extreme achievement, impatience, and perfectionism.

A variety of *personal factors* are also sources of potential stress for people at work. A **Type A personality** is high in achievement orientation, impatience, and perfectionism. Type A persons are likely to bring stress on themselves, even in situations others may find relatively stress free. The stressful behavior patterns of *Type A personalities* include:[51]

- Always moving, walking, and eating rapidly.
- Acting impatiently, hurrying others, disliking waiting.
- Doing, or trying to do, several things at once.
- Feeling guilty when relaxing.

RESEARCH BRIEF

Business students more satisfied with their lives overall are higher performing

Wondering if "a happy student is a high performing student," Joseph C. Rode, Marne L. Arthaud-Day, Christine H. Mooney, Janet P. Near, Timothy T. Baldwin, William H. Bommer, and Robert S. Rubin hypothesized that satisfaction with both "life and student domains" would, along with cognitive abilities, have a positive influence on student academic performance. They created a predictive model from what they called "an integrative life" perspective, meaning that a person's performance is influenced by his or her overall state of life satisfaction.

A sample of 673 business students completed satisfaction and IQ questionnaires, and their academic performance was measured by self-reported GPAs and performance on a 3-hour simulation exercise. The findings confirmed the expected relationships between students' leisure and family satisfaction and overall life satisfaction. Also confirmed were links between both life satisfaction and IQ scores, and self-reported GPA and simulation performance. Expected relationships between students' university and housing satisfaction and overall life satisfaction proved not to be significant.

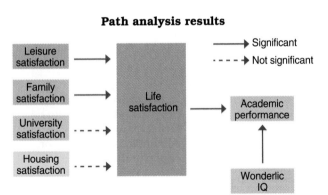

Path analysis results

Rode, et al. point out that "it is time to more fully acknowledge that college students also live 'integrated lives' and are heavily influenced by the milieu that surrounds them."

QUESTIONS & APPLICATIONS

Does your everyday experience as a student support these results or contradict them? Build a model that describes how you would predict student academic performance, not limiting yourself to directions used in this study. If it is true that students' academic performance is influenced by overall life satisfaction, what does this mean to an instructor? To a college administrator? Now that we know it may be important, what can we do about it? How could any lessons of this study carry over to work situations?

Reference: Joseph C. Rode, Marne L. Arthaud-Day, Christine H. Mooney, Janet P. Near, Timothy T. Baldwin, William H. Bommer, and Robert S. Rubin, "Life Satisfaction and Student Performance, *Academy of Management Learning & Education*, vol. 4 (2005), pp. 421–433.

- Trying to schedule more in less time.
- Using nervous gestures such as a clenched fist.
- Hurrying or interrupting the speech of others.

Also, stress from *non-work factors* can have spillover effects that affect people at work. Stressful life situations, including such things as family events (e.g., the birth of a new child), economics (e.g., a sudden loss of extra income), and personal affairs (e.g., a preoccupation with a bad relationship), are often sources of emotional strain. Depending on the individual and his or her ability to deal with them, preoccupation with such situations can affect one's work and add to the stress of work-life conflicts.

CONSEQUENCES OF STRESS

The discussion of stress so far may give the impression that it always acts as a negative influence on our lives. But it actually has two faces—one constructive and one destructive.[52] Consider the analogy of a violin.[53] When a violin string is too loose, the sound produced by even the most skilled player is weak and raspy. When the string is too tight, however, the sound gets shrill and the string might even snap. But when the tension on the string is just right, neither too loose or too tight, a most beautiful sound is created. With just enough stress, in other words, performance is optimized.

The same argument tends to hold in the workplace. **Constructive stress**, sometimes called *eustress*, acts in a positive way for the individual and/or the organization. It occurs in moderation and proves energizing and performance enhancing.[54] The stress is sufficient to encourage increased effort, stimulate creativity, and enhance diligence in one's work while not overwhelming the individual and causing negative outcomes. Individuals with a Type A personality, for example, are likely to work long hours and to be less satisfied with poor performance. For them, challenging task demands imposed by a supervisor may elicit higher levels of task accomplishment. Even non-work stressors such as new family responsibilities may cause them to work harder in anticipation of greater financial rewards.

Just like tuning the violin string, however, achieving the right balance of stress for each person and situation is difficult. **Destructive stress,** or *distress*, is dysfunctional. It occurs as intense or long-term stress that, as shown in *Figure 15.3*, overloads and breaks down a person's physical and mental systems.

Destructive stress can lead to **job burnout**—a form of physical and mental exhaustion that can be incapacitating both personally and with respect to one's work. Productivity suffers when people react to very intense stress through turnover, absenteeism, errors, accidents, dissatisfaction, and reduced performance. Today, there is also increased concern for another potential stress

■ **Constructive stress** acts in a positive way to increase effort, stimulate creativity, and encourage diligence in one's work.

■ **Destructive stress** impairs the performance of an individual.

■ **Job burnout** is physical and mental exhaustion from work stress.

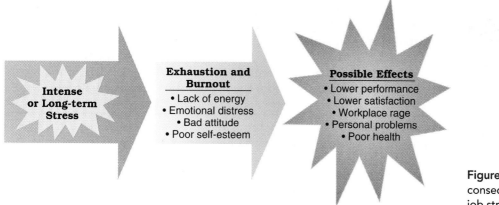

Figure 15.3 Potential negative consequences of a destructive job stress–burnout cycle.

■ **Workplace rage** is aggressive behavior toward co-workers or the work setting.

byproduct, **workplace rage**—overtly aggressive behavior toward co-workers and the work setting in general. Lost tempers are common examples; the unfortunate extremes are tragedies that result in physical harm to others.[55]

Medical research is concerned that too much stress can reduce resistance to disease and increase the likelihood of physical and/or mental illness. It may contribute to health problems such as hypertension, ulcers, substance abuse, overeating, depression, and muscle aches, among others.[56]

Also important to understand is that excessive work stress can have *spillover effects* into one's personal life. A study of dual-career couples found that one partner's work experiences can have psychological consequences for the other; as one's work stress increases, the partner is likely to experience stress, too.[57] The bottom line is that any stress we experience at work is contagious; it can affect one's spouse, family, and friends. The wife of a company controller, for example, went through a time when her husband was stressed by a boss who was overly critical. "He was angry, really angry when he came home," she says. His mood affected her and their young child, and created what she called "one of the worst times in our seven-year marriage."[58]

STRESS MANAGEMENT

The best stress management strategy is to prevent it from reaching excessive levels in the first place. Stressors emerging from personal and nonwork factors can be identified so that action can be taken to prevent them or minimize their negative consequences. Family difficulties, for example, may be relieved by a change in work schedule, or the anxiety they cause may be reduced by an understanding supervisor. Also, people sometimes need help in combating the tendency toward "working too much." Reminders from bosses, co-workers, and friends not to forgo vacations or not to work excessive overtime can be very helpful.

■ **Personal wellness** is the pursuit of one's full potential through a personal health-promotion program.

Among work factors with potential to cause excessive stress are role ambiguities, conflicts, and overloads. They can sometimes be dealt with by *role clarification* through a management-by-objectives approach. By bringing together the communication between supervisors and subordinates, MBO offers an opportunity both to spot stressors and to take action to reduce or eliminate them. Job redesign can also be helpful when there is a poor fit between individual abilities and job demands.

Personal wellness is a term used to describe the pursuit of one's physical and mental potential through a personal health-promotion program. This form of preventative stress management recognizes the individual's responsibility to enhance his or her personal health through a disciplined approach to such things as smoking, alcohol use, diet, exercise, and physical fitness.

The essence of personal wellness is a lifestyle that reflects a true commitment to health. And it makes a great deal of sense. Those who aggressively maintain their personal wellness are better prepared to deal with the inevitable stresses of work, work-life conflicts, and organizational changes. Many employers now sponsor wellness programs that help employees with such things as smoking control, health risk appraisals, back care, stress management, exercise/physical fitness, nutrition education, high blood pressure control, and weight control. The expectations are that investments in wellness programs benefit both the organization and its employees.

| **Learning Check 4** | *Be sure you can* ■ define the terms emotion, mood and stress ■ explain how emotions and moods influence behavior ■ identify the common stressors found in work and in personal life ■ describe a person with a Type A personality ■ differentiate constructive and destructive stress ■ discuss personal wellness as a stress management strategy |

CHAPTER 15 STUDY GUIDE

STUDY QUESTIONS SUMMARY

1 How does perception influence behavior?

- Perception acts as a filter through which all communication passes as it travels from one person to the next.
- Because people tend to perceive things differently, the same situation may be interpreted and responded to differently by different people.
- A healthy psychological contract occurs when an individual perceives a fair balance between their work contributions—such as time and effort, and inducements received—such as pay and respect.
- Fundamental attribution error occurs when we blame others for performance problems while excluding possible external causes; self-serving bias occurs when, in judging our own performance. we take personal credit for successes and blame failures on external factors.
- Stereotypes, projections, halo effects, and selective perception can distort perceptions and result in errors as people communicate and relate with one another.

2 What should we know about personalities in the workplace?

- Personality is a set of traits and characteristics that cause people to behave in unique ways.
- The personality factors in the Big Five model are extraversion, agreeableness, conscientiousness, emotional stability, and openness to experience.
- Additional personality dimensions of special work significance are locus of control, authoritarianism, Machiavellianism, problem-solving style, and behavioral self-monitoring.

3 How do attitudes influence individual behavior?

- An attitude is a predisposition to respond in a certain way to people and things.

- Cognitive dissonance occurs when a person's attitude and behavior are inconsistent.
- Job satisfaction is an important work attitude, reflecting a person's evaluation of the job, co-workers, and other aspects of the work setting.
- Job satisfaction influences work attendance and turnover, and is related to other attitudes such as job involvement and organizational commitment.
- Three possible explanations for the job satisfaction and performance relationship are: satisfaction causes performance, performance causes satisfaction, and rewards cause both performance and satisfaction.

4 What are the dynamics of emotions, moods, and stress?

- Emotions are strong feelings directed at someone or something, and that influence behavior often with intensity and for short periods of time.
- Moods are generalized positive or negative states of mind that can be persistent influences on one's behavior.
- Stress occurs as the tension accompanying extraordinary demands, constraints, or opportunities.
- Stress can be destructive or constructive; a moderate level of stress typically has a positive impact on performance.
- Stressors are found in a variety of work, personal, and non-work situations.
- For some people, having a Type A personality creates stress as a result of continuous feelings of impatience and pressure.
- Stress can be effectively managed through both prevention and coping strategies, including a commitment to personal wellness.

KEY TERMS REVIEW

SELF-TEST 15

MULTIPLE-CHOICE QUESTIONS:

1. In the psychological contract, security is considered a/an _____ while loyalty is considered a/an _____.
   (a) satisfier factor, hygiene factor (b) intrinsic reward, extrinsic reward (c) inducement, contribution (d) attitude, personality trait

2. Self-serving bias is a form of attribution error that involves _____.
   (a) blaming yourself for problems caused by others (b) blaming the environment for problems you caused (c) poor emotional intelligence (d) authoritarianism

3. If a new team leader changes job designs for persons on her work team mainly "because I would prefer to work the new way rather than the old," the chances are that she is committing a perceptual error known as _____.
   (a) halo effect (b) stereotype (c) selective perception (d) projection

4. If a manager allows one characteristic of person, say a pleasant personality, to bias performance ratings of that individual overall, the manager is falling prey to a perceptual distortion known as _____.
   (a) halo effect (b) stereotype (c) selective perception (d) projection

5. Use of special dress, manners, gestures, and vocabulary words when meeting a prospective employer in a job interview are all examples of how people use _____ in daily life.
   (a) projection (b) selective perception (c) impression management (d) self-serving bias

6. A person with a/an _____ personality would most likely act unemotionally and manipulatively when trying to influence others to achieve personal goals.
   (a) extraverted (b) sensation-thinking (c) self-monitoring (d) Machiavellian

7. When a person tends to believe that he or she has little influence over things that happen in life, this indicates a _____ personality.
   (a) low emotional stability (b) external locus of control (c) high self monitoring (d) intuitive-thinker

8. Among the Big Five personality traits, _____ indicates someone who is responsible, dependable, and careful with respect to tasks.
   (a) authoritarianism (b) agreeableness (c) conscientiousness (d) emotional stability

9. The _____ component of an attitude is what indicates a person's belief about something, while the _____ component indicates a specific positive or negative feeling about it.
   (a) cognitive, affective (b) emotional, affective (c) cognitive, attributional (d) behavioral, attributional

10. The term used to describe the discomfort someone feels when his or her behavior is inconsistent with an expressed attitude is _____.
    (a) alienation (b) cognitive dissonance (c) job dissatisfaction (d) person-job imbalance

11. Job satisfaction is known from research to be a reasonable predictor of _____.
    (a) job performance (b) job burnout (c) conscientiousness (d) absenteeism

12. In terms of individual psychology, a/an _____ represents a rather intense but short-lived feeling about a person or a situation, while a/an _____ describes a more generalized positive or negative state of mind.
    (a) stressor, role ambiguity (b) external locus of control, internal locus of control (c) self-serving bias, halo effect (d) emotion, mood

13. Through _____, the stress people experience in their personal lives can create problems for them at work, and the stress experienced at work can create problems for their personal lives.
    (a) eustress (b) self-monitoring (c) spillover effects (d) selective perception

14. As a stress management strategy, MBO would be especially useful in helping people deal with _____.
    (a) role conflicts (b) workplace rage (c) personal wellness (d) resistance to change

15. At what level is stress most likely functional or positive in terms of impact on individual performance?
    (a) zero (b) low (c) moderate (d) high

SHORT-RESPONSE QUESTIONS:

16. What is a healthy psychological contract?

17. What is the difference between self-serving bias and fundamental attribution error?

18. Which three of the Big Five personality traits do you believe most affect how well people work together in organizations, and why?

19. Why is it important for a manager to understand the Type A personality?

APPLICATION QUESTION:

20. When Scott Tweedy picked up a magazine article on how to manage health care workers, he was pleased to find some advice. Scott was concerned about poor or mediocre performance on the part of several respiratory therapists in his clinic. The author of the article said that the "best way to improve performance is to make your workers happy." Scott was glad to have read this and made a pledge to himself to start doing a much better job of making workers happy. But should Scott follow this advice? What do we know about the relationship between job satisfaction and performance, and how can this apply to the performance problems at Scott's clinic?

CHAPTER 15 APPLICATIONS

CASE 15

MySpace: The Kids Are Online

Arriving in 2003 and quickly taking charge of the growing social networking movement, MySpace.com has earned the rapt attention of parents, marketers, and a sizeable portion of 14- to 34-year-old Internet users. Why are all eyes on MySpace? And how long will it last?

A profound shift in youth behavior has occurred. Irreversibly transformative, it has affected millions under the age of 25 and continues to change the lives of more every day. They disappear for hours at a time, locked away in bedrooms, dorm rooms, or home offices. And concerned friends and family wonder what could be causing this extreme form of self-imposed isolation.

Behind it all are two young Internet impresarios from California. Tom Anderson and Chris DeWolfe have transformed the time-honored youth ritual of spending hours on the phone. Their social networking Web site, MySpace.com, has quickly become the hottest place on the Internet for teens and young adults to define themselves and satisfy their curiosity about everyone else.

Creative Chaos

Most MySpace users are between the ages of 14 and 34. And, according to MySpace SVP Shawn Gold, their ranks are growing by 2 million a week.[59] They frequently spend hours a day navigating this tangled web of interpersonal connectivity: Users create personal pages on which they post pictures and songs, list their vital stats and likes/dislikes, and send instant messages to other users.

For some it's just a passing fancy; others fall deeper under the MySpace Spell, describing it as "an addiction" and claiming they "get sucked in."

"I'm into every day for like two hours at a minimum," said 18-year-old Shanda Edstrom. "It's just crazy."[60]

Crazy like a fox, maybe. In only two years, MySpace's membership has skyrocketed beyond 84 million members, having 48 million unique visitors a month in the U.S. alone.[61] Founders DeWolfe and Anderson are still president and CEO, respectively, even after it was bought out for $580 million in 2005 by media mogul Rupert Murdoch's News Corporation. Retaining that degree of control is rated in dot-com buyouts, but News corporation has allowed the two to maintain creative control of their effervescent brand.[62]

This creative control, marked by the outward appearance of chaos, has made MySpace a hit. Straying from the template-based page designs that typify other blogging or social networking sites, MySpace gives users the freedom to use whatever colors, fonts, or images they like (though profanity and nudity are banned), no matter how much the results might make your average Web designer cringe.

This free-expression philosophy complements DeWolfe and Anderson's initial strategy: to make MySpace a place where bands sing for free. R.E.M., the Black Eyed Peas, Weezer, and Billy Corgan have all hosted "listening parties," streaming new albums exclusively to users well before the street release date. To date, there are approximately 1.8 million music profiles on MySpace.[63]

And though MySpace has grown well beyond its initial scope, the strategy proves that its founders know the compulsions of their users. According to the Pew Internet & American Life Project, 87 percent of 12- to 17-year-olds use the Internet. And 15- to 18-year-olds average nearly 6.5 hours a day watching TV, playing video games, and surfing the Web, according to a recent Kaiser Family Foundation survey. How does MySpace size up? According to NetNielsen, the site reaches 51% of 13–17-year-olds who are online.[64]

Looking for Friends in All the New Places

MySpace inhabitants are tech-savvy, but they're also curious types. The social networking aspect of MySpace allows users to browse pages of their friends, learn more (and freely communicate with) about friends of their friends, and search out other users with similar backgrounds or interests. Considering the site's primitive design, the search interface is surprisingly complex, giving users a myriad of ways to peruse the multitudes. Offer this technology to Internet-wise curiosity-seekers with time on their hands, and it's easy to see why MySpace users speak of their activity as an addiction.

MySpace is not alone in offering such services to the young and socially mobile. Both Friendster, a social networking predecessor to MySpace, and Facebook, a competitor intended exclusively for high school and college students, allow users to see who their friends are friends with, and to browse for others with shared qualities.

As with Friendster, you can attribute some of MySpace's success—and addictive properties—to the thrill of the chase. Both services allow visitors to a page to see how many "friends" a person has collected. Many users, young or otherwise, feel their merit is decided by their prowess in acquisition. Once upon a time, yearbook signatures, baseball cards, or rare 45s were symbols of social potency. Now everybody has to have friends, which is ironic, considering that cruising social networking sites is usually a solo endeavor.

Some of it you can chalk up to kids just being kids. "Teens are narcissistic and exhibitionist," said Anastasia Goodstein, publisher of the online Genera-

tion Y news and commentary site Ypulse. "For teens, especially, who are going through this stage where they're constantly looking for that affirmation and validation and response for everything they are, it's just addictive."[65]

According to James Katz, professor of communications at Rutgers University, MySpace "is the kind of place that in earlier generations, kids dreamed about—where they could go and be with their friends, meet new people with similar tastes and find out what's cool, what's hot and what's not."[66]

Turning the Corner on a Bigger, Better Brand

Clearly, what's hot is the MySpace business model. Having derived profits largely from advertising to this point, MySpace is finally in a position to extend its brand and develop a range of products and services. The site recently teamed with music label Interscope to create MySpace Records, an imprint intended to release several albums a year from bands first found on its site.[67]

And for the future, DeWolfe and Anderson are planning big. They plan to extend the brand offline by widening services to include local event planning, ultimately including festivals and large-scale concerts. Before long, MySpace is planning to reach satellite radio, mobile devices, and even the big screen; MySpace Films (with a little help from News Corporation) hopes to back a few independent films a year and draw big buzz by flooding the premieres with MySpace denizens.[68] "It costs us nothing to get millions of MySpace users to show up at event," noted Dewolfe.[69]

And as the brand eventually extends into a larger multimedia portal, as planned, MySpace will find eager competition from the big players. Yahoo!, Microsoft, and AOL all have social networking projects in development. Yahoo! has more than 112 million registered users, and MSN has more than 88 million. By starting with such tremendous membership numbers, the existing portals feel they've got a fighting chance.[70]

"Don't I Know You From Somewhere?"

This assumes, of course, that users will stick around for the long term. Some privacy and safety advocates worry that in the largely no-rules environment of MySpace and other similar sites, the temptation exists to present oneself in a way that future employers, coworkers, or even romantic prospects may find less than appealing.

Web archiving makes it relatively easy for interested parties to dig up outdated personal Web pages and posting them, even if you've taken them off the site. "If you've been out there talking about yourself and posting photos for 10 years, it can have an impact on your job hunt," said Pam Dixon, executive director of the World Privacy Forum. She notes that HR departments already routinely Google candidates. "To say that it won't affect employment prospects is naive."[71]

Fad or Forever?

In just a short time, MySpace has skyrocketed to incredible heights of cultural popularity because of its ease of use, customizability, and seeming omnipresence among teens. But is its use merely a trend—like the popularity AOL once enjoyed—or can MySpace continue to develop its business model to keep both users and investors satisfied?

REVIEW QUESTIONS

1. Is there a "psychological contract" between MySpace users and the company?

2. What role do issues of emotions and moods play in the success of MySpace?

3. Many schools are instituting programs to communicate to their students that they should be discreet about the personal details they post to their MySpace profile. Review the MySpace of several of your friends or classmates. Does it appear to you as if college students are self-monitoring the material they post to their pages?

TEAM PROJECT

Job Satisfaction Around the World

A Gallup poll finds that only 30% of people report having a "best friend" at work. But it also shows that when people have close friends at work their job satisfaction is some 50% higher than for those that don't.

Question: Are workers more satisfied in the United States or elsewhere in the world?

Research Directions:

■ Gather together recent reports on job satisfaction, its sources and consequences, among workers in the United States.

■ Gather similar data regarding workers in other countries, such as Canada, United Kingdom, Germany, Japan, and India.

■ Compare the job satisfaction data across countries to answer the project question.

■ Consider going further by researching how the various countries compare on working conditions, labor laws, and related matters. Use this information to add context to your job satisfaction findings.

PERSONAL MANAGEMENT

Problem-Solving Style

Your **PROBLEM-SOLVING STYLE** is likely to differ from those of people you study and work with. It is important to understand your style and learn about problems that can occur as styles clash. Which of the four master problem-solving styles shown here best describes you?

■ *Sensation-Thinker:* STs take a realistic approach to problem solving, preferring "facts," clear goals, and certainty.

■ *Intuitive-Thinker:* NTs are comfortable with abstraction and unstructured situations, tending to be idealistic and to avoid details.

■ *Intuitive-Feeler:* NFs are insightful, like to deal with broad issues, and value flexibility and human relationships.

■ *Sensation-Feeler:* SFs emphasize analysis using facts, while being open communicators and respectful of feelings and values.

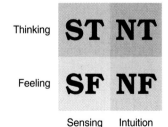

	Thinking	Feeling
	ST **NT**	
	SF **NF**	

Sensing   Intuition

Building the Brand Called "You"   Go to the Management Learning Workbook and complete Self-Assessment #25. Use the results to plot your style on the graph. Ask someone with whom you work to do the same; try to pick someone who you believe may have a different personality. Compare the two graphs and talk together about the implications for how well you work together.

NEXT STEPS: MANAGEMENT LEARNING WORKBOOK

Self-Assessments
- Assertiveness (#12)
- Are You Cosmopolitan? (#18)
- Cognitive Style (#25)
- Internal/External Control (#26)

Experiential Exercises
- What Do You Value in Work? (#7)
- Work vs. Family (#17)
- Why Do We Work? (#21)

Teams and Teamwork

16

Working Together, Falling Apart

Synergy is one of the most elusive of workplace conditions. It's easy to talk about but much harder to achieve. In the absence of synergy, frustration often besets workers. So how do successful companies achieve synergy? And is frustration always a bad thing?

Ask just about any managers whether their employees work well together, and unless you've caught them in an extraordinarily candid moment, the reply will most likely be yes.

But fewer managers could truthfully say that their employees are working in *synergy*—that is, working to produce a combined effect greater than the sum of their separate effects. Companies that accomplish this feat of synchronicity are often described as "working with one mind."

What distinguishes a group whose divisions work in synergy? For one, it's the way that interrelated employees or teams work with one another to achieve common goals. A vivid example of this would be a NASCAR pit crew. When a driver pulls in for a pit stop, multiple teams must jump in to perform their tasks flawlessly and in perfect order and unison. The advantage of a fraction of a

What *They* Think

"This is the time for women to start being the leaders of organizations and helping organizations to become more nurturing and effective environments."
Connie Gersick, UCLA's Women's Leadership Institute.

SYNERGY: *"This conglomerate concept doesn't work, there is no synergy—just a bunch of people spending a large amount of money that should be spent on running different companies well."*
Carl Icahn, corporate raider and Blockbuster Inc. director.

FRUSTRATION: *"We started the company out of frustration with the employer that we had because we were building great stuff and there was no way that this stuff was ever going to get into the hands of the people who could use it."*
John Warnock, co-founder of Adobe Systems.

second can be crucial to a NASCAR driver, so pit teams must be well trained and rehearsed to efficiently perform their complex, interwoven tasks.

Timing is also crucial to achieving synergy. In manufacturing assembly lines, each line worker must perform his or her task exactly when needed, or else the whole line slows down. Manufacturing operations thrive on continual production, so an environment where work constantly stops to allow workers to wait for or catch up to one another cannot succeed competitively.

When companies are not working in the pursuit of common goals, or when the needs of individuals are not being met, workers experience *frustration* in lieu of synergy. Frustration can be positive when it indicates the need for change, but unless either management is attuned to this or employees are empowered to fix their own problems, it is unlikely that frustration would lead to productivity or improvement.

In the 1970s and 1980s, when women started entering companies' executive teams in greater numbers, corporations found that many women were leaving the workforce to have children and not returning to work, or ended up working in other industries. This produced mutual frustration: Women executives were frustrated because they felt the rigorous demands of corporate life forced them to choose between motherhood and a career, and corporations were frustrated because they felt they were losing the significant investment of time and energy they put into these employees.

Wisely, some companies began to add flexibility to the job description and benefits of female executives to find a happy medium where mothers could keep their jobs and still feel connected to their growing children. Once taken for granted, hundreds of companies now offer such perks as flex-time and in-house day-care.

"Women who are now ripe for senior positions have spent their careers fitting themselves into organizations designed by and for men with wives," said Connie Gersick of UCLA's Women's Leadership Institute. "This is the time for women to start being the leaders of organizations and helping organizations to become more nurturing and effective environments."

Federated Department Stores encourages women to work part-time and still keep their management positions. And Procter & Gamble has an innovative "phase-back" plan that allows mothers to work a reduced schedule but still be connected to their job and the office.[1]

The Numbers

American Management Association Ranks Most Frustrating Work Circumstances

1. more tasks and responsibilities than time to do them
2. time spent on correspondence and in meetings
3. dealing with others' incompetence
4. poor communication from top management
5. lack of recognition for personal accomplishments

Quick Facts

* Racing pit crew members can earn more than $100,000.[2]
* Kurt Busch's team won the National Pit Crew Championship in 2006 with a mistake-free 16.342 second stop.[3]
* NASCAR pit crews now strive for sub-13-second pit stops, almost half the time it took a world-class team to simply change two tires in 1967.[4]
* To purchase an advertiser's decal logo for a NASCAR vehicle, the racing organization charges $200,000 for a 3 × 5 inch decal. That equals $13,333 per square inch.[5]

What do *you* think?

1. What does it take for employee frustration to create positive organizational change?
2. Why do some managers of fast-food restaurants seem to get synergy from their crews, while others do not?

Teams and Teamwork			
Study Question 1 **Teams in Organizations**	**Study Question 2** **Trends in the Use of Teams**	**Study Question 3** **How Teams Work**	**Study Question 4** **Decision Making in Teams**
■ What is teamwork? ■ Teamwork pros Teamwork cons ■ Meetings, meetings, meetings ■ Formal and informal groups	■ Committees, project teams, task forces ■ Cross-functional teams ■ Virtual teams ■ Self-managing teams	■ Team effectiveness ■ Stages of development ■ Norms and cohesiveness ■ Task and maintenance needs ■ Communication networks ■ Team building	■ How groups make decisions ■ Assets and liabilities of group decisions ■ Groupthink ■ Creativity in team decision making
Learning Check 1	**Learning Check 2**	**Learning Check 3**	**Learning Check 4**

People have the need to work in teams. There is a desire to work with others and enjoy the benefits of your work and your successes together. These . . . satisfactions are as important today as they have ever been.
Andy Grove, former Chairman of Intel Inc.

I learned a long time ago that in team sports or in business, a group working together can always defeat a team of individuals even if the individuals, by themselves, are better than your team . . . If you're going to empower people and you don't have teamwork, you're dead.
John Chambers, CEO of Cisco Systems

As these opening quotations suggest, the new workplace is rich in teams and teamwork.[6] But even so, we have to admit that just the words *"group"* and *"team"* elicit both positive and negative reactions in the minds of many people. Although it is said that "two heads are better than one," we are also warned that "too many cooks spoil the broth." The true skeptic can be heard to say: "A camel is a horse put together by a committee." Against this somewhat humorous background lies a most important point. Teams are both rich in performance potential and very complex in the way they work.[7] Consider, too, these realities. Many people prefer to work in teams rather than independently; over 60 percent of the average worker's time is spent in a team environment; even though most workers spend at least some time in teams, less than half receive training in group dynamics.[8]

TEAMS IN ORGANIZATIONS

Most tasks in organizations are well beyond the capabilities of individuals alone. Managerial success is always earned in substantial part through success at mobilizing, leading, and supporting people as they work together in groups. The new organizational designs and cultures require it, as does any true commitment to empowerment and employee involvement.[9] The question for managers, and the guiding theme of this chapter, thus becomes: How do we make sure that teams and teamwork are utilized to everyone's best advantage?

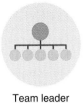
Team leader

Network facilitator

Helpful participant

External coach

How managers get involved with teams and teamwork

Figure 16.1 Team and teamwork roles for managers.

WHAT IS TEAMWORK?

A **team** is a small group of people with complementary skills, who work together to accomplish shared goals while holding themselves mutually accountable for performance results.[10] **Teamwork** is the process of people working together to accomplish these goals. And as shown in *Figure 16.1*, managers must perform at least four important roles in order to fully master the challenges of teams and teamwork. These roles, along with examples, are (1) *team leader* or *supervisor*—serving as the appointed head of a team or work unit; (2) *facilitator*—serving as the peer leader and networking hub for a special task force; (3) *participant*—serving as a helpful contributing member of a project team; and (4) *coach*—serving as the external convenor or sponsor of a problem-solving team staffed by others.

▪ A **team** is a collection of people who regularly interact to pursue common goals.

▪ **Teamwork** is the process of people actively working together to accomplish common goals.

TEAMWORK PROS

Teamwork in our society makes available everything from aircraft to the Internet to music videos to, as featured in the Topic Chapter opener, a really successful pit stops for the leader of a NASCAR race. It all happens because of **synergy**, the creation of a whole that is greater than the sum of its parts. Synergy pools individual talents and efforts to create extraordinary results. It occurs when a team uses its membership resources to the fullest and thereby achieves through collective action far more than could otherwise be achieved. This is very good for organizations and it can also be very good for their members.

Being part of a team can have a strong influence on individual attitudes and behaviors. When the experience is positive, working in and being part of a team helps satisfy important individual needs. Sometimes these are needs that may be difficult to meet in the regular work setting. Thus, in terms of both performance and satisfaction, the usefulness of teams is extensive.[11]

▪ **Synergy** is the creation of a whole greater than the sum of its individual parts.

- More resources for problem solving.
- Improved creativity and innovation.
- Improved quality of decision making.
- Greater commitments to tasks.
- Higher motivation through collective action.
- Better control and work discipline.
- More individual need satisfaction.

TEAMWORK CONS

Experience has taught all of us that achieving synergy isn't always easy, and that things don't always work out as intended. Teams and teamwork are not problem free. Who, for example, hasn't encountered **social loafing**? This is the presence of "free-riders" who slack off because respon-

▪ **Social loafing** is the tendency of some people to avoid responsibility by "free-riding" in groups.

sibility is diffused in teams and others are present to do the work.[12]

Things don't have to be this way. The time we spend in groups can be productive and satisfying, but to make it so we must understand the complex nature of groups and their internal dynamics.[13] Take social loafing as an example. What can a leader or other concerned team member do when someone is free-riding? It's not easy, but the problem can be addressed. Actions can be taken to make individual contributions more visible, reward individuals for their contributions, make task assignments more interesting, and keep group size small so that free-riders are more visible to peer pressure and leader evaluation.[14]

Other problems are also common when we work in groups and teams. Personality conflicts and individual differences in work styles can disrupt the team. Tasks are not always clear. Ambiguous agendas or ill-defined problems can cause teams to work too long on the wrong things. Not everyone is always ready to work. Sometimes the issue is lack of motivation, but it may also be conflicts with other deadlines and priorities. Low enthusiasm for group work may also be caused by a lack of team organization or progress, as well as by meetings that lack purpose and members who come unprepared.[15] These and other difficulties can easily turn the great potential of teams into frustration and failure.

MEETINGS, MEETINGS, MEETINGS

What do you think when someone says: "Let's have a meeting." Are you ready, apprehensive, or even perturbed? Meetings are a hard fact of the workplace, especially in today's horizontal, flexible, and team-oriented structures. And all too often, those who must attend do not view the call to yet another meeting enthusiastically.

A survey by Office Team found that 27 percent of respondents viewed meetings as their biggest time wasters, ranking ahead of unnecessary interruptions.[16] "We have the most ineffective meetings of any company," says a technology executive. "We just seem to meet and meet and meet and we never seem to do anything," says another in the package delivery industry. "We realize our meetings are unproductive. A consulting firm is trying to help us. But we've got a long way to go," says yet another corporate manager.[17]

Consider the list of typical meeting problems described in *Management Smarts 16.1.*[18] You might even be able to add to the list from personal experience in student groups and work teams. But remember, meetings can and should be places where information is shared, decisions get made, and people gain understanding of issues and one another. And this can be accomplished without "wasting" time. But as with all group activities in organizations, good things don't happen by chance. People have to work hard and work together to make meetings productive and rewarding.

MANAGEMENT SMARTS 16.1

Spotting sins of deadly meetings

1. People arrive late, leave early, and don't take things seriously.
2. The meeting is too long, sometimes twice as long as necessary.
3. People don't stay on topic; they digress and are easily distracted.
4. The discussion lacks candor; people are unwilling to tell the truth.
5. The right information isn't available, so decisions are postponed.
6. Nothing happens when the meeting is over; no one puts decisions into action.
7. Things never get better; the same mistakes are made meeting after meeting.

FORMAL AND INFORMAL GROUPS

The teams officially designated and supported by the organization are **formal groups.** They fulfill a variety of essential operations as part of the formal organizational structure.

Rensis Likert describes organizations as interlocking networks of formal groups in which managers and leaders serve important "linking pin" roles.[19] Each manager or leader serves as a superior in one work group and as a subordinate in the next-higher-level one. Such work groups exist in various sizes and go by different labels. They may be called *departments* (e.g., market research department), *units* (e.g., audit unit), *teams* (e.g., customer service team), or *divisions* (e.g., office products division), among other possibilities.

Although they are not depicted on organization charts, **informal groups** are present and important in all organizations. They emerge from natural or spontaneous relationships among people. Some informal groups are *interest groups*, in which workers band together to pursue a common cause such as better working conditions. Some emerge as *friendship groups* that develop for a wide variety of personal reasons, including shared non-work interests. Others exist as *support groups*, in which the members basically help one another do their jobs.

Two points about informal groups are especially important for managers to understand. First, informal groups are not necessarily bad; they can have a positive impact on work performance. The relationships and connections made possible by informal groups may actually help speed the workflow or allow people to "get things done" in ways not possible within the formal structure. Second, informal groups can help satisfy social needs that are otherwise thwarted or left unmet. Among other things, informal groups often offer their members social satisfactions, security, support, and a sense of belonging.

■ A **formal group** is officially recognized and supported by the organization.

■ An **informal group** is unofficial and emerges from relationships and shared interests among members.

REAL ETHICS

Social Loafing

1. Psychology study: A German researcher asked people to pull on a rope as hard as they could. First, individuals pulled alone. Second, they pulled as part of a group. The results showed that people pull harder when working alone than when working as part of a team. Such "social loafing" is the tendency to reduce effort when working in groups.

2. Faculty office: A student wants to speak with the instructor about his team's performance on the last group project. There were 4 members, but 2 did almost all of the work. The other 2 largely disappeared, showing up only at the last minute to be part of the formal presentation. His point is that the team was disadvantaged because two "free-riders" caused reduced performance capacity.

3. Telephone call from the boss: "John, I really need you to serve on this committee. Will you do it? Let me know tomorrow." In thinking about this, I ponder: I'm overloaded, but I don't want to turn down the

boss. I'll accept but let the committee members know about my situation. I'll be active in discussions and try to offer viewpoints and perspectives that are helpful. However, I'll let them know up front that I can't be a leader or volunteer for any extra work.

FURTHER INQUIRY

Whether you call it "social loafing, "free-riding" or just plain old "slacking off," the issue is the same: what right do some people have to sit back in team situations and let other people do all the work? Is this ethical? And when it comes to John, does the fact that he is going to be up front with the other committee members make any difference? Isn't he still going to be a loafer and yet earn credit with the boss for serving on the committee?

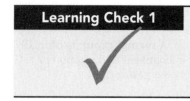

Be sure you can ▪ define the terms team and teamwork ▪ identify four roles managers perform in groups ▪ explain synergy ▪ explain teamwork pros and cons ▪ discuss the implications of social loafing ▪ differentiate formal and informal groups ▪ explain the potential benefits of informal groups

TRENDS IN THE USE OF TEAMS

The trend toward greater empowerment in organizations includes an emphasis on committees, project teams, task forces, and cross-functional teams. Organizations today also increasingly use computer-mediated or virtual teams, and self-managing teams.

COMMITTEES, PROJECT TEAMS, AND TASK FORCES

▪ A **committee** is designated to work on a special task on a continuing basis.

A **committee** brings people together outside of their daily job assignments to work in a small team for a specific purpose. The task agenda is typically narrow, focused, and ongoing. For example, organizations usually have a variety of permanent or standing committees dedicated to a wide variety of concerns such as diversity and compensation. Committees are led by a designated head or chairperson, who is held accountable for performance results.

▪ A **project team** or **task force** is convened for a specific purpose and disbands when its task is completed.

Project teams or **task forces** bring together people to work on common problems, but on a temporary rather than on a permanent basis. The task assignments for project teams and task forces are specific; completion deadlines are clearly defined. Creativity and innovation are sometimes very important. Project teams, for example, might be formed to develop a new product or service, redesign an office layout, or provide specialized consulting for a client.[20]

CROSS-FUNCTIONAL TEAMS

▪ A **cross-functional team** operates with members who come from different functional units of an organization.

The **cross-functional team,** whose members come from different functional units, is indispensable to organizations that emphasize adaptation and horizontal integration. Members of cross-functional teams work together on specific projects or tasks, and with the needs of the whole organization in mind. They are expected to share information, explore new ideas, seek creative solutions, and meet project deadlines. They are expected to knock down the "walls" that otherwise separate departments and people in the organization. At Tom's of Maine, for example, "Acorn Groups"—symbolizing the fruits of the stately oak tree—have been used to help launch new products. They bring together members of all departments to work on new ideas from concept to finished product. The goal is to minimize problems and maximize efficiency through cross-departmental cooperation.[21]

VIRTUAL TEAMS

▪ Members of a **virtual team** work together and solve problems through computer-based interactions.

A form of group that is increasingly common in today's organizations is the **virtual team**. This is a team of people who work together largely through computer-mediated rather than face-to-face interactions. The use of virtual teams is changing the way many committees, task forces, and other problem-solving teams function. Although working in electronic environments, team members in dispersed locations can easily address problems and seek consensus on how to best deal with them. Virtual teams operate like other teams in respect to what gets done. Just how things get done, however, is different, and this can be a source of both potential advantages and disadvantages.[22]

In terms of potential advantages, virtual teams can save time and travel expenses. They can allow members to work collectively in a time-efficient fashion and without interpersonal difficulties that might otherwise occur—especially when the issues are controversial. A vice president for human resources at Marriott, for example, once called electronic meetings "the quietest, least stressful, most productive meetings you've ever had."[23] Virtual teams can also be easily expanded to include additional members, and the discussions and information shared among members can be stored online for continuous updating and access.

When problems do occur in virtual teams, they often arise because members have difficulty establishing good working relationships. Relations among team members can become depersonalized as the lack of face-to-face interaction limits the role of emotions and nonverbal cues in the communication process.[24] But, following some basic guidelines can help ensure that the advantages of virtual teams outweigh their disadvantages. The critical ingredients relate to the creation of positive impressions and the development of trust among team members with limited face-to-face meeting opportunities. Among the tips for leading successful virtual teams are:[25]

- Begin with social messaging that allows members to exchange information about each other to personalize the process.
- Assign clear roles so that members can focus while working alone and also know what others are doing.
- Choose members who will join and engage the team with positive attitues and willingness to work hard to meet team goals.

SELF-MANAGING TEAMS

In a growing number of organizations, traditional work units consisting of first-level supervisors and their immediate subordinates are being replaced with **self-managing work teams.** Sometimes called *autonomous work groups*, these are teams of workers whose jobs have been redesigned to create a high degree of task interdependence, and that have been given group authority to make many decisions about how they work.[26]

■ Members of a **self-managing work team** have the authority to make decisions about how they share and complete their work.

Self-managing teams operate with participative decision making, shared tasks, and responsibility for many of the managerial tasks performed by supervisors in more traditional settings. The "self-management" responsibilities include planning and scheduling work, training members in various tasks, distributing tasks, meeting performance goals, ensuring high quality, and solving day-to-day operating problems. In some settings the team's authority may even extend to "hiring" and "firing" its members when necessary. A key feature is *multitasking*, in which team members each have the skills to perform several different jobs. As shown in *Figure 16.2*, typical characteristics of self-managing teams are as follows:

- Members are held collectively accountable for performance results.
- Members have discretion in distributing tasks within the team.
- Members have discretion in scheduling work within the team.
- Members are able to perform more than one job on the team.
- Members train one another to develop multiple job skills.
- Members evaluate one another's performance contributions.
- Members are responsible for the total quality of team products.

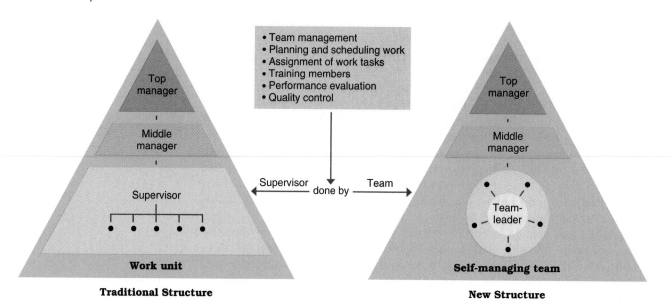

Figure 16.2 Organizational and management implications of self-managing work teams.

Within a self-managing team the emphasis is always on participation. The leader and members are expected to jointly decide how the work gets done. A true self-managing team emphasizes team decision making, shared tasks, high involvement, and collective responsibility for accomplished results. The expected advantages include better performance, decreased costs, and higher morale. Of course, these results are not guaranteed. Managing the transition to self-managing teams from more traditional work settings isn't always easy. The process requires leadership committed to both empowerment and a lot of support for those learning to work in new ways. As the concept of self-managing teams spreads globally, researchers are also examining the receptivity of different cultures to self-management concepts.[27] Such cultural dimensions as high-power distance and individualism, for example, may generate resistance that must be considered when implementing team-based organizational practices.

Learning Check 2

Be sure you can ■ differentiate a committee from a task force ■ explain the expected benefits of cross-functional teams ■ explain the potential advantages and disadvantages of virtual teams ■ list the characteristics of self-managing work teams ■ explain how self-managing teams are changing organizations

HOW TEAMS WORK

Regardless of its form and purpose, any team should achieve three key results—perform its tasks well, satisfy its members, and remain viable for the future.[28] On the task *performance* side, a work group or team is expected to transform resource inputs (such as ideas, materials, and objects) into product outputs (such as a report, decision, service, or commodity) that have some value to the organization. The members of a team should also be able to experience *satisfaction* both from these performance results and from their participation in the process. And, in respect to *future viability*, the team should have a social fabric and work climate that makes members willing and able to work well together in the future, again and again as needed.

FOUNDATIONS OF TEAM EFFECTIVENESS

An **effective team** is one that achieves and maintains high levels of task performance, member satisfaction, and viability for future action.[29] *Figure 16.3* shows how any team can be viewed as an open system that transforms various resource inputs into these outcomes. Among the important inputs are such things as the organizational setting, the nature of the task, the team size, and the membership characteristics.[30] Each of these factors influences the group process and helps set the stage for team effectiveness.

▪ An **effective team** achieves high levels of task performance, membership satisfaction, and future viability.

Group Inputs

The *nature of the task* is always important. It affects how well a team can focus its efforts and how intense the group process needs to be to get the job done. Clearly defined tasks make it easier for team members to combine their work efforts. Complex tasks require more information exchange and intense interaction than do simpler tasks.

The *organizational setting* can also affect how team members relate to one another and apply their skills toward task accomplishment. A key issue is the amount of support provided in terms of information, material resources, technology, organization structures, available rewards, and spatial arrangements. Increasingly, for example, organizations are being architecturally designed to directly facilitate teamwork. At SEI Investments, employees work in a large, open

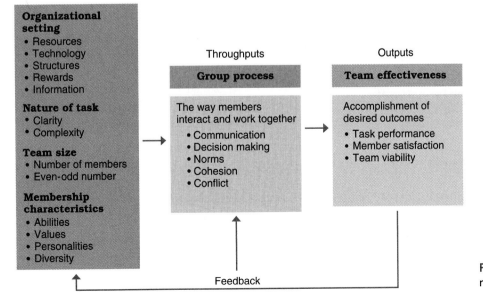

Figure 16.3 An open-systems model of team effectiveness.

space without cubicles or dividers; each has a private set of office furniture and fixtures—but all on wheels; all technology easily plugs and unplugs from suspended power beams that run overhead. Project teams convene and disband as needed, and people easily meet and converse intensely within the ebb and flow of daily work.[31]

Team size affects how members work together, handle disagreements, and reach agreements. The number of potential interactions increases geometrically as teams increase in size, and communications become more congested. Teams larger than about six or seven members can be difficult to manage for the purpose of creative problem solving. When voting is required, teams with odd numbers of members help prevent "ties."

In all teams, the *membership characteristics* are also important. Teams must have members with the right abilities, or skill mix, to master and perform tasks well. They must also have values and personalities that are sufficiently compatible for everyone to work well together.

RESEARCH BRIEF

Demographic faultlines pose implications for managing teams

Membership of organizations is becoming more diverse, and teams are becoming more important. According to Dora Lau and Keith Murnighan, these trends raise some important research issues. They believe that strong "faultlines" occur when demographic diversity results in the formation of two or more subgroups whose members are similar to and strongly identify with one another. Examples include teams with subgroups forming around age, gender, race, ethnic, occupational, or tenure differences. When strong faultlines are present, members tend to identify more strongly with their subgroups than with the team as a whole. Lau and Murnighan predict that this affects what happens within the team in terms of conflict, politics, and performance.

Using subjects from 10 organizational behavior classes at a university, the researchers created different conditions of faultline strengths by randomly assigning students to case work groups based on sex and ethnicity. After working on cases the students completed questionnaires about group processes and outcomes. Results showed members of strong faultline groups evaluated those in their subgroups more favorably than did members of weak faultline groups. Members of strong faultline groups also experienced less conflict, more psychological safety, and more satisfaction than did those in weak faultline groups.

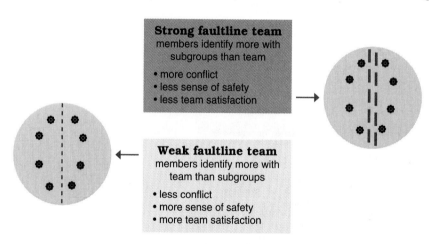

QUESTIONS & APPLICATIONS

Can demographic faultlines affect groups working together over long periods, not just on short-term tasks such as a case study? How might faultlines operate in groups of different sizes and in the contexts of different organizational cultures?

When and if demographic faultlines exist, we should know how to best deal with and manage them. Are faultlines influencing the processes and outcomes of groups in which you participate—at the university and at work? And, if you are a member or leader of a team with strong faultlines, what could you do to help minimize any negative effects?

Reference: Dora C. Lau and J. Keith Murnighan, "Interactions within Groups and Subgroups: The Effects of Demographic Faultlines," *Academy of Management Journal*, vol. 48 (2005), pp. 645–659; "Demographic Diversity and Faultlines: The Compositional Dynamics of Organizational Groups," *Academy of Management Review*, vol. 23 (1998), pp. 325–340.

Group Process and Diversity

Although having the right inputs available to a team is important, it is not a guarantee of effectiveness. **Group process** counts too. This is the way the members of any team actually work together as they transform inputs into outputs. Also called *group dynamics*, the process aspects of any group or team include how members communicate with one another, make decisions, handle conflicts, and share norms. When the process breaks down and the internal dynamics fail in any way, team effectiveness can suffer.[32] This *Team Effectiveness Equation* is a helpful reminder: Team effectiveness=quality of inputs+ (process gains−process losses).

■ **Group process** is the way team members work together to accomplish tasks.

Team diversity, in the form of different values, personalities, experiences, demographics, and cultures among the membership, can present significant group process challenges. The more homogeneous the team— the more similar the members are to one another—the easier it is to manage relationships. As team diversity increases, so, too, does the complexity of interpersonal relationships among members. But with the complications also come special opportunities. The more heterogeneous the team—the more diversity among members—the greater the variety of ideas, perspectives, and experiences that can add value to problem solving and task performance.

In teamwork, as with organizations at large, the diversity lesson is clear. There is a lot to gain when membership diversity is valued and well managed. The process challenge is to maximize the advantages of team diversity while minimizing its potential disadvantages. In the international arena, for example, research indicates that culturally diverse work teams have more difficulty learning how to work well together than do culturally homogeneous teams.[33] They tend to struggle more in the early stages of working together. But once the process challenges are successfully mastered, the diverse teams eventually prove to be more creative than the homogeneous ones.

STAGES OF TEAM DEVELOPMENT

A synthesis of research on small groups suggests that there are five distinct phases in the life cycle of any team:[34]

1. *Forming*—a stage of initial orientation and interpersonal testing.
2. *Storming*—a stage of conflict over tasks and working as a team.
3. *Norming*—a stage of consolidation around task and operating agendas.
4. *Performing*—a stage of teamwork and focused task performance.
5. *Adjourning*—a stage of task completion and disengagement.

Forming Stage

The forming stage involves the first entry of individual members into a team. This is a stage of initial task orientation and interpersonal testing. As people come together for the first time or two, they ask a number of questions: "What can or does the team offer me?" "What will I be asked to contribute?" "Can my needs be met while my efforts serve the task needs of the team?"

In the forming stage, people begin to identify with other members and with the team itself. They are concerned about getting acquainted, establishing interpersonal relationships, discovering what is considered acceptable behavior, and learning how others perceive the team's task. This may also be a time when some members rely on or become temporarily dependent on others who appear "powerful" or especially "knowledgeable." Such things as prior experience with team members in other contexts and individual impressions of organization philosophies, goals, and policies may also affect member relationships in new work teams. Difficulties in the forming stage tend to be greater in more culturally and demographically diverse teams.

Storming Stage

The storming stage of team development is a period of high emotionality. Tension often emerges between members over tasks and interpersonal concerns. There may be periods of outright hostility and infighting. Coalitions or cliques may form around personalities or interests. Subteams may form around areas of agreement and disagreement involving group tasks and/or the manner of operations. Conflict may develop as individuals compete to impose their preferences on others and to become influential in the group's status structure.

Important changes occur in the storming stage as task agendas become clarified and members begin to understand one another's interpersonal styles. Here attention begins to shift toward obstacles that may stand in the way of task accomplishment. Efforts are made to find ways to meet team goals while also satisfying individual needs. Failure in the storming stage can be a lasting liability, whereas success in the storming stage can set a strong foundation for later team effectiveness.

KAFFEEKLATSCH

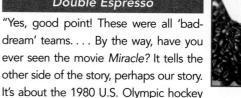

Bad-Dream Teams

First Cup

"What do you think of the CEO's new hiring initiative? Recruit from only business schools ranked in the top 25 internationally we're being told; don't interview anyone whose GPA is under 3.5 and who doesn't have at least one significant leadership position in a student organization. When I pointed out that some of us, me included, didn't fit that bill when we were hired, I was told: 'Don't take this new strategy as personal criticism. We're talking about going forward from today; it's time to build the dream team for the future.' "

Studying the Grounds

■ When the United States fielded a team of baseball superstars for the last summer Olympics, most everyone looked in awe. But the combination of Derek Jeter, Alex Rodriquez, Roger Clemens, Johnny Damon, and others couldn't pass the test—losing to Mexico, Canada, and South Korea.

■ Investors were sure they had a super-sized winner in the movie *Ocean's Twelve*, with a cast including Julia Roberts, Brad Pitt, Catherine Zeta-Jones, and George Clooney. It was soundly beaten in the ratings by an upstart with a no-name cast: *My Big Fat Greek Wedding*.

■ Enron's former CEO, Jeffrey Skilling, has an MBA from Harvard; former CFO Andrew Fastow's MBA is from Northwestern; both men were convicted of crimes contributing to the firm's financial collapse.

Double Espresso

"Yes, good point! These were all 'bad-dream' teams.... By the way, have you ever seen the movie *Miracle*? It tells the other side of the story, perhaps our story. It's about the 1980 U.S. Olympic hockey team that won the gold medal by beating favorite Russia and then going on to defeat Finland. The movie is a stunner, and it's a lesson in team building, leadership, and motivation all in one. The coach, Herb Brooks, passed over many of the year's college superstars in picking the team. He was looking for 'personal chemistry' since he believed that the great international teams could only be beaten through superb teamwork. Brooks has a great line in the movie; perhaps our top management people might do well to listen: 'I'm not looking for the best players; I'm looking for the right players'. That isn't the message we're hearing, is it?"

Your Turn

There's quite a bit at stake in this conversation. One of the speakers seems defensive because she or he doesn't meet the credentials being established for new hires. Then there's the point about creating a dream team or dream cast or dream organization out of a group of superstars. Maybe superstars will be more interested in working for themselves than for the team. Also, there's the question about college recruiting. When an employer uses school rankings, GPAs, and student activities as screening criteria, don't a lot of potentially top recruits get missed?

Norming Stage

Cooperation is an important issue for teams in the norming stage. At this point, members of the team begin to become coordinated as a working unit and tend to operate with shared rules of conduct. The team feels a sense of leadership, with each member starting to play useful roles. Most interpersonal hostilities give way to a precarious balancing of forces as norming builds initial integration. Harmony is emphasized, but minority viewpoints may be discouraged.

In the norming stage, members are likely to develop initial feelings of closeness, a division of labor, and a sense of shared expectations. This helps protect the team from disintegration. Holding the team together may become even more important than successful task accomplishment.

Performing Stage

Teams in the performing stage are more mature, organized, and well functioning. This is a stage of total integration, in which team members are able to deal in creative ways with both complex tasks and any interpersonal conflicts. The team operates with a clear and stable structure, and members are motivated by team goals.

The primary challenges of teams in the performing stage are to continue refining the operations and relationships essential to working as an integrated unit. Such teams need to remain coordinated with the larger organization and adapt successfully to changing conditions over time. A team that has achieved total integration will score high on the criteria of team maturity shown in *Figure 16.4*.[35]

Adjourning Stage

The final stage of team development is adjourning, when team members prepare to achieve closure and disband. Ideally, temporary committees, task forces, and project teams disband with a sense that important goals have been accomplished. This may be an emotional time. When members have worked together intensely for a period of time, breaking up the close relationships may be painful. In all cases, the team would like to disband with

	Very poor			Very good	
1. Trust among members	1	2	3	4	5
2. Feedback mechanisms	1	2	3	4	5
3. Open communications	1	2	3	4	5
4. Approach to decisions	1	2	3	4	5
5. Leadership sharing	1	2	3	4	5
6. Acceptance of goals	1	2	3	4	5
7. Valuing diversity	1	2	3	4	5
8. Member cohesiveness	1	2	3	4	5
9. Support for each other	1	2	3	4	5
10. Performance norms	1	2	3	4	5
	Where you don't want to be			Where you do want to be	

Figure 16.4 Criteria for assessing the maturity of a team.

members feeling they would work with one another again sometime in the future. Members should be acknowledged for their contributions and praised for the group's overall success.

NORMS AND COHESIVENESS

■ A **norm** is a behavior, rule, or standard expected to be followed by team members.

A **norm** is a behavior expected of team members.[36] It is a "rule" or "standard" that guides their behavior. When violated, a norm may be enforced with reprimands and other sanctions. In the extreme, violation of a norm can result in a member being expelled from a team or socially ostracized by other members.

The *performance norm*, which defines the level of work effort and performance that team members are expected to contribute, is extremely important. In general, work groups and teams with positive performance norms are more successful in accomplishing task objectives than are teams with negative performance norms. Other important team norms relate to such things as helpfulness, participation, timeliness, quality, and innovation.

Team leaders should help and encourage members to develop positive norms. During forming and storming steps of development, for example, norms relating to membership issues such as expected attendance and levels of commitment are important. By the time the stage of performing is reached, norms relating to adaptability and change become most relevant. Guidelines for *how to build positive group norms* are:[37]

- Act as a positive role model.
- Reinforce the desired behaviors with rewards.
- Control results by performance reviews and regular feedback.
- Train and orient new members to adopt desired behaviors.
- Recruit and select new members who exhibit the desired behaviors.
- Hold regular meetings to discuss progress and ways of improving.
- Use team decision-making methods to reach agreement.

■ **Cohesiveness** is the degree to which members are attracted to and motivated to remain part of a team.

Team members vary in the degree to which they accept and adhere to group norms. Conformity to norms is largely determined by the strength of group **cohesiveness,** the degree to which members are attracted to and motivated to remain part of a team.[38] Persons in a highly cohesive team value their membership and strive to maintain positive relationships with other team members. They experience satisfaction from team identification and interpersonal relationships. Because of this they tend to conform to the norms.

Look at *Figure 16.5*. When the performance norm of a team is positive, high cohesion and the resulting conformity to norms has a beneficial effect on overall team performance. This is a "best-case" scenario. Competent team members work hard and reinforce one another's task accomplishments while experiencing satisfaction with the team. But when the performance

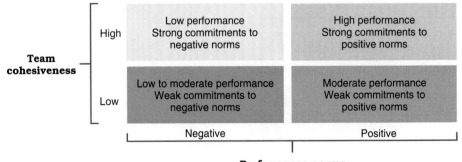

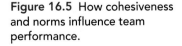

Figure 16.5 How cohesiveness and norms influence team performance.

norm is negative in a cohesive team, high conformity to the norm can have undesirable results. The figure shows this as a "worst-case" scenario where team performance suffers from restricted work efforts by members.

To achieve and maintain the best-case scenario shown in the figure, managers should be skilled at building positive norms as previously discussed, and building high cohesiveness. Guidelines on *how to increase group cohesion* include:

- Induce agreement on team goals.
- Increase membership homogeneity.
- Increase interactions among members.
- Decrease team size.
- Introduce competition with other teams.
- Reward team rather than individual results.
- Provide physical isolation from other teams.

TASK AND MAINTENANCE NEEDS

Research on the social psychology of groups identifies two types of activities that are essential if team members are to work well together.[39] **Task activities** contribute directly to the team's performance purpose, and **maintenance activities** support the emotional life of the team as an ongoing social system.

Although the team leader or supervisor will often handle them, the responsibility for both types of activities should be shared and distributed among all team members. Anyone can help lead a team by acting in ways that satisfy its task and maintenance needs. This concept of *distributed leadership in teams* makes every member continually responsible for both recognizing when task or maintenance activities are needed and taking actions to provide them.

Figure 16.6 offers useful insights on distributed leadership in teams. Leading through task activities involves making an effort to define and solve problems and to advance work toward performance results. Without the relevant task activities, such as initiating agendas, sharing information, and others listed in the figure, teams will have difficulty accomplishing their objectives. Leading through maintenance activities, by contrast, helps strengthen the team as a social system. When maintenance activities such as encouraging others and reducing tensions are performed well, good interpersonal relationships are achieved and the ability of the team to stay together over the longer term is ensured.

Both team task and maintenance activities stand in distinct contrast to the *disruptive activities* also described in *Figure 16.6*. Activities such as

▨ A **task activity** is an action taken by a team member that directly contributes to the group's performance purpose.

▨ A **maintenance activity** is an action taken by a team member that supports the emotional life of the group.

Distributed leadership roles in teams

Team leaders provide task activities
- Initiating
- Information sharing
- Summarizing
- Elaborating
- Opinion giving

Team leaders provide maintenance activities
- Gatekeeping
- Encouraging
- Following
- Harmonizing
- Reducing tension

Team leaders avoid disruptive activities
- Being aggressive
- Blocking
- Self-confessing
- Seeking sympathy
- Competing
- Withdrawal
- Horsing around
- Seeking recognition

Figure 16.6 Distributed leadership helps teams meet task and maintenance needs.

withdrawing and horsing around are usually self-serving to the individual member. They detract from, rather than enhance, team effectiveness. Unfortunately, very few teams are immune to dysfunctional behavior by members. Everyone shares in the responsibility for minimizing its occurrence and meeting the distributed leadership needs of a team by contributing functional task and maintenance behaviors.

COMMUNICATION NETWORKS

Figure 16.7 depicts three interaction patterns and communication networks that are common in teams.[40] Each is important in the life of any group.

When team members must interact intensively and work closely together on tasks this need is best met by a **decentralized communication network** in which all members communicate directly with one another. Sometimes this is called the *all-channel* or *star communication network*. At other times and in other situations team members work on tasks independently, with the required work being divided up among them. Activities are coordinated and results pooled by a central point of control. Most communication flows back and forth between individual members and this hub or center point. This creates a **centralized communication network,** as shown in the figure. Sometimes this is called a *wheel* or *chain communication structure*.

When teams are composed of subgroups experiencing issue-specific disagreements, such as a temporary debate over the best means to achieve a goal, the resulting interaction pattern often involves a *restricted communication network*. Here, polarized subgroups contest one another and may even engage in antagonistic relations. Communication between the subgroups is limited and biased, with negative consequences for group process and effectiveness.

■ A **decentralized communication network** allows all members to communicate directly with one another.

■ In a **centralized communication network**, communication flows only between individual members and a hub or center point.

Figure 16.7 Interaction patterns and communication networks in teams. *Source:* John R. Schermerhorn Jr., James G. Hunt, and Richard N. Osborn, *Organizational Behavior*, 8th ed. (Hoboken: Wiley, 2003), p. 347. Used by permission.

Pattern	Diagram	Characteristics
Interacting Group _____ Decentralized communication network		High interdependency around a common task _____ Best at complex tasks
Co-acting Group _____ Centralized communication network		Independent individual efforts on behalf of common task _____ Best at simple tasks
Counteracting Group _____ Restricted communication network		Subgroups in disagreement with one another _____ Slow task accomplishment

The best teams use communication networks in the right ways, at the right times, and for the right tasks. Centralized communication networks seem to work better on simple tasks.[41] These tasks require little creativity, information processing, and problem solving and lend themselves to more centralized control. The reverse is true for more complex tasks, where interacting groups do better. Here, the decentralized networks work well since they are able to support the more intense interactions and information sharing required to perform complicated tasks. When teams get complacent, the conflict among co-acting groups can be a source of creativity and critical evaluation. But when subgroups have difficulty communicating with one another, task accomplishment typically suffers, for the short run at least.

TEAM BUILDING

Continuing effort to refine and apply creative team concepts is high on most executives' action agendas. But whether the group or team is working at the top, bottom, cross-functionally, or in direct customer service, high-performance results can't be left to chance. There are too many forces in the environment and group dynamics that can lead teams astray. Team success is only achieved through the special efforts of leaders and members alike. We know, for example, that high-performance teams generally share these characteristics:[42]

- a clear and elevating goal
- a task-driven and results-oriented structure
- competent and committed members who work hard
- a collaborative climate
- high standards of excellence
- external support and recognition
- strong, principled leadership

One of the ways to build capacity for long term-team effectiveness from such factors is a practice known as **team building.** This is a sequence of planned activities used to analyze the functioning of a team, and then make constructive changes to increase its operating effectiveness.[43] Most systematic approaches to team building begin with awareness that a problem may exist or may develop within the team. Members then work together to gather data and fully understand the problem. Action plans are made by members and collectively implemented. Results are evaluated by team members working together. As difficulties or new problems are discovered, the team-building process recycles.

■ **Team building** is a sequence of collaborative activities to gather and analyze data on a team and make changes to increase its effectiveness.

There are many ways to gather data on team functioning, including structured and unstructured interviews, questionnaires, and team meetings. Regardless of the method used, the basic principle of team building remains the same. The process requires a careful and collaborative assessment of the team's inputs, processes, and results. All members should participate in data gathering, assist in data analysis, and collectively decide on actions to be taken.

Sometimes teamwork can be improved when people share the challenges of unusual and even physically demanding experiences. On one fall day, for example, a team of employees from American Electric Power (AEP) went to an outdoor camp for a day of

team-building activities. They worked on problems like how to get six members through a spider-web maze of bungee cords strung 2 feet above the ground. When her colleagues lifted Judy Gallo into their hands to pass her over the obstacle, she was nervous. But a trainer told the team this was just like solving a problem together at the office. The spider web was just another performance constraint, like the difficult policy issues or financial limits they might face at work. After "high-fives" for making it through the web, Judy's team jumped tree stumps together, passed hula hoops while holding hands, and more. Says one team trainer, "We throw clients into situations to try and bring out the traits of a good team."[44]

Learning Check 3 ✓	*Be sure you can* ■ define the term group effectiveness ■ identify inputs that influence group effectiveness ■ discuss how membership diversity influences team effectiveness ■ list five stages of group development ■ define the term group norm and list ways to build positive group norms ■ define the term cohesiveness and list ways to increase group cohesion ■ explain how norms and cohesiveness influence group performance ■ differentiate between task, maintenance, and disruptive activities ■ describe use of decentralized and centralized communication networks ■ explain how team building works

DECISION MAKING IN TEAMS

Decision making, discussed extensively in Chapter 7, is the process of making choices among alternative possible courses of action. It is one of the most important group processes, but one that is complicated by the fact that teams can make decisions in different ways.

HOW TEAMS MAKE DECISIONS

Edgar Schein, a respected scholar and consultant, notes that teams make decisions by at least 6 methods: lack of response, authority rule, minority rule, majority rule, consensus, and unanimity.[45]

In *decision by lack of response*, one idea after another is suggested without any discussion taking place. When the team finally accepts an idea, all others have been bypassed and discarded by simple lack of response rather than by critical evaluation. In *decision by authority rule*, the leader, manager, committee head, or some other authority figure makes a decision for the team. This can be done with or without discussion and is very time efficient. Whether the decision is a good one or a bad one, however, depends on whether the authority figure has the necessary information and on how well this approach is accepted by other team members. In *decision by minority rule*, two or three people are able to dominate or "railroad" the team into making a mutually agreeable decision. This is often done by providing a suggestion and then forcing quick agreement by challenging the team with such statements as "Does anyone object? . . . Let's go ahead, then."

One of the most common ways teams make decisions, especially when early signs of disagreement arise, is *decision by majority rule*. Here, formal voting may take place, or members may be polled to find the majority viewpoint. This method parallels the democratic political system and is often used without awareness of its potential problems. The very process of voting can create coalitions; that is, some people will be "winners" and others will be "losers." Those in the minority—the "losers"—may feel left out or discarded without having had a fair say. They may be unenthusiastic about implementing the decision of the "majority," and lingering resentments may impair team effectiveness in the future. There is no better example of the dynamics associated with close voting than the American presidential elections of 2000, and the lingering controversy over Bush/Gore vote tallies in Florida.

Teams are often encouraged to follow *decision by consensus*. This is where full discussion leads to one alternative being favored by most members and the other members agree to support it. When a consensus is reached, even those who may have opposed the chosen course of action know that they have been heard and have had an opportunity to influence the decision outcome. Such consensus does not require unanimity. But it does require that team members be able to argue, engage in reasonable conflict, and still get along with and respect one another.[46] And it requires the opportunity for dissenting members to know that they have been able to speak and that they have been listened to.

A *decision by unanimity* may be the ideal state of affairs. Here, all team members agree on the course of action to be taken. This is a logically perfect method for decision making in teams, but it is also extremely difficult to attain in actual practice. One of the reasons that teams sometimes turn to authority decisions, majority voting, or even minority decisions, in fact, is the difficulty of managing the team process to achieve consensus or unanimity.

INSIGHTS

Teams Are Worth the Hard Work

Toy Story, Toy Story II, A Bug's Life, Monsters Inc., Finding Nemo Cars?—you surely recognize the names of these popular animated films. All, by the way, share a common heritage: being created, brought to life if you will, at Pixar Animation Studios. To create the best animated films, Pixar's leadership, knows it can only be as good as the talents of its team members. The firm does its best to attract great people with a challenging, satisfying, and re-

All seems to be working according to plans at Pixar. The firm's talented employees have won 15 Academy Awards, and the hits keep coming. Its technical teams have created three major proprietary software packages—Marionette, Ringmaster, and RenderMan.

warding workplace. In a setting that depends on creativity and teamwork, the building spaces and the culture encourage personal expression and interaction. Founding CEO Steve Jobs says: "Even though we use computers, our films are handmade, and we wanted the building to reflect that."

The firm, now owned by the Walt Disney Company, is self described as providing "an environment that is irresistible in its professional challenges, creative output and open, collaborative spirit." The collaborative team spirit that drives the Pixar work culture also means "fun." The headquarters in Emeryville, California, has been described as a "fun house." Hallways are art galleries featuring employees' work; the lunchroom has a trattoria; roller scooters are allowed in the building; offices are outfitted to individual tastes.

ASSETS AND LIABILITIES OF GROUP DECISIONS

The best teams don't limit themselves to just one decision-making method. A very important team leadership skill is the ability to help a team choose the "best" decision method—one that provides for a timely and quality decision and one to which the members are highly committed. This reasoning is consistent with the Vroom-Jago leader-participation model discussed in Chapter 13.[47] You should recall that this model describes how leaders should utilize a range of individual, consultative, and group decision methods as they resolve daily problems. To do this well, however, team leaders must understand the potential assets and potential liabilities of group decisions.[48]

The potential *advantages of group decision making* are significant. Because of this, the general argument is that group decisions should be made whenever time and other circumstances permit. Group decisions make greater amounts of information, knowledge, and expertise available to solve problems. They expand the number of action alternatives that are examined; they help teams avoid tunnel vision and tendencies to consider only a limited range of options. Group decisions increase the understanding and acceptance of outcomes by members. And importantly, they increase the commitments of members to follow through to implement the decision once made.

The potential *disadvantages of group decision making* largely trace to the difficulties that can be experienced in group process. In a group decision there may be social pressure to conform. Individual members may feel intimidated or compelled to go along with the apparent wishes of others. There may be minority domination, where some members feel forced or "railroaded" to accept a decision advocated by one vocal individual or small coalition. Also, the time required to make group decisions can sometimes be a disadvantage. As more people are involved in the dialogue and discussion, decision making takes longer. This added time may be costly, even prohibitively so, in certain circumstances.[49]

GROUPTHINK

Although it may seem counterintuitive, a high level of cohesiveness can sometimes be a disadvantage during decision making. Members of very cohesive teams may feel so strongly about the group that they may not want to do anything that might detract from feelings of goodwill. This might cause them to publicly agree with actual or suggested courses of action, while privately having serious doubts about them. Strong feelings of team loyalty can make it hard for members to criticize and evaluate one another's ideas and suggestions. Unfortunately, there are times when desires to hold the team together at all costs and avoid disagreements may result in poor decisions.

Groupthink is a tendency for highly cohesive teams to lose their evaluative capabilities.

Psychologist Irving Janis calls this phenomenon **groupthink,** the tendency for highly cohesive groups to lose their critical evaluative capabilities.[50] You should be alert to spot the following *symptoms of groupthink* when they occur in your decision-making teams:

■ *Illusions of invulnerability:* Members assume that the team is too good for criticism or beyond attack.
■ *Rationalizing unpleasant and disconfirming data:* Members refuse to accept contradictory data or to thoroughly consider alternatives.
■ *Belief in inherent group morality:* Members act as though the group is inherently right and above reproach.

- *Stereotyping competitors as weak, evil, and stupid:* Members refuse to look realistically at other groups.
- *Applying direct pressure to deviants to conform to group wishes:* Members refuse to tolerate anyone who suggests the team may be wrong.
- *Self-censorship by members:* Members refuse to communicate personal concerns to the whole team.
- *Illusions of unanimity:* Members accept consensus prematurely, without testing its completeness.
- *Mind guarding:* Members protect the team from hearing disturbing ideas or outside viewpoints.

Groupthink can occur anywhere. In fact, Janis ties a variety of well-known historical blunders to the phenomenon, including the lack of preparedness of the United States's naval forces for the Japanese attack on Pearl Harbor, the Bay of Pigs invasion under President Kennedy, and the many roads that led to the United States' difficulties in the Vietnam war. When and if you encounter groupthink, Janis suggests taking action along the lines shown in *Management Smarts 16.2*.

MANAGEMENT SMARTS 16.2

How to avoid groupthink

- Assign the role of critical evaluator to each team member; encourage a sharing of viewpoints.
- As a leader, don't seem partial to one course of action; do absent yourself from meetings at times to allow free discussion.
- Create subteams to work on the same problems and then share their proposed solutions.
- Have team members discuss issues with outsiders and report back on their reactions.
- Invite outside experts to observe team activities and react to team processes and decisions.
- Assign one member to play a "devil's advocate" role at each team meeting.
- Hold a "second-chance" meeting after consensus is apparently achieved to review the decision.

ISSUES & SITUATIONS

Team Building Novelties

The next time you fly on United Airlines, check out the ground crews. Top management hopes you notice some similarities with the teams handling pit stops for NASCAR racers. In fact, there's a good chance the members of the ramp crews have been through "Pit Crew U." United is among many organizations that are sending employees to Pit Instruction & Training in Mooresville, North Carolina. At this facility, where real racing crews train, United's ramp workers learn to work intensely and under pressure while meeting the goals of teamwork, safety, and job preparedness. The goal is better teamwork to reduce aircraft delays and service inadequacies.

Pit Crew U is just one example of many team-building alternatives that break people out of their normal work settings and help them learn from entirely new experiences. Seagate Technology's CEO Bill Watkins takes this to the extreme. He spends some $9,000 per person to send employees to New Zealand for Eco Seagate. Participants spend a week doing team building in a variety of outdoor settings and activities. One includes a Maori *haka* dance with everyone chanting in the Maori language, "Seagate is powerful. Seagate is powerful." At the grand finale, teams compete in an all-day race of kayaking, cycling, swimming, and cliff rappelling.

Critical Response

Habit is a strong influence on behavior, and the work habits of teams can become complacent and lackadaisical. It can be a real challenge to break people out of existing habits and switch into new mindsets that reinvigorate teamwork. Seagate's Bill Watkins says that one of the best ways to do this is to put them in team situations that are so novel and new that they're forced to learn new ways of working together. He says: "You put them in an environment where they have to ask for help."

What about it? Are Pit Crew U and Eco Seagate onto something? And, what about less extreme alternatives? How can organizations facilitate inspired teamwork at less expense and in less sensational ways?

CREATIVITY IN TEAM DECISION MAKING

Among the potential benefits that teams can bring to organizations is increased creativity. Two techniques that are particularly helpful for tapping creativity in group decision making are brainstorming and the nominal group technique.[51] Both can now be pursued in computer-mediated or virtual team discussions, as well as in face-to-face formats.

▪ **Brainstorming** engages group members in an open, spontaneous discussion of problems and ideas.

In **brainstorming,** teams of 5 to 10 members meet to generate ideas. Brainstorming teams typically operate within these guidelines: *All criticism is ruled out*—judgment or evaluation of ideas must be withheld until the idea-generation process has been completed. *"Freewheeling" is welcomed*—the wilder or more radical the idea, the better. *Quantity is important*—the greater the number of ideas, the greater the likelihood of obtaining a superior idea. *Building on one another's ideas is encouraged*—participants should suggest how ideas of others can be turned into better ideas, or how two or more ideas can be joined into still another hybrid idea.

▪ The **nominal group technique** structures interaction among team members discussing problems and ideas.

By prohibiting criticism, the brainstorming method reduces fears of ridicule or failure on the part of individuals. Ideally, this results in more enthusiasm, involvement, and a freer flow of ideas among members. But there are times when team members have very different opinions and goals. The differences may be so extreme that a brainstorming meeting might deteriorate into antagonistic arguments and harmful conflicts. In such cases, a **nominal group technique** could help. This approach uses a highly structured meeting agenda to allow everyone to contribute ideas without the interference of evaluative comments by others. Participants are first asked to work alone and respond in writing with possible solutions to a stated problem. Ideas are then shared in round-robin fashion without any criticism or discussion; all ideas are recorded as they are presented. Ideas are next discussed and clarified in round-robin sequence, with no evaluative comments allowed. Next, members individually and silently follow a written voting procedure that allows for all alternatives to be rated or ranked in priority order. Finally, the last two steps are repeated as needed to further clarify the process.

Learning Check 4

✓

Be sure you can ▪ illustrate how groups make decisions by authority rule, minority rule, majority rule, consensus, and unanimity ▪ list advantages and disadvantages of group decision making ▪ define the term groupthink and identify its symptoms ▪ illustrate how brainstorming and the nominal group techniques can improve creativity in decision making

CHAPTER 16 STUDY GUIDE

STUDY QUESTIONS SUMMARY

1 How do teams contribute to organizations?

- A team is a collection of people working together to accomplish a common goal.
- Teams help organizations through synergy in task performance, the creation of a whole that is greater than the sum of its parts.
- Teams help satisfy important needs for their members, providing various types of job support and social satisfactions.
- Social loafing and other problems can limit the performance of teams.
- Organizations operate as networks of formal and informal groups.

2 What are current trends in the use of teams?

- Teams are important mechanisms of empowerment and participation in the workplace.
- Committees and task forces are used to facilitate operations and accomplish special projects.
- Cross-functional teams bring members together from different departments and help improve lateral relations and integration in organizations.
- New developments in information technology are making virtual teams more common.
- Self-managing teams are changing organizations as team members perform many tasks previously done by their supervisors.

3 How do teams work?

- An effective team achieves high levels of task performance, member satisfaction, and team viability.

- Important team inputs include the organizational setting, nature of the task, size, and membership characteristics.
- A team matures through various stages of development, including forming, storming, norming, performing, and adjourning.
- Norms are the standards or rules of conduct that influence the behavior of team members; cohesion is the attractiveness of the team to its members.
- In highly cohesive teams, members tend to conform to norms; the best situation is a team with positive performance norms and high cohesiveness.
- Distributed leadership occurs as members share in meeting a team's task and maintenance needs.
- Effective teams make use of alternative communication networks to best complete tasks.

4 How do teams make decisions?

- Teams can make decisions by lack of response, authority rule, minority rule, majority rule, consensus, and unanimity.
- The potential advantages of group decision making include having more information available and generating more understanding and commitment.
- The potential liabilities of group decision making include social pressures to conform and greater time requirements.
- Groupthink is a tendency of members of highly cohesive teams to lose their critical evaluative capabilities and make poor decisions.
- Techniques for improving creativity in teams include brainstorming and the nominal group technique.

KEY TERMS REVIEW

Brainstorming (p. 416)
Centralized communication
   network (p. 410)
Cohesiveness (p. 408)
Committee (p. 400)
Cross-functional team (p. 400)
Decentralized communication
   network (p. 410)
Effective team (p. 403)

Formal group (p. 399)
Group process (p. 405)
Groupthink (p. 414)
Informal group (p. 399)
Maintenance activity (p. 409)
Nominal group technique (p. 416)
Norm (p. 408)
Project team (p. 400)
Self-managing team (p. 401)

Social loafing (p. 397)
Synergy (p. 397)
Task activity (p. 409)
Task force (p. 400)
Team (p. 397)
Team building (p. 411)
Teamwork (p. 397)
Virtual team (p. 400)

SELF-TEST 16

MULTIPLE-CHOICE QUESTIONS:

1. When a group of people is able to achieve more than what its members could by working individually, this is called _____.
   (a) social loafing   (b) consensus   (c) viability   (d) synergy

2. In an organization operating with self-managing teams, the traditional role of _____ is replaced by the role of team leader.
   (a) chief executive officer   (b) first-line supervisor   (c) middle manager   (d) general manager

3. An effective team is defined as one that achieves high levels of task performance, member satisfaction, and _____.
   (a) resource efficiency   (b) future viability   (c) consensus   (d) creativity

4. In the open-systems model of teams, the _____ is an important input factor.
   (a) communication network   (b) decision-making method   (c) performance norm   (d) set of membership characteristics

5. A basic rule of team dynamics states that the greater the _____ in a team, the greater the conformity to norms.
   (a) membership diversity   (b) cohesiveness   (c) task structure   (d) competition among members

6. Groupthink is most likely to occur in teams that are _____.
   (a) large in size   (b) diverse in membership   (c) high performing   (d) highly cohesive

7. Gatekeeping is an example of a _____ activity that can help teams work effectively over time.
   (a) task   (b) maintenance   (c) team-building   (d) decision-making

8. Members of a team tend to become more motivated and able to deal with conflict during the _____ stage of team development.
   (a) forming   (b) norming   (c) performing   (d) adjourning

9. One way for a manager to build positive norms within a team is to _____.
   (a) act as a positive role model   (b) increase group size   (c) introduce groupthink   (d) isolate the team from others

10. When teams are highly cohesive, _____.
    (a) members are high performers   (b) members tend to be satisfied with their team membership   (c) members have positive norms   (d) the group achieves its goals

11. When members of a group share commitments to being on time for all meetings, on-time behavior has become _____.
    (a) symptom of groupthink   (b) synergy   (c) a norm   (d) activity maintenance

12. It would be common to find members of self-managing work teams engaged in _____.
    (a) social loafing   (b) multitasking   (c) centralized communication   (d) decision by authority rule

13. The team effectiveness equation states the following: Team effectiveness=quality of inputs+ (_____–process losses).
    (a) process gains   (b) leadership impact   (c) membership ability   (d) problem complexity

14. A _____ decision is one in which all members agree on the course of action to be taken.
    (a) consensus   (b) unanimity   (c) majority   (d) synergy

15. To increase the cohesiveness of a group, a manager would be best off _____.
    (a) starting competition with other groups   (b) increasing the group size   (c) acting as a positive role model   (d) introducing a new member

SHORT-RESPONSE QUESTIONS:

16. How can a manager improve team effectiveness by modifying inputs?
17. What is the relationship among a team's cohesiveness, performance norms, and performance results?
18. How would a manager know that a team is suffering from groupthink (give two symptoms) and what could the manager do about it (give two responses)?
19. What makes a self-managing team different from a traditional work team?

APPLICATION QUESTION:

20. Marcos Martinez has just been appointed manager of a production team operating the 11 P.M. to 7 A.M. shift in a large manufacturing firm. An experienced manager, Marcos is pleased that the team members really like and get along well with one another, but they also appear to be restricting their task outputs to the minimum acceptable levels. What could Marcos do to improve things in this situation, and why should he do them?

CHAPTER 16 APPLICATIONS

NASCAR: Fast Cars, Passion Motivate Top Drivers

By only his second full year of NASCAR Winston Cup Series racing, the young Ryan Newman was rapidly becoming a racing phenomenon. He has had several spectacular consecutive racing seasons. As of late, Newman had competed in almost 175 Winston Cup races, finishing among the top ten 82 times while winning 37 pole positions and 12 races.[52] Ryan Newman appears driven to succeed. What motivates someone like Ryan Newman?

In a sport that measures victory in hundredths of a second, NASCAR drivers need every competitive edge they can get. And Ryan Newman, number 0, claims a unique advantage among his racing peers: his education. Committed to succeeding as a racer, Ryan graduated from Purdue University with a degree in vehicle structural engineering. Did it make a difference? That season, Ryan earned almost $500,000 in NASCAR winnings. One year later, he'd earned nearly ten times as much.

Ryan Newman's Racing Passion

A self-admitted car buff, Ryan Newman loves to drive cars and work on them.[53] His passion for fast cars developed at an early age. Encouraged by his parents, he started racing quarter midgets when he was only four-and-a-half years old. Newman amassed more than 100 midget car victories. Later he raced midget cars and sprint cars, achieving extraordinary success there as well. He won Rookie of the Year honors in 1993 for the All-American Midget Series, in 1995 for the USAC National Midget Series, in 1996 for USAC Silver Crown Racing, and in 1999 for sprint cars.[54]

When Newman joined the Penske Racing Team in late 1999, the team's co-owners hired Buddy Baker, a former race car driver and subsequently a race car driving instructor, to work with Newman. Being very selective about the drivers he works with, Baker insisted on meeting Newman and his family before accepting the job offer. Baker says: "When I started talking to Ryan, I could feel the energy that he had, and the passion he had for the sport. Then, I met his dad, and right there I knew, OK, he's got a good background. His father's been with him in go-carts, midgets. He turned the wrenches for his son. It was an automatic fit for me." Baker thinks of Newman as though he were one of his own sons, both of whom briefly tried racing but neither of whom had a passion for it. Baker says that he never wanted to do anything but race, and Newman is just like him. Referring to Newman, Baker says: "From the time he was 5 years old until now, he's never wanted to be anything else."[55]

Referring to his pre–Winston Cup racing days, Newman says: "I always worked on my own cars and maintained them, did the set-ups, things like that. Obviously, I also drove them so I was always a hands-on,

involved, seat of the pants driver." As a Winston Cup driver, Newman acknowledges that he misses working on the cars, "but when you have great guys doing that work, you don't feel like you have to do it yourself."[56]

"For all my life, my family has been my crew," Newman also says." "To come to an organization like Penske, and have so many more people behind you fighting for the same goals, it's like being in a bigger family. When you're with people you like, you have the confidence to do things well."[57] Most of the people who work on Newman's crew are engineers, and all of them are computer whizzes—significant talents for building and maintaining today's race cars.[58] Newman and the crew try to learn from the problem situations that they encounter so they can "keep the freak things from happening."[59]

Newman enters every race with the attitude that he can and will win it.[60]

Newman asserts that his racing team does the best job it can with what they have. "When there's an opportunity to try and stretch it to the end, we're going to try to stretch to the end," says Newman.[61]

Working together as a team and optimizing every mechanical advantage, Ryan Newman and his team have beat the odds to generate a successful record in the ultracompetitive NASCAR circuit. And though victory brings the loyalty of fans and big prize winnings, it can also create tension among fellow racers, many of whom have been racing decades longer than Newman. Does this young driver have the talent, know-how, and commitment to make it in NASCAR for the long haul?

REVIEW QUESTIONS

1. How does Ryan Newman's passion for racing affect his Nascar team?
2. What is the link between Newman's defeats and the success of his racing team?
3. How do the professional actions of Ryan Newman and his team constitute synergy?

TEAM PROJECT

Superstars on the Team

During a period of reflection following a down cycle for his teams, Sasho Cirovski, head coach of the University of Maryland's men's soccer, came to a realization. "I was recruiting talent," he said, "I wasn't doing a very good job of recruiting leaders." With a change of strategy his teams moved back to top-ranked national competition.

Question: What do you do with a "superstar" on your team?

Research Directions:

■ Everywhere you look—in entertainment, in sports, and in business—a lot of attention these days goes to the superstars. What is the record of teams and groups with superstars? Do they really outperform the rest?

■ What is the real impact of a superstar's presence on a team or in the workplace? What do they add? What do they cost? Consider the potential costs of having a superstar on a team in the equation. Benefits−Costs=Value. What is the bottom line of having a superstar on the team?

■ Interview the athletic coaches on your campus. Ask them the previous questions about superstars. Compare and contrast their answers. Interview players from various teams. Ask them the same questions.

■ Develop a set of guidelines for creating team effectiveness in a situation where a superstar is present. Be thorough and practical.

PERSONAL MANAGEMENT

Team Contributions

No one can deny that teams are indispensable in today's organizations. And importantly, you cannot deny that a large part of your career success will depend on your skills at working in and leading teams. Are you ready for truly valuable **TEAM CONTRIBUTIONS**? Consider this list of must have skills for top team contributors. Good at:

■ encouraging and motivating others.
■ accepting suggestions.
■ listening to different points of view.
■ communicating information and ideas.
■ persuasion.
■ conflict resolution and negotiating.
■ building consensus.
■ fulfilling commitments.

Building the Brand Called "You" In your classes and/or at work, are you making these contributions to the teams in which you are asked to participate? Push the question even further. Ask others who know and work with you to assess your performance and contributions as a group member. What suggestions do they have for how you could improve your team contributions? Take the self-assessments. What do they say?

NEXT STEPS: MANAGEMENT LEARNING WORKBOOK

Self-Assessments
■ Emotional Intelligence (#2)
■ T-t Leadership Style (#21)
■ Team Leader Skills (#27)

Experiential Exercises
■ Leading through Participation (#16)
■ Lost at Sea (#26)
■ Work Team Dynamics (#27)

Communication, Conflict, and Negotiation

17

Building Up or Breaking Down?

Though it seems hard to believe, not all managers are doing the best for their organizations. While some lead in ways that unify and strengthen their employees, others find themselves embroiled in almost constant conflict and dissension. Why the disparity?

"He has achieved success . . . who has filled his niche and accomplished his task; who has left the world better than he found it."

These lines from American poet Bessie Anderson Stanley encapsulate the essence of *constructive management*; that is, management that seeks not only to keep an organization running, but also to grow it and improve upon its strengths.

It isn't the easiest way to govern. Constructive management employs open communication, respect, diplomacy, tact, and negotiation to develop trust among participating groups and overcome conflict within and outside the organization.

To millions around the world, the United Nations (UN) embodies both the spirit and the reality of constructive management. The organization brings together 191 countries to defend human rights, conduct peacekeeping missions, fight dangerous diseases, and reduce poverty worldwide.[1]

What *They* Think

"We work in an organization where one usually tries to avoid conflict, but when the issues are that important and also that persistent, one needs to find a way of getting them debated, and move forward in a rational and perhaps more organized manner."
Kofi Annan, former secretary-general of the UN

CONSTRUCTIVE: *"Good management is the art of making problems so interesting and their solutions so constructive that everyone wants to get to work and deal with them."*
Paul Hawken, environmentalist and author.

DESTRUCTIVE: *"We need leadership, and I don't think we're getting it. To sit back and just push it away and say we'll deal with it sometime down the road is dishonest to the people and self-destructive."*
Russell Train, chairman emeritus of the World Wildlife Fund.

The UN is led by a secretary-general who heads internal matters and acts as a spokesperson to the outside world. During his 10-year tenure as secretary-general, Kofi Annan gained a reputation as a soft-spoken leader. The native of Ghana earned the respect of member states by aggressively but diplomatically pursuing positive change both within the organization and in countries that needed it the most.

"Kofi Annan's courage in assuming personal responsibility, as well as responsibility for the Secretariat for its role in Rwanda, is nothing short of revolutionary at the United Nations," said David Malone, president of the International Peace Academy, a New York-based independent research organization that offers counsel to diplomats.[2] Annan received equal parts appreciation and ire for his tendency to shine a spotlight on the UN's blemishes in order to improve the organization.

"We work in an organization where one usually tries to avoid conflict," Annan said, "but when the issues are that important and also that persistent, one needs to find a way of getting them debated, and move forward in a rational and perhaps more organized manner."[3]

In contrast, *destructive management*, while perhaps well intentioned, causes enough harm or ill will to generate concern among employees, investors and other stakeholders.

When Hewlett-Packard picked Carly Fiorina to lead the company in 1999, it was thought that her management style would help carry HP into a new century of competitive business. But in a short time, she made a number of decisions that provoked those who should have been her allies – among them, replacing portraits of HP's founders in office lobbies with her own,[4] accelerating layoffs to increase quarterly profits,[5] and charging to HP the cost of transporting her yacht from coast to coast.[6]

Many struggled to match Fiorina's decisions with the company's best interests. Not too long after a controversial takeover of Compaq Computer, Fiorina was asked to step down by HP's board. Later, as luck would have it, Fiorina released a tell-all book describing her tenure at HP while the company was in the midst of a corporate espionage scandal. In it, she describes the board of directors—with whom she frequently clashed in her years at the top—as divided and "dysfunctional."[7]

What about it? Will you have what it takes to be a constructive leader?

The Numbers

Hewlett-Packard Stock Price with Carly Fiorina as CEO

July 1999 (Fiorina starts)	$37.16
July 2000	$49.95
July 2001	$22.78
July 2002	$13.29
July 2003	$20.27
July 2004	$19.58
February 2005 (Fiorina departs)	$20.38

Quick Facts

* In 2000, the UN reported: the three richest persons in the world had assets valued greater than the GNP of the world's 48 poorest nations; the cost of ice cream consumed by Europeans, $11 billion, could provide clean water and safe sewers for the world.[8]
* During its existence, the UN has sponsored more than 500 multilateral agreements designed to improve international law.[9]
* HP's takeover of Compaq was the biggest in corporate history, valued at $120 billion.[10]
* The son of HP founder Bill Hewlett and a board member fought the purchase of Compaq for over a year.[11]
* HP's stock jumped 7 percent on news of Carly Fiorina's departure.[12]

What Do *You* Think?

1. If he was responsible for instituting positive change at the United Nations, why did Kofi Annan provoke resentment for exposing the UN's shortcomings?

2. Was Carly Fiorina's leadership good or bad for HP in the long run?

423

Communication, Conflict, and Negotiation			
Study Question 1 The Communication Process	**Study Question 2** Improving Communication	**Study Question 3** Conflict	**Study Question 4** Negotiation
■ What is effective communication? ■ Persuasion and credibility in communication ■ Communication barriers	■ Active listening ■ Constructive feedback ■ Space design ■ Channels and technology ■ Interactive management ■ Valuing culture and diversity	■ Functional and dysfunctional conflict ■ Causes of conflict ■ How to deal with conflict ■ Conflict management styles	■ Negotiation goals and approaches ■ Gaining integrative agreements ■ Negotiation pitfalls ■ Third-party dispute resolution
Learning Check 1	**Learning Check 2**	**Learning Check 3**	**Learning Check 4**

hen recruiters are asked what attributes are most important for graduates of business schools, "Communication and interpersonal skills" tops the list.[13] And anyone heading into the new workplace must understand just how important this finding is. Whether you work at the top, building support for strategies and organizational goals, or at lower levels, interacting with others to support their work efforts and your own, communication and interpersonal skills are essential to your personal tool kit.

Think back to the descriptions of managerial work by Henry Mintzberg, John Kotter, and others as discussed in Chapter 1. For Mintzberg, managerial success involves performing well as an information "nerve center," gathering information from and disseminating information to internal and external sources.[14] For Kotter, it depends largely on one's ability to build and maintain a complex web of interpersonal networks with insiders and outsiders so as to implement work priorities and agendas.[15] Says Pam Alexander, CEO of Ogilvy Public Relations Worldwide: "Relationships are the most powerful form of media. Ideas will only get you so far these days. Count on personal relationships to carry you further."[16]

THE COMMUNICATION PROCESS

■ **Communication** is the process of sending and receiving symbols with meanings attached.

Communication is an interpersonal process of sending and receiving symbols with messages attached to them. In more practical terms, the key elements in the communication process are shown in *Figure 17.1*. They include a *sender*, who is responsible for encoding an intended *message* into meaningful symbols, both verbal and nonverbal. The message is sent through a *communication channel* to a *receiver*, who then decodes or interprets its *meaning*. This interpretation may or may not match the sender's original intentions. *Feedback*, when present, reverses the process and conveys the receiver's response back to the sender. Another way to view the communication process is as a series of questions. "Who?" (sender) "says what?" (message) "in what way?" (channel) "to whom?" (receiver) "with what result?" (interpreted meaning).

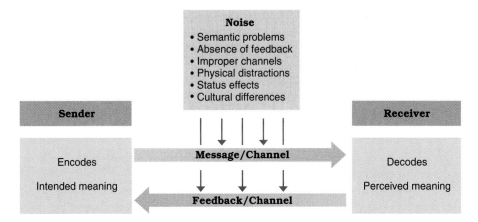

Figure 17.1 The interactive two-way process of interpersonal communication.

WHAT IS EFFECTIVE COMMUNICATION?

The ability to communicate well both orally and in writing is a critical managerial skill and the foundation of effective leadership. Through communication, people exchange and share information with one another, and influence one another's attitudes, behaviors, and understandings. Communication allows managers to establish and maintain interpersonal relationships, listen to others, deal with conflicts, negotiate, and otherwise gain the information needed to create an inspirational workplace.

Effective communication occurs when the sender's message is fully understood by the receiver. As we all know, effectiveness in communication is not always achieved; sometimes efficiency is traded for effectiveness. **Efficient communication** occurs at minimum cost in terms of resources expended. Time, in particular, is an important resource in the communication process. Picture your instructor taking the time to communicate individually with each student about this chapter. It would be virtually impossible. Even if it were possible, it would be costly. This is why managers often leave voice-mail messages and interact by e-mail rather than visit people personally. These alternatives are more efficient than one-on-one and face-to-face communications. But, they may not be effective.

A low-cost approach such as an e-mail note to a distribution list may save time, but it does not always result in everyone getting the same meaning from the message. Without opportunities to ask questions and clarify the message, erroneous interpretations are possible. By the same token, an effective communication may not always be efficient. If a work team leader visits each team member individually to explain a new change in procedures, this may guarantee that everyone truly understands the change. But it may also be very costly in the demands it makes on the leader's time. A team meeting would be more efficient. In these and other ways, potential trade-offs between effectiveness and efficiency must be recognized in communication.

PERSUASION AND CREDIBILITY IN COMMUNICATION

Communication is not always just about sharing information or being "heard"; it often includes the desire of one party to influence or motivate the other in a desired way. Especially in management, one of the most important purposes of communication is **persuasion,** getting someone else to support the message being presented.[17]

In today's organizations managers get things done by working with and persuading others who are their peers, teammates, and co-workers. They often

■ In **effective communication** the intended meaning is fully understood by the receiver.

■ **Efficient communication** occurs at minimum cost.

■ **Persuasion** is presenting a message in a manner that casues the other person to support it.

get things done more by convincing than by order giving. Furthermore, they must be able to persuade others over and over again; once is not enough.

Among the power bases discussed in Chapter 13 on leadership, personal powers of expertise and reference are essential to the art of effective persuasion. Scholar and consultant Jay Conger says that many managers "confuse persuasion with taking bold stands and aggressive arguing." He points out that this often leads to "counter persuasion" responses and to questions regarding the managers' credibility.[18] And without **credibility**—trust, respect, and integrity in the eyes of others—he sees little chance that persuasion can be successful. Conger's advice is to build credibility for persuasive communication through expertise and relationships.

> ■ **Credibility** is trust, respect, and integrity in the eyes of others.

To build *credibility through expertise*, you must be knowledgeable about the issue in question and/or have a successful track record in dealing with similar issues in the past. In a hiring situation where you are trying to persuade team members to select candidate A rather than B, for example, you had better be able to defend your reasons. And it will always be better if your past recommendations turned out to be good ones.

To build *credibility through relationships*, you must have a good working relationship with the person to be persuaded. The iron rule of reference power should be remembered: it is always easier to get someone to do what you want if that person likes you. To return to the prior example, if you have to persuade your boss to support a special bonus package to attract candidates, having a good relationship with your boss will add credibility to your request.

COMMUNICATION BARRIERS

Noise, as previously shown in *Figure 17.1*, is anything that interferes with the effectiveness of the communication process. For example, when Yoshihiro

INSIGHTS

Lead the Way with Communication

Communication and interpersonal skills are mainstream in leadership development at the internationally regarded Center for Creative Leadership. Headquartered in Greensboro, North Carolina, the center's mission is "to advance the understanding, practice and development of leadership for the benefit of society worldwide." It has a global reputation for excellence and has

been ranked number 1 by *Business Week* for executive education in leadership.

> *The Center for Creative Leadership was founded on the initiative of H. Smith Richardson, Jr., a successful executive. He believed that "what organizations needed was not just leadership for the present and the near future, but a kind of innovative leadership with a broader focus and a longer view. Such leadership would be concerned not with profits, markets and business strategies alone, but with the place of business in society."*

When Richard S. Herlich came to the Center, he had been recently promoted to director of marketing for his firm. "I thought I had the perfect style," he said. He learned through role-playing that others viewed him as an aloof and poor communicator. After returning to his job and meeting with his subordinates to discuss his style, Herlich became more involved in their work projects. Another participant, Robert Siddall, received feedback that he was too structured and domineering. Center instructors worked with him to develop more positive relationships and to display a more "coaching" style of management. After he returned to his job, Siddall's performance ratings went up, and his relationships with co-workers improved. He says, "If I start screaming and yelling, they say—'Old Bob, old Bob.' "

Wada was president of Mazda Corporation, he once met with representatives of the firm's American joint venture partner, Ford. But he had to use an interpreter. He estimated that 20 percent of his intended meaning was lost in the exchange between himself and the interpreter; another 20 percent was lost between the interpreter and the Americans, with whom he was ultimately trying to communicate.[19] In addition to the obvious problems when different languages are involved, common sources of noise in communication include poor choice of channels, poor written or oral expression, failure to recognize nonverbal signals, physical distractions, and status effects.

Poor Choice of Channels

A *communication channel* is the medium through which a message is conveyed from sender to receiver. Good managers choose the right communication channel, or combination of channels, to accomplish their intended purpose.[20] In general, *written channels*, paper or electronic, are acceptable for simple messages that are easy to convey and for those that require extensive dissemination quickly. They are also important as documentation when formal policies or directives are being conveyed. *Spoken channels* work best for messages that are complex and difficult to convey, where immediate feedback to the sender is valuable. They are also more personal and can create a supportive, even inspirational, emotional climate.

Poor Written or Oral Expression

Communication will be effective only to the extent that the sender expresses a message in a way that can be clearly understood by the receiver. This means that words must be well chosen and properly used to express the sender's intentions. Consider the following "bafflegab" found among some executive communications.

> A business report said: "Consumer elements are continuing to stress the fundamental necessity of a stabilization of the price structure at a lower level than exists at the present time." (*Translation:* Consumers keep saying that prices must go down and stay down.)

> A manager said: "Substantial economies were effected in this division by increasing the time interval between distribution of data-eliciting forms to business entities." (*Translation:* The division saved money by sending out fewer questionnaires.)

Both written and oral communication require skill. It isn't easy, for example, to write a concise, clear and understandable e-mail. Like any written message, the e-mail can easily be misunderstood. It takes practice and hard work to express yourself well. The same holds true for oral communication that takes place in telephone calls, face-to-face meetings, formal briefings, video conferences, and the like. *Management Smarts 17.1* identifies guidelines for an important communication situation—the executive briefing or formal presentation.[21]

MANAGEMENT SMARTS 17.1

How to make a successful presentation

- *Be prepared:* Know what you want to say; know how you want to say it; rehearse saying it.
- *Set the right tone:* Act audience centered; make eye contact; be pleasant and confident.
- *Sequence points:* State your purpose; make important points; follow with details; then summarize.
- *Support your points:* Give specific reasons for your points; state them in understandable terms.
- *Accent the presentation:* Use good visual aids; provide supporting handouts when possible.
- *Add the right amount of polish:* Attend to details; have room, materials, and arrangements ready to go.
- *Check your technology:* Check everything ahead of time; make sure it works and know how to use it.
- *Don't bet on the Internet:* Beware of plans to make real-time Internet visits; save sites on a disk and use a browser to open the file.
- *Be professional:* Be on time; wear appropriate attire; act organized, confident, and enthusiastic.

Failure to Recognize Nonverbal Signals

■ **Nonverbal communication** takes place through gestures and body language.

Nonverbal communication takes place through such things as hand movements, facial expressions, body posture, eye contact, and the use of interpersonal space. It can be a powerful means of transmitting messages. Eye contact or voice intonation can be used intentionally to accent special parts of an oral communication. The astute observer notes the "body language" expressed by other persons. At times our body may be "talking" for us even as we otherwise maintain silence. And when we do speak, our body may sometimes "say" different things than our words convey.

A **mixed message** occurs when a person's words communicate one message while his or her actions, body language, appearance, or use of interpersonal space communicate something else. Watch how people behave in a meeting. A person who feels under attack may move back in a chair or lean away from the presumed antagonist, even while expressing verbal agreement. All of this is done quite unconsciously, but it sends a message to those alert enough to pick it up.

Nonverbal channels probably play a more important part in communication than most people recognize. One researcher indicates that gestures alone may make up as much as 70 percent of communication.[22] In fact, a potential side effect of the growing use of electronic mail, computer networking, and other communication technologies is that gestures and other nonverbal signals that can add important meaning to the communication event are lost.

■ A **mixed message** results when words communicate one message while actions, body language, or appearance communicate something else.

Physical Distractions

Any number of physical distractions can interfere with communication effectiveness. Some of these distractions, such as telephone interruptions, drop-in visitors, and lack of privacy, are evident in the following conversation between an employee, George, and his manager:

> Okay, George, let's hear your problem [phone rings, boss picks it up, promises to deliver a report "just as soon as I can get it done"]. Uh, now, where were we—oh, you're having a problem with your technician. She's [manager's secretary brings in some papers that need his immediate signature; secretary leaves] . . . you say she's overstressed lately, wants to leave. . . . I tell you what, George, why don't you [phone rings again, lunch partner drops by] . . . uh, take a stab at handling it yourself. . . . I've got to go now.[23]

Besides what may have been poor intentions in the first place, the manager in this example did not do a good job of communicating with George. This problem could be easily corrected; many communication distractions can be avoided or at least minimized through proper planning. If George has something important to say, the manager should set aside adequate time for the meeting. Additional interruptions such as telephone calls and drop-in visitors could be eliminated by issuing appropriate instructions to the secretary.

Status Effects

"Criticize my boss? I don't have the right to." "I'd get fired." "It's her company, not mine." As these comments suggest, the hierarchy of authority in organizations creates another potential barrier to effective communications.

Consider the "corporate cover-up" once discovered at an electronics company. Product shipments were being predated and papers falsified to meet unrealistic sales targets set by the president. His managers knew the targets were impossible to attain, but at least 20 persons in the organization cooperated in the deception. It was months before the top found out. What happened in this case was **filtering**—the intentional distortion of information to make it appear favorable to the recipient.

> ▨ **Filtering** is the intentional distortion of information to make it appear most favorable to the recipient.

The presence of information filtering is often found in communications between lower and higher levels in organizations. Tom Peters, management author and consultant, has called information distortion "Management Enemy Number 1."[24] Simply put, it most often involves someone "telling the boss what he or she wants to hear." Whether the reason behind this is a fear of retribution for bringing bad news, an unwillingness to identify personal mistakes, or just a general desire to please, the end result is the same. The person receiving filtered communications can end up making poor decisions because of a biased and inaccurate information base.

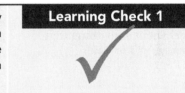

Be sure you can ■ describe the communication process and identify its key components ■ differentiate between effective and efficient communication ■ explain the role of credibility in persuasive communication ■ list the common sources of noise that inhibit effective communication ■ explain how mixed messages and filtering interfere with communication

Learning Check 1

IMPROVING COMMUNICATION

A number of things can be done to reduce noise, overcome barriers and improve the process of communication. They include active listening, constructive use of feedback, opening upward communication channels, understanding the use of space, utilizing technology, and valuing diversity.

ACTIVE LISTENING

Managers must be very good at listening. When people "talk," they are trying to communicate something. That "something" may or may not be what they are saying. **Active listening** is the process of taking action to help someone say exactly what he or she really means.[25] It involves being sincere and trying to find out the full meaning of what is being said. It also involves being disciplined in controlling emotions and withholding premature evaluations or interpretations.

> ▨ **Active listening** helps the source of a message say what he or she really means.

Different responses to the following two questions contrast how a "passive" listener and an "active" listener might act in real workplace conversations. Question 1: "Don't you think employees should be promoted on the basis of seniority?" *Passive listener's response:* "No, I don't!" *Active listener's response:* "It seems to you that they should, I take it?" Question 2: "What does the supervisor expect us to do about these out-of-date computers?" *Passive listener's response:* "Do the best you can, I guess." *Active listener's response:* "You're pretty disgusted with those machines, aren't you?"

These examples help show how active listening can facilitate communication in difficult circumstances, rather than discourage it. As you think further about active listening, keep these rules in mind.[26]

1. *Listen for message content:* Try to hear exactly what content is being conveyed in the message.
2. *Listen for feelings:* Try to identify how the source feels about the content in the message.
3. *Respond to feelings:* Let the source know that her or his feelings are being recognized.
4. *Note all cues:* Be sensitive to nonverbal and verbal messages; be alert for mixed messages.
5. *Paraphrase and restate:* State back to the source what you think you are hearing.

CONSTRUCTIVE FEEDBACK

■ **Feedback** is the process of telling someone else how you feel about something that person did or said.

The process of telling other people how you feel about something they did or said, or about the situation in general, is called **feedback.** The art of giving feedback is an indispensable skill, particularly for managers who must regularly give feedback to other people. Often this takes the form of performance feedback given as evaluations and appraisals. When poorly done, such feedback can be threatening to the recipient and cause resentment. When properly done, feedback—even performance criticism—can be listened to, accepted, and used to good advantage by the receiver.[27] When Lydia Whitfield, a marketing vice president at Avaya, asked one of her managers for feedback she was surprised. He said: "You're angry a lot." Whitfield learned from the experience, saying: "What he and other employees saw as my anger, I saw as my passion."[28]

There are ways to help ensure that feedback is useful and constructive rather than harmful. To begin, one must learn to recognize when the feedback will really benefit the receiver, and when it will mainly satisfy some personal need. A supervisor who berates a computer programmer for errors, for example, may actually be angry about personally failing to give clear instructions in the first place. A manager should also make sure that any feedback is understandable, acceptable, and plausible. *Some guidelines for giving "constructive" feedback* are:[29]

- Give feedback directly and with real feeling, based on trust between you and the receiver.
- Make sure that feedback is specific rather than general; use good, clear, and preferably recent examples to make your points.
- Give feedback at a time when the receiver seems most willing or able to accept it.
- Make sure the feedback is valid; limit it to things the receiver can be expected to do something about.
- Give feedback in small doses; never give more than the receiver can handle at any particular time.

SPACE DESIGN

An important but sometimes neglected part of communication involves *proxemics,* or the use of space.[30] The distance between people conveys varying intentions in terms of intimacy, openness, and status. And the physical layout of an office is an often-overlooked form of nonverbal communication.

Check it out. Offices with chairs available for side-by-side seating convey different messages than those where the manager's chair sits behind the desk, and those for visitors sit facing it in front.

Office or workspace architecture is an important influence on communication and behavior. Architects and consultants specializing in *organizational ecology* are helping executives build offices conducive to the intense communication needed today. When Sun Microsystems built its San Jose, California, facility, public spaces were designed to encourage communication among persons from different departments. Many meeting areas had no walls, and most walls were glass. As manager of planning and research, Ann Bamesberger said: "We were creating a way to get these people to communicate with each other more." Importantly, the Sun project involved not only the assistance of expert architectural consultants, but also extensive inputs and suggestions from the employees themselves.[31] At Google headquarters, or googleplex, telecommuters work in specially designed office "tents." These are made of acrylics to allow both the sense of private personal space and transparency.[32]

KAFFEEKLATSCH

Difficult Employees

First Cup

"We just got a new transfer into our office. Whew, he's a handful. Some days he comes in happy and pleasant; most days he's a real bear. Technically his work is fine, but his behavior is getting very disruptive. The others are starting to complain that his 'bad days' are becoming 'bad days' for everyone. And, I'm starting to notice that on his bad days everyone else's performance also drops."

Studying the Grounds

■ Sometimes managers transfer their "problem workers" to other departments. Although this isn't fair to the receiving unit, it is an easy, although self-centered, solution for the sending unit.

■ Different management styles apply best in different situations. This is point of contingency leadership thinking. "Calm and supportive" may fit one employee type or situation; "directive and firm" might be better for others.

■ People's work and non-work lives don't always fall into neat and separate compartments. Things that happen at work can spill over to affect one's behavior outside of work, and vice versa.

■ Managers are supposed to engage in "performance management" discussions with their direct reports. This is easy when things are all positive, but it's a lot harder to hold the conversation with an employee who has a performance problem.

Double Espresso

"I've tried to be supportive and understanding with the guy, but I'm starting to lose patience. I've got to do something or the situation will get out of hand. As a manager, am I supposed to be a 'boss' or a 'therapist'? Or, should I be both?"

Your Turn

What are the best ways to deal with a disruptive employee like this? Is it time for constructive feedback or active listening, or are things past the point where they would be useful? And let's not forget the other members of the team. How can they be best dealt with, or even brought into the "solution?"

CHANNELS AND TECHNOLOGY UTILIZATION

■ **Channel richness** is the capacity of a communication channel to effectively carry information.

People communicate with one another using a variety of channels. Choice of channels is important, since they vary in **channel richness**, the capacity to carry information in an effective manner.[33] *Figure 17.2* shows that face-to-face communication is very high in richness, enabling two-way interaction and real-time feedback. Things like written reports, memos, and text messages are very low in richness because of impersonal, one-way interaction with limited opportunity for feedback. Managers need to understand the limits of the possible channels and choose wisely when using them for communication.

When IBM surveyed employees to find out how they learned what was going on at the company, executives were not surprised that co-workers were perceived as credible and useful sources. But they were surprised that the firm's intranet ranked equally high. IBM's internal Web sites were ranked higher than news briefs, company memos, and information from managers.[34] The new age of communication is one of e-mail, voice-mail, instant messaging, teleconferencing, online discussions, videoconferencing, virtual or computer-mediated meetings, intranets, and Web portals. And the many implications for technology utilization must be understood.

Knowing how and when to use e-mail is a major communication issue for people in organizations today. Purpose and privacy are concerns. Employers are concerned that too much work time gets spent handling personal e-mail; employees are concerned that employers are eavesdropping on their e-mail messages. The best advice comes down to this: (1) find out the employer's policy on personal e-mail and follow it; (2) don't assume that you ever have e-mail privacy at work. E-mail workload, which can be overwhelming, is also a concern. At Intel, for example, managers discovered that some employees faced up to 300 e-mail messages a day and spent some 2.5 hours per day dealing with them. The firm initiated a training program to improve e-mail utilization and efficiency.[35] Tips on managing your e-mail are presented in *Management Smarts 17.2.*[36]

Another thing to remember is that technology offers the power of the *electronic grapevine*, speeding messages and information from person to person. When the members of a sixth-grade class in Taylorsville, North Carolina (population 1,566) sent out the e-mail message "Hi! . . . We are curious to see where in the world our e-mail will travel," they were surprised. Over a half-million replies flooded in, overwhelming not only the students but the school's

---

MANAGEMENT SMARTS 17.2

Tips on Handling E-mail

- Read items only once.
- Take action immediately to answer, move to folders, or delete.
- Purge folders regularly of useless messages.
- Send group mail and use "reply to all" only when really necessary.
- Get off distribution lists that are without value to your work.
- Send short messages in the subject line, avoiding a full-text message.
- Put large files on Web sites, instead of sending them as attachments.
- Use instant messaging as an e-mail alternative.
- Don't forget the basic rule of e-mail privacy: there isn't any.

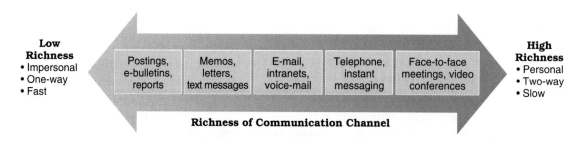

Low Richness						High Richness
• Impersonal • One-way • Fast	Postings, e-bulletins, reports	Memos, letters, text messages	E-mail, intranets, voice-mail	Telephone, instant messaging	Face-to-face meetings, video conferences	• Personal • Two-way • Slow

Richness of Communication Channel

Figure 17.2 Channel richness and the use of communication media.

computer system.[37] Messages fly with equal speed and intensity around organizations. The results can be both functional—when the information is accurate and useful—and dysfunctional—when the information is false, distorted, or simply based on rumor. Managers need to be quick to correct such misimpressions and inaccuracies; they should be alert to use electronic grapevines to quickly move factual and relevant information to organizational members.

INTERACTIVE MANAGEMENT

Interactive management approaches use a variety of means to keep communication channels open between organizational levels. A popular choice is **management by wandering around (MBWA)**—dealing directly with subordinates by regularly spending time walking around and talking with them. MBWA involves finding out for yourself what is going on in face-to-face communications. The basic objectives are to break down status barriers, increase the frequency of interpersonal contact, and get more and better information from lower-level sources. Of course, this requires a trusting relationship. Patricia Gallup, CEO of PC Connection, became known for her interactive style of leadership and emphasis on communication. By making herself available by e-mail and by spending as much time as possible out of her office, she made MBWA part of her style.[38]

■ In **management by wandering around (MBWA)** managers spend time outside their offices to meet and talk with workers at all levels.

Management practices designed to open channels and improve upward communications have traditionally involved *open office hours,* whereby busy senior executives like Gallup set aside time in their calendars to welcome walk-in visits during certain hours each week. Today this approach is often expanded to include *online discussion forums* and "chat rooms" that are open at certain hours. Regular *employee group meetings* are also helpful. Here, a rotating schedule of "shirtsleeve" meetings can bring top managers into face-to-face contact with mixed employee groups throughout an organization. The face-to-face groups can be supplemented by *video conferences,* which serve similar purposes, overcoming time and distance limitations to communication. In some cases, a comprehensive communications program includes an *employee advisory council,* composed of members elected by their fellow employees. Such councils meet with management on a regular schedule to discuss and react to new policies and programs that will affect employees.

When executives suspect that they are having communication problems, *communication consultants* can be hired to conduct interviews and surveys of employees on their behalf. Marc Brownstein, president of a public relations and advertising firm, for example, was surprised when managers complained in an anonymous survey that he was a poor listener that gave them insufficient feedback. They also felt poorly informed about the firm's financial health. In other words, poor communication was hurting staff morale. With help from consultants, Brownstein started to hold more meetings and work more aggressively to share information and communicate regularly with the firm's employees.[39]

VALUING CULTURE AND DIVERSITY

Communicating under conditions of diversity, where the sender and receiver are part of different cultures, is certainly a significant challenge. For years, cultural challenges have been recognized by international travelers and executives. But as we know, you don't have to travel abroad to come face-to-

face with cultural diversity. The importance of cross-cultural applies at home just as much as it does in a foreign country. The workplace abounds with subcultures based on gender, age, ethnicity, race, and other factors. All are a source of different perspectives, experiences, values, and expectations that can complicate the communication process. When the sender and receiver are unable to empathize with one another's cultures, they will have difficulties understanding when and why certain words, gestures, and messages are misinterpreted.

It is useful to recall that a major source of cross-cultural difficulties is **ethnocentrism,** the tendency to consider one's culture superior to any and all others. Ethnocentrism can adversely affect communication in at least three major ways: (1) it may cause someone to not listen well to what others have to say; (2) it may cause someone to address or speak with others in ways that alienate them; and (3) it may lead to the use of inappropriate stereotypes when dealing with persons from another culture.[40]

■ **Ethnocentrism** is the tendency to consider one's culture superior to any and all others.

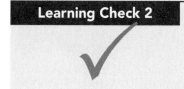

Learning Check 2

Be sure you can ■ define active listening and list active listening rules ■ illustrate the guidelines for constructive feedback ■ explain how and why space design influences communication ■ discuss the influence of technology utilization on communication ■ explain how MBWA can improve upward communication ■ explain the impact of ethnocentrism on communication

CONFLICT

Among your communication and related interpersonal skills, the ability to deal with conflicts is critical. **Conflict** is a disagreement between people on substantive or emotional issues.[41] And, managers and leaders spend a lot of time dealing with conflicts of various forms. **Substantive conflicts** involve disagreements over such things as goals and tasks; the allocation of resources; the distribution of rewards, policies, and procedures; and job assignments. **Emotional conflicts** result from feelings of anger, distrust, dislike, fear, and resentment, as well as from personality clashes and relationship problems. Both forms of conflict can cause difficulties. But when managed well, they can also be helpful in promoting creativity and high performance.

■ **Conflict** is a disagreement over issues of substance and/or an emotional antagonism.

■ **Substantive conflict** involves disagreements over goals, resources, rewards, policies, procedures, and job assignments.

■ **Emotional conflict** results from feelings of anger, distrust, dislike, fear, and resentment, as well as from personality clashes.

FUNCTIONAL AND DYSFUNCTIONAL CONFLICT

It is important to remember that not all conflict is bad, and the absence of conflict is not always good. In Chapter 16, for example, the phenomenon described as groupthink is associated with highly cohesive groups whose members make bad decisions because they are unwilling to engage in conflict. But whether or not conflict benefits people and organizations depends on two factors: (1) the intensity of the conflict and (2) how well the conflict is managed.

The inverted "U" curve depicted in *Figure 17.3* shows that conflict of moderate intensity can be good for performance. This **functional conflict,** or *constructive conflict,* stimulates people toward greater work efforts, cooperation, and creativity. It helps groups achieve their goals. At very low or very high intensities, **dysfunctional conflict,** or *destructive conflict,* occurs.

■ **Functional conflict** is constructive and helps task performance.

■ **Dysfunctional conflict** is destructive and hurts task performance.

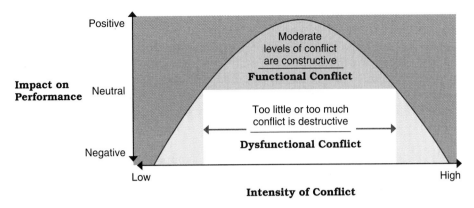

Figure 17.3 The relationship between conflict and performance.

This makes it difficult for groups to achieve their goals. Too much conflict is distracting and interferes with other more task-relevant activities; too little conflict promotes complacency and the loss of a creative, high-performance edge. The goal, as suggested in The Topic chapter opener is to keep conflict constructive and avoid its destructive consequences.

CAUSES OF CONFLICT

A number of antecedent conditions can make the eventual emergence of conflict very likely. *Role ambiguities* set the stage for conflict. Unclear job expectations and other task uncertainties increase the probability that some people will be working at cross purposes, at least some of the time. *Resource*

REAL ETHICS

Bloggers Beware

It is easy and tempting to set up your own Weblog. Writing about experiences and impressions, . . . and then sharing it with others online? So, why not do it?

Catherine Sanderson might have asked this question before launching her blog, *Le Petite Anglaise*. A Britain living and working in Paris, her blog at one point was so "successful" that she had 3,000 readers. But, you see, her Internet diary included reports on her experiences at work. And her employer, the accounting firm Dixon Wilson, wasn't at all happy when it became public knowledge.

Even though Sanderson was blogging anonymously, her photo was on the site, and the connection was eventually discovered. Noticed, too, was her running commentary about bosses, colleagues, and life at the office. One boss, she wrote, "calls secretaries 'typists.' " A Christmas party was described in detail, including an executive's "unforgivable faux pas." Under the heading "Titillation" she told how she displayed cleavage during a video conference at the office.

It's all out now. News reports said that one of the firm's partners was "incandescent with rage" after learning what Sanderson had written about him. Now Sander-

son is upset. She says that she was "dooced"—a new term being used to describe being fired for what one writes in a blog. She wants financial damages and confirmation of her rights, on principle, to have a private blog.

FURTHER INQUIRY

What are bloggers' rights to communicate? Would you agree with the observer who asked this question based on the Sanderson case: "Say you worked for a large corporation, and in your spare time you wrote an anonymous 'insider's view' column for the *Financial Times*. Would you expect anything less than termination upon discovery?" Or, would you agree with another who asks: "Where does the influence your employer has on your day-to-day life stop?"

Just what are the ethics issues here—from the blogger's and the employer's perspectives? Who has what rights when it comes to communicating in public about one's work experiences and impressions?

scarcities cause conflict. Having to share resources with others and/or compete directly with them for resource allocations creates a potential situation conflict, especially when resources are scarce. *Task interdependencies* cause conflict. When individuals or groups must depend on what others do to perform well themselves, conflicts often occur. *Competing objectives* are opportunities for conflict. When objectives are poorly set or reward systems are poorly designed, individuals and groups may come into conflict by working to one another's disadvantage. *Structural differentiation* breeds conflict. Differences in organization structures and in the characteristics of the people staffing them may foster conflict because of incompatible approaches toward work. And *unresolved prior conflicts* tend to erupt in later conflicts. Unless a conflict is fully resolved, it may remain latent and later emerge as a basis for more conflict over the same or related matters.

HOW TO DEAL WITH CONFLICT

■ **Conflict resolution** is the removal of the substantial and/or emotional reasons for a conflict.

When any one or more of these antecedent conditions are present, conflicts are likely to occur. And when they do, they can either be "resolved," in the sense that the sources are corrected, or "suppressed," in that the sources remain but the conflict behaviors are controlled. Suppressed conflicts tend to fester and recur at a later time. True **conflict resolution** eliminates the underlying causes of conflict and reduces the potential for similar conflicts in the future.

Managers use various approaches to deal with conflicts between individuals or groups. There are times when *appealing to superordinate goals* can focus the attention on one mutually desirable end state. The appeal to higher-level goals offers all parties a common frame of reference against which to analyze differences and reconcile disagreements. Conflicts whose antecedents lie in the competition for scarce resources can be resolved by *making more resources available* to everyone. Although costly, this technique removes the reasons for the continuing conflict. By *changing the people,* that is, by replacing or transferring one or more of the conflicting parties, conflicts caused by poor interpersonal relationships can be eliminated. The same holds true for *altering the physical environment.* Facilities, work space, or workflows can be rearranged to physically separate conflicting parties and decrease opportunities for contact with one another.

The *integrating devices* introduced in Chapter 10 as ways to improve coordination in an organization can also be used to deal with conflicts. Using liaison personnel, special task forces, cross-functional teams, and even the matrix form of organization can change interaction patterns and assist in conflict reduction. *Changing reward systems* may reduce competition between individuals and groups for rewards. Creating systems that reward cooperation can encourage behaviors and attitudes that promote teamwork and reduce conflict. *Changing policies and procedures* may redirect behavior in ways that minimize the likelihood of known conflict-prone situations. Finally, *training in interpersonal skills* can help prepare people to communicate and work more effectively in situations where conflict is likely.

CONFLICT MANAGEMENT STYLES

Interpersonally, people respond to conflict through different combinations of cooperative and assertive behaviors.[42] *Cooperativeness* is the desire to satisfy another party's needs and concerns; *assertiveness* is the desire to satisfy one's own needs and concerns. *Figure 17.4* shows five interpersonal styles of conflict management that result from various combinations of these two tendencies.

- **Avoidance** or *withdrawal*—being uncooperative and unassertive, downplaying disagreement, withdrawing from the situation, and/or staying neutral at all costs.
- **Accommodation** or *smoothing*—being cooperative but unassertive, letting the wishes of others rule, smoothing over or overlooking differences to maintain harmony.
- **Competition** or *authoritative command*—being uncooperative but assertive, working against the wishes of the other party, engaging in win-lose competition, and/or forcing through the exercise of authority.
- **Compromise**—being moderately cooperative and assertive, bargaining for "acceptable" solutions in which each party wins a bit and loses a bit.
- **Collaboration** or *problem solving*—being cooperative and assertive, trying to fully satisfy everyone's concerns by working through differences, finding and solving problems so that everyone gains.[43]

The five conflict management styles should be selected and used with caution, and with the requirements of each unique conflict situation carefully considered.[44] Conflict management by *avoiding* or *accommodating* often creates **lose-lose conflict.** No one achieves her or his true desires, and the underlying reasons for conflict often remain unaffected. Although a lose-lose conflict may appear settled or may even disappear for a while, it tends to recur in the future. Avoidance is an extreme form of nonattention. Everyone withdraws and pretends that conflict doesn't really exist, hoping that it will simply go away. Accommodation plays down differences and highlights similarities and areas of agreement. Peaceful coexistence through a recognition of common interests is the goal. In reality, such smoothing may ignore the real essence of a conflict.

Competing and *compromising* tend to create **win-lose conflict.** Here, each party strives to gain at the other's expense. In extreme cases, one party achieves its desires to the complete exclusion of the other party's desires. Because win-lose methods fail to address the root causes of conflict, future conflicts of the same or a similar nature are likely to occur. In competition, one party wins, as superior skill or outright domination allows his or her desires to be forced on the other. This also occurs in the form of authoritative command, where the forcing is accomplished by a higher-level supervisor who simply dictates a solution to subordinates. Compromise occurs when trade-offs are made such that each party to the conflict gives up and gains something of value. But, because each party loses something, antecedents for future conflicts are established.

■ **Avoidance** pretends that a conflict doesn't really exist.

■ **Accommodation** or smoothing plays down differences and highlights similarities to reduce conflict.

■ **Competition** or authoritative command uses force, superior skill, or domination to "win" a conflict.

■ **Compromise** occurs when each party to the conflict gives up something of value to the other.

■ **Collaboration** or problem solving involves working through conflict differences and solving problems so everyone wins.

■ In **lose-lose conflict** no one achieves his or her true desires, and the underlying reasons for conflict remain unaffected.

■ In **win-lose conflict** one party achieves its desires, and the other party does not.

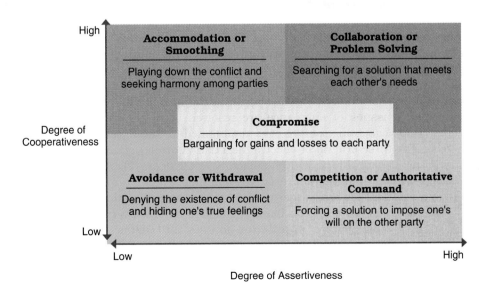

Figure 17.4 Alternative conflict management styles.

▨ In **win-win conflict** the conflict is resolved to everyone's benefit.

Collaborating in true problem solving tries to reconcile underlying differences and is often the most effective conflict management style. It is a form of **win-win conflict** wherein issues are resolved to the mutual benefit of all conflicting parties. This is typically achieved by confronting the issues and through the willingness of everyone involved to recognize that something is wrong and needs attention. Win-win conditions are created by eliminating the underlying causes of the conflict. All relevant issues are raised and discussed openly. Win-win methods are clearly the most preferred of the interpersonal styles of conflict management.

Learning Check 3 ✓	*Be sure you can* ▪ differentiate substantive and emotional conflict ▪ differentiate functional and dysfunctional conflict ▪ explain the common causes of conflict ▪ list the possible approaches to conflict resolution ▪ explain the conflict management styles of avoidance, accommodation, competition, compromise, and collaboration ▪ discuss how these styles create lose-lose, win-lose, and win-win conflicts

NEGOTIATION

Put yourself in the following situations.[45] How would you behave, and what would you do? (1) You have been offered a promotion and would really like to take it. However, the pay raise being offered is less than you hoped. (2) You have enough money to order a new computer for your team, but two members have each requested new computers.

▨ **Negotiation** is the process of making joint decisions when the parties involved have different preferences.

These are examples of the many work situations that lead to **negotiation**—the process of making joint decisions when the parties involved have different preferences. Stated a bit differently, negotiation is a way of reaching agreement. People negotiate over salary, merit raises, performance evaluations, job assignments, work schedules, work locations, and many other considerations. All such negotiations are susceptible to conflict and test the communication and interpersonal skills of those involved.

NEGOTIATION GOALS AND APPROACHES

There are two important goals in negotiation. *Substance goals* are concerned with outcomes; they are tied to the content issues of the negotiation. *Relationship goals* are concerned with processes; they are tied to the way people work together while negotiating, and how they (and any constituencies they represent) will be able to work together again in the future. Effective negotiation occurs when issues of substance are resolved, and working relationships among the negotiating parties are maintained or even improved in the process. The three criteria of effective negotiation are (1) *quality*—negotiating a "wise" agreement that is truly satisfactory to all sides; (2) *cost*—negotiating efficiently, using up minimum resources and time; and (3) *harmony*—negotiation in a way that fosters, rather than inhibits, interpersonal relationships.[46]

▨ **Distributive negotiation** focuses on win-lose claims made by each party for certain preferred outcomes.

The way each party approaches a negotiation can have a major impact on the results.[47] **Distributive negotiation** focuses on "claims" made by each party for certain preferred outcomes. This can take a competitive form in which one party can gain only if the other loses. In such win-lose conditions, relationships are often sacrificed as the negotiating parties focus only on their respective self-interests. It may also become accommodative if the parties defer to one another's wishes simply "to get it over with."

Principled negotiation, often called **integrative negotiation,** is based on a win-win orientation. The focus on substance is still important, but the interests of all parties are considered. The goal is to base the final outcome on the merits of individual claims and to try to find a way for all claims to be satisfied if at all possible. No one should lose, and relationships should be maintained in the process.

■ **Principled/integrative negotiation** uses a "win-win" orientation to reach solutions acceptable to each party.

GAINING INTEGRATIVE AGREEMENTS

In their book *Getting to Yes*, Roger Fisher and William Ury point out that truly integrative agreements are obtained by following 4 negotiation rules:[48]

1. Separate the people from the problem.
2. Focus on interests, not on positions.
3. Generate many alternatives before deciding what to do.
4. Insist that results be based on some objective standard.

ISSUES AND SITUATIONS

Buzzwords and Mixed Messages

There's a new vocabulary developing for today's work environments. But what do the buzzwords really mean? Here is a sampling of what you might be hearing.

BHAGs – big, hairy, audacious goals, ones that stretch aspirations upwards
Execution – putting the strategy into action; actually getting things done
Knowledge acquisition – hiring new people that bring major new talents
Process flow analysis – cutting costs by cutting unnecessary work activities
Skills development – training existing staff to adapt and raise talents
Sox – short for Sarbanes-Oxley corporate governance legislation
Unsiloing – getting people who work in different areas to cooperate more.

While it's good to know the lingo, management professor and consultant Warren Bennis says we should be careful about using buzzwords as we communicate: "Too often people use buzzwords to muddy or cover up what they are actually saying." He might be talking about these examples:

Rightsizing – It used to be called "downsizing," but that had lots of negative pushback. Rightsizing is supposedly defined more positively: reducing size and shrinking resources to fit new circumstances.
Delayering – It used to be called "lay offs," "cutbacks," or "staff reduction." When a firm delayers, it lets go of middle managers; the positive spin is that delayering reduces management levels and increases efficiency.

And while we're talking about management talk, let's not forget the possibility that there might be a lot of mixed messages floating around when higher-ups say one thing but act quite differently. *Business Week*, for example, reported a survey showing that mixed ethics messages are common. Although 68 percent of respondents said that unethical conduct resulting in personal gain is reprimanded, only 51 percent said that it was reprimanded when corporate gain was involved.

Critical Response

In your reading of the news and from listening in conversations, what other buzzwords would you add to this listing? Among the buzzwords, which ones, as Bennis suggests, are really attempts to put positive new twists or spins on practices that have negatives attached to them? And how about mixed messages? What other examples can you describe where people in organizations are talking one thing but acting out quite another?

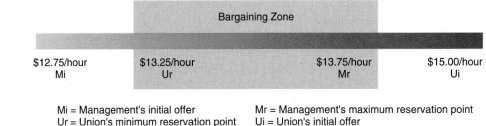

Figure 17.5 The bargaining zone in classic two-party negotiation.

Mi = Management's initial offer
Ur = Union's minimum reservation point

Mr = Management's maximum reservation point
Ui = Union's initial offer

■ **BATNA** is the best alternative to a negotiated agreement.

■ A **bargaining zone** is the area between one party's minimum reservation point and the other party's maximum reservation point.

Proper attitudes and good information are necessary foundations for integrative agreements. The attitudinal foundations involve the willingness of each negotiating party to trust, share information with, and ask reasonable questions of the other party. The informational foundations involve both parties knowing what is really important to them and finding out what is really important to the other party. In addition, each should understand his or her personal **best alternative to a negotiated agreement (BATNA).** This is an answer to the question "What will I do if an agreement can't be reached?"

Figure 17.5 introduces a typical case of labor–management negotiations over a new contract and salary increase. This helps to illustrate elements of classic two-party negotiation as they occur in many contexts.[49] To begin, look at the figure and case from the labor union's perspective. The union negotiator has told her management counterpart that the union wants a new wage of $15.00 per hour. This expressed preference is the union's *initial offer.* However, she also has in mind a *minimum reservation point* of $13.25 per hour. This is the lowest wage rate that she is willing to accept for the union. But the management negotiator has a different perspective. His *initial offer* is $12.75 per hour, and his *maximum reservation point,* the highest wage he is prepared eventually to offer to the union, is $13.75 per hour.

In classic two-party negotiation of this type, the **bargaining zone** is defined as the zone between one party's minimum reservation point and the other party's maximum reservation point. The bargaining zone of $13.25 per hour to $13.75 per hour in this case is a "positive" one since the reservation points of the two parties overlap. If the union's minimum reservation point were greater than management's maximum reservation point, no room would exist for bargaining. Whenever a positive bargaining zone exists, there is room for true negotiation. A key task for any negotiator is to discover the other party's reservation point. Until this is known, and each party becomes aware that a positive bargaining zone exists, it is difficult to proceed effectively.

AVOIDING NEGOTIATION PITFALLS

The negotiation process is admittedly complex, and negotiators must guard against common pitfalls. The first is *falling prey to the myth of the "fixed pie."* This involves acting on the distributive assumption that in order for you to gain, the other person must give something up. Negotiating this way fails to recognize the integrative assumption that the "pie" can sometimes be expanded and/or utilized to everyone's advantage. A second negotiation error is *nonrational escalation of conflict.* The negotiator in this case becomes committed to previously stated "demands" and allows personal needs for "ego" and "face saving" to increase the perceived importance of satisfying them.

A third common negotiating error is *overconfidence and ignoring the other's needs.* The negotiator becomes overconfident, believes his or her position is the only correct one, and fails to see the needs of the other party and the merits in its position. The fourth error is *too much "telling" and too little "hearing."* When committing the "telling" error, parties to a negotiation don't really make themselves understood to each other. When committing the "hearing" error, they fail to listen well enough to understand what each other is saying.[50]

RESEARCH BRIEF

Words used affect outcomes in online dispute resolution

A study of dispute resolution among eBay buyers and sellers found that using words that "give face" were more likely than words that "attack face" to result in the settlement of online disputes. Jeanne Brett, Marla Olekans, Ray Friedman, Nathan Goates, Cameron Anderson, and Cara Cherry Lisco studied real disputes being addressed through Square Trade, an online dispute resolution service to which eBay refers unhappy customers. The researchers note a study by the National Consumer League reporting that 41 percent of participants in online trading had problems, often associated with late deliveries. For purposes of the study a "dispute" was defined as a form of conflict in which one party to a transaction makes a claim that the other party rejects.

The researchers adopted what they call a "language-based" approach using the perspectives of "face theory," essentially arguing that how participants use language to give and attack the face of the other party will have a major impact on results. For example, in filing a claim, an unhappy buyer might use polite words that preserve the positive self-image, or face, of the seller, or the buyer might use negative words that attack this sense of face. Examples of negative words are *"agitated, angry, apprehensive, despise, disgusted, frustrated, furious, and hate."*

On-Line Dispute Resolution

Dispute resolution less likely when	Dispute resolution more likely when
• Negative emotions are expressed • Commands are issued	• Causal explanations given • Suggestions are offered • Communications are firm

This study examined 386 eBay-generated disputes processed through Square Trade. Results showed that expressing negative emotions and giving commands to the other party inhibited dispute resolution, whereas providing a causal explanation, offering suggestions, and communicating firmness all made dispute resolution more likely. An hypothesis that expressing positive emotions would increase the likelihood of dispute resolution was not supported. The study also showed that the longer a dispute played out, the less likely it was to be resolved.

In terms of practical implications, the researchers say: "Watch your language: avoid attacking the other's face either by showing your anger toward them, or expressing contempt; avoid signaling weakness, be firm in your claim. Provide causal accounts that take responsibility and give face."

QUESTIONS & APPLICATIONS

Why is it that using words that express negative emotions seems to have adverse effects on dispute resolution, but the use of words expressing positive emotions does not have positive effects? How might this result be explained? Also, why is it that using words that communicate "firmness" seem important in resolving disputes?

Take these ideas and findings and try to apply them to other contexts. Suppose a student is unhappy about a grade. How does dispute resolution with the course instructor play out? Suppose an employee is unhappy about a performance evaluation or pay raise. How does dispute resolution with the boss proceed?

References: Jeanne Brett, Marla Olekans, Ray Friedman, Nathan Goates, Cameron Anderson, and Cara Cherry Lisco, "Sticks and Stones: Language and On-Line Dispute Resolution," *Academy of Management Journal*, Vol. 50 (February 2007).

Another potential negotiation pitfall, and one increasingly important in our age of globalization, is *premature cultural comfort*. This occurs when a negotiator is too quick to assume that he or she understands the intentions, positions, and meanings being communicated by a negotiator from a different culture. Scholar Jeanne Brett says, for example, that negotiators from low-context cultures can run into difficulties when dealing with ones from high-context cultures. The low-context negotiator is used to getting information through direct questions and answers; the high-context negotiator is likely to communicate indirectly and not explicitly state positions.[51]

Finally, managers, and anyone else involved in negotiation, should avoid the trap of *ethical misconduct*. The motivation to behave unethically sometimes arises from an undue emphasis on the profit motive. This may be experienced as a desire to "get just a bit more" or to "get as much as you can" from a negotiation. The motivation to behave unethically may also result from a sense of competition. This may be experienced as a desire to "win" a negotiation just for the sake of winning it, or in the misguided belief that someone else must "lose" in order for you to gain.

When unethical behavior occurs in negotiation, the persons involved may try to explain it away with inappropriate rationalizing: "It was really unavoidable," "Oh, it's harmless," "The results justify the means," or "It's really quite fair and appropriate."[52] Of course these excuses for questionable behavior are morally unacceptable. Such practices and viewpoints can also be challenged by the possibility that any short-run gains will be accompanied by long-run losses. Negotiators using unethical tactics will incur lasting legacies of distrust, disrespect, and dislike. They can also expect to be targeted for "revenge" in later negotiations.

THIRD-PARTY DISPUTE RESOLUTION

Even with the best of intentions it may not always be possible to achieve integrative agreements. When disputes reach the point of impasse, third-party assistance with dispute resolution can be useful.

■ In **mediation** a neutral party tries to help conflicting parties improve communication to resolve their dispute.

Mediation involves a neutral third party, who tries to improve communication between negotiating parties and keep them focused on relevant issues. The *mediator* does not issue a ruling or make a decision but can take an active role in discussions. This may include making suggestions in an attempt to move the parties toward agreement. **Arbitration,** such as salary arbitration in professional sports, is a stronger form of dispute resolution. It involves a neutral third party, the *arbitrator,* who acts as a "judge" and issues a binding decision. This usually includes a formal hearing, in which the arbitrator listens to both sides and reviews all facets of the case before making a ruling.

■ In **arbitration** a neutral third party issues a binding decision to resolve a dispute.

Some organizations formally provide for a process called *alternative dispute resolution*. This approach utilizes mediation and/or arbitration, but only after direct attempts to negotiate agreements between the conflicting parties have failed. Often an *ombudsperson*, or designated neutral third party who listens to complaints and disputes, plays a key role in the process.

Learning Check 4	*Be sure you can* ■ define negotiation ■ differentiate between distributive and principled negotiation ■ list 4 rules of principled negotiation ■ define BATNA and bargaining zone ■ use these terms to illustrate a labor–management wage negotiation ■ describe the potential pitfalls in negotiation ■ differentiate between mediation and arbitration

CHAPTER 17 STUDY GUIDE

STUDY QUESTIONS SUMMARY

1 What is the communication process?

- Communication is the interpersonal process of sending and receiving symbols with messages attached to them.
- Effective communication occurs when the sender and the receiver of a message both interpret it in the same way.
- Efficient communication occurs when the message is sent at low cost for the sender.
- Persuasive communication results in the recipient acting as intended by the sender; credibility earned by expertise and good relationships is essential to persuasive communication.
- Noise is anything that interferes with the effectiveness of communication; common examples are poor utilization of channels, poor written or oral expression, physical distractions, and status effects.

2 How can communication be improved?

- Active listening, through reflecting back and paraphrasing, can help overcome barriers and improve communication.
- Constructive feedback is specific, direct, well-timed, and limited to things the receiver can change.
- Office architecture and space designs can be used to improve communication in organizations.
- Proper choice of channels and use of information technology can improve communication in organizations.
- Interactive management through MBWA and use of structured meetings, suggestion systems, and advisory councils can improve upward communication.
- The negative influences of ethnocentrism on communication can be offset by greater cross-cultural awareness and sensitivity.

3 How can we deal positively with conflict?

- Conflict occurs as disagreements over substantive or emotional issues.
- Moderate levels of conflict are functional for performance and creativity; too little or too much conflict becomes dysfunctional.
- Conflict may be managed through structural approaches that involve changing people, goals, resources, or work arrangements.
- Personal conflict management styles include avoidance, accommodation, compromise, competition, and collaboration.
- True conflict resolution involves problem solving through a win-win collaborative approach.

4 How can we negotiate successful agreements?

- Negotiation is the process of making decisions in situations in which the participants have different preferences.
- Both substance goals, those concerned with outcomes, and relationship goals, those concerned with processes, are important in successful negotiation.
- Effective negotiation occurs when issues of substance are resolved, and the process results in good working relationships.
- Distributive approaches to negotiation emphasize win-lose outcomes; integrative approaches to negotiation emphasize win-win outcomes.
- Common negotiation pitfalls include, among other possibilities, myth of the fixed pie, overconfidence, too much telling, too little hearing, and ethical misconduct.
- Mediation and arbitration are structured approaches to third-party dispute resolution.

KEY TERMS REVIEW

Accommodation (p. 437)

Active listening (p. 429)

Arbitration (p. 442)

Avoidance (p. 437)

Bargaining zone (p. 440)

BATNA (p. 440)

Channel richness (p. 432)

Collaboration (p. 437)

Communication (p. 424)

Competition (p. 437)

Compromise (p. 437)

Conflict (p. 434)

Conflict resolution (p. 436)

Credibility (p. 426)

Distributive negotiation (p. 438)

Dysfunctional conflict (p. 434)

Effective communication (p. 425)

Efficient communication (p. 425)

Emotional conflict (p. 434)

Ethnocentrism (p. 434)

Feedback (p. 430)

Filtering (p. 429)

Functional conflict (p. 434)

Integrative negotiation (p. 439)

Lose-lose conflict (p. 437)

Management by wandering around (p. 433)

Mediation (p. 442)

Mixed message (p. 428)

Negotiation (p. 438)

Nonverbal communication (p. 428)

Persuasion (p. 425)

Principled negotiation (p. 439)

Substantive conflict (p. 434)

Win-lose conflict (p. 437)

Win-win conflict (p. 433)

SELF-TEST 17

MULTIPLE-CHOICE QUESTIONS:

1. The use of paraphrasing and reflecting back what someone else says in communication is characteristic of _____.
   (a) mixed messages   (b) active listening   (c) projection   (d) lose-lose conflict

2. When the intended meaning of the sender and the interpreted meaning of the receiver are the same, communication is _____.
   (a) effective   (b) persuasive   (c) selective   (d) efficient

3. Constructive feedback is _____.
   (a) general rather than specific   (b) indirect rather than direct   (c) given in small doses   (d) given any time the sender is ready

4. When a manager uses e-mail to send a message that is better delivered in person, the communication process suffers from _____.
   (a) semantic problems   (b) a poor choice of communication channels   (c) physical distractions   (d) information overload

5. _____ is a form of interactive management that helps improve upward communication.
   (a) Attribution   (b) Mediation   (c) MBWA   (d) BATNA

6. Cross-cultural communication may run into difficulties because of _____, or the tendency to consider one's culture superior to others.
   (a) selective perception   (b) ethnocentrism   (c) mixed messages   (d) projection

7. An appeal to superordinate goals is an example of a(n) _____ approach to conflict management.
   (a) avoidance   (b) structural   (c) dysfunctional   (d) self-serving

8. The conflict management style with the greatest potential for true conflict resolution involves _____.
   (a) compromise   (b) competition   (c) smoothing   (d) collaboration

9. When a person is highly cooperative but not very assertive in approaching conflict, the conflict management style is referred to as _____.
   (a) avoidance   (b) authoritative   (c) smoothing   (d) collaboration

10. The three criteria of an effective negotiation are quality, cost, and _____.
    (a) harmony   (b) timeliness   (c) efficiency   (d) effectiveness

11. In order to be consistently persuasive when communicating with others in the workplace, a manager should build credibility by _____.
    (a) making sure the rewards for compliance are clear   (b) making sure the penalties for noncompliance are clear   (c) making sure that they know who is the boss   (d) making sure that good relationships have been established with them

12. A manager who understands the importance of proxemics in communication would be likely to _____.
    (a) avoid sending mixed messages   (b) arrange work spaces so as to encourage interaction   (c) be very careful in the choice of written and spoken words   (d) make frequent use of e-mail messages to keep people well informed

13. A conflict is most likely to be functional and have a positive impact on performance when it is _____.
    (a) based on emotions   (b) resolved by arbitration   (c) caused by resource scarcities   (d) of moderate intensity

14. In classic two-party negotiation, the difference between one party's minimum reservation point and the other party's maximum reservation point is known as the _____.
    (a) BATNA   (b) arena of indifference   (c) myth of the fixed pie   (d) bargaining zone

15. The first rule of thumb for gaining integrative agreements in negotiations is to _____.
    (a) separate the people from the problems   (b) focus on positions   (c) deal with a minimum number of alternatives   (d) avoid setting standards for measuring outcomes

SHORT-RESPONSE QUESTIONS:

16. Briefly describe how a manager would behave as an active listener when communicating with subordinates.

17. Explain the "inverted U" curve of conflict intensity.

18. How do tendencies toward assertiveness and cooperativeness in conflict management result in win-lose, lose-lose, and win-win outcomes?

19. What is the difference between substance and relationship goals in negotiation?

APPLICATION QUESTION:

20. After being promoted to store manager for a new branch of a large department store chain, Kathryn was concerned about communication in the store. Six department heads reported directly to her, and 50 full-time and part-time sales associates reported to them. Given this structure, Kathryn worried about staying informed about all store operations, not just those coming to her attention as senior manager. What steps might Kathryn take to establish and maintain an effective system of upward communication in this store?

CHAPTER 17 APPLICATIONS

AFL-CIO and the Teamsters: Communicating the Benefits of Change

Once the preeminent labor organization, the AFL-CIO has been fragmented in recent years by the dissent within its ranks. Yet, this is nothing new to organized labor. Learn how differing opinions within the labor movement aided the information of both the AFL and CIO and caused their eventual merger.

Representing nearly nine million laborers in the United States, the American Federation of Labor and Congress of Industrial Organizations (AFL-CIO) advocates for the rights of the majority of unionized American workers. The AFL-CIO is not a union itself; it is a voluntary coalition of 53 national and international labor unions whose members are ultimately represented by union chapters on the local level. The AFL-CIO represents a diverse group of workers whose vocations include farm workers, day laborers, musicians and actors, public workers, pilots, transport drivers, medical workers, printers, and many more occupations.[53]

The Roots of the AFL

The American Federation of Labor (AFL) was one of the earliest federations of labor unions in the United States. Founded in Columbus, Ohio, by Samuel Gompers in 1886, it was originally created as a reorganization of its precursor, Federation of Organized Trades and Labor Unions. At the time, many leaders of existing trade unions were unsatisfied with the Knights of Labor, an organization that had successfully led some of the era's largest strikes for workers' rights, but whose leadership was known to also support multiple rival unions whose members were willing to work for lower wages and to work as scabs during strikes.[54]

To distinguish itself from the Knights, Gompers's new AFL focused attention on the independence and autonomy of each affiliated trade union. In addition, the AFL limited its membership to workers and their organizations, in contrast with the Knights' policy of also admitting workers' employers.[55]

Once the Knights of Labor dissolved in the 1890s, the AFL was left as the sole major national union body.

To swell its ranks, the AFL widened its scope to include several major unions formed on industrial union lines, including the United Mine Workers, International Ladies' Garment Workers' Union, and the United Brewery Workers. Despite this, the craft unions of the AFL, who were among its earlier members, still held the balance of power within the organization.[56]

Bureaucracy Fosters a Split

As the AFL grew in size and scope throughout the early 1900s, so inevitably did its bureaucracy and, to some degree, its effectiveness. Strikes were becoming an increasingly effective tool to resolve gaps the workers perceived in their rights, but because of its growing size and scope of its concerns, the AFL found itself increasingly unable to win strikes. This was especially of concern to steel and auto workers, who found strikes a useful tool to gain power.

So shortly after the 1934 convention, John L. Lewis of the United Mine Workers of America called together heads of or representatives from the International Typographical Union; the Amalgamated Clothing Workers of America; the International Ladies' Garment Workers' Union (ILGWU); the United Textile Workers; the Mine, Mill, and Smelter Workers Union; the Oil Workers Union; and the Hatters, Cap, and Millinery Workers to consider forming a new group within the AFL to spearhead the growing efforts for industrial organizing. One year later, on November 8, 1935, the creation of the Congress of Industrial Organizations (CIO) was announced.[57]

Though the CIO was announced and intended as simply a group within the AFL gathered to support industrial unionism, the AFL responded with disapproval to the group's formation, refusing to deal with the CIO and demanding that it dissolve. But by doing so, the AFL only increased the authority and commitment to organizing with which affiliated workers perceived the burgeoning CIO; many of these workers were disillusioned by what they saw as the AFL's disaffected and weak efforts to support industrial unionizing.[58]

Within a year, the CIO effectively organized rubber workers who had gone on strike and formed the Steel Workers Organizing Committee (SWOC). And by 1937, the CIO was showing considerable momentum. The United Auto Workers, a powerful faction within the CIO, won union recognition from General Motors after a turbulent 43-day sit-down strike. And the SWOC negotiated the signing of a collective bargaining agreement with U.S. Steel, who had until then successfully resisted such efforts.[59]

Coming Full Circle

But the CIO was not without its troubles. It formally established itself as a rival to the AFL in 1938; shortly thereafter, the ILGWU and the Millinery Workers left the CIO to return to the AFL. And internal tensions limited the organization's external influence; CIO President John L. Lewis clashed with Philip Murray, his long-time assistant and head of the SWOC, over both the CIO's own activities and its relationship with FDR's administration. In 1941, Lewis resigned as president and chose Murray to succeed him. And in 1942, the Mine Workers, who came to the CIO with Lewis, dropped out.[60]

Walter Reuther succeeded Murray as head of the CIO in 1952. Coincidentally, William Green, who had headed the AFL since the 1920s, died that same month. His successor, George Meany, came together with Reuther to discuss a merger of their organizations. Many of the deal-breaking issues that had separated the groups had faded in the approximately 15 years since the CIO's conception. In that time, the AFL had embraced both industrial organizing and large industrial unions, such as the Association of Machinists. And so in 1955, the AFL-CIO was created by the joining of American Federation of Labor and the Congress of Industrial Organizations.[61]

Considerable Challenges to the Present

In the approximately 50 years since the joining of the AFL and the CIO, the merged organization has continued to struggle to maintain a unified charter and body of members. Recalling the initial formation of the CIO, a loose group of some of the AFL-CIO's largest unions came together as a coalition called the New Unity Partnership (NUP). After the 2004 defeat of Democratic presidential candidate John Kerry, who had been heavily supported by labor interests, the NUP's quest for reform began to intensify.[62] The NUP called for a reduction of the AFL-CIO's central bureaucracy, reallocating resources to the organization of new members instead of supporting electoral politics. It also sought to restructure the relationship between unions and local chapters, eliminating smaller local units and refocusing energy on unified industrial unionism.[63]

The NUP was replaced in scope by the Change to Win Coalition, whose members threatened to secede from the AFL-CIO if its demands for major reorganization were not met. On the eve of the AFL-CIO's 50th anniversary celebration (and surely not by coincidence), three of the organization's four largest unions announced their withdrawal: the Service Employees International Union (SEIU), the International Brotherhood of Teamsters, and the United Food and Commercial Workers International Union (UFCW). In addition, two other unions, the Laborers' International Union of North America and the United Farm Workers, claim dual loyalty with both the AFL-CIO and Change to Win.[64] This split was especially troublesome to the AFL-CIO leadership because SEIU president Andy Stern, an outspoken leader of Change to Win, was formerly considered the protégé of former SEIU president and current AFL-CIO president John J. Sweeney.[65]

Divided We Fall

Whether united or divided, the component factions of the AFL-CIO have been able to reshape working conditions for millions of industrial workers, laborers, and other tradespeople for more than 100 years. As is common for large, diverse organizations, it has been challenging for the federation to present a consistently unified front, resulting in factions splitting off to advance alternative agendas. The most recent split by the Change to Win Coalition will severely challenge the AFL-CIO's authority among millions of previously loyal members and diminish the federation's political clout. Will this spell the end of the AFL-CIO? Or will the organization adapt to focus on its remaining membership base? Is it possible that years from now, the Change to Win Coalition might be reabsorbed into the AFL-CIO? Millions of hard-working Americans will be waiting to see.

REVIEW QUESTIONS

1. List some issues of significance that have kept the AFL-CIO from maintaining a unified front.

2. Do you believe the recent tension within the AFL-CIO exemplifies functional or dysfunctional conflict? Explain your answer.

3. How does internal conflict and tension within the AFL-CIO influence its capabilities to represent labor interests in negotiations with large employers?

At BMW's plant in Leipzig, Germany, the firm can increase production without having to pay overtime. The company provides job security and has never had layoffs. It gives workers a share of profits, and in return the autoworker's union is flexible.

Labor–Management Relations

Question: What is the future for labor unions and labor–management relations in America?

Research Direction:
- Identify the trends in labor union membership in the United States over the past 20 to 30 years; focus in particular on areas where unions are gaining and losing strength in the new economy.
- Analyze news reports of labor–management relations. Find and study examples showing cooperation and others showing only conflict and dissagreement. See what patterns might exist.
- Consider talking with members of labor unions and managers who deal with unions to gather their viewpoints on labor union trends and labor–management cooperation.
- Consider examining union trends and labor–management relations in other countries.
- Prepare a report that uses the results of your research to answer the project question.

PERSONAL MANAGEMENT

COMMUNICATION skills top most lists of characteristics looked for in employment candidates by corporate recruiters today. Yet there are some worrisome statistics out there. An amazing 81 percent of college professors in one survey rated high school graduates as "fair" or "poor" in writing clearly; 78 percent rated students the same in spelling and use of grammar. In an American Management Association survey, managers rated their bosses only slightly above average (3.51 on a 5-point scale) on transforming ideas into words, being credible, listening and asking questions, and giving written and oral presentations. There is no doubt that we are in very challenging times when it comes to finding internships and full-time jobs in a streamlined economy. Strong communication and interpersonal skills could differentiate you from others wanting the same job.

Communication

Building the Brand Called "You" Use the self-assessments to check aspects of your communication tendencies. What about it? Can you convince a recruiter that you have the skills you need to run effective meetings, write informative reports, use e-mail correctly, deliver persuasive presentations, conduct job interviews, work well with others on a team, keep conflicts constructive and negotiations positive, network with peers and mentors, and otherwise communicate enthusiasm to the people with whom you work?

NEXT STEPS: MANAGEMENT LEARNING WORKBOOK

Self-Assessments
- Assertiveness (#12)
- Performance Appraisal (#19)
- Conflict Management Style (#28)

Experiential Exercises
- Upward Appraisal (#24)
- How to Give, Take Criticism (#25)
- Feedback and Assertiveness (#28)

Controlling–Processes and Systems

18

Planning Ahead

Who Has Control?

Most organizations recognize the importance of maintaining control of their employees. But how is this best done? Some industries give employees the freedom to control their own decisions. Others prefer to schedule their workers' every task and responsibility. Is one approach better than the other?

At this point in your life, chances are that you've had at least one job where a supervisor or business tried to micromanage your time. Whether it was scheduling coffee breaks down to the minute or showing you the "proper" way to put a hamburger on a bun, perhaps it seemed that your manager—or employer—felt as if you might not be able to do anything right, and thus you needed to be told exactly what to do at all times.

With experience, didn't you come to ask: "Is this necessary? Are there truly some industries or workers whose time must be so precisely controlled?"

Thus goes the managerial debate over worker control. Some companies would advocate that their employees are sufficiently managed by *internal control*—that is, by self-direction. Meanwhile, other industries might be equally valid when they argue that their workforce requires *external control*—through exterior rules monitored by a supervisor or a bureaucracy.

What *They* Think

"Even though worker capacity and motivation are destroyed when leaders choose power over productivity, it appears that bosses would rather be in control than have the organization work well."
Margaret J. Wheatley, management consultant

INTERNAL: *"You have to be a self-starter out here at a certain point. It's important to take the reigns or, otherwise, you can be relegated to obscurity so quickly."*
Bill Paxton, actor and screenwriter.

EXTERNAL: *"Those who follow orders to commit such crimes will be found and they will be punished. War crimes will be prosecuted. And it will be no excuse to say, 'I was just following orders.' "*
Donald Rumsfeld, U.S. Secretary of Defense.

Consider the operations of a nuclear power plant. How much discretion do you want individual employees to have? Just one small error can cause a disaster. Nuclear plants are set up to carefully govern each step in the process. The rules are carefully developed to ensure safety; we expect employees to follow the rules and we expect rule breakers to be removed from the system without fail.

Compare this with the situation of real estate agents. If there's one universal adjective for a real estate agent, it's "self-starter." The role of the job necessitates that agents be self-driven; if agents can't get themselves to work on time or can't stay on top of their listings, their agency must work overtime to compensate for their lack of motivation.

Thus, it seems that in the real estate industry, the greater liability is that agents might lack enough internal control, and would thus require unnecessary external control from the home office or other agents in order to remain profitable. Also, there is the suggestion that too much control may be tantamount to micromanagement.

Yet there's a lot of micromanagement around. "Even though worker capacity and motivation are destroyed when leaders choose power over productivity," said Margaret J. Wheatley, a management consultant who studies organization "it appears that bosses would rather be in control than have the organization work well."[1]

In some fields, the very nature of the work may determine the relational effects on external control. For real estate agents, the goal is straightforward, if not always simple: Represent your clients to the best of your ability and as profitably as possible. Beyond that, exactly how to close a sale is largely at an agent's discretion.

In contrast, the military's chain of command dictates that personnel have very little discretion over how to execute their orders. In their training, soldiers are taught simply to execute orders, not to deliberate how best to do so. Because success in a military campaign requires absolute attention to the details of orders, the armed forces enforces high external control to ensure that specific orders are followed precisely. But, what if the orders are immoral or illegal?

Are the advantages of maintaining complete control over a workforce worth the potential disadvantages? As a manager, just how do you decide on the balance of control you strike with your employees?

The Numbers

Survey Reports Top 10 Boss Sins

1. Trying to be everyone's friend	2. Micromanaging
3. Ignoring conflict	4. Being arrogant
5. Being wishy-washy	6. Impulsive
7. Unable to delegate	8. Impatient
9. Stubborn	10. Unprofessional

Quick Facts

* The U.S. Nuclear Regulatory Commission monitors security at the country's 103 private nuclear power plants operating in 31 states; they are an average of 24 years old.[2]
* IN 2006 there were 442 nuclear power plants in the world, located in 30 countries; there were 12 new plants under construction.[3]
* Nuclear power provides 20% of electricity in the United States and 16% worldwide; it is the world's largest source of emission free energy.[4]
* Real Estate agents typically earn between $21,000 and $70,000 annually.[5]
* Despite the many other forms of control they are afforded, employers have no responsibility to monitor an employee to ensure that they are keeping a serious disease, such as diabetes, under control.[6]

What Do *You* Think?

1. If you ran a real estate office, what kinds of controls might you use to allowing your employees' freedom while ensuring that your firm's requirements are also met?

2. Besides nuclear power and the military, what other organizations tend to operate using a high degree of employee control?

Controlling		
Study Question 1	**Study Question 2**	**Study Question 3**
Why and How Managers Control	**Steps in the Control Process**	**Control Systems and Techniques**
■ Importance of controlling ■ Types of controls ■ Internal and external control	■ Establish objectives and standards ■ Measure performance results ■ Compare results with objectives and standards ■ Take corrective action	■ Employee discipline systems ■ Project management ■ Information and financial controls
Learning Check 1	**Learning Check 2**	**Learning Check 3**

People in the ever-changing technology industry know that CEO T. J. Rodgers of Cypress Semiconductor Corp. values both performance and accountability. Cypress employees work with clear and quantified work goals, which they help set. Rodgers believes that this system helps find problems before they interfere with performance. He says: "Managers monitor the goals, look for problems, and expect people who fall behind to ask for help before they lose control of or damage a major project."[7]

Rodgers is all about planning—setting goals, and controlling—keeping things on track to accomplish them. Control is important for any organization, and we practice a lot of control quite naturally. Think of fun things you do—playing golf or tennis or Frisbee, reading, dancing, driving a car, or riding a bike. You may be surprised to know that through them you've already become quite expert in the control process. How? Most probably by having an objective in mind, always checking to see how well you were doing, and making continuous adjustments until you got it right.

WHY AND HOW MANAGERS CONTROL

"Keeping in touch . . . Staying informed . . . Being in control." These are important responsibilities for every manager. But "control" is a word like "power." If you aren't careful when and how the word is used, it leaves a negative connotation. But control plays a positive and necessary role in the management process. To have things "under control" is good; for things to be "out of control" is generally bad.

IMPORTANCE OF CONTROLLING

■ **Controlling** is the process of measuring performance and taking action to ensure desired results.

In management, **controlling** is a process of measuring performance and taking action to ensure desired results. Its purpose is straightforward—to make sure that plans are achieved, that actual performance meets or sur-

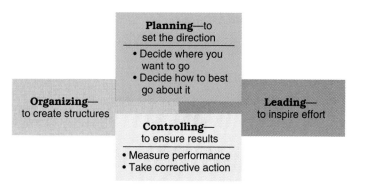

Figure 18.1 The role of controlling in the management process.

passes objectives. The foundation of control is information. Henry Schacht, former CEO of Cummins Engine Company, once discussed control in terms of what he called "friendly facts." He stated; "Facts that reinforce what you are doing . . . are nice, because they help in terms of psychic reward. Facts that raise alarms are equally friendly, because they give you clues about how to respond, how to change, where to spend the resources."[8]

Figure 18.1 shows how controlling fits in with the other management functions. Planning sets the directions and allocates resources. Organizing brings people and material resources together in working combinations. Leading inspires people to best utilize these resources. Controlling sees to it that the right things happen, in the right way, and at the right time. It helps ensure that performance is consistent with plans, and that accomplishments throughout an organization are coordinated in a means-ends fashion. It also helps ensure that people comply with organizational policies and procedures.

Effective control is also important to organizational learning. It offers the great opportunity of learning from experience. Consider, for example, the program of **after-action review** pioneered by the U.S. Army and now utilized in many corporate settings. This is a structured review of lessons learned and results accomplished through a completed project, task force assignment, or special operation. Participants are asked to answer questions like: "What was the intent?" "What actually happened?" "What did we learn?"[9] The after-action review helps make continuous improvement a part of the organizational culture. It encourages everyone involved to take responsibility for their performance efforts and accomplishments.

Improving performance through learning is one of the great opportunities offered by the control process. However, the potential benefits are realized only when learning is translated into corrective actions. After setting up Diversity Network Groups (DNGs) worldwide, for example, IBM executives learned that male attitudes were major barriers to the success of female managers. They addressed this finding by making senior executives report annually on the progress of women managers in their divisions. This action is credited with substantially increasing the percentage of women in IBM's senior management ranks.[10]

■ An **after-action review** identifies lessons learned through a completed project, task force assignment, or special operation.

TYPES OF CONTROLS

Figure 18.2 shows how feedforward, concurrent, and feedback controls link with different phases of the organization's input-throughput-output cycle.[11] Each type of control offers significant opportunities for managers to act in ways that increase the likelihood for high performance.

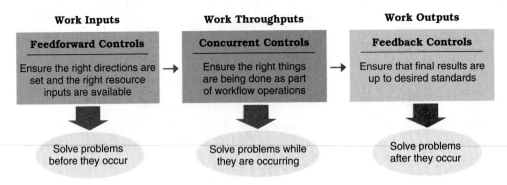

Figure 18.2 Feedforward, concurrent, and feedback controls.

Feedforward Controls

■ **Feedforward control** ensures that directions and resources are right before the work begins.

Feedforward controls, also called *preliminary controls*, take place before a work activity begins. They ensure that objectives are clear, that proper directions are established, and that the right resources are available to accomplish them. Feedforward controls are preventive in nature. The goal is to solve problems before they occur by asking an important but often-neglected question: "What needs to be done before we begin?" This is a forward-thinking and proactive approach to control. At McDonald's, for example, preliminary control of food ingredients plays an important role in the firm's quality program. The company requires that suppliers of its hamburger buns produce them to exact specifications, covering everything from texture to uniformity of color. Even in overseas markets, the firm works hard to develop local suppliers that can offer dependable quality.[12]

Concurrent Controls

■ **Concurrent control** focuses on what happens during the work process.

Concurrent controls focus on what happens during the work process. Sometimes called *steering controls*, they make sure things are being done according to plan. The goal of concurrent controls is to solve problems as they are occurring. The key question is "What can we do to improve things right now?" At McDonald's, ever-present shift leaders provide concurrent control through direct supervision. They constantly observe what is taking place even while helping out with the work. They are trained to intervene immediately when something is not done right and to correct things on the spot. Detailed instruction manuals also "steer" workers in the right directions as their jobs are performed.

Feedback Controls

■ **Feedback control** takes place after an action is completed.

Feedback controls, also called *postaction controls*, take place after work is completed. They focus on the quality of end results rather than on inputs and activities. Feedback controls are largely reactive; the goals are to solve problems after they occur and prevent future ones. They ask the question "Now that we are finished, how well did we do?" Restaurants, for example, ask how you liked a meal . . . after it is eaten; final course evaluations tell instructors how well they performed . . . after the course is over; a budget summary identifies cost overruns . . . after a project is completed. In these and other circumstances the feedback provided by the control process is useful information for improving things in the future.

INTERNAL AND EXTERNAL CONTROL

As suggested in The Topic chapter opener, managers have two broad options with respect to control. They can rely on people to control their own behavior. This strategy of **internal control** allows motivated individuals and groups to exercise self-discipline in fulfilling job expectations. Alternatively, managers can take direct action to control the behavior of others. This strategy of **external control** occurs through personal supervision and the use of formal administrative systems. Effective control typically involves a combination of both. However, the new workplace, with its emphasis on participation, empowerment, and involvement, places increased reliance on internal control.

■ **Internal control** occurs through self-discipline and self-control.

■ **External control** occurs through direct supervision or administrative systems.

An internal control strategy requires a high degree of trust. When people are expected to work on their own and exercise self-control, managers must give them the freedom to do so. According to Douglas McGregor's Theory Y perspective, introduced in Chapter 3, people are ready and willing to exercise self-control in their work.[13] But he also points out that they are most likely to do this when they participate in setting performance objectives and standards. Furthermore, the potential for self-control is increased when capable people have a clear sense of organizational mission, know their goals, and have the resources necessary to do their jobs well. It is also enhanced by participative organizational cultures in which everyone treats each other with respect and consideration.

Many jobs today require large amounts of internal control. Writers are an interesting example. When asked by a friend "How do you develop discipline to sit alone in front of a computer all day," one replied that "writing is a process, a messy process with very few rules or boundaries." He went on to say that writing begins with an assignment and ends in a finished article, but what happens in between is hard to specify. The writer thinks about the

INSIGHTS

Courteous Service, Well-Treated Staff Fuel Growth at Chick-fil-A

Great! But don't plan on stopping in for a chicken sandwich on a Sunday; all the chain's 1270 stores are closed. It has been a tradition started by 85-year old founder Truett Cathy, who believes that employees deserve a day of rest. Called someone who believes in placing "people before profits," Truett has built a successful, and fast growing, fast-food franchise.

Chick-fil-A's turnover among restaurant operators is only 3%, compared to an industry average as high as 50%. It is also a relatively inexpensive franchise, costing $5,000, compared to $50,000 that is typical of its competitors.

Chick-fil-A, headquartered in Atlanta where its first restaurant was opened, is wholly owned by Truett's family, and is now headed by his son. It has a reputation as a great business, processing about 10,000 inquiries each year for 100 restaurant franchise opportunities. The president of the national Restaurant Association Educational Foundation says: "I don't think there's any chain that creates such a wonderful culture around the way they treat their people and the respect they have for their employees."

Truett asks his employees to always say "my pleasure" when thanked by a customer. He says: "It's important to keep people happy." The results seem to speak for themselves. Chick-fil-A is the 25th largest restaurant chain in the U.S., and reached over $2 billion sales in 2006.

topic no matter what he or she is doing, and works it over in his or her mind all the time, not just when at the computer. This self-control over one's work contrasts with what the writer once experienced as an office worker. Then, he says, "even trips to the office cooler were discouraged."[14]

Learning Check 1

Be sure you can ■ define controlling as a management function ■ explain benefits of after-action reviews ■ illustrate how a fast-food restaurant utilizes feedforward, concurrent, and feedback controls ■ differentiate internal control and external control

STEPS IN THE CONTROL PROCESS

The control process involves the four steps shown in *Figure 18.3*: (1) establish performance objectives and standards; (2) measure actual performance; (3) compare actual performance with objectives and standards; and (4) take corrective action as needed. While essential to management, the process applies equally well to personal affairs and careers. Think about it. Without career objectives, how do you know where you really want to go? How can you allocate your time and other resources to take best advantage of available opportunities? Without measurement, how can you assess any progress being made? How can you adjust current behavior to improve prospects for future results?

STEP 1: ESTABLISH OBJECTIVES AND STANDARDS

The control process begins with planning, when performance objectives and standards for measuring them are set. It can't start without them. Performance objectives should represent key results that one wants to accomplish. The word "key" in the prior sentence is important. The focus in planning should be on describing "critical" or "essential" results that

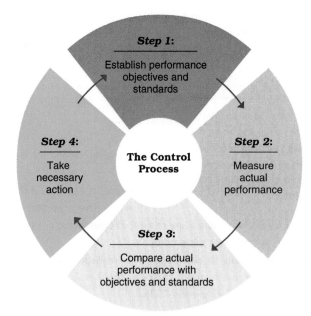

Figure 18.3 Four steps in the control process.

will make a substantial performance difference. Standards are important, too. As key results are identified, one also has to specify the standards and measures that will be used to evaluate their accomplishment.

Standards for measuring business performance that we often hear are things like earnings per share, sales growth, and market share. Others include quantity and quality of production, costs incurred, service or delivery time, and error rates. But how about other types of organizations, like a symphony orchestra? When the Cleveland Orchestra wrestled with performance standards, the members weren't willing to rely on vague generalities like "we played well," "the audience

KAFFEEKLATSCH

Computer Addiction

First Cup

"Do you ever turn off the computer at home? I mean not for power saving, I mean for '*life saving*'. Sometimes I wonder who's in control: is it me, or is it the computer? It used to be that we took work home in a briefcase, did a bit, closed the case up, and took it back to work the next day. Now work is always there, on the computer, on the Internet, in our e-mails. And it's habit forming. I go home and turn the computer on—and it holds me captive for most of the night. I just can't seem to allocate a period of time for 'homework' and then shut the thing down and relax with the family."

Studying the Grounds

■ In San Jose, California, Elizabeth Safran works virtually; that's the way the 13-member public relations firm operates—by e-mails and instant messaging. But she is concerned about work/life balance, saying: "It [technology] makes us more productive, but everybody is working all the time—weekends, evenings. It's almost overkill."

■ In London, England, Paul Renucci is managing director of a systems integration firm. He works at home on Fridays, saving two hours of traffic time and staying connected by computer. At 5 P.M. he turns the machine off, his workday over. He says: "I can work pretty hard but at 5 P.M. exactly I stop working and the weekend starts."

■ In Cambridge, Massachusetts, MIT Professor Lotte Bailyn notes that few people think about the impact of technology on personal lives when it arrives, but that "it is the top people that need to model the right behavior . . . set the example."

Double Espresso

"You're getting close to 'computer addiction.' You've got to get back in control; remember to use the 'off' button and take charge of your time. For me technology is an office tool, not a lifestyle. But when it comes to our kids the story may be different—they're always instant messaging, text messaging from one minute to the next. We'll have to see what happens when they enter the workplace. Maybe they'll be so comfortable with technology in their lives that they won't have any problems with it. But for people like us, we're learning how to deal with it at the same time we're learning how to use it. So don't let it trap you. Just use the 'off' button the way I do and don't worry."

Your Turn

Who is in control when it comes to technology and our personal time? In management there is a lot of talk about self-control, about people understanding themselves, being vigilant about their work and lifestyles, and making sure to keep things running "right." But is technology one of those things that silently and effortlessly creeps into our lives and, before we know it, takes control? And in this respect, is the MIT professor correct? Is it up to those in charge, top managers, to set the norms and provide examples that show others how to take full advantage of technology for work while still staying in personal control of work-life balance?

seemed happy," or "not too many mistakes were made." Rather, they decided to track standing ovations, invitations to perform in other countries, and how often other orchestras copied their performance styles.[15]

■ An **output standard** measures performance results in terms of quantity, quality, cost, or time.

These have all been examples of **output standards** that measure actual outcomes or work results. Businesses use many output standards; we have already discussed a couple. Based on your experience at work and as a customer, you can probably come up with even more examples. When Allstate Corporation launched a new diversity initiative, it created a "diversity index" to quantify performance on diversity issues. The standards included how well employees met the goals of bias-free customer service, and how well managers met the firm's diversity expectations.[16] When General Electric became concerned about managing ethics in its 320,000 member global workforce, it created measurement standards to track compliance. Each business unit reports quarterly on how many of its members attended ethics training sessions, and what percentage signed the firm's "Spirit and Letter" ethics guide.[17]

■ An **input standard** measures work efforts that go into a performance task.

Not all standards are based on outputs. The control process also uses **input standards** that measure work efforts. These are often used in situations where outputs are difficult or expensive to measure. Examples of input standards for a college professor might be the existence of an orderly course syllabus, meeting all class sessions, and returning exams and assignments in a timely fashion. Of course, as this example might suggest, measuring inputs doesn't mean that outputs, such as high quality teaching and learning, are necessarily achieved. Other examples of input standards in the workplace include conformance with rules and procedures, efficiency in the use of resources, and work attendance or punctuality.

REAL ETHICS

Privacy and Censorship

Washington—A U.S. spy agency secretly collects the phone records of millions of Americans as telephone companies turn over private data on their customers. International financial transfers are also electronically monitored in an attempt to detect terrorist networks. David Sobel of the Electronic Privacy Information Center says: "The climate has changed, and many companies give less weight to the privacy interests of their customers."

London—Amnesty International claims that Yahoo, Microsoft, and Google are violating human rights in China by complying with government requests for censorship. Amnesty says that "corporate values and policies" are being compromised in the quest for profits. A spokesperson for Yahoo's China business, Alibaba.com, counters: "By creating opportunities for entrepreneurs and connecting China's exporters to buyers around the world, Alibaba.com and Yahoo China are having an overwhelmingly positive impact on the lives of average people in China."

Beijing—The Skype company is told by the Chinese government that its software must filter words that the Chi-

nese leadership considers offensive from text messages. If the company doesn't, it can't do business in the country. After refusing at first, company executives finally agree; phrases like "Falun Gong" and "Dalai Lama" no longer appear in text messages delivered through Skype's Chinese joint venture partner, Tom Online.

FURTHER INQUIRY

Skype cofounder Niklas Zennstrom says: "I may like or not like the laws and regulations to operate businesses in the UK or Germany or the U.S., but if I do business there I choose to comply. . . . " What do you think? Do company executives have any choice but to comply with the requests of governments—American or otherwise? At what point, or when, should business executives stand up and challenge "laws and regulations" used to deny customers the privacy they expect?

STEP 2: MEASURE PERFORMANCE RESULTS

The second step in the control process is to measure actual performance. The goal is to assess results based on output standards and/or input standards. Measurement must be accurate enough to spot significant differences between what is really taking place and what was originally planned. Without it, effective control is not possible. And a willingness to measure has its rewards: what gets measured tends to happen.

When Linda Sanford was appointed head of IBM's sales force, she came with an admirable performance record earned during a 22-year career with the company. Notably, Sanford grew up on a family farm, where she developed an appreciation for measuring results. "At the end of the day, you saw what you did, knew how many rows of strawberries you picked." At IBM she was known for walking around the factory just to see "at the end of the day how many machines were going out of the back dock."[18]

STEP 3: COMPARE RESULTS WITH OBJECTIVES AND STANDARDS

Step 3 in the control process is to compare objectives with results. You can remember its implications by this *control equation:*

Need for action = Desired performance − Actual performance.

Dealing with an identified need for action is like any other problem solving. It can point toward *performance threat or deficiency*—when actual is less than desired. Or it can point toward a possible *performance opportunity*—when actual is more than desired.

The question of what constitutes "desired" performance plays an important role in the control equation and its implications. Some organizations use *engineering comparisons.* One example is United Parcel Service (UPS). The firm carefully measures the routes and routines of its drivers to establish the times expected for each delivery. When a delivery manifest is scanned as completed, the driver's time is registered in a performance log that is closely monitored by supervisors. Organizations make use of *historical comparisons* also. They use past experience as a basis for evaluating current performance. Similarly, *relative comparisons* are also common. These benchmark performance against that being achieved by other people, work units, or organizations.

STEP 4: TAKE CORRECTIVE ACTION

The final step in the control process is to take any action necessary to correct problems or make improvements. **Management by exception** is the practice of giving attention to situations that show the greatest need for action. It can save valuable time, energy, and other resources by focusing attention on high-priority areas. Managers should be alert to two types of exceptions. The first is a *problem situation* that must be understood so corrective action can restore performance to the desired level. The second is an *opportunity situation* that must be understood with the goal of continuing or increasing the high level of accomplishment in the future.

■ **Management by exception** focuses attention on substantial differences between actual and desired performance.

Be sure you can ■ list the steps in the control process ■ explain where and why planning is important to controlling ■ explain the difference between output standards and input standards ■ state the control equation ■ explain management by exception

Learning Check 2

✓

CONTROL SYSTEMS AND TECHNIQUES

Most organizations use a variety of control systems and techniques. Among them, employee discipline systems are important in human resource management. Special techniques also facilitate control in project management. And, organizations often use information and financial controls on a systems wide basis.

EMPLOYEE DISCIPLINE SYSTEMS

Absenteeism . . . tardiness . . . sloppy work . . . the list of undesirable conduct can go on to even more extreme actions: falsifying records . . . sexual harassment . . . embezzlement. All are examples of behaviors that can and should be formally addressed in human resource management through **discipline,** the act of influencing behavior through reprimand.

> ▨ **Discipline** is the act of influencing behavior through reprimand.

When discipline is handled in a fair, consistent, and systematic way, it is a useful form of managerial control. One way to be consistent in disciplinary situations is to remember the "hot stove rules" in *Management Smarts 18.1*. They rest on a simple understanding: "When a stove is hot, don't touch it." Everyone knows that when this rule is violated, you get burned—immediately, consistently, but usually not beyond the possibility of repair.[19]

Progressive discipline ties reprimands to the severity and frequency of the employee's infractions. Penalties for misbehavior vary according to the significance of the problem. A progressive discipline system takes into consideration such things as the seriousness of the problem, how frequently it has occurred, how long it lasts, and past experience in dealing with the person who has caused the problem. The goal is to achieve compliance with organizational expectations through the least extreme reprimand possible. For example, the ultimate penalty of "discharge" would be reserved for the most severe behaviors (e.g., any felony crime) or for repeated infractions of a less severe nature (e.g., being continually late for work and failing to respond to a series of written reprimands and/or suspensions).

MANAGEMENT SMARTS 18.1

"Hot stove rules" of employee discipline

- A reprimand should be immediate; a hot stove burns the first time you touch it.
- A reprimand should be directed toward someone's actions, not the individual's personality; a hot stove doesn't hold grudges, doesn't try to humiliate people, and doesn't accept excuses.
- A reprimand should be consistently applied; a hot stove burns anyone who touches it, and it does so every time.
- A reprimand should be informative; a hot stove lets a person know what to do to avoid getting burned in the future—"don't touch."
- A reprimand should occur in a supportive setting; a hot stove conveys warmth but with an inflexible rule: "don't touch."
- A reprimand should support realistic rules; the don't-touch-a-hot-stove rule isn't a power play, a whim, or an emotion of the moment; it is a necessary rule of reason.

PROJECT MANAGEMENT

> ▨ **Progressive discipline** ties reprimands to the severity and frequency of misbehavior.
>
> ▨ **Projects** are unique one-time events that occur within a defined time period.
>
> ▨ **Project management** is the overall planning, supervision, and control of projects.

It might be something personal like an anniversary party for one's parents, a renovation to your home, or the launch of a new product or service at your place of work. What these examples and others like them share in common is that they are relatively complex tasks with multiple components that have to happen in a certain sequence, and that must be completed by a specified date. In management we call them **projects,** one-time events with unique components and an objective that must be met within a defined time period.

Project management is responsibility for the overall planning, supervision, and control of projects. Basically, a project manager's job is to ensure

Activities

A Complete research and development work

B Complete engineering design

C Prepare budgets

D Build prototype

E Test prototype

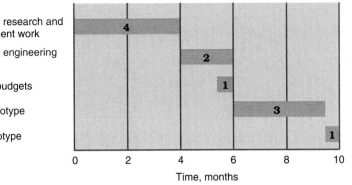

Figure 18.4 Simplified Gantt chart for a new cell phone prototype.

that a project is completed on time, within budget, and consistent with objectives. In addition to the general managerial responsibilities discussed throughout this book, two of the major issues in project management involve project scheduling and control. Both are assisted by two special techniques—Gantt charts and CPM/PERT.

A **Gantt chart,** depicted in *Figure 18.4,* graphically displays the scheduling of tasks required to complete a project. This approach was developed in the early twentieth century by Henry Gantt, an industrial engineer, and it has become a mainstay of project management ever since. In the figure, the left column lists major activities required to complete a new cell phone prototype. The bars extending from the right indicate the time required to complete each activity.

■ A **Gantt chart** graphically displays the scheduling of tasks required to complete a project.

The Gantt chart provides a visual overview of what needs to be done on the project. This allows for progress checks to be made at different time intervals. It also assists with event or activity sequencing, making sure that things get accomplished in time for later work to build upon them. One of the biggest problems with projects, for example, is when delays in early activities create problems for later ones. A project manager who actively uses Gantt charts is trying to avoid such difficulties. Obviously, the one in the prior figure is oversimplified; an actual project to develop a new cell phone, even a product modification like the newest Palm, for example, is exceedingly complex. However, with computer assistance, Gantt charts play a useful role in helping project managers track progress even through such high levels of complexity.

A step up from the Gantt chart in its ability to handle greater project complexity is **CPM/PERT**, a combination of the *critical path method* and the *program evaluation and review technique*. Both CPM and PERT are network modeling approaches that originated separately and have now converged. A network chart such as that shown in *Figure 18.5* is central to CPM/PERT. Such a chart is developed by breaking a service or production project into a series of small sub activities that each have clear beginning and end points. These points are shown in the chart as "nodes" and the arrows between them indicate precedence relationships, showing basically in what order things must be completed.

■ **CPM/PERT** is a combination of the *critical path method* and the *program evaluation and review technique.*

When the events associated with various activities are plotted, the result is a diagram showing the necessary interrelationships that are required for the entire project to be successfully completed. Use of CPM/PERT analysis helps project managers track activities, making sure activities happen in the right sequence and on time. These activities can be listed on the arrows for tacking purposes, known as the *activity-on-arrows* or AOA diagram; they can also be listed on the nodes, resulting in *activity-on-nodes* or AON diagrams.

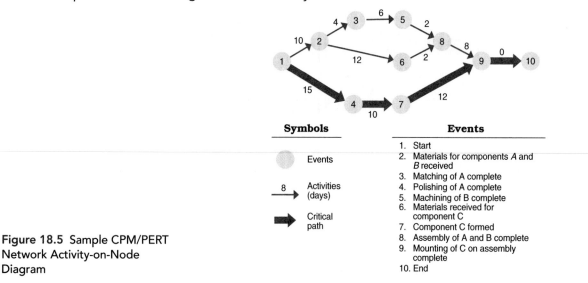

Symbols		Events
Events		1. Start 2. Materials for components *A* and *B* received 3. Matching of A complete 4. Polishing of A complete 5. Machining of B complete 6. Materials received for component C 7. Component C formed 8. Assembly of A and B complete 9. Mounting of C on assembly complete 10. End

Figure 18.5 Sample CPM/PERT Network Activity-on-Node Diagram

The network in the figure is an AON diagram. If you look again at it, you should notice that the time required for each activity can be easily computed and tracked. Among all the paths required for the project, the one having the longest time requirements is called the *critical path*. This represents the shortest possible time in which the entire project can be finished, assuming everything goes according to schedule and plans. In the example, the critical path is 37 days. Excellent computer programs are now available for CPM/PERT analyses to help managers track progress even under the most complex project conditions.

INFORMATION AND FINANCIAL CONTROLS

The pressure is ever present for all organizations to use their financial resources well and to achieve high performance. In business the analysis of a firm's financial performance is an important aspect of managerial control. At a minimum, managers should be able to understand the following financial performance measures: (1) *liquidity*—ability to generate cash to pay bills; (2) *leverage*—ability to earn more in returns than the cost of debt; (3) *asset management*—ability to use resources efficiently and operate at minimum cost; and (4) *profitability*—ability to earn revenues greater than costs.

These financial performance indicators can be assessed using a variety of financial ratios, including those listed below. Notice in the list that up and down arrows show the preferred directions that a manager would like the ratios to move.

Liquidity
- *Current Ratio* = Current Assets / Current Liabilities
- ↑ You want more assets and fewer liabilities.

Leverage
- *Debt Ratio* = Total Debts/Total Assets
- ↓ You want fewer debts and more assets.

Asset Management
- *Inventory Turnover* = Sales/Average Inventory
- ↑ You want more sales and lower inventory.

RESEARCH BRIEF

Restating corporate financial performance foreshadows significant turnover among corporate executives and directors

Control and accountability are core issues in research by Marne L. Arthaud-Day, S. Travis Certo, Catherine M. Dalton, and Dan R. Dalton. Using a technique known as event history analysis, the researchers say that what happens subsequent to financial misstatements is an "opportunity to study the accountability of leaders for organizational outcomes, independent of firm performance."

Arthaud-Day et al. examined what happened in a 2-year period for 116 firms that restated financials in comparison with 116 others that did not. The firms were chosen from the Financial Statement Restatement Database and matched in pairs by industry and sizes for control purposes. The basic hypothesis was that higher turnover in all positions would be experienced by firms that restated their earnings. These results were confirmed in the data analysis, with CEOs, CFOs, outside directors, and audit committee members more likely to turn over in the misstatement firms.

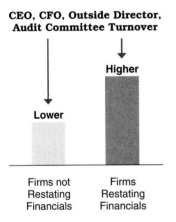

CEO, CFO, Outside Director, Audit Committee Turnover

In discussing the findings, the researchers point out that financial misstatements harm a firm's legitimacy in the eyes of key stakeholders, and this harm threatens the firm's ability to obtain resources and external support. Because financial misstatements are considered to be direct management failures, holding executives accountable is more likely here than in generally poor performance of an organization overall, even for bankruptcy, which might be explained by adverse external factors.

The researchers note that "companies often couch involuntary departures in nice sounding clichés (i.e., an executive "retires"), making it nearly impossible to determine the true reason for turnover." But, they also go on to point out that the data are highly "suggestive" that a cause and effect relationship does exist. In terms of future research Arthaud-Day et al. recommend looking at what happens after "tainted" leadership is removed. Does the firm regain stakeholder legitimacy and do better in the future, or not?

QUESTIONS & APPLICATIONS

If one looked at not just financial misstatements, but share price declines, profit and loss trends, and product successes and failures, would similar patterns of control and accountability for top managers be found? Given the increased concern for tightening financial controls and holding business executives accountable for performance, what is happening in governments, schools, and nonprofits? Are there cases in your community and local news where executives in these types of organizations have been held accountable for major errors in organizational leadership?

Reference: Marne L. Arthaud-Day, S. Travis Certo, Catherine M. Dalton, and Dan R. Dalton, "A Changing of the Guard: Executive and Director Turnover Following Corporate Financial Restatements," *Academy of Management Journal* , Vol. 49 (December 2006).

Profitability
- *Net Margin* = Net Profit after Taxes/Sales
- *Return on Assets* (RAO) = Net Profit after Taxes/Total Assets
- ↑ You want as much profit as possible.

Such financial ratios provide an information framework for historical comparisons within the firm and for external benchmarking relative to industry performance. They can also be used to set financial targets or goals to be shared with employees and tracked to indicate success or failure in their accomplishment. At Civco Medical Instruments, for example, a financial scorecard is distributed monthly to all employees. They always know factually how well the firm is doing. This helps them focus on what they can do differently and better, and strengthens personal commitments to future improvements in the firm's "bottom line."[20]

ISSUES AND SITUATIONS

Balanced Scorecards

What gets measured happens, the old adage says. And it is true. If an instructor takes class attendance and assigns grades based on it, students tend to come to class; if an employer tracks the number of customers each employee serves per day, employees tend to serve more customers. Do the same principles hold for organizations?

Strategic management consultants Robert S. Kaplan and David P. Norton think so. They advocate what is called the "balanced scorecard." It gives top managers, as they say, "a fast but comprehensive view of the business." The basic principle is that to do well and to win, you have to keep score.

Developing a balanced scorecard for any organization begins with a clarification of the organization's mission and vision—what it wants to be, and how it wants to be perceived by its key stakeholders. Then, the questions used to develop balanced scorecard goals and measures are the following:

Financial Performance—To improve financially, how should we appear to our shareholders? Sample goals: survive, succeed, prosper. Sample measures: cash flow, sales growth and operating income, increased market share and return on equity.

Customer Satisfaction—To achieve our vision, how should we appear to our customers? Sample goals: new products, responsive supply. Sample measures: percentage sales from new products, percentage on-time deliveries.

Internal Process Improvement—To satisfy our customers and shareholders, at what internal business processes should we excel? Sample goals: manufacturing excellence, design productivity, new product introduction. Sample measures: cycle times, engineering efficiency, new product time.

Innovation and Learning—To achieve our vision, how will we sustain our ability to change and improve? Sample goals: technology leadership, time to market. Sample measures: time to develop new technologies, new product introduction time versus competition.

When balanced scorecard measures are taken and routinely recorded for critical managerial review, Kaplan and Norton expect organizations to perform better in those areas. In other words, what gets measured happens.

Critical Response

How can the balanced scorecard approach be used by the following organizations: an elementary school, a hospital, a community library, a mayor's office, a fast food restaurant? How do the performance dimensions and indicators vary among these different types of organizations? And if your scorecards make sense, why is it that more organizations don't use them?

CHAPTER 18 STUDY GUIDE

STUDY QUESTIONS SUMMARY

1 Why and how do managers control?

- Controlling is the process of measuring performance and taking corrective action as needed.
- Feedforward controls are accomplished before a work activity begins; they ensure that directions are clear, and that the right resources are available to accomplish them.
- Concurrent controls make sure that things are being done correctly; they allow corrective actions to be taken while the work is being done.
- Feedback controls take place after an action is completed; they address the question "Now that we are finished, how well did we do, and what did we learn for the future?"
- External control is accomplished through personal supervision and administrative systems; internal control is self-control and occurs as people take personal responsibility for their work.

2 What are the steps in the control process?

- The first step in the control process is to establish performance objectives and standards, to create targets against which later performance can be evaluated.
- The second step in the control process is to measure actual performance, to specifically identify what results are being achieved.

- The third step in the control process is to compare performance results with objectives to determine how well things are going.
- The fourth step in the control process is to take action to resolve problems or explore opportunities that are identified when results are compared with objectives.

3 What are common control systems and techniques?

- Discipline is the process of influencing behavior through reprimand; progressive discipline systems vary reprimands according to the severity of infractions.
- A project is a unique event that must be completed by a specified date; project management is the process of ensuring that projects are completed on time, on budget, and according to objectives.
- Gantt charts assist in project management and control by displaying how various tasks must be scheduled in order to complete a project on time.
- CPM/PERT analysis assists in project management and control by describing the complex networks of activities that must be completed in various sequences in order for a project to be completed successfully.
- Financial control of business performance is facilitated by analysis of financial ratios, such as those dealing with liquidity, leverage, assets, and profitability.

KEY TERMS REVIEW

After-action review (p. 453)
CPM/PERT (p. 461)
Concurrent control (p. 454)
Controlling (p. 452)
Discipline (p. 460)
External control (p. 455)

Feedback control (p. 454)
Feedforward control (p. 454)
Gantt chart (p. 461)
Input standards (p. 458)
Internal control (p. 455)
Management by exception (p. 459)

Output standards (p. 458)
Progressive discipline (p. 460)
Project (p. 460)
Project management (p. 460)

SELF-TEST 18

MULTIPLE-CHOICE QUESTIONS:

1. After objectives and standards are set, what step comes next in the control process? _____
   (a) measure results   (b) take corrective action   (c) compare results with objectives   (d) modify standards to fit circumstances

2. When a soccer coach tells her players at the end of a losing game, "You really played well and stayed with the game plan," she is using a/an _____ as a measure of performance.
   (a) input standard   (b) output standard   (c) historical comparison   (d) relative comparison

3. When an automobile manufacturer is careful to purchase only the highest-quality components for use in production, this is an example of an attempt to ensure high performance through _____ control.

   (a) concurrent   (b) statistical   (c) inventory   (d) feedforward

4. Management by exception means _____.

   (a) managing only when necessary   (b) focusing attention where the need for action is greatest   (c) the same thing as concurrent control   (d) the same thing as just-in-time delivery

5. When a supervisor working along side of an employee corrects him or her when a mistake is made, this is an example of _____ control.

   (a) feedforward   (b) external   (c) internal   (d) preliminary

6. If an organization's top management establishes a target of increasing new hires of minority and female candidates by 15% in the next six months, this is an example of a/an _____ standard for control purposes.

   (a) input   (b) output   (c) management by exception   (d) concurrent

7. The control equation states: _____ = Desired Performance – Actual Performance.

   (a) Problem Magnitude   (b) Management Opportunity   (c) Planning Objective   (d) Need for Action

8. When a UPS manager compares the amount of time a driver takes to accomplish certain deliveries against a standard set through scientific analysis of her delivery route, this is known as _____.

   (a) an historical comparison   (b) an engineering comparison   (c) relative benchmarking   (d) concurrent control

9. Projects are unique one-time events that _____.

   (a) have unclear objectives   (b) must be completed by a specific time   (c) have unlimited budgets   (d) are largely self-managing

10. The _____ chart graphically displays the scheduling of tasks required to complete a project.

    (a) exception   (b) Taylor   (c) Gantt   (d) after action

11. In CPM/PERT, "CPM" stands for _____.

    (a) critical path method   (b) control planning management   (c) control plan map   (d) current planning method

12. In a CPM/PERT analysis the focus is on _____ and the event _____ that link them together with the finished project.

    (a) costs, budgets   (b) activities, sequences   (c) timetables, budgets   (d) goals, costs

13. A manager following the "hot stove rules" of progressive discipline would _____.

    (a) avoid giving too much information when reprimanding someone   (b) reprimand at random   (c) focus the reprimand on actions, not personality   (d) delay reprimands until something positive can also be discussed.

14. Among the financial ratios often used for control purposes, Current Assets / Current Liabilities is known as the _____.

    (a) debt ratio   (b) net margin   (c) current ratio   (d) inventory turnover ratio

15. In respect to Return on Assets (ROA) and the Debt Ratio, the preferred directions when analyzing them from a control standpoint are _____.

    (a) decrease ROA, increase Debt   (b) increase ROA, increase Debt   (c) increase ROA, decrease Debt   (d) decrease ROA, decrease Debt

SHORT-RESPONSE QUESTIONS:

16. List the four steps in the controlling process and give examples of each.

17. How might feedforward control be used by the owner/manager of a local bookstore?

18. How does Douglas McGregor's Theory Y relate to the concept of internal control?

19. How does a progressive discipline system work?

APPLICATION QUESTION:

20. Assume that you are given the job of project manager for building a new student center on your campus. List just five of the major activities that need to be accomplished to complete the new building in two years. Draw an AON network diagram that links the activities together in required event scheduling and sequencing. Make an estimate for the time required for each sequence to be completed and identify the critical path.

Take2 Interactive; How Much Is Too Much?

Ask any kid to name who's making the edgiest video games on the market right now, and they'll likely point you toward Take2 Interactive. Along with subsidiary RockStar Games, this rising star of the gaming circuit produces some of the most popular and most graphic game titles, including the Grand Theft Auto series State of Emergency. But are its games too hot for consumers to handle? And can the company overcome its own financial challenges to continue producing gritty, innovative game titles?

Quick question: How many cars have you stolen?

Ever shot someone over a simple disagreement? Or driven through a storefront window just to see the glass shatter?

More American teens than you might suspect have, and most share the same partner in crime: Take2 Interactive Software.

Living on the Edge

Loved by gamers but abhorred by parents, many of Take2's video-game titles have enabled a new degree of on-screen recklessness among digital devotees. Take2 subsidiary RockStar Games may be the most famous arm, publishing well-known titles like the *Grand Theft Auto series* and *State of Emergency*. And Take2's 2K Games division has produced the popular ESPN 2K line of sports games.

Take2 came under fire not long ago when clever gamers discovered they could access some pretty racy content in the latest installment of its hit *Grand Theft Auto Series—GTA: San Andreas*—with the help of a downloadable software modification called Hot Coffee. Though Take2 initially claimed the scenes had been inserted by the modification, investigators later concluded that the explicit content had existed in the game all along, but could only be unlocked with the third-party software.

The company known for its edgy content meekly complied with Federal Trade Commission investigators and vowed to internally apply a more stringent game-editing process.

But for Take2, content is king. And as the video-game maker has learned, especially contentious content drives ambitious game scales. Since their respective releases, *Grand Theft Auto III* and *GTA: Vice City* have sold approximately 11 and 13 million games annually. *San Andreas* has done just as well, selling over 12 million copies in its first year and creating approximately $600 million in revenue for Take2.[21]

Ever since the release of the first *Grand Theft Auto*, Take2's major title releases have heralded an uptick in stock activity.[22]

An Unexpected Twist

With all the attention surrounding Take2's frequent game releases, you'd think that the company's financial outlook would be most rosy. But not necessarily. Not too long ago, when, Take2 announced that an anticipated fiscal quarterly loss would be even greater than Wall Street had imagined, the news sent Take2 stock down 8%. The company has had to fend off media inquiries about an internal investigation concerning its stock option grant practices. All of this created some loss of credibility in the eyes of stock analysts.[23]

Mike Hickey, an analyst for Janco Partners and longtime Take2 stock advocate said: "We believe management's continued inability to provide guidance is either from inadequate internal financial controls and/or guidance too undesirable to report, neither of which leaves us with much confidence." Hickey's report on Take2 stock, entitled "Pain, Disgust, and Agony," lambasted the company's lack of guidance for coming quarterly revenues and its "spiraling chaos of continued bad news. Surprisingly, not all analysts were downtrodden about Take2's challenging prospects. A writer on *Seeking Alpha*, a stock opinion and analysis Web site, wrote, "Personally I don't consider this a significant event for long-term holders."

Betting on the *Bully*

Luckily for Take2, gamers and analysts alike have poor short-term memory, and their future prospects are likely to be evaluated by the success of their next game. So how does Take2 plan to retake the video-game industry?

With an old-fashioned schoolyard beating, of course.

As usual, Take2 subsidiary RockStar Games is responsible for all the commotion. RockStar's game, *Bully*, is a digital take on the classic growing pains of adolescence. Its main character is a 15-year-old boy who deals with teen archetypes (jocks, authoritarian types) while avoiding getting beat up at his fictional boarding school.[24]

Even before its release, Take2 had already been given its fair share of publicity surrounding this game. School and parental groups clamored for retailers to restrict children from purchasing *Bully*. More than six months before its release, the Florida Miami-Dade County School Board asked retailers not to sell the game to minors and asked the schools to warn parents about harmful effects of playing violent video games.[25]

According to the *New York Times*, "Anti-game activists claimed that it would encourage players to become bullies themselves. Even some executives at other game companies feared that *Bully*, coming from Rockstar, a company that has long been a lightning rod for politicians and others fearful of video games, would drag the entire industry into yet another quagmire of criticism."[26]

Gaming's Unrepentant Bad-Boy

Take2 has no plans to back off of any other contentious components of its games, which are frequently distinguished by how easy they make it for gamers to carry out excessively violent acts. Considering how many gamers are teens, some critics find the company straddling an ethical line, and wonder about the longevity of a game shop that banks its future on edgy content.

RockStar Games' vice president Dan Houser, who rarely sits down for interviews, is characteristically oblique when discussing Take2's status as a lightning rod for social criticism.

"Certainly it's frustrating when people don't wish to understand what you do and don't wish to learn," Houser said. "Anyone who plays any of our games and wishes to criticize it, having played it, experienced it and thought about it, they are of course welcome to do that. But when large numbers of people criticize something and haven't even done it, it's very frustrating. There's a large amount of the population that lives in relative ignorance and only hears scary stories about what we do."[27] But is this vague criticism of critics enough to soothe concerned parents and administrators over the coming *Bully* brouhaha? More importantly, can Take2 find a way to regain the attention of suddenly disinterested investors and analysts? Perhaps most tellingly, it is the gaming public who will decide this. So pull up a chair, grab a controller, and decide for yourself whether Take2 Interactive has what it takes to stay in the game.

REVIEW QUESTIONS

1. Is Take2's strategy of producing news-grabbing, edgy video games sustainable in the long-term? Should the company break out of this model?
2. When concerned groups protest the content in a video game well before its release, is this more helpful to the protestors or the video-game maker?
3. Is Take2 a firm that seems to be on the verge of operating out of control?

TEAM PROJECT

Top Job Checkup

There's lot of internal control or self-management involved in being a student. Part of that control involves having a clear direction against which one's progress can be measured. Think of your career direction and the extent to which internal control is working for you or against you.

Question: What are the "best" jobs in today's employment markets and what makes them great?

Research Directions:

- Develop a set of criteria for rating jobs. In your mind what makes the difference between a "great" and "poor" job?
- Brainstorm a list of the top 10 jobs that you and your peers are likely to be seeking. For each of those jobs rate them according to the criteria you just developed.
- Look at *Money* magazine and other sources to find actual ratings of jobs. Compare the criteria they use to rate jobs with your own. Add their criteria to yours and expand the ratings of the jobs you have on your listing. Have any of your ratings changed overall, and, if so, why?
- Identify what *Money* magazine and other sources consider the "top" jobs. Compare these jobs to the ones you and your peers are seeking. Are you going after the right ones? Would you make any changes in your job aspirations based on the published rankings?
- Summarize your investigation in a report that your college or university placement center might use as an information or advice piece for its student clients. Title the report this way: What College Graduates Should Consider When Rating Alternative Job Opportunities.

PERSONAL MANAGEMENT

It may strike you as odd to talk here about personal **STRENGTH AND ENERGY**. But the fact is that it isn't easy to work today and to always exercise the self-control needed to balance work and personal responsibilities. One national survey of American workers, for example, found 54 percent feel overworked, 55 percent feel overwhelmed by their workloads, 56 percent say they do not have enough time to complete their work, 59 percent do not have enough time for reflection, and 45 percent have to do too many things at once. At a minimum this reminds us that work in the 21st century can be very stressful. And just as with playing tennis or some other sport, we have to get and stay in shape for work. This means building strength and energy to best handle the inevitable strains and anxieties of organizational changes, job pressures, and the potential conflicts between work demands and personal affairs. Some personal questions are:

Strength and Energy

- Is it hard to relax after a day in class?
- Does it take effort to concentrate in your spare time?
- Do you lay awake thinking and worrying about events of the day?
- Are you so tired that you are unable to join friends or family in leisure activities?

Building the Brand Called "You"   Take the above 4-question test. Any yes answer indicates the need to do a better job of building and sustaining your capacities to handle heavy workloads. And if you think things are tough as a student, get ready. The real challenges lie ahead! What does the recommended self-assessment suggest about your readiness to act?

NEXT STEPS: MANAGEMENT LEARNING WORKBOOK

Self-Assessments
- Internal/External Control (#26)

Experiential Exercises
- After Meeting/Project Review (#20)

Operations Management and Services

19

Planning Ahead

Chapter 19 Study Questions

1 What are the essentials of operations management?

2 How do organizations manage customer service and product quality?

3 How can work processes be designed for productivity?

Value . . . at What Cost?

Wal-Mart has long been a paradigm of operational efficiency, earning the loyalty of shoppers, the respect of CEOs, and the ire of penny-pinched suppliers. But the retailer knows that despite all its deals, everything comes at a cost. How is Wal-Mart's unwavering quest for value affecting its customers?

Wal-Mart's no-holds-barred campaign for market dominance has but one goal: value. Wal-Mart's leadership strategy defines true value as a "fair" price. The fair prices are underpinned by lean, ultra-efficient logistics, ruthless negotiation tactics with suppliers, and cost-conscious labor practices.

Now if you jump into the always unfolding "Wal-Mart" story, you'll find that the firm, its leaders, its strategy and its overall impact on people and communities are well debated. It's a long way from the days when Wal-Mart, led by its founder Sam Walton, was marching squarely and securely at the head of the pack. It's still the world's largest retailer, but there's lot of competition breathing down the company's neck. Just stop by your local Target store for one example.

The Bentonville, Arkansas, company's relentless pursuit of the "lowest possible price" has resulted in an ever-narrower customer base: the consumer who shops by price alone. Value is not always determined by price perceptions, so Wal-Mart is

What *They* Think?

"Our position is to give our customers the best value, and value is a combination of price, quality, and time-saving."
Gail Lavielle, senior director of corporate communications at Wal-Mart

EFFICIENCY: *"One of the ravages of inflation is that it affects those who have the least. And Wal-Mart is a great inflation fighter. It challenges the norms in terms of what people pay for high-quality goods."*
Jack Welch, former General Electric CEO

CUSTOMERS: *"It's an empty public relations stunt. Wal-Mart knows that it doesn't have to spend much on this health-care coverage because hardly anyone will sign up."*
Chris Kofinis, communications director at WakeUpWalMart.com

expanding its product lines in hopes that more consumers will find something to buy on their next trip, improving both their in-store experience and the company's profit margins.

"We don't want to give [the impression] we're abandoning low price," said Gail Lavielle, senior director of corporate communications at Wal-Mart. "Our position is to give our customers the best value, and value is a combination of price, quality, and time-saving"[1]

The repositioning to emphasize "value" over low prices—Wal-Mart's traditional badge of honor—is emblematic of the larger image overhaul that Wal-Mart is undertaking.

Historically, the company has been able to present customers with rock-bottom prices. Some claim this is only possible because Wal-Mart is able to pay noncompetitive wages and avoids offering benefits whenever possible.

In its defense, each new Wal-Mart adds an average of nearly 100 net jobs to its county.[2]

But some communities—and workers—targeted for the latest Wal-Mart expansion have begun to wonder whether the jobs are the kind they want to import. Wal-Mart may be creating a built-in base of customers in every town because so many of its workers are hard pressed to shop on any basis other than price. Ironically, denying workers a living wage and benefits ultimately hurts productivity because of lost time resulting from illness and lost efficiency resulting from low morale.

To combat allegations of unfriendliness and to highlight its pursuit of value for all, the retailer known for its smiley-faced mascot is trying to put on a compassionate face.

Wal-Mart is enabling its workers to remain its customers by offering them substantial discounts on produce to encourage healthy eating. It is also making an inexpensive "value plan" health insurance available to workers: high-deductible catastrophic coverage is tempered by low co-pays for a limited number of office visits.[3]

In the end, the company insists that taking care of workers is not Wal-Mart's problem, but America's problem. CEO Lee Scott recently told the National Governors Association, "The soaring cost of health care in America cannot be sustained over the long term by any business that offers health benefits to its employees."[4]

The Numbers

Wal-Mart vs. Target

	Wal-Mart	Target
Market Cap	$204.16B	$49.96B
Employees	1,800,000	338,000
Revenue	$329.86B	$55.36B
Gross Margin	23.22%	32.37%
Earnings per Share	$2.557	$2.884

Quick Facts

* When Wal-Mart petitioned the Federal Deposit Insurance Corporation (FDIC) to create the Wal-Mart Bank to process credit and debit-card transactions, the application generated 3,600 comment letters. For the first time in its history, the FDIC held public hearings on a deposit application.[5]
* More than 20 states have introduced legislation intended to force Wal-Mart to spend more on its employees' health care.[6]
* A recently leaked memo shows that Wal-Mart's 1.3 million employees, who make an average of $20,000 a year, spend 8 percent of their income on health care, nearly twice the national average.[7]
* Forty-six percent of Wal-Mart employees' children are either uninsured or on Medicaid.[8]
* China's seventh-largest export market is one U.S. company: Wal-Mart.[9]

What Do You Think?

1. In what ways might Wal-Mart's pursuit of cost efficiencies have a negative impact on customer satisfaction and loyalties?
2. How does Wal-Mart's pledge of "best value" for its customers translate into actual store operations?

Services and operations management		
Study Question 1	**Study Question 2**	**Study Question 3**
Operations Management Essentials	**Service and Product Quality**	**Work Processes**
■ Productivity and competitive advantage ■ Manufacturing and services technology ■ Value and supply chain management ■ Inventory management ■ Break-even analysis	■ Customer relationship management ■ Quality management ■ Statistical quality control	■ Work process analysis ■ Process reengineering ■ Process-driven organizations
Learning Check 1	**Learning Check 2**	**Learning Check 3**

Managers today are learning to operate in a world that places a premium on productivity, technology utilization, quality, customer service, and speed. Businesses of all types and sizes are struggling and innovating as they try to succeed in a world of intense competition, continued globalization of markets and business activities, and rapid technological change. Just how top executives approach these challenges differs from one organization to the next, but they all focus on moving services and products into the hands of customers in ways that create loyalty and profits.

At Xerox Corporation, CEO Anne Mulcahy believes that competition is an opportunity to focus one's operations and keep employees' eyes on the target—winning ground against strong competitors. And in that regard she believes customers are center stage, saying: "The toughest customers are the ones that embed themselves in customer relationships . . . that's what we're trying to do." And when in the field, she advises her sales force to emphasize Xerox's strengths rather than bad-mouthing the competition.[10]

At BMW, where customers are also foremost, a major thrust is on continuous innovation. CEO Norbert Reithofer says: "We push change through the organization to ensure its strength. There are always better solutions." One of those solutions is state-of-the-art manufacturing: the firm's facilities produce 1.3 million customized vehicles a year.[11]

At Ann Taylor, when the firm was struggling to reassert its women's clothing brand and market position, new CEO Kay Krill started with a 54-point action plan. It covered everything from processes to products to marketing. Although criticized for identifying so many things to address, she said: "There were 54 things we needed to fix. We fixed every one of them. All 54 were important to me."[12]

OPERATIONS MANAGEMENT ESSENTIALS

In one way or another, all organizations must master the challenges of **operations management**—getting work done by managing productive systems that transform resources into finished products, goods, and services for customers and clients.[13] Typical operations management decisions address such things as resource acquisition, inventories, facilities, workflows, technologies, and product quality. In all respects the core issues come down to "productivity" and "competitive advantage" through effective management of the multiple processes through which resources, in the form of people, materials, equipment, and capital, are turned into goods and services.

It is important to remember that the essentials of operations management apply to all types of organizations, not just to product manufacturers. Yes, Xerox transforms resource inputs into quality photocopy manchines; BMW transforms them into attractive, high-performance automobiles; and Ann Taylor transforms them into fashionable clothing and accessories. But also in the services sector, Southwest Airlines transforms resource inputs into low-cost, dependable air travel; American Express transforms them into financial services; Mayo Clinic transforms them into health care services; and governments transform them into public services. And as we all know, some organizations, be they in manufacturing or services, do perform much better than others in these respects.

■ **Operations management** is the process of managing productive systems that transform resources into finished products.

PRODUCTIVITY AND COMPETITIVE ADVANTAGE

Operations management in both manufacturing and services is very concerned with **productivity**—a quantitative measure of the efficiency with which inputs are transformed into outputs. The basic *productivity equation* is:

$$Productivity = Output/Input$$

If, for example, a local Red Cross center collects 100 units of donated blood in one 8-hour day, its productivity would be 10.25 units per hour. If we were in

■ **Productivity** is the efficiency with which inputs are transformed into outputs.

INSIGHTS

Flexible Manufacturing New Push by Fashion Benchmark

Pressures from upstart retailers excelling at "fast fashion"—getting new designs into stores quickly, has brought changes to Louis Vuitton. The maker of high-fashion handbags and other accessories is revamping production techniques to increase speed without sacrificing quality. A tote bag used to take up to 30 craftpersons some 8 days to make. The bag was passed from hand-to-hand, with each worker performing a separate and highly specialized task. That all changed when Vuitton executives, advised by consultants from McKinsey & Company, benchmarked Toyota's production processes and decided that they could do things a lot faster. The company reorganized workers into teams of 6 to 12 people, working at U-shaped work stations. The people in each team perform more than one task, pass the in-process tote bag back and forth, and complete a tote bag in just 1 day.

Workers in Louis Vuitton's Pégase teams are less specialized than before. They are able to perform different tasks and make different kinds of bags, allowing production to switch quickly from one design to another.

The new production system is called "Pégase" after the mythical flying horse, a symbol of speed and power. Since it was introduced, Louis Vuitton has been able to ship new designs every 6 weeks, more than twice as fast as previously. This was a major shift of mindset in the high-end fashion industry previously ruled by design; now it's ruled by design and execution. Says Patrick Louis Vuitton of the founding family: "It's about finding the best ratio between quality and speed."[49]

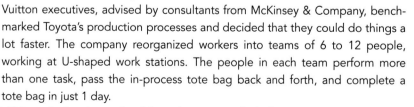

charge of centers in several locations, the productivity of the centers could be compared on this measure. Alternatively, one might compare the centers using a productivity measure based not on hours of inputs but on numbers of full-time staff. Using this input measure, a center that collects 500 units per week with two full-time staff members (250 units per person) is more productive than one that collects 600 units per week with three (200 units per person).

When Microsoft studied productivity of office workers, the online survey of 38,000+ people across 200 countries showed a variety of productivity shortfalls.[14] Although people reported working 47 hours per week, they were unproductive during 17 of the hours: 69 percent said time spent in meetings was unproductive. Productivity obstacles included unclear objectives and priorities as well as procrastination and poor communication.

Inefficiencies like those reported by Microsoft are costly. Productivity by any measure is one of the components of organizational competitiveness. The concept of **competitive advantage** was initially defined in Chapter 4 as a core competency that allows an organization to outperform competitors.[15] Operating efficiencies that increase productivity are among the ways organizations may gain competitive advantage. Others include such things as the ability to outperform based on product innovation, customer service, speed to market, manufacturing flexibility, and product or service quality. But regardless of how competitive advantage is achieved, the key result is the same: an ability to consistently do something of high value that one's competitors cannot replicate quickly or do as well.

■ **Competitive advantage** is the ability to outperform one's competitors.

TECHNOLOGY IN MANUFACTURING AND SERVICES

Standing at the core of any transformation process is *technology*, the combination of knowledge, skills, equipment, and work methods used to transform resource inputs into organizational outputs. It is the way tasks are accomplished using tools, machines, techniques, and human know-how. The availability of appropriate technology is a cornerstone of productivity, and the nature of the core technologies in use is an important element in competitive advantage.

It is common to classify *manufacturing technology* into three categories.[16] In **small-batch production,** such as in a racing bicycle shop, a variety of custom products are tailor-made to order. Each item or batch of items is made somewhat differently to fit customer specifications. The equipment used may not be elaborate, but a high level of worker skill is often needed. In **mass production,** the organization produces a large number of uniform products in an assembly-line system. Workers are highly dependent on one another as the product passes from stage to stage until completion. Equipment may be sophisticated, and workers often follow detailed instructions while performing simplified jobs. Organizations using **continuous-process production** are highly automated. They produce a few products by continuously feeding raw materials—such as liquids, solids, and gases—through a highly automated production system with largely computerized controls. Such systems are equipment intensive, but they can often be operated by a relatively small labor force. Classic examples are automated chemical plants, steel mills, oil refineries, and power plants.

■ **Small-batch production** manufactures a variety of products crafted to fit customer specifications.

■ **Mass production** manufactures a large number of uniform products with an assembly-line system.

■ In **continuous-process production,** raw materials are continuously transformed by an automated system.

Among the directions in manufacturing technology today, the following trends are evident:

■ There is increased use of *robotics*, where computer-controlled machines perform physically repetitive work with consistency and efficiency. If you visit any automobile manufacturer today, chances are that robotics is a major feature of the operations.

- There is also increased use of *flexible manufacturing systems* that allow automated operations to quickly shift from one task or product type to another. The goal is to combine flexibility with efficiency, allowing what is sometimes called *mass customization* that results in efficient mass production of products meeting specific customer requirements.

- There is increased use of *cellular layouts* that place together machines doing different work so that the movement of materials from one to the other is as efficient as possible. Celluar layouts also accommodate more teamwork on the part of machine operators.

- There is increased use of *computer-integrated manufacturing*, in which product designs, process plans, and manufacturing are driven from a common computer platform. Such CIM approaches are now integrated with the Internet so that customer purchasing trends in retail locations can be spotted and immediately integrated into production schedules in a manufacturing location.

- There is increased focus on *lean production* that continuously innovates and employs best practices to keep increasing production efficiencies. A master of this approach is Toyota, featured in the end-of-chapter case.

- There is increased attention to *design for disassembly.* The goal here is to design and manufacture products in ways that consider how their component parts will be recycled at the end of their lives.

- There is increased value to be found in *remanufacturing.* Instead of putting things together, remanufacturing takes used items apart and rebuilds them as products to be used again. One estimate is that using remanufactured materials saves up to 30 percent on costs.[17]

When it comes to *service technology*, the classifications are slightly different.[18] In health care, education, and related services, **intensive technology** focuses the efforts of many people with special expertise on the needs of patients or clients. In banks, real estate firms, insurance companies, employment agencies, and others like them, **mediating technology** links together parties seeking a mutually beneficial exchange of values—typically a buyer and seller. Finally, **long-linked technology** can function like mass production, where a client is passed from point to point for various aspects of service delivery.

VALUE AND SUPPLY CHAIN MANAGEMENT

Figure 19.1 shows how the **value chain** might be described for a typical organization. This is the specific sequence of activities that result in the creation of finished good or services with value for customers. Part of the logic of being able to identify and diagram the components of the value chain is to

▨ **Intensive technology** focuses the efforts and talents of many people to serve clients.

▨ **Mediating technology** links together people in a beneficial exchange of values.

▨ In **long-linked technology** a client moves from point to point during service delivery.

▨ The **value chain** is the specific sequence of activities that creates goods and services with value for customers.

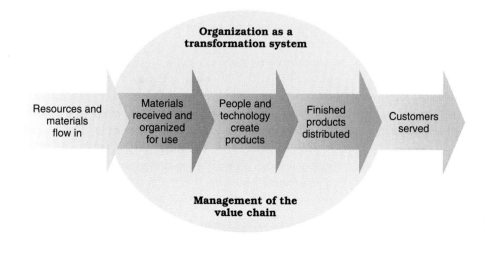

Figure 19.1 Elements in an organization's value chain.

focus attention on two major questions: (1) What value is being created for customers in each step? (2) How efficient is each step as a contributor to overall organizational productivity?

As the customer of an online retailer, like Amazon.com for example, you can think of this value in such terms as the price you pay, the quality you receive, and the timeliness of the delivery. From the standpoint of Amazon's management, the value creation process can be examined from the point of book purchases, to their transportation and warehousing, to electronic inventorying and order processing, to packaging and distribution to the ultimate customer.

Just as organizations need to manage their customers on the output side, supplier relationships on the input side must also be well managed. The concept of **supply chain management**, or SCM, involves strategic management of all operations linking an organization and its suppliers, including such areas as purchasing, manufacturing, transportation, and distribution.[19] The goals of supply chain management are to achieve efficiency in all aspects of the supply chain while ensuring on-time availability of quality resources and products. Wal-Mart, featured in the Hot Topic chapter opener, is considered a master of supply chain management. As one example, the firm uses an advanced information system that continually updates inventory records and sales forecasts based on point-of-sale computerized information collection. Suppliers access this information electronically, allowing them to adjust their operations and rapidly ship replacement products to meet the retailer's needs.

■ **Supply chain management** strategically links all operations dealing with resource supplies.

REAL ETHICS

Fair Trade Fashion

Perhaps you're one of a growing number of consumers that like to shop "fair trade." Doesn't it feel good when you buy coffee, for example, that is certified as grown by persons who were paid fairly for their labors? But, can we say the same about clothing? How do we know that what we're wearing right now wasn't made under sweatshop conditions or by children?

There is at least one retailer that wants to be considered as selling fair trade fashion. Fair Indigo, launched by former executives of major fashion retailers, presents itself as "a new clothing company with a different way of doing business" that wants to "create stylish, high-quality clothes while paying a fair and meaningful wage to the people who produce them." Pointing out that there is no certifying body for fair trade apparel, Fair Indigo offers this guarantee: "We will therefore guarantee that every employee who makes our clothing is paid a fair wage, not just a legal minimum wage, as is the benchmark in the industry."

The firm's representatives travel the globe searching for small factories and cooperatives that meet their standards. By doing so, they're bucking industry trends in outsourcing and contract manufacturing. Fair Indigo's CEO,

Bill Bass, says: "The whole evolution of the clothing and manufacturing industry has been to drive prices and wages down, shut factories and move work to countries with lower wages. We said 'we're going to reverse this and push wages up.' "

FURTHER INQUIRY

How do you define "fair" as in "fair trade"? Are you willing to pay a bit more for a fair trade product? And, what do you think about Fair Indigo's business model? Is it "fashion" that sells apparel, or factory and conditions of origin? Will consumers pay more for fair trade fashion?

As of yet, Fair Indigo has not disclosed its list of suppliers, claiming that this is a competitive asset for the firm. But it also makes it harder for activist groups and others to investigate how closely their suppliers stack up against Indigo's stated standards. What's your reading of all this? Is Fair Indigo on the forefront of the next new wave of innovation in fashion retailing?

INVENTORY MANAGEMENT

Rising costs of materials are a fact of life in today's economy. Controlling these costs through efficient purchasing management is an important productivity tool in value and supply chain management. Just as any individual would be, a thrifty organization must be concerned about how much it pays for what it buys. To leverage buying power, more organizations are centralizing purchasing to allow buying in volume. They are focusing on a small number of suppliers with whom they negotiate special contracts, gain quality assurances, and get preferred service. They are also finding ways to work together in supplier-purchaser partnerships. It is now more common, for example, that parts suppliers maintain warehouses in their customer's facilities. The customer provides the space; the supplier does the rest. The benefits to the customer are lower purchasing costs and preferred service; the supplier gains an exclusive customer contract and more sales volume.

Inventory is the amount of materials or products kept in storage. Organizations maintain inventories of raw materials, work in process, and finished goods. The goal of inventory control is to make sure that an inventory is just the right size to meet performance needs, thus minimizing the cost. The **economic order quantity** (EOQ) method of inventory control involves ordering a fixed number of items every time an inventory level falls to a predetermined point. When this point is reached, as shown in *Figure 19.2*, a decision is automatically made (typically by computer) to place a standard order to replenish the stock. The order sizes are mathematically calculated to minimize costs of inventory. The best example is the local supermarket, where hundreds of daily orders are routinely made on this basis.

■ Inventory control by **economic order quantity** orders replacements whenever inventory level falls to a predetermined point.

Another approach to inventory control is **just-in-time scheduling** (JIT), made popular by the Japanese. JIT systems reduce costs and improve workflow by scheduling materials to arrive at a workstation or facility "just in time" to be used. Since almost no inventories are maintained, the just-in-time approach is an important productivity tool. Because JIT nearly eliminates the carrying costs of inventories, this system is an important business productivity tool. When a major hurricane was predicted to hit Florida, Wal-Mart's computer database anticipated high demand for, of all things, strawberry Pop-Tarts. JIT kicked in to deliver them to the stores "just in time" for the storm.[20]

■ **Just-in-time scheduling** minimizes inventory by outing materials to workstations "just in time" to be used.

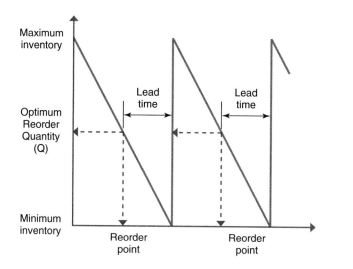

Figure 19.2 Inventory control by economic order quantity (EOQ).

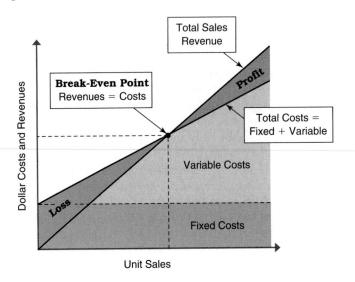

Figure 19.3 Graphical approach to break-even analysis.

BREAK-EVEN ANALYSIS

■ The **break-even point** is where revenues = costs.

When business executives are deliberating new products or projects, a frequent question is: "What is the **break-even point**?" The graph in *Figure 19.3* shows this as the point where revenues just equal costs. You can also think of it as the point where losses end and profit begins. The formula for calculating break-even points is

Break-Even Point=Fixed Costs/(Price−Variable Costs).

■ **Break-even analysis** calculates the point at which revenues cover costs under different "what if" conditions.

Managers use **break-even analysis** to improve control and perform "what if" calculations under different projected cost and revenue conditions. See if you can calculate some break-even points. What if the proposed target price for a new product is $8 per unit, fixed costs are $10,000, and variable costs are $4 per unit? What sales volume is required to break even? (*Answer:* the break-even point is at 2500 units.) What happens if you are good at cost control and can keep variable costs to $3 per unit? (*Answer:* the break-even point is at 2000 units.) Now, suppose you can only produce 1000 units in the beginning and at the original costs. At what price must you sell them to break even? (*Answer:* $14.) These are the types of analyses that business executives perform every day.

Be sure you can ■ define operations management ■ state the productivity equation ■ define competitive advantage ■ list alternative types of manufacturing and service technologies ■ describe the value chain for an organization ■ illustrate how supply chain management applies to an organization ■ calculate an EOQ ■ explain JIT ■ calculate break even points

CUSTOMER SERVICE AND PRODUCT QUALITY

Some years ago, at a time when American industry was first coming to grips with fierce competition from Japanese products, American quality pioneer J. M. Juran challenged an audience of Japanese executives with a prediction. He warned them against complacency, suggesting that America would bounce back in business competitiveness and that the words "Made in

KAFFEEKLATSCH

Cost Cutting Backfires

First Cup

"Here we go again—cut costs, cut costs, cut costs. How far can you cut costs and still have a viable operation? I think these top managers must have all graduated from the same MBA program, one that was dominated by 'numbers crunchers.' All they seem to know is how to cut costs. But where is it getting us? I see low morale, increasing problems meeting targets because we're all so overloaded, and corners being trimmed that could well turn into major quality problems at some point. I don't know about you, but I'm about fed up with it all."

Studying the Grounds

■ Dell Computer suffered a major customer backlash when some 3,000 callers to its customer service lines in one week had to wait at least 30 minutes before being able to speak with a real person.

■ Northwest Airlines once left passengers stranded inside a plane for 8 hours because of a snowstorm in Detroit.

■ Customer satisfaction at Home Depot fell 8.2 percent in a year that sales surged at its rival Lowe's, known for its customer service.

Double Espresso

"I know, just look at the wait lines at some service establishments. How long does it take you to get to the car rental counter or to cash a check at the bank? Most service establishments these days are cutting back so far on staff that there are few people left to actually serve their customers. And the next time you're in a restaurant, keep your eyes open. The chances are that the servers are being run ragged because there just aren't enough of them. Don't you wonder how much could be added to the bottom lines of these firms if they would just pay more to staff at levels that customers would appreciate?"

Your Turn

What is the real cost of customer dissatisfaction for the businesses you patronize? Northwest Airlines, for example, doesn't have much competition in some markets and may not have lots of incentives to respond to customer dissatisfaction. Does a lack of competition like this hurt customer services? Or, is it really a management philosophy of cost-cutting that creates conditions for poor service delivery?

America" would once again symbolize world-class quality.[21] There seems little doubt today that Juran's prediction was accurate.

A *Harvard Business Review* survey reports that American business leaders rank customer service and product quality as the first and second most important goals in the success of their organizations.[22] In a survey by the market research firm Michelson & Associates, poor service and product dissatisfaction were also ranked number 1 and number 2 as reasons why customers abandon a retail store. Reaching the twin goals of providing great service and quality products isn't always easy. But when pursued relentlessly, striving to reach these goals can be an important source of competitive advantage. Bill Gates once said: "Your most unhappy customers are your greatest source of learning."[23]

Just imagine the ramifications if every customer or client contact for an organization was positive. Not only would these customers and clients return again and again, but they would also tell others and expand the customer base.

CUSTOMER RELATIONSHIP MANAGEMENT

Figure 19.4 expands the open-systems view of organizations to depict the complex internal operations of the organization as well as its interdependence with the external environment. In this figure the organization's *external*

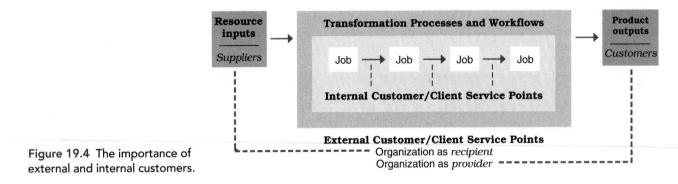

Figure 19.4 The importance of external and internal customers.

customers purchase the goods produced or utilize the services provided. They may be industrial customers—other firms that buy a company's products for use in their own operations—or they may be retail customers or clients who purchase or use the goods and services directly. *Internal customers*, by contrast, are found within the organization. They are the individuals and groups who use or otherwise depend on one another's work in order to do their own jobs well. The notion of customer service applies equally well to external and internal customers.

When customers are respected and treated as key stakeholders of any organization, they sit at the top of the upside-down pyramid originally described in Chapter 1. And without any doubt, customers put today's organizations to a very stiff test, wanting (1) high quality, (2) low price, and (3) on-time delivery in the goods and services they buy.

Many organizations now use the principles of **customer relationship management** to establish and maintain high standards of customer service.[24] Known as CRM, this approach uses the latest information technologies to maintain intense communication with customers as well as to gather and utilize data regarding their needs and desires. At Marriott International, for example, CRM is supported by special customer management software that tracks information on customer preferences. When you check in, the likelihood is that your past requests for things like a king-size bed, no smoking room, and computer modem access are already in your record. Says Marriott's chairman: "It's a big competitive advantage."[25]

■ **Customer relationship management** strategically tries to build lasting relationships with and to add value to customers.

QUALITY MANAGEMENT

The quality theme first introduced in Chapter 1 is closely connected with customer service and customer relationship management.[26] Managers that are customer and quality conscious understand the basic link between competitive advantage and the ability to always deliver quality goods and services. High performance organizational cultures include service and quality as core values to be reinforced in all aspects of value and supply chain management.

One indicator of how embedded quality objectives have become in operations management and services is the importance of **ISO certification** by the International Standards Organization in Geneva, Switzerland. It has been adopted by many countries of the world as a quality benchmark. Businesses that want to compete as "world-class companies" are increasingly expected to have ISO certification at various levels. To do so, they must refine and upgrade quality in all operations, and then undergo a rigorous assessment by outside auditors to determine whether they meet ISO requirements.

■ **ISO certification** indicates conformance with a rigorous set of international quality standards.

The work of W. Edwards Deming is a cornerstone of the quality movement. His story begins in 1951 when he was invited to Japan to explain quality control techniques that had been developed in the United States. The result was a lifelong relationship epitomized in the Deming Application Prize, which is still awarded annually in Japan for companies achieving extraordinary excellence in quality. "When Deming spoke," we might say, "the Japanese listened." The principles he taught the Japanese were straightforward . . . and they worked: tally defects, analyze and trace them to the source, make corrections, and keep a record of what happens afterward.[27] Deming's approach to quality emphasizes constant innovation, use of statistical methods, and commitment to training in the fundamentals of quality assurance.

One outgrowth of Deming's work was the emergergence of **total quality management**, or TQM. This is a process that makes quality principles part of the organization's strategic objectives, applying them to all aspects of operations and striving to meet customers' needs by doing things right the first time. Most TQM approaches begin with an insistence that the total quality commitment applies to everyone in an organization, from resource acquisition and supply chain management, through production and into the distribution of finished goods and services, and ultimately to customer relationship management.

This search for quality is closely tied to the emphasis on **continuous improvement**—always looking for new ways to improve on current performance.[28] The notion is that one can never be satisfied; something always can and should be improved on. Another important aspect of total quality operations is *cycle time*—the elapsed time between receipt of an order and delivery of the finished product. The quality objective here is to reduce cycle time by finding ways to serve customer needs more quickly.

▪ **Total quality management** is managing with an organization-wide commitment to continuous improvement, product quality, and customer needs.

▪ **Continuous improvement** involves always searching for new ways to improve work quality and performance.

STATISTICAL QUALITY CONTROL

An easy way to understand the notion of systematic **quality control** is through *control charts*, such as the one shown in *Figure 19.5*. Control charts are graphical ways of displaying trends so that exceptions to quality standards can be identified for special attention. In the figure, for example, an *upper control limit* and a *lower control limit* specify the allowable tolerances for measurements of a machine part. As long as the manufacturing process produces parts that fall within these limits, things are "in control." However, as soon as parts start to fall outside the limits, it is clear that something is going wrong that is affecting quality. The process can then be investigated, even shut down, to identify the source of the errors and correct them.

The same logic is extended further with sophisticated *statistical quality control* procedures that use rigorous statistical analysis for checking

▪ **Quality control** checks processes, materials, products, and services to ensure that they meet high standards.

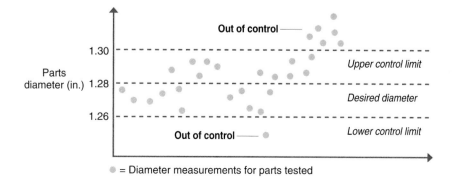

= Diameter measurements for parts tested

Figure 19.5 Sample control chart showing upper and lower control limits.

processes, materials, products, and services to ensure that they meet high standards. Many would consider statistical quality control a basic foundation for any quality management program, and advances in computer technologies make it highly accessible in many operations. Typically, statistical quality control begins by taking samples of work, measuring the quality in the samples, and then determining the acceptability of results. Unacceptable results in a sample trigger the need for investigation and corrective action.

The power of statistics allows sampling to be efficiently used as the basis for decision making and quality management. Many manufacturers now use a **Six Sigma** program, meaning that statistically the firm's quality performance will tolerate no more than 3.4 defects per million units of goods produced or services completed. This translates to a perfection rate of 99.9997 percent. As tough as it sounds, Six Sigma is a common quality standard for many, if not most, major competitors in our demanding global marketplace.

■ **Six Sigma** is a quality standard of 3.4 defects less per million products or service deliveries.

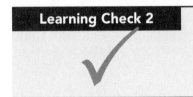

Learning Check 2

Be sure you can ■ explain the difference between internal and external customers of a firm ■ discuss the importance of customer relationship management in a competitive business environment ■ explain ISO certification ■ define the terms TQM and continuous improvement ■ illustrate how control charts and Six Sigma programs enhance quality management

WORK PROCESSES

■ **Process reengineering** systematically analyzes work processes to design new and better ones.

The emphasis on productivity and competitive advantage through strategic operations management includes a development known as business **process reengineering**.[29] This is defined by consultant Michael Hammer as the systematic and complete analysis of work processes and the design of new and better ones.[30] The goal of a reengineering effort is to break old work habits and focus attention on new and better ways of doing things.

WORK PROCESS ANALYSIS

■ A **work process** is a related group of tasks that together create a value for the customer.

In his book *Beyond Reengineering*, Michael Hammer defines a **work process** as "a related group of tasks that together create a result of value for the customer."[31] These tasks are what people do to turn resource inputs into goods or services for customers. Hammer highlights the following key words as implications of his definition: (1) *group*—tasks are viewed as part of a group rather than in isolation; (2) *together*—everyone must share a common goal; (3) *result*—the focus is on what is accomplished, not on activities; (4) *customer*—processes serve customers, and their perspectives are the ones that really count.

■ **Workflow** is the movement of work from one point to another in a system.

The concept of **workflow,** or the way work moves from one point to another in manufacturing or service delivery, is central to the understanding of processes.[32] The various parts of a work process must all be completed to achieve the desired results, and they must typically be completed in a given order. An important starting point for a reengineering effort is to diagram or map these workflows as they actually take place. Then each step can be systematically analyzed to determine whether it is adding value, to consider ways of eliminating or combining steps, and to find ways to use technology to improve efficiency. At People-Soft, now merged with Oracle, paper forms were largely driven out of the system some time ago. The firm's chief information officer once said: "Nobody jumps out of bed in the morning and says, 'I want to go to work and fill out forms.' We create systems that let people be brilliant rather than push paper."[33]

ISSUES AND SITUATIONS

Lean Production

You may have heard the term before: "lean production." It's another of the production innovations Japan has offered to the world. As a *Business Week* headline recently said, "No One Does Lean Like the Japanese." A great example is Matsushita Electric Industries. The firm's plant in Saga, Japan, was considered a model of efficiency in making telephones, fax machines, and security cameras. Its productivity doubled in a four-year period. But even this didn't satisfy Matsushita executives.

A huge set of conveyers was removed and robots were brought in, along with sophisticated software to operate them. The robots quickly adjust to one another and are even able to shift work to another robot if one breaks down. Plant manager Hitoshi Hirata says: "It used to be 2.5 days into a production run before we had our first finished product. But now the first is done in 40 minutes." One might be tempted to compliment Hirata on a job well done and sit back to watch the results. Not so. He goes on to say: "Next year we'll try to shorten the cycle even more."

The Saga plant has become an internal benchmark for Matsushita. Saga's group alone has 7 factories around the world. They serve different markets and make different products. But even with this complexity, the Saga innovations were copied and the robotic approach was moved to all plants. The firm experiments and works with local staff to achieve the right design to best fit each plant's products and circumstances.

Critical Response

The lean production notion is an interesting model. In the case of Japan's electronics manufacturers, it helps keep them a step ahead of other low-cost producers in China and other countries. But does going "lean" have limitations? Just how far can you go in trying to squeeze the "fat" out of a system without losing product or service quality? And what is the impact of "lean" methods on the employees?

PROCESS REENGINEERING

Given the mission, objectives, and strategies of an organization, business process reengineering can be used to regularly assess and fine-tune work processes to ensure that they directly add value to operations. Through a technique called **process value analysis,** core processes are identified and carefully evaluated for their performance contributions. Each step in a workflow is examined. Unless a step is found to be important, useful, and contributing to value-added results, it is eliminated. Process value analysis typically involves the following steps:[34]

■ **Process value analysis** identifies and evaluates core processes for their performance contributions.

1. Identify the core processes.
2. Map the core processes with respect to workflows.
3. Evaluate all core process tasks.
4. Search for ways to eliminate unnecessary tasks or work.
5. Search for ways to eliminate delays, errors, and misunderstandings.
6. Search for efficiencies in how work is shared and transferred among people and departments.

Figure 19.6 shows an example of how reengineering and better use of computer technology can streamline a purchasing operation. A purchase order should result in at least three value-added outcomes: order fulfillment, a paid bill, and a satisfied supplier. Work to be successfully accomplished includes such things as ordering, shipping, receiving, billing, and payment. A traditional business system might have purchasing, receiving, and accounts payable as separate functions, with each function communicating with each other and with the supplier. Alternatively, process value analysis might result in reengineering the workflow and redesigning a new purchasing support team whose members handle the same work more efficiently with the support of the latest computer technology.[35]

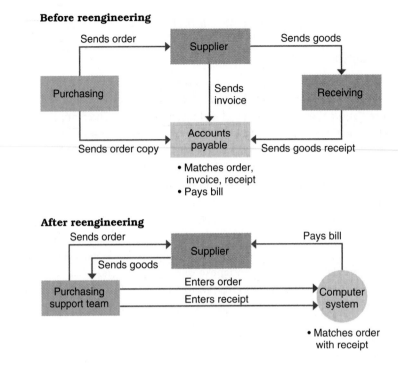

Figure 19.6 How reengineering can streamline work processes.

PROCESS-DRIVEN ORGANIZATIONS

Customers, teamwork, and efficiency are central to Hammer's notion of process reengineering. He describes the case of Aetna Life & Casualty Company, where a complex system of tasks and processes once took as much as 28 days to accomplish.[36] Customer service requests were handled in a step-by-step fashion by many different people. After an analysis of workflows, the process was redesigned into a "one and done" format, where a single customer service provider handled each request from start to finish. One of Aetna's customer account managers said after the change was made: "Now we can see the customers as individual people. It's no longer 'us' and 'them.' "[37]

Hammer also describes reengineering at a unit of Verizon Communications. Before reengineering, customer inquiries for telephone service and repairs required extensive consultation between technicians and their supervisors. After process value analysis, technicians were formed into geographical teams that handled their own scheduling, service delivery, and reporting. They were given cellular telephones and laptop computers to assist in managing their work, resulting in the elimination of a number of costly supervisory jobs. The technicians enthusiastically responded to the changes and opportunities. "The fact that you've got four or five people zoned in a certain geographical area," said one, "means that we get personally familiar with our customers' equipment and problems."[38]

The essence of process reengineering is to locate control for processes with an identifiable group of people, and to focus each person and the entire system on meeting customer needs and expectations. It tries to eliminate duplication of work and systems bottlenecks to reduce costs, increase efficiency, and build capacity for change. As Hammer says about the process-driven organization:

> Its intrinsic customer focus and its commitment to outcome measurement make it vigilant and proactive in perceiving the need for change; the process owner, freed from other responsibilities and wielding the power of process design, is an institutionalized agent of change; and employees who have an appreciation for customers and who are measured on outcomes are flexible and adaptable.[39]

RESEARCH BRIEF

How do you improve the productivity of a sales force?

That's the question asked by Dianne Ledingham, Mark Kovac, and Heidi Locke Simon. Writing in the *Harvard Business Review*, they use a series of case examples to illustrate how companies have used data and analytical methods to raise sales. They contrast the newer, data-driven approaches with what they call a "wing-and-a-prayer" style, in which salespersons are given goals and then simply told to go out and meet them.

One case involves U.S. Equipment Financing, headed by Michael Pilot and a division of GE Commercial Finance. Pilot's approach was to focus on raising the performance of existing sales representatives by helping them sell more—called the "productivity improvement approach"—in contrast to simply hiring more reps—what they call the "capacity increase approach."

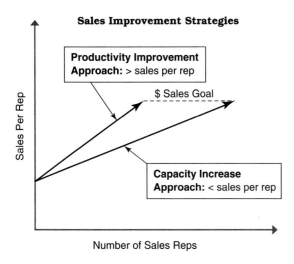

Pilot attributes some $300 million in new business to his scientific approach to sales-force productivity. He began with a new database that inventoried past transactions. He then asked sales reps to come up with criteria that would indicate the likelihood of a customer doing business with GE. He next ran regression analyses that tested these criteria against the past transactions. The result was a set of 6 criteria that correlated well with past successes.

When new prospects were scored using the criteria, Pilot found 50 percent more top-prospect sales candidates than had previously been identified. Using this set of top prospects, he redesigned the sales force to maximize attention to those prospects, and he provided reps with information and tools to better deal with their customers. The result was a 19 percent increase in the "conversion" rate, or sales closings.

The researchers conclude that Pilot's scientific method is a "best practice" approach to improve sales force productivity. They recommend the TOPSales approach, focusing on (1) targeted offerings by market segment, (2) optimized technology tools and procedures, (3) performance management metrics and systems, and (4) systematic sales force deployment.

QUESTIONS & APPLICATIONS

Once a goal is set to achieve a certain outcome target, be it sales or something else, resources must be mobilized to accomplish it. Some might be satisfied to just say that "we/I reached the target." Others will be more demanding, wanting to know "how much did it cost you to get there?"

This article describes a vigorous productivity improvement approach to reaching a higher sales goal. Can you find examples in your experience or community where goals are reached but the costs of doing so are very high? In these examples, can you identify ways that the same goals could be reached with lower costs and higher productivity?

Reference: Dianne Ledingham, Mark Kovac, and Heidi Locke Simon, "The New Science of Sales Force Productivity," *Harvard Business Review*, Vol. 84 (September 2006), pp. 124–133.

Be sure you can ■ define the terms process reengineering and work process ■ draw a map of the workflow in an organization familiar to you ■ explain how process value analysis can be used to streamline workflows and improve work performance

Learning Check 3

CHAPTER 19 STUDY GUIDE

STUDY QUESTIONS SUMMARY

1 What are the essentials of operations management and services?

- The challenges of operations management relate to getting work done by managing productive systems that transform resources into finished goods and services for customers and clients.

- Productivity measures the efficiency with which inputs are transformed into outputs: Productivity = Output/Input.

- Technology, including the use of knowledge, equipment, and work methods in the transformation process, is an important consideration in operations management.

- The value chain is the specific sequence of activities that create value at each stage involved in producing goods or services.

- Supply chain management, or SCM, is the process of managing all operations linking an organization and its suppliers, including purchasing, manufacturing, transportation, and distribution.

- Efficent purchasing and inventory management techniques such as just-in-time and economic order quantities are important forms of cost control.

- Break-even analysis identifies the point where revenues will equal costs under different pricing and cost conditions.

2 How do organizations manage customer service and product quality?

- Customer relationship management builds and maintains strategic relationships with customers.

- Quality management addresses the needs of both internal customers and external customers.

- To compete in the global economy, organizations seek to meet ISO 9000 quality standards.

- Total quality management tries to meet customers' needs—on time, the first time, and all the time.

- Organizations often use statistical techniques such as the Six Sigma system to measure quality of work samples for quality control purposes.

3 How can work processes be designed for productivity?

- A work process is a related group of tasks that together create value for a customer.

- Process engineering is the systematic and complete analysis of work processes and the design of new and better ones.

- In process value analysis all elements of a process and its workflows are examined to identify their exact contributions to key performance results.

- Reengineering eliminates unnecessary worksteps, combines others, and uses technology to gain efficiency and reduce costs.

KEY TERMS REVIEW

Break-even analysis (p. 480)
Break-even point (p. 480)
Competitive advantage (p. 476)
Continuous improvement (p. 483)
Continuous-process production (p. 476)
Customer relationship management (p. 482)
Economic order quantity (p. 479)

ISO certification (p. 482)
Intensive technology (p. 477)
Just-in-time scheduling (p. 479)
Long-linked technology (p. 477)
Mass production (p. 476)
Mediating technology (p. 477)
Operations management (p. 475)
Process reengineering (p. 484)
Process value analysis (p. 485)

Productivity (p. 475)
Quality control (p. 483)
Six Sigma (p. 484)
Small-batch production (p. 476)
Supply chain management (p. 478)
Total quality management (p. 483)
Value chain (p. 477)
Workflow (p. 484)
Work process (p. 484)

MULTIPLE-CHOICE QUESTIONS:

1. Productivity in a typical organization is computed using the formula Productivity =_____/Input.
   (a) Profit   (b) Cost   (c) Output   (d) Revenue
2. If you conducted a value chain analysis of a business, you would study _____.
   (a) customer satisfaction with products   (b) how much TQM affects profits   (c) the flow of activities that transform resources into goods and services   (d) the links between performance and rewards
3. New computer technologies have made possible _____ that quickly and efficiently produces individualized products for customers.
   (a) flexible manufacturing   (b) mass production   (c) mass customization   (d) design for disassembly
4. In remanufacturing the focus is on _____.
   (a) breaking down used products and using the parts to make new ones   (b) arranging machines in cellular layouts   (c) mass customization   (d) replacing people with robots
5. Wal-Mart's suppliers electronically access inventory data and sales forecasts in the stores and automatically ship replacement products. This is an example of IT utilization in _____.
   (a) supply chain management   (b) customer relationship management   (c) total quality management   (d) strategic constituencies analysis
6. An economic order quantity approach to inventory control _____.
   (a) uses computer control to accomplish JIT scheduling   (b) reorders inventory automatically when a certain point is reached   (c) allows for inventory to be purchased only when suppliers grant quantity discounts   (d) means that inventory levels never exceed a preset reorder amount
7. In a break-even analysis, the break-even point occurs when _____.
   (a) fixed costs = variable costs   (b) profits = expenses   (c) assets = liabilities   (d) revenues = total costs
8. Benchmarking, continuous improvement, and reduced cycle times are examples of organizational practices that show a commitment to _____.
   (a) affirmative action   (b) total quality management   (c) cost containment   (d) supply chain management
9. A quality standard that has become essential for world-class companies competing in global markets is _____.
   (a) the Deming prize   (b) upper control limit   (c) CRM   (d) ISO certification
10. _____ is an example of a statistical quality control technique.
    (a) Design for dissassembly   (b) SCM   (c) Six Sigma   (d) Quality circle
11. A work process is defined as a related group of tasks that together create value for _____.
    (a) shareholders   (b) customers   (c) workers   (d) society
12. The first step in process value analysis is to _____.
    (a) look for ways to eliminate unnecessary tasks   (b) map or diagram the workflows   (c) identify core processes   (d) look for efficiencies in transferring work among people and departments
13. In addition to operating efficiency, competitive advantage is often pursued through operations management initiatives that _____.
    (a) increase use of minimum-wage workers   (b) provide for customer service improvements   (c) cut product quality to allow for lower pricing   (d) use the same product designs over and over again
14. A major difference between operations management in manufacturing and in services is that _____.
    (a) service organizations don't measure productivity   (b) manufacturing organizations don't offer services   (c) service organizations often use different technologies than do manufacturing organizations   (d) supply chain management doesn't work in services
15. The techniques of operations management are closely aligned with the concept of the organization as a/an _____.
    (a) open system   (b) closed system   (c) top-down pyramid   (d) machine-driven rather than people-driven system

SHORT-RESPONSE QUESTIONS:

16. What operating objectives are appropriate for an organization seeking competitive advantage through improved customer service?
17. What is the difference between an organization's external customers and its internal customers?
18. Why is supply chain management considered important in operations management?
19. If you were a reengineering consultant, how would you describe the steps in a typical approach to process value analysis?

APPLICATION QUESTION:

20. What would be possible productivity measures for the following organizations?
    (a) United States Postal Service   (b) university   (c) hospital   (d) amusement park   (e) restaurant

CHAPTER 19 APPLICATIONS

CASE 19

Toyota: Looking Far into the Future

By borrowing the best ideas from American brands and in-novating the rest, Toyota has become a pinnacle of auto manufacturing efficiency. Its vehicles are widely known for their quality and longevity. And though Toyota's sales numbers don't yet approach those of the American Big Three, they're edging ever closer. How did Toyota get so efficient at producing high-quality automobiles?

What does "Buy American" mean these days?

It used to be a well-known slogan encouraging U.S. car buyers to "keep it in the family" by purchasing domestic models assembled in America. But times have changed, and many domestic lines have left the United States to seek cheaper factories just outside its borders. Those who still tout the motto have likely done a good bit of head-scratching over how to classify Toyota—a Japanese company sited in rural America, using American workers and American-made parts to produce vehicles to be sold in the United States. And what to think when this Japanese brand using American workers achieves a product quality far superior to long-known American brands?

While selling almost 1.3 million cars, Toyota recently held 13.3 percent of the American automotive market, just shy of third-place Chrysler.[40] And it did so with a sales force far more consolidated than those of its domestic counterparts: Toyota has approximately 1 U.S. dealership for every 10 domestic outlets. So it's no surprise that Toyota franchises sell more cars per outlet than any other manufacturer. In an era when the

Big Three are fighting to consolidate dealerships, cut costs, and reduce distribution centers, Toyota has kept mediocrity among dealers at bay.

Quality by Design

Toyota's continued success and growth in the American auto market is no accident. With admirable discipline, the company has enforced a set of strategies since the 1950s that aim to earn and retain customer satisfaction by producing vehicles of superior quality within a highly efficient production environment.

Initially important was Toyota's commitment to produce only automobiles. Unfettered by the responsibilities and complex supply chains of larger manufacturing concerns that were also making heavier vehicles, like Honda, Toyota could thus dedicate itself to pursuing success within a narrow niche of production.

From the home office to factories to showrooms, two core philosophies guide most of Toyota's business: creating fair, balanced, mutually beneficial relationships with both suppliers and employees, and strictly adhering to a just-in-time (JIT) manufacturing principle.

Collaboration over Competition

Over the decades, American auto manufacturers have developed relationships with their suppliers that emphasize tense competition, price-cutting, and the modification of suppliers' production capacities to meet the changing needs of the domestic market. Year after year, parts suppliers must bid to renew their contracts with U.S. manufacturers in a process that inherently values year-to-year price savings over long-term relationships.

Domestic manufacturers are notorious for changing production demands mid-season to comply with late-breaking market dynamics or customer feedback. This forces suppliers to turn to double or triple shifts to keep capacity up, and to face the inevitable problems—quality slips, recalls, line shutdowns, layoffs—that ultimately slow the final assembly of vehicles. When a car-maker doesn't know what it wants, suppliers have little chance of keeping up.

In contrast, the Toyota model of supply chain management displays an exclusive commitment to parts suppliers, well-forecast parts orders not subject to sways in the market, and a genuine concern for the success of the supplier.

In the *Financial Times*, M. Reza Vaghefi noted that supply chain relationships among Asian manufacturers are based on a complex system of cooperation and equity interests. "Asian values, more so than in western cultures, traditionally emphasize the collective good over the goals of the individual," he said. "This attitude clearly supports the synergistic approach of supply chain management and has encouraged concern for quality and productivity."[41]

Visiting American auto plants and seeing months' worth of excess parts waiting to be installed helped Toyota realize the cost benefits of having only enough supplies on hand to fulfill a given production batch. To realize this degree of efficiency, Toyota plans its production schedules months in advance, dictating regularly scheduled parts shipments from its suppliers. In turn, the supplier benefits by being able to predict long-range demand for its products and schedule its production accordingly, which builds mutual loyalty between supplier and carmaker. It is almost as if the suppliers are a part of Toyota, not competing for its business.

The end result of this relationship—insisted upon by Toyota—is the quality of the final product. The fit and finish in Toyota vehicles is so precise because its suppliers can afford to focus on the quality of their parts. And the consumer notices this as well: Toyota vehicles consistently rate highly for customer satisfaction, and they retain their resale value better than almost any other line.[42]

Keep It Lean

Early Toyota presidents Toyoda Kiichiro and Ohno Taiichi are considered to be the fathers of the Toyota Production System (TPS), known widely by the JIT moniker or as "lean production." Emphasizing quality and efficiency at all levels, TPS drives nearly all aspects of decision making at Toyota.[43]

Simply put, TPS is "all about producing only what's needed and transferring only what's needed," said Teruyuki Minoura, senior managing director at Toyota. He likened it to a "pull" system—in which workers fetch only that which is immediately needed—as opposed to a traditional "push" system.[44]

"Producing what's needed means producing the right quantity of what's needed," he continued. "The answer is a flexible system that allows the line to produce what's necessary when it's necessary. If it takes six people to make a certain quantity of an item and there is a drop in the quantity required, then your system should let one or two of them drop out and get on with something else."[45]

To achieve maximum efficiency, workers at Toyota plants must be exceptionally knowledgeable about all facets of a vehicle's production and able to change responsibilities as needed.

"An environment where people have to think brings with it wisdom, and this wisdom brings with it *kaizen* [the notion of continuous improvement]," noted Minoura. "If asked to produce only one unit at a time, to produce according to the flow, a typical line worker is likely to be flummoxed. It's a basic characteristic of human beings that they develop wisdom from being put under pressure."[46]

Quiet Strength

Unlike the characters in its "Oh, What a Feeling!" ads from years past, Toyota has never been a company to make much noise about itself. Today, as domestic carmakers compound rebates by thousands of dollars to attract a diminishing pool of customers, Toyota has never needed to offer discounts to boost its quarterly profits. (Toyota does quietly offer dealers' sales incentives, but this practice is widespread in the industry.)

Part of the reason is that there is less competition among Toyota dealers simply because there are fewer dealers. Toyota has cautiously kept its number of retail outlets low. Instead, dealers are expected to service a wider customer base than are their domestic counterparts. Again, the Toyota model of preferring collaboration to competition means that dealers have more energy to focus on serving customers, and they have survey numbers to back up their results.

Because of its commitment to its suppliers and workers, Toyota is also reluctant to exceed production expectations. Most recently, the company chose not to increase production after the unexpected success of its Sienna minivan. Critics more familiar with U.S. terms of production might say that Toyota missed a golden opportunity. Yet it managed to maintain a steady relationship with its suppliers and still sell out of Siennas without padding the numbers through sales to fleet or rental car companies, as U.S. car companies often do.

"They are what an American company should be," said Jeffrey K. Liker, a University of Michigan professor and the author of *The Toyota Way*. "Is it realistic for American car companies to be like Toyota? No. They would have had to have been different 20 years ago. Now they're trying to pull themselves together and survive."[47]

Gaining the Lead, One Vehicle at a Time

By substituting discipline and efficiency for fanfare, Toyota has quietly earned a long-standing reputation for the reliability and quality of all of its models. And although the company's domestic competition has taken notice, they're too mired in financial difficulties to put up much of a fight. But in such a fierce market, can Toyota maintain the self-control to beat the Big Three at their own game? Take a test drive and see if Toyota has what it takes to earn *your* business.

REVIEW QUESTIONS

1. What are the advantages to parts suppliers of Toyota's preferred partner relationships?

2. How might Toyota's just-in-time (JIT) parts availability strategy work to its disadvantage?

3. What are the preconditions needed for success with JIT systems?

TEAM PROJECT

**Design for the
Competitive Edge**

Xerox CEO Anne Mulcahy says: "Competition gives you focus . . . We take apart every element of a competitive [product] to assess the strengths and weaknesses and how we can compete to win."[48]

Question: What does it take for a product design to provide competitive advantage?

Research Directions:

■ Choose two competing products—disposable pens, disposable razors, toothbrushes, pocket breath fresheners, book bags, sun glasses, for example.

■ Study the two products to identify aspects of their respective designs that are pluses and minuses in terms of attracting customer interests.

■ Examine the products closely, even taking them apart if possible, to estimate the various steps involved in the production process. Try to discover which product design is easier or harder to produce, which is more or less expensive to produce, and which can be produced both efficiently and with necessary quality.

■ Consider the "green" implications of the two products. How "costly" are they in terms of the impact of materials and production processes on the environment? Is either one better designed for disposability? Can any of the components or the entire product be recycled/reused in any way?

■ Summarize your investigation in a report on the implications of product designs for competitive advantage based on customer appeal, operating efficiencies, and environmental impact.

PERSONAL MANAGEMENT

Networking

Even as you develop expertise with operations management techniques, don't forget the importance of relationships. Work is also an interpersonal process. You often do well or poorly as a result of your ability to relate well to other people. This involves **NETWORKING**. Within teams, across functions, and in day-to-day work encounters, people get things done by building and maintaining positive working relationships with others. In the social context of organizations, there is very little you can do by yourself; other people in networks have to help you out. For some of us, networking is as natural as walking down the street. For others, it is a big challenge.

Building the Brand Called "You" Don't underestimate the challenge; be prepared for the human side of operations management. Develop confidence in these networking skills: *Network identification*—knowing and finding the right people to work with. *Network building*—engaging others and relating to them in positive ways. *Network maintenance*—actively nurturing and supporting others in their work.

NEXT STEPS: MANAGEMENT LEARNING WORKBOOK

Self-Assessments
■ Managerial Assumptions (#4)
■ Job Design Choices (#24)

Experiential Exercises
■ Defining Quality (#3)
■ Best Job Design (#23)

eXperiential

MANAGEMENT

LEARNING

WORKBOOK

Self-

Assessments

MANAGEMENT LEARNING WORKBOOK

EXPERIENTIAL EXERCISES

1. My Best Manager
2. What Managers Do
3. Defining Quality
4. What Would the Classics Say?
5. The Great Management History Debate
6. Confronting Ethical Dilemmas
7. What Do You Value in Work?
8. Which Organizational Culture Fits You?
9. Beating the Time Wasters
10. Personal Career Planning
11. Decision-Making Biases
12. Strategic Scenarios
13. The MBO Contract
14. The Future Workplace
15. Dots and Squares Puzzle
16. Leading through Participation
17. Work vs. Family—You Be the Judge
18. Compensation and Benefits Debate
19. Sources and Uses of Power
20. After Meeting/Project Review
21. Why Do We Work?
22. The Case of the Contingency Workforce
23. The "Best" Job Design
24. Upward Appraisal
25. How to Give, and Take, Criticism
26. Lost at Sea
27. Work Team Dynamics
28. Feedback and Assertiveness
29. Creative Solutions
30. Force-Field Analysis

SELF-ASSESSMENTS

1. A 21st-Century Manager?
2. Emotional Intelligence
3. Learning Tendencies
4. What Are Your Managerial Assumptions?
5. Terminal Values Survey
6. Instrumental Values Survey
7. Diversity Awareness
8. Global Readiness Index
9. Time Orientation
10. Entrepreneurship Orientation
11. Your Intuitive Ability
12. Assertiveness
13. Time Management Profile
14. Facts and Inferences
15. Empowering Others
16. Turbulence Tolerance Test
17. Organizational Design Preference
18. Are You Cosmopolitan?
19. Performance Appraisal Assumptions
20. "T-P" Leadership Questionnaire
21. "T-t" Leadership Style
22. Least-Preferred Co-worker Scale
23. Student Engagement Survey
24. Job Design Choices
25. Cognitive Style
26. Internal/External Control
27. Team Leader Skills
28. Conflict Management Styles
29. Stress Self-Test
30. Work-Life Balance

eXperiential

EXERCISES

EXERCISE 1

My Best Manager

Preparation

Working alone, make a list of the *behavioral attributes* that describe the *best* manager you have ever worked for. This could be someone you worked for in a full-time or part-time job, summer job, volunteer job, student organization, or whatever. If you have trouble identifying an actual manager, make a list of behavioral attributes of the type of manager you would most like to work for in your next job.

Instructions

Form into groups as assigned by your instructor, or work with a nearby classmate. Share your list of attributes and listen to the lists of others. Be sure to ask questions and make comments on items of special interest. Work together to create a master list that combines the unique attributes of the "best" managers experienced by members of your group. Have a spokesperson share that list with the rest of the class.

Source: Adapted from John R. Schermerhorn Jr., James G. Hunt, and Richard N. Osborn, *Managing Organizational Behavior,* 3rd ed. (New York: Wiley, 1988), pp. 32–33. Used by permission.

What Managers Do

Preparation

Think about the questions that follow. Record your answers in the spaces provided.

1. How much of a typical manager's time would you expect to be allocated to these relationships? (total should = 100%)

    _____ % of time working with subordinates

    _____ % of time working with boss

    _____ % of time working with peers and outsiders

2. How many hours per week does the average manager work? _____ hours

3. What amount of a manager's time is typically spent in the following activities? (total should = 100%)

    _____ % in scheduled meetings

    _____ % in unscheduled meetings

    _____ % doing desk work

    _____ % talking on the telephone

    _____ % walking around the organization/work site

Instructions

Talk over your responses with a nearby classmate. Explore the similarities and differences in your answers. Be prepared to participate in a class discussion led by your instructor.

Defining Quality

Preparation

Write your definition of the word *quality* here. QUALITY =

Instructions

Form groups as assigned by your instructor. (1) Have each group member present a definition of the word *quality*. After everyone has presented, come up with a consensus definition of *quality*. That is, determine and write down one definition of the word with which every member can agree. (2) Next, have the group assume the position of top manager in each of the following organizations. Use the group's *quality* definition to state for each organization a *quality objective* that can guide the behavior of members in producing high-quality goods and/or services for customers or clients. Elect a spokesperson to share group results with the class as a whole.

Organizations:

a. A university

b. A community hospital

c. A retail sporting goods store

d. A fast-food franchise restaurant

e. A United States post office branch

f. A full-service bank branch

g. A student apartment rental company

h. A used textbook store

i. A computer software firm

What Would the Classics Say?

Preparation

Consider this situation:

Six months into his new job, Bob, a laboratory worker, is performing just well enough to avoid being fired. When hired, he had been carefully selected and had the abilities required to do the job really well. At first Bob was enthusiastic about his new job, but now he isn't performing up to this high potential. Fran, his supervisor, is concerned and wonders what can be done to improve this situation.

Instructions

Assume the identity of one of the following persons: Frederick Taylor, Henri Fayol, Max Weber, Abraham Maslow, Chris Argyris. Assume that *as this person* you have been asked by Fran for advice on the management situation just described. Answer these questions as you think your assumed identity would respond. Be prepared to share your answers in class and to defend them based on the text's discussion of this person's views.

1. As (*your assumed identity*), what are your basic beliefs about good management and organizational practices?

2. As (*your assumed identity*), what do you perceive may be wrong in this situation that would account for Bob's low performance?

3. As (*your assumed identity*), what could be done to improve Bob's future job performance?

The Great Management History Debate

Preparation

Consider the question "What is the best thing a manager can do to improve productivity in her or his work unit?"

Instructions

The instructor will assign you, individually or in a group, to one of the following positions. Complete the missing information as if you were the management theorist referred to. Be prepared to argue and defend your position before the class.

- Position A: "Mary Parker Follett offers the best insight into the question. Her advice would be to . . . " (advice to be filled in by you or the group).

- Position B: "Max Weber's ideal bureaucracy offers the best insight into the question. His advice would be to . . . " (advice to be filled in by you or the group).

- Position C: "Henri Fayol offers the best insight into the question. His advice would be to . . . " (advice to be filled in by you or the group).

- Position D: "The Hawthorne studies offer the best insight into the question. Elton Mayo's advice would be to . . . " (advice to be filled in by you or the group).

EXERCISE 6

Confronting Ethical Dilemmas

Preparation

Read and indicate your response to each of the situations below.

a. Ron Jones, vice president of a large construction firm, receives in the mail a large envelope marked "personal." It contains a competitor's cost data for a project that both firms will be bidding on shortly. The data are accompanied by a note from one of Ron's subordinates saying: "This is the real thing!" Ron knows that the data could be a major advantage to his firm in preparing a bid that can win the contract. *What should he do?*

b. Kay Smith is one of your top-performing subordinates. She has shared with you her desire to apply for promotion to a new position just announced in a different division of the company. This will be tough on you since recent budget cuts mean you will be unable to replace anyone who leaves, at least for quite some time. Kay knows this and, in all fairness, has asked your permission before she submits an application. It is rumored that the son of a good friend of your boss is going to apply for the job. Although his credentials are less impressive than Kay's, the likelihood is that he will get the job if she doesn't apply. *What will you do?*

c. Marty Jose got caught in a bind. She was pleased to represent her firm as head of the local community development committee. In fact, her supervisor's boss once held this position and told her in a hallway conversation, "Do your best and give them every support possible." Going along with this, Marty agreed to pick up the bill (several hundred dollars) for a dinner meeting with local civic and business leaders. Shortly thereafter, her supervisor informed everyone that the entertainment budget was being eliminated in a cost-saving effort. Marty, not wanting to renege on supporting the community development committee, was able to charge the dinner bill to an advertising budget. Eventually, an internal auditor discovered the mistake and reported it to you, the personnel director. Marty is scheduled to meet with you in a few minutes. *What will you do?*

Instructions

Working alone, make the requested decisions in each of these incidents. Think carefully about your justification for the decision. Meet in a group assigned by your instructor. Share your decisions and justifications in each case with other group members. Listen to theirs. Try to reach a group consensus on what to do in each situation and why. Be prepared to share the group decisions, and any dissenting views, in general class discussion.

EXERCISE 7

What Do You Value in Work?

Preparation

Rank order the nine items in terms of how important (9 = most important) they would be to you in a job.

How important is it to you to have a job that

_____ Is respected by other people?

_____ Encourages continued development of knowledge and skills?

_____ Provides job security?

_____ Provides a feeling of accomplishment?

_____ Provides the opportunity to earn a high income?

_____ Is intellectually stimulating?

_____ Rewards good performance with recognition?

_____ Provides comfortable working conditions?

_____ Permits advancement to high administrative responsibility?

Instructions

Form into groups as designated by your instructor. Within each group, the *men in the group* will meet to develop a consensus ranking of the items as they think the *women* in the Beutell and Brenner survey ranked them. The reasons for the rankings should be shared and discussed so they are clear to everyone. The *women in the group* should not participate in this ranking task. They should listen to the discussion and be prepared to comment later in class discussions. A spokesperson for the men in the group should share the group's rankings with the class.

Optional Instructions
Form into groups as designated by your instructor but with each group consisting entirely of men or women. Each group should meet and decide which of the work values members of the *opposite* sex ranked first in the Beutell and Brenner survey. Do this again for the work value ranked last. The reasons should be discussed, along with the reasons why each of the other values probably was not ranked first . . . or last. A spokesperson for each group should share group results with the rest of the class.

Source: Adapted from Roy J. Lewicki, Donald D. Bowen, Douglas T. Hall, and Francine S. Hall, *Experiences in Management and Organizational Behavior,* 3rd ed. (New York: Wiley, 1988), pp. 23–26. Used by permission.

EXERCISE 8

Which Organizational Culture Fits You?

Instructions
Indicate which one of the following organizational cultures you feel most comfortable working in.

1. A culture that values talent, entrepreneurial activity, and performance over commitment; one that offers large financial rewards and individual recognition.

2. A culture that stresses loyalty, working for the good of the group, and getting to know the right people; one that believes in "generalists" and step-by-step career progress.

3. A culture that offers little job security; one that operates with a survival mentality, stresses that every individual can make a difference, and focuses attention on "turnaround" opportunities.

4. A culture that values long-term relationships; one that emphasizes systematic career development, regular training, and advancement based on gaining functional expertise.

Interpretation
These labels identify the four different cultures: 1 = "the baseball team," 2 = "the club," 3 = "the fortress," and 4 = "the academy."

Discuss results in work groups assigned by your instructor. To some extent, your future career success may depend on working for an organization in which there is a good fit between you and the prevailing corporate culture. This exercise can help you learn how to recognize various cultures, evaluate how well they can serve your needs, and recognize how they may change with time. A risk taker, for example, may be out of place in a "club" but fit right in with a "baseball team." Someone who wants to seek opportunities wherever they may occur may be out of place in an "academy" but fit right in with a "fortress."

Source: Developed from Carol Hymowitz, "Which Corporate Culture Fits You?" *Wall Street Journal* (July 17, 1989), p. B1.

Beating the Time Wasters

Preparation

1. Make a list of all the things you need to do tomorrow. Prioritize each item in terms of *how important it is to creating outcomes that you can really value.* Use this classification scheme:

   (A) Most important, top priority

   (B) Important, not top priority

   (C) Least important, low priority

   Look again at all activities you have classified as "B." Reclassify any that are really "As" or "Cs." Look at your list of "As." Reclassify any that are really "Bs" or "Cs." Double-check to make sure you are comfortable with your list of "Cs."

2. Make a list of all the "time wasters" that often interfere with your ability to accomplish everything you want to on any given day.

Instructions

Form into groups as assigned by the instructor. Have all group members share their lists and their priority classifications. Members should politely "challenge" each other's classifications to make sure that only truly "high-priority" items receive an "A" rating. They might also suggest that some "C" items are of such little consequence that they might not be worth doing at all. After each member of the group revises his or her "to do" list based on this advice, go back and discuss the time wasters identified by group members. Develop a master list of time wasters and what to do about them. Have a group spokesperson be prepared to share discussion highlights and tips on beating common time wasters with the rest of the class.

Source: Developed from Roy J. Lewicki, Donald D. Bowen, Douglas T. Hall, and Francine S. Hall, *Experiences in Management and Organizational Behavior,* 3rd ed. (New York: Wiley, 1988), pp. 314–316.

Personal Career Planning

Preparation

Complete the following three activities and bring the results to class. Your work should be in a written form suitable for your instructor's review.

Step 1. *Strengths and Weaknesses Inventory.* Different occupations require special talents, abilities, and skills if people are to excel in their work. Each of us, you included, has a repertoire of existing strengths and weaknesses that are "raw materials" we presently offer a potential employer. Of course, actions can (and should!) be taken over time to further develop current strengths and to turn weaknesses into strengths. Make a list identifying your most important strengths and weaknesses at the moment in relation to the career direction you are most likely to pursue upon graduation. Place a * next to each item you consider most important to address in your courses and student activities *before* graduation.

Step 2. *Five-Year Career Objectives.* Make a list of 3 to 5 career objectives that are appropriate given your list of personal strengths and weaknesses. Limit these objectives to ones that can be accomplished within 5 years of graduation.

Step 3. *Five-Year Career Action Plans.* Write a specific action plan for accomplishing each of the 5 objectives. State exactly what you will do, and by when, in order to meet each objective. If you will need special support or assistance, identify it *and* state how you will obtain it. Remember, an outside observer should be able to read your action plan for each objective and end up feeling confident that (a) he or she knows exactly what you are going to do and (b) why.

Instructions

Form into groups as assigned by the instructor. Share your career-planning analysis with the group; listen to those of others. Participate in a discussion that examines any common patterns and major differences among group members. Take advantage of any opportunities to gather feedback and advice from others. Have one group member be prepared to summarize the group discussion for the class as a whole. Await further class discussion led by the instructor.

Source: Developed in part from Roy J. Lewicki, Donald D. Bowen, Douglas T. Hall, and Francine S. Hall, *Experiences in Management and Organizational Behavior*, 3rd ed. (New York: Wiley, 1988), pp. 261–267. Used by permission.

EXERCISE 11

Decision-Making Biases

Instructions

How good are you at avoiding potential decision-making biases? Test yourself by answering the following questions:

1. Which is riskier:

    (a) driving a car on a 400-mile trip?

    (b) flying on a 400-mile commercial airline flight?

2. Are there more words in the English language

    (a) that begin with *r*?

    (b) that have *r* as the third letter?

3. Mark is finishing his MBA at a prestigious university. He is very interested in the arts and at one time considered a career as a musician. Is Mark more likely to take a job

    (a) in the management of the arts?

    (b) with a management consulting firm?

4. You are about to hire a new central-region sales director for the fifth time this year. You predict that the next director should work out reasonably well since the last four were "lemons," and the odds favor hiring at least 1 good sales director in 5 tries. Is this thinking

    (a) correct?

    (b) incorrect?

5. A newly hired engineer for a computer firm in the Boston metropolitan area has 4 years' experience and good all-round qualifications. When asked to estimate the starting salary for this employee, a chemist with very little knowledge about the profession or industry guessed an annual salary of $35,000. What is your estimate?

    $ _____ per year

Scoring

Your instructor will provide answers and explanations for the assessment questions.

Interpretation

Each of the preceding questions examines your tendency to use a different judgmental heuristic. In his book *Judgment in Managerial Decision Making*, 3rd ed. (New York: Wiley, 1994), pp. 6–7, Max Bazerman calls these heuristics "simplifying strategies, or rules of thumb" used in making decisions. He states; "In general, heuristics are helpful, but their use can sometimes lead to severe errors. . . . If we can make managers aware of the potential adverse impacts of using heuristics, they can then decide when and where to use them." This assessment offers an initial insight into your use of such heuristics. An informed decision maker understands the heuristics, is able to recognize when they appear, and eliminates any that may inappropriately bias decision making.

Test yourself further. Write next to each item the name of the judgmental heuristic that you think applies (see Chapter 7).

Source: Incidents from Max H. Bazerman, *Judgment in Managerial Decision Making*, 3rd ed. (New York: Wiley, 1994), pp. 13–14. Used by permission.

Strategic Scenarios

Preparation

In today's turbulent environment, it is no longer safe to assume that an organization that was highly successful yesterday will continue to be so tomorrow—or that it will even be in existence. Changing times exact the best from strategic planners. Think about the situations currently facing the following well-known organizations. Think, too, about the futures they may face.

McDonald's

Apple Computer

Yahoo.com

Ann Taylor

Ford

Nordstrom's

National Public Radio

The New York Times

Instructions

Form into groups as assigned by your instructor. Choose one or more organizations from the prior list (as assigned) and answer for the organization the following questions:

1. What in the future might seriously threaten the success, perhaps the very existence, of this organization? (As a group develop at least three such *future scenarios*.)

2. Estimate the probability (0 to 100 percent) of each future scenario occurring.

3. Develop a strategy for each scenario that will enable the organization to successfully deal with it.

Thoroughly discuss these questions within the group and arrive at your best possible consensus answers. Be prepared to share and defend your answers in general class discussion.

Source: Suggested by an exercise in John F. Veiga and John N. Yanouzas, *The Dynamics of Organization Theory: Gaining a Macro Perspective* (St. Paul, MN: West, 1979), pp. 69–71.

The MBO Contract

Listed below are performance objectives from an MBO contract for a plant manager, Chris Atkins.

a. To increase deliveries to 98% of all scheduled delivery dates

b. To reduce waste and spoilage to 3% of all raw materials used

c. To reduce lost time resulting from accidents to 100 work days/year

d. To reduce operating cost to 10% below budget

e. To install a quality-control system at a cost of less than $53,000

f. To improve production scheduling and increase machine utilization time to 95% capacity

g. To complete a management development program this year

h. To teach a community college course in human resource management

1. Study this MBO contract. In the margin write one of the following symbols to identify each objective as an improvement, maintenance, or personal development objective.

   I = Improvement objective

   M = Maintenance objective

   P = Personal development objective

2. Assume that this MBO contract was actually developed and implemented under the following circumstances. After each statement, write yes if the statement reflects proper MBO procedures and write no if it reflects poor MBO procedures.

   (a) The president drafted the 8 objectives and submitted them to Atkins for review.

   (b) The president and Atkins thoroughly discussed the 8 objectives in proposal form before they were finalized.

   (c) The president and Atkins scheduled a meeting in 6 months to review Atkins's progress on the objectives.

(d) The president didn't discuss the objectives with Atkins again until the scheduled meeting was held.

(e) The president told Atkins the annual raise would depend entirely on the extent to which these objectives were achieved.

3. Share and discuss your responses to parts 1 and 2 of the exercise with a nearby classmate. Reconcile any differences of opinion by referring back to the Chapter 8 discussion of MBO. Await further class discussion.

EXERCISE 14

The Future Workplace

Instructions

Form groups as assigned by the instructor. Brainstorm to develop a master list of the major characteristics you expect to find in the future workplace in the year 2020. Use this list as background for completing the following tasks:

1. Write a one-paragraph description of what the typical "Workplace 2020" manager's workday will be like.

2. Draw a "picture" representing what the "Workplace 2020" organization will look like.

Choose a spokesperson to share your results with the class as a whole *and* explain their implications for the class members.

EXERCISE 15

Dots and Squares Puzzle

1. Shown here is a collection of 16 dots. Study the figure to determine how many "squares" can be created by connecting the dots.

2. Draw as many squares as you can find in the figure while making sure a dot is at every corner of every square. Count the squares and write this number in the margin to the right of the figure.

3. Share your results with those of a classmate sitting nearby. Indicate the location of squares missed by either one of you.

4. Based on this discussion, redraw your figure to show the maximum number of possible squares. Count them and write this number to the left of the figure.

5. Await further class discussion led by your instructor.

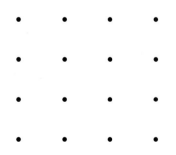

Leading through Participation

Preparation

Read each of the following vignettes. Write in the margin whether you think the leader should handle the situation with an individual decision (I), consultative decision (C), or group decision (G).

Vignette I

You are the leader of a large team laying an oil pipeline. It is now necessary to estimate your expected rate of progress in order to schedule material deliveries to the next field site. You know the nature of the terrain you will be traveling and have the historical data needed to compute the mean and variance in the rate of speed over the type of terrain. Given these two variables, it is a simple matter to calculate the earliest and latest times at which materials and support facilities will be needed at the next site. It is important that your estimate be reasonably accurate; underestimates result in idle teams, and overestimates result in materials being tied up for a period of time before they are to be used. Progress has been good, and your team stands to receive substantial bonuses if the project is completed ahead of schedule.

Vignette II

You are supervising the work of 12 engineers. Their formal training and work experience are very similar, permitting you to use them interchangeably on projects. Yesterday, your manager informed you that a request had been received from an overseas affiliate for 4 engineers to go abroad on extended loan for a period of 6 to 8 months. He argued and you agreed that for a number of reasons this request should be filled from your group. All your engineers are capable of handling this assignment, and from the standpoint of present and future projects, there is no particular reason that any one should be retained over any other. The problem is complicated by the fact that the overseas assignment is in what is generally regarded in the company as an undesirable location.

Vignette III

You are the head of a staff unit reporting to the vice president of finance. He has asked you to provide a report on the firm's current portfolio, including recommendations for changes in the *selection criteria* currently employed. Doubts have been raised about the efficiency of the existing system in the current market conditions, and there is considerable dissatisfaction with prevailing rates of return. You plan to write the report, but at the moment you are quite perplexed about the approach to take. Your own specialty is the bond market, and it is clear to you that a detailed knowledge of the equity market, which you lack, would greatly enhance the value of the report. Fortunately, 4 members of your staff are specialists in different segments of the equity market. Together, they possess a vast amount of knowledge about the intricacies of investment. However, they seldom agree on the best way to achieve anything when it comes to the stock market. Although they are obviously conscientious as well as knowledgeable, they have major differences when it comes to investment philosophy and strategy. The report is due in 6 weeks. You have already begun to familiarize yourself with the firm's current portfolio and have been provided by management with a specific set of constraints that any portfolio must satisfy. Your immediate problem is to come up with some alternatives to the firm's present practices and select the most promising ones for detailed analysis in your report.

Vignette IV

You are on the division manager's staff and work on a wide variety of problems of both an administrative and technical nature. You have been given the assignment of developing a universal method to be used in each of the 5 plants in the division for manually reading equipment registers, recording the readings, and transmitting the scoring to a centralized information system. All plants are located in a relatively small geographical region. Until now there has been a high error rate in the reading and/or transmittal of the data. Some locations have considerably higher error rates than others, and the methods used to record and transmit the data vary among plants. It is probable, therefore, that part of the error variance is a function of specific local conditions rather than anything else, and this will complicate the establishment of any system common to all plants. You have the information on error rates but no information on the local practices that generate these errors or on the local conditions that necessitate the different practices. Everyone would benefit from an improvement in the quality of the data because they are used in a number of important decisions. Your contacts with the plants are through the quality control supervisors responsible for collecting the data. They are a conscientious group committed to doing their jobs well, but they are highly sensitive to interference on the part of higher management in their own operations. Any solution that does not receive the active support of the various plant supervisors is unlikely to reduce the error rate significantly.

Instructions

Form groups as assigned by the instructor. Share your choices with other group members and try to achieve a consensus on how the leader should best handle each situation. Refer back to the discussion of the Vroom-Jago "leader-participation" theory presented in Chapter 13. Analyze each vignette according to their ideas. Do you come to any different conclusions? If so, why? Nominate a spokesperson to share your results in general class discussion.

Source: Victor H. Vroom and Arthur G. Jago, *The New Leadership* (Englewood Cliffs, NJ: Prentice-Hall, 1988). Used by permission.

EXERCISE 17

Work vs. Family—You Be the Judge

1. Read the following situation.

   Joanna, a single parent, was hired to work 8:15 A.M. to 5:30 P.M. weekdays selling computers for a firm. Her employer extended her workday until 10 P.M. weekdays and from 8:15 A.M. to 5:30 P.M. on Saturdays. Joanna refused to work the extra hours, saying that she had a 6-year old son and that so many work hours would lead to neglect. The employer said this was a special request during a difficult period, and that all employees needed to share in helping out during the "crunch." Still refusing to work the extra hours, Joanna was fired. She sued the employer.

2. You be the judge in this case. Take an individual position on the following questions: Should Joanna be allowed to work only the

hours agreed to when she was hired? Or was the employer correct in asking all employees, regardless of family status, to work the extra hours? Why?

3. Form into groups as assigned by the instructor. Share your responses to the questions and try to develop a group consensus. Be sure to have a rationale for the position the group adopts. Appoint a spokesperson who can share results with the class. Be prepared to participate in an open class discussion.

Source: This case scenario is from Sue Shellenbarger, "Employees Challenge Policies on Family and Get Hard Lessons," *Wall Street Journal* (December 17, 1997), p. B1.

EXERCISE 18

Compensation and Benefits Debate

Preparation

Consider the following quotations:

On compensation: "A basic rule of thumb should be—pay at least as much, and perhaps a bit more, in base wage or salary than what competitors are offering."

On benefits: "When benefits are attractive or at least adequate, the organization is in a better position to employ highly qualified people."

Instructions

Form groups as assigned by the instructor. Each will be given *either* one of the preceding position statements *or* one of the following alternatives.

On compensation: "Given the importance of controlling costs, organizations can benefit by paying as little as possible for labor."

On benefits: "Given the rising cost of health care and other benefit programs and the increasing difficulty many organizations have staying in business, it is best to minimize paid benefits and let employees handle more of the cost on their own."

Each group should prepare to debate a counterpoint group on its assigned position. Af-ter time is allocated to prepare for the debate, each group will present its opening positions. Each will then be allowed one rebuttal period to respond to the other group. General class dis-cussion on the role of compensation and bene-fits in the modern organization will follow.

EXERCISE 19

Sources and Uses of Power

Preparation

Consider *the way you have behaved* in each of the situations described below. These behav-iors may be from a full-time or part-time job, student organization or class group, sports team, or whatever. If you have not had an expe-rience of the type described, try to imagine yourself in one; think about how you would ex-pect yourself to behave.

1. You needed to get a peer to do something you wanted that person to do but were worried he or she didn't want to do it.

2. You needed to get a subordinate to do some-thing you wanted her or him to do but were worried the subordinate didn't want to do it.

3. You needed to get your boss to do some-thing you wanted him or her to do but were worried the boss didn't want to do it.

Instructions

Form into groups as assigned by the instructor. Start with situation 1 and have all members of the group share their approaches. Determine what specific sources of power (see Chapter 13) were used. Note any patterns in group mem-bers' responses. Discuss what is required to be successful in this situation. Do the same for situations 2 and 3. Note any special differences in how situations 1, 2, and 3 should be or could be handled. Choose a spokesperson to share results in general class discussion.

EXERCISE 20

After Meeting/Project Review

After participating in a meeting or a group proj-ect, complete the following assessment:

1. How satisfied are *you* with the outcome of the meeting project?

   Not at all   Totally
   satisfied   satisfied
      1   2   3   4   5   6   7

2. How do you think *other members of the meeting/project group would rate you* in terms of your *influence* on what took place?

     No   Very high
   influence   influence
      1   2   3   4   5   6   7

3. In your opinion, how *ethical* was any deci-sion that was reached?

    Highly   Highly
   unethical   ethical
      1   2   3   4   5   6   7

4. To what extent did you feel "*pushed into*" going along with the decision?

   Not pushed
     into it
     at all   Very pushed
                              into it
      1   2   3   4   5   6   7

5. How *committed* are *you* to the agreements reached?

Not at all   Highly
committed   committed

    1   2   3   4   5   6   7

6. Did you understand what was expected of you as a member of the meeting or project group?

Not at all   Perfectly
  clear   clear

    1   2   3   4   5   6   7

7. Were participants in the meeting/project group discussions listening to each other?

Never   Always

    1   2   3   4   5   6   7

8. Were participants in the meeting/project group discussions honest and open in communicating with one another?

Never   Always

    1   2   3   4   5   6   7

9. Was the meeting/project completed efficiently?

Not at all   Very much

    1   2   3   4   5   6   7

10. Was the outcome of the meeting/project something that you felt proud to be a part of?

Not at all   Very much

    1   2   3   4   5   6   7

Instructions

In groups (actual meeting/project group or as assigned by the instructor), share results and discuss their implications (a) for you and (b) for the effectiveness of meetings and group project work in general.

Source: Developed from Roy J. Lewicki, Donald D. Bowen, Douglas T. Hall, and Francine S. Hall, *Experiences in Management and Organizational Behavior,* 4th ed. (New York: Wiley, 1997), pp. 195–197.

EXERCISE 21

Why Do We Work?

Preparation

Read the following "ancient story."

In days of old, a wandering youth happened upon a group of men working in a quarry. Stopping by the first man, he said: "What are you doing?" The worker grimaced and groaned as he replied: "I am trying to shape this stone, and it is backbreaking work." Moving to the next man, the youth repeated the question. This man showed little emotion as he answered: "I am shaping a stone for a building." Moving to the third man, our traveler heard him singing as he worked. "What are you doing?" asked the youth. "I am helping to build a cathedral," the man proudly replied.

Instructions

In groups assigned by your instructor, discuss this short story. Ask and answer the question: "What are the lessons of this ancient story for (a) workers and (b) managers of today?" Ask members of the group to role-play each of the stonecutters, respectively, while they answer a second question asked by the youth: "Why are you working?" Have someone in the group be prepared to report and share the group's responses with the class as a whole.

Source: Developed from Brian Dumaine, "Why Do We Work?" *Fortune* (December 26, 1994), pp. 196–204.

The Case of the Contingency Workforce

Preparation

Part-time and contingency work is a rising percentage of the total employment in the United States. Go to the library and read about the current use of part-time and contingency workers in business and industry. Ideally, go to the Internet, enter a government database, and locate some current statistics on the size of the contingent labor force, the proportion that is self-employed and employed part-time, and the proportion of part-timers that is voluntary and involuntary.

Instructions

In your assigned work group, pool the available information on the contingency workforce. Discuss the information. Discuss one another's viewpoints on the subject as well as its personal and social implications. Be prepared to participate in a classroom "dialogue session" in which your group will be asked to role-play one of the following positions:

a. Vice president for human resources of a large discount retailer hiring contingency workers.

b. Owner of a local specialty music shop hiring contingency workers.

c. Recent graduate of your college or university working as a contingency employee at the discount retailer in (a).

d. Single parent with two children in elementary school, working as a contingency employee of the music shop in (b).

The question to be answered by the (a) and (b) groups is "What does the contingency workforce mean to me?" The question to be answered by the (c) and (d) groups is "What does being a contingency worker mean to me?"

The "Best" Job Design

Preparation

Use the left-hand column to rank the following job characteristics in the order most important *to you* (1 = highest to 10 = lowest). Then use the right-hand column to rank them in the order in which you think they are most important *to others.*

____ Variety of tasks

____ Performance feedback

____ Autonomy/freedom in work

____ Working on a team

____ Having responsibility

____ Making friends on the job

____ Doing all of a job, not part

____ Importance of job to others

____ Having resources to do well

____ Flexible work schedule

Instructions

Form work groups as assigned by your instructor. Share your rankings with other group members. Discuss where you have different individual preferences and where your impressions differ from the preferences of others. Are there any major patterns in your group—for either the "personal" or the "other" rankings? Develop group consensus rankings for each column. Designate a spokesperson to share the group rankings and results of any discussion with the rest of the class.

Source: Developed from John M. Ivancevich and Michael T. Matteson, *Organizational Behavior and Management,* 2nd ed. (Homewood, IL: BPI/Irwin, 1990), p. 500. Used by permission.

Upward Appraisal

Instructions

Form into work groups as assigned by the instructor. The instructor will then leave the room. As a group, complete the following tasks:

1. Within each group create a master list of comments, problems, issues, and concerns about the course experience to date that members would like to communicate to the instructor.

2. Select one person from the group to act as spokesperson who will give your feedback to the instructor when he or she returns to the classroom.

3. Before the instructor returns, the spokespersons from each group should meet to decide how the room should be physically arranged (placement of tables, chairs, etc.) for the feedback session. This arrangement should allow the spokespersons and instructor to communicate while they are being observed by other class members.

4. While the spokespersons are meeting, members remaining in the groups should discuss what they expect to observe during the feedback session.

5. The classroom should be rearranged. The instructor should be invited in.

6. Spokespersons should deliver feedback to the instructor while observers make notes.

7. After the feedback session is complete, the instructor will call on observers for comments, ask the spokespersons for their reactions, and engage the class in general discussion about the exercise and its implications.

Source: Developed from Eugene Owens, "Upward Appraisal: An Exercise in Subordinate's Critique of Superior's Performance," *Exchange: The Organizational Behavior Teaching Journal,* vol. 3 (1978), pp. 41–42.

How to Give, and Take, Criticism

Preparation

The "criticism session" may well be the toughest test of a manager's communication skills. Picture Setting 1—you and a subordinate are meeting to review a problem with the subordinate's performance. Now picture Setting 2—you and your boss are meeting to review a problem with *your* performance. Both situations require communication skills in giving and receiving feedback. Even the most experienced person can have difficulty, and the situations can end as futile gripe sessions that cause hard feelings. The question is "How can such 'criticism sessions' be handled in a positive manner that encourages improved performance . . . and good feelings?"

Instructions

Form into groups as assigned by the instructor. Focus on either Setting 1, Setting 2, or both as assigned by the instructor. First, answer the question from the perspective assigned. Second, develop a series of action guidelines that could best be used to handle situations of this type. Third, prepare and present a mini-management training session to demonstrate the (a) unsuccessful and (b) successful use of these guidelines. If time permits, outside of class prepare a more extensive management training session that includes a videotape demonstration of your assigned criticism setting being handled first poorly and then very well. Support the videotape with additional written handouts and an oral presentation to help your classmates better understand the communication skills needed to successfully give and take criticism in work settings.

Lost at Sea

	A	B	C
Sextant	___	___	___
Shaving mirror	___	___	___
5 gallons water	___	___	___
Mosquito netting	___	___	___
1 survival meal	___	___	___
Maps of Pacific Ocean	___	___	___
Flotable seat cushion	___	___	___
2 gallons oil-gas mix	___	___	___
Small transistor radio	___	___	___
Shark repellent	___	___	___
20 square feet black plastic	___	___	___
1 quart 20-proof rum	___	___	___
15 feet nylon rope	___	___	___
24 chocolate bars	___	___	___
Fishing kit	___	___	___

Consider This Situation

You are adrift on a private yacht in the South Pacific when a fire of unknown origin destroys the yacht and most of its contents. You and a small group of survivors are now in a large raft with oars. Your location is unclear, but you estimate that you are about 1,000 miles south-southwest of the nearest land. One person has just found in her pockets 5 $1 bills and a packet of matches. Everyone else's pockets are empty. The items at the left are available to you on the raft.

Instructions

1. *Working alone,* rank in Column **A** the 15 items in order of their importance to your survival ("1" is most important and "15" is least important).

2. *Working in an assigned group,* arrive at a "team" ranking of the 15 items and record this ranking in Column **B**. Appoint one person as group spokesperson to report your group rankings to the class.

3. *Do not write in Column **C** until further instructions are provided by your instructor.*

Source: Adapted from "Lost at Sea: A Consensus-Seeking Task," in *The 1975 Handbook for Group Facilitators.* Used with permission of University Associates, Inc.

Work Team Dynamics

Preparation

Think about your course work group, a work group you are involved in for another course, or any other group suggested by your instructor. Indicate how often each of the following statements accurately reflects your experience in the group. Use this scale:

1 = Always   2 = Frequently   3 = Sometimes
4 = Never

1. ____ My ideas get a fair hearing.
2. ____ I am encouraged to give innovative ideas and take risks.
3. ____ Diverse opinions within the group are encouraged.
4. ____ I have all the responsibility I want.
5. ____ There is a lot of favoritism shown in the group.
6. ____ Members trust one another to do their assigned work.
7. ____ The group sets high standards of performance excellence.
8. ____ People share and change jobs a lot in the group.
9. ____ You can make mistakes and learn from them in this group.
10. ____ This group has good operating rules.

Instructions

Form groups as assigned by your instructor. Ideally, this will be the group you have just rated. Have all group members share their ratings, and then make one master rating for the group as a whole. Circle the items over which there are the biggest differences of opinion. Discuss those items and try to find out why they exist. In general, the better a group scores on this instrument, the higher its creative potential. If everyone has rated the same group, make a list of the five most important things members can do to improve its operations in the future. Nominate a spokesperson to summarize the group discussion for the class as a whole.

Source: Adapted from William Dyer, *Team Building*, 2nd ed. (Reading, MA: Addison-Wesley, 1987), pp. 123–125.

Feedback and Assertiveness

Preparation

Indicate the degree of discomfort you would feel in each situation below by circling the appropriate number:

1. high discomfort
2. some discomfort
3. undecided
4. very little discomfort
5. no discomfort

1 2 3 4 5 **1.** Telling an employee who is also a friend that she or he must stop coming to work late.

1 2 3 4 5 **2.** Talking to an employee about his or her performance on the job.

1 2 3 4 5 **3.** Asking an employee if she or he has any comments about your rating of her or his performance.

1 2 3 4 5 **4.** Telling an employee who has problems in dealing with other employees that he or she should do something about it.

1 2 3 4 5 **5.** Responding to an employee who is upset over your rating of his or her performance.

1 2 3 4 5 **6.** Responding to an employee's becoming emotional and defensive when you tell her or him about mistakes on the job.

1 2 3 4 5 **7.** Giving a rating that indicates improvement is needed to an employee who has failed to meet minimum requirements of the job.

1 2 3 4 5 **8.** Letting a subordinate talk during an appraisal interview.

1 2 3 4 5 **9.** Having an employee challenging you to justify your evaluation in the middle of an appraisal interview.

1 2 3 4 5 **10.** Recommending that an employee be discharged.

1 2 3 4 5 **11.** Telling an employee that you are uncomfortable with the role of having to judge his or her performance.

1 2 3 4 5 **12.** Telling an employee that her or his performance can be improved.

1 2 3 4 5 **13.** Telling an employee that you will not tolerate his or her taking extended coffee breaks.

1 2 3 4 5 **14.** Telling an employee that you will not tolerate her or his making personal telephone calls on company time.

Instructions

Form three-person teams as assigned by your instructor. Identify the 3 behaviors with which each person indicates the most discomfort. Then each team member should practice performing these behaviors with another member, while the third member acts as an observer. Be direct, but try to perform the behavior in an appropriate way. Listen to feedback from the observer and try the behaviors again, perhaps with different members of the group practicing each behavior. When finished, discuss the overall exercise. Be prepared to participate in further class discussion.

Source: Feedback questionnaire is from Judith R. Gordon, *A Diagnostic Approach to Organizational Behavior*, 3rd ed. (Boston: Allyn & Bacon, 1991), p. 298. Used by permission.

Creative Solutions

Preparation

Complete these 5 tasks while working alone. Be prepared to present and explain your responses in class.

1. Divide the following shape into four pieces of exactly the same size.

2. Without lifting your pencil from the paper, draw no more than 4 lines that cross through all of the following dots.

```
•    •    •

•    •    •

•    •    •
```

3. Draw the design for a machine that will turn the pages of your textbook so you can eat a snack while studying.

4. Why would a wheelbarrow ever be designed this way?

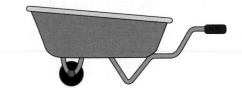

5. Turn the following into words.
   (a) ____ program
   (b) r\e\a\d\i\n\g
   (c) ECNALG
   (d)   j
           u
       yousme
          t
   (e) stand
          i

Instructions

After working alone, share your responses with a nearby classmate or with a group. See if you can develop different and/or better solutions based on this exchange of ideas.

Source: Ideas 3 and 5 found in Russell L. Ackoff, *The Art of Problem Solving* (New York: Wiley, 1978); ideas 1 and 4 found in Edward De Bono, *Lateral Thinking: Creativity Step by Step* (New York: Harper & Row, 1970); source for 5 is unknown.

Force-Field Analysis

Instructions

1. Form into your class discussion groups.
2. Review the concept of force-field analysis—the consideration of forces driving in support of a planned change and forces resisting the change.

Driving forces ⟩ Resisting forces

Current state ●●●●⟩ Desired future state

3. Use this force-field analysis worksheet in the assignment:

List of Driving Forces (those supporting the change)

——
____ . . . list as many as you can think of

List of Resisting Forces (those working against the change)

——
____ . . . list as many as you can think of

4. Apply force-field analysis and make your lists of driving and resisting forces for one of the following situations:

(a) Because of rapid advances in Web-based computer technologies, the possibility exists that the course you are presently taking could be, in part, offered online. This would mean a reduction in the number of required class sessions but an increase in students' responsibility for completing learning activities and assignments through computer mediation.

(b) A new owner has just taken over a small walk-in-and-buy-by-the-slice pizza shop in a college town. There are presently eight employees, three of whom are full-time and five of whom are part-time. The shop is presently open 7 days a week from 10:30 A.M. to 10:30 P.M. The new owner believes there is a market niche available for late-night pizza and would like to stay open each night until 2 a.m.

(c) A situation assigned by the instructor.

5. Choose the three driving forces that are most significant for the proposed change. For each force develop ideas on how it could be further increased or mobilized in support of the change.

6. Choose the three resisting forces that are most significant for the proposed change. For each force develop ideas on how it could be reduced or turned into a driving force.

7. Be prepared to participate in a class discussion led by your instructor.

Self

Assessments

ASSESSMENT 1

A 21st-Century Manager?

Instructions

Rate yourself on the following personal characteristics. Use this scale.

S = Strong, I am very confident with this one.

G = Good, but I still have room to grow.

W = Weak, I really need work on this one.

U = Unsure, I just don't know.

1. *Resistance to stress:* The ability to get work done even under stressful conditions.

2. *Tolerance for uncertainty:* The ability to get work done even under ambiguous and uncertain conditions.

3. *Social objectivity:* The ability to act free of racial, ethnic, gender, and other prejudices or biases.

4. *Inner work standards:* The ability to personally set and work to high performance standards.

5. *Stamina:* The ability to sustain long work hours.

6. *Adaptability:* The ability to be flexible and adapt to changes.

7. *Self-confidence:* The ability to be consistently decisive and display one's personal presence.

8. *Self-objectivity:* The ability to evaluate personal strengths and weaknesses and to understand one's motives and skills relative to a job.
9. *Introspection:* The ability to learn from experience, awareness, and self-study.
10. *Entrepreneurism:* The ability to address problems and take advantage of opportunities for constructive change.

Scoring

Give yourself 1 point for each S, and 1/2 point for each G. Do not give yourself points for W and U responses. Total your points and enter the result here [PMF = _____].

Interpretation

This assessment offers a self-described *profile of your management foundations (PMF).* Are you a perfect 10, or is your PMF score something less than that? There shouldn't be too many 10s around. Ask someone who knows you to assess you on this instrument. You may be surprised at the differences between your PMF score as you described it and your PMF score as described by someone else. Most of us, realistically speaking, must work hard to continually grow and develop in these and related management foundations. This list is a good starting point as you consider where and how to further pursue the development of your managerial skills and competencies. The items on the list were recommended by the Association to Advance Collegiate Schools of Business (AACSB) as the skills and personal characteristics that should be nurtured in college and university students of business administration. Their success—and yours—as 21st-century managers may well rest on (1) an initial awareness of the importance of these basic management foundations and (2) a willingness to continually strive to strengthen them throughout the work career.

_____

Source: See *Outcome Measurement Project,* Phase I and Phase II Reports (St. Louis: American Assembly of Collegiate Schools of Business, 1986 and 1987).

ASSESSMENT 2

Emotional Intelligence

Instructions

Rate yourself on how well you are able to display the abilities for each item listed below. As you score each item, try to think of actual situations in which you have been called upon to use the ability. Use the following scale:

| 1 | 2 | 3 | 4 | 5 | 6 | 7 |

Low Ability   Neutral   High Ability

1 2 3 4 5 6 7   **1.** Identify changes in physiological arousal.

1 2 3 4 5 6 7   **2.** Relax when under pressure in situations.

1 2 3 4 5 6 7   **3.** Act productively when angry.

1 2 3 4 5 6 7   **4.** Act productively in situations that arouse anxiety.

1 2 3 4 5 6 7   **5.** Calm yourself quickly when angry.

1 2 3 4 5 6 7   **6.** Associate different physical cues with different emotions.

1 2 3 4 5 6 7   **7.** Use internal "talk" to affect your emotional states.

1 2 3 4 5 6 7   **8.** Communicate your feelings effectively.

1 2 3 4 5 6 7   **9.** Reflect on negative feelings without being distressed.

1 2 3 4 5 6 7   **10.** Stay calm when you are the target of anger from others.

1 2 3 4 5 6 7   **11.** Know when you are thinking negatively.

1 2 3 4 5 6 7   **12.** Know when your "self-talk" is instructional.

1 2 3 4 5 6 7   **13.** Know when you are becoming angry.

1 2 3 4 5 6 7   **14.** Know how you interpret events you encounter.

1 2 3 4 5 6 7   **15.** Know what senses you are currently using.

1 2 3 4 5 6 7   **16.** Accurately communicate what you experience.

1 2 3 4 5 6 7   **17.** Identify what information influences your interpretations.

1 2 3 4 5 6 7   **18.** Identify when you experience mood shifts.

1 2 3 4 5 6 7 **19.** Know when you become defensive.

1 2 3 4 5 6 7 **20.** Know the impact your behavior has on others.

1 2 3 4 5 6 7 **21.** Know when you communicate incongruently.

1 2 3 4 5 6 7 **22.** "Gear up" at will.

1 2 3 4 5 6 7 **23.** Regroup quickly after a setback.

1 2 3 4 5 6 7 **24.** Complete long-term tasks in designated time frames.

1 2 3 4 5 6 7 **25.** Produce high energy when doing uninteresting work.

1 2 3 4 5 6 7 **26.** Stop or change ineffective habits.

1 2 3 4 5 6 7 **27.** Develop new and more productive patterns of behavior.

1 2 3 4 5 6 7 **28.** Follow words with actions.

1 2 3 4 5 6 7 **29.** Work out conflicts.

1 2 3 4 5 6 7 **30.** Develop consensus with others.

1 2 3 4 5 6 7 **31.** Mediate conflict between others.

1 2 3 4 5 6 7 **32.** Exhibit effective interpersonal communication skills.

1 2 3 4 5 6 7 **33.** Articulate the thoughts of a group.

1 2 3 4 5 6 7 **34.** Influence others, directly or indirectly.

1 2 3 4 5 6 7 **35.** Build trust with others.

1 2 3 4 5 6 7 **36.** Build support teams.

1 2 3 4 5 6 7 **37.** Make others feel good.

1 2 3 4 5 6 7 **38.** Provide advice and support to others, as needed.

1 2 3 4 5 6 7 **39.** Accurately reflect people's feelings back to them.

1 2 3 4 5 6 7 **40.** Recognize when others are distressed.

1 2 3 4 5 6 7 **41.** Help others manage their emotions.

1 2 3 4 5 6 7 **42.** Show empathy to others.

1 2 3 4 5 6 7 **43.** Engage in intimate conversations with others.

1 2 3 4 5 6 7 **44.** Help a group to manage emotions.

1 2 3 4 5 6 7 **45.** Detect incongruence between others' emotions or feelings and their behaviors.

Scoring

This instrument measures 6 dimensions of your emotional intelligence. Find your scores as follows.

Self-awareness—Add scores for items 1, 6, 11, 12, 13, 14, 15, 16, 17, 18, 19, 20, 21

Managing emotions—Add scores for items 1, 2, 3, 4, 5, 7, 9, 10, 13, 27

Self-motivation—Add scores for items 7, 22, 23, 25, 26, 27, 28

Relating well—Add scores for items 8, 10, 16, 19, 20, 29, 30, 31, 32, 33, 34, 35, 36, 37, 38, 39, 42, 43, 44, 45

Emotional mentoring—Add scores for items 8, 10, 16, 18, 34, 35, 37, 38, 39, 40, 41, 44, 45

Interpretation

The prior scoring indicates your self-perceived abilities in these dimensions of emotional intelligence. To further examine your tendencies, go back to each dimension and sum the number of responses you had that were 4 and lower (suggesting lower ability), and then sum the number of responses you had that were 5 or better (suggesting higher ability). This gives you an indication by dimension of where you may have room to grow and develop your emotional intelligence abilities.

Source: Scale from Hendrie Weisinger, *Emotional Intelligence at Work* (San Francisco: Jossey-Bass, 1998), pp. 214–215. Used by permission.

ASSESSMENT 3

Learning Tendencies

Instructions

In each of the following pairs, distribute 10 points between the two statements to best describe how you like to learn. For example:

3 (a) I like to read.
7 (b) I like to listen to lectures.

1. _____ (a) I like to learn through working with other people and being engaged in concrete experiences.

_____ (b) I like to learn through logical analysis and systematic attempts to understand a situation.

2. _____ (a) I like to learn by observing things, viewing them from different perspectives, and finding meaning in situations.

_____ (b) I like to learn by taking risks, getting things done, and influencing events through actions taken.

Scoring

Place "dots" on the following graph to record the above scores: "Doing"=2b. "Watching"=1b. "Feeling" =1a. "Thinking"=2a. Connect the dots to plot your learning tendencies.

Interpretation

This activity provides a first impression of your learning tendencies or style. Four possible learning styles are identified on the graph—convergers, accommodators, divergers, and assimilators. Consider the following descriptions for their accuracy in describing you. For a truly good reading on your learning tendencies, ask several others to complete the Step 1 questions for you, and then assess how their results compare with your own perceptions.

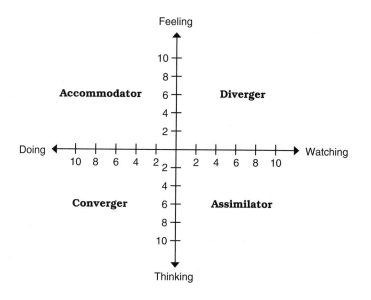

Convergers—combine tendencies toward abstract conceptualization (thinking) and active experimentation (doing). They like to learn in practical situations. They prefer to deal with technical issues and solve problems through systematic investigation of alternatives. Good at experimentation, finding new ways of doing things, making decisions.

Accommodators—combine concrete experience (feeling) with active experimentation (doing). They like to learn from hands-on experience. They prefer "gut" responses to problems rather than systematic analysis of alternatives. Good at influencing others, committing to goals, seeking opportunities.

Divergers—combine concrete experience (feeling) with reflective observation (watching). They like to learn from observation. They prefer to participate in brainstorming and imaginative information gathering. Good at listening, imagining, and being sensitive to feelings.

Assimilators—combine abstract conceptualization (thinking) with reflective observation (watching). They like to learn through information. They prefer ideas and concepts to people, and they value logical reasoning. Good at organizing information, building models, and analyzing data.

Source: Developed from David A. Kolb, "Learning Style Inventory" (Boston, MA: McBer & Company, 1985); see also his article "On Management and the Learning Process," in David A. Kolb, Irwin M. Rubin, and James M. McIntyre, eds., *Organizational Psychology: A Book of Readings*, 2nd ed. (Englewood Cliffs, NJ: Prentice-Hall, 1974), pp. 27–42.

ASSESSMENT 4

What Are Your Managerial Assumptions?

Instructions

Read the following statements. Use the space in the margins to write Yes if you agree with the statement, or No if you disagree with it. Force yourself to take a yes or no position. Do this for every statement.

1. Are good pay and a secure job enough to satisfy most workers?

2. Should a manager help and coach subordinates in their work?

3. Do most people like real responsibility in their jobs?

4. Are most people afraid to learn new things in their jobs?

5. Should managers let subordinates control the quality of their work?

6. Do most people dislike work?

7. Are most people creative?

8. Should a manager closely supervise and direct the work of subordinates?

9. Do most people tend to resist change?

10. Do most people work only as hard as they have to?

11. Should workers be allowed to set their own job goals?

12. Are most people happiest off the job?

13. Do most workers really care about the organization they work for?

14. Should a manager help subordinates advance and grow in their jobs?

Scoring

Count the number of yes responses to items 1, 4, 6, 8, 9, 10, 12; write that number here as [X = _____]. Count the number of yes responses to items 2, 3, 5, 7, 11, 13, 14; write that score here [Y = _____].

Interpretation

This assessment provides insight into your orientation toward Douglas McGregor's Theory X (your "X" score) and Theory Y (your "Y" score) assumptions. You should review the discussion of McGregor's thinking in Chapter 3 and consider further the ways in which you are likely to behave toward other people at work. Think, in particular, about the types of "self-fulfilling prophecies" you are likely to create.

ASSESSMENT 5

Terminal Values Survey

Instructions

Rate each of the following values in terms of its importance to you. Think about each value *in terms of its importance as a guiding principle in your life.* As you work, consider each value in relation to all the other values listed in the survey.

Terminal Values

1. A comfortable life   1   2   3   4   5   6   7
Of lesser importance   Of greater importance

2. An exciting life   1   2   3   4   5   6   7
Of lesser importance   Of greater importance

3. A sense of accomplishment   1   2   3   4   5   6   7
Of lesser importance   Of greater importance

4. A world at peace   1   2   3   4   5   6   7
Of lesser importance   Of greater importance

5. A world of beauty   1   2   3   4   5   6   7
Of lesser importance   Of greater importance

6. Equality   1   2   3   4   5   6   7
Of lesser importance   Of greater importance

7. Family security   1   2   3   4   5   6   7
Of lesser importance   Of greater importance

8. Freedom   1   2   3   4   5   6   7
Of lesser importance   Of greater importance

9. Happiness   1   2   3   4   5   6   7
Of lesser importance   Of greater importance

10. Inner harmony   1   2   3   4   5   6   7
Of lesser importance   Of greater importance

11. Mature love   1   2   3   4   5   6   7
Of lesser importance   Of greater importance

12. National security   1   2   3   4   5   6   7
Of lesser importance   Of greater importance

13. Pleasure   1   2   3   4   5   6   7
Of lesser importance   Of greater importance

14. Salvation   1   2   3   4   5   6   7
Of lesser importance   Of greater importance

15. Self-respect   1   2   3   4   5   6   7
Of lesser importance   Of greater importance

16. Social recognition   1   2   3   4   5   6   7
Of lesser importance   Of greater importance

17. True friendship   1   2   3   4   5   6   7
Of lesser importance   Of greater importance

18. Wisdom   1   2   3   4   5   6   7
Of lesser importance   Of greater importance

Interpretation

Terminal values reflect a person's preferences concerning the "ends" to be achieved. They are the goals individuals would like to achieve in their lifetimes. Different value items receive different weights in this scale. (Example: "A comfortable life" receives a weight of "5" while "Freedom" receives a weight of "1.") Subtract your Social Values score from your Personal Values score to determine your Terminal Values score.

Scoring

To score this instrument, multiply your score for each item times a "weight"—e.g., $(\#3 \times 5)$ = your new question 3 score.

1. Calculate your Personal Values Score as:
$(\#1 \times 5) + (\#2 \times 4) + (\#3 \times 4) + (\#7) + (\#8) + (\#9 \times 4) + (\#10 \times 5) + (\#11 \times 4) + (\#13 \times 5) + (\#14 \times 3) + (\#15 \times 5) + (\#16 \times 3) + (\#17 \times 4) + (\#18 \times 5)$

2. Calculate your Social Values Score as
$(\#4 \times 5) + (\#5 \times 3) + (\#6 \times 5) + (\#12 \times 5)$

3. Calculate your Terminal Values Score as Personal Values-Social Values

---

Source: Adapted from James Weber, "Management Value Orientations: A Typology and Assessment," *International Journal of Value Based Management*, vol. 3, no. 2 (1990), pp. 37–54.

ASSESSMENT 6

Instrumental Values Survey

Instructions

Rate each of the following values in terms of its importance to you. Think about each value *in terms of its importance as a guiding principle in your life.* As you work, consider each value in relation to all the other values listed in the survey.

Instrumental Values

1. Ambitious

1	2	3	4	5	6	7
Of lesser importance					Of greater importance	

2. Broadminded

1	2	3	4	5	6	7
Of lesser importance					Of greater importance	

3. Capable

1	2	3	4	5	6	7
Of lesser importance					Of greater importance	

4. Cheerful

1	2	3	4	5	6	7
Of lesser importance					Of greater importance	

5. Clean

1	2	3	4	5	6	7
Of lesser importance					Of greater importance	

6. Courageous

1	2	3	4	5	6	7
Of lesser importance					Of greater importance	

7. Forgiving

1	2	3	4	5	6	7
Of lesser importance					Of greater importance	

8. Helpful

1	2	3	4	5	6	7
Of lesser importance					Of greater importance	

9. Honest

1	2	3	4	5	6	7
Of lesser importance					Of greater importance	

10. Imaginative

1	2	3	4	5	6	7
Of lesser importance					Of greater importance	

11. Independent

1	2	3	4	5	6	7
Of lesser importance					Of greater importance	

12. Intellectual

1	2	3	4	5	6	7
Of lesser importance					Of greater importance	

13. Logical

1	2	3	4	5	6	7
Of lesser importance					Of greater importance	

14. Loving

1	2	3	4	5	6	7
Of lesser importance					Of greater importance	

15. Obedient

1	2	3	4	5	6	7
Of lesser importance					Of greater importance	

16. Polite

1	2	3	4	5	6	7
Of lesser importance					Of greater importance	

17. Responsible

1	2	3	4	5	6	7
Of lesser importance					Of greater importance	

18. Self-controlled

1	2	3	4	5	6	7
Of lesser importance					Of greater importance	

Interpretation

Instrumental Values are defined as the "means" for achieving desired ends. They represent how you might go about achieving your important end states, depending on the relative importance you attach to the instrumental values.

Different value items receive different weights in this scale. (Example: "Ambitious" receives a weight of "5" while "Obedient" receives a weight of "1.") Subtract your Moral Values score from your Competence Values score to determine your Instrumental Values score.

Scoring

To score this instrument, multiply your score for each item times a "weight"—e.g., (#3×5) = your new question 3 score.

1. Calculate your Competence Values Score as (#1×5)+(#2×2)+(#3×5) +(#10×5)+(#11×5)+(#12×5)+(#13×5)+(#17×4)+(18×4)

2. Calculate your Moral Values Score as (#4×4)+(#5×3)+(#6×2)+(#7×5) +(#8×5)+(#9×2)+(#14×5)+(#15)+(#16×3)

3. Calculate your Instrumental Values Score as Competence Values−Moral Values

Source: Adapted from James Weber, "Management Value Orientations: A Typology and Assessment," *International Journal of Value Based Management,* vol. 3, no. 2 (1990), pp. 37–54.

Diversity Awareness

Instructions

Complete the following questionnaire:

Diversity Awareness Checklist

Consider where you work or go to school as the setting for the following questions. Indicate "O" for often, "S" for sometimes, and "N" for never in response to each of the following questions as they pertain to the setting.

_____ 1. How often have you heard jokes or remarks about other people that you consider offensive?

_____ 2. How often do you hear men "talk down" to women in an attempt to keep them in an inferior status?

_____ 3. How often have you felt personal discomfort as the object of sexual harassment?

_____ 4. How often do you work or study with African Americans or Hispanics?

_____ 5. How often have you felt disadvantaged because members of ethnic groups other than yours were given special treatment?

_____ 6. How often have you seen a woman put in an uncomfortable situation because of unwelcome advances by a man?

_____ 7. How often does it seem that African Americans, Hispanics, Caucasians, women, men, and members of other minority demographic groups seem to "stick together" during work breaks or other leisure situations?

_____ 8. How often do you feel uncomfortable about something you did and/or said to someone of the opposite sex or a member of an ethnic or racial group other than yours?

_____ 9. How often do you feel efforts are made in this setting to raise the level of cross-cultural understanding among people who work and/or study together?

_____10. How often do you step in to communicate concerns to others when you feel actions and/or words are used to the disadvantage of minorities?

Scoring

There are no correct answers for the Diversity Awareness Checklist.

Interpretation

In the diversity checklist, the key issue is the extent to which you are "sensitive" to diversity issues in the workplace or university. Are you comfortable with your responses? How do you think others in your class responded? Share your responses with others and examine different viewpoints on this important issue.

Source: Items for the WV Cultural Awareness Quiz selected from a longer version by James P. Morgan Jr. and published by University Associates, 1987. Used by permission.

Global Readiness Index

Instructions

Rate yourself on each of the following items to establish a baseline measurement of your readiness to participate in the global work environment.

Rating Scale

1 = Very Poor
2 = Poor
3 = Acceptable
4 = Good
5 = Very Good

_____ 1. I understand my own culture in terms of its expectations, values, and influence on communication and relationships.

_____ 2. When someone presents me with a different point of view, I try to understand it rather than attack it.

_____ 3. I am comfortable dealing with situations where the available information is incomplete and the outcomes unpredictable.

_____ 4. I am open to new situations and am always looking for new information and learning opportunities.

5. I have a good understanding of the attitudes and perceptions toward my culture as they are held by people from other cultures.

6. I am always gathering information about other countries and cultures and trying to learn from them.

7. I am well informed regarding the major differences in the government, political, and economic systems around the world.

8. I work hard to increase my understanding of people from other cultures.

9. I am able to adjust my communication style to work effectively with people from different cultures.

10. I can recognize when cultural differences are influencing working relationships and adjust my attitudes and behavior accordingly.

Interpretation

To be successful in the 21st-century work environment, you must be comfortable with the global economy and the cultural diversity that it holds. This requires a *global mindset* that is receptive to and respectful of cultural differences, *global knowledge* that includes the continuing quest to know and learn more about other nations and cultures, and *global work skills* that allow you to work effectively across cultures.

Scoring

The goal is to score as close to a perfect "5" as possible on each of the three dimensions of global readiness. Develop your scores as follows.

Items (1+2+3+4)/4 = _____ Global Mindset Score

Items (5+6+7)/3 = _____ Global Knowledge Score

Items (8+9+10)/3 = _____ Global Work Skills Score

Source: Developed from "Is Your Company Really Global?" *Business Week* (December 1, 1997).

ASSESSMENT 9

Time Orientation

Instructions

This instrument examines your tendencies to favor "monochronic" or "polychronic" time orientations. Rate your tendencies for each item below using the following scale:

Rating Scale

1 = Almost never   2 = Seldom
3 = Sometimes   4 = Usually
5 = Almost always

1. I like to do one thing at a time.

2. I have a strong tendency to build lifetime relationships.

3. I concentrate on the job at hand.

4. I base my level of promptness on the particular relationship.

5. I take time commitments (deadlines, schedules) seriously.

6. I borrow and lend things often and easily.

7. I am committed to the job.

8. Intimacy with family and friends is more important than respecting their privacy.

9. I adhere closely to plans.

10. I put obligations to family and friends before work concerns.

11. I am concerned about not disturbing others (follow rules of privacy).

12. I change plans often and easily.

13. I emphasize promptness in meetings.

14. I am committed to people and human relationships.

15. I show great respect for private property (seldom borrow or lend).

16. I am highly distractible and frequently interrupt what I am doing.

17. I am comfortable with short-term relationships.

18. I like to do many things at once.

Scoring

To obtain your *monochronic time orientation* score, sum results for items 1, 3, 5, 7, 9, 11, 13, 15, 17. To obtain your *polychronic time orientation* score, sum results for items 2, 4, 6, 8, 10, 12, 14, 16, 18.

Interpretation

A person high in monochronic time orientation approaches time in a linear fashion, with things dealt with one at a time in an orderly fashion. Time is viewed as a precious commodity, not to be wasted; this person values punctuality and promptness.

A person high in polychronic time orientation tends to do a number of things at once, intertwining them together in a dynamic process that considers changing circumstances. Commitments are viewed as objectives, but capable of adjustment when necessary.

Cultural differences in orientations toward time can be observed. Tendencies toward monochronic time orientation are common to North America and northern European cultures. Tendencies toward polychronic time orientation are common in cultures of the Middle East, Asia, and Latin America.

Source: Adapted from J. Ned Seelye and Alan Seelye-James. _Culture Clash_ (Lincolnwood, IL: NTC Business Books, 1996).

ASSESSMENT 10

Entrepreneurship Orientation

Instructions

Answer the following questions:

1. What portion of your college expenses did you earn (or are you earning)?
   (a) 50 percent or more
   (b) less than 50 percent
   (c) none

2. In college, your academic performance was/is
   (a) above average.
   (b) average.
   (c) below average.

3. What is your basic reason for considering opening a business?
   (a) I want to make money.
   (b) I want to control my own destiny.
   (c) I hate the frustration of working for someone else.

4. Which phrase best describes your attitude toward work?
   (a) I can keep going as long as I need to; I don't mind working for something I want.
   (b) I can work hard for a while, but when I've had enough, I quit.
   (c) Hard work really doesn't get you anywhere.

5. How would you rate your organizing skills?
   (a) superorganized
   (b) above average
   (c) average
   (d) I do well to find half the things I look for.

6. You are primarily a(n)
   (a) optimist.
   (b) pessimist.
   (c) neither.

7. You are faced with a challenging problem. As you work, you realize you are stuck. You will most likely
   (a) give up.
   (b) ask for help.
   (c) keep plugging; you'll figure it out.

8. You are playing a game with a group of friends. You are most interested in
   (a) winning.
   (b) playing well.
   (c) making sure that everyone has a good time.
   (d) cheating as much as possible.

9. How would you describe your feelings toward failure?
   (a) Fear of failure paralyzes me.
   (b) Failure can be a good learning experience.
   (c) Knowing that I might fail motivates me to work even harder.
   (d) "Damn the torpedoes! Full speed ahead."

10. Which phrase best describes you?
    (a) I need constant encouragement to get anything done.
    (b) If someone gets me started, I can keep going.

(c) I am energetic and hard-working—a self-starter.

11. Which bet would you most likely accept?
(a) a wager on a dog race
(b) a wager on a racquetball game in which you play an opponent
(c) Neither. I never make wagers.

12. At the Kentucky Derby, you would bet on
(a) the 100-to-1 long shot.
(b) the odds-on favorite.
(c) the 3-to-1 shot.
(d) none of the above.

Scoring

Give yourself 10 points for each of the following answers: 1a, 2a, 3c, 4a, 5a, 6a, 7c, 8a, 9c, 10c, 11b, 12c; total the scores and enter the results here [I = _____]. Give yourself 8 points for each of the following answers: 3b, 8b, 9b; total the scores and enter the results here [II = _____]. Give yourself 6 points for each of the following answers: 2b, 5b; total the scores and enter the results here [III = _____]. Give yourself 5 points for this answer: 1b; enter the result here [IV = _____]. Give yourself 4 points for this answer:

5c; enter the result here [V = _____]. Give yourself 2 points for each of the following answers: 2c, 3a, 4b, 6c, 9d, 10b, 11a, 12b; total the scores and enter the results here [VI = _____]. Any other scores are worth 0 points. Total your summary scores for I+II+III+IV+V+VI and enter the result here [EP = _____].

Interpretation

This assessment offers an impression of your *entrepreneurial profile*, or EP. It compares your characteristics with those of typical entrepreneurs. Locate your EP score in the following table.

100+ = Entrepreneur extraordinaire
80–99 = Entrepreneur
60–79 = Potential entrepreneur
0–59 = Entrepreneur in the rough

Your instructor can provide further information on each question as well as some additional insights into the backgrounds of entrepreneurs.

───────────

Source: Instrument adapted from Norman M. Scarborough and Thomas W. Zimmerer, *Effective Small Business Management,* 3rd ed. (Columbus: Merrill, 1991), pp. 26–27. Used by permission.

ASSESSMENT 11

Your Intuitive Ability

Instructions

Complete this survey as quickly as you can. Be honest with yourself. For each question, select the response that most appeals to you.

1. When working on a project, do you prefer to
(a) be told what the problem is but be left free to decide how to solve it?
(b) get very clear instructions for how to go about solving the problem before you start?

2. When working on a project, do you prefer to work with colleagues who are
(a) realistic?
(b) imaginative?

3. Do you most admire people who are
(a) creative?
(b) careful?

4. Do the friends you choose tend to be
(a) serious and hard working?
(b) exciting and often emotional?

5. When you ask a colleague for advice on a problem you have, do you
(a) seldom or never get upset if he or she questions your basic assumptions?
(b) often get upset if he or she questions your basic assumptions?

6. When you start your day, do you
(a) seldom make or follow a specific plan?
(b) usually first make a plan to follow?

7. When working with numbers, do you find that you
(a) seldom or never make factual errors?
(b) often make factual errors?

8. Do you find that you
(a) seldom daydream during the day and really don't enjoy doing so when you do it?
(b) frequently daydream during the day and enjoy doing so?

9. When working on a problem, do you
   (a) prefer to follow the instructions or rules that are given to you?
   (b) often enjoy circumventing the instructions or rules that are given to you?

10. When you are trying to put something together, do you prefer to have
    (a) step-by-step written instructions on how to assemble the item?
    (b) a picture of how the item is supposed to look once assembled?

11. Do you find that the person who irritates you *the most* is the one who appears to be
    (a) disorganized?
    (b) organized?

12. When an unexpected crisis comes up that you have to deal with, do you
    (a) feel anxious about the situation?
    (b) feel excited by the challenge of the situation?

Scoring

Total the number of "a" responses circled for questions 1, 3, 5, 6, 11; enter the score here [A = ____]. Total the number of "b" responses for questions 2, 4, 7, 8, 9, 10, 12; enter the score here [B = ____]. Add your "a" and "b" scores and enter the sum here [A+B = ____]. This is your *intuitive score*. The highest possible intuitive score is 12; the lowest is 0.

Interpretation

In his book *Intuition in Organizations* (Newbury Park, CA: Sage, 1989), pp. 10–11, Weston H. Agor states, "Traditional analytical techniques . . . are not as useful as they once were for guiding major decisions. . . . If you hope to be better prepared for tomorrow, then it only seems logical to pay some attention to the use and development of intuitive skills for decision making." Agor developed the preceding survey to help people assess their tendencies to use intuition in decision making. Your score offers a general impression of your strength in this area. It may also suggest a need to further develop your skill and comfort with more intuitive decision approaches.

――――――

Source: AIM Survey (El Paso, TX: ENFP Enterprises, 1989). Copyright (c)1989 by Weston H. Agor. Used by permission.

ASSESSMENT 12

Assertiveness

Instructions

This instrument measures tendencies toward aggressive, passive, and assertive behaviors in work situations. For each statement below, decide which of the answers best fits you. Use the following rating scale:

       1 = Never true
       2 = Sometimes true
       3 = Often true
       4 = Always true

____ 1. I respond with more modesty than I really feel when my work is complimented.

____ 2. If people are rude, I will be rude right back.

____ 3. Other people find me interesting.

____ 4. I find it difficult to speak up in a group of strangers.

____ 5. I don't mind using sarcasm if it helps me make a point.

____ 6. I ask for a raise when I feel I really deserve it.

____ 7. If others interrupt me when I am talking, I suffer in silence.

____ 8. If people criticize my work, I find a way to make them back down.

____ 9. I can express pride in my accomplishments without being boastful.

____10. People take advantage of me.

____11. I tell people what they want to hear if it helps me get what I want.

____12. I find it easy to ask for help.

____13. I lend things to others even when I don't really want to.

____14. I win arguments by dominating the discussion.

____15. I can express my true feelings to someone I really care for.

____16. When I feel angry with other people, I bottle it up rather than express it.

_____ 17. When I criticize someone else's work, they get mad.

_____ 18. I feel confident in my ability to stand up for my rights.

Scoring

Obtain your scores as follows:

Aggressiveness tendency score—Add items 2, 5, 8, 11, 14, and 17

Passive tendency score—Add items 1, 4, 7, 10, 13, and 16

Assertiveness tendency score—Add items 3, 6, 9, 12, 15, and 18

Interpretation

The maximum score in any area is 24. The minimum score is 6. Try to find someone who knows you well. Have this person complete the instrument as it relates to you. Compare his or her impression of you with your own score. What is this telling you about your behavior tendencies in social situations?

_____

Source: From Douglas T. Hall, Donald D. Bowen, Roy J. Lewicki, and Francine S. Hall, *Experiences in Management and Organizational Behavior,* 2nd ed. (New York: Wiley, 1985). Used by permission.

ASSESSMENT 13

Time Management Profile

Instructions

Complete the following questionnaire by indicating "Y" (yes) or "N" (no) for each item. Force yourself to respond yes or no. Be frank and allow your responses to create an accurate picture of how you tend to respond to these kinds of situations.

_____ 1. When confronted with several items of similar urgency and importance, I tend to do the easiest one first.

_____ 2. I do the most important things during that part of the day when I know I perform best.

_____ 3. Most of the time I don't do things someone else can do; I delegate this type of work to others.

_____ 4. Even though meetings without a clear and useful purpose upset me, I put up with them.

_____ 5. I skim documents before reading them and don't complete any that offer a low return on my time investment.

_____ 6. I don't worry much if I don't accomplish at least one significant task each day.

_____ 7. I save the most trivial tasks for that time of day when my creative energy is lowest.

_____ 8. My workspace is neat and organized.

_____ 9. My office door is always "open"; I never work in complete privacy.

_____ 10. I schedule my time completely from start to finish every workday.

_____ 11. I don't like "to do" lists, preferring to respond to daily events as they occur.

_____ 12. I "block" a certain amount of time each day or week that is dedicated to high-priority activities.

Scoring

Count the number of "Y" responses to items 2, 3, 5, 7, 8, 12. Enter that score here [_____.] Count the number of "N" responses to items 1, 4, 6, 9, 10, 11. Enter that score here [_____.] Add the two scores together.

Interpretation

The higher the total score, the closer your behavior matches recommended time management guidelines. Reread those items where your response did not match the desired one. Why don't they match? Do you have reasons why your behavior in this instance should be different from the recommended time management guideline? Think about what you can do (and how easily it can be done) to adjust your behavior to be more consistent with these guidelines. For further reading, see Alan Lakein, *How to Control Your Time and Your Life* (New York: David McKay), and William Oncken, *Managing Management Time* (Englewood Cliffs, NJ: Prentice-Hall, 1984).

_____

Source: Suggested by a discussion in Robert E. Quinn, Sue R. Faerman, Michael P. Thompson, and Michael R. McGrath, *Becoming a Master Manager: A Contemporary Framework* (New York: Wiley, 1990), pp. 75–76.

Facts and Inferences

Preparation

Often, when we listen or speak, we don't distinguish between statements of fact and those of inference. Yet, there are great differences between the two. We create barriers to clear thinking when we treat inferences (guesses, opinions) as if they are facts. You may wish at this point to test your ability to distinguish facts from inferences by taking the accompanying fact-inference test based on those by Haney (1973).

Instructions

Carefully read the following report and the observations based on it. Indicate whether you think the observations are true, false, or doubtful on the basis of the information presented in the report. Write "T" if the observation is definitely true, "F" if the observation is definitely false, and "?" if the observation may be either true or false. Judge each observation in order. Do not reread the observations after you have indicated your judgment, and do not change any of your answers.

A well-liked college instructor had just completed making up the final examinations and had turned off the lights in the office. Just then a tall, broad figure with dark glasses appeared and demanded the examination. The professor opened the drawer. Everything in the drawer was picked up, and the individual ran down the corridor. The president was notified immediately.

_____ 1. The thief was tall, broad, and wore dark glasses.

_____ 2. The professor turned off the lights.

_____ 3. A tall figure demanded the examination.

_____ 4. The examination was picked up by someone.

_____ 5. The examination was picked up by the professor.

_____ 6. A tall, broad figure appeared after the professor had turned off the lights in the office.

_____ 7. The man who opened the drawer was the professor.

_____ 8. The professor ran down the corridor.

_____ 9. The drawer was never actually opened.

_____ 10. Three persons are referred to in this report.

When told to do so by your instructor, join a small work group. Now, help the group complete the same task by making a consensus decision on each item. Be sure to keep a separate record of the group's responses and your original individual responses.

Scoring

Your instructor will read the correct answers. Score both your individual and group responses.

Interpretation

To begin, ask yourself if there was a difference between your answers and those of the group for each item. If so, why? Why do you think people, individually or in groups, may answer these questions incorrectly? Good planning depends on good decision making by the people doing the planning. Being able to distinguish "facts" and understand one's "inferences" are important steps toward improving the planning process. Involving others to help do the same can frequently assist in this process.

Source: Joseph A. Devito, *Messages: Building Interpersonal Communication Skills*, 3rd ed. (New York: HarperCollins, 1996), referencing William Haney, *Communicational Behavior: Text and Cases*, 3rd ed. (Homewood, IL: Irwin, 1973). Reprinted by permission.

Empowering Others

Instructions

Think of times when you have been in charge of a group—this could be a full-time or part-time work situation, a student work group, or whatever. Complete the following questionnaire by recording how you feel about each statement according to this scale:

1 = Strongly disagree 2 = Disagree 3 = Neutral
4 = Agree 5 = Strongly agree

When in charge of a group, I find that

_____ 1. Most of the time other people are too inexperienced to do things, so I prefer to do them myself.

_____ 2. It often takes more time to explain things to others than to just do them myself.

_____ 3. Mistakes made by others are costly, so I don't assign much work to them.

_____ 4. Some things simply should not be delegated to others.

_____ 5. I often get quicker action by doing a job myself.

_____ 6. Many people are good only at very specific tasks and so can't be assigned additional responsibilities.

_____ 7. Many people are too busy to take on additional work.

_____ 8. Most people just aren't ready to handle additional responsibilities.

_____ 9. In my position, I should be entitled to make my own decisions.

Scoring

Total your responses: enter the score here [_____].

Interpretation

This instrument gives an impression of your *willingness to delegate.* Possible scores range from 9 to 45. The lower your score, the more willing you appear to be to delegate to others. Willingness to delegate is an important managerial characteristic: It is essential if you—as a manager—are to "empower" others and give them opportunities to assume responsibility and exercise self-control in their work. With the growing importance of empowerment in the new workplace, your willingness to delegate is worth thinking about seriously. Be prepared to share your results and participate in general class discussion.

Source: Questionnaire adapted from L. Steinmetz and R. Todd, *First Line Management*, 4th ed. (Homewood, IL: BPI/Irwin, 1986), pp. 64–67. Used by permission.

Turbulence Tolerance Test

Instructions

The following statements were made by a 37-year-old manager in a large, successful corporation. How would you like to have a job with these characteristics? Using the following scale, write your response to the left of each statement.

0 = This feature would be very unpleasant for me.

1 = This feature would be somewhat unpleasant for me.

2 = I'd have no reaction to this feature one way or another.

3 = This would be enjoyable and acceptable most of the time.

4 = I would enjoy this very much; it's completely acceptable.

_____ 1. I regularly spend 30 to 40 percent of my time in meetings.

_____ 2. Eighteen months ago my job did not exist, and I have been essentially inventing it as I go along.

_____ 3. The responsibilities I either assume or am assigned consistently exceed the authority I have for discharging them.

_____ 4. At any given moment in my job, I have on the average about a dozen phone calls to be returned.

_____ 5. In my job, there seems to be very little relation between the quality of my performance and my actual pay and fringe benefits.

_____ 6. About 2 weeks a year of formal management training is needed in my job just to stay current.

_____ 7. Because we have very effective equal employment opportunity (EEO) in my company and because it is thoroughly multinational, my job consistently brings me into close working contact at a professional level with people of many races, ethnic groups, and nationalities, and of both sexes.

_____ 8. There is no objective way to measure my effectiveness.

_____ 9. I report to three different bosses for different aspects of my job, and each has an equal say in my performance appraisal.

_____ 10. On average about a third of my time is spent dealing with emergencies that force all scheduled work to be postponed.

_____ 11. When I have to have a meeting of the people who report to me, it takes my secretary most of a day to find a time when we are all available, and even then I have yet to have a meeting where everyone is present for the entire meeting.

_____ 12. The college degree I earned in preparation for this type of work is now obsolete, and I probably should go back for another degree.

_____ 13. My job requires that I absorb 100–200 pages of technical material per week.

_____ 14. I am out of town overnight at least 1 night per week.

_____ 15. My department is so interdependent with several other departments in the company that all distinctions about which departments are responsible for which tasks are quite arbitrary.

_____ 16. In about a year I will probably get a promotion to a job in another division that has most of these same characteristics.

_____ 17. During the period of my employment here, either the entire company or the division I worked in has been reorganized every year or so.

_____ 18. While there are several possible promotions I can see ahead of me, I have no real career path in an objective sense.

_____ 19. While there are several possible promotions I can see ahead of me, I think I have no realistic chance of getting to the top levels of the company.

_____ 20. While I have many ideas about how to make things work better, I have no direct influence on either the business policies or the personnel policies that govern my division.

_____ 21. My company has recently put in an "assessment center" where I and all other managers will be required to go through an extensive battery of psychological tests to assess our potential.

_____ 22. My company is a defendant in an antitrust suit, and if the case comes to trial, I will probably have to testify about some decisions that were made a few years ago.

_____ 23. Advanced computer and other electronic office technology is continually being introduced into my division, necessitating constant learning on my part.

_____ 24. The computer terminal and screen I have in my office can be monitored in my bosses' offices without my knowledge.

Scoring

Add up all of your scores and then divide the total by 24. This is your "Turbulence Tolerance Test" (TTT) score.

Interpretation

This instrument gives an impression of your tolerance for managing in turbulent times—something likely to characterize the world of work well into the new century. In general, the higher your TTT score, the more comfortable you seem to be with turbulence and change—a positive sign.

For comparison purposes, the average TTT scores for some 500 MBA students and young managers was 1.5–1.6. The test's author suggests TTT scores may be interpreted much like a grade point average in which 4.0 is a perfect A. On this basis, a 1.5 is below a C! How did you do?

_____

Source: Peter B. Vail, *Managing as a Performance Art: New Ideas for a World of Chaotic Change* (San Francisco: Jossey-Bass, 1989), pp. 8–9. Used by permission.

ASSESSMENT 17

Organizational Design Preference

Instructions

In the margin near each item, write the number from the following scale that shows the extent to which the statement accurately describes your views.

5 = strongly agree
4 = agree somewhat
3 = undecided
2 = disagree somewhat
1 = strongly disagree

I prefer to work in an organization where

1. goals are defined by those in higher levels.
2. work methods and procedures are specified.
3. top management makes important decisions.
4. my loyalty counts as much as my ability to do the job.
5. clear lines of authority and responsibility are established.
6. top management is decisive and firm.
7. my career is pretty well planned out for me.
8. I can specialize.
9. my length of service is almost as important as my level of performance.
10. management is able to provide the information I need to do my job well.
11. a chain of command is well established.
12. rules and procedures are adhered to equally by everyone.
13. people accept the authority of a leader's position.
14. people are loyal to their boss.
15. people do as they have been instructed.
16. people clear things with their boss before going over his or her head.

Scoring

Total your scores for all questions. Enter the score here [_____].

Interpretation

This assessment measures your preference for working in an organization designed along "organic" or "mechanistic" lines (see Chapter 4). The higher your score (above 64), the more comfortable you are with a mechanistic design; the lower your score (below 48), the more comfortable you are with an organic design. Scores between 48 and 64 can go either way. This organizational design preference represents an important issue in the new workplace. Indications are that today's organizations are taking on more and more organic characteristics. Presumably, those of us who work in them will need to be comfortable with such designs.

_____

Source: John F. Veiga and John N. Yanouzas. *The Dynamics of Organization Theory: Gaining a Macro Perspective* (St. Paul, MN: West, 1979), pp. 158–160. Used by permission.

Are You Cosmopolitan?

Instructions

Answer the following questions:

1. You believe it is the right of the professional to make his or her own decisions about what is to be done on the job.
   Strongly disagree 1 2 3 4 5 Strongly agree

2. You believe a professional should stay in an individual staff role regardless of the income sacrifice.
   Strongly disagree 1 2 3 4 5 Strongly agree

3. You have no interest in moving up to a top administrative post.
   Strongly disagree 1 2 3 4 5 Strongly agree

4. You believe that professionals are better evaluated by professional colleagues than by management.
   Strongly disagree 1 2 3 4 5 Strongly agree

5. Your friends tend to be members of your profession.
   Strongly disagree 1 2 3 4 5 Strongly agree

6. You would rather be known or get credit for your work outside rather than inside the company.
   Strongly disagree 1 2 3 4 5 Strongly agree

7. You would feel better making a contribution to society than to your organization.
   Strongly disagree 1 2 3 4 5 Strongly agree

8. Managers have no right to place time and cost schedules on professional contributors.
   Strongly disagree 1 2 3 4 5 Strongly agree

Scoring

Add your score for each item to get a total score between 8 and 40.

Interpretation

A "cosmopolitan" identifies with the career profession, and a "local" identifies with the employing organization. A score of 30–40 suggests a "cosmopolitan" work orientation, 10–20 a "local" orientation, and 20–30 a "mixed" orientation.

Source: Developed from Joseph A. Raelin, *The Clash of Cultures, Managers and Professionals* (Boston: Harvard Business School Press, 1986).

Performance Appraisal Assumptions

Instructions

In each of the following pairs of statements, check off the statement that best reflects your assumptions about performance evaluation. Performance evaluation is

1. (a) a formal process that is done annually.
   (b) an informal process done continuously.

2. (a) a process that is planned for subordinates.
   (b) a process that is planned with subordinates.

3. (a) a required organizational procedure.
   (b) a process done regardless of requirements.

4. (a) a time to evaluate subordinates' performance.
   (b) a time for subordinates to evaluate their manager.

5. (a) a time to clarify standards.
   (b) a time to clarify the subordinate's career needs.

6. (a) a time to confront poor performance.
   (b) a time to express appreciation.

7. (a) an opportunity to clarify issues and provide direction and control.
   (b) an opportunity to increase enthusiasm and commitment.

8. (a) only as good as the organization's forms.

   (b) only as good as the manager's coaching skills.

Scoring

There is no formal scoring for this assessment, but there may be a pattern to your responses. Check them again.

Interpretation

In general, the "a" responses represent a more traditional approach to performance appraisal that emphasizes its *evaluation* function. This role largely puts the supervisor in the role of documenting a subordinate's performance for control and administrative purposes. The "b" responses represent a more progressive approach that includes a strong emphasis on the *counseling* or *development* role. Here, the supervisor is concerned with helping the subordinate do better and with learning from the subordinate what he or she needs to be able to do better. There is more of an element of reciprocity in this role. It is quite consistent with new directions and values emerging in today's organizations.

_____

Source: Developed in part from Robert E. Quinn, Sue R. Faerman, Michael P. Thompson, and Michael R. McGrath, *Becoming a Master Manager: A Contemporary Framework* (New York: Wiley, 1990), p. 187. Used by permission.

-- -- -- ■ ASSESSMENT 20 ■ -- -- -- -- -- -- -- -- -- -- -- -- --

"T-P" Leadership Questionnaire

Instructions

The following items describe aspects of leadership behavior. Respond to each item according to the way you would most likely act if you were the leader of a work group. Circle how you would most likely behave in the described way: always (A), frequently (F), occasionally (O), seldom (S), or never (N).

A F O S N   **1.** I would most likely act as the spokesperson of the group.

A F O S N   **2.** I would encourage overtime work.

A F O S N   **3.** I would allow members complete freedom in their work.

A F O S N   **4.** I would encourage the use of uniform procedures.

A F O S N   **5.** I would permit the members to use their own judgment in solving problems.

A F O S N   **6.** I would stress being ahead of competing groups.

A F O S N   **7.** I would speak as a representative of the group.

A F O S N   **8.** I would push members for greater effort.

A F O S N   **9.** I would try out my ideas in the group.

A F O S N   **10.** I would let the members do their work the way they think best.

A F O S N   **11.** I would be working hard for a promotion.

A F O S N   **12.** I would tolerate postponement and uncertainty.

A F O S N   **13.** I would speak for the group if there were visitors present.

A F O S N   **14.** I would keep the work moving at a rapid pace.

A F O S N   **15.** I would turn the members loose on a job and let them go to it.

A F O S N   **16.** I would settle conflicts when they occur in the group.

A F O S N   **17.** I would get swamped by details.

A F O S N   **18.** I would represent the group at outside meetings.

A F O S N   **19.** I would be reluctant to allow the members any freedom of action.

A F O S N   **20.** I would decide what should be done and how it should be done.

A F O S N   **21.** I would push for increased performance.

A F O S N   **22.** I would let some members have authority which I could otherwise keep.

A F O S N   **23.** Things would usually turn out as I had predicted.

A F O S N   **24.** I would allow the group a high degree of initiative.

A F O S N **25.** I would assign group members to particular tasks.

A F O S N **26.** I would be willing to make changes.

A F O S N **27.** I would ask the members to work harder.

A F O S N **28.** I would trust the group members to exercise good judgment.

A F O S N **29.** I would schedule the work to be done.

A F O S N **30.** I would refuse to explain my actions.

A F O S N **31.** I would persuade others that my ideas are to their advantage.

A F O S N **32.** I would permit the group to set its own pace.

A F O S N **33.** I would urge the group to beat its previous record.

A F O S N **34.** I would act without consulting the group.

A F O S N **35.** I would ask that group members follow standard rules and regulations.

Interpretation

Score the instrument as follows.

a. Write a "1" next to each of the following items if you scored them as S (seldom) or N (never):

8, 12, 17, 18, 19, 30, 34, 35

b. Write a "1" next to each of the following items if you scored them as A (always) or F (frequently):

1, 2, 3, 4, 5, 6, 7, 9, 10, 11, 13, 14, 15, 16, 20, 21, 22, 23, 24, 25, 26, 27, 28, 29, 31, 32, 33

c. Circle the "1" scores for the following items, and then add them up to get your TOTAL "P" SCORE = _____.

3, 5, 8, 10, 15, 18, 19, 22, 23, 26, 28, 30, 32, 34, 35

d. Circle the "1" scores for the following items, and then add them up to get your TOTAL "T" SCORE = _____.

1, 2, 4, 6, 7, 9, 11, 12, 13, 14, 16, 17, 20, 21, 23, 25, 27, 29, 31, 33

e. Record your scores on the following graph to develop an indication of your tendencies toward task-oriented leadership, people-oriented leadership, and shared leadership. Mark your "T" and "P" scores on the appropriate lines, and then draw a line between these two points to determine your shared leadership score.

———————

Source: Modified slightly from "T-P Leadership Questionnaire," University Associates, Inc., 1987. Used by permission.

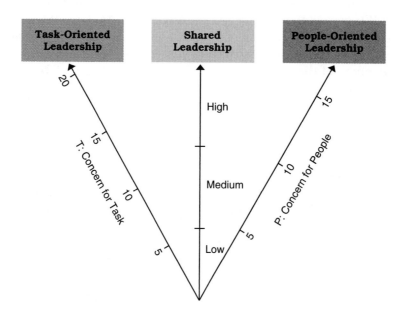

"T-t" Leadership Style

Instructions

For each of the following 10 pairs of statements, divide 5 points between the two according to your beliefs or perceptions of yourself or according to which of the two statements characterizes you better. The 5 points may be divided between the "a" and "b" statements in any one of the following ways: 5 for a, 0 for b; 4 for a, 1 for b; 3 for a, 2 for b; 1 for a, 4 for b; 0 for a, 5 for b, but not equally (2–1/2) between the two. Weigh your choices between the two according to which one characterizes you or your beliefs better.

1. (a) As leader I have a primary mission of maintaining stability.
   (b) As leader I have a primary mission of change.

2. (a) As leader I must cause events.
   (b) As leader I must facilitate events.

3. (a) I am concerned that my followers are rewarded equitably for their work.
   (b) I am concerned about what my followers want in life.

4. (a) My preference is to think long range: what might be.
   (b) My preference is to think short range: what is realistic.

5. (a) As a leader I spend considerable energy in managing separate but related goals.
   (b) As a leader I spend considerable energy in arousing hopes, expectations, and aspirations among my followers.

6. (a) Although not in a formal classroom sense, I believe that a significant part of my leadership is that of teacher.
   (b) I believe that a significant part of my leadership is that of facilitator.

7. (a) As leader I must engage with followers on an equal level of morality.
   (b) As leader I must represent a higher morality.

8. (a) I enjoy stimulating followers to want to do more.
   (b) I enjoy rewarding followers for a job well done.

9. (a) Leadership should be practical.
   (b) Leadership should be inspirational.

10. (a) What power I have to influence others comes primarily from my ability to get people to identify with me and my ideas.
    (b) What power I have to influence others comes primarily from my status and position.

Scoring

Circle your points for items 1b, 2a, 3b, 4a, 5b, 6a, 7b, 8a, 9b, 10a and add up the total points you allocated to these items; enter the score here [**T** = _____]. Next, add up the total points given to the uncircled items 1a, 2b, 3a, 4b, 5a, 6b, 7a, 8b, 9a, 10b; enter the score here [**t** = _____].

Interpretation

This instrument gives an impression of your tendencies toward "transformational" leadership (your "**T**" score) and "transactional" leadership (your "**t**" score). You may want to refer to the discussion of these concepts in Chapter 13. Today, a lot of attention is being given to the transformational aspects of leadership—those personal qualities that inspire a sense of vision and the desire for extraordinary accomplishment in followers.

Source: Questionnaire by W. Warner Burke, PhD. Used by permission.

Least-Preferred Co-worker Scale

Instructions

Think of all the different people with whom you have ever worked—in jobs, in social clubs, in student projects, or whatever. Next think of the *one person* with whom you could work *least* well—that is, the person with whom you had the most difficulty getting a job done. This is the one person—a peer, boss, or subordinate—with whom you would least want to work. Describe this person by circling numbers at the appropriate points on each of the following pairs of bipolar adjectives. Work rapidly. There are no right or wrong answers.

Pleasant	8 7 6 5 4 3 2 1	Unpleasant
Friendly	8 7 6 5 4 3 2 1	Unfriendly
Rejecting	1 2 3 4 5 6 7 8	Accepting
Tense	1 2 3 4 5 6 7 8	Relaxed
Distant	1 2 3 4 5 6 7 8	Close
Cold	1 2 3 4 5 6 7 8	Warm
Supportive	8 7 6 5 4 3 2 1	Hostile
Boring	1 2 3 4 5 6 7 8	Interesting
Quarrelsome	1 2 3 4 5 6 7 8	Harmonious
Gloomy	1 2 3 4 5 6 7 8	Cheerful
Open	8 7 6 5 4 3 2 1	Guarded
Backbiting	1 2 3 4 5 6 7 8	Loyal
Untrustworthy	1 2 3 4 5 6 7 8	Trustworthy
Considerate	8 7 6 5 4 3 2 1	Inconsiderate
Nasty	1 2 3 4 5 6 7 8	Nice
Agreeable	8 7 6 5 4 3 2 1	Disagreeable
Insincere	1 2 3 4 5 6 7 8	Sincere
Kind	8 7 6 5 4 3 2 1	Unkind

Scoring

This is called the "least-preferred co-worker scale" (LPC). Compute your LPC score by totaling all the numbers you circled; enter that score here [LPC = ____].

Interpretation

The LPC scale is used by Fred Fiedler to identify a person's dominant leadership style (see Chapter 13). Fiedler believes that this style is a relatively fixed part of one's personality and is therefore difficult to change. This leads Fiedler to his contingency views, which suggest that the key to leadership success is finding (or creating) good "matches" between style and situation. If your score is 73 or above, Fiedler considers you a "relationship-motivated" leader; if your score is 64 or below, he considers you a "task-motivated" leader. If your score is between 65 and 72, Fiedler leaves it up to you to determine which leadership style is most like yours.

Source: Fred E. Fiedler and Martin M. Chemers, *Improving Leadership Effectiveness: The Leader Match Concept,* 2nd ed. (New York: Wiley, 1984). Used by permission.

Student Engagement Survey

Instructions

Use the following scale to indicate the degree to which you agree with the statements that follow.

1—No agreement
2—Weak agreement
3—Some agreement
4—Considerable agreement
5—Very strong agreement

In the margin, write the number from the scale that best represents your level of agreement.

1. Do you know what is expected of you in this course?

2. Do you have the resources and support you need to do your coursework correctly?

3. In this course, do you have the opportunity to do what you do best all the time?

4. In the last week, have you received recognition or praise for doing good work in this course?

5. Does your instructor seem to care about you as a person?

6. Is there someone in the course who encourages your development?

7. In this course, do your opinions seem to count?

8. Does the mission/purpose of the course make you feel your study is important?

9. Are other students in the course committed to doing quality work?

10. Do you have a best friend in the course?

11. In the last six sessions, has someone talked to you about your progress in the course?

12. In this course, have you had opportunities to learn and grow?

Scoring

Score the instrument by adding up all your responses. A score of 0–24 suggests you are "actively disengaged" from the learning experience; a score of 25–47 suggests you are "moderately engaged"; a score of 48–60 indicates you are "actively engaged."

Interpretation

This instrument suggests the degree to which you are actively "engaged" or "disengaged" from the learning opportunities of your course. It is a counterpart to a survey used by the Gallup Organization to measure the "engagement" of American workers. The Gallup results are surprising—indicating that up to 19 percent of U.S. workers are actively disengaged, with the annual lost productivity estimated at some $300 billion per year. One has to wonder: What are the costs of academic disengagement by students?

Source: This survey was developed from a set of "Gallup Engagement Questions" presented in John Thackray, "Feedback for Real," *Gallup Management Journal* (March 15, 2001), retrieved from http:// gmj.gallup.com/management_articles/employee_engagement/article.asp?i=238&p= 1, June 5, 2003; data reported from James K. Harter, "The Cost of Disengaged Workers," Gallup Poll (March 13, 2001).

Job Design Choices

Instructions

People differ in what they like and dislike about their jobs. Listed below are 12 pairs of jobs. For each pair, indicate which job you would prefer. Assume that everything else about the jobs is the same—pay attention only to the characteristics actually listed for each pair of jobs. If you would prefer the job in Column A, indicate how much you prefer it by putting a check mark in a blank to the left of the Neutral point. If you prefer the job in Column B, check one of the blanks to the right of Neutral. Check the Neutral blank only if you find the two jobs equally attractive or unattractive. Try to use the Neutral blank sparingly.

Column A   **Column B**

1. A job that offers little or no challenge.

Strongly   Neutral   Strongly
prefer A   prefer B

A job that requires you to be completely isolated from co-workers.

2. A job that pays well.

Strongly   Neutral   Strongly
prefer A   prefer B

A job that allows considerable opportunity to be creative and innovative.

3. A job that often requires you to make important decisions.

Strongly   Neutral   Strongly
prefer A   prefer B

A job in which there are many pleasant people to work with.

4. A job with little security in a somewhat unstable organization.

Strongly   Neutral   Strongly
prefer A   prefer B

A job in which you have little or no opportunity to participate in decisions that affect your work.

5. A job in which greater responsibility is given to those who do the best work.

Strongly   Neutral   Strongly
prefer A   prefer B

A job in which greater responsibility is given to loyal employees who have the most seniority.

6. A job with a supervisor who sometimes is highly critical.

Strongly   Neutral   Strongly
prefer A   prefer B

A job that does not require you to use much of your talent.

7. A very routine job.

Strongly   Neutral   Strongly
prefer A   prefer B

A job in which your co-workers are not very friendly.

8. A job with a supervisor who respects you and treats you fairly.

Strongly   Neutral   Strongly
prefer A   prefer B

A job that provides constant opportunities for you to learn new and interesting things.

9. A job that gives you a real chance to develop yourself personally.

Strongly   Neutral   Strongly
prefer A   prefer B

A job with excellent vacation and fringe benefits.

10. A job in which there is a real chance you could be laid off.

Strongly   Neutral   Strongly
prefer A   prefer B

A job that offers very little chance to do challenging work.

11. A job that gives you little freedom and independence to do your work in the way you think best.

Strongly   Neutral   Strongly
prefer A   prefer B

A job with poor working conditions.

12. A job with very satisfying teamwork.

Strongly   Neutral   Strongly
prefer A   prefer B

A job that allows you to use your skills and abilities to the fullest extent.

Interpretation

People differ in their need for psychological growth at work. This instrument measures the degree to which you seek growth-need satisfaction. Score your responses as follows:

For items 1, 2, 7, 8, 11, and 12 give yourself the following points for each item:

1	2	3	4	5	6	7

Strongly   Neutral   Strongly
prefer A   prefer B

For items 3, 4, 5, 6, 9, and 10 give yourself the following points for each item:

7	6	5	4	3	2	1

Strongly   Neutral   Strongly
prefer A   prefer B

Add up all of your scores and divide by 12 to find the average. If you score above 4.0, your desire for growth-need satisfaction through work tends to be high, and you are likely to prefer an enriched job. If you score below 4.0, your desire for growth-need satisfaction through work tends to be low, and you are likely to not be satisfied or motivated with an enriched job.

Source: Reprinted by permission from J. R. Hackman and G. R. Oldham, _The Job Diagnostic Survey: An Instrument for the Diagnosis of Jobs and the Evaluation of Job Redesign Projects, Technical Report 4_ (New Haven, CT: Yale University, Department of Administrative Sciences, 1974).

ASSESSMENT 25

Cognitive Style

Instructions

This assessment is designed to get an impression of your cognitive style, based on the work of psychologist Carl Jung. For each of the following 12 pairs, place a "1" next to the statement that best describes you. Do this for each pair even though the description you choose may not be perfect.

1. ___ (a) I prefer to learn from experience.
   ___ (b) I prefer to find meanings in facts and how they fit together.

2. ___ (a) I prefer to use my eyes, ears, and other senses to find out what is going on.
   ___ (b) I prefer to use imagination to come up with new ways to do things.

3. ___ (a) I prefer to use standard ways to deal with routine problems.
   ___ (b) I prefer to use novel ways to deal with new problems.

4. ___ (a) I prefer ideas and imagination.
   ___ (b) I prefer methods and techniques.

5. ___ (a) I am patient with details but get impatient when they get complicated.
   ___ (b) I am impatient and jump to conclusions but am also creative, imaginative, and inventive.

6. ___ (a) I enjoy using skills already mastered more than learning new ones.
   ___ (b) I like learning new skills more than practicing old ones.

7. ___ (a) I prefer to decide things logically.
   ___ (b) I prefer to decide things based on feelings and values.

8. ___ (a) I like to be treated with justice and fairness.
   ___ (b) I like to be praised and to please other people.

9. ___ (a) I sometimes neglect or hurt other people's feelings without realizing it.
   ___ (b) I am aware of other people's feelings.

10. ___ (a) I give more attention to ideas and things than to human relationships.
    ___ (b) I can predict how others will feel.

11. ___ (a) I do not need harmony; arguments and conflicts don't bother me.
    ___ (b) I value harmony and get upset by arguments and conflicts.

12. ___ (a) I am often described as analytical, impersonal, unemotional, objective, critical, hard-nosed, rational.
    ___ (b) I am often described as sympathetic, people-oriented, unorganized, uncritical, understanding, ethical.

Scoring

Sum your scores as follows, and record them in the space provided. (Note that the Sensing and Feeling scores will be recorded as negatives.)

(–) *Sensing (S Type)* = 1a+2a+3a+4a+5a+6a

( ) *Intuitive (N Type)* = 1b+2b+3b+4b+5b+6b

( ) *Thinking (T Type)* = 7a+8a+9a+10a+11a+12a

(–) *Feeling (F Type)* = 7b+8b+9b+10b+11b+12b

Plot your scores on the following graph. Place an "X" at the point that indicates your suggested problem-solving style.

Interpretation

This assessment examines cognitive style through the contrast of personal tendencies toward information gathering (sensation vs. intuition) and information evaluation (feeling vs. thinking) in one's approach to problem solving. The result is a classification of four master cognitive styles and their characteristics. Read the descriptions and consider the implications of your suggested style, including how well you might work with persons whose styles are very different.

Sensation Thinkers: STs tend to emphasize the impersonal rather than the personal and take a realistic approach to problem solving. They like hard "facts," clear goals, certainty, and situations of high control.

Intuitive Thinkers: NTs are comfortable with abstraction and unstructured situations. They tend to be idealistic, prone toward intellectual and theoretical positions; they are logical and impersonal but also avoid details.

Intuitive Feelers: NFs prefer broad and global issues. They are insightful and tend to avoid details, being comfortable with intangibles; they value flexibility and human relationships.

Sensation Feelers: SFs tend to emphasize both analysis and human relations. They tend to be realistic and prefer facts; they are open communicators and sensitive to feelings and values.

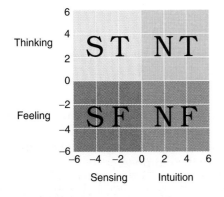

Source: Developed from Donald Bowen, "Learning and Problem-Solving: You're Never Too Jung," in Donald D. Bowen, Roy J. Lewicki, Donald T. Hall, and Francine S. Hall, eds., *Experiences in Management and Organizational Behavior,* 4th ed. (New York: Wiley, 1997), pp. 7–13; and John W. Slocum Jr., "Cognitive Style in Learning and Problem Solving," ibid., pp. 349–353.

ASSESSMENT 26

Internal/External Control

Instructions

Circle either "a" or "b" to indicate the item you most agree with in each pair of the following statements.

1. (a) Promotions are earned through hard work and persistence.
   (b) Making a lot of money is largely a matter of breaks.

2. (a) Many times the reactions of teachers seem haphazard to me.
   (b) In my experience I have noticed that there is usually a direct connection between how hard I study and the grades I get.

3. (a) The number of divorces indicates that more and more people are not trying to make their marriages work.
   (b) Marriage is largely a gamble.

4. (a) It is silly to think that one can really change another person's basic attitudes.
   (b) When I am right I can convince others.

5. (a) Getting promoted is really a matter of being a little luckier than the next guy.
   (b) In our society an individual's future earning power is dependent upon his or her ability.

6. (a) If one knows how to deal with people, they are really quite easily led.
   (b) I have little influence over the way other people behave.

7. (a) In my case the grades I make are the results of my own efforts; luck has little or nothing to do with it.
   (b) Sometimes I feel that I have little to do with the grades I get.

8. (a) People like me can change the course of world affairs if we make ourselves heard.
(b) It is only wishful thinking to believe that one can really influence what happens in society at large.

9. (a) Much of what happens to me is probably a matter of chance.
(b) I am the master of my fate.

10. (a) Getting along with people is a skill that must be practiced.
(b) It is almost impossible to figure out how to please some people.

Scoring

Give yourself 1 point for 1a, 2b, 3a, 4b, 5b, 6a, 7a, 8a, 9b, 10a.
8–10 = high *internal* locus of control
6–7 = moderate *internal* locus of control
5 = mixed locus of control
3–4 = moderate *external* locus of control

Interpretation

This instrument offers an impression of your tendency toward an *internal locus of control* or an *external locus of control*. Persons with a high internal locus of control tend to believe they have control over their own destinies. They may be most responsive to opportunities for greater self-control in the workplace. Persons with a high external locus of control tend to believe that what happens to them is largely in the hands of external people or forces. They may be less comfortable with self-control and more responsive to external controls in the workplace.

Source: Instrument from Julian P. Rotter, "External Control and Internal Control," *Psychology Today* (June 1971), p. 42. Used by permission.

ASSESSMENT 27

Team Leader Skills

Instructions

Consider your experience in groups and work teams. Ask: "What skills do I bring to team leadership situations?" Then, complete the following inventory by rating yourself on each item using this scale:

1 = Almost Never
2 = Seldom
3 = Sometimes
4 = Usually
5 = Almost Always

1 2 3 4 5   **1.** I facilitate communications with and among team members between team meetings.

1 2 3 4 5   **2.** I provide feedback/coaching to individual team members on their performance.

1 2 3 4 5   **3.** I encourage creative and "out-of-the-box" thinking.

1 2 3 4 5   **4.** I continue to clarify stakeholder needs/expectations.

1 2 3 4 5   **5.** I keep team members' responsibilities and activities focused within the team's objectives and goals.

1 2 3 4 5   **6.** I organize and run effective and productive team meetings.

1 2 3 4 5   **7.** I demonstrate integrity and personal commitment.

1 2 3 4 5   **8.** I have excellent persuasive and influencing skills.

1 2 3 4 5   **9.** I respect and leverage the team's cross-functional diversity.

1 2 3 4 5   **10.** I recognize and reward individual contributions to team performance.

1 2 3 4 5   **11.** I use the appropriate decision-making style for specific issues.

1 2 3 4 5   **12.** I facilitate and encourage border management with the team's key stakeholders.

1 2 3 4 5   **13.** I ensure that the team meets its team commitments.

1 2 3 4 5   **14.** I bring team issues and problems to the team's attention and focus on constructive problem solving.

1 2 3 4 5   **15.** I provide a clear vision and direction for the team.

Scoring

The inventory measures seven dimensions of team leadership. Add your scores for the items listed next to each dimension below to get an indication of your potential strengths and weaknesses.

1,9   Building the Team
2,10   Developing People
3,11   Team Problem Solving/Decision Making
4,12   Stakeholder Relations
5,13   Team Performance
6,14   Team Process
7,8,15   Providing Personal Leadership

Interpretation

The higher the score, the more confident you are on the particular skill and leadership capability. When considering the score, ask yourself if others would rate you the same way. Consider giving this inventory to people who have worked with you in teams and have them rate you. Compare the results to your self-assessment. Also, remember that it is doubtful that any one team leader is capable of exhibiting all the skills listed above. More and more, organizations are emphasizing "top-management teams" that blend a variety of skills, rather than depending on the vision of the single, heroic leader figure. As long as the necessary leadership skills are represented within the membership, it is more likely that the team will be healthy and achieve high performance. Of course, the more skills you bring with you to team leadership situations, the better.

Source: Developed from Lynda McDermott, Nolan Brawley, and William Waite, *World-Class Teams: Working across Borders* (New York: Wiley, 1998).

ASSESSMENT 28

Conflict Management Styles

Instructions

Think of how you behave in conflict situations in which your wishes differ from those of one or more other persons. In the space to the left of each of the following statements, write the number from the following scale that indicates how likely you are to respond that way in a conflict situation.

1=very unlikely   2=unlikely
3=likely   4=very likely

_____ 1. I am usually firm in pursuing my goals.

_____ 2. I try to win my position.

_____ 3. I give up some points in exchange for others.

_____ 4. I feel that differences are not always worth worrying about.

_____ 5. I try to find a position that is intermediate between the other person's and mine.

_____ 6. In approaching negotiations, I try to be considerate of the other person's wishes.

_____ 7. I try to show the logic and benefits of my positions.

_____ 8. I always lean toward a direct discussion of the problem.

_____ 9. I try to find a fair combination of gains and losses for both of us.

_____ 10. I attempt to work through our differences immediately.

_____ 11. I try to avoid creating unpleasantness for myself.

_____ 12. I try to soothe the other person's feelings and preserve our relationship.

_____ 13. I attempt to get all conerns and issues immediately out in the open.

_____ 14. I sometimes avoid taking positions that would create controversy.

_____ 15. I try not to hurt others' feelings.

Scoring

Total your scores for items 1, 2, 7; enter that score here [*Competing=____*]. Total your scores for items 8, 10, 13; enter that score here [*Collab-*

orating=____]. Total your scores for items 3, 5, 9; enter that score here [*Compromising*=____]. Total your scores for items 4, 11, 14; enter that score here [*Avoiding*=____]. Total your scores for items 6, 12, 15; enter that score here [*Accommodating*=____].

Interpretation

Each of the scores above corresponds to one of the conflict management styles discussed in Chapter 17. Research indicates that each style has a role to play in management but that the best overall conflict management approach is collaboration; only it can lead to problem solving and true conflict resolution. You should consider any patterns that may be evident in your scores and think about how to best handle the conflict situations in which you become involved.

Source: Adapted from Thomas-Kilmann, *Conflict Mode Instrument.* Copyright (c) 1974, Xicom, Inc., Tuxedo, NY 10987. Used by permission.

ASSESSMENT 29

Stress Self-Test

Instructions

Complete the following questionnaire. Circle the number that best represents your tendency to behave on each bipolar dimension.

Am casual about appointments	1 2 3 4 5 6 7 8	Am never late
Am not competitive	1 2 3 4 5 6 7 8	Am very competitive
Never feel rushed	1 2 3 4 5 6 7 8	Always feel rushed
Take things one at a time a time	1 2 3 4 5 6 7 8	Try to do many things at once
Do things slowly	1 2 3 4 5 6 7 8	Do things fast
Express feelings	1 2 3 4 5 6 7 8	"Sit" on feelings
Have many interests	1 2 3 4 5 6 7 8	Have few interests except work

Scoring

Total the numbers circled for all items, and multiply this by 3; enter the result here [____].

Interpretation

This scale is designed to measure your personality tendency toward Type A or Type B behaviors. As described in Chapter 15, a Type A personality is associated with high stress. Persons who are Type A tend to bring stress on themselves even in situations where others are relatively stress-free. This is an important characteristic to be able to identify in yourself and in others.

Points	Personality
120+	A+
106–119	A
100–105	A–
90–99	B+
below 90	B

Source: Adapted from R. W. Bortner. "A Short Rating Scale as a Potential Measure of Type A Behavior," *Journal of Chronic Diseases,* vol. 22 (1966), pp. 87–91. Used by permission.

Work-Life Balance

Instructions

Complete this inventory by circling the number that indicates the extent to which you agree or disagree with each of the following statements.

1. How much time do you spend on non-work-related activities such as taking care of family, spending time with friends, participating in sports, enjoying leisure time?
   Almost none/never   1 2 3 4 5   Very much/always

2. How often do family duties and non-work responsibilities make you feel tired out?
   Almost none/never   1 2 3 4 5   Very much/always

3. How often do you feel short of time for family-related and non-work activities?
   Almost none/never   1 2 3 4 5   Very much/always

4. How difficult is it for you to do everything you should as a family member and friend to others?
   Almost none/never   1 2 3 4 5   Very much/always

5. I often feel that I am being run ragged, with not enough time in a day to do everything and do it well.
   Completely disagree   1 2 3 4 5   Completely agree

6. I am given entirely too much work to do.
   Strongly disagree   1 2 3 4 5   Strongly agree

7. How much conflict do you feel there is between the demands of your job, your family, and the non-work activities in your life?
   Not at all/never   1 2 3 4 5   A lot/very often

8. How much does your job situation interfere with your family life?
   Not at all/never   1 2 3 4 5   A lot/very often

9. How much do your family life and nonwork activities interfere with your job?
   Not at all/never   1 2 3 4 5   A lot/very often

Scoring

1. Life Demand Score: Total items 1, 2, 3, and 4 and divide by 4.
2. Work Demand Score: Total items 5 and 6 and divide by 2.
3. Work-Life Conflict Score: Total items 7, 8, and 9 and divide by 3.

Your responses to items 1 through 4 are totaled and divided by 4, giving you the Life Demand score. Your responses to items 5 and 6 are totaled and divided by 2, resulting in your Work Demand score. Responses to items 7 through 9 are totaled and divided by 3, giving your Work-Life conflict score.

Interpretation

Compare yourself to these scores from a sample of Chinese and American workers. Are there any suprises in this comparison?

	U.S.	Chinese	Your Scores
Life Demand	3.53	2.58	_____
Work Demand	2.83	2.98	_____
Work-Life Conflict	2.53	2.30	_____

Work-life conflict is defined as "a form of interrole conflict in which the role pressures from the work and family nonwork domains are mutually noncompatible in some respect." Demands of one role make it difficult to satisfy demands of the others.

Source: Based on Nini Yang, Chao. D. Chen, Jaepil Choi, and Yimin Zou, "Sources of Work-Family Conflict: A Sino–U.S. Comparison of the Effects of Work and Family Demands," *Academy of Management Journal*, vol. 43, no. 1, pp. 113–123.

Chapter 1

1. d
2. c
3. a
4. b
5. a
6. a
7. c
8. a
9. b
10. b
11. c
12. a
13. b
14. c
15. c
16. Managers must value people and respect subordinates as mature, responsible, adult human beings. This is part of their ethical and social responsibility as persons to whom others report at work. The work setting should be organized and managed to respect the rights of people and their human dignity. Included among the expectations for ethical behavior would be actions to protect individual privacy, provide freedom from sexual harassment, and offer safe and healthy job conditions. Failure to do so is socially irresponsible. It may also cause productivity losses due to dissatisfaction and poor work commitments.
17. The manager is held accountable by her boss for performance results of her work unit. The manager must answer to her boss for unit performance. By the same token, the manager's subordinates must answer to her for their individual performance. They are accountable to her.
18. If the glass ceiling effect operates in a given situation, it would act as a hidden barrier to advancement beyond a certain level. Managers controlling promotions and advancement opportunities in the firm would not give them to African-American candidates, regardless of their capabilities. Although the newly hired graduates may progress for a while, sooner or later their upward progress in the firm would be halted by this invisible barrier.
19. Kenichi Ohmae uses the term "borderless world" to describe how more businesses are operating on a global scale. Globalization means that the countries and peoples of the world are increasingly interconnected and that business firms increasingly cross national boundaries in acquiring resources, getting work accomplished, and selling their products. This internationalization of work will affect most everyone in the new economy. People will be working with others from different countries, working in other countries, and certainly buying and using products and services produced in whole or in part in other countries. As countries become more interdependent economically, products are sold and resources purchased around the world, and business strategies increasingly target markets in more than one country.
20. One approach to this question is through the framework of essential management skills offered by Katz. At the first level of management, technical skills are important and I would feel capable in this respect. However, I would expect to learn and refine these skills through my work experiences. Human skills, the ability to work well with other people, will also be very important. Given the diversity anticipated for this team, I will need good human skills. Included here would be my emotional intelligence, or ability to understand my emotions and those of others when I am interacting with them. I will also have a leadership responsibility to help others on the team develop and utilize these skills so that the team itself can function effectively. Finally, I would expect opportunities to develop my conceptual or analytical skills in anticipation of higher-level appointments. In terms of personal development, I should recognize that the conceptual skills will increase in importance relative to the technical skills as I move upward in management responsibility. The fact that the members of the team will be diverse, with some of different demographic and cultural backgrounds from my own, will only increase the importance of my abilities in the human skills area. It will be a challenge to embrace and value differences to create the best work experience for everyone and to fully value everyone's potential contributions to the audits we will be doing. Conceptually I will need to understand the differences and try to utilize them to solve problems faced by the team, but in human relationships I will need to excel at keeping the team spirit alive and everyone committed to working well together over the life of our projects.

Chapter 2

1. b
2. a
3. c
4. c
5. c
6. d
7. b
8. a
9. c
10. b
11. d
12. c
13. d
14. b
15. d
16. The individualism view is that ethical behavior is that which best serves long-term interests. The justice view is that ethical behavior is fair and equitable in its treatment of people.
17. The rationalizations are believing that: (1) the behavior is not really illegal, (2) the behavior is really in everyone's best interests, (3) no one will find out, and (4) the organization will protect you.
18. The socioeconomic view of corporate social responsibility argues that socially responsible behavior is in a firm's long-run best interests. It should be good for profits, it creates a positive public image, it helps avoid government regulation, it meets public expectations, and it is an ethical obligation.
19. A Board of Directors of a business is ultimately responsible for the decisions and actions of the top management and the performance of the organization as a whole. The board members would normally be involved in such decisions as hiring/firing top management, setting compensation of top management, verifying and approving financial records and reports, and approving corporate strategies.
20. The manager could make a decision based on any one of the strategies. As an obstructionist, the manager may assume that Bangladesh needs

the business and that it is a local matter as to who will be employed to make the gloves. As a defensive strategy, the manager may decide to require the supplier to meet the minimum employment requirements under Bangladeshi law. Both of these approaches represent cultural relativism. As an accommodation strategy, the manager may require that the supplier go beyond local laws and meet standards set by equivalent laws in the United States. A proactive strategy would involve the manager in trying to set an example by operating in Bangladesh only with suppliers who not only meet local standards but also actively support the education of children in the communities in which they operate. These latter two approaches would be examples of universalism.

Chapter 3

1. c
2. b
3. d
4. a
5. a
6. b
7. a
8. c
9. a
10. a
11. c
12. a
13. d
14. c
15. b
16. Theory Y assumes that people are capable of taking responsibility and exercising self-direction and control in their work. The notion of self-fulfilling prophecies is that managers who hold these assumptions will act in ways that encourage workers to display these characteristics, thus confirming and reinforcing the original assumptions. The emphasis on greater participation and involvement in the modern workplace is an example of Theory Y assump-

tions in practice. Presumably, by valuing participation and involvement, managers will create self-fulfilling prophecies in which workers behave this way in response to being treated with respect. The result is a positive setting where everyone gains.
17. According to the deficit principle, a satisfied need is not a motivator of behavior. The social need will only motivate if it is deprived or in deficit. According to the progression principle, people move step by step up Maslow's hierarchy as they strive to satisfy needs. For example, once the social need is satisfied, the esteem need will be activated.
18. Contingency thinking takes an "if-then" approach to situations. It seeks to modify or adapt management approaches to fit the needs of each situation. An example would be to give more customer contact responsibility to workers who want to satisfy social needs at work, while giving more supervisory responsibilities to those who want to satisfy their esteem or ego needs.
19. The external environment is the source of the resources an organization needs to operate. In order to continue to obtain these resources, the organization must be successful in selling its goods and services to customers. If customer feedback is negative, the organization must make adjustments or risk losing the support needed to obtain important resources.
20. A bureaucracy operates with a strict hierarchy of authority, promotion based on competency and performance, formal rules and procedures, and written documentation. Enrique can do all of these things in his store, since the situation is probably quite stable and most work requirements are routine and predictable. However, bureaucracies are quite rigid and may

deny employees the opportunity to make decisions on their own. Enrique must be careful to meet the needs of the workers and not to make the mistake—identified by Argyris—of failing to treat them as mature adults. While remaining well organized, the store manager should still be able to help workers meet higher-order esteem and self-fulfillment needs as well as assume responsibility as would be consistent with McGregor's Theory Y assumptions.

Chapter 4

1. a
2. c
3. b
4. d
5. a
6. c
7. c
8. a
9. b
10. a
11. b
12. b
13. c
14. d
15. b
16. Possible operating objectives reflecting a commitment to competitive advantage through customer service include: (1) providing high-quality goods and services, (2) producing at low cost so that goods and services can be sold at low prices, (3) providing great service and short waiting times for goods and services, and (4) providing goods and services meeting unique customer needs.
17. Core values indicate important beliefs that underlie organizational expectations about the behavior and contributions of members. Sample values for high performance organizations might include expressed commitments to honesty and integrity, innovation, customer service, quality and respect for people.
18. The core culture of the organization consists of the values that shape and direct the behavior of members. Examples would be "honesty" and "quality" in everything that people do. Value-based management actively models such core values, communicates them, and encourages others to live up to them in their work. Responsibility for value-based management is shared by all managers from senior executives to first-level supervisors and team leaders.
19. Subcultures are important in organizations because of the many aspects of diversity found in the workforce. Although working in the same organization and sharing the same organizational culture, members differ in subculture affiliations based on such aspects as gender, age, and ethnic differences, as well as in respect to occupational and functional affiliations. It is important to understand how subculture differences may influence working relationships. For example, a 40-year-old manager of 20-year-old workers must understand that the values and behaviors of the younger workforce may not be totally consistent with what she or he believes in, and vice versa.
20. I disagree with this statement since a strong organizational or corporate culture can be a positive influence on any organization, large or small. Also, issues of diversity, inclusiveness, and multiculturalism apply as well. In fact, such things as a commitment to pluralism and respect for diversity should be part of the core values and distinguishing features of the organization's culture. The woman working for the large company is mistaken in thinking that the concepts do not apply to her friend's small business. In fact, the friend as owner and perhaps founder of the business should be working hard to establish the values and other elements that will create a strong and continuing culture and respect for diversity. Employees of any organization should have core organizational values to serve as reference points for their attitudes and behavior. The rites and rituals of everyday organizational life are also important ways to recognize positive accomplishments and add meaning to the employment relationships. It may even be that the friend's roles as creator and sponsor of the corporate culture and diversity leader are more magnified in the small-business setting. As the owner and manager, she is visible every day to all employees. How she acts will have a great impact on any "culture" that is established in her business.

Chapter 5

1. c
2. d
3. b
4. d
5. a
6. a
7. d
8. c
9. a
10. d
11. d
12. a
13. c
14. c
15. c
16. The relationship between an MNC and a host country should be mutually beneficial. Sometimes, however, host countries complain that MNCs take unfair advantage of them and do not include them in the benefits of their international operations. The complaints against MNCs include taking excessive profits out of the host country, hiring the best local labor, not respecting local laws and customs, and dominating the local economy. Engaging in corrupt practices is another important concern.

17. The power-distance dimension of national culture reflects the degree to which members of a society accept status and authority inequalities. Since organizations are hierarchies with power varying from top to bottom, the way power differences are viewed from one setting to the next is an important management issue. Relations between managers and subordinates or team leaders and team members will be very different in high-power-distance cultures than in low-power-distance ones. The significance of these differences is most evident in international operations when a manager from a high-power-distance culture has to perform in a low-power-distance one, or vice versa. In both cases, the cultural differences can cause problems as the manager deals with local workers.

18. In Project GLOBE the cultural dimension of institutional collectivism describes the degree to which members of a society emphasize and reward group as opposed to individual actions. In-group collectivism describes a society in which members take pride in family and their group or organizational memberships.

19. For each region of the world you should identify a major economic theme or issue or element. For example: Europe—the European Union should be discussed for its economic significance to member countries and to outsiders; the Americas—NAFTA should be discussed for its current implications as well as potential significance once Chile and other nations join; Asia—the Asia-Pacific Economic Forum should be identified as a platform for growing regional economic cooperation among a very economically powerful group of countries; Africa—the new nonracial democracy in South Africa should be cited as a stimulus to broader outside investor interest in Africa.

20. Kim must recognize that the cultural differences between the United States and Japan may affect the success of group-oriented work practices such as quality circles and work teams. The United States was the most individualistic culture in Hofstede's study of national cultures; Japan is much more collectivist. Group practices such as the quality circle and teams are natural and consistent with the Japanese culture. When introduced into a more individualistic culture, these same practices might cause difficulties or require some time for workers to get used to. At the very least, Kim should proceed with caution, discuss ideas for the new practices with the workers before making any changes, and then monitor the changes closely so that adjustments can be made to improve them as the workers gain familiarity with them and have suggestions of their own.

Chapter 6

1. c
2. a
3. b
4. b
5. b
6. a
7. d
8. a
9. b
10. a
11. b
12. d
13. c
14. b
15. d
16. Entrepreneurship is rich with diversity. It is an avenue for business entry and career success that is pursued by many women and members of minority groups. Data show almost 40 percent of U.S. businesses are owned by women. Many report leaving other employment because they had limited opportunities. For them, entrepreneurship made available the opportunities for career success that they lacked. Minority-owned businesses are one of the fastest-growing sectors, with the growth rates highest for Hispanic-owned, Asian-owned, and African-American-owned businesses in that order.

17. The three stages in the life cycle of an entrepreneurial firm are birth, breakthrough, and maturity. In the birth stage, the leader is challenged to get customers, establish a market, and find the money needed to keep the business going. In the breakthrough stage, the challenges shift to becoming and staying profitable, and managing growth. In the maturity stage, a leader is more focused on revising/maintaining a good business strategy and more generally managing the firm for continued success and possibly more future growth.

18. The limited partnership form of small business ownership consists of a general partner and one or more "limited partners." The general partner(s) play an active role in managing and operating the business; the limited partners do not. All contribute resources of some value to the partnership for the conduct of the business. The advantage of any partnership form is that the partners may share in profits, but their potential for losses is limited by the size of their original investments.

19. A venture capitalist, often a business, makes a living by investing in and taking ownership interests in fledgling companies with the goal eventually of large financial gains when the company is sold. An angel investor is an individual who is willing to make a financial investment in return for some ownership in the new firm.

20. My friend is right—it takes a lot of forethought and planning to prepare the launch of

a new business venture. In response to the question of how to ensure that I am really being customer-focused, I would ask and answer for myself the following questions. In all cases I would try to frame my business model so that the answers are realistic but still push my business toward a strong customer orientation. The "customer" questions might include: "Who are my potential customers? What market niche am I shooting for? What do the customers in this market really want? How do these customers make purchase decisions? How much will it cost to produce and distribute my product/service to these customers? How much will it cost to attract and retain customers?" Following an overall executive summary, which includes a commitment to this customer orientation, I would address the following areas in writing up my initial business plan. The plan would address such areas as company description—mission, owners, and legal form—as well as an industry analysis, product and services description, marketing description and strategy, staffing model, financial projections with cash flows, and capital needs.

Chapter 7

1. c
2. c
3. a
4. a
5. c
6. c
7. b
8. a
9. c
10. b
11. c
12. a
13. a
14. d
15. a
16. An optimizing decision is one that represents the absolute "best" choice of alternatives. It is selected from a set of all known alternatives. A satisficing decision selects the first alternative that offers a "satisfactory" choice, not necessarily the absolute best choice. It is selected from a limited or incomplete set of alternatives.
17. The ethics of a decision can be checked with the "spotlight" question: "How would you feel if your family found out?" "How would you feel if this were published in the local newspaper?" Also, one can test the decision by evaluating it on four criteria. (1) Utility—does it satisfy all stakeholders? (2) Rights—does it respect everyone's rights? (3) Justice—is it consistent with fairness and justice? (4) Caring—does it meet responsibilities for caring?
18. A manager using systematic thinking is going to approach problem solving in a logical and rational fashion. The tendency will be to proceed in a linear step-by-step fashion, handling one issue at a time. A manager using intuitive thinking will be more spontaneous and open in problem solving. He or she may jump from one stage in the process to the other and deal with many different things at once.
19. It almost seems contradictory to say that one can prepare for crisis, but it is possible. The concept of crisis management is used to describe how managers and others prepare for unexpected high-impact events that threaten an organization's health and well-being. Crisis management involves both anticipating possible crises and preparing teams and plans ahead of time for how to handle them if they do occur. Many organizations today, for example, are developing crisis management plans to deal with terrorism and computer "hacking" attacks.
20. This is what I would say in the mentoring situation—Continuing developments in information technology are changing the work setting for most employees. An important development for the traditional white-collar worker falls in the area of office automation—the use of computers and related technologies to facilitate everyday office work. In the "electronic office" of today and tomorrow, you should be prepared to work with and take full advantage of the following: smart workstations supported by desktop computers; voice messaging systems whereby computers take dictation, answer the telephone, and relay messages; database and word processing software systems that allow storage, access, and manipulation of data as well as the preparation of reports; electronic mail systems that send mail and data computer to computer; electronic bulletin boards for posting messages; and computer conferencing and videoconferencing that allow people to work with one another every day over great distances. These are among the capabilities of the new workplace. To function effectively, you must be prepared not only to use these systems to full advantage but also to stay abreast of new developments as they become available.

Chapter 8

1. d
2. a
3. b
4. d
5. b
6. c
7. a
8. d
9. a
10. b
11. a
12. c
13. c
14. d
15. a
16. The five steps in the formal planning process are: (1) Define your objectives, (2) determine where you stand relative to objectives, (3) develop premises

about future conditions, (4) identify and choose among action alternatives to accomplish objectives, (5) implement action plans and evaluate results.

17. Benchmarking is the use of external standards to help evaluate one's own situation and develop ideas and directions for improvement. The bookstore owner/manager might visit other bookstores in other towns which are known for their success. By observing and studying the operations of those stores and then comparing her store to them, the owner/manager can develop plans for future action.

18. Planning helps improve focus for organizations and for individuals. Essential to the planning process is identifying your objectives and specifying exactly where it is you hoped to get in the future. Having a clear sense of direction helps keep us on track by avoiding getting sidetracked on things that might not contribute to accomplishing our objectives. It also helps us to find discipline in stopping periodically to assess how well we are doing. With a clear objective, present progress can be realistically evaluated and efforts refocused on its accomplishment.

19. Very often plans fail because the people who make the plans aren't the same ones that must implement them. When people who will be implementing are allowed to participate in the planning process, at least two positive results may happen that help improve implementation. 1) Through involvement they better understand the final plans. 2) Through involvement they become more committed to making those plans work.

20. I would begin the speech by describing MBO as an integrated planning and control approach. I would also clarify that the key elements in MBO are objectives and participation. Any objectives should be clear, measurable, and time-defined. In addition, these objectives should be set with the full involvement and participation of the employees; they should not be set by the manager and then told to the employees. Given this, I would describe how each business manager should jointly set objectives with each of his or her employees and jointly review progress toward their accomplishment. I would suggest that the employees should work on the required activities while staying in communication with their managers. The managers, in turn, should provide any needed support or assistance to their employees. This whole process could be formally recycled at least twice per year.

Chapter 9

1. a
2. b
3. c
4. c
5. d
6. b
7. c
8. a
9. b
10. a
11. d
12. c
13. d
14. b
15. a
16. A corporate strategy sets long-term direction for an enterprise as a whole. Functional strategies set directions so that business functions such as marketing and manufacturing support the overall corporate strategy.
17. A SWOT analysis is useful during strategic planning. It involves the analysis of organizational strengths and weaknesses, and of environmental opportunities and threats.
18. An e-business strategy uses the Internet to help achieve sustainable competitive advantage. This can be done through B2B strategies that link businesses electronically with one another in business-to-business relationships. A good example is B2B in supply chain management, where suppliers are linked by the Internet and extranets to customers' information systems. They follow sales and track inventories in real time and ship new orders as needed. The B2C approach is more of a retailing model linking businesses to customers. An example is Amazon. com, which uses online sales and online customer interaction to sell its products.

19. Strategic leadership is the ability to enthuse people to participate in continuous change, performance enhancement, and the implementation of organizational strategies. The special qualities of the successful strategic leader include the ability to make trade-offs, create a sense of urgency, communicate the strategy, and engage others in continuous learning about the strategy and its performance responsibilities.

20. Porter's competitive strategy model involves the possible use of three alternative strategies: differentiation, cost leadership, and focus. In this situation, the larger department store seems better positioned to follow the cost leadership strategy. This means that Kim may want to consider the other two alternatives. A differentiation strategy would involve trying to distinguish Kim's products from those of the larger store. This might involve a "made in America" theme or an emphasis on leather or canvas or some other type of clothing material. A focus strategy might specifically target college students and try to respond to their tastes and needs rather than those of the the larger community population. This

might involve special orders and other types of individualized service for the college student market.

Chapter 10

1. b
2. a
3. b
4. a
5. b
6. c
7. b
8. b
9. a
10. a
11. c
12. b
13. b
14. c
15. b

16. The functional structure is prone to problems of internal coordination. One symptom may be that the different functional areas, such as marketing and manufacturing, are not working well together. This structure is also slow in responding to changing environmental trends and challenges. If the firm finds that its competitors are getting to market faster with new and better products, this is another potential indicator that the functional structure is not supporting operations properly.

17. A network structure often involves one organization "contracting out" aspects of its operations to other organizations that specialize in them. The example used in the text was of a company that contracted out its mailroom services. Through the formation of networks of contracts, the organization is reduced to a core of essential employees whose expertise is concentrated in the primary business areas. The contracts are monitored and maintained in the network to allow the overall operations of the organization to continue even though they are not directly accomplished by full-time employees.

18. The term "contingency" is used in management to indicate that management strategies and practices should be tailored to fit the unique needs of individual situations. There is no universal solution that fits all problems and circumstances. Thus, in organizational design, contingency thinking must be used to identify and implement particular organizational points in time. What works well at one point in time may not work well in another as the environment and other conditions change. For example, the more complex, variable, and uncertain the elements in the environment, the more difficult it is for the organization to operate. This situation calls for a more organic design. In a stable and more certain environment the mechanistic design is appropriate, since operations are more routine and predictable.

19. Differentiation and integration are somewhat conflicting in organizational design. As differentiation increases—that is, as more differences are present in the complexity of the organization—more integration is needed to ensure that everything functions together to the betterment of the whole organization. However, the greater the differentiation, the harder it is to achieve integration. Thus, when differentiation is high, organization design tends to shift toward the use of more complex horizontal approaches to integration and away from the vertical ones such as formal authority and rules or policies. In horizontal integration, the focus is on such things as cross-functional teams and matrix structures.

20. Faisal must first have confidence in the two engineers—he must trust them and respect their capabilities. Second, he must have confidence in himself—trusting his own judg-

ment to give up some work and allow these others to do it. Third, he should follow the rules of effective delegation. These include being very clear on what must be accomplished by each engineer. Their responsibilities should be clearly understood. He must also give them the authority to act in order to fulfill their responsibility, especially in relationship to the other engineers. And he must not forget his own final accountability for the results. He should remain in control and, through communication, make sure that work proceeds as planned.

Chapter 11

1. a
2. b
3. c
4. d
5. b
6. c
7. d
8. b
9. b
10. c
11. a
12. a
13. b
14. a
15. d

16. Internal recruitment deals with job candidates who already know the organization well. It is also a strong motivator because it communicates to everyone the opportunity to advance in the organization through hard work. External recruitment may allow the organization to obtain expertise not available internally. It also brings in employees with new and fresh viewpoints who are not biased by previous experience in the organization.

17. Orientation activities introduce a new employee to the organization and the work environment. This is a time when the individual may develop key attitudes and when performance expectations will also be established. Good orientation communicates positive attitudes and expectations

and reinforces the desired organizational culture. It formally introduces the individual to important policies and procedures that everyone is expected to follow.

18. The graphic rating scale simply asks a supervisor to rate an employee on an established set of criteria, such as quantity of work or attitude toward work. This leaves a lot of room for subjectivity and debate. The behaviorally anchored rating scale asks the supervisor to rate the employee on specific behaviors that had been identified as positively or negatively affecting performance in a given job. This is a more specific appraisal approach and leaves less room for debate and disagreement.

19. Mentoring is when a senior and experienced individual adopts a newcomer or more junior person with the goal of helping him or her develop into a successful worker. The mentor may or may not be the individual's immediate supervisor. The mentor meets with the individual and discusses problems, shares advice, and generally supports the individual's attempts to grow and perform. Mentors are considered very useful for persons newly appointed to management positions.

20. As Sy's supervisor, you face a difficult but perhaps expected human resource management problem. Not only is Sy influential as an informal leader, he also has considerable experience on the job and in the company. Even though he is experiencing performance problems using the new computer system, there is no indication that he doesn't want to work hard and continue to perform for the company. Although retirement is an option, Sy may also be transferred, promoted, or simply terminated. The latter response seems unjustified and may cause legal problems. Transferring Sy, with his agreement, to another position could be a positive move; promoting Sy to a supervisory position in which his experience and networks would be useful is another possibility. The key in this situation seems to be moving Sy out so that a computer-literate person can take over the job, while continuing to utilize Sy in a job that better fits his talents. Transfer and/or promotion should be actively considered both in his and in the company's interest.

Chapter 12

1. b
2. a
3. b
4. c
5. c
6. b
7. c
8. a
9. d
10. a
11. a
12. d
13. b
14. a
15. a
16. A product innovation is one that results in a new or substantially modified product that an organization can sell or offer to its customers. A process innovation is a new or improved way of getting work done in the organization. A business model innovation is a new way to earn money as a business or earn clients as nonprofit.

17. Lewin's three phases of planned change are: Unfreezing—preparing a system for change; changing—moving or creating change in a system; and refreezing—stabilizing and reinforcing change once it has occurred.

18. In general, managers can expect that others will be more committed and loyal to changes that are brought about through shared power strategies. Rational persuasion strategies can also create enduring effects if they are accepted. Force-coercion strategies tend to have temporary effects only.

19. The statement that "OD equals planned change plus" basically refers to the fact that OD tries both to create change in an organization and to make the organization members capable of creating such change for themselves in the future.

20. In any change situation, it is important to remember that successful planned change occurs only when all three phases of change—unfreezing, changing, and refreezing—have been taken care of. Thus, I would not rush into the changing phase. Rather, I would work with the people involved to develop a felt need for change based on their ideas and inputs as well as mine. Then I would proceed by supporting the changes and helping to stabilize them into everyday routines. I would also be sensitive to any resistance and respect that resistance as a signal that something important is being threatened. By listening to resistance, I would be in a position to better modify the change to achieve a better fit with the people and the situation. Finally, I would want to take maximum advantage of the shared power strategy, supported by rational persuasion, and with limited use of force-coercion (if it is used at all). By doing all of this, I would like my staff to feel empowered and committed to constructive improvement through planned change.

Chapter 13

1. d
2. d
3. b
4. a
5. c
6. a
7. b
8. c
9. b

10. a
11. b
12. a
13. d
14. a
15. b
16. Position power is based on reward, coercion or punishment, and legitimacy or formal authority. Managers, however, need to have more power than that made available to them by the position alone. Thus, they have to develop personal power through expertise and reference. This personal power is essential in helping managers to get things done beyond the scope of their position power alone.
17. Leader-participation theory suggests that leadership effectiveness is determined in part by how well managers or leaders handle the many different problem or decision situations that they face every day. Decisions can be made through individual or authority, consultative, or group-consensus approaches. No one of these decision methods is always the best; each is a good fit for certain types of situations. A good manager or leader is able to use each of these approaches and knows when each is the best approach to use in various situations.
18. The three variables used in Fiedler's model to diagnose situational favorableness are: (1) Position power—how much power the leader has in terms of rewards, punishments, and legitimacy. (2) Leader-member relations—the quality of relationships between the leader and followers. (3) Task structure—the degree to which the task is clear and well defined, or open-ended and more ambiguous.
19. Drucker says that good leaders have more than the "charisma" or "personality" being popularized in the concept of transformational leadership. He reminds us that good leaders work hard to accomplish some basic things in their everyday activities. These include: (1) establishing a clear sense of mission, (2) accepting leadership as a responsibility, not a rank, and (3) earning and keeping the respect of others.
20. In his new position, Marcel must understand that the transactional aspects of leadership are not sufficient to guarantee him long-term leadership effectiveness. He must move beyond the effective use of task-oriented and people-oriented behaviors and demonstrate through his personal qualities the capacity to inspire others. A charismatic leader develops a unique relationship with followers in which they become enthusiastic, highly loyal, and high achievers. Marcel needs to work very hard to develop positive relationships with the team members. He must emphasize in those relationships high aspirations for performance accomplishments, enthusiasm, ethical behavior, integrity, and honesty in all dealings, and a clear vision of the future. By working hard with this agenda and by allowing his personality to positively express itself in the team setting, Marcel should make continuous progress as an effective and moral leader.

Chapter 14

1. c
2. d
3. d
4. b
5. b
6. d
7. c
8. d
9. a
10. b
11. c
12. a
13. b
14. a
15. b
16. People high in need for achievement will prefer work settings and jobs in which they have (1) challenging but achievable goals, (2) individual responsibility, and (3) performance feedback.
17. Participation is important to goal-setting theory because, in general, people tend to be more committed to the accomplishment of goals they have helped to set. When people participate in the setting of goals, they also understand them better. Participation in goal setting improves goal acceptance and understanding.
18. Maslow, McClelland, and Herzberg would likely find common agreement in respect to a set of "higher order" needs. For Maslow these are self-actualization and ego; they correspond with Alderfer's growth needs, and with McClelland's needs for achievement and power. Maslow's social needs link up with relatedness needs in Alderfer's theory and need for affiliation in McClelland's theory. Maslow's safety needs correspond to Alderfer's existence needs.
19. The compressed workweek, or 4-40 schedule, offers employees the advantage of a three-day weekend. However, it can cause problems for the employer in terms of ensuring that operations are covered adequately during the normal five workdays of the week. Labor unions may resist, and the compressed workweek will entail more complicated work scheduling. In addition, some employees find that the schedule is tiring and can cause family adjustment problems.
20. It has already been pointed out in the answer to question 16 that a person with a high need for achievement likes moderately challenging goals and performance feedback. Participation of both manager and subordinate in goal setting offers an opportunity to choose goals to which the subordinate will respond and which also will serve the organization.

Furthermore, through goal setting, the manager and individual subordinates can identify performance standards or targets. Progress toward these targets can be positively reinforced by the manager. Such reinforcements can serve as indicators of progress to someone with high need for achievement, thus responding to their desires for performance feedback.

Chapter 15

1. c
2. b
3. d
4. a
5. c
6. d
7. b
8. c
9. a
10. b
11. d
12. d
13. c
14. a
15. c
16. A psychological contract is the individual's view of the inducements he or she expects to receive from the organization in return for his or her work contributions. The contract is healthy when the individual perceives that the inducements and contributions are fair and in a state of balance.
17. Self-serving bias is the attribution tendency to blame the environment when things go wrong—"It's not my fault, 'they' caused all this mess." Fundamental attribution error is the tendency to blame others for problems that they have—"It's something wrong with 'you' that's causing the problem."
18. All the Big Five personality traits are relevant to the workplace. To give some basic examples, consider the following. Extraversion suggests whether or not a person will reach out to relate and work well with others. Agreeableness suggests whether or not

a person is open to the ideas of others and willing to go along with group decisions. Conscientiousness suggests whether someone can be depended on to meet commitments and perform agreed-upon tasks. Emotional stability suggests whether or not someone will be relaxed and secure, or uptight and tense, in work situations. Openness to experience suggests whether someone will be open to new ideas or resistant to change.
19. The Type A personality is characteristic of people who bring stress on themselves by virtue of personal characteristics. These tend to be compulsive individuals who are uncomfortable waiting for things to happen, who try to do many things at once, and who generally move fast and have difficulty slowing down. Type A personalities can be stressful for both the individuals and the people around them. Managers must be aware of Type A personality tendencies in their own behavior and among others with whom they work. Ideally, this awareness will help the manager take precautionary steps to best manage the stress caused by this personality type.
20. Scott needs to be careful. Although there is modest research support for the relationship between job satisfaction and performance, there is no guarantee that simply doing things to make people happier at work will cause them to be higher performers. Scott needs to take a broader perspective on this issue and his responsibilities as a manager. He should be interested in job satisfaction for his therapists and do everything he can to help them to experience it. But he should also be performance oriented and understand that performance is achieved through a combination of skills, support, and motivation. He

should be helping the therapists to achieve and maintain high levels of job competency. He should also work with them to find out what obstacles they are facing and what support they need—things that perhaps he can deal with in their behalf. All of this relates as well to research indications that performance can be a source of job satisfaction. And finally, Scott should make sure that the therapists believe they are being properly rewarded for their work since rewards are shown by research to have an influence on both job satisfaction and job performance.

Chapter 16

1. d
2. b
3. b
4. d
5. b
6. d
7. b
8. c
9. a
10. b
11. c
12. b
13. a
14. b
15. a
16. Input factors can have a major impact on group effectiveness. In order to best prepare a group to perform effectively, a manager should make sure that the right people are put in the group (maximize available talents and abilities), that these people are capable of working well together (membership characteristics should promote good relationships), that the tasks are clear, and that the group has the resources and environment needed to perform up to expectations.
17. A group's performance can be analyzed according to the interaction between cohesiveness and performance norms. In a highly cohesive group, members tend to conform to group norms. Thus, when the

performance norm is positive and cohesion is high, we can expect everyone to work hard to support the norm-high performance is likely. By the same token, high cohesion and a low performance norm will act similarly—low performance is likely. With other combinations of norms and cohesion, the performance results will be more mixed.

18. The textbook lists several symptoms of groupthink along with various strategies for avoiding groupthink. For example, a group whose members censure themselves from contributing "contrary" or "different" opinions and/or whose members keep talking about outsiders as "weak" or the "enemy" may be suffering from groupthink. This may be avoided or corrected, for example, by asking someone to be the "devil's advocate" for a meeting and by invitingin an outside observer to help gather different viewpoints.

19. In a traditional work group, the manager or supervisor directs the group. In a self-managing team, the members of the team provide self-direction. They plan, organize, and evaluate their work, share tasks, and help one another develop skills; they may even make hiring decisions. A true self-managing team does not need the traditional "boss" or supervisor, since the team as a whole takes on the supervisory responsibilities.

20. Marcos is faced with a highly cohesive group whose members conform to a negative or low-performance norm. This is a difficult situation that is ideally resolved by changing the performance norm. In order to gain the group's commitment to a high-performance norm, Marcos should act as a positive role model for the norm. He must communicate the norm clearly and positively to the group. He should not assume that

everyone knows what he expects of them. He may also talk to the informal leader and gain his or her commitment to the norm. He might carefully reward high-performance behaviors within the group. He may introduce new members with high-performance records and commitments. And he might hold group meetings in which performance standards and expectations are discussed, with an emphasis on committing to new high-performance directions. If his attempts to introduce a high-performance norm fail, Marcos may have to take steps to reduce group cohesiveness so that individual members can pursue higher-performance results without feeling bound by group pressures to restrict their performance.

Chapter 17

1. b
2. a
3. c
4. b
5. c
6. b
7. b
8. d
9. c
10. a
11. d
12. b
13. d
14. d
15. a
16. The manager's goal in active listening is to help the subordinate say what he or she really means. To do this, the manager should carefully listen for the content of what someone is saying, paraphrase or reflect back what the person appears to be saying, remain sensitive to nonverbal cues and feelings, and not be evaluative.
17. The inverted "U" curve of conflict intensity shows that as conflict intensity increases from low to moderate levels, performance increases. This is the zone of constructive

conflict. As conflict intensity moves into extreme levels, performance tends to decrease. This is the zone of destructive conflict.

18. Win-lose outcomes are likely when conflict is managed through high-assertiveness and low-cooperativeness styles. In this situation of competition, the conflict is resolved by one person or group dominating another. Lose-lose outcomes occur when conflict is managed through avoidance (where nothing is resolved) and possibly when it is managed through compromise (where each party gives up something to the other). Win-win outcomes are associated mainly with problem solving and collaboration in conflict management, which is a result of high assertiveness and high cooperativeness.

19. In a negotiation, both substance and relationship goals are important. Substance goals relate to the content of the negotiation. A substance goal, for example, may relate to the final salary agreement between a job candidate and a prospective employer. Relationship goals relate to the quality of the interpersonal relationships among the negotiating parties. Relationship goals are important because the negotiating parties most likely have to work together in the future. For example, if relationships are poor after a labor-management negotiation, the likelihood is that future problems will occur.

20. Kathy can do a number of things to establish and maintain a system of upward communication for her department store branch. To begin, she should, as much as possible, try to establish a highly interactive style of management based upon credibility and trust. Credibility is earned through building personal power through expertise and reference. With credibility, she might set the tone for the

department managers by using MBWA—"managing by wandering around." Once this pattern is established, trust will build between her and other store employees, and she should find that she learns a lot from interacting directly with them. Kathy should also set up a formal communication structure, such as bimonthly store meetings, where she communicates store goals, results, and other issues to the staff, and in which she listens to them in return. An e-mail system whereby Kathy and her staff could send messages to one another from their workstation computers would also be beneficial.

Chapter 18

1. a
2. b
3. d
4. b
5. b
6. a
7. d
8. b
9. b
10. c
11. a
12. b
13. c
14. c
15. c
16. The four steps in the formal planning process are: (1) establish objectives and standards, (2) measure actual performance, (3) compare actual performance with objectives and standards and (4) take necessary action.
17. Feedforward control involves the careful selection of system inputs to assure that outcomes are of the desired quality and up to all performance standards. In the case of a local bookstore, one of the major points of influence over performance and customer satisfaction is the relationship between the customers and the persons in the store's employ that serve them. Thus, a good example of feedforward

control is exercising great care when the manager hires new employees and then trains them to work according to the store's expectations.
18. Douglas McGregor's concept of Theory Y involves the assumption that people can be trusted to exercise self-control in their work. This is the essence of internal control— people controlling their own work by taking personal responsibility for results. If managers approach work with McGregor's Theory Y assumptions, they will, according to him, promote more self-control or internal control by people at work.
19. A progressive discipline system works by adjusting the discipline to fit the severity and frequency of the inappropriate behavior. In the case of a person who comes late to work, for example, progressive discipline might involve a verbal warning after 3 late arrivals, a written warning after 5, and a pay-loss penalty after 7. In the case of a person who steals money from the business, there would be immediate dismissal after the first such infraction.
20. There are a very large number of activities required to complete a new student center building on a college campus. Among them one might expect the following to be core requirements—(1) land surveys—and planning permissions from local government, (2) architect plans developed and approved, (3) major subcontractors hired, (4) site excavation completed, (5) building exterior completed, (6) building interior completed and furnishings installed. Use Figure 18.5 from the chapter as a guide for developing your AON diagram.

Chapter 19

1. c
2. c
3. c
4. a

5. a
6. b
7. d
8. d
9. b
10. c
11. b
12. c
13. b
14. c
15. a
16. Possible operating objectives reflecting a commitment to competitive advantage through customer service include: (1) providing high-quality goods and services, (2) producing at low cost so that goods and services can be sold at low prices, (3) providing short waiting times for goods and services, and (4) providing goods and services meeting unique customer needs.
17. External customers are the consumers or clients in the specific environment who buy the organization's goods or use its services. Internal customers are found internally in the workflows among people and subsystems in the organization. They are individuals or groups within the organization who utilize goods and services produced by others also inside the organization.
18. Douglas McGregor's concept of Theory Y involves the assumption that people can be trusted to exercise self-control in their work. This is the essence of internal control—people controlling their own work by taking personal responsibility for results. If manager's approach work with McGregor's Theory Y assumptions, they will, according to him, promote more self-control or internal control by people at work.
19. The focus of process reengineering is on reducing costs and streamlining operations efficiency while improving customer service. This is accomplished by closely examining core business processes through the following sequence of activities: (1) iden-

tify the core processes; (2) map them in a workflows diagram; (3) evaluate all tasks involved; (4) seek ways to eliminate unnecessary tasks; (5) seek ways to eliminate delays, errors, and misunderstandings in the workflows; and (6) seek efficiencies in how work is shared and transferred among people and departments.

20. Although the appropriateness of the measure would vary by department or area of each organization that one is addressing, possible productivity measures are:

(a) U.S. Post Office—# letters delivered per day / # letter carriers on payroll

(b) University—# students enrolled / (# full-time + part-time faculty)

(c) Hospital—# patients per day / # available hospital beds

(d) Amusement Park—# paid admissions per day / # available rides

(e) Restaurant—# meals served per day / # servers on payroll

Glossary

Accommodation or smoothing plays down differences and highlights similarities to reduce conflict.

An **accommodative strategy** accepts social responsibility and tries to satisfy economic, legal, and ethical critera.

Accountability is the requirement to show performance results to a supervisor.

Action research is a collaborative process of collecting data, using it for action planning, and valuating the results.

Active listening helps the source of a message say what he or she really means.

An **adaptive organization** operates with a minimum of bureaucratic features and encourages worker empowerment and teamwork.

An **administrator** is a manager in a public or nonprofit organization.

Affirmative action is an effort to give preference in employment to women and minority group members.

An **after-action review** identifies lessons learned through a completed project, task force assignment, or special operation.

Agreeableness is being good-natured, cooperative, and trusting.

An **amoral manager** fails to consider the ethics of her or his behavior.

An **angel investor** is a wealthy individual willing to invest in return for equity in a new venture.

In **arbitration** a neutral third party issues a binding decision to resolve a dispute.

An **assessment center** examines how job candidates handle simulated work situations.

An **attitude** is a predisposition to act in a certain way.

Attribution is a process of explaining events.

Fundamental **attribution error** overestimates internal factors and underestimates external factors as influences on someone's behavior.

Authentic leadership activates positive psychological states to achieve self-awareness and positive self-regulation.

Authoritarianism is the degree to which a person tends to defer to authority.

An **authority decision** is made by the leader and then communicated to the group.

A leader with an **autocratic style** acts in a unilateral, command-and-control fashion.

Automation is the total mechanization of a job.

Avoidance pretends that a conflict doesn't really exist.

B

A **B2B business strategy** uses IT and Web portals to link organizations vertically in supply chains.

A **B2C business strategy** uses IT and Web portals to link businesses with customers.

A **bargaining zone** is the area between one party's minimum reservation point and the other party's maximum reservation point.

Base compensation is a salary or hourly wage paid to an individual.

The **BCG matrix** analyzes business opportunities according to market growth rate and market share.

The **behavioral decision model** describes decision making with limited information and bounded rationality.

A **behaviorally anchored rating scale** uses specific descriptions of actual behaviors to rate various levels of performance.

Benchmarking uses external comparisons to gain insights for planning.

BATNA is the best alternative to a negotiated agreement.

Best practices are things that lead to superior performance.

Biculturalism is when minority members adopt characteristics of majority cultures in order to succeed.

Bona fide occupational qualifications are employment criteria justified by capacity to perform a job.

In **bottom-up change**, change initiatives come from all levels in the organization.

A **boundaryless organization** eliminates internal boundaries among subsystems and external boundaries with the external environment.

Brainstorming engages group members in an open, spontaneous discussion of problems and ideas.

Break-even analysis calculates the point at which revenues cover costs under different "what if" conditions.

The **break-even point** is where revenues=costs.

A **budget** is a plan that commits resources to projects or activities.

A **bureaucracy** is a rational and efficient form of organization founded on logic, order, and legitimate authority.

A **bureaucracy** emphasizes formal authority, order, fairness, and efficiency.

Business model innovation results in ways for firms to make money.

A **business plan** describes the direction for a new business and the financing needed to operate it.

A **business strategy** identifies how a division or strategic business unit will compete in its product or service domain.

C

A **career** is a sequence of jobs that constitutes what a person does for a living.

Career planning is the process of matching career goals and individual capabilities with opportunities for their fulfillment.

A **career plateau** is a position from which someone is unlikely to move to a higher level of work responsibility.

Centralization is the concentration of authority for most decisions at the top level of an organization.

In a **centralized communication network**, communication flows only between individual members and a hub or center point.

A **certain environment** offers complete information on possible action alternatives and their consequences

The **chain of command** links all persons with successively higher levels of authority.

A **change leader** is a *change agent* who tries to change the behavior of another person or social system.

Changing is the phase where a planned change actually takes place.

Channel richness is the capacity of a communication channel to effectively carry information.

A **charismatic leader** develops special leader-follower relationships and inspires followers in extraordinary ways.

Child labor is the full-time employment of children for work otherwise done by adults.

The **classical decision model** describes decision making with complete information.

Coaching occurs as an experienced person offers performance advice to a less-experienced person.

A **code of ethics** is a formal statement of values and ethical standards.

Coercive power is the capacity to punish or withhold positive outcomes as a means of influencing other people.

Cognitive dissonance is discomfort felt when attitude and behavior are inconsistent.

Cohesiveness is the degree to which members are attracted to and motivated to remain part of a team.

Collaboration or problem solving involves working through conflict differences and solving problems so everyone wins.

Collective bargaining is the process of negotiating, administering, and interpreting a labor contract.

Commercializing innovation turns ideas into economic value added.

A **committee** is designated to work on a special task on a continuing basis.

Communication is the process of sending and receiving symbols with meanings attached.

Comparable worth holds that persons performing jobs of similar importance should be paid at comparable levels.

Comparative management studies how management practices differ among countries and cultures.

Competition or authoritative command uses force, superior skill, or domination to "win" a conflict.

A **competitive advantage** allows an organization to deal with market and environmental forces better than its competitors.

A **competitive advantage** comes from operating in successful ways that are difficult to imitate.

Competitive advantage is the ability to outperform one's competitors.

A **compressed work week** allows a full-time job to be completed in less than five days.

Compromise occurs when each party to the conflict gives up something of value to the other.

Growth through **concentration** is within the same business area.

A **conceptual skill** is the ability to think analytically and solve complex problems.

Concurrent control focuses on what happens during the work process.

Conflict is a disagreement over issues of substance and/or an emotional antagonism.

Conflict resolution is the removal of the substantial and/or emotional reasons for a conflict.

Conscientiousness is being responsible, dependable, and careful.

Constructive stress acts in a positive way to increase effort, stimulate creativity, and encourage diligence in one's work.

A **consultative decision** is made by a leader after receiving information, advice, or opinions from group members.

Contingency planning identifies alternative courses of action to take when things go wrong.

Contingency thinking tries to match management practices with situational demands.

Contingency workers are employed on a part-time and temporary basis to supplement a permanent workforce.

Continuous improvement is a process of always looking for new ways to improve.

Continuous improvement involves always searching for new ways to improve work quality and performance.

In **continuous-process production** raw materials are continuously transformed by an automated system.

Controlling is the process of measuring performance and taking action to ensure desired results.

Co-opetition is the strategy of working with rivals on projects of mutual benefit.

A **core competency** is a special strength that gives an organization a competitive advantage.

Core values are beliefs and values shared by organization members.

Corporate governance is oversight of a company's management by a board of directors.

A **corporate strategy** sets long-term direction for the total enterprise.

A **corporation** is a legal entity that exists separately from its owners.

Corruption involves illegal practices to further one's business interests.

A **cost leadership strategy** seeks to operate with lower costs than competitors

Cost-benefit analysis involves comparing the costs and benefits of each potential course of action.

CPM/PERT is a combination of the *critical path method* and the *Program evaluation and review technique.*

Creativity is the generation of a novel idea or unique approach that solves a problem or crafts an opportunity.

Credibility is trust, respect, and integrity in the eyes of others.

A **crisis** is an unexpected problem that can lead to disaster if not resolved quickly and appropriately.

Crisis management is preparation for the management of crises that threaten an organization's health and well-being.

The **critical-incident technique** keeps a log of someone's effective and ineffective job behaviors.

A **cross-functional team** operates with members who come from different functional units of an organization.

Cultural intelligence is the ability to accept and adopt to new cultures.

Cultural relativism suggests there is no one right way to behave; ethical behavior is determined by its cultural context.

Culture is a shared set of beliefs, values, and patterns of behavior common to a group of people.

Culture shock is the confusion and discomfort a person experiences when in an unfamiliar culture.

Customer relationship management strategically tries to build lasting relationships with, and to add value to, customers.

A **customer structure** groups together people and jobs that serve the same customers or clients.

D

Data are raw facts and observations.

Debt financing involves borrowing money that must be repaid over time with interest.

Decentralization is the dispersion of authority to make decisions throughout all organization levels.

A **decentralized communication network** allows all members to communicate directly with one another.

A **decision** is a choice among possible alternative courses of action.

The **decision-making process** begins with identification of a problem and ends with evaluation of implemented solutions.

A **defensive strategy** seeks protection by doing the minimum legally required.

Delegation is the process of distributing and entrusting work to other persons.

A leader with a **democratic style** encourages participation with an emphasis on both task accomplishment and development of people.

Departmentalization is the process of grouping together people and jobs into work units.

Destructive stress impairs the performance of an individual.

Differentiation is the degree of difference between subsystems in an organization.

A **differentiation strategy** offers products that are unique and different from the competition.

Discipline is the act of influencing behavior through reprimand.

Discrimination actively denies minority members the full benefits of organizational membership.

Discrimination occurs when someone is denied a job or job assignment for reasons not job relevant.

Distributive justice is concerned that people are treated the same regardless of personal characteristics.

Distributive negotiation focuses on win-lose claims made by each party for certain preferred outcomes.

Growth through **diversification** is by acquisition of or investment in new and different business areas.

The term **diversity** describes race, gender, age, and other individual differences.

Divestiture sells off parts of the organization to refocus attention on core business areas.

A **divisional structure** groups together people working on the same product, in the same area, with similar customers, or on the same processes.

Downsizing decreases the size of operations.

Dysfunctional conflict is destructive and hurts task performance.

E

An **e-business strategy** strategically uses the Internet to gain competitive advantage.

Inventory control by **economic order quantity** orders replacements whenever inventory level falls to a predetermined point.

In **effective communication** the intended meaning is fully understood by the receiver.

An **effective team** achieves high levels of task performance, membership satisfaction, and future viability.

Efficient communication occurs at minimum cost.

An **emergent strategy** develops over time as managers learn from and respond to experience

Emotions are strong feelings directed toward someone or something.

Emotional conflict results from feelings of anger, distrust, dislike, fear, and resentment, as well as from personality clashes.

Emotional intelligence is the ability to manage ourselves and our relationships effectively.

Emotional intelligence is the ability to manage our emotions in social relationships.

Emotional stability is being relaxed, secure, and unworried.

Employee assistance programs help employees cope with personal stresses and problems.

Empowerment enables others to gain and use decision-making power.

An **entrepreneur** is willing to pursue opportunities in situations others view as problems or threats.

Entrepreneurship is dynamic, risk-taking, creative, growth-oriented behavior.

Environmental uncertainty is a lack of complete information about the environment.

Equal employment opportunity is the right to employment and advancement without regard to race, sex, religion, color, or national origin.

Equity financing involves exchanging ownership shares for outside investment monies.

Escalating commitment is the continuation of a course of action even though it is not working.

Ethical behavior is "right" or "good" in the context of a governing moral code.

An **ethical dilemma** is a situation that offers potential benefit or gain and is also unethical.

Ethical imperialism is an attempt to impose one's ethical standards on other cultures.

Ethics set moral standards of what is "good" and "right" in one's behavior.

Ethics sets standards of good or bad, or right or wrong, in one's conduct.

Ethics mindfulness is enriched awareness that leads to consistent ethical behavior.

Ethics training seeks to help people understand the ethical aspects of decision making and to incorporate high ethical standards into their daily behavior.

Ethnocentrism is the belief that one's membership group or subculture is superior to all others.

The **Euro** is the new common European currency.

The **European Union** is a political and economic alliance of European countries.

Expectancy is a person's belief that working hard will result in high task performance.

Expert power is the capacity to influence other people because of specialized knowledge.

In **exporting,** local products are sold abroad.

External control occurs through direct supervision or administrative systems.

Extinction discourages a behavior by making the removal of a desirable consequence contingent on its occurrence.

Extraversion is being outgoing, sociable, and assertive.

F

A **family business** is owned and controlled by members of a family.

Family-friendly benefits help employees achieve better work-life balance.

Feedback is the process of telling someone else how you feel about something that person did or said.

Feedback control takes place after an action is completed.

Feedforward control ensures that directions and resources are right before the work begins.

Filtering is the intentional distortion of information to make it appear most favorable to the recipient.

A **first-mover advantage** comes from being first to exploit a niche or enter a market.

Flexible benefits programs allow employees to choose from a range of benefit options.

Flexible working hours give employees some choice in daily work hours.

A **focused cost leadership** strategy seeks the lowest costs of operations within a special market segment.

A **focused differentiation** strategy offers a unique product to a special market segment.

A **force-coercion strategy** pursues change through formal authority and/or the use of rewards or punishments.

Forecasting attempts to predict the future.

A **foreign subsidiary** is a local operation completely owned by a foreign firm.

A **formal group** is officially recognized and supported by the organization.

Formal structure is the official structure of the organization.

Framing error is solving a problem in the context perceived.

A **franchise** is when one business owner sells to another the right to operate the same business in another location.

In **franchising** a fee is paid for rights to use another firm's name and operating methods.

Fringe benefits are nonmonetary forms of compensation such as health insurance and retirement plans.

The **functional chimneys problem** is a lack of communication and coordination across functions.

Functional conflict is constructive and helps task performance.

Functional managers are responsible for one area of activity, such as finance, marketing, production, personnel, accounting, or sales.

A **functional strategy** guides activities within one specific area of operation.

A **functional structure** groups together people with similar skills who perform similar tasks.

G

A **Gantt chart** graphically displays the scheduling of tasks required to complete a project.

The **general environment** is comprised of cultural, economic, legal-political, and educational conditions.

General managers are responsible for complex, multifunctional units.

A **geographical structure** groups together people and jobs performed in the same location.

The **glass ceiling** is a hidden barrier to the advancement of women and minorities.

The **glass ceiling effect** is an invisible barrier limiting career advancement of women and minorities.

In the **global economy** resources, markets, and competition are worldwide in scope.

A **global manager** is culturally aware and informed on international affairs.

In **global sourcing,** materials or services are purchased around the world for local use.

Globalization is the process of growing interdependence among elements of the global economy.

A **globalization strategy** adopts standardized products and advertising for use worldwide.

Globalization is the worldwide interdependence of resource flows, product markets, and business competition.

A **graphic rating scale** uses a checklist of traits or characteristics to evaluate performance.

A **group decision** is made by group members themselves.

Group process is the way team members work together to accomplish tasks.

Groupthink is a tendency for highly cohesive teams to lose their evaluative capabilities.

A **growth strategy** involves expansion of the organization's current operations.

H

A **halo effect** occurs when one attribute is used to develop an overall impression of a person or situation.

The **Hawthorne effect** is the tendency of persons singled out for special attention to perform as expected.

Heuristics are strategies for simplifying decision making.

In a **hierarchy of objectives**, lower-level objectives are means to accomplishing higher level ones.

High-context cultures rely on nonverbal and situational cues as well as on spoken or written words in communication.

Higher-order needs are esteem and self-actualization needs in Maslow's hierarchy.

A **high-performance organization** consistently achieves excellence while creating a high-quality work environment.

Human capital is the economic value of people with job-relevant abilities, knowledge, ideas, energies, and commitments.

The **human relations movement** suggested that managers using good human relations will achieve productivity.

A leader with a **human relations style** emphasizes people over task.

Human resource management is the process of attracting, developing, and maintaining a high-quality workforce.

Human resource planning analyzes staffing needs and identifies actions to fill those needs.

A **human skill** is the ability to work well in cooperation with other people.

A **hygiene factor** is found in the job context, such as working conditions, interpersonal relations, organizational policies, and salary.

I

An **immoral manager** chooses to behave unethically.

Importing is the process of acquiring products abroad and selling them in domestic markets.

Impression management is the systematic attempt to influence how others perceive us.

Incremental change bends and adjusts existing ways to improve performance.

Independent contractors are hired as needed and are not part of the organization's permanent workforce.

In the **individualism view**, ethical behavior advances long-term self-interests.

An **informal group** is unofficial and emerges from relationships and shared interests among members.

Informal structure is the set of unofficial relationships among an organization's members.

Information is data made useful for decision making.

Information systems use IT to collect, organize, and distribute data for use in decision making.

An **initial public offering (IPO)** is an initial selling of shares of stock to the public at large.

Innovation is the process of taking a new idea and putting it into practice.

An **input standard** measures work efforts that go into a performance task.

Instrumental values are preferences regarding the means to desired ends.

Instrumentality is a person's belief that various outcomes will occur as a result of task performance.

Integration is the level of coordination achieved between subsystems in an organization.

Integrity in leadership is honesty, credibility, and consistency in putting values into action.

Intellectual capital is the collective brainpower or shared knowledge of a workforce.

Intensive technology focuses the efforts and talents of many people to serve clients.

Interactional justice is the degree to which others are treated with dignity and respect.

Internal control occurs through self-discipline and self-control.

An **international business** conducts commercial transactions across national boundaries.

International management involves managing operations in more than one country.

Intuitive thinking approaches problems in a flexible and spontaneous fashion.

ISO certification indicates conformance with a rigorous set of international quality standards.

J

A **job analysis** studies exactly what is done in a job, and why.

Job burnout is physical and mental exhaustion from work stress.

A **job description** details the duties and responsibilities of a job holder.

Job design is arranging work tasks for individuals and groups.

Job enlargement increases task variety by combining into one job two or more tasks previously assigned to separate workers.

Job enrichment increases job depth by adding work planning and evaluating duties normally performed by the supervisor.

Job involvement is the extent to which an individual is dedicated to a job.

Job rotation increases task variety by periodically shifting workers between different jobs.

Job satisfaction is the degree to which an individual feels positive or negative about a job.

Job sharing splits one job between two people.

Job simplification employs people in clearly defined and very specialized tasks.

Job specifications list the qualifications required of a job holder.

A **joint venture** operates in a foreign country through co-ownership with local partners.

In the **justice view,** ethical behavior treats people impartially and fairly.

Just-in-time scheduling minimizes inventory by outing materials to workstations "just in time" to be used.

K

Knowledge management is the process of using intellectual capital for competitive advantage.

A **knowledge worker** is someone whose mind is a critical asset to employers.

L

A **labor contract** is a formal agreement between a union and employer about the terms of work for union members.

A **labor union** is an organization that deals with employers on the workers' collective behalf.

A leader with a **laissez-faire style** displays a "do the best you can and don't bother me" attitude.

The **law of effect** states that behavior followed by pleasant consequences is likely to be repeated; behavior followed by unpleasant consequences is not.

Leadership is the process of inspiring others to work hard to accomplish important tasks.

Leadership style is the recurring pattern of behaviors exhibited by a leader.

Leading is the process of arousing enthusiasm and inspiring efforts to achieve goals.

A **learning organization** continuously changes and improves, using the lessons of experience.

Legitimate power is the capacity to influence other people by virtue of formal authority, or the rights of office.

In a **licensing agreement** one firm pays a fee for rights to make or sell another company's products.

Lifelong learning is continuous learning from daily experiences.

A **limited liability corporation (LLC)** is a hybrid business form combining advantages of the sole proprietorship, partnership, and corporation.

Line managers directly contribute to the production of the organization's basic goods or services.

Locus of control is the extent to which one believes that what happens is within one's control.

In **long-linked technology** a client moves from point to point during service delivery.

In **lose-lose conflict** no one achieves his or her true desires, and the underlying reasons for conflict remain unaffected.

Low-context cultures emphasize communication via spoken or written words.

Lower-order needs are physiological, safety, and social needs in Maslow's hierarchy.

M

Machiavellianism describes the extent to which someone is emotionally detached and manipulative.

A **maintenance activity** is an action taken by a team member that supports the emotional life of the group.

Management is the process of planning, organizing, leading, and controlling the use of resources to accomplish performance goals.

Management by exception focuses attention on substantial differences between actual and desired performance.

MBO is a process of joint objective setting between a superior and subordinate.

In **management by wandering around (MBWA),** managers spend time outside their offices to meet and talk with workers at all levels.

Management development is training to improve knowledge and skills in the management process.

Management information systems meet the information needs of managers in making daily decisions.

A **managerial competency** is a skill-based capability for high performance in a management job.

A **manager** is a person who supports and is responsible for the work of others.

Managing diversity is building an inclusive work environment that allows everyone to reach their full potential.

Mass production manufactures a large number of uniform products with an assembly-line system.

A **matrix structure** combines functional and divisional approaches to emphasize project or program teams.

A **mechanistic design** is centralized with many rules and procedures, a clear-cut division of labor, narrow spans of control, and formal coordination.

Mediating technology links together people in a beneficial exchange of values.

In **mediation** a neutral party tries to help conflicting parties improve communication to resolve their dispute.

Mentoring assigns early career employees as protégés to more senior ones.

Middle managers oversee the work of large departments or divisions.

The **mission** is the organization's reason for existence in society.

A **mixed message** results when words communicate one message while actions, body language, or appearance communicate something else.

Modeling uses personal behavior to demonstrate performance expected of others.

In **monochronic cultures** people tend to do one thing at a time.

Moods are generalized positive and negative feelings or states on mind.

Moral leadership is always "good" and "right" by ethical standards.

A **moral manager** makes ethical behavior a personal goal.

In the **moral-rights view** ethical behavior respects and protects fundamental rights.

Most favored nation status gives a trading partner most favorable treatment for imports and exports.

Motion study is the science of reducing a task to its basic physical motions.

Motivation accounts for the level, direction, and persistence of effort expended at work.

A **multicultural organization** is based on pluralism and operates with inclusivity and respect for diversity.

Multiculturalism involves pluralism and respect for diversity.

A **multidomestic strategy** customizes products and advertising to best fit local needs.

A **multinational corporation** is a business with extensive international operations in more than one foreign country.

A **multiperson comparison** compares one person's performance with that of others.

N

NAFTA is the North American Free Trade Agreement linking Canada, the United States, and Mexico in an economic alliance.

Necessity-based entrepreneurship takes place because other employment options don't exist.

A **need** is a physiological or psychological deficiency that a person wants to satisfy.

Need for Achievement is the desire to do something better, to solve problems, or to master complex tasks.

Need for Affiliation is the desire to establish and maintain good relations with people.

Need for Power is the desire to control, influence, or be responsible for other people.

A **need** is an unfulfilled physiological or psychological desire.

Negative reinforcement strengthens a behavior by making the avoidance of an undesirable consequence contingent on its occurrence.

Negotiation is the process of making joint decisions when the parties involved have different preferences.

A **network structure** uses IT to link with networks of outside suppliers and service contractors.

The **nominal group technique** structures interaction among team members discussing problems and ideas.

A **nonprogrammed decision** applies a specific solution crafted for a unique problem.

Nonverbal communication takes place through gestures and body language.

A **norm** is a behavior, rule, or standard expected to be followed by team members.

O

Objectives are specific results that one wishes to achieve.

An **obstructionist strategy** avoids social responsibility and reflects mainly economic priorities.

An **OD intervention** is a structured activity that helps create change for organization development.

An **open system** interacts with its environment and transforms resource inputs into outputs.

Openness is being curious, receptive to new ideas, and imaginative.

Operant conditioning is the control of behavior by manipulating its consequences.

Operating objectives are specific results that organizations try to accomplish.

An **operational plan** identifies activities to implement strategic plans.

Operations management is the study of how organizations produce goods and services.

An **optimizing decision** chooses the alternative giving the absolute best solution to a problem.

An **organic design** is decentralized with fewer rules and procedures, open divisions of labor, wide spans of control, and more personal coordination.

An **organization** is a collection of people working together to achieve a common purpose.

An **organization chart** describes the arrangement of work positions within an organization.

Organization development is a comprehensive effort to improve an organization's ability to solve problems and improve performance.

Organization structure is a system of tasks, reporting relationships, and communication linkages.

Organizational behavior is the study of individuals and groups in organizations.

Organizational citizenship behaviors are things people do above and beyond basic job requirements.

Organizational commitment is the loyalty of an individual to the organization.

Organizational culture is the system of shared beliefs and values that guides behavior in organizations.

Organizational design is the process of creating structures that accomplish mission and objectives.

Organizational stakeholders are directly affected by the behavior of the organization and hold a stake in its performance.

Organizing is the process of assigning tasks, allocating resources, and coordinating work activities.

Orientation familiarizes new employees with jobs, co-workers, and organizational policies and services.

An **output standard** measures performance results in terms of quantity, quality, cost, or time.

P

Participatory planning includes the persons who will be affected by plans and/or who will implement them.

A **partnership** is when two or more people agree to contribute resources to start and operate a business together.

Part-time work is temporary employment for less than the standard 40-hour work week.

Perception is the process through which people receive, organize, and interpret information from the environment.

Performance appraisal is the process of formally evaluating performance and providing feedback to a job holder.

Performance effectiveness is an output measure of task or goal accomplishment.

Performance efficiency is an input measure of resource cost associated with goal accomplishment.

A **performance gap** is a discrepancy between a desired and actual state of affairs.

A **performance management system** sets standards, assesses results, and plans for performance improvements.

Personal wellness is the pursuit of one's full potential through a personal-health promotion program.

Personality is the profile of characteristics making a person unique from others.

Persuasion is presenting a message in a manner that casues the other person to support it.

A **plan** is a statement of intended means for accomplishing objectives.

Planned change aligns the organization with anticipated future challenges.

Planning is the process of setting objectives and determining what should be done to accomplish them.

A **policy** is a standing plan that communicates broad guidelines for decisions and action.

In **polychronic cultures** time is used to accomplish many different things at once.

A **portfolio planning** approach seeks the best mix of investments among alternative business opportunities.

Positive reinforcement strengthens a behavior by making a desirable consequence contingent on its occurrence.

Power is the ability to get someone else to do something you want done or to make things happen the way you want.

Prejudice is the display of negative, irrational attitudes toward members of diverse populations.

principled/integrative negotiation uses a "win-win" orientation to reach solutions acceptable to each party.

A **proactive strategy** meets all the criteria of social responsibility, including discretionary performance.

Problem solving involves identifying and taking action to resolve problems.

Problem-solving style is the way people gather and evaluate information.

Procedural justice is concerned that policies and rules are fairly applied.

Process innovations result in better ways of doing things.

Process reengineering systematically analyzes work processes to design new and better ones.

A **process structure** groups jobs and activities that are part of the same processes.

Process value analysis identifies and evaluates core processes for their performance contributions.

Product innovations result in new or improved goods or services.

A **product structure** groups together people and jobs focused on a single product or service.

Productivity is the efficiency with which inputs are transformed into outputs.

A **programmed decision** applies a solution from past experience to a routine problem.

Progressive discipline ties reprimands to the severity and frequency of misbehavior.

Project management makes sure that activities required to complete a project are accomplished on time and correctly.

Project teams are convened for a particular task or project and disband once it is completed.

A **project team** or **task force** is convened for a specific purpose and disbands when its task is completed.

Projection is the assignment of personal attributes to other individuals.

Projects are unique one time events that occur within a defined time period

Protectionism is a call for tariffs and favorable treatments to protect domestic firms from foreign competition.

Proxemics is how people use space to communicate.

A **psychological contract** is the set of individual expectations about the employment relationship.

Punishment discourages a behavior by making an unpleasant consequence contingent on its occurrence.

Q

Quality control checks processes, materials, products, and services to ensure that they meet high standards.

Quality of work life is the overall quality of human experiences in the workplace.

R

A **rational persuasion strategy** pursues change through empirical data and rational argument.

Reactive change responds to events as or after they occur.

Realistic job previews provide job candidates with all pertinent information about a job and organization.

Recruitment is a set of activities designed to attract a qualified pool of job applicants.

Referent power is the capacity to influence other people because of their desire to identify personally with you.

Refreezing is the phase at which change is stabilized.

Reliability means a selection device gives consistent results over repeated measures.

Restructuring reduces the scale and/or mix of operations.

A **retrenchment strategy** changes operations to correct weaknesses.

Reward power is the capacity to offer something of value as a means of influencing other people.

A **risk environment** lacks complete information but offers "probabilities" of the likely outcomes for possible action alternatives.

A procedure or **rule** precisely describes actions that are to be taken in specific situations.

S

A **satisficing decision** chooses the first satisfactory alternative that comes to one's attention.

A **satisfier factor** is found in job content, such as a sense of achievement, recognition, responsibility, advancement, or personal growth.

Scenario planning identifies alternative future scenarios and makes plans to deal with each.

Scientific management emphasizes careful selection and training of workers and supervisory support.

Selection is choosing individuals to hire from a pool of qualified job applicants.

Selective perception is the tendency to define problems from one's own point of view.

A **self-fulfilling prophecy** occurs when a person acts in ways that confirm another's expectations.

Members of a **self-managing work team** have the authority to make decisions about how they share and complete their work.

Self-monitoring is the degree to which someone is able to adjust behavior in response to external factors.

Self-serving bias explains personal success by internal causes and personal failures by external causes.

Servant leadership is follower-centered and committed to helping others in their work.

Sexual harassment is behavior of a sexual nature that affects a person's employment situation.

Shaping is positive reinforcement of successive approximations to the desired behavior.

A **shared power strategy** pursues change by participation in assessing change needs, values, and goals.

Six Sigma is a quality standard of 3.4 defects or less per million products or service deliveries.

A **skill** is the ability to translate knowledge into action that results in desired performance.

A **small business** has fewer than 500 employees, is independently owned and operated, and does not dominate its industry.

Small-batch production manufactures a variety of products crafted to fit customer specifications.

The **social contract** reflects expectations in the employee-employer relationship.

social entrepreneurship has a mission to solve pressing social problems.

Social loafing is the tendency of some people to avoid responsibility by "free-riding" in groups.

Social responsibility is the obligation of an organization to serve its own interests and those of society.

A **social responsibility audit** assesses an organization's accomplishments in areas of social responsibility.

Socialization systematically influences the expectations, behavior, and attitudes of new employees.

A **sole proprietorship** is an individual pursuing business for a profit.

Span of control is the number of subordinates directly reporting to a manager.

The **specific environment** includes the people and groups with whom an organization interacts.

Staff managers use special technical expertise to advise and support line workers.

Staff positions provide technical expertise for other parts of the organization.

Stakeholders are individuals and groups directly affected by an organization and its accomplishments.

A **stereotype** is when attributes commonly associated with a group are assigned to an individual.

In a **strategic alliance** organizations join together in partnership to pursue an area of mutual interest.

Strategic human resource management mobilizes human capital to implement organizational strategies.

Strategic intent focuses and applies organizational energies on a unifying and compelling goal.

Strategic leadership inspires people to continuously change, refine, and improve strategies and their implementation.

Strategic management is the process of formulating and implementing strategies.

Strategic opportunism focuses on long-term objectives while being flexible in dealing with short-term problems.

A **strategic plan** identifies long-term directions for the organization.

A **strategy** is a comprehensive plan guiding resource allocation to achieve long-term organization goals.

Strategy formulation is the process of creating strategies.

Strategy implementation is the process of putting strategies into action.

Stress is a state of tension experienced by individuals facing extraordinary demands, constraints, or opportunities.

A **stressor** is anything that causes stress.

Structured problems are straightforward and clear in information needs.

Organizational **subcultures** exist among people with similar values and beliefs based on shared work responsibilities and personal characteristics.

Substantive conflict involves disagreements over goals, resources, rewards, policies, procedures, and job assignments.

Substitutes for leadership are factors in the work setting that direct work efforts without the involvement of a leader.

A **subsystem** is a work unit or smaller component within a larger organization.

A **succession plan** describes how the leadership transition and related financial matters will be handled.

The **succession problem** is the issue of who will run the business when the current head leaves.

Supply chain management strategically links all operations dealing with resource supplies.

Sustainable development meets the needs of the present without hurting future generations.

Sweatshops employ workers at very low wages for long hours and in poor working conditions.

A **SWOT analysis** examines organizational strengths and weaknesses and environmental opportunities and threats.

A **symbolic leader** uses symbols to establish and maintain a desired organizational culture.

Synergy is the creation of a whole greater than the sum of its individual parts.

A **system** is a collection of interrelated parts working together for a purpose.

Systematic thinking approaches problems in a rational and analytical fashion.

T

A **task activity** is an action taken by a team member that directly contributes to the group's performance purpose.

A **team** is a collection of people who regularly interact to pursue common goals.

Team building is a sequence of collaborative activities to gather and analyze data on a team and make changes to increase its effectiveness.

Team leaders or **supervisors** report to middle managers and directly supervise nonmanagerial workers.

A **team structure** uses permanent and temporary cross-functional teams to improve lateral relations.

Teamwork is the process of people actively working together to accomplish common goals.

A **technical skill** is the ability to use expertise to perform a task with proficiency.

Telecommuting involves using IT to work at home or outside the office.

Terminal values are preferences about desired end states.

Theory X assumes people dislike work, lack ambition, are irresponsible, and prefer to be led.

Theory Y assumes people are willing to work, accept responsibility, and are self-directed and creative.

Top managers guide the performance of the organization as a whole or of one of its major parts.

In **top-down change**, the change initiatives come from senior management.

Total quality management is a process of making a commitment to quality part of all operations.

Total quality management is managing with an organization-wide commitment to continuous improvement, product quality, and customer needs.

Training provides learning opportunities to acquire and improve job-related skills.

Transactional leadership directs the efforts of others through tasks, rewards, and structures.

Transformational change results in a major and comprehensive redirection of the organization.

Transformational leadership is inspirational and arouses extraordinary effort and performance.

A **transnational corporation** is an MNC that operates worldwide on a borderless basis.

A **transnational strategy** seeks efficiencies of global operations with attention to local markets.

A **Type A personality** is a person oriented toward extreme achievement, impatience, and perfectionism.

U

An **uncertain environment** lacks so much information that it is difficult to assign probabilities to the likely outcomes of alternatives.

Unfreezing is the phase during which a situation is prepared for change.

Universalism suggests ethical standards apply absolutely across all cultures.

Unstructured problems have ambiguities and information deficiencies.

In the **utillitarian view,** ethical behavior delivers the greatest good to the most people.

V

Valence is the value a person assigns to work-related outcomes.

Validity means scores on a selection device have demonstrated links with future job performance.

The **value chain** is the specific sequence of activities that creates goods and services with value for customers.

Value creation is creating value for and satisfying needs of constituencies.

Value-based management actively develops, communicates, and enacts shared values.

Values are broad beliefs about what is appropriate behavior.

Venture capitalists make large investments in new ventures in return for an equity stake in the business.

Growth through **vertical integration** is by acquiring suppliers or distributors.

A **virtual organization** uses IT and the Internet to engage a shifting network of strategic alliances.

Members of a **virtual team** work together and solve problems through computer-based interactions.

A **vision** is a clear sense of the future.

Visionary leadership brings to the situation a clear sense of the future and an understanding of how to get there.

W

A **whistleblower** exposes the misdeeds of others in organizations.

In **win-lose conflict** one party achieves its desires, and the other party does not.

In **win-win conflict** the conflict is resolved to everyone's benefit.

A **work process** is a related group of tasks that together create a value for the customer.

In **work sampling,** applicants are evaluated while performing actual work tasks.

Workflow is the movement of work from one point to another in a system.

Workforce diversity describes difference among workers in gender, race, age, ethnicity religion sexual orientation, and able-bodiedness.

Work-life balance involves balancing career demands with personal and family needs.

Workplace privacy is the right to privacy while at work.

Workplace rage is aggressive behavior toward co-workers or the work setting.

World Trade Organization member nations agree to negotiate and resolve disputes about tariffs and trade restrictions.

Z

A **zero-based budget** allocates resources as if each budget was brand new.

360° feedback includes in the appraisal process superiors, subordinates, peers, and even customers.

Chapter 1

[1] Martin Piszczalski. "eBay & autos: a new model?" *Automotive Design and Production,* March, 2003, Accessed August 21, 2006, at http://www.find-articles.com/p/articles/mi_m0KJI/is_3_115/ai_98901441.

[2] William Meyers. "Keeping a Gentle Grip on Power." *U.S. News and World Report,* October 31, 2005. Accessed January 27, 2006, from EBSCOhost.

[3] Microsoft Corporation. "eBay Consolidates E-Mail Servers 71 Percent, Supports Rapid Growth While It Cuts Costs." Microsoft Windows Server System Customer Solution Case Study, September 2005. Accessed August 21, 2006 at download.Microsoft.com/documents/customerevidence/11780_ebay_wss_case_study.doc.

[4] Margaret Kane. "eBay picks up PayPal for $1.5 billion." Cnet News.com. Accessed August 21, 2006, at http://news.com.com/2100-1017-941964.html.

[5] Robert Hof and Sarah Lacy. "Big Waves from 'Google Base.'" Business Week Online, October 27, 2005. Accessed January 27, 2006, from EBSCOhost.

[6] "eBay." Wikipedia entry. Accessed June 12, 2006, at http://en.wikipedia.org/wiki/eBay.

[7] eBay Investor Relations. "Frequently Asked Questions." Accessed June 11, 2006 at http://investor.ebay.com/faq.cfm.

[8] Adam Ginsberg. Accessed June 11, 2006, at http://www.the automatic-moneymachine.com/.

[9] "eBay Consolidates E-Mail Servers 71 Percent, Supports Rapid Growth While It Cuts Costs."

[10] Information from the *Fast Company* website: www.fastcompany.com.

[11] Charles O'Reilly III and Jeffrey Pfeffer, *Hidden Value: How Great Companies Achieve Extraordinary Results with Ordinary People* (Boston: Harvard Business School Press, 2000), p. 2.

[12] Max DePree's books include *Leadership Is an Art* (New York: Dell, 1990) and *Leadership Jazz* (New York: Dell, 1993). See also Herman Miller's home page at www.hermanmiller.com.

[13] Thomas A. Stewart, *Intellectual Capital: The Wealth of Organizations* (New York: Bantam, 1998).

[14] See Peter F. Drucker, *The Changing World of the Executive* (New York: T.T. Times Books, 1982), and *The Profession of Management* (Cambridge, MA: Harvard Business School Press, 1997); and Francis Horibe, *Managing Knowledge Workers: New Skills and Attitudes to Unlock the Intellectual Capital in Your Organization* (New York: Wiley, 1999).

[15] Kenichi Ohmae's books include *The Borderless World: Power and Strategy in the Interlinked Economy* (New York: Harper, 1989); *The End of the Nation State* (New York: Free Press, 1996); *The Invisible Continent: Four Strategic Imperatives of the New Economy* (New York: Harper, 1999); and, *The Next Global Stage: Challenges and Opportunities in Our Borderless World* (Philadelphia: Wharton School Publishing, 2006).

[16] For a discussion of globalization see Thomas L. Friedman, *The Lexus and the Olive Tree: Understanding Globalization* (New York: Bantam Doubleday Dell, 2000). *The World is Flat: A Brief History of the Twenty-First Century* (New York: Farrar, Straus and Giroux, 2005).

[17] Alfred E. Eckes, Jr., and Thomas W. Zeiler, *Globalization and the American Century* (Cambridge, UK: Cambridge University Press, 2003), pp. 1, 2.

[18] Michael E. Porter, *The Competitive Advantage of Nations: With a New Introduction* (New York: Free Press, 1998).

[19] *Workforce 2000: Work and Workers for the 21st Century* (Indianapolis: Towers Perrin/Hudson Institute, 1987); Richard W. Judy and Carol D' Amico (eds.), *Work and Workers for the 21st Century* (Indianapolis Hudson Institute, 1997); See Richard D. Bucher, *Diversity Consciousness: Opening Our Minds to People, Cultures, and Opportunities* (Upper Saddle River, NJ: Prentice-Hall, 2000); R. Roosevelt Thomas, "From Affirmative Action to Affirming Diversity," *Harvard Business Review* (March–April 1990), pp. 107–17; and *Beyond Race and Gender: Unleashing the Power of Your Total Workforce by Managing Diversity* (New York: AMACOM, 1992).

[20] June Dronholz, "Hispanics Gain in Census," *The Wall Street Journal* (May 10, 2006), p. A6; Phillip Toledano, "Demographics: The Population Hourglass," *Fast Company* (March, 2006), p. 56.

[21] Quotations from Thomas, op cit. (1990); and *Business Week* (August 8, 1990), p. 50, emphasis added.

[22] Thomas, op cit.

[23] Information from "Racism in Hiring Remains, Study Says," *Columbus Dispatch* (January 17, 2003), p. B2.

[24] For discussions of the glass ceiling effect see Ann M. Morrison, Randall P. White, and Ellen Van Velso, *Breaking the Glass Ceiling* (Reading, MA: Addison-Wesley, 1987); Anne E. Weiss, *The Glass Ceiling: A Look at Women in the Workforce* (New York: Twenty First Century, 1999); and Debra E Meyerson and Joyce K. Fletcher, "A Modest Manifesto for Shattering the Glass Ceiling," *Harvard Business Review* (January–February 2000).

[25] Judith B. Rosener, "Women *Make* Good Managers. So What?" *Business Week* (December 11, 2000), p. 24.

[26] Information from Patricia M. Flynn and Susan M. Adams, "Women on Board," *BizEd* (September/October, 2004), pp. 34–39; and, "Gender Pay Gap," *The Columbus Dispatch* (January 2, 2005), p. Fl; "Carol Hymowitz, "Too Many Women Fall for Stereotypes of Selves, Study Says," *The Wall Street Journal* (October 24, 2005), p. Bl; Carol Hymowitz, "The New Diversity," *The Wall Street Journal* (November 14, 2005), pp. R1, R3; "Equal Pay: It's Time for Working Women to Earn Equal Pay," www.AFL-CIO.org/issues

(retrieved March 13, 2006); "Breaking into the Boardroom," *The Wall Street Journal* (March 27, 2006), p. B3; Carol Hymowitz, "Women Smell Ranker as Middle Manager," The *Wall Street Journal* (July 24, 2006), p. B1.

[27]Sue Shellenbarger, "Number of Women Managers Rises," *Wall Street Journal* (September 30, 2003), p. D2; "Women of Color," Working Mother Media website: www.workingmother.com/pr.chicagol.shtml.

[28]Portions adapted from John W. Dienhart and Terry Thomas, "Ethical Leadership: A Primer on Ethical Responsibility in Management," in John R. Schermerhorn, Jr., (ed.), *Management*, 7th ed. (New York: Wiley, 2002).

[29]See Judith Burns, "Everything You Wanted to Know About Corporate Governance . . . But Didn't Know How to Ask," *The Wall Street Journal* (October 27, 2003), pp. R1. R7.

[30]Charles Handy, *The Age of Unreason* (Cambridge, MA: Harvard Business School Press, 1990).

[31]"Is Your Job Your Calling?" *Fast Company* (February–March 1998), p. 108.

[32]Robert Reich, "The Company of the Future," *Fast Company* (November 1998), p. 124ff.

[33]Tom Peters, "The New Wired World of Work," *Business Week* (August 28, 2000), pp. 172–73.

[34]For an overview of organizations and organization theory, see W. Richard Scott, *Organizations: Rational, Natural and Open Systems*, 4th ed. (Englewood Cliffs, NJ: Prentice-Hall, 1998).

[35]Developed in part from Jay A. Conger, *Winning 'em Over: A New Model for Managing in the Age of Persuasion* (New York: Simon & Schuster, 1998), pp. 180–81; Stewart D. Friedman, Perry Christensen, and Jessica De-Groot, "Work and Life: The End of the Zero-Sum Game," *Harvard Business Review* (November–December 1998), pp. 119–29, Chris Argyris, "Empowerment: The Emperor's New Clothes," *Harvard Business Review* (May–June 1998), pp. 98–105, and John A. Byrne, "Management by Web," *Business Week* (August 28, 2000), pp. 84–98.

[36]Jeffrey Pfeffer and John F. Veiga, "Putting People First for Organizational Success," *Academy of Management Executive*, vol. 13 (May 1999), pp. 37–48, and Jeffrey Pfeffer, *The Human Equation: Building Profits by Putting People First* (Boston: Harvard Business School Press, 1998).

[37]Henry Mintzberg, "The Manager's Job: Folklore and Fact," *Harvard Business Review*, vol. 53 (July–August 1975), p. 61. See also his book, *The Nature of Managerial Work* (New York: Harper & Row, 1973, and HarperCollins, 1997).

[38]Information from David Whitford, "A Human Place to Work," *Fortune* (January 8, 2001), pp. 108–20.

[39]For a perspective on the first-level manager's job, see Leonard A. Schlesinger and Janice A. Klein, "The First-Line Supervisor: Past, Present and Future," pp. 370–82, in Jay W. Lorsch (ed.), *Handbook of Organizational Behavior* (Englewood Cliffs, NJ: Prentice-Hall, 1987). Research reported in "Remember Us?" *Economist* (February 1, 1992), p. 71.

[40]Whitford, op cit.

[41]Stewart D. Friedman, Perry Christensen, and Jessica De Groot, "Work and Life: The End of the Zero-Sum Game," *Harvard Business Review* (November–December 1998), pp. 119–29.

[42]This running example is developed from information from "Accountants Have Lives, Too, You Know," *Business Week* (February 23, 1998), pp. 88–90, and the Ernst & Young website: www.ey.com. See also Jaclyne Badal, "To Retain Valued Women Employees Companies Pitch Flextime as Macho," *The Wall Street Journal* (December 11, 2006), pp. B1, B3.

[43]Mintzberg, op cit. (1973/1997), p. 30.

[44]See Mintzberg, op cit (1973/1997); and Henry Mintzberg, "Covert Leadership: The Art of Managing Professionals," *Harvard Business Review* (November–December 1998), pp. 140–47; and, Jonathan Gosling and Henry Mintzberg, "The Five Minds of a Manager," *Harvard Business Review* (November, 2003), pp. 1–9.

[45]Mintzberg, op cit. (1973/1997), p. 60.

[46]For research on managerial work see Morgan W. McCall, Jr., Ann M. Morrison, and Robert L. Hannan, *Studies of Managerial Work: Results and Methods. Technical Report #9* (Greensboro, NC: Center for Creative Leadership, 1978), pp. 7–9. See also John P. Kotter, "What Effective General Managers Really Do," *Harvard Business Review* (November–December 1982), pp. 156–57.

[47]Kotter, op cit. p. 164. See also his book, *The General Managers* (New York: Free Press, 1986); and David Barry, Catherine Durnell Crampton, and Stephen J. Carroll, "Navigating the Garbage Can: How Agendas Help Managers Cope with Job Realities," *Academy of Management Executive*, vol. II (May 1997), pp. 43–56.

[48]Robert L. Katz, "Skills of an Effective Administrator," *Harvard Business Review* (September–October 1974), p. 94.

[49]See Daniel Goleman's books *Emotional Intelligence* (New York: Bantam, 1995) and *Working with Emotional Intelligence* (New York: Bantam, 1998); and his articles "What Makes a Leader," *Harvard Business Review* (November–December 1998), pp. 93–102, and "Leadership That Makes a Difference," *Harvard Business Review* (March–April 2000), pp. 79–90, quote from p. 80.

[50]Daniel Pink, A *Whole New Mind: Moving from the Information Age to the Conceptual Age* (New York: Riverhead Books, 2005), pp. 2–3.

[51]Richard E. Boyatzis, *The Competent Manager: A Model for Effective Performance* (New York: Wiley, 1982). See also Jon P. Briscoe and Douglas T. Hall, "Grooming and Picking Leaders Using Competency Frameworks: Do They Work?" *Organizational Dynamics* (Autumn 1999), pp. 37–52.

[52] Gary Hamel, "Bringing Silicon Valley Inside," *Harvard Business Review* (September—October 1999), pp. 71–84.

[53] Jill Rosenfeld, "Training to Work," *Fast Company* (August 2000), pp. 77.

[54] "Richard Branson's Virgin Success: The Incredible Triumph of an Enigmatic Entrepreneur," www.execpc.com/~shepler/ branson.html.

[55] Michael S. Hopkins. "Because He's Game for Anything. In Fact, Everything." *Inc.*, April, 2005. vol. 27, Issue 4.

[56] "Richard Branson," Askmen.com, www.askmen.com/men/december99/6_richard_branson.html.

[57] http://www.hrmreport.com/pastissue/article.asp?art=26645&issue=162.

[58] www.virgin.com.

[59] Hamel.

[60] "The Virgin Story," www.virgin.com/aboutus.

[61] Kerry Capell, "Virgin Takes E-Wing," *Business Week e. biz* (January 22, 2001), pp. EB30-EB34.

[62] Ibid.

[63] Ibid.

[64] Ibid.

65 "Business Proposals," www.virgin.com/aboutus.
66 Ibid.

Features:
Insights: eBay Annual Reports, 2001 & 2005; https://gsbapps.stanford.edu/cases/documents/P-33%20.pdf. Quote from "Monster.com Ranked #1 According to Media Metrix," *Business Wire* (June 20, 2000). See also www.monster.com.
Issues & Situations: Information from Nanette Byrnes, "Star Search," *Business Week* (October 10, 2005), pp. 68–78.
Kaffeeklatsch: Jeffrey Pfeffer and Robert I. Sutton, *Hard Facts: Dangerous Half-Truths & Total Nonsense* (Cambridge, Mass.: Harvard Business School Press, 2006); Jena McGregor, "Forget Going with Your Gut," *Business Week* (March 20, 2006), p. 112; Carol Hymowitz, "Today's Bosses Find Mentoring Isn't Worth the Time and Risks," *The Wall Street Journal* (March 13, 2006), p. B1.
Personal Management: Quote from Allan H. Church, Executive Commentary, *Academy of Management Executive* (February , 2002), p. 74.
Real Ethics: Information from Brian Bergstein, "Hundred Dollar Laptop Project: Founder Expects Distribution by 2007," *The Columbus Dispatch* (April 10, 2006), p. F5; and, "Waking Up a Laptop Revolution," *Financial Times* (March 29, 2006), p. 1; Bruce Einhorn, "In Search of a PC for the People," *Business Week* (June 12, 2006), pp. 40–41.

Chapter 2

1 Stephanie Thompson. "Exec Brings Focus and Free Spirit to Build Buzz around natural beauty." *Advertising Age*, September 26, 2005. Accessed January 11, 2006, from EBSCOhost.
2 Susan Donovan. "Roxanne Quimby: How I Did It." *Inc.*, January 2004. Volume 26, Issue 1, p. 77.
3 Ibid.
4 Vicki Lee Parker, "Dressing Babies, Going Organic," The News Observer, retrieved from *www.newsobserver.com* (November 3, 2006).
5 Donovan, p. 76.
6 Carez press release, www.csswire.com (August 2, 2006).
7a Ibid www.pbs.org/newshour/bb/business/july-dec02/garments_10-10.html.
7b Stacey Burling, "Survey: MBA Students More Likely to Cheat,"

Philadelphia Inquirer, retrieved from *www.philly.com/mld/inquirer* (November 1, 2006).
8 Desmond Tutu, "Do More Than Win," *Fortune* (December 30, 1991), p. 59.
9 For an overview, see Linda K. Treviño and Katherine A. Nelson, *Managing Business Ethics*, 3rd ed. (New York: Wiley, 2003).
10 See for example James Oliver Horter and Lois E. Horton, *Slavery and the Making of America* (New York: Oxford University Press, 2004).
11 Treviño and Nelson, op cit.
12 Milton Rokeach, *The Nature of Human Values* (New York: Free Press, 1973). See also W. C. Frederick and J. Weber, "The Values of Corporate Executives and Their Critics: An Empirical Description and Normative Implications," in W. C. Frederick and L. E. Preston (eds.), *Business Ethics: Research Issues and Empirical Studies* (Greenwich, CT: JAI Press, 1990).
13 See Gerald F. Cavanagh, Dennis J. Moberg, and Manuel Velasquez, "The Ethics of Organizational Politics," *Academy of Management Review*, vol. 6 (1981), pp. 363–74; Justin G. Locknecker, Joseph A. McKinney, and Carlos W. Moore, "Egoism and Independence: Entrepreneurial Ethics," *Organizational Dynamics* (winter 1988), pp. 64–72; and Justin G. Locknecker, Joesph A. McKinney, and Carlos W. Moore, "The Generation Gap in Business Ethics," *Business Horizons* (September-October 1989), pp. 9–14.
14 Raymond L. Hilgert, "What Ever Happened to Ethics in Business and in Business Schools," *The Diary of Alpha Kappa Psi* (April 1989), pp. 4–8.
15 Jerald Greenburg, "Organizational Justice: Yesterday, Today, and Tomorrow," *Journal of Management*, vol. 16, (1990), pp. 399–432; and Mary A. Konovsky, "Understanding Procedural Justice and Its Impact on Business Organizations," *Journal of Management*, vol. 26 (2000), pp. 489–511.
16 Interactional justice is described by Robert J. Bies, "The Predicament of Injustice: The Management of Moral Outrage," in L. L. Cummings & B. M. Staw (eds.). *Research in Organizational Behavior*, vol. 9 (Greenwich, CT: JAI Press, 1987), pp. 289–319. The example is from Carol T. Kulik & Robert L. Holbrook, "Demographics in Service Encounters: Effects of Racial and Gender Congruence on Perceived Fair-

ness," *Social Justice Research*, vol. 13 (2000), pp. 375–402.
17 Robert D. Haas, "Ethics—A Global Business Challenge," *Vital Speeches of the Day* (June 1, 1996), pp. 506–9.
18 This discussion based on Thomas Donaldson, "Values in Tension: Ethics Away from Home," *Harvard Business Review*, vol. 74 (September-October 1996), pp. 48–62.
19 Ibid; Thomas Donaldson and Thomas W. Dunfee, "Towards a Unified Conception of Business Ethics: Integrative Social Contracts Theory," *Academy of Management Review*, vol. 19 (1994), pp. 252–85.
20 Developed from Donaldson, op cit.
21 Reported in Barbara Ley Toffler, "Tough Choices: Managers Talk Ethics," *New Management*, vol. 4 (1987), pp. 34–39. See also Barbara Ley Toffler, *Tough Choices: Managers Talk Ethics* (New York: Wiley, 1986).
22 See discussion by Treviño and Nelson, op cit., pp. 47–62.
23 Information from Steven N. Brenner and Earl A. Mollander, "Is the Ethics of Business Changing?" *Harvard Business Review*, vol. 55 (January-February 1977).
24 Saul W. Gellerman, "Why 'Good' Managers Make Bad Ethical Choices," *Harvard Business Review*, vol. 64 (July-August, 1986), pp. 85–90.
25 Survey results from Del Jones, "48% of Workers Admit to Unethical or Illegal Acts," *USA Today* (April 4, 1997), p. A1.
26 Reported in Adam Smith, "Wall Street's Outrageous Fortunes," *Esquire* (April 1987), p. 73.
27 The Body Shop came under scrutiny over the degree to which its business practices actually live up to this charter and the company's self-promoted green image. See, for example, John Entine, "Shattered Image," *Business Ethics* (September-October 1994), pp. 23–28. Quote with photo from www.anitaroddick.com (retrieved September 9, 2006).
28 Information on this case from William M. Carley, "Antitrust Chief Says CEOs Should Tape All Phone Calls to Each Other," *Wall Street Journal* (February 15, 1983), p. 23; "American Air, Chief End Antitrust Suit, Agree Not to Discuss Fares with Rivals," *Wall Street Journal* (July 15, 1985), p. 4; "American Airlines Loses Its Pilot," *Economist* (April 18, 1998), p. 58.
29 Alan L. Otten, "Ethics on the Job: Companies Alert Employees to Potential

Dilemmas," *Wall Street Journal* (July 14, 1986), p. 17; and "The Business Ethics Debate," *Newsweek* (May 25, 1987), p. 36.

30 See "Whistle-Blowers on Trial," *Business Week* (March 24, 1997), pp. 172–78; and "NLRB Judge Rules for Massachusetts Nurses in Whistle-Blowing Case," *American Nurse* (January-February 1998), p. 7.

31 For a review of whistleblowing, see Marcia P. Micelli and Janet P. Near, *Blowing the Whistle* (Lexington, MA: Lexington Books, 1992); see also Micelli and Near, "Whistleblowing: Reaping the Benefits," *Academy of Management Executive*, vol. 8 (August 1994), pp. 65–72.

32 Information from James A. Waters, "Catch 20.5: Mortality as an Organizational Phenomenon," *Organizational Dynamics*, vol. 6 (spring 1978), pp. 3–15.

33 Information from Ethics Resource Center, "Major Survey of America's Workers Finds Substantial Improvements in Ethics": www.ethics.org/releases/nr_20030521_nbes.html.

34 Information from "Gifts of Gab: A Start-up's Social Conscience Pays Off," *Business Week* (February 5, 2001), p. F38.

35 Information from www.josephsoninstitute.org/MED/MED-2sixpillars.htm.

36 Information from corporate website: www.gapinc.com/community sourcing/vendor_conduct.htm.

37 Archie B. Carroll, "In Search of the Moral Manager," *Business Horizons* (March/April, 2001), pp. 7–15.

38 See Terry Thomas, John R. Schermerhorn, Jr., and John W. Dienhart, "Leading Toward Ethical Behavior in Business," *Academy of Management Executive*, vol. 18 (May 2004), pp. 56–66.

39 See Thomas Donaldson and Lee Preston, "The Stakeholder Theory of the Corporation," *Academy of Management Review*, vol. 20 (January 1995), pp. 65–91.

40 Quote from corporate website: http//www.tomsofmaine.com.

41 Mary Miller, "Ben Cohen's Hot Fudge Venture Fund," *Business Ethics*, vol. 16 (January-February 2002), p. 6.

42 Information from "The Socially Correct Corporate," *Fortune* special advertising section (July 24, 2000), pp. S32–S34; Joseph Pereiva, "Doing Good and Doing Well at Timberland,"

Wall Street Journal (September 9, 2003), pp. B1, B10.

43 See Joel Makower: Putting Social Responsibility to Work for Your Business and the World (New York: Simon & Schuster, 1994), pp. 17–18.

44 The historical framework of this discussion is developed from Keith Davis, "The Case for and against Business Assumption of Social Responsibility," *Academy of Management Journal* (June 1973), pp. 312–22; Keith Davis and William Frederick, *Business and Society: Management: Public Policy, Ethics*, 5th ed. (New York: McGraw-Hill, 1984). The debate is also discussed by Makower, op. cit., pp. 28–33. See also, "Civics 101," *Economist* (May 11, 1996), p. 61.

45 The Friedman quotation is from Milton Friedman, *Capitalism and Freedom* (Chicago: University of Chicago Press, 1962); see also, Henry G. Manne, "Milton Friedman Was Right," *The Wall Street Journal* (November 24, 2006), p. A12. The Samuelson quotation is from Paul A. Samuelson, "Love That Corporation," *Mountain Bell Magazine* (spring 1971). Both are cited in Davis, op. cit.

46 Davis and Frederick, quoted in op. cit.

47 See James K. Glassman, "When Ethics Meet Earnings," *International Herald Tribune* (May 24–25, 2003), p. 15.

48 See Makower, op cit. (1994), pp. 71–75; Sandra A. Waddock and Samuel B. Graves, "The Corporate Social Performance-Financial Performance Link," *Strategic Management Journal* (1997), pp. 303–19; Michael E. Porter and Mark R. Kramer, "Strategy & Society: The Link Between Competitive Advantage and Corporate Social Responsibility," *Harvard Business Review* (December, 2006), pp. 78–92.

49 The "compliance—conviction" distinction is attributed to Mark Goyder in Martin Waller, "Much Corporate Responsibility Is Box-Ticking," *The Times Business* (July 8, 2003), p. 21.

50 Archie B. Carroll, "A Three-Dimensional Model of Corporate Performance," *Academy of Management Review*, vol. 4 (1979), pp. 497–505. Carroll's continuing work in this area is most recently reported in Mark S. Schwartz and Archie B, Carroll, "Corporate Social Responsibility: A Three

Domain Approach, "*Business Ethics Quarterly,* vol. 13 (2003), pp. 503–530.

51 Elizabeth Gatewood and Archie B. Carroll, "The Anatomy of Corporate Social Response," *Business Horizons,* vol. 24 (September-October 1981), pp. 9–16.

52 Judith Burns, "Everything You Wanted to Know About Corporate Governance. . . But Didn't Know How to Ask," *The Wall Street Journal* (October 27, 2003), pp. R1, R7.

53 Ibid.

54 "Warming to Corporate Reform," *The Wall Street Journal* (October 25, 2005), p. R2.

55 Laura Zinn, "Tom Chappell: Sweet Success from Unsweetened Toothpaste," *Business Week* (September 2, 1991), p. 52.

56 Janet Bamford, "Changing Business as Usual," *Working Women*, vol. 18 (November, 1993), p. 106.

57 Craig Cox, "Interview: Tom Chappell, Minister of Commerce," *Business Ethics*, vol. 8 (January 1994), p. 42.

58 Judy Quinn, "Tom's of Maine," *Incentive* (December 1993), p. A4.

59 Ibid.

60 Mary Martin, "Toothpaste and Theology," *Boston Globe* (October 10, 1993), p. A4.

61 Cox.

62 Mary Martin, "A 'Nuisance' to Rivals," *Boston Globe* (October 10, 1993), p. A4.

63 Cox.

64 Ibid.

65 "The Tom's of Maine Mission": www.tomsofmaine.com/about/mission.asp.

66 Quinn.

67 Ellyn E. Spragins, "Paying Employees to Work Elsewhere," *Inc.* (February 1993), p. 29.

68 Quinn.

69 Ibid.

70 Martin Everett, "Profiles in Marketing: Katie Shisler," *Sales and Marketing Management* (March 1993), p. 12.

71 Quinn.

72 Cox.

73 Ibid.

74 Ibid.

75 Tom's of Maine home page: www.tomsofmaine.com

76 Ibid.

77 K. W. Meyers, "Tom's of Maine Business Plan Includes People," *Denver Rocky Mountain News* (October 5, 2000), p. 3B.

78 http://www.usatoday.com/money/industries/retail/2006-03-21-colgate-toms_x.htm

79 http://www.tomsofmaine.com/about/press/2006_03 21_Colgate.asp

Features:

Insights: Information from www.benandjerrys. com, including timeline.

Issues and Situations: Information from Erin White, "What Would You Do? Ethics Courses Get Context," *The Wall Street Journal* (June 12, 2006), p. B3.

Kaffeeklatsch*: Information from John R. Emshwiller, Gary McWilliams, and Ann Davis, "Symbol of an Era: Lay, Skilling Convicted of Conspiracy," *The Wall Street Journal* (May 26, 2006), pp. A1, A9; and, Bethany McLean and Peter Elkind, "The Guiltiest Guys in the Room," *Fortune* (May 29, 2006), retrieved from CNNMoney.com (May 29, 2006). Quotes from McLean and Elkind.

Team Project: Information from Jeffrey Seglin, "Cheating Student Converts After Pal Goes Too Far," *Columbus Dispatch* (September 10, 2006), p. 62; "Report Card on the Ethics of American Youth," The Josephson Institute of Ethics, http://www.josephsoninstitute.org (retrieved September 10, 2006).

Personal Management: Information on the Josephson Institute of Ethics from http://www.josephsoninstitute.org/MED/MED-2sixpillars.htm (retrieved September 10, 2006).

Real Ethics: Information from Cheryl Soltis, *The Wall Street Journal* (March 21, 2006), p. B7.

Chapter 3

1 Robert D. Hof, "Jeff Bezos' Risky Bet," *Business Week* (November 13, 2006), pp. 52–58. See also "Jeffrey P. Bezos." Academy of Accomplishment. Accessed June 13, 2006, at http://www.achievement.org/autodoc/page/bez0bio-1.

2 Daniel Pink. "Revenge of the Right Brain," *Wired*, February 2005. Accessed June 22 at http://www.wired.com/wired/archive/13.02/brain.html.

3 "Information Age: People, Information & Technology." Smithsonian Institution. Accessed June 13, 2006, at http://photos.si.edu/infoage/infoage.html.

4 Smithsonian.

5 "In Computer Science a growing gender gap," *The Boston Globe* (December 18, 2005).

6 Not used.

7 A thorough review and critique of the history of management thought, in-cluding management in ancient civilizations, is provided by Daniel A. Wren, *The Evolution of Management Thought*, 4th ed. (New York: Wiley, 1993).

8 Pauline Graham, *Mary Parker Follett—Prophet of Management: A Celebration of Writings from the 1920s* (Boston: Harvard Business School Press, 1995).

9 For a timeline of twentieth-century management ideas see "75 Years of Management Ideas and Practices: 1922–1997," *Harvard Business Review*, supplement (September-October 1997).

10 For a sample of this work see Henry L. Gantt, *Industrial Leadership* (Easton, MD: Hive, 1921; Hive edition published in 1974); Henry C. Metcalfe and Lyndall Urwick (eds.), *Dynamic Administration: The Collected Papers of Mary Parker Follett* (New York: Harper & Brothers, 1940); James D. Mooney, *The Principles of Administration*, rev. ed. (New York: Harper & Brothers, 1947); Lyndall Urwick, *The Elements of Administration* (New York: Harper & Brothers, 1943); and *The Golden Book of Management* (London: N. Neame, 1956).

11 References on Taylor's work are from Frederick W. Taylor, *The Principles of Scientific Management* (New York: W. W. Norton, 1967), originally published by Harper & Brothers in 1911. See Charles W. Wrege and Amedeo G. Perroni, "Taylor's Pig-Tale: A Historical Analysis of Frederick W. Taylor's Pig Iron Experiments," *Academy of Management Journal*, vol. 17 (March 1974), pp. 6–27, for a criticism; see Edwin A. Lock, "The Ideas of Frederick W. Taylor. An Evaluation," *Academy of Management Review*, vol. 7 (1982), p. 14, for an examination of the contemporary significance of Taylor's work. See also the biography, Robert Kanigel, *The One Best Way* (New York: Viking, 1997).

12 Kanigel, op cit. See also Cynthia Crossen, "Early Industry Expert Soon Realized a Staff Has Its Own Efficiency," *The Wall Street Journal* (November 6, 2006), p. B1.

13 See Frank B. Gilbreth, *Motion Study* (New York: Van Nostrand, 1911).

14 Available in the English language as Henri Fayol, *General and Industrial Administration* (London: Pitman, 1949); subsequent discussion is based on M. B. Brodie, *Fayol on Administration* (London: Pitman, 1949).

15 A.M. Henderson and Talcott Parsons (eds. and trans.), *Max Weber: The Theory of Social Economic Organization* (New York: Free Press, 1947).

16 Ibid., p. 337.

17 M.P. Follett, *Freedom and Coordination* (London: Management Publications Trust, 1949).

18 Judith Garwood, "A Review of *Dynamic Administration: The Collected Papers of Mary Parker Follett*," *New Management*, vol. 2 (1984), pp. 61–62; eulogy from Richard C. Cabot, *Encyclopedia of Social Work*, vol. 15, "Follett, Mary Parker," p. 351.

19 The Hawthorne studies are described in detail in F. J. Roethlisberger and William J. Dickson, *Management and the Worker* (Cambridge, MA: Harvard University Press, 1966); and G. Homans, *Fatigue of Workers* (New York: Reinhold, 1941). For an interview with three of the participants in the relay-assembly test-room studies, see R. G. Greenwood, A. A. Bolton, and R. A. Greenwood, "Hawthorne a Half Century Later: 'Relay Assembly Participants Remember'", *Journal of Management*, vol. 9 (1983), pp. 217–31.

20 The criticisms of the Hawthorne studies are detailed in Alex Carey, "The Hawthorne Studies: A Radical Criticism," *American Sociological Review*, vol. 32 (1967), pp. 403–16; H.M. Parsons, "What Happened at Hawthorne?" *Science*, vol. 183 (1974), pp. 922–32; and B. Rice, "The Hawthorne Defect: Persistence of a Flawed Theory," *Psychology Today*, vol. 16(1982), pp. 70–74. See also Wren, op cit.

21 This discussion of Maslow's theory is based on Abraham H. Maslow, *Eupsychian Management* (Homewood, IL: Richard D. Irwin, 1965); and Abraham H. Maslow, *Motivation and Personality*, 2nd ed. (New York: Harper & Row, 1970).

22 Douglas McGregor, *The Human Side of Enterprise* (New York: McGraw-Hill, 1960).

23 See Gary Heil, Deborah F. Stevens, and Warren G. Bennis, *Douglas McGregor on Management: Revisiting the Human Side of Enterprise* (New York: Wiley, 2000).

24 Chris Argyris, *Personality and Organization* (New York: Harper & Row, 1957).

25 The ideas of Ludwig von Bertalanffy contributed to the emergence of this

systems perspective on organizations. See his article, "The History and Status of General Systems Theory," *Academy of Management Journal*, vol. 15 (1972), pp. 407–26. This viewpoint is further developed by Daniel Katz and Robert L. Kahn in their classic book, *The Social Psychology of Organizations* (New York: Wiley, 1978). For an integrated systems view see Lane Tracy, *The Living Organization* (New York: Quorum Books, 1994). For an overview, see W. Richard Scott, *Organizations: Rational, Natural, and Open Systems*, 4th ed. (Upper Saddle River, NJ: Prentice-Hall, 1998).

[26] Chester I. Barnard, *Functions of the Executive* (Cambridge, MA: Harvard University Press, 1938).

[27] For an overview, see Scott, op cit., pp. 95–97.

[28] Thomas J. Peters and Robert H. Waterman, Jr., *In Search of Excellence: Lessons from America's Best-Run Companies* (New York: Harper & Row, 1982). For a retrospective see William C. Bogner, "Tom Peters on the Real World of Business" and "Robert Waterman on Being Smart and Lucky," *Academy of Management Executive*, vol. 16(2002), pp. 40–50.

[29] Based on a discussion in John R. Schermerhorn, Jr., James G. Hunt, and Richard N. Osborn, *Organizational Behavior*, 9th Ed. (Hoboken, NJ: John Wiley & Sons, 2005), pp. 24–25. See also Jim Collins and Jerry I. Porras, *Built to Last* (New York: HarperCollins, 1994) and Jim Collins, *Good to Great* (New York: Harper-Collins, 2001);

[30] Peter Senge, *The Fifth Discipline* (New York: Harper, 1990).

[31] Apple Computer home page: http://www.apple.com.

[32] Ibid.

[33] Pixar home page: http://www.pixar.com/.

[34] Apple Computer home page.

Features:

Insights: Quote from "How Good is Google?" *The Economist* (November 1, 2003). See also www.google.com/corporate.

Kaffeeklatsch: Data from Louis Lavelle, "Is the MBA Overrated?" *Business Week* (March 20, 2006), pp. 78–80.

Personal Management: Quote from Allan H. Church, Executive Commentary, *Academy of Management Executive* (February, 2002), p. 74

Real Ethics: Reported in *The Columbus Dispatch* (March 8, 2006), p. D2. Quote from Allan H. Church, Executive Commentary, *Academy of Management Executive* (February, 2002), p. 74.

Chapter 4

[1] Michele Conlin, "Smashing the Clock," *Business Week* (December 11, 2006), pp. 60–38. Arvind Sarma, "Agency-Related Matters: Creating a Creative Culture." Strategic Thinking. Accessed August 6, 2006, at http://www.etstrategicmarketing.com/smmar-apr2/agency.htm.

[2] Ibid.

[3] http://www.pgcareers.com/index.asp?11=4&12=8&13=37&14=75&profile=223&mode=2. Accessed August 24, 2006.

[4] Warren Bennis, "Making Staffs Creative, and Keeping Them That Way." *CIO Insight*, June 5, 2005. Accessed August 30, 2006, from http://www.cioinsight.com/article2/0.1540.1926226.00.asp.

[5] http://www.blankgarments.com/factsnstats.php. Accessed August 22, 2006.

[6] "Fuzzy Maths," *The Economist*, May 15, 2006. Vol. 379, Issue 8477.

[7a] http://www.busreslab.com/quick-polls/poll7.htm.

[7b] Robert Reich, *The Future of Success* (New York: Knopf, 2001), p. 7.

[8] Quote from *The New Blue* (IBM Annual Report, 1997), p.8.

[9] Reich, op cit.

[10] See Michael E. Porter, *Competitive Strategy: Techniques for Analyzing Industries and Competitors* (New York: Free Press, 1980), and *Competitive Advantage: Creating and Sustaining Superior Performance* (New York: Free Press, 1986); also, Richard A. D'Aveni, *Hyper-Competition: Managing the Dynamics of Strategic Maneuvering* (New York: Free Press, 1994).

[11] See Richard D. Bucher, *Diversity Consciousness: Opening Our Minds to People, Cultures, and Opportunities* (Upper Saddle River, NJ: Prentice-Hall, 2000), p. 201.

[12] Information from "Ivory Tower: How an MBA Can Bend Your Mind," *Business Week* (April 1, 2002), p. 12.

[13] James D. Thompson, *Organizations in Action* (New York: McGraw-Hill, 1967); and Robert B. Duncan, "Characteristics of Organizational Environments and Perceived Environmental Uncertainty," *Administrative Science Quarterly*, vol. 17 (1972), pp. 313–27. For discussion of the implications of uncertainty see Hugh Courtney, Jane Kirkland, and Patrick Viguerie, "Strategy Under Uncertainty," *Harvard Business Review* (November-December 1997), pp. 67–79.

[14] Quotation from a discussion by Richard J. Shonberger and Edward M. Knod Jr., *Operations Management: Serving the Customer*, 3rd ed. (Plano, TX: Business Publications, 1988), p. 4.

[15] Quote from *The Vermont Teddy Bear Company Gazette*, op cit., p. 3.

[16] Rosabeth Moss Kanter, "Transcending Business Boundaries: 12,000 World Managers View Change," *Harvard Business Review* (May–June 1991), pp. 151-64.

[17] Reported in Jennifer Steinhauer, "The Undercover Shoppers," *New York Times* (February 4, 1998), pp. C1, C2.

[18] Information from "How Marriott Never Forgets a Guest," *Business Week* (February 21, 2000), p. 74; and Melissa Campanell, "Proof Gamble Apples RightNow to Be Online Consumer Experience"

[19] Roger D. Blackwell and Kristina Blackwell, "The Century of the Consumer: Converting Supply Chains into Demand Chains," *Supply Chain Management Review* (fall 1999).

[20] Edgar H. Schein, "Organizational Culture," *American Psychologist*, vol. 45 (1990), pp. 109-19. See also Schein's *Organizational Culture and Leadership*, 2nd ed. (San Francisco: Jossey-Bass, 1997); and *The Corporate Culture Survival Guide* (San Francisco: Jossey-Bass, 1999).

[21] In their book *Corporate Culture and Performance* (New York: Macmillan, 1992), John P. Kotter and James L. Heskett make the point that strong cultures have the desired effects over the long term only if they encourage adaptation to a changing environment. See also Collins and Porras, op cit. (1994).

[22] James Collins and Jerry Porras, *Built to Last* (New York: Harper Business, 1994).

[23] Schein, op. cit. (1997); Terrence E. Deal and Alan A. Kennedy, *Corporate Cultures: The Rites and Rituals of Corporate Life* (Reading, MA: Addison-Wesley, 1982); and Ralph Kilmann,

Beyond the Quick Fix (San Francisco: Jossey-Bass, 1984).

[24] This is a simplified model developed from Schein, op cit. (1997).

[25] James C. Collins and Jerry I. Porras, "Building Your Company's Vision," *Harvard Business Review* (September-October 1996), pp. 65–77.

[26] This case is reported in Jenny C. McCune, "Making Lemonade," *Management Review* (June 1997), pp. 49–53.

[27] Ralph H. Kilmann, Mary J. Saxton, and Roy Serpa, "Issues in Understanding and Changing Corporate Culture," *California Management Review*, vol. 28 (1986), pp. 87–94.

[28] See Mary Kay Ash, *Mary Kay: You Can Have It All* (New York: Roseville, CA: Prima Publishing, 1995).

[29] Thomas R. Roosevelt Jr., *Beyond Race and Gender* (New York: AMACOM, 1992), p. 10; see also Thomas R. Roosevelt Jr., "From 'Affirmative Action' to 'Affirming Diversity,'" *Harvard Business Review*, (November-December 1990), pp. 107–17; Thomas R. Roosevelt Jr., with Marjorie I. Woodruff, *Building a House for Diversity* (New York: AMACOM, 1999).

[30] Thomas Kochan, Katerina Bezrukova, Robin Ely, Susan Jackson, Aparna Joshi, Karen Jehn, Jonathan Leonard, David Levine, and David Thomas, "The Effects of Diversity on Business Performance: Report of the Diversity Research Network," reported in SHRM Foundation Research Findings, retrieved from www.shrm.org/ foundation/findings.asp. Full article published in *Human Resource Management* (2003).

[31] Gardenswartz and Anita Rowe, *Managing Diversity: A Complete Desk Reference and Planning Guide* (Chicago: Irwin, 1993).

[32] Taylor Cox, Jr., *Cultural Diversity in Organizations* (San Francisco: Berrett Koehler, 1994).

[33] See Joseph A. Raelin, *Clash of Cultures* (Cambridge, MA: Harvard Business School Press, 1986).

[34] See Anthony Robbins and Joseph McClendon III, *Unlimited Power: A Black Choice* (New York: Free Press, 1997), and Augusto Failde and William Doyle, *Latino Success: Insights from America's Most Powerful Latino Executives* (New York: Free Press, 1996).

[35] Barbara Benedict Bunker, "Appreciating Diversity and Modifying Organizational Cultures: Men and Women at Work," Chapter 5 in Suresh Srivastva and David L. Cooperrider, *Appreciative Management and Leadership* (San Francisco: Jossey-Bass, 1990).

[36] See Gary N. Powell, *Women & Men in Management* (Thousand Oaks, CA: Sage, 1993) and Cliff Cheng (ed.), *Masculinities in Organizations* (Thousand Oaks, CA: Sage, 1996). For added background, see also Sally Helgesen, *Everyday Revolutionaries: Working Women and the Transformation of American Life* (New York: Doubleday, 1998).

[37] Stephanie N. Mehta, "What Minority Employees Really Want," *Fortune* (July 10, 2000), pp. 181–86.

[38] Ibid.

[39] Thomas, op cit. (1992).

[40] Ibid.

[41] This section is based on ideas set forth by Thomas, op cit. (1992); and Thomas and Woodruff, op cit. (1999).

[42] Survey reported in "The Most Inclusive Workplaces Generate the Most Loyal Employees," *Gallup Management Journal* (December 2001), retrieved from http://gmj.gallup.com/press_room/ release.asp?i=117.

[43] "Diversity Today: Corporate Recruiting Practices in Inclusive Workplaces," *Fortune* (June 12, 2000), p. S4.

[44] http://www.panera.com/ about_co_history.aspx. Accessed August 2, 2006.

[45] http://www.bakingbusiness.com/ bs/channel.asp?ArticleID=73003. Accessed August 2, 2006.

[46] http://www.panera.com/ about_co. aspx. Accessed August 2, 2006.

[47] "Panera Bread Introduces Panera Kids." Panera Bread press release, June 2, 2006.

[48] "Panera Bread Removes Trans Fat from Menu." Panera Bread press release. February 23, 2006.

[49] Ron Shaich. Speech at Annual Meeting 2006, Temple Israel, June 28, 2006.

[50] Ron Miller. "Wi-Fi Continues Its Extended Coffee Break." *Information Week*, January 4, 2006. Accessed August 2, 2006, at http://www.informationweek.com/story/showArticle.jhtml?articleID=175801232.

[51] Jefferson Graham. "As Wi-Fi spreads, more free locations popping up." *USA Today*, December 8, 2005. Accessed August 2, 2006, at www.us- atoday.com/tech/wireless/2005-12-08-wi-fi-free_x.htm.

[52] "Panera Bread Recognized as the Top Performer in Restaurant Category for One-, Five and Ten-Year Returns to Shareholders." Panera Bread press release, May 4, 2006.

Features:
Insights: David Rocks, "Reinventing Herman Miller," *Business Week eBiz* (April 2, 2000), pp. E88-E96; www.hermanmiller.com.

Issues and Situations: Information from "The Immelt Revolution," *Business Week* (March 28, 2005), pp. 64–73.

Kaffeeklatsch: Data from "How We Picked the Best Jobs: We Started with the Growing Fields . . . and then Started Cutting," cnn.com/money (April 12, 2006).

Personal Management: Quote from T. S. Eliot, *Little Gidding*.

Real Ethics: Based on incident reported in "FBI Nabs 3 Over Coca-Cola Secrets," cnn.com (retrieved July 6, 2006); and Betsy McKay, "Coke Employee Faces Charges in Plot to Sell Secrets," *The Wall Street Journal* (July 6, 2006), p. B1.

Chapter 5

[1] Roger Parloff, Clay Chandler, and Alice Fung. "Not Exactly Counterfeit." *Fortune (Europe)*, May 15, 2006. Volume 15, Issue 8.

[2] Ibid.

[3] Ibid.

[4] Ibid.

[5] Parloff, et al.

[6] http://news.com.com/Commentary+ The+IT+diaspora/2009-1069_3-980632. html. Accessed June 21, 2006.

[7] Melanie Klettner. "New Balance Sprinting with Apparel at 100." *Women's Wear Daily*, March 16, 2006. Volume 191, Issue 57.

[8] "Survey: Intellectual Property Theft now accounts for 31% of Global Counterfeiting." Gieschen Consultancy, February 25, 2005. Accessed June 21, 2006 at http://express-press-release.com/10/Survey%20intellectual% 20Property%20Theft%20now%20 accounts%2031%25%20of%20Global% 20Counterfeiting.php.

[9] http://www.thirdworldtraveler.com/ Globalization/Globalization_FactsFigures.html. Accessed August 23, 2006.

[10] Kenichi Ohmae's books include *The Borderless World: Power and Strategy*

in the Interlinked Economy (New York: Harper, 1989); The End of the Nation State (New York: Free Press, 1996); and The Invisible Continent: Four Strategic Imperatives of the New Economy (New York: Harper, 1999); and, The Next Global Stage: Challenges and Opportunities in Our Borderless World (Philadelphia: Wharton School Publishing, 2006).

[11] For a discussion of globalization see Thomas L. Friedman. The Lexus and the Olive Tree: Understanding Globalization (New York: Bantam Doubleday Dell, 2000); and John Micklethwait and Adrian Woodridge, A Future Perfect: The Challenges and Hidden Promise of Globalization (New York: Crown, 2000); and Thomas L. Friedman, The World is Flat: A Brief History of the Twenty-First Century (New York: Farrar, Straus and Giroux, 2005).

[12] Rosabeth Moss Kanter, World Class: Thinking Locally in the Global Economy (New York: Simon & Schuster, 1995), preface.

[13] Quote from Jeffrey E. Garten, "The Mind of the CEO," Business Week (February 5, 2001), p. 106.

[14] Information from Mark Niquette, "Honda's 'Bold Move' Paid Off," Columbus Dispatch (November 16, 2002), pp. C1, C2.

[15] Quote from John A. Byrne, "Visionary vs. Visionary," Business Week (August 28, 2000), p. 210.

[16] Business Week (February 29, 1988), pp. 63–66; further information on corporate website: www.falconproducts.com/.

[17] "Best Practices for Global Competitiveness," Fortune (March 30, 1998), pp. S1–S3, special advertising

[18] The Economist is a good weekly source of information on Europe. See www.economist.com.

[19] A monthly publication that covers NAFTA's maquiladora industries is the Twin Plant News (El Paso, Texas); see website at: www.twin-plant-news.com/.

[20] The Economist is a good weekly source of information on Africa. See www.economist.com. See also "Embracing Africa," Business Week (December 18, 2006), p. 101.

[21] James A. Austin and John G. McLean, "Pathways to Business Success in Sub-Saharan Africa," Journal of African Finance and Economic Development, vol. 2 (1996), pp. 57–76.

[22] See Alex Taylor III, "This Year's Model," Fortune (June 12, 2006), pp. 41–42.

[23] See Peter F. Drucker, "The Global Economy and the Nation-State," Foreign Affairs, vol. 76 (September-October 1997), pp. 159–71.

[24] R. Hall Mason. "Conflicts between Host Countries and Multinational Enterprise," California Management Review, vol. 17 (1974), pp. 6, 7.

[25] Information from corporate website: www.nikeBiz.com/labor/toc_monitoring.html.

[26] "An Industry Monitors Child Labor," New York Times (October 16, 1997), pp. B1, B9; and Rugmark International website: www.rugmark.de.

[27] Definition from World Commission on Environment and Development, Our Common Future (Oxford: Oxford University Press, 1987); reported on International Institute for Sustainable Development website: www.iisdl.iisd.ca.

[28] Based on Barbara Benedict Bunker, "Appreciating Diversity and Modifying Organizational Cultures: Men and Women at Work," in Suresh Srivastiva and David L. Cooperrider (eds), Appreciative Management and Leadership: The Power of Positive Thought and Action in Organizations (San Francisco: Jossey-Bass, 1990), pp. 127–49.

[29] Examples reported in Neil Chesanow, The World-Class Executive (New York: Rawson Associates, 1985).

[30] P. Christopher Earley and Elaine Mosakowski, "Toward Cultural Intelligence: Turning Cultural Differences Into Workplace Advantage," Academy of Management Executive, Vol. 18 (2004), pp. 151–157.

[31] For a good overview of the practical issues, see Richard D. Lewis, The Cultural Imperative: Global Trends in the 21st Century (Yarmouth, ME: Intercultural Press, 2002); and Martin J. Gannon, Understanding Global Cultures (Thousand Oaks, CA: Sage, 1994).

[32] Edward T. Hall, The Silent Language (New York: Anchor Books, 1959).

[33] Edward T. Hall, Beyond Culture (New York: Doubleday, 1976).

[34] Edward T. Hall, The Hidden Dimension (New York: Anchor Books, 1969); and, Hidden Differences (New York: Doubleday, 1990).

[35] Geert Hofstede, Culture's Consequences (Beverly Hills: Sage, 1984).

[36] This dimension is explained more thoroughly by Geert Hofstede et al., Masculinity and Feminity: The Taboo Dimension of National Cultures (Thousand Oaks, CA: Sage, 1998).

[37] For an introduction to the fifth dimension, see Geert Hofstede and Michael H. Bond, "The Confucius Connection: From Cultural Roots to Economic Growth," Organizational Dynamics, vol. 16 (1988), pp. 4–21, which presents comparative data from Bond's "Chinese Values Survey."

[38] Robert J. House, Paul J. Hanges, Mansour Javidan, Peter W. Dorfman, and Vipin Gupta, (eds.), Culture, Leadership and Organizations: The GLOBE Study of 62 Societies (Thousand Oaks, CA: Sage Publications, Inc., 2004). Further issues on Project GLOBE are developed in George B. Graen, "In the Eye of the Beholder: Cross-Cultural Lesson in Leadership from Project GLOBE: A Response Viewed from the Third Culture Bonding (TCB) Model of Cross Cultural Leadership," Academy of Management Perspectives, Vol. 20 (November, 2006), pp. 95–101; and, Robert J. House, Mansour Javidan, Peter W. Dorfman, and Mary Sully de Luque, "A Failure of Scholarship: response to George Graen's Critique of GLOBE," Academy of Management Perspectives, Vol. 20 (November, 2006), pp. 102–114.

[39] This summary is based on Ibid. and Mansour Javidan, P. Dorfman, Mary Sully de Luque, and Robert J. House, "In the Eye of the Beholder: Cross Cultural Lessons in Leadership from Project GLOBE," Academy of Management Perspectives (February 2006), pp. 67–90.

[40] For additional cultural models and research see the summary in House, op cit., as well as Fons Trompenaars, Riding the Waves of Culture: Understanding Cultural Diversity in Business (London: Nicholas Brealey Publishing, 1993); Harry C. Triandis, Culture and Social Behavior (New York: McGraw-Hill, 1994); Steven H. Schwartz, "A Theory of Cultural Values and Some Implications for Work," Applied Psychology: An International Review, vol. 48 (1999), pp. 23–47; Martin J. Gannon, Understanding Global Cultures, 3rd ed. (Thousand Oaks, CA: Sage, 2004).

[41] Geert Hofstede, "Motivation, Leadership, and Organization," p. 43. See also Hofstede's "Cultural Constraints in Management Theories," Academy of Management Review, vol. 7 (1993), pp. 81–94.

[42] The classics are William Ouchi, Theory Z: How American Business Can Meet the Japanese Challenge (Reading, MA:

Addison-Wesley, 1981), and Richard Tanner Pascale and Anthony G. Athos, *The Art of Japanese Management: Applications for American Executives* (New York: Simon & Schuster, 1981). See also J. Bernard Keys, Luther Tray Denton, and Thomas R. Miller, " The Japanese Management Theory Jungle—Revisited," *Journal of Management*, vol. 20 (1994), pp. 373–402.

[43] See Chapters 4 and 5 in Miriam Erez and P. Christopher Early, *Culture, Self-Identity, and Work* (New York: Oxford University Press, 1993).

[44] For a good discussion of the historical context of Japanese management practices see Makoto Ohtsu, *Inside Japanese Business: A Narrative History 1960–2000* (Armonk, NY: M.E. Sharpe, 2002), pp. 39–41.

[45] Quote from Kenichi Ohmae, "Japan's Admiration for U.S. Methods Is an Open Book," *Wall Street Journal* (October 10, 1983), p. 21. See also his book *The Borderless World: Power and Strategy in the Interlinked Economy*, (New York, Harper, 1989).

[46] See for example Mzamo P. Mangaliso, "Building Competitive Advantage from *ubuntu*: Management Lessons from South Africa," *Academy of Management Executive*, vol. 15 (2001), pp. 23–33.

[47] Geert Hofstede, "A Reply to Goodstein and Hunt," *Organizational Dynamics*, vol. 10 (summer 1981), p. 68.

[48] Harley-Davidson home page: www. harley-davidson.com.

[49] Malia Boyd, "Harley-Davidson Motor Company," *Incentive* (September 1993), pp. 26&ndah;27.

[50] Shrader et al., "Harley-Davidson, Inc.—1991," in Fred David, ed., *Strategic Management*, 4th ed. (New York: Macmillan, 1993), p. 655.

[51] Ibid.

[52] Martha H. Peak, "Harley-Davidson: Going Whole Hog to Provide Stakeholder Satisfaction," *Management Review*, vol. 82 (June 1993), p. 53

[53] Harley-Davidson home page.

[54] Peak.

[55] Harley-Davidson home page.

[56] Kevin Kelly and Karen Miller, "The Rumble Heard Round the World: Harleys," *Business Week* (May 24, 1993) p. 60.

[57] Ibid.

[58] Harley-Davidson home page.

[59] Sandra Dallas and Emily Thornton, "Japan's Bikers: The Tame Ones," *Business Week* (October 20, 1997), p. 159.

[60] "H-D Cautiously Upbeat Over Beijing Dealer." *Dealer News*, May 2006, p. 67.

[61] Harley-Davidson home page.

Features:

Insights: Information from corporate website: www.limited.com; quotes from www.limited.com/feature.jsp and www.limited.com/who/index. jsp. See also Les Wekner, "How I Conquered the Women's Retail Clothing Industry (and an Ulcer), *Fortune Small Business* (September, 2003), pp. 40–43.

Issues and Situations: Information from Peter Burrows, "Stalking High-Tech Sweatshops" *Business Week* (June 19, 2006), pp. 62–63.

Kaffeeklatsch: Information from Richard Milne, "Unions Face VW Threat in Dispute Over Pay" *Financial Times* (June 15, 2006), p. 18; "Europe Auto Relations Get Testy," *The Wall Street Journal* (June 15, 2006), p. A8. Real Ethics: Information from Raul Burgoa, "Bolivia Seizes Control of Oil and Gas Fields," *Bangkok Post* (May 3, 2006), p. B5.

Personal Management: Richard D. Lewis, *The Cultural Imperative: Global Trends in the 21st Century* (Yarmouth, ME: Intercultural Press, 2002); Makoto Ohtsu, *Inside Japanese Business: A Narrative History 1960–2000* (Armonk, NY: M.E. Sharpe, 2002).

Team Project: Thomas L. Friedman, *The World Is Flat: A Brief History of the Twenty-First Century* (New York: Farrar, Straus and Giroux, 2005), p. 325. Source: http://express-press-release. com/10/Survey%20Intellectual%20Pr operty%20Theft%20now%20accounts% 20for%2031%25%20of%20Global%20 Counterfeiting.php

Chapter 6

[1] Kevin Maney. "Ice cream arrives in a flash, but MooBella's start took time." *USA Today*, April 19, 2006, p. 3b.

[2] Ibid.

[3] Peter Lewis. "Cream of the Crop." *Fortune, March 6, 2006. Vol. 153, Issue 4.*

[4] Ibid.

[5] "Vending Technology Looks to Ice Cream." *Dairy Foods*, June 1, 2006.

[6] "Ice Cream Consumption," *http://www.sendicecream.com/contriv.html.*

[7] Ibid.

[8] http://www.dama.org/public/pages/ index.cfm?pageid=461

[9] Speech at the Lloyd Greif Center for Enterpreneurial Studies, Marshall School of Business, University of Southern California, 1996.

[10] Information from the corporate websites and from The Entrepreneur's Hall of Fame: www.1tbn.com/halloffame.html.

[11] For a review and discussion of the entrepreneurial mind see Jeffry A. Timmons, *New Venture Creation: Entrepreneurship for the 21st Century* (New York: Irwin/McGraw-Hill, 1999), pp. 219–25.

[12] See the review by Robert D. Hisrich and Michael P. Peters, *Entrepreneurship*, 4th ed. (New York: Irwin/McGraw-Hill, 1998), pp. 67–70; and Paulette Thomas. "Entrepreneurs' Biggest Problems and How They Solve Them," *Wall Street Journal Reports* (March 17, 2003), pp. R1, R2.

[13] Based on research summarized by Hisrich and Peters, op. cit., pp. 70–74.

[14] Information from Jim Hopkins, "Serial Entrepreneur Strikes Again at Age 70," *USA Today* (August 15, 2000).

[15] Timothy Butler and James Waldroop, "Job Sculpting: The Art of Retaining Your Best People," *Harvard Business Review* (September-October 1999), pp. 144–52.

[16] This list is developed from Timmons, op cit, pp. 47–48; and Hisrich and Peters, op cit., pp. 67–70.

[17] "Smart Talk: Start-Ups and Schooling," *Wall Street Journal* (September 7, 2004), p. B4.

[18] *Paths to Entrepreneurship: New Directions for Women in Business* (New York: Catalyst, 1998) and Eve Hayek, "Report Shatters Myths About U.S. Women's Equality" (October 1, 2005); both available on the National Foundation for Women Business Owners Web site: www.nfwbo.org/key.html.

[19] Data from Ibid. and "Smart Talk: Start-Ups and Schooling," *Wall Street Journal* (September 7, 2004), p. B4.

[20] Data from *Paths to Entrepreneurship: New Directions for Women in Business* (New York: Catalyst, 1998) as summarized on the National Foundation for Women Business Owners website: www.nfwbo.org/key.html.

[21] National Foundation for Women Business Owners, *Women Business Owners of Color: Challenges and Accomplishments* (1998).

[22] Data reported by Karen E. Klein, "Minority Start Ups: A Measure of Progress,"

Business Week (August 25, 2005), retrieved from www.businessweekonline.

23 David Bornstein, *How to Change the World: Social Entrepreneurs and the Power of New Ideas* (Oxford, U.K.: Oxford University Press, 2004).

24 See Laura D' Andrea Tyson, "Good Works—With a Business Plan," *Business Week* (May 3, 2004), retrieved from Business Week Online (November 14, 2005) at www.businessweek.com.

25 Information from "Chapter 2," *Kellogg* (Winter, 2004), p. 6; See also *Leaving Microsoft to Change the World* (New York: Harper Collins), 2006.

26 *The Facts About Small Business 1999* (Washington, DC: U.S. Small Business Administration, Office of Advocacy).

27 See U.S. Small Business Administration website: www.sba.gov; and *Statistical Abstract of the United States* (Washington, DC: U.S. Census Bureau, 1999).

28 Information reported in "The Rewards," *Inc. State of Small Business* (May 20–21, 2001), pp. 50–51.

29 "Small Business Expansions in Electronic Commerce," U.S. Small Business Administration, Office of Advocacy (June 2000).

30 Information from Will Christensen, "Rod Spencer's Sports-Card Business Has Migrated Cyberspace Marketplace," *Columbus Dispatch* (July 24, 2000), p. F1.

31 Data reported by The Family Firm Institute: www.ffi.org/looking/factsfb. html.

32 Conversation from the case "Am I My Uncle's Keeper?" by Paul I. Karofsky (Northeastern University Center for Family Business) and published at: www.fambiz.com/contprov.cfm? ContProvCode=NECFB&ID=140.

33 Survey of Small and Mid-Sized Businesses: Trends for 2000 (Arthur Andersen, 2000).

34 Ibid.

35 See U.S. Small Business Administration website: www.sba.gov.

36 George Gendron, "The Failure Myth," *Inc.* (January 2001), p. 13.

37 Discussion based on "The Life Cycle of Entrepreneurial Firms," in Ricky Griffin (ed.), *Management*, 6th ed. (New York: Houghton Mifflin, 1999), pp. 309–10; and Neil C. Churchill and Virginia L. Lewis, "The Five Stages of Small Business Growth," *Harvard Business Review* (May-June 1993), pp. 30–50.

38 Developed from William S. Sahlman, "How to Write a Great Business Plan," *Harvard Business Review* (July-August 1997), pp. 98–108.

39 Marcia H. Pounds, "Business Plan Sets Course for Growth," *Columbus Dispatch* (March 16, 1998), p. 9; see also firm website: www.calcustoms.com.

40 Standard components of business plans are described in many text sources such as Linda Pinson and Jerry Jinnett, *Anatomy of a Business Plan: A Step-by-Step Guide to Starting Smart, Building the Business, and Securing Your Company's Future*, 4th ed. (Dearborn Trade, 1999), and Scarborough and Zimmerer, op. cit.; and on websites such as: American Express Small Business Services, Business Town.com., and Bizplanlt.com.

41 "You've Come a Long Way Baby," *Business Week Frontier* (July 10, 2000).

42 Domino's Pizza home page: www. dominos.com.

43 Ibid.

44 "Tom Monaghan," The American Dreams Collection, www.usdreams.com/ Monaghan7677. html, March 1, 2001.

45 Ibid.

46 Domino's Pizza home page.

47 "Tom Monaghan."

48 Amy Zuber, "Tom Monaghan," Nation's Restaurant News (September 13, 1999), pp. 139–141.

49 "Tom Monaghan."

50 Domino's Pizza home page.

51 "Pizza Magnate Backs Off Catholic Town Plan." Church & State, May 2006, p.21.

52 http://www.pizzatoday.com.

53 Ibid.

54 Domino's Pizza home page.

Features:

Insights: Information from "Women Business Owners Receive First-Ever Micro Loans Via the Internet," *Business Wire* (August 9, 2000); Jim Hopkins, "Non-Profit Loan Group Takes Risks on Women in Business," *USA Today* (August 9, 2000), p. 2B; and "Women's Group Grants First Loans to Entrepreneurs," *Columbus Dispatch* (August 10, 2000), p. B2.

Issues and Situations: Information from Kelly Greene, "Tapping Talent, Experience of Those Age 60-Plus" *The Wall Street Journal* (November 29, 2005), p. B7.

Kaffeeklatsch: Information from Sally Beatty, "Staffing Up to Give Billions Away," *The Wall Street Journal* (June 30, 2006), p. W2; "Gates Foundation to Get Bulk of Buffett's Fortune," *Washington Post Online* (6/30/2006); Jim Hopkins, "A Philanthropic Powerhouse: Buffet's Gift to Gates will 'Deepen' Efforts," *USA Today* (June 27, 2006).

Team Project: Quote from http://www. woopidoo.com/businessquotes/authors/ michaelgerber/index.htm (retrieved September 16, 2006); see also Michael Gerber, *The E-Myth Revisited: Why Most Small Businesses Don't Work and What to Do About It* (New York: Harper-Collins, 2001).

Real Ethics: Information from Francis Lam, "Pizza With Passion," *Financial Times* (May 7, 2006), p. W9.

Chapter 7

1 "The Un-Google." *The Economist*, June 15, 2006. Vol.379, Issue 8482.

2 www.google.com/press/funfacts. html.

3 Gary Stix. "A Farewell to Keywords." *Scientific American*, July 2006. Vol. 295, Issue 1.

4 Om Malik. "The Rush to Feed the Internet Giants." *Business 2.0*, June, 2006. Vol. 7, Issue 5.

5 Ibid.

6 Matt Woodward. "Google: Facts, Figures, and a Little Fiction." Accessed August 27, 2006, at http://arstechnica.com/news.ars/post/20040224-3461.html.

7 www.quotedb.com.

8 Peter F. Drucker, "Looking Ahead: Implications of the Present," *Harvard Business Review* (September–October 1997), pp. 18–32. See also Shaker A. Zahra, "An Interview with Peter Drucker," *Academy of Management Executive*, vol. 17 (August 2003), pp. 9–12.

9 Thomas A. Stewart, *Intellectual Capital: The Wealth of Organizations* (New York: Doubleday, 1997).

10 See Susan G. Cohen and Don Mankin, "The Changing Nature of Work: Managing the Impact of Information Technology," Chapter 6 in Susan Albers Mohrman, Jay R. Galbraith, Edward E. Lawler III and Associates, *Tomorrow's Organization: Crafting Winning Capabilities in a Dynamic World* (San Francisco: Jossey-Bass, 1988), pp. 154–78.

11 Jaclyn Fierman, "Winning Ideas from Maverick Managers," *Fortune* (February 6, 1995), pp. 66–80.

[12] Henry Mintzberg, *The Nature of Managerial Work* (New York: Harper-Collins, 1997).

[13] Developed from Anna Muoio, "Where There's Smoke It Helps to Have a Smoke Jumper," *Fast Company*, vol. 33, p. 290.

[14] For scholarly reviews, see Dean Tjosvold, "Effects of Crisis Orientation on Managers' Approach to Controversy in Decision Making," *Academy of Management Journal*, vol. 27 (1984), pp. 130–38; and Jan 1. Mitroff, Paul Shrivastava, and Firdaus E. Udwadia, "Effective Crisis Management," *Academy of Management Executive*, vol. 1 (1987), pp. 283–92.

[15] See David Greisling, *I'd Like to Buy the World a Coke: The Life and Leadership of Roberto Goizueta* (New York: Wiley, 1998).

[16] See Hugh Courtney, Jane Kirkland, and Patrick Viguerie, "Strategy Under Uncertainty," *Harvard Business Review* (November-December 1997), pp. 67–79.

[17] For a good discussion, see Watson H. Agor, *Intuition in Organizations: Leading and Managing Productively* (Newbury Park, CA: Sage, 1989); Herbert A. Simon, "Making Management Decisions: The Role of Intuition and Emotion," *Academy of Management Executive*, vol. 1 (1987), pp. 57–64; Orlando Behling and Norman L. Eckel, "Making Sense Out of Intuition," *Academy of Management Executive*, vol. 5 (1991), pp. 46–54.

[18] Daniel J. Isenberg, "How Senior Managers Think," *Harvard Business Review*, vol. 62 (November–December 1984), pp. 81–90.

[19] Daniel J. Isenberg, "The Tactics of Strategic Opportunism," *Harvard Business Review*, vol. 65 (March–April 1987), pp. 92–97.

[20] See George P. Huber, *Managerial Decision Making* (Glenview, IL: Scott, Foresman 1975). For a comparison, see the steps in Xerox's problem-solving process as described in David A. Garvin, "Building a Learning Organization," *Harvard Business Review* (July–August 1993), pp. 78–91; and the Josephson model for ethical decision making described at www.josephsoninstitute.org/MED/MED-4seven-steppath.htm.

[21] Peter F. Drucker, *Innovation and Entrepreneurship: Practice and Principles* (New York: Harper & Row, 1985).

[22] For a sample of Simon's work, see Herbert A. Simon, *Administrative Behavior* (New York: Free Press, 1947); James G. March and Herbert A. Simon *Organizations* (New York: Wiley, 1958); Herbert A. Simon, *The New Science of Management Decision* (New York: Harper, 1960).

[23] This presentation is based on the work of R. H. Hogarth, D. Kahneman, A. Tversky, and others, as discussed in Max H. Bazerman, *Judgment in Managerial Decision Making*, 3rd ed. (New York: Wiley, 1994).

[24] Barry M. Staw, "The Escalation of Commitment to a Course of Action," *Academy of Management Review*, vol. 6 (1981), pp. 577–87; and Barry M. Staw and Jerry Ross, "Knowing When to Pull the Plug," *Harvard Business Review*, vol. 65 (March–April 1987), pp. 68–74.

[25] The classic work is Norman R. Maier, "Assets and Liabilities in Group Problem Solving," *Psychological Review*, vol. 74 (1967), pp. 239–49.

[26] Josephson, op. cit.

[27] Based on Gerald F. Cavanagh, *American Business Values*, 4th ed. (Upper Saddle River, NJ: Prentice-Hall, 1998).

[28] Peter F. Drucker, "The Future That Has Already Happened," *Harvard Business Review*, vol. 75 (September–October 1997), pp. 20–24; and Peter F. Drucker, Esther Dyson, Charles Handy, Paul Daffo, and Peter M. Senge, "Looking Ahead: Implications of the Present," *Harvard Business Review*, vol. 75 (September–October, 1997).

[29] See, for example, Thomas H. Davenport and Laurence Prusak, *Working Knowledge: How Organizations Manage What They Know* (Cambridge, MA: Harvard Business School Press, 1997).

[30] See Eric Schmidt and Hal Varian, "Google: Ten Golden Rules," *Newsweek* (December 2, 2005).

[31] Peter Senge, *The Fifth Discipline* (New York: Harper, 1990).

[32] http://www.amazon.com.

[33] http://www.jumpstart-it.com/jumpstart-iot_on_amazon.html.

[34] Sean O'Neill. "Indulge Your Literary Urge." *Kiplinger's Personal Finance*, August 2005. Vol. 59, Issue 8.

[35] Jeffrey Ressner. "10 Questions for Jeff Bezos." *Time*, August 1, 2005. Vol. 166, Issue 5.

[36] "Sit Back and Watch Your Amazon.com." *USA Today*, January 19, 2006.

[37] "Amazon CEO Takes Long View." *USA Today*, July 6, 2005.

[38] David Meerman Scott. "The Flip Side of Free." *eContent*, October 2005. Vol. 28, Issue 10.

[39] Thomas Pack and Loraine Page. "Amazon.com Still Amazes." *Information Today*, July/August 2005. Vol. 22, Issue 7.

[40] David Meerman Scott. "Amazon and the Hard Sell." *eContent*, September 2005. Vol. 28, Issue 9.

[41] Gordon Flagg. "Amazon, Random House, Microsoft Announce Online-Books Initiative." *American Libraries*, December 2005. Vol. 36, Issue 11.

[42] Jim Milliott and Rachel Deahl. "Setting the Stage." *Publishers Weekly*, November 7, 2005. Vol. 252, Issue 44.

[43] "Long View."

[44] Ibid.

[45] Stephen Foley. "Amazon's aPod Takes on the Big Apple." The *Independent* (UK), February 17, 2006.

[46] Ibid.

[47] "10 Questions."

[48] "Long View."

Features:

Insights: Information from www.sandiego.edu/gen/recording/motown.html; www.history-of-rock.com/motown_records.htm; and, www.motown.com/classicmotown.

Issues and Situations: Lauren Foswter and David Ibison, "Spike the Robot Helps Lego Rebuild Strategy," *Financial Times* (June 22, 2006), p. 18.

AOL utilizes Google's search technology Source: *Economist*, (June 17, 2006), vol. 379, issue 8482, pp. 65–66, 2p, 1c.

Kaffeeklatsch: Information from Dale Dauten, "The Best Coworkers Share Three Dimensions," *St. Louis Post-Dispatch*, (March 19, 2006), p. E2.

Team Project: Paul F. Roberts, "Dell, Sony Discussed Battery Problem 10 Months Ago," *Computerworld* (September 18, 2006), retrieved from www.computerworld.com.au (September 18, 2006); quote from http:// hardware.slashdot.org/article.pl?sid=06/08/19/0146221.

Personal Management: Example and quotes from Information from Carol Hymowitz, "Independent Program Puts College Students on Leadership Paths," *Wall Street Journal* (January 14, 2003), p. B1.

Real Ethics: Information from "Little Surprise Man was Left to Die on Everest," *MSNBC.com* (May 26, 2006); Steve McMorran, "Everest Pioneer Appalled that Clmber was Left to Die," *The Seattle Times*, online edition (May 25, 2006); Thomas Bell, "Everest Climber Left to Die Alone," *London Daily Telegraph*, online edition (May 23, 2006).

Chapter 8

1 Brett Clanton. "GM Puts Squeeze on Suppliers." *Detroit News*, September 9, 2005.

2 General Motors. "Current Offers for Customers Residing in the Northeast Region." Accessed August 27, 2006, at http://www.gm.com/automotive/vehicle_shopping/currentoffers/NE_Consumer_IOU.html.

3 "GM: Money to Burn—And It's Burning." *Business Week*, June 5, 2006. Accessed June 26, 2006, at http://www.businessweek.com/magazine/content/06_23/b3987078.htm.

4 Robert Sherefkin. "Suppliers: Big 3 Relationships Are Getting Better." *Automotive News*, June 12, 2006. Vol. 80, Issue 6207.

5 Matthew Neundorf. "Ford Death Watch 4: Death by a Thousand Cuts." *The Truth About Cars*, August 24, 2006. Accessed August 30, 2006, at http://www.thetruthaboutcars.com/?p=2075.

6 "Ford Names Boeing's Alan Mulally President & CEO; Bill Ford is Executive Chairman," Ford Motor Company Press Release (September 5, 2006).

7 Bryce G. Hoffman, "Half Take Ford Buyout," *The Detroit News* (November 29, 2006).

8 T. J. Rodgers, with William Taylor and Rick Foreman, "No Excuses Management," *World Executive's Digest* (May 1994) pp. 26–30.

9 Eaton Corporation Annual Report, 1985.

10 Henry Mintzberg, "The Manager's Job: Folklore and Fact," *Harvard Business Review*, vol. 53 (July–August 1975), pp. 54–67; and Henry Mintzberg, "Planning on the Left Side and Managing on the Right," *Harvard Business Review*, vol. 54 (July–August 1976), pp. 46–55.

11 Quote from Stephen Covey and Roger Merrill, "New Ways to Get Organized at Work," *USA Weekend* (February 6–8, 1998), p. 18. Books by Stephen R. Covey include: *The 7 Habits of Highly Effective People: Powerful Lessons in Personal Change* (New York: Fireside, 1990), and Stephen R. Covey and Sandra Merril Covey, *The 7 Habits of Highly Effective Families: Building a Beautiful Family Culture in a Turbulent World* (New York: Golden Books, 1996).

12 See Stanley Thune and Robert House, "Where Long-Range Planning Pays Off," *Business Horizons*, vol. 13 (1970), pp. 81–87. For a critical review of the literature, see Milton Leontiades and Ahmet Teel, "Planning Perceptions and Planning Results," *Strategic Management Journal*, vol. 1 (1980), pp. 65–75; and J. Scott Armstrong. "The Value of Formal Planning for Strategic Decisions," *Strategic Management Journal*, vol. 3 (1982), pp. 197–211. For special attention to the small business setting, see Richard B. Robinson Jr., John A. Pearce II, George S. Vozikis, and Timothy S. Mescon, "The Relationship Between Stage of Development and Small Firm Planning and Performance," *Journal of Small Business Management*, vol. 22 (1984), pp. 45–52; and Christopher Orphen, "The Effects of Long-Range Planning on Small Business Performance: A Further Examination," *Journal of Small Business Management*, vol. 23 (1985), pp. 16–23. For an empirical study of large corporations, see Vasudevan Ramanujam and N. Venkataraman, "Planning and Performance: A New Look at an Old Question," *Business Horizons*, vol. 30 (1987), pp. 19–25.

13 Quotes from *Business Week* (August 8, 1994), pp. 78–86.

14 See William Oncken, Jr., and Donald L. Wass, "Management Time: Who's Got the Monkey?" *Harvard Business Review*, vol. 52 (September–October 1974), 75–80, and featured as an HBR classic, *Harvard Business Review* (November–December 1999).

15 See Elliot Jaques, *The Form of Time* (New York: Russak & Co., 1982). For an executive commentary on his research, see Walter Kiechel III, "How Executives Think," *Fortune* (December 21, 1987), pp. 139–44.

16 See Henry Mintzberg, "Rounding Out the Manager's Job," *Sloan Management Review* (fall 1994), pp. 1–25.

17 Information from "Avoiding a Time Bomb: Sexual Harassment," *Business Week*. Enterprise issue (October 13, 1997), pp. ENT20–21.

18 For a thorough review of forecasting, see J. Scott Armstrong, *Long-Range Forecasting*, 2nd ed. (New York: Wiley, 1985).

19 Information from Associated Press, "Cola Jihad Bubbling in Europe," *Columbus Dispatch* (February 11, 2003), pp. C1, C2.

20 The scenario-planning approach is described in Peter Schwartz, *The Art of the Long View* (New York: Double-day/Currency, 1991): and Arie de Geus, *The Living Company: Habits for Survival in a Turbulent Business Environment* (Boston, MA: Harvard Business School Press, 1997).

21 See, for example, Robert C. Camp, *Business Process Benchmarking* (Milwaukee: ASQ Quality Press 1994); Michael J. Spendolini, *The Benchmarking Book* (New York: AMACOM, 1992); and Christopher E. Bogan and Michael J. English, *Benchmarking for Best Practices: Winning Through Innovative Adaptation* (New York: McGraw-Hill, 1994).

22 Rachel Tiplady, "Taking the Lead in Fast-Fashion," *Business Week Online* (August 29, 2006).

23 Carol Hymowitz, "Two More CEO Ousters Underscore the Need to Better Strategizing," *The Wall Street Journal* (September 11, 2006), p. 81.

24 See Dale D. McConkey, *How to Manage by Results*, 3rd ed. (New York: AMACOM, 1976); Stephen J. Carroll, Jr., and Henry J. Tosi, Jr., *Management by Objectives: Applications and Research* (New York: Macmillan, 1973); and Anthony P. Raia, *Managing by Objectives* (Glenview, IL: Scott, Foresman, 1974).

25 For a discussion of research, see Carroll and Tosi, op.cit.; Raia, op.cit; and Steven Kerr, "Overcoming the Dysfunctions of MBO," *Management by Objectives*, vol. 5, no. I (1976). Information in part from Dylan Loeb McClain, "Job Forecast: Internet's Still Hot," *New York Times* (January 30, 2001), p. 9.

26 See Douglas McGregor, *The Human Side of Enterprise* (New York: McGraw-Hill, 1960).

27 The work on goal-setting theory is well summarized in Edwin A. Locke and Gary P. Latham, *Goal Setting: A Motivational Technique That Works!* (Englewood Cliffs, NJ: Prentice Hall, 1984). See also Edwin A. Locke, Kenneth N. Shaw, Lisa A. Saari, and

Gary P. Latham, "Goal Setting and Task Performance 1969–1980," *Psychological Bulletin*, vol. 90 (1981), pp. 125–52; Mark E. Tubbs, "Goal Setting: A Meta-Analytic Examination of the Empirical Evidence," *Journal of Applied Psychology*, vol. 71 (1986), pp. 474–83; and Terence R. Mitchell, Kenneth R. Thompson, and Jane George-Falvy, "Goal Setting: Theory and Practice," Chapter 9 in Cary L. Cooper and Edwin A. Locke (eds.), *Industrial and Organizational Psychology: Linking Theory with Practice* (Malden, MA: Blackwell Business, 2000), pp. 211–249.

[28] "Store Openings." WalMartFacts.com. Downloaded September 6, 2006, at http://www.walmartfacts.com/Fact-Sheets/8262006_Store_Openings.pdf.

[29] "Financial Results." WalMartFacts.com. Downloaded September 6, 2006, at http://www.walmartfacts.com/Fact-Sheets/8262006_Financial_Results.pdf

[30] "Wal-Mart Picks Up the PACE," Business Week (November 15, 1993), p. 45.

[31] http://www.walmartstores.com/Global WMStores Web/ navigate. do? catg =369.

[32] Wal-Mart home page: http://www.walmartstores.com.

[33] 2003 Annual Report, op. cit., p. 3.

[34] Barbara Marsh, "Merchants Mobilize to Battle Wal-Mart in a Small Community," Wall Street Journal (June 5, 1991), p. A1.

[35] Victoria Colliver. "Health Insurance for $25." San Francisco Chronicle, October 25, 2006. Accessed September 5, 2006. at http://www.sfgate.com/ cgi-bin/article.cgi?file=/chronicle/ archive/2005/10/25/BUGV7FDB421.DTL&type=business

[36] Bill Saporito, "David Glass Won't Crack Under Fire," Fortune (February 8, 1993), pp. 75, 78.

[37] 2003 Annual Report, op cit., p. 5.

[38] Wal-Mart homepage, op cit.

[39] Wal-Mart homepage, op cit.

[40] 2003 Annual Report, op cit., p. 9.

Features:

Insights: Information from Joseph B. White and Lee Hawkins, Jr., "GM Cuts Deeper in North America," *The Wall Street Journal* (November 22, 2005), p. A3; see also www.kinkos.com/about_us.

Issues and Situations: Information from Moon Ihlwan, "Camp Samsung: to Develop Winning Products, the Korean Giant Isolates Artists and Techies for Months on End," *Business Week* (July 3, 2006), pp. 46-48.

Kaffeeklatsch: Information from Spencer E. Ante, "The Science of Desire," *Business Week* (June 5, 2006), pp. 106.

Team Project: News reports on Ford's restructuring started appearing in September, 2006.

Personal Management: Survey results from "Hurry Up and Decide," *Business Week* (May 14, 2001), p. 16.

Real Ethics: Information from "Trial and Error," *Forbes* (June 19, 2006), pp. 128-130; Drake Bennett, "Measures of Success," *Boston Globe Online* (July 2, 2006).

Chapter 9

[1] "Firefox Wings to the Rescue." *The Economist*, December 17, 2005, Vol. 377, Issue 8457.

[2] Ibid.

[3] "About Mozilla Corporation." Mozilla Corporation. Accessed January 6, 2006, at 2http://www.mozilla.com/about/.

[4] "Firefox Swings."

[5] Ibid.

[6] http://www.spreadfirefox.com/fifty/

[7] Steve Hamm. "The Gnat Nipping at Microsoft." *Business Week*, January 24, 2005. Issue 3917.

[8] Nielse/NetRatings, reported by ZD-net.com (retrieved September 26, 2006).

[9] "Firefox Swings."

[10] McDither, Soutbaw. "Men Blast Women in Browser Battle Wars." The Inquirer.net, April 13, 2005. Accessed June 24, 2006, 2006, at http://www.theinquirer.net/default.aspx? Article=22510,

[11] www.mozilla.org/about/.

[12] Ibid.

[13] Ibid.

[14] For an overview of Wal-Mart see Charles Fishman, *The Wal-Mart Effect* (New York: Penguin, 2006).

[15] Michael Barbaro and Reed Abelson, "Despite Some Holes, Wal-Mart's Plan to Cut Drug Prices is Lauded by Most," *The New York Times* (September 22, 2006), p. C3.

[16] Jim Collins, "Bigger, Better, Faster," *Fast Company*, vol. 71 (June 2003), p. 74; and www.fastcompany.com/magazine/71/walmart.html.

[17] See Michael E. Porter, *Competitive Strategy: Techniques for Analyzing Industries and Competitors* (New York: Free Press, 1980), and *Competitive Advantage: Creating and Sustaining Superior Performance* (New York: Free Press, 1986): and Richard A. D'Aveni, *Hyper-Competition: Managing the Dynamics of Strategic Maneuvering* (New York: Free Press. 1994).

[18] Gary Hamel and C.K. Prahalad, "Strategic Intent." *Harvard Business Review* (May–June 1989), pp. 63–76.

[19] www.pepsico.com/PEP_company.

[20] Information and quotes from Marcia Stepanek, "How Fast Is Net Fast?" *Business Week E-Biz* (November 1, 1999), pp. EB52–EB54.

[21] For research support, see Daniel H. Gray, "Uses and Misuses of Strategic Planning," *Harvard Business Review*, vol. 64 (January–February 1986), pp. 89–97.

[22] Peter F. Drucker, "Five Questions." *Executive Excellence* (November 6, 1994), pp. 6–7.

[23] Peter F. Drucker, *Management: Tasks, Responsibilities, Practices* (New York: Harper & Row, 1973), p. 122.

[24] See Laura Nash. "Mission Statements—Mirrors and Windows," *Harvard Business Review* (March–April 1988). pp. 155–56; James C. Collins and Jerry I. Porras, "Building Your Company's Vision," *Harvard Business Review* (September–October 1996), pp. 65–77; and James C. Collins and Jerry I. Porras. *Built to Last: Successful Habits of Visionary Companies* (New York: Harper Business, 1997).

[25] Gary Hamel. *Leading the Revolution* (Boston, MA: Harvard Business School Press, 2000), pp. 72–73.

[26] Steve Hamm, "A Passion for the Plan," *Business Week* (August 21/28, 2006), pp. 92–94.

[27] Ibid.

[28] www.patagonia.com

[29] Terrence E. Deal and Allen A. Kennedy, *Corporate Cultures: The Rites and Rituals of Corporate Life* (Reading, MA: Addison-Wesley, 1982), p. 22. For more on organizational culture see Edgar H. Schein, *Organizational Culture and Leadership*, 2nd ed. (San Francisco: Jossey-Bass, 1997).

[30] www.patagonia.com

[31] Peter F. Drucker's views on organizational objectives are expressed in his classic books: *The Practice of Management* (New York: Harper & Row, 1954), and *Management: Tasks, Responsibilities, Practices* (New York: Harper & Row, 1973). For a more

recent commentary, see his article, "Management: The Problems of Success," *Academy of Management Executive*, vol. 1 (1987), pp. 13–19.

[32] Hamm, op cit., 2006.

[33] C.K. Prahalad and Gary Hamel, "The Core Competencies of the Corporation," *Harvard Business Review* (May–June 1990), pp. 79–91; see also Hitt et al., op. cit., pp. 99–103.

[34] For a discussion of Michael Porter's approach to strategic planning, see his books *Competitive Strategy* and *Competitive Advantage*; his article, "What Is Strategy? *Harvard Business Review* (November–December, 1996), pp. 61–78; and Richard M. Hodgetts' interview "A Conversation with Michael E. Porter. A Significant Extension Toward Operational Improvement and Positioning," *Organizational Dynamics* (summer 1999), pp. 24–33.

[35] The four grand strategies were originally described by William F. Glueck, *Business Policy: Strategy Formulation and Management Action*. 2nd ed. (New York: McGraw-Hill, 1976).

[36] Michael A. Hitt. R. Duane Ireland, and Robert E. Hoskisson, *Strategic Management: Competitiveness and Globalization* (Minneapolis: West, 1997), p. 197

[37] See William McKinley, Carol M. Sanchez, and A. G. Schick. "Organizational Downsizing: Constraining, Cloning, Learning," *Academy of Management Executive*, vol. 9 (August 1995), pp. 32–44.

[38] Kim S. Cameron. Sara J. Freeman, and A. K. Mishra, "Best Practices in White-Collar Downsizing: Managing Contradictions," *Academy of Management Executive*, vol. 4 (August 1991), pp. 57–73.

[39] This strategy classification is found in Hitt et al., op. cit.; the attitudes are from a discussion by Howard V. Perlmutter, "The Tortuous Evolution of the Multinational Corporation," *Columbia Journal of World Business*, vol. 4 (January-February 1969).

[40] See Adam M. Brandenburger and Barry J. Nalebuff, *Co-Opetition: A Revolution Mindset that Combines Competition and Cooperation* (New York: Bantam, 1996).

[41] Peter Coy, "Sleeping with the Enemy," *Business Week* (August 21/28, 2006), pp. 96–97.

[42] See Michael E. Porter, "Strategy and the Internet," *Harvard Business Review* (March 2001), pp. 63–78; Michael Rappa, *Business Models on the Web* (www.ecommerce.ncsu.edu/business_models.html. February 6, 2001).

[43] Hammond, op cit.

[44] Porter, op cit. (1980), (1986), (1996).

[45] Information from www.polo.com.

[46] Richard G. Hammermesh, "Making Planning Strategic," *Harvard Business Review*, vol. 64 (July-August 1986), pp. 115–120; and Richard G. Hammermesh, *Making Strategy Work* (New York: Wiley, 1986).

[47] See Gerald B. Allan, "A Note on the Boston Consulting Group Concept of Competitive Analysis and Corporate Strategy," Harvard Business School, Intercollegiate Case Clearing House, ICCH9–175–175 (Boston: Harvard Business School, June 1976).

[48] James Brian Quinn, "Strategic Change: Logical Incrementalism," *Sloan Management Review*, vol. 20 (fall 1978), pp. 7–21.

[49] Henry Mintzberg, *The Nature of Managerial Work* (New York: Harper & Row, 1973); and John R. P. Kotter, *The General Managers* (New York: Free Press, 1982).

[50] Henry Mintzberg, "Planning on the Left Side and Managing on the Right," *Business Review*, vol. 54 (July-August 1976), pp. 46–55; Henry Mintzberg and James A. Waters, "Of Strategies, Deliberate and Emergent," *Strategic Management Journal*, vol. 6 (1985), pp. 257–72; Henry Mintzberg, "Crafting Strategy," *Harvard Business Review*, vol. 65 (July-August 1987), pp. 66–75.

[51] For research support, see Daniel H. Gray, "Uses and Misuses of Strategic Planning," *Harvard Business Review*, vol. 64 (January-February 1986), pp. 89–97.

[52] See Judith Burns, "Everything You Wanted to Know About Corporate Governance . . . But Didn't Know How to Ask," *The Wall Street Journal* (October 27, 2003), pp. R1. R7.

[53] See Carol Hymowitz, "GE Chief Is Charting His Own Strategy, Focusing on Technology," *Wall Street Journal* (September 23, 2003), p. B1.

[54] See R. Duane Ireland and Michael A. Hitt. "Achieving and Maintaining Strategic Competitiveness in the 21st Century," *Academy of Management Executive*, vol. 13 (1999), pp. 43–57.

[55] Hammond, op cit.

[56] Michael Dell quotes from Matt Murray, "As Huge Companies Keep Growing, CEOs Struggle to Keep Pace," *Wall Street Journal* (February 8, 2001), pp. A1, A6. See also Dell facts at *www.dell.com*.

[56a] https://dunkindonuts.com/aboutus/company/products/CoffeeConsFacts.aspx?Section=company

[57] https://www.dunkindonuts.com/aboutus/company/.

[58] https://www.dunkindonuts.com/aboutus/company/Global.aspx.

[59] Susan Spielberg. "For Snack Chains, Coffee Drinks the Best Way to Sweeten Profits." *Nation's Restaurant News*, June 27, 2005.

[60] "Dunkin Donuts Unveils Plan for 230-Store Expansion." *Boston Business Journal*, May 24, 2005.

[61] https://dunkindonuts.com/aboutus/company/products/Breakfast-SandFacts.aspx?Section=company

[62] Kara Kridler. "Dunkin Donuts To Add 150 Stores in Baltimore-Washington Area." *Daily Record* (Baltimore), May 26, 2005.

[63] https://dunkindonuts.com/aboutus/company/products/EspressoRevolution.aspx?Section=company

Features:

Insights: Information from "Starbucks: Making Values Pay," *Fortune* (September 29, 1997), pp. 261–72; Howard Schultz and Dori Jones Yang, *Pour Your Heart into It* (San Francisco: Hyperion, 1997); and www.starbucks.com.

Issues and Situations: Information from Nick Wingfield, "Master of the Universe," *The Wall Street Journal* (May 27–28, 2006), pp. A1, A8.

Kaffeeklatsch: Information from Spencer E. Ante, "The Science of Desire," *Business Week* (June 5, 2006), p. 106. See also Lawrence J. Peter, *The Peter Principle* (New York: Buccaneer Books, 1993).

Real Ethics: Information from David Welch, "Go Bankrupt, Then Go Overseas," *Business Week* (April 24, 2006), pp. 52–54.

Chapter 10

[1] http://nucor.com/indexinner.aspx?finpage=aboutus

[2] Ibid.

[3] http://www.emoryleadership.org/2006/02/polarity_management.htm.

[4] http:www.factorylogic.com/article_jpg_research.html.

[5] http://www.jhu.edu/~gazette/1999/oct2599/25ford.html.

6 "Most Inspiring Steel Boss," *Business Week* (December 18, 2006), p. 61.

7 World Coal Institute, *www.world-coal.org.*

8a Ibid.

8b Ibid.

9 Henry Mintzberg and Ludo Van der Heyden, "Organigraphs: Drawing How Companies Really Work," *Harvard Business Review* (September–October 1999), pp. 87–94.

10 The classic work is Alfred D. Chandler, *Strategy and Structure* (Cambridge, MA: MIT Press, 1962).

11 See Alfred D. Chandler, Jr., "Origins of the Organization Chart," *Harvard Business Review* (March–April 1988), pp. 156–57.

12 See David Krackhardt and Jeffrey R. Hanson, "Informal Networks: The Company Behind the Chart," *Harvard Business Review* (July–August 1993), pp. 104–11.

13 See Kenneth Noble, "A Clash of Styles: Japanese Companies in the U.S." *New York Times* (January 25, 1988), p. 7.

14 For a discussion of departmentalization, see H. I. Ansoff and R. G. Bradenburg, "A Language for Organization Design," *Management Science*, vol. 17 (August 1971), pp. B705–B731; Mariann Jelinek, "Organization Structure: The Basic Conformations," in Mariann Jelinek, Joseph A. Litterer, and Raymond E. Miles, eds., *Organizations by Design: Theory and Practice* (Plano, TX: Business Publications, 1981), pp. 293–302; Henry Mintzberg, "The Structuring of Organizations," in James Brian Quinn, Henry Mintzberg, and Robert M. James (eds.), *The Strategy Process: Concepts, Contexts, and Cases* (Englewood Cliffs, NJ: Prentice-Hall, 1988), pp. 276–304.

15 Robert L. Simison, "Jaguar Slowly Sheds Outmoded Habits," *Wall Street Journal* (July 26, 1991), p. A6; and Richard Stevenson, "Ford Helps Jaguar Get Back Old Sheen," *International Herald Tribune* (December 14, 1994), p. 11.

16 These alternatives are well described by Mintzberg, op cit.

17 The focus on process is described in Michael Hammer, *Beyond Reengineering* (New York: Harper Business, 1996).

18 Excellent reviews of matrix concepts are found in Stanley M. Davis and Paul R. Lawrence, *Matrix* (Reading, MA: Addison-Wesley, 1977); Paul R. Lawrence, Harvey F. Kolodny, and Stanley M. Davis, "The Human Side of the Matrix," *Organizational Dynamics*, vol. 6 (1977), pp. 43–61; and Harvey F. Kolodny, "Evolution to a Matrix Organization," *Academy of Management Review*, vol. 4 (1979), pp. 543–53.

19 Davis and Lawrence, op cit.

20 Developed from Frank Ostroff, *The Horizontal Organization: What the Organization of the Future Looks Like and How It Delivers Value to Customers* (New York: Oxford University Press, 1999).

21 The nature of teams and teamwork is described in Jon R. Katzenbach and Douglas K. Smith, "The Discipline of Teams," *Harvard Business Review* (March–April 1993), pp. 111–20.

22 Susan Albers Mohrman, Susan G. Cohen, and Allan M. Mohrman, Jr., *Designing Team-Based Organizations* (San Francisco: Jossey-Bass, 1996).

23 See Glenn M. Parker, *Cross-Functional Teams* (San Francisco: Jossey-Bass, 1995).

24 Information from William Bridges, "The End of the Job," *Fortune* (September 19, 1994), pp. 62–74; Alan Deutschman. "The Managing Wisdom of High-Tech Superstars," *Fortune* (October 17, 1994), pp. 197–206.

25 See the discussion by Jay R. Galbraith. "Designing the Networked Organization: Leveraging Size and Competencies," in Susan Albers Mohrman, Jay R. Galbraith, Edward E. Lawler III and Associates, *Tomorrow's Organizations: Crafting Winning Strategies in a Dynamic World* (San Francisco: Jossey-Bass, 1998), pp. 76–102. See also Rupert F. Chisholm, *Developing Network Organizations: Learning from Practice and Theory* (Reading, MA: Addison-Wesley, 1998).

26 See Jerome Barthelemy, "The Seven Deadly Sins of Outsourcing," *Academy of Management Executive*, vol. 17 (2003), pp. 87–98.

27 See Ron Ashkenas, Dave Ulrich, Todd Jick, and Steve Kerr, *The Boundaryless Organization: Breaking the Chains of Organizational Structure* (San Francisco: Jossey-Bass, 1996).

28 Information from "Scott Livengood and the Tasty Tale of Krispy Kreme," *BizEd* (May/June 2003), pp. 16–20.

29 Information from John A. Byrne, "Management by Web," *Business Week* (August 28, 2000), pp. 84–97; See the collection of articles by Cary L. Cooper and Denise M. Rousseau, eds., *The Virtual Organization: Vol. 6, Trends in Organizational Behavior* (New York: Wiley, 2000).

30 For a classic work see Jay R. Galbraith, *Organizational Design* (Reading, MA: Addison Wesley, 1977).

31 This framework is based on Harold J. Leavitt, "Applied Organizational Change in Industry," in James G. March, *Handbook of Organizations* (New York: Rand McNally, 1965), pp. 1144–70; and Edward E. Lawler III, *From the Ground Up: Six Principles for the New Logic Corporation* (San Francisco: Jossey-Bass Publishers, 1996), pp. 44–50.

32 Max Weber, *The Theory of Social and Economic Organization*, A. M. Henderson, trans., and H. T. Parsons (New York: Free Press, 1947).

33 For classic treatments of bureaucracy, see Alvin Gouldner, *Patterns of Industrial Bureaucracy* (New York: Free Press, 1954); and Robert K. Merton, *Social Theory and Social Structure* (New York: Free Press, 1957).

34 Tom Burns and George M. Stalker, *The Management of Innovation* (London: Tavistock, 1961; republished by Oxford University Press, London, 1994).

35 See Henry Mintzberg, *Structure in Fives: Designing Effective Organizations* (Englewood Cliffs, NJ: Prentice-Hall, 1983).

36 See Rosabeth Moss Kanter, *The Changing Masters* (New York: Simon & Schuster, 1983). Quotation from Rosabeth Moss Kanter and John D. Buck, "Reorganizing Part of Honeywell: From Strategy to Structure," *Organizational Dynamics*, vol. 13 (winter 1985), p. 6.

37 See for example, Jay R. Galbraith, Edward E. Lawler III, and Associates, *Organizing for the Future* (San Francisco: Jossey-Bass Publishers, 1993); and Susan Albers Mohrman, Jay R. Galbraith, Edward E. Lawler III, and Associates, *Tomorrow's Organizations: Crafting Winning Strategies in a Dynamic World* (San Francisco: Jossey-Bass, 1998).

38 Peter Senge, *The Fifth Discipline: The Art and Practice of the Learning Organization* (New York: Doubleday, 1994).

39 Paul R. Lawrence and Jay W. Lorsch, *Organizations and Environment* (Boston: Division of Research, Graduate School of Business Administration, Harvard University, 1967).

[40] Burns and Stalker, op cit.

[41] See Jay R. Galbraith, op cit., and Susan Albers Mohrman, "Integrating Roles and Structure in the Lateral Organization," chapter 5 in Jay R. Galbraith, Edward E. Lawler III, and Associates, *Organizing for the Future* (San Francisco: Jossey-Bass Publishers, 1993).

[42] For a good discussion of coordination and integration approaches, see Scott, op.cit., pp. 231–39.

[43] David Van Fleet, "Span of Management Research and Issues," *Academy of Management Journal*, vol. 26 (1983), pp. 546–52.

[44] www.nucor.com/aboutus.htm (refriened September 29, 2006).

[45] "Adidas-Reebok Merger Lets Rivals Nip at Nike's Heels." *USA Today*, August 4, 2005.

[46] Ibid.

[47] Rich, Thomaselli. "Deal Sets Stage for Full-Scale War with Nike." *Advertising Age*, August 8, 2005. Vol. 76, Issue 32.

[48] "Adidas-Reebok Merger."

[49] Aaron Bernstein. "Nike Names Names." *Business Week Online*, April 13, 2005.

[50] Ibid.

[51] Rich Thomaselli. "Nike Launches Upscale Urban Street Wear Line." *Advertising Age*, August 1, 2005. Vol. 76, Issue 31.

[52] Stanley Holmes, "Green Foot Forward." *Business Week*, November 28, 2005. Issue 3961.

[53] "Nike Replaces CEO After 13 Months." *USA Today*, January 24, 2006.

[54] "Just Doing It." *Economist*, August 6, 2005. Vol. 376, Issue 8438.

[55] "Adidas-Reebok Merger."

[56] "Deal Sets Stage."

[57] "Adidas-Reebok Merger."

Features:

Insights: Information from Stacy Perman, "Scones and Social Responsibility," *Business Week* (August 21/28, 2006), p. 38.
Issues and Situations: Information from What Ails Microsoft?" *Business Week* (September 26, 2005), p. 101; "Should Microsoft Break Up, on Its Own?" *The Wall Street Journal* (November 26–27, 2005), p. B16; and, Peter Burrows, "Microsoft Singing its Own iTune," *Business Week Online* (July 7, 2006).
Kaffeeklatsch: Information from Jena McGregor, "The Office Chart that Really Counts," *Business Week* (February 27, 2006), pp. 48–49.

Chapter 11

[1] http://www.marketingpower.com/content16577.php.

[2] http://discuss.fogcreek.com/joelonsoftware/default.asp?cmd=show&ixPost=17864.

[3] http://www.jockbio.com/Bios/Bryant/Bryant_numbers.html.

[4] http://www.baselinemag.com/article2/0,1540,1996741,00.asp.

[5] http://wwww.pokersourceonline.com/superstars/phil-hellmuth.asp.

[6] http://www.buffalo.edu/news/fast-execute.cgi/article-page.html?article=56420009.

[7] http://childrensbooks.about.com/b/a/102387.htm.

[8] Robert Reich, *The Future of Success* (New York: Knopf, 2000); Robert B. Reich, "The Company of the Future," *Fast Company* (November 1998), pp. 124ff;

[9] See Jeffrey Pfeffer, *The Human Equation: Building Profits by Putting People First* (Boston: Harvard University Press, 1998); and James O'Toole and Edward E. Lawler III, (*Workers As Self Managers* New York: Palgrave Macmillan, 2006).

[10] See, for example, Charles Handy, *The Age of Unreason* (Cambridge, MA: Harvard Business School Press, 1990); and Tom Peters, "The Brand Called *You,*" *Fast Company* (August 1997), pp. 83ff.

[11] Quote from William Bridges, "The End of the Job," *Fortune* (September 19, 1994), p. 68.

[12] Jeffrey Pfeffer and John F. Veiga, "Putting People First for Organizational Success," *Academy of Management Executive*, vol. 13 (May 1999), pp. 37–48.

[13] James N. Baron and David M. Kreps, *Strategic Human Resources: Framework for General Managers* (New York: Wiley, 1999).

[14] Quotes from Kris Maher, "Human-Resources Directors Are Assuming Strategic Roles," *Wall Street Journal* (June 17, 2003), p. B8.

[15] Ibid.

[16] Pfeffer, op cit., p. 292.

[17] Lawrence Otis Graham, *Perversity: Getting Past Face Value and Finding the Soul of People* (New York: Wiley, 1997).

[18] See also R. Roosevelt Thomas, Jr. 's books, *Beyond Race and Gender* (New York: AMACOM, 1999); and (with Marjorie I. Woodruff) *Building a House for Diversity* (New York: AMACOM, 1999); and Richard D. Bucher, *Diversity Consciousness* (Englewood Cliffs, NJ: Prentice-Hall, 2000).

[19] For a discussion of affirmative action see R. Roosevelt Thomas, Jr., "From 'Affirmative Action' to 'Affirming Diversity,'" *Harvard Business Review* (November–December 1990), pp. 107–17; and Thomas, op. cit. (1998).

[20] See the discussion by David A. DeCenzo and Stephen P. Robbins, *Human Resource Management,* 6th ed. (New York: Wiley, 1999), pp. 66–68 and 81–83.

[21] Ibid., pp. 77–79.

[22] See discussion by DeCenzo and Robbins, op cit., pp. 79–90.

[23] See Frederick S. Lane, *The Naked Employee: How Technology is Compromising Workplace Privacy* (New York: AMACOM, 2003).

[24] Quote from George Myers, "Bookshelf," *Columbus Dispatch* (June 9, 2003), p. E6.

[25] See Ernest McCormick, "Job and Task Analysis," in Marvin Dunnette (ed.), *Handbook of Industrial and Organizational Psychology* (Chicago: Rand McNally, 1976), pp. 651–96.

[26] Information from Gautam Naik, "India's Technology Whizzes Find Passage to Nokia," *Wall Street Journal* (August 1, 2000), p. B1.

[27] See David Greising, *I'd Like to Buy the World a Coke: The Life and Leadership of Roberto Goizueta* (New York: Wiley, 1998).

[28] See John P. Wanous, *Organizational Entry: Recruitment, Selection, and Socialization of Newcomers* (Reading, MA: Addison-Wesley, 1980), pp. 34–44.

[29] Information from Justin Martin, "Mercedes: Made in Alabama," *Fortune* (July 7, 1997), pp. 150–58.

[30] Reported in "Would You Hire This Person Again?" *Business Week*, Enterprise issue (June 9, 1997), pp. ENT32.

[31] For a scholarly review, see John Van Maanen and Edgar H. Schein. "Toward a Theory of Socialization," in Barry M. Staw (ed.), *Research in Organizational Behavior*, vol. 1 (Greenwich, CT: JAI Press, 1979), pp. 209–64; for a practitioner's view, see Richard Pascale, "Fitting New Employees into the Company Culture," *Fortune* (May 28, 1984), pp. 28–42.

[32] Quote from Ronald Henkoff, "Finding, Training, and Keeping the Best Service Workers," *Fortune* (October 3, 1994), pp. 110–22.

33 This involves the social information processing concept as discussed in Gerald R. Salancik and Jeffrey Pfeffer, "A Social Information Processing Approach to Job Attitudes and Task Design," *Administrative Science Quarterly*, vol. 23 (June 1978), pp. 224–53.

34 Quote from Peter Petre, "Games That Teach You to Manage," *Fortune* (October 29, 1984), pp. 65–72; see also, the "Looking Glass" description on the Center for Creative Leadership website: www.ccl.org.

35 See Larry L. Cummings and Donald P. Schwab, *Performance in Organizations: Determinants and Appraisal* (Glenview, IL: Scott, Foresman, 1973).

36 Dick Grote, "Performance Appraisal Reappraised," *Harvard Business Review Best Practice* (1999), Reprint F00105.

37 Ibid.

38 See Mark R. Edwards and Ann J. Ewen, *360-Degree Feedback: The Powerful New Tool for Employee Feedback and Performance Improvement* (New York: AMACOM, 1996).

39 Information from "What Are the Most Effective Retention Tools?" *Fortune* (October 9, 2000), p. S7.

40 Charles Handy, *The Age of Unreason* (Cambridge, MA: Harvard Business School Press, 1990), p. 55.

41 O'Toole and towfer, op. cit, 2006.

42 See Thomas P. Ference, James A. F. Stoner, and E. Kirby Warren, "Managing the Career Plateau," *Academy of Management Review*, vol. 2 (October 1977), pp. 602–12.

43 Timothy Butler and James Waldroop, "Job Sculpting: The Art of Retaining Your Best People," *Harvard Business Review* (September–October 1999), pp. 144–52.

44 See Betty Friedan, *Beyond Gender: The New Politics of Work and the Family* (Washington, DC: Woodrow Wilson Center Press, 1997); and James A. Levine, *Working Fathers: New Strategies for Balancing Work and Family* (Reading, MA: Addison-Wesley, 1997).

45 For reviews see Richard B. Freeman and James L. Medoff, *What Do Unions Do?* (New York: Basic Books, 1984); Charles C. Heckscher, *The New Unionism* (New York: Basic Books, 1988); and Barry T. Hirsch, *Labor Unions and the Economic Performance of Firms* (Kalamazoo, MI: W.E. Upjohn Institute for Employment Research, 1991).

46 Yochi J. Dreazen, "Percentage of U.S. Workers in a Union Sank to Record Low of 13.5% Last Year," *Wall Street Journal* (January 19, 2001), p. A2; Ellen Simon, "Ford Buyouts Demonstrate UAW's Decline," *The Columbus Dispatch* (September 17, 2006), p. G1.

47 Connie Mabin, "UAW Works to Help Save Ford," *The Columbus Dispatch* (September 27, 2006), p. D1.

48 http://www.hp.com/hpinfo/abouthp/histnfacts/timeline/hist_30s.html.

49 Ibid.

50 http://www.algebra.com/algebra/about/history/Hewlett-Packard.

51 www.agi/eat.com/about

52 http://www.hp.com/hpinfo/abouthp/histnfacts/museum/personalsystems/0021/index.html.

53 http://www.hpmuseum.org/.

54 http://www.hp.com/hpinfo/abouthp/histnfacts/timeline/hist_80s.html.

55 http://www.hp.com/hpinfo/newsroom/facts.html.

56 www.computertakeback.com/document.cfm?documentID=21.

57 http://www.hp.com/hpinfo/abouthp/histnfacts/timeline/hist_00s.html.

58 HP Fast Facts.

59 http://www.algebra.com/algebra/about/history/Hewlett-Packard.

60 Information and quotes from Peter Waldman and Don Clark, "Probing the Pretexters," *The Wall Street Journal* (September 29, 2006), pp. B1, B2.

61 Greg Sandoval. "Greenpeace: HP stands for 'Harmful Products.'" CNET News.com, December 6, 2005.

62 http://www.hp.com/hpinfo/newsroom/feature_stories/2006/06tradein.html.

63 http://www.hp.com/hpinfo/newsroom/feature_stories/2006/06restore. html.

Features:

Insights: Information from www.workingmother.com (retrieved September 29, 2006).

Issues and Situations: Michael Orey, "Trouble at Toyota," *Business Week* (May 22, 2006), pp. 46–48; Joan S. Lublin, "U.S. Harassment Laws Are Strict, Foreigners Find," *The Wall Street Journal* (May 15, 2006), pp. B1, B3.

Kaffeeklatsch: Information from "The Pause that Refreshes," *Business Week* (January 9, 2006), p. 57; Sue Schellenbarger, "Taking Back the Weekend: Companies Help Employees Cut Back

on Overwork," *The Wall Street Journal* (May 18, 2006), p. D1.
Source: http://www.baseballprospectus.com/glossary/index.php?search=Stars.
Personal Management: Information from "SHRM Code of Ethical and Professional Standards in Human Resource Management," retrieved from www.shrm.org/ethics/code-of-ethics.asp.
Real Ethics: Information from Jennifer Saranow, "Car Dealers Recruit Saleswomen at the Mall," *The Wall Street Journal* (April 12, 2006), pp. B1, B3.

Chapter 12

1 Jeanne C. Meister. "Does Your Learning Department Operate at the Speed of Business?" *Chief Learning Officer*. http://www.clomedia.com/content/templates/clo_article.asp?articleid=1434&zoneid=53.

2 "Speed Demons." *Business Week*, March 27, 2006. Accessed August 11, 2006, at http://www.businessweek.com/magazine/sontent/06_13/b3977001.htm.

3 Ibid.

4 Ibid.

5 Ibid.

6 http:www.trendwatching.com/trends/CUSTOMER-MADE.htm.

7 "Does Your Learning Department"

8 Ibid.

9 Speed Demons"

10 Michael Beer and Nitin Nohria, "Cracking the Code of Change," *Harvard Business Review* (May–June 2000), pp. 133–41.

11 Quote from John A. Byrne, "Visionary vs. Visionary," *Business Week* (August 28, 2000), p. 210.

12 Tom Peters, *The Circle of Innovation* (New York: Knopf, 1997).

13 R. Duane Ireland and Michael A. Hitt, "Achieving and Maintaining Strategic Competitiveness in the 21st Century: The Role of Strategic Leadership," *Academy of Management Executive* (February 1999), pp. 43–57.

14 Byme, op. cit.

15 See, for example, Roger von Oech, *A Whack on the Side of the Head* (New York: Warner Books, 1983) and *A Kick in the Seat of the Pants* (New York: Harper & Row, 1986).

16 Examples from "Providing Rural Phone Service Profitably in Poor Countries," *Business Week* (December 18, 2000),

special advertising section, and Michael M. Phillips, Marcus Walker and Mark Whitehouse, "Financial Pioneer of 'Microloans' Wins Nobel Prize," *The Wall Street Journal* (October 14, 2006), pp. B1, B5 and, Aubrey Henvetty "Seeds of Change," *Kellogg* (Summer, 2006), p. 13.

[17] See Peter F. Drucker, "The Discipline of Innovation," *Harvard Business Review* (November–December 1998), pp. 3–8.

[18] Peter F. Drucker, *Management: Tasks, Responsibilities, and Practices* (New York: Harper & Row, 1973), p. 797.

[19] See Cortis R. Carlson and William W. Wilmont, *Getting to "Aha"* (New York: Crown Business, 2006).

[20] Information from Jena McGregor, "The World's Most Innovative Companies," *Business Week* (April 24, 2006), pp. 63–74.

[21] Based on Edward B. Roberts, "Managing Invention and Innovation," *Research Technology Management* (January–February 1988), pp. 1–19, and Hamel, op cit.

[22] This discussion is stimulated by James Brian Quinn, "Managing Innovation Controlled Chaos," *Harvard Business Review*, Vol. 63 (May–June 1985).

[23] Quotations from Kenneth Labich. "The Innovators," *Fortune* (June 6, 1988), pp. 49–64.

[24] Peter F. Drucker, "Best R&D Is Business Driven," *Wall Street Journal*, (February 10, 1988), p. 11.

[25] See Roberts, op cit.

[26] Reported in Carol Hymowitz, "Task of Managing Changes in Workplace Takes a Careful Hand," *Wall Street Journal* (July 1, 1997), p. B1.

[27] Reported in G. Christian Hill and Mike Tharp, "Stumbling Giant—Big Quarterly Deficit Stuns Bank America, Adds Pressure on Chief," *Wall Street Journal*, (July 18, 1985), pp. 1–16.

[28] Beer and Nohria, op cit.; and "Change Management, An Inside Job," *Economist* (July 15, 2000), p. 61.

[29] Reported in Robert Rose, "Kentucky Plant Workers Are Cranking Out Good Ideas," *Wall Street Journal* (August 13, 1996), p. B1.

[30] Beer & Nohria, op. cit.

[31] For a review of scholarly work on organizational change, see Arthur G. Bedian, "Organizational Change: A Review of Theory and Research," *Journal of Management*, vol. 25 (1999), pp. 293–315.

[32] For a discussion of alternative types of change, see David A. Nadler and Michael L. Tushman, *Strategic Organizational Design* (Glenview, II: Scott, Foresman, 1988); John P. Kotter, "Leading Change: Why Transformations Efforts Fail," *Harvard Business Review* (March–April 1995), pp. 59–67; and W. Warner Burke, *Organization Change* (Thousand Oaks, CA.: Sage, 2002).

[33] "FEMA to See Radical Change Homeland Security Chief Says," *The Columbus Dispatch* (December 21, 2005), p. A5.

[34] Based on Gary Hamel, *Leading the Revolution* (Boston, MA: Harvard Business School Press, 2000), pp. 293–95

[35] Based on Kotter, op. cit.

[36] See Edward E. Lawler III, "Strategic Choices for Changing Organizations," chapter 12 in Allan M. Mohrman Jr., Susan Albers Mohrman, Gerald E. Ledford Jr., Thomas G. Cummings, Edward E. Lawler III, and Associates, *Large Scale Organizational Change* (San Francisco; Jossey-Bass, 1989).

[37] The classic description of organizations on these terms is by Harold J. Leavitt, "Applied Organizational Change in Industry: Structural, Technological and Humanistic Approaches," in James G. March (ed.), *Handbook of Organizations* (Chicago: Rand McNally, 1965), pp. 1144–70.

[38] Kurt Lewin, "Group Decision and Social Change," in G. E. Swanson, T. M. Newcomb, and E. L. Hartley (eds.), *Readings in Social Psychology* (New York: Holt, Rinehart, 1952), pp. 459–73.

[39] This discussion is based on Robert Chin and Kenneth D. Benne, "General Strategies for Effecting Changes in Human Systems," in Warren G. Bennis, Kenneth D. Benne, Robert Chin, and Kenneth E. Corey (eds.), *The Planning of Change*, 3rd ed. (New York: Holt, Rinehart; 1969), pp. 22–45.

[40] The change agent descriptions here and following are developed from an exercise reported in J. William Pfeiffer and John E. Jones, *A Handbook of Structured Experiences for Human Relations Training*, vol. 2 (La Jolla, CA: University Associates, 1973).

[41] Ram N. Aditya, Robert J. House, and Steven Kerr, "Theory and Practice of Leadership: Into the New Millennium," Chapter 6 in Cary L. Cooper and Edwin A. Locke, *Industrial and Organizational Psychology: Linking Theory with Practice* (Malden, MA: Blackwell, 2000).

[42] Information from Mike Schneider, Disney Teaching Exces Magic of Customer Service," *Columbus Dispatch* (December 17, 2000), p. G9.

[43] Teresa M. Amabile, "How to Kill Creativity, *Harvard Business Review*, (September–October, 1998), pp. 77–87.

[44] Sue Shellenbarger, "Some Employers Find Way to Ease Burden of Changing Shifts," *Wall Street Journal* (March 25, 1998), p. B1.

[45] Ibid.

[46] John P. Kotter and Leonard A. Schlesinger, "Choosing Strategies for Change," *Harvard Business Review*, vol. 57 (March–April 1979); 109–12. Example from *Fortune* (December, 1991), pp. 56–62; additional information from corporate website: www.toro.com.

[47] Wanda J. Orlikowski and J. Debra Hofman, "An Improvisational Model for Change Management: The Case of Groupware Technologies," *Sloan Management Review* (winter 1997), pp. 11–21.

[48] Ibid.

[49] Overviews of organization development are provided by W. Warner Burke, *Organization Development: A Normative View* (Reading, MA: Addison-Wesley, 1987); William Rothwell, Roland Sullivan, and Gary N. McLean, *Practicing Organization Development* (San Francisco: Jossey-Bass, 1995); and Wendell L. French and Cecil H. Bell Jr., *Organization Development*, 6th ed. (Englewood Cliffs, NJ: Prentice-Hall, 1998).

[50] See French and Bell, op. cit.

[51] Jennifer LeClaire. "Skype Calls on EMI, Sony, Warner in Ringtone Deal." TechNewsWorld, April 27, 2006. Accessed August 1, 2006, at http:// www.technewsworld.com/story/50210.html.

[52] Steve Rosenbush. "Kazaa, Skype, and Now 'The Venice Project.' " *Business Week Online*, July 24, 2006.

[53] http://about.skype.com/.

[54] http://us.accessories.skype.com/direct/skypeusa/welcome.jsp.

[55] Olga Kharif. "Voice over Microsoft Protocol?" *Business Week Online*, February 1, 2006.

[56] Trevor Zion Bauknight. "Speaking Freely." *Business & Economic Review*, July–September 2006.

[57] Ron Condon. "Should You Switch to VoIP?" *Management Today*, July 2006.

58 http://www.skype.com/business/.

59 http://www.skype.com/security/.

60 "The Venice Project."

61 http://about.skype.com/skypeebay.html

62 "The Venice Project."

Features:

Insights: Information from "'Mosh Pits' of Creativity," *Business Week* (November 7, 2005), pp. 98–99; "Edward Zander: Motorola," *Business Week* (December 19, 2005), p. 63; and, Adam Lashinsky, "Razr's Edge," *Fortune* (June 12, 2006), pp 124–131.

Issues and Situations: Information from Jena McGregor, "The World's Most Innovative Companies," *Business Week* (April 24, 2006), pp. 63–74; "Innovation: The View from the Top," *Business Week* (April 3, 2006), pp. 52–53; "The Enemies of Innovation," *Business Week* (April 24, 2006), p. 68.

Kaffeeklatsch: See "Change Management: An Inside Job," *The Economist* (July 15, 2000), p. 61; Michael Beer and Nitin Nohria, "Cracking the Code of Change," *Harvard Business Review* (May–June 2000), pp. 133–41.

Real Ethics: Information from "Can Business Be Cool?" *The Economist* (June 10, 2006), pp. 59–60; and, Aubrey Henretty, "A Brighter Day," *Kellogg* (Summer, 2006), pp. 32–34; Competitive Enterprise Institute, http://www.cei.org/pages/co2.cfm (retrieved September 29, 2006). Quotes from Henretty, op cit., and Joseph Stiglitz, *Making Globalization Work* (New York: Norton, 2006), p. 172.

Chapter 13

1 David Casserly. "Mutual Fund Leaders Aim to Repair Trust." *Governance Weekly.* Accessed August 11, 2006, at http://www.issproxy.com/governance/publications/2004archived/059.jsp.

2 Joseph Guinto. "Wheels Up." *Southwest Airlines Spirit*, June 2006, p. 116.

3 Seana Mulcahy. "Bomb-Proof Branding." OnlineSPIN, November 14, 2005. Accessed August 11, 2006, at http://publications.mediapost.com/index.cfm?fuseaction=Articles.showArticle&art_aid=36268.

4 www.boozallen.com, op cit.

5 Robert Heller. "Management and Statistics: Never Ignore the Power of Statistics in Business Management." *Thinking Managers.* Accessed September 7, 2006, at http://www.thinking managers.com/management/management-statistics.php.

6 Maria Marsala. "Going Public: Is It the Best Option for You?" Accessed September 7, 2006, at http://www.coachmaria.com/articles/goingpublic.html.

7 http://icmr.icfai.org/casestudies/catalogue/Leadership%20and%20Entrepreneurship/LDEN021.htm

8 Manfred Davidmann. "Style of Management and Leadership." Case study. Accessed September 8, 2006, at http://www.solbaram.org/articles/clm2.html.

9 Max DePree. "An Old Pro's Wisdom: It Begins with a Belief in People," *New York Times* (September 10, 1989), p. F2. (New York: Doubleday, 2004), see also David Woodruff, "Herman Miller: How Green Is My Factory," *Business Week* (September 16, 1991), pp. 54–56; and, Max DePree, *Leadership Jazz* (New York: Doubleday, 1992); and *Leadership Is an Art.*

10 Tom Peters, "Rule #3: Leadership Is Confusing as Hell," *Fast Company* (March 2001), pp. 124–40.

11 Abraham Zaleznick, "Leaders and Managers: Are They Different?" *Harvard Business Review* (May–June 1977), pp. 67–78.

12 Quote from Marshall Loeb, "Where Leaders Come From," *Fortune* (September 19, 1994), pp. 241–42. For additional thoughts, see Warren Bennis, *Why Leaders Can't Lead* (San Francisco: Jossey-Bass, 1996).

13 See Jean Lipman-Blumen, *Connective Leadership: Managing in a Changing World* (New York: Oxford University Press, 1996), pp. 3–11.

14 Rosabeth Moss Kanter, "Power Failure in Management Circuits," *Harvard Business Review* (July–August 1979), pp. 65–75.

15 For a good managerial discussion of power, see David C. McClelland and David H. Burnham, "Power Is the Great Motivator," *Harvard Business Review*, (March–April 1976), pp. 100–10.

16 The classic treatment of these power bases is John R. P. French Jr. and Bertram Raven, "The Bases of Social Power," in Darwin Cartwright, ed., *Group Dynamics: Research and Theory* (Evanston, IL: Row, Peterson, 1962), pp. 607–13. For managerial applications of this basic framework, see Gary Yukl and Tom Taber, "The Effective Use of Managerial Power," *Personnel*, vol. 60 (1983), pp. 37–49; and Robert C. Benfari. Harry E. Wilkinson, and Charles D. Orth, "The Effective Use of Power," *Business Horizons*, vol. 29 (1986), pp. 12–16. Gary A. Yukl, *Leadership in Organizations*, 4th ed. (Englewood Cliffs, NJ: Prentice-Hall, 1998); includes "information" as a separate, but related, power source.

17 James M. Kouzes and Barry Z. Posner, "The Leadership Challenge," *Success* (April 1988), p. 68. See also their books *Credibility: How Leaders Gain and Lose It; Why People Demand It* (San Francisco: Jossey-Bass, 1996); *Encouraging the Heart: A Leader's Guide to Rewarding and Recognizing Others* (San Francisco: Jossey-Bass, 1999); and *The Leadership Challenge: How to Get Extraordinary Things Done in Organizations, Third Edition* (San Francisco: Jossey-Bass, 2002).

18 Burt Nanus, *Visionary Leadership: Creating a Compelling Sense of Vision for Your Organization* (San Francisco: Jossey-Bass, 1992).

19 Lorraine Monroe, "Leadership Is About Making Vision Happen—What I Call 'Vision Acts,'" *Fast Company* (March 2001), p. 98; School Leadership Academy website: www.lorrainemonroe.com.

20 Robert K. Greenleaf and Larry C. Spears, *The Power of Servant Leadership: Essays* (San Francisco: Berrett-Koehler, 1996).

21 Jay A. Conger, "Leadership: The Art of Empowering Others," *Academy of Management Executive*, vol. 3 (1989), pp. 17–24.

22 Max DePree, op cit., 1989, 1992, 2004.

23 Lorraine Monroe, "Leadership Is about Making Vision Happen—What I Call 'Vision Acts,'" *Fast Company* (March 2001), p. 98; School Leadership Academy Web site: www.lorrainemonroe.com.

24 Greenleaf and Spears, op cit., p. 78.

25 The early work on leader traits is well represented in Ralph M. Stogdill, "Personal Factors Associated with Leadership: A Survey of the Literature," *Journal of Psychology*, vol. 25 (1948), pp. 35–71. See also Edwin E. Ghiselli, *Explorations in Management Talent* (Santa Monica, CA: Goodyear, 1971); and Shirley A. Kirkpatrick and Edwin A. Locke, "Leadership: Do Traits Really Matter?" *Academy of*

Management Executive (1991), pp. 48–60.

26 See also John W. Gardner's article, "The Context and Attributes of Leadership," *New Management*, vol. 5 (1988), pp. 18–22; John P. Kotter, *The Leadership Factor* (New York: Free Press, 1988); and Bernard M. Bass, *Stogdill's Handbook of Leadership* (New York: Free Press, 1990).

27 Kirkpatrick and Locke, op cit. (1991).

28 This work traces back to classic studies by Kurt Lewin and his associates at the University of Iowa. See, for example, K. Lewin and R. Lippitt, "An Experimental Approach to the Study of Autocracy and Democracy: A Preliminary Note," *Sociometry*, vol. 1 (1938), pp. 292–300; K. Lewin, "Field Theory and Experiment in Social Psychology: Concepts and Methods," *American Journal of Sociology*, vol. 44 (1939), pp. 886–896; and K. Lewin, R. Lippitt, and R. K. White, "Patterns of Aggressive Behavior in Experimentally Created Social Climates," *Journal of Social Psychology*, vol. 10 (1939), pp. 271–301.

29 The original research from the Ohio State studies is described in R.M. Stogdill and A.E. Coons (Eds.), *Leader Behavior: Its Description and Measurement*, Research Monograph No. 88 (Columbus, OH: Ohio State University Bureau of Business Research, 1951); see also Chester A. Schreisham, Claudia C. Cogliser, and Linda L. Neider, "Is It 'Trustworthy'? A Multiple-Levels-of-Analysis Reexamination of an Ohio State Leadership Study with Implications for Future Research," *Leadership Quarterly* Vol. 2 (Summer, 1995), pp. 111–145. For the University of Michigan studies see Robert Kahn and Daniel Katz, "Leadership Practices in Relation to Productivity and Morale," in Dorwin Cartwright and Alvin Alexander (Eds.), *Group Dynamics: Research and Theory*, Third Edition (New York: Harper & Row, 1968).

30 See Bass, op cit., 1990.

31 Robert R. Blake and Jane Srygley Mouton, *The New Managerial Grid III* (Houston: Gulf Publishing, 1985).

32 See Lewin and Lippitt, op cit., 1938.

33 For a good discussion of this theory, see Fred E. Fiedler, Martin M. Chemers, and Linda Mahar, *The Leadership Match Concept* (New York: Wiley, 1978); Fiedler's current contin-

gency research with the cognitive resource theory is summarized in Fred E. Fiedler and Joseph E. Garcia, *New Approaches to Effective Leadership* (New York: Wiley, 1987).

34 Paul Hersey and Kenneth H. Blanchard, *Management and Organizational Behavior* (Englewood Cliffs, NJ: Prentice-Hall, 1988). For an interview with Paul Hersey on the origins of the model, see John R. Schermerhorn, Jr., "Situational Leadership: Conversations with Paul Hersy," *Mid-American Journal of Business* (fall 1997), pp. 5–12.

35 See Claude L. Graeff, "The Situational Leadership Theory: A Critical View," *Academy of Management Review*, vol. 8 (1983), pp. 285–91; and, Carmen F. Fenandez and Robert P. Vecchio, "Situational Leadership Theory Revisited: A Test of an Across-Jobs Perspective," *Leadership Quarterly*, vol. 8 (Summer, 1997), pp. 67–84.

36 See, for example, Robert J. House, "A Path-Goal Theory of Leader Effectiveness," *Administrative Sciences Quarterly*, vol. 16 (1971), pp. 321–38; Robert J. House and Terrence R. Mitchell, "Path-Goal Theory of Leadership," *Journal of Contemporary Business* (Autumn 1974), pp. 81–97; the path-goal theory is reviewed by Bass, op cit., and Yukl, op cit. A supportive review of research is offered in Julie Indvik. "Path-Goal Theory of Leadership; A Meta-Analysis," in John A. Pearce II and Richard B. Robinson Jr. eds., *Academy of Management Best Paper Proceedings* (1986), pp. 189–92. The theory is reviewed and updated in Robert J. House, "Path-Goal Theory of Leadership: Lessons, Legacy and a Reformulated Theory," *Leadership Quarterly*, vol. 7 (Autumn, 1996), pp. 323–352.

37 See the discussions of path-goal theory in Yukl, op cit.; and Bernard M. Bass, "Leadership: Good, Better, Best," *Organizational Dynamics* (winter 1985), pp. 26–40.

38 See Steven Kerr and John Jermier, "Substitutes for Leadership: Their Meaning and Measurement", *Organizational Behavior and Human Performance*, vol. 22 (1978), pp. 375–403; Jon P. Howell and Peter W. Dorfman, "Leadership and Substitutes for Leadership among Professional and Non-professional Workers," *Journal of Applied Behavioral Science*," vol. 22 (1986), pp. 29–46.

39 Victor H. Vroom and Arthur G. Jago, *The New Leadership: Managing Participation in Organizations* (Englewood Cliffs, NJ: Prentice-Hall, 1988). This is based on earlier work by Victor H. Vroom, "A New Look in Managerial Decision-Making," *Organizational Dynamics* (spring 1973), pp. 66–80; and Victor H. Vroom and Phillip Yetton, *Leadership and Decision-Making* (Pittsburgh: University of Pittsburgh Press, 1973).

40 For a related discussion see Edgar H. Schein, *Process Consultation Revisited: Building the Helping Relationship* (Reading, MA: Addison-Wesley, 1999).

41 Vroom and Jago, op cit.

42 For a review see Yukl, op cit.

43 See the discussion by Victor H. Vroom, "Leadership and the Decision Making Process," *Organizational Dynamics*, vol. 28 (2000), pp. 82–94.

44 Among popular books Warren Bennis and Burt Nanus, *Leaders: The Strategies for Taking Charge* (New York: Harper Business 1997); Max De-Pree, *Leadership Is an Art*, op cit; Kotter, *The Leadership Factor*, op cit.; Kouzes and Posner, *The Leadership Challenge*, op cit., 2002.

45 The distinction was originally made by James McGregor Burns, *Leadership* (New York: Harper & Row, 1978), and was further developed by Bernard Bass, *Leadership and Performance Beyond Expectations* (New York: Free Press, 1985) and Bernard M. Bass, "Leadership: Good, Better, Best," *Organization Dynamics* (winter 1985), pp. 26–40.

46 This list is based on Kouzes and Posner, op cit.; Gardner, op cit.

47 Daniel Goleman, "Leadership That Gets Results," *Harvard Business Review* (March–April 2000), pp. 78–90. See also his books *Emotional Intelligence* (New York: Bantam Books, 1995) and *Working with Emotional Intelligence* (New York: Bantam Books, 1998).

48 Daniel Goleman, "What Makes a Leader?" *Harvard Business Review* (November–December 1998), pp. 93–102.

49 Goleman, op cit. 1998.

50 Information from "Women and Men, Work and Power," *Fast Company*, Issue 13 (1998), p. 71.

51 Jane Shibley Hyde, "The Gender Similarities Hypothesis," *American Psychologist*, vol. 60, no. 6 (2005), pp. 581–592.

52 A. H. Eagley, S. J. Daran, and M. G. Makhijani, "Gender and the Effectiveness of Leaders: A Meta-Analysis," *Psychological Bulletin*, vol. 117 (1995), pp. 125–45.

53 Research on gender issues in leadership is reported in Sally Helgesen, *The Female Advantage: Women's Ways of Leadership* (New York: Doubleday, 1990); Judith B. Rosener, "Ways Women Lead," *Harvard Business Review* (November–December 1990), pp. 119–125; and Alice H. Eagley, Steven J. Karau, and Blair T. Johnson, "Gender and Leadership Style Among School Principals: A Meta-Analysis," *Administrative Science Quarterly*, vol. 27 (1992), pp. 76–102; Jean Lipman-Blumen, *Connective Leadership: Managing in a Changing World* (New York: Oxford University Press, 1996); Alice H. Eagley, Mary C. Johannesen-Smith, and Marloes L. van Engen, "Transformational, Transactional and Laissez-Faire Leadership: A Meta-Analysis of Women and Men, *Psychological Bulletin*, vol. 124 (4), 2003: pp. 569–591; Carol Hymowitz, "Too Many Women Fall for Stereotypes of Selves, Study Says," *Wall Street Journal* (October 24, 2005), p. B.1.

54 Vroom, op cit. (2000).

55 Data reported by Rochelle Sharpe, "As Women Rule," *Business Week* (November 20, 2000), p. 75.

56 Eagley, et al., op cit.; Hymowitz, op cit.; Rosener, op cit.; Vroom, op cit.

57 Rosener, op cit. (1990).

58 For debate on whether some transformational leadership qualities tend to be associated more with female than male leaders, see "Debate: Ways Women and Men Lead," *Harvard Business Review* (January–February 1991), pp. 150–60.

59 Quote from "As Leaders, Women Rule," *Business Week* (November 20, 2000), pp. 75–84. Rosabeth Moss Kanter is the author of *Men and Women of the Corporation*, 2nd ed. (New York: Basic Books, 1993).

60 Hyde, op cit.; Hymowitz, op cit.

61 Peter F. Drucker, "Leadership: More Doing than Dash," *Wall Street Journal* (January 6, 1988), p. 16. For a compendium of writings on leadership sponsored by the Drucker Foundation, see Frances Hesselbein, Marshall Goldsmith, and Richard Beckhard, *Leader of the Future* (San Francisco: Jossey-Bass, 1997).

62 Quotes from Ibid.

63 Based on the discussion by John W. Dienhart and Terry Thomas, "Ethical Leadership: A Primer on Ethical Responsibility" in John R. Schermerhorn, Jr., *Management*, 7th ed. (New York: Wiley, 2003).

64 James MacGregor Burns, *Transforming Leadership: A New Pursuit of Happiness* (New York: Atlantic Monthly Press, 2003); information from Christopher Caldwell, book review, *International Herald Tribune* (April 29, 2003), p. 18.

65 Fred Luthans and Bruce Avolio, "Authentic Leadership: A Positive Development Approach", in K. S. Cameron, J. E. Dutton, and R. E. Quinn (eds.), *Positive Organizational Scholarship* (San Francisco, Berrett-Koehler, 2003), pp. 241–258.

66 Doug May, Adrian Chan, Timothy Hodges, and Bruce Avolio point out ("Developing the Moral Component of Authentic Leadership", *Organizational Dynamics*, 2003, vol. 32, pp. 247–60).

67 Kenneth Lablich, "Is Herb Kelleher America's Best CEO"? *Fortune* (May 2, 1994), p. 45.

68 "Little Giant." *Southwest Airlines Spirit*, June 2006. p. 154.

69 James Campbell Quick, "Crafting an Organizational Culture: Herb's Hand at Southwest Airlines," *Organizational Dynamics*, vol. 21 (August 1992), p. 47.

70 Richard S. Teitelbaum, "Where Service Flies Right," *Fortune* (August 24, 1992), p. 115.

71 Colleen Barrett, "Pampering Customers on a Budget," *Working Woman* (April 1993), pp. 19–22.

72 Justin Martin, "So, You Want to Work for the Best . . . " *Fortune* (January 12, 1998), p. 77.

73 Southwest Airlines home page, op cit.

74 Southwest Airlines home page, op cit.

75 "Did We Say Cheap?" *Inc.* (October 1997), p. 60.

76 "Little Giant."

77 Teitelbaum, op cit., p. 116.

78 "Colleen's Corner," (June 27, 2003), Southwest Airlines home page: www.southwest.com. Column written June 27, 2003.

Features:

Insights: Information and quotes from Sharon Shinn, "Luv, Colleen," *BizEd* (March–April 2003), pp. 18–23; corporate website: www.southwestairlines.com.

Kaffeeklatsch: Based on Carol Hymowitz, "Too Many Women Fall for Stereotypes of Selves, Study Says," *The Wall Street Journal* (October 24, 2005), p. B1.

Team Project: Survey reported in "The Big Picture," *Business Week* (October 2, 2006), p. 9.

Personal Management: List developed from S. Bartholomew Craig and Gigrid B. Qustafson, "Perceived Leader Integrity Scale: An Instrument for Assessing Employee Perceptions of Leader Integrity," *Leadership Quarterly*, vol. 9 (1998), pp. 127–145.

Real Ethics: Suggested by Jeffrey Seglin, "Request Puts Employees in a Tough Spot," *The Columbus Dispatch* (May 28, 2006), p. B3.

Chapter 14

1 Mark Edmondson. "The ABCs of Rank and File Management." LEAN Affiliates. Accessed September 6, 2006, at http://www.leanlibrary.com/rank_and_file_management.htm.

2 http://www.1000ventures.com/business_guide/crosscuttings/cs_leadership_welch.html

3 *Business Week* (August 21/28, 2006), p. 44.

4 http://www.bizactions.com/index.cfm/ba/e100/fa/49057140G1554J1105539P6P16T1/

5 http://www.mspb.gov/studies/newsletters/04sepnws/04sepnws.htm

6 www.calpelra.org/pdf/Alert06-04.pdf

7 http://www.msstate.edu/president/odep/myths.php

8 Quotes from Charles O'Reilly III and Jeffrey Pfeffer, *Hidden Value: How Great Companies Achieve Extraordinary Results Through Ordinary People* (Boston, MA: Harvard Business School Press, 2000).

9 See Abraham H. Maslow, *Eupsychian Management* (Homewood, IL: Richard D. Irwin, 1965); Abraham H. Maslow, *Motivation and Personality*, 2d ed. (New York: Harper & Row, 1970). For a research perspective, see Mahmoud A. Wahba and Lawrence G. Bridwell, "Maslow Reconsidered: A Review of Research on the Need Hierarchy," *Organizational Behavior and Human Performance*, vol. 16 (1976), pp. 212–40.

10 Teresa M. McAleavy, "Worker Dissatisfaction Up, Survey Finds," *The Columbus Dispatch* (September 3, 2006), p. F2.

11 See Clayton P. Alderfer, *Existence, Relatedness, and Growth* (New York: Free Press, 1972).

12 The complete two-factor theory is in Frederick Herzberg, Bernard Mausner, and Barbara Block Synderman, *The Motivation to Work*, 2d ed. (New York: Wiley, 1967); Frederick Herzberg, "One More Time: How Do You Motivate Employees?" *Harvard Business Review* (January–February 1968), pp. 53–62, and reprinted as an *HBR classic* (September–October 1987), pp. 109–20.

13 Critical reviews are provided by Robert J. House and Lawrence A. Wigdor, "Herzberg's Dual-Factor Theory of Job Satisfaction and Motivation: A Review of the Evidence and a Criticism," *Personnel Psychology*, vol. 20 (winter 1967), pp. 369–89; Steven Kerr, Anne Harlan, and Ralph Stogdill, "Preference for Motivator and Hygiene Factors in a Hypothetical Interview Situation," *Personnel Psychology*, vol. 27 (winter 1974), pp. 109–24.

14 Frederick Herzberg, "Workers' Needs: The Same around the World," *Industry Week* (September 21, 1987), pp. 29–32.

15 For a collection of McClelland's work, see David C. McClelland, *The Achieving Society* (New York: Van Nostrand, 1961); "Business Drive and National Achievement," *Harvard Business Review*, vol. 40 (July–August 1962), pp. 99–112; David C. McClelland and David H. Burnham, "Power is the Great Motivator," *Harvard Business Review* (March–April 1976), pp. 100–10; David C. McClelland, *Human Motivation* (Glenview, IL: Scott, Foresman, 1985); David C. McClelland and Richard E. Boyatsis, "The Leadership Motive Pattern and Long-Term Success in Management," *Journal of Applied Psychology*, vol. 67 (1982), pp. 737–43.

16 See, for example, J. Stacy Adams, "Toward an Understanding of Inequity," *Journal of Abnormal and Social Psychology*, vol. 67 (1963), pp. 422–36; J. Stacy Adams, "Inequity in Social Exchange," in vol. 2, L. Berkowitz (ed.), *Advances in Experimental Social Psychology*, (New York: Academic Press, 1965), pp. 267–300.

17 See, for example, J. W. Harder, "Play for Pay: Effects of Inequity in a Pay-for-Performance Context," *Administrative Science Quarterly*, vol. 37 (1992), pp. 321–35.

18 Sarah Anderson, "Wal-Mart's Pay Gap," Institute for Policy Studies (April 19, 2005).

19 Diane Stafford, "Gap Between Wonder Executive Pay Criticized in Annual Report" the *Columbus Dispatch* (September 4, 2006), p. F6.

20 Victor H. Vroom, *Work and Motivation* (New York: Wiley, 1964; republished by Jossey-Bass, 1994).

21 The work on goal-setting theory is well summarized in Edwin A. Locke and Gary P. Latham, *Goal Setting: A Motivational Technique That Works!* (Englewood Cliffs, NJ: Prentice Hall, 1984). See also Edwin A. Locke, Kenneth N. Shaw, Lisa A. Saari, and Gary P. Latham, "Goal Setting and Task Performance 1969–1980," *Psychological Bulletin*, vol. 90 (1981), pp. 125–52; Mark E. Tubbs, "Goal Setting: A Meta-Analytic Examination of the Empirical Evidence," *Journal of Applied Psychology*, vol. 71 (1986), pp. 474–83; and Terence R. Mitchell, Kenneth R. Thompson, and Jane George-Falvy, "Goal Setting: Theory and Practice," Chapter 9 in Cary L. Cooper and Edwin A. Locke (eds.), *Industrial and Organizational Psychology: Linking Theory with Practice* (Malden, MA: Blackwell Business, 2000), pp. 211–249.

22 Gary P. Latham and Edwin A. Locke, "Self-Regulation Through Goal Setting," *Organizational Behavior and Human Decision Processes*, vol. 50 (1991), pp. 212–47.

23 E. L. Thorndike, *Animal Intelligence* (New York: Macmillan, 1911), p. 244.

24 See B. F. Skinner, *Walden Two* (New York: Macmillan, 1948); *Science and Human Behavior* (New York: Macmillan, 1953); *Contingencies of Reinforcement* (New York: Appleton-Century-Crofts, 1969).

25 Fred Luthans and Robert Kreitner, *Organizational Behavior Modification* (Glenview, IL: Scott, Foresman, 1975); and Fred Luthans and Robert Kreitner, *Organizational Behavior Modification and Beyond* (Glenview, IL: Scott, Foresman, 1985); see also Fred Luthans and Alexander D. Stajkovic, "Reinforce for Performance: The Need to Go Beyond Pay and Even Rewards," *Academy of Management Executive*, vol. 13 (1999), pp. 49–57.

26 For the Mary Kay story and philosophy see Mary Kay Ash, *Mary Kay on People Management* (New York: Warner Books, 1985); see also information at the corporate website: http://www.marykay.com.

27 Information from David Whitford, "A Human Place to Work," *Fortune* (January 8, 2001), pp. 108–20.

28 See Frederick Herzberg, Bernard Mausner, and Barbara Block Synderman, *The Motivation to Work*, 2d ed. (New York: Wiley, 1967). The quotation is from Frederick Herzberg, "One More Time: Employees?" *Harvard Business Review* (January–February 1968), pp. 53–62, and reprinted as an HBR Classic in September–October 1987, pp. 109–20.

29 For a complete description of the core characteristics model, see J. Richard Hackman and Greg R. Oldham, *Work Redesign* (Reading, MA: Addison-Wesley, 1980).

30 Barney Olmsted and Suzanne Smith, *Creating a Flexible Workplace: How to Select and Manage Alternative Work Options* (New York: American Management Association, 1989).

31 See Allen R. Cohen and Herman Gadon, *Alternative Work Schedules: Integrating Individual and Organizational Needs* (Reading, MA: Addison-Wesley, 1978), p. 125; Simcha Ronen and Sophia B. Primps, "The Compressed Work Week as Organizational Change: Behavioral and Attitudinal Outcomes," *Academy of Management Review*, vol. 6 (1981), pp. 61–74.

32 Information from Lesli Hicks, "Workers, Employers Praise Their Four-Day Workweek," *Columbus Dispatch* (August 22, 1994), p. 6; and Walsh, op cit. (2001).

33 Business for Social Responsibility Resource Center: www.bsr.org/resourcecenter (January 24, 2001); Anusha Shrivastava, "Flextime is Now Key Benefit for Mom-Friendly Employers," *The Columbus Dispatch* (September 23, 2003), p. C2; Sue Shellenbarger, "Number of Women Managers Rises," *The Wall Street Journal* (September 30, 2003), p. D2.

34 "Networked Workers," *Business Week* (October 6, 1997), p. 8; and Diane E. Lewis, "Flexible Work Arrangements as Important as Salary to Some," *Columbus Dispatch* (May 25, 1998), p. 8.

35 For a review see Wayne F. Cascio, "Managing a Virtual Workplace," *Academy of Management Executive*, vol. 14 (2000), pp. 81–90.

36 Quote from Phil Porter, "Telecommuting Mom Is Part of a National Trend," *Columbus Dispatch* (November 29, 2000), pp. H1, H2.

37 See "Report on the American Workforce 1999" (Washington: U.S. Bureau of Labor Statistics); "1999 AMA Survey of Contingent Workers" (New York: American Management Association, 1999).

38 "About Us." Nucor Steel. Accessed August 9, 2006, at http://nucor.com/indexinner.aspx? finpage=aboutus.

39 Nanette Byrnes, and Michal Arndt. "The Art of Motivation." *Business Week Online*, May 1, 2006. Accessed August 9, 2006, at http://www.businessweek.com/magazine/content/06_18/b3982075.htm.

40 "About Us."

41 Ibid.

42 Ibid.

43 Ibid.

44 Ibid.

45 Ibid.

46 Ibid.

47 Ibid.

48 Tom Terez. "The Soft Side of a Steel Company." Accessed August 10, 2006, at http://www.betterworkplacenow.com/iverson.html.

49 "About Us."

50 Ibid.

Features:

Insights: Information and quotes from Julie Flaherty, "A Parting Gift from the Boss Who Cared," *New York Times* (September 28, 2000), pp. C1, C25; Business Wire Press Release, "Employees of the Butcher Company Share over $18 Million as Owner Shares Benefits of Success" (September 21, 2000).

Issues and Situations: "It's Not So Easy to Shame a CEO," *Business Week* (March 20, 2006), p. 14; Anne Teresen, "How Much Are CEOs Really Paid?" *Business Week* (March 20, 2006), pp. 96–98; "Occidental Chief Irani, Board Redefine Pay Bloat: Graef Crystal," Bloomberg.com (March 13, 2006); "State of Working America 2004/2005: CEO Pay," Economic Policy Institute www.epinet.org; "What's the Difference Between a Living Wage and the Minimum Wage?" AFL-CIO: www.aflcio.org/issues/jobseconomy.; "Huge Gap in U.S. CEO/Worker Pay," *Financial Times* (June 22, 2006), p. 4.

Kaffeeklatsch: Information from Len Boselovic, "Few Workers Go the Extra Mile, Study Says," *The Columbus Dispatch* (December 14, 2005), p. G1; Steve Hamm, "A Passion for the Plan," *Business Week* (August 21/28, 2006), pp. 92–93.

Team Project: CEO pay from "Best-Paid CEOs" *USA Today* (October 5, 2006), p. 2B.

Real Ethics: Information from Jared Sandberg, "Why You May Regret Looking at Papers Left on the Office Copier," *The Wall Street Journal* (June 20, 2006), p. B1.

Chapter 15

1 http://money.cnn.com/magazines/fortune/fortune_archive/2006/09/04/8384727/index.htm

2 http://www.thevirtualhandshake.com/blog/2006/06/23

3 http://www.nytimes.com/2006/06/11/us/11recruit.html?ei=5090&en=ddfbele3b386090b&ex=1307678400

4 Virtual Handshake.

5 Jessi Hempel, and Paula Lehman. "The MySpace Generation." *Business Week*, December 12, 2005.

6 Ibid.

7 Ibid.

8 Ibid.

9 Charles O'Reilly III and Jeffrey Pfeffer *Hidden Value: How Great Companies Achieve Extraordinary Results Through Ordinary People* (Boston: MA: Harvard Business School Publishing, 2000), quotes from p. 2.

10 This example is reported in *Esquire* (December 1986), p. 243. Emphasis is added to the quotation. *Note:* Nussbaum became director of the Labor Department's Women's Bureau during the Clinton administration and subsequently moved to the AFL-CIO as head of the Women's Bureau.

11 See H. R. Schiffman, *Sensation and Perception: An Integrated Approach*, 3d ed. (New York: Wiley, 1990).

12 John P. Kotter, "The Psychological Contract: Managing the Joining Up Process," *California Management Review*, vol. 15 (spring 1973), 91–99; Denise Rousseau (ed.), *Psychological Contracts in Organizations* (San Francisco: Jossey-Bass, 1995); Denise Rousseau, "Changing the Deal While Keeping the People," *Academy of Management Executive*, vol. 10 (1996), pp. 50–59; and Denise Rousseau and Rene Schalk (eds.), *Psychological Contracts in Employment: Cross-Cultural Perspectives* (San Francisco: Jossey-Bass, 2000).

13 A good review is E. L. Jones (ed.), *Attribution: Perceiving the Causes of Behavior* (Morristown, NJ: General Learning Press, 1972). See also John H. Harvey and Gifford Weary, "Current Issues in Attribution Theory and Research," *Annual Review of Psychology*, vol. 35 (1984), pp. 427–59.

14 See, for example, Stephan Thernstrom and Abigail Thernstrom, *America in Black and White* (New York: Simon & Schuster, 1997); and David A. Thomas and Suzy Wetlaufer, "A Question of Color: A Debate on Race in the U.S. Workplace," *Harvard Business Review* (September–October 1997), pp. 118–32.

15 Information from "Misconceptions About Women in the Global Arena Keep Their Numbers Low," Catalyst study: www.catalystwomen.org/home.html.

16 These examples are from Natasha Josefowitz, *Paths to Power* (Reading, MA: Addison-Wesley, 1980), p. 60. For more on gender issues see Gray N. Powell (ed.), *Handbook of Gender and Work* (Thousand Oaks, CA: Sage, 1999).

17 Survey reported in Kelly Greene, "Age Is Still More Than a Number," *Wall Street Journal* (April 10, 2003), p. D2.

18 The classic work is Dewitt C. Dearborn and Herbert A. Simon, "Selective Perception: A Note on the Departmental Identification of Executives," *Sociometry*, vol. 21 (1958), pp. 140–44. See also, J. P. Walsh, "Selectivity and Selective Perception: Belief Structures and Information Processing, *Academy of Management Journal*, vol. 24 (1988), pp. 453–70.

19 Quotation from Sheila O'Flanagan, Underestimate Casual Dressers at Your Peril," *Irish Times* (July 22, 2005).

20 See William L. Gardner and Mark J. Martinko, "Impression Management in Organizations," *Journal of Management* (June 1988), p. 332.

21 Sandy Wayne and Robert Liden, "Effects of Impression Management on Performance Ratings," *Academy of Management Journal* (February 2005), pp. 232–252.

[22] See M. R. Barrick and M. K. Mount, "The Big Five Personality Dimensions and Job Performance: A Meta-Analysis," *Personnel Psychology*, vol. 44 (1991), pp. 1–26.

[23] This discussion based in part on Schermerhorn et. al, op cit., pp. 54–60.

[24] J. B. Rotter, "Generalized Expectancies for Internal Versus External Control of Reinforcement," *Psychological Monographs*, vol. 80 (1966), pp. 1–28; see also Thomas W. Ng, Kelly L. Sorensen, and Lillian T. Eby, "Cocos of Control at Work: A Meta-Analysis, *Journal of Organizational Behavior*, Press (2006).

[25] T. W. Adorno, E. Frenkel-Brunswick, D. J. Levinson, and R. N. Sanford, *The Authoritarian Personality* (New York: Harper & Row, 1950).

[26] Niccolo Machiavelli, *The Prince*, trans. George Bull (Middlesex, UK: Penguin, 1961).

[27] Richard Christie and Florence L. Geis, *Studies in Machiavellianism* (New York: Academic Press, 1970).

[28] See Donald Bowen, "Learning and Problem-Solving: You're Never Too Jung," in Donald D. Bowen, Roy J. Lewicki, Donald T. Hall, and Francine S. Hall, *Experiences in Management and Organizational Behavior*, 4th ed. (New York: Wiley 1997), pp. 7–13.

[29] I. Briggs-Myers, *Introduction to Type* (Palo Alto, CA: Consulting Psychologists Press, 1980); William L. Gardner and Mark J. Martinko, "Using the Myers-Briggs Type Indicator to Study Managers: A Literature Review and Research Agenda," *Journal of Management*, vol. 22 (1996), pp. 45–83; Naomi L. Quenk, *Essentials of Myers-Briggs Type Indicator Assessment* (New York: Wiley, 2000).

[30] See M. Snyder, *Public Appearances/Private Realities: The Psychology of Self-Monitoring* (New York: Freeman, 1987).

[31] Information and quote from Joann S. Lublin, "How One Black Woman Lands Her Top Jobs: Risks and Networking," *Wall Street Journal* (March 4, 2003), p. B1.

[32] Martin Fishbein and Icek Ajzen, *Belief, Attitude, Intention and Behavior: An Introduction to Theory and Research* (Reading, MA: Addison-Wesley, 1973).

[33] See Leon Festinger, *A Theory of Cognitive Dissonance* (Palo Alto, CA: Stanford University Press, 1957).

[34] Timothy A. Judge and Allan H. Church, "Job Satisfaction: Research and Practice," Chapter 7 in Cary L. Cooper and Edwin A. Locke (eds.), *Industrial and Organizational Psychology: Linking Theory with Practice* (Malden, MA: Blackwell Business, 2000); and, Timothy A. Judge, "Promote Job Satisfaction Through Mental Challenge, Chapter 6 in Edwin A. Locke (ed.), *the Blackwell Handbook of Organizational Behavior* (Malden, MA: Blackwell, 2004).

[35] Linda Grant, "Happy Workers, High Returns," *Fortune* (January 12, 1998), p. 81.

[36] Dennis W. Organ, *Organizational Citizenship Behavior: The Good Soldier Syndrome* (Lexington, MA: Lexington Books, 1988).

[37] Information from Sue Shellenbarger, "Employers Are Finding It Doesn't Cost Much to Make a Staff Happy," *Wall Street Journal* (November 19, 1997), p. B1. See also, "Job Satisfaction on the Decline," The Conference Board (July, 2002).

[38] Judge and Church, op cit., (2000; Judge, op cit., 2004.

[39] Data reported in "When Loyalty Erodes, So Do Profits," *Business Week* (August 13, 2001), p. 8.

[40] These relationships are discussed in Charles N. Greene, "The Satisfaction-Performance Controversy," *Business Horizons*, vol. 15 (1982), p. 31; Michelle T. Iaffaldano and Paul M. Muchinsky, "Job Satisfaction and Job Performance: A Meta-Analysis," *Psychological Bulletin*, vol. 97 (1985), pp. 251–273; Judge, op cit., 2004.

[41] This discussion follows conclusions in Judge, op cit., 2004.

[42] Damon Darlin and Matt Richtel, "Chairwoman Leaves Hewlett in Spying Furor," *The Wall Street Journal* (September 23, 2006), pp. A1, A9.

[43] Daniel Goleman, "Leadership that Gets Results," *Harvard Business Review* (March–April, 2000), pp. 78–90.

[44] See Robert G. Lord, Richard J. Klimoski and Ruth Knafer (Eds.), *Emotions in the Workplace; Understanding the Structure and Role of Emotions in Organizational Behavior* (San Francisco: Jossey-Bass, 2002); and, Roy L. Payne and Cary L. Cooper (Eds.), *Emotions at Work: Theory Research and Applications for Management* (Chichester, UK: John Wiley & Sons, 2004).

[45] Joyce E. Bono and Remus Ilies, "Charisma, Positive Emotions and Mood Contagion," *Leadership Quarterly*, Vol. 17 (2006), pp. 317–334.

[46] See Arthur P. Brief, Randall S. Schuler, and Mary Van Sell, *Managing Job Stress* (Boston: Little, Brown, 1981), pp. 7, 8.

[47] Robert B. Reich, *The Future of Success* (New York: Knopf, 2000), p. 8.

[48] Michael Weldholz, "Stress Increasingly Seen as Problem with Executives More Vulnerable," *Wall Street Journal*, (September 28, 1982), p. 31.

[49] Sue Shellenbarger, "Do We Work More or Not? Either Way, We Feel Frazzled," *Wall Street Journal* (July 30, 1997), p. B1.

[50] Carol Hymowitz, "Impossible Expectations and Unfulfilling Work Stress Managers, Too," *Wall Street Journal* (January 16, 2001), p. B1.

[51] The classic work is Meyer Friedman and Ray Roseman, *Type A Behavior and Your Heart* (New York: Knopf, 1974).

[52] See Hans Selye, *Stress in Health and Disease* (Boston: Butterworth, 1976).

[53] Carol Hymowitz, "Can Workplace Stress Get *Worse*?" *Wall Street Journal* (January 16, 2001), pp. B1, B3.

[54] See Steve M. Jex, *Stress and Job Performance* (San Francisco: Jossey-Bass, 1998).

[55] See "workplace violence" discussed by Richard V. Denenberg and Mark Braverman, *The Violence-Prone Workplace* (Ithaca, NY: Cornell University Press, 1999).

[56] See Daniel C. Ganster and Larry Murphy, "Workplace Interventions to Prevent Stress-Related Illness: Lessons from Research and Practice," Chapter 2 in Cooper and Locke (eds.), op cit. (2000); Long working hours linked to high blood pressure," www.Gn.com/2006/Health (retrieved August 29, 2006).

[57] Reported in Sue Shellenbarger, "Finding Ways to Keep a Partner's Job Stress from Hitting Home," *Wall Street Journal*, (November 29, 2000), p. B1.

[58] Quote from Shellenbarger, op cit.

[59] David Teten. "Shawn Gold, SVP, MySpace: Marketing in a Networked Culture," Accessed August 15, 2006, at http://www.thevirtualhandshake.com/blog/2006/06/23.

[60] "Teens Hang Out at MySpace." *USA Today*, January 9, 2006.

[61] "Marketing in a Networked Culture."

[62] Steve Rosenbush. "Users Crowd into MySpace." *Business Week Online*, November 15, 2005.

[63] Antony Bruno. "MySpace Is the (Online) Place." *Billboard*, July 2, 2005. Vol. 117, Issue 27.

[64] Jessi Hempel and Paula Lehman. "The MySpace Generation," *Business Week*, December 12, 2005.

[65] "Teens Hang Out."

[66] Ibid.

[67] Brad Stone. "The MySpace.com Guys." *Newsweek*, December 26, 2005.

[68] Ibid.

[69] Ibid.

[70] Rosenbush Steve. "Why MySpace Is the Hot Place." *Business Week Online*, May 31, 2005.

[71] Scott Medintz. "Talkin' 'bout MySpace Generation." *Money*, February 2006. Vol. 35, Issue 2.

Features:

Insights: Information on Whole Foods Market reported on www.wholefoodsmarket.com. Additional survey information from Lindsey Gerdes, "Get Ready for a Pickier Workforce," *Business Week* (September 18, 2006), p. 82. Issues and Situations: Information from "Meet the New Boss," *Business Week* (June 26, 2006), p. 78; Diane Brady, "Charm Offensive," *Business Week* (June 26, 2006), pp. 76–80; and, Del Jones, "Not All Successful CEOs Are Extroverts," *The Wall Street Journal* (June 7, 2006), pp. 18–19.

Kaffeeklatsch: Information from Erin White, "Typecast at Work? Here's How to Fix Your Image," *The Wall Street Journal* (February 28, 2006), p. 29.

Team Project: Gallup data from "Kerry Hannon, "People with Pals at Work More Satisfied, Productive," *USA Today* (August 14, 2006), p. 4B; see also, Tom Rath, *Vital Friends: The People You Can't Afford to Live Without* (Princeton, NJ: Gallup Press, 2006).

Real Ethics: Information from Victoria Knight, "Personality Tests as Hiring Tools," *The Wall Street Journal* (March 15, 2006), p. B3C.

Chapter 16

[1] "NAFE's Employers of Choice Groom Women for Crucial Bottom-Line Positions." National Association for Female Executives. Accessed August 18, 2006, at 5http://www.nafe.com/mag_1stqtr05_cover.shtml.

[2] Viv Bernstein. "On Pit Row, It's First and Tire Change." *New York Times*, August 15, 2006. Accessed August 18, 2006, at 4http://www.nytimes.com/2006/08/15/sports/othersports/15pit.html?_r=1 &oref=slogin&pagewanted=print.

[3] "Busch's Team Wins Pit Crew Championship," Auto Racing New Wine: Sports.espn.go.com.

[4] Bernstein, op cit.

[5] http://www.jcs-group.com/trickle/manual/monawd2.html

[6] Grove quote from John A. Bryne, "Visionary vs. Visionary," *Business Week* (August 28, 2000), pp. 210–14; Chambers quote from Charles O'Reilly III and Jeffrey Pfeffer, *Hidden Value: How Great Companies Achieve Extraordinary Results Through Ordinary People* (Boston, MA: Harvard Business School Publishing, 2000), p. 4.

[7] Jon R. Katzenbach and Douglas K. Smith, *The Wisdom of Teams: Creating the High Performance Organization* (Boston: Harvard Business School Press, 1993).

[8] Cited in Lynda C. McDermott, Nolan Brawley, and William A. Waite, *World-Class Teams: Working Across Borders* (New York: Wiley, 1998), p. 5.

[9] See, for example, Edward E. Lawler III, Susan Albers Mohrman, and Gerald E. Ledford Jr., *Employee Involvement and Total Quality Management: Practices and Results in Fortune 1000 Companies* (San Francisco: Jossey-Bass, 1992); Susan A. Mohrman, Susan A. Cohen, and Monty A. Mohrman, *Designing Team-based Organizations: New Forms for Knowledge Work* (San Francisco: Jossey-Bass, 1995).

[10] Katzenbach and Smith, op cit.

[11] See Leavitt, op cit.

[12] A classic work is Bib Latane, Kipling Williams, and Stephen Harkins, "Many Hands Make Light the Work: The Causes and Consequences of Social Loafing, *Journal of Personality and Social Psychology*, vol. 37 (1978), pp. 822–32.

[13] See Marvin E. Shaw, *Group Dynamics: The Psychology of Small Group Behavior*, 2d ed. (New York: McGraw-Hill, 1976); Harold J. Leavitt, "Suppose We Took Groups More Seriously," in Eugene L. Cass and Frederick G. Zimmer (eds.), *Man and Work in Society* (New York: Van Nostrand Reinhold, 1975), pp. 67–77.

[14] John M. George, "Extrinsic and Intrinsic Origins of Perceived Social Loafing in Organizations," *Academy of Management Journal* (March, 1992), pp. 191–202; and W. Jack Duncan, "Why Some People Loaf in Groups While Others Loaf Alone," *Academy of Management Executive*, vol. 8 (1994), pp. 79–80.

[15] For insights on how to conduct effective meetings see Mary A. De Vries, *How to Run a Meeting* (New York: Penguin, 1994).

[16] Survey reported in "Meetings Among Top Ten Time Wasters," *San Francisco Business Times* (April 7, 2003): www.bizjournals.com/sanfrancisco/stories/2003/04/07/daily21.html.

[17] Quotes from Eric Matson, "The Seven Sins of Deadly Meetings," *Fast Company* (April/May, 1996), p. 122.

[18] Developed from ibid.

[19] The "linking pin" concept is introduced in Rensis Likert, *New Patterns of Management* (New York: McGraw-Hill, 1962).

[20] See Susan D. Van Raalte, "Preparing the Task Force to Get Good Results," *S.A.M. Advanced Management Journal*, vol. 47 (winter, 1982), pp. 11–16; Walter Kiechel III, "The Art of the Corporate Task Force," *Fortune* (January 28, 1991), pp. 104–6.

[21] Information from Jenny C. McCune, "Making Lemonade," *Management Review* (June, 1997), pp. 49–53.

[22] See Wayne F. Cascio, "Managing a Virtual Workplace," *Academy of Management Executive*, vol. 14 (2000), pp. 81–90; Sheila Simsarian Webber, "Virtual Teams: A Meta-Analysis,": http://www.shrm.org/foundation/findings.asp.

[23] William M. Bulkeley, "Computerizing Dull Meetings Is Touted as an Antidote to the Mouth That Bored," *Wall Street Journal* (January 28, 1992), pp. B1, B2.

[24] R. Brent Gallupe and William H. Cooper, "Brainstorming Electronically," *Sloan Management Review* (winter, 1997), pp. 11–21; Cascio, op cit.

[25] Cascio, op cit.

[26] See, for example, Paul S. Goodman, Rukmini Devadas, and Terri L. Griffith Hughson, "Groups and Productivity: Analyzing the Effectiveness of Self-Managing Teams," Chapter 11 in John R. Campbell and Richard J. Campbell,

Productivity in Organizations (San Francisco: Jossey-Bass, 1988); Jack Orsbrun, Linda Moran, Ed Musslewhite, and John H. Zenger, with Craig Perrin, *Self-Directed Work Teams: The New American Challenge* (Homewood, IL: Business One Irwin, 1990); Dale E. Yeatts and Cloyd Hyten, *High Performing Self-Managed Work Teams* (Thousand Oaks, CA: Sage, 1997).

27 Bradley L. Kirkman and Debra L. Shapiro, "The Impact of Cultural Values on Employee Resistance to Teams: Toward a Model of Globalized Self-Managing Work Team Effectiveness," *Academy of Management Review*, vol. 22 (1997), pp. 730–57.

28 For a discussion of effectiveness in the context of top management teams, see Edward E. Lawler III, David Finegold, and Jay A. Conger, "Corporate Boards: Developing Effectiveness at the Top," in Mohrman, op cit. (1998), pp. 23–50.

29 For a review of research on group effectiveness, see J. Richard Hackman, "The Design of Work Teams," in Jay W. Lorsch (ed.), *Handbook of Organizational Behavior* (Englewood Cliffs, NJ: Prentice-Hall, 1987), pp. 315–42; and J. Richard Hackman, Ruth Wageman, Thomas M. Ruddy, and Charles L. Ray, "Team Effectiveness in Theory and Practice," Chapter 5 in Cary L. Cooper and Edwin A. Locke, *Industrial and Organizational Psychology: Linking Theory with Practice* (Malden, MA: Blackwell, 2000).

30 Ibid; Lawler et al., op cit., 1998.

31 Example from "Designed for Interaction," *Fortune* (January 8, 2001), p. 150.

32 Marvin E. Shaw, *Group Dynamics: The Psychology of Small Group Behavior* (New York: McGraw-Hill, 1976).

33 See Warren Watson, "Cultural Diversity's Impact on Interaction Process and Performance," *Academy of Management Journal*, vol. 16 (1993); Christopher Earley and Elaine Mosakowski, "Creating Hybrid Team Structures: An Empirical Test of Transnational Team Functioning," *Academy of Management Journal*, vol. 5 (February, 2000), pp. 26–49; Jeanne Brett, Kristin Behfar, and Mary C. Kern, "Managing Multicultural Teams," *Harvard Business Review* (November, 2006), pp. 84–91.

34 J. Steven Heinen and Eugene Jacobson, "A Model of Task Group Development in Complex Organizations and a Strategy of Implementation," *Academy of Management Review*, vol. 1 (1976), pp. 98–111; Bruce W. Tuckman, "Developmental Sequence in Small Groups," Psychological Bulletin, vol. 63 (1965), pp. 384–99; Bruce W. Tuckman and Mary Ann C. Jensen, "Stages of Small-Group Development Revisited," *Group & Organization Studies*, vol. 2 (1977), pp. 419–27.

35 See for example, Edgar Schein, *Process Consultation* (Reading, MA: Addison-Wesley, 1988); and Linda C. McDermott, Nolan Brawley, and William A. Waite, *World-Class Teams: Working Across Borders* (New York: Wiley, 1998).

36 For a good discussion, see Robert F. Allen and Saul Pilnick, "Confronting the Shadow Organization: How to Detect and Defeat Negative Norms," *Organizational Dynamics* (Spring 1973), pp. 13–16.

37 See Schein, op cit., pp. 76–79.

38 Ibid., Show, op cit.

39 A classic work in this area is K. Benne and P. Sheets, *Journal of Social Issues*, vol. 2 (1948), pp. 42–47; see also, Likert, op cit., pp. 166–69; Schein, op cit. pp. 49–56.

40 Based on John R. Schermerhorn Jr., James G. Hunt, and Richard N. Osborn, *Organizational Behavior*, 9th ed. (New York: Wiley, 2005).

41 Research on communication networks is found in Alex Bavelas, "Communication Patterns in Task-Oriented Groups," *Journal of the Acoustical Society of America*, vol. 22 (1950), pp. 725–30; Shaw, op cit.

42 Schein, op cit., pp. 69–75.

43 A very good overview is William D. Dyer, *Team-Building* (Reading MA: Addison-Wesley, 1977).

44 Dennis Berman, "Zap! Pow! Splat!" *Business Week*, Enterprise issue (February 9, 1998), p. ENT22.

45 Schein, op. cit.

46 See Kathleen M. Eisenhardt, Jean L. Kahwajy, and L. J. Bourgeois III, "How Management Teams Can Have a Good Fight," *Harvard Business Review* (July–August 1997), pp. 77–85.

47 Victor H. Vroom and Arthur G. Jago, *The New Leadership: Managing Participation in Organizations* (Englewood Cliffs, NJ: Prentice-Hall, 1988); Victor H. Vroom, "A New Look in Managerial Decision-Making," *Organizational Dynamics* (spring 1973), pp. 66–80; Victor H. Vroom and Phillip Yetton, *Leadership and Decision-Making* (Pittsburgh: University of Pittsburgh Press, 1973).

48 Norman F. Maier, "Assets and Liabilities in Group Problem Solving," *Psychological Review*, vol. 74 (1967), pp. 239–49.

49 Ibid.

50 See Irving L. Janis, "Groupthink," *Psychology Today* (November 1971), pp. 43–46; *Victims of Groupthink*, 2d ed. (Boston: Houghton Mifflin, 1982).

51 These techniques are well described in Andre L. Delbecq. Andrew H. Van de Ven, and David H. Gustafson, *Group Techniques for Program Planning* (Glenview, IL: Scott, Foresman, 1975).

52. "Ryan Newman: Career Statistics." Yahoo! Sports. Accessed August 15, 2006, at http://sports.yahoo.com/nascar/nextel/drivers/176/career

53. Mike Harris, "Baker: Newman the Perfect Protégé," Associated Press (April 10, 2003).

54. "Ryan Newman Biography": www.penskeracing.com/newman.

55. Harris, op cit.

56. Dave Rodman, "Conversation: Ryan Newman." Turner Sports Interactive (June 9, 2003): http://www.nascar.com.

57. "Ryan Newman Biography," op. cit.

58. Harris, op cit.

59. Rodman, op cit.

60. "Newman Looking Forward to Speedweeks Experience": http://www.nascar.com.

61. Stove Bresidine, "Bottomless Tank Gives Newman Win," Associated Press (October 6, 2003).

Features:

Insights: Information from Brend Schlender, "Pixar's Fun House," *Fortune* (July 23, 2001); corporate website: http://www.pixar.com.

Issues and Situations: Information from Susan Carey, "Racing to Improve," *The Wall Street Journal* (March 24, 2006), pp. B1, B6; and, Sarah Max, "Seagate's Morale-athon," *Business Week* (April 3, 2006), pp. 110–111.

Kaffeeklatsch: Information from Geoffrey Colvin, "Why Dream Teams Fail," *Business Week* (June 12, 2006), pp. 87–92.

Team Project: Quote from Jena McGregor, "Game Plan: First Find the

Leaders," *Business Week* (August 21/28, 2006), pp. 102–103.

Real Ethics: For research see Bib Latané, Kipling Williams, and Stephen Harkins, "Many Hands Make Light the Work: The Causes and Consequences of Social Loafing," *Journal of Personality and Social Psychology*, vol. 37 (1978), pp. 822–832; and, W. Jack Duncan, "Why Some People Loaf in Groups and Others Loaf Alone," *Academy of Management Executive*, Vol. 8 (1994), pp. 79–80.

Chapter 17

[1] http://www.un.org/Overview/unin-brief/

[2] http://www.globalpolicy.org/secgen/kofi2.htm

[3] Ibid.

[4] http://www.nytimes.com/2005/02/10/technology/10carly.html?

[5] http://experts.about.com/e/c/ca/Carly_Fiorina.htm

[6] http://experts.about.com/e/c/ca/Carly_Fiorina.htm

[7] http://news.zdnet.com/2100-9595_22-6123609.html

[8] http://www.countdown.org/end_articles/fam_kofi_annans_astonishing_facts.htm

[9] http://www.un.org/aboutun/basic-facts/inetlaw.htm

[10] Peter Burrows, *Backfire – Carly Fiorina's High-Stakes Battle for the Soul of Hewlett-Packard* (Hoboken, NJ: John Wiley & Sons, 2003).

[11] Ibid.

[12] http://www.usatoday.com/money/companies/management/2005-02-10-departing-ceos-usat_x.htm

[13] "Ranking the Attributes," *The Wall Street Journal* (September 20, 2006), p. R3.

[14] Henry Mintzberg, *The Nature of Managerial Work* (New York: Harper & Row, 1973).

[15] John P. Kotter, "What Effective General Managers Really Do," *Harvard Business Review*, vol. 60 (November–December 1982), pp. 156–57; and *The General Managers* (New York: Macmillan, 1986).

[16] "Relationships Are the Most Powerful Form of Media," *Fast Company* (March 2001), p. 100.

[17] Jay A. Conger, *Winning 'Em Over: A New Model for Managing in the Age of Persuasion* (New York: Simon & Schuster, 1998), pp. 24–79.

[18] This discussion developed from ibid.

[19] *Business Week* (February 10, 1992), pp. 102–8.

[20] See Robert H. Lengel and Richard L. Daft, "The Selection of Communication Media as an Executive Skill," *Academy of Management Executive*, vol. 2 (August 1988), pp. 225–32.

[21] See Eric Matson, "Now That We Have Your Complete Attention," *Fast Company* (February–March 1997), pp. 124–32.

[22] David McNeill, *Hand and Mind: What Gestures Reveal about Thought* (Chicago: University of Chicago Press, 1992).

[23] Adapted from Richard V. Farace, Peter R. Monge, and Hamish M. Russell, *Communicating and Organizing* (Reading, MA: Addison-Wesley, 1977), pp. 97–98.

[24] Tom Peters and Nancy Austin, *A Passion for Excellence* (New York: Random House, 1985).

[25] This discussion is based on Carl R. Rogers and Richard E. Farson, "Active Listening" (Chicago: Industrial Relations Center of the University of Chicago, n.d.).

[26] Ibid.

[27] A useful source of guidelines is John J. Gabarro and Linda A. Hill, "Managing Performance," Note 9-96-022 (Boston, MA: Harvard Business School Publishing, n.d.).

[28] Carol Hymowitz, "Managers See Feedback from Their Staffers as Most Valuable," *Wall Street Journal* (August 22, 2000), p. B1.

[29] Developed from John Anderson, "Giving and Receiving Feedback," in Paul R. Lawrence, Louis B. Barnes, and Jay W. Lorsch (eds.), *Organizational Behavior and Administration*, 3d ed. (Homewood, IL: Richard D. Irwin, 1976), p. 109.

[30] A classic work on proxemics is Edward T. Hall's book, *The Hidden Dimension* (Garden City, NY: Doubleday, 1986).

[31] Mirand Wewll, "Alternative Spaces Spawning Desk-Free Zones," *Columbus Dispatch* (May 18, 1998), pp. 10–11.

[32] "Tread: Rethinking the Workplace," *Business Week* (September 25, 2006), p. IN.

[33] See Lengel and Daft, op cit. (1988).

[34] Information from Susan Stellin, "Intranets Nurture Companies from the Inside," *New York Times* (January 21, 2001), p. C4.

[35] Alison Overholt, "Intel's Got (Too Much) Mail; *Fortune* (March, 2001), pp. 56–58.

[36] Developed from *Working Woman* (November 1995), p. 14; and Elizabeth Weinstein, "Help! I'm Drowning in E-Mail!" *Wall Street Journal* (January 10, 2002), pp. B1, B4.

[37] Example from Heidi A. Schuessler, "Social Studies Class Finds How Far E-Mail Travels," *New York Times* (February 22, 2001), p. D8.

[38] Information from Esther Wachs Book, "Leadership for the Millennium," *Working Woman* (March 1998), pp. 29–34.

[39] Information from Hilary Stout, "Self-Evaluation Brings Change to a Family's Ad Agency," *Wall Street Journal* (January 6, 1998), p. B2.

[40] See Edward T. Hall, *The Silent Language* (New York: Doubleday, 1973).

[41] Richard E. Walton, *Interpersonal Peacemaking: Confrontations and Third-Party Consultation* (Reading, MA: Addison-Wesley, 1969), p. 2.

[42] See Kenneth W. Thomas, "Conflict and Conflict Management," in M. D. Dunnett (ed.), *Handbook of Industrial and Organizational Behavior* (Chicago; Rand McNally, 1976), pp. 889–935.

[43] See Robert R. Blake and Jane Strygley Mouton, "The Fifth Achievement," *Journal of Applied Behavioral Science*, vol. 6 (1970), pp. 413–27; Alan C. Filley, *Interpersonal Conflict Resolution* (Glenview, IL: Scott, Foresman, 1975).

[44] This discussion is based on Filley, op cit.

[45] Portions of this treatment of negotiation originally adapted from John R. Schermerhorn, Jr., James G. Hunt, and Richard N. Osborn, *Managing Organizational Behavior*, 4th ed. (New York: Wiley, 1991), pp. 382–87. Used by permission.

[46] See Roger Fisher and William Ury; *Getting to Yes: Negotiating Agreement Without Giving In* (New York: Penguin, 1983); James A. Wall, Jr., *Negotiation: Theory and Practice* (Glenview, IL: Scott, Foresman, 1985); and William L. Ury, Jeanne M. Brett, and Stephen B. Goldberg, *Getting Disputes Resolved* (San Francisco: Jossey-Bass, 1997).

[47] Fisher and Ury, op cit.

[48] Ibid.

[49] Developed from Max H. Bazerman, *Judgment in Managerial Decision Making*, 4th ed. (New York: Wiley, 1998), Chapter 7.

50 Fisher and Ury, op cit.

51 "*A classes grapher's Care*," Kellogg (Summer, 2006), p. 40.

52 Roy J. Lewicki and Joseph A. Litterer, *Negotiation* (Homewood, IL: Irwin, 1985).

53 "This Is the AFL-CIO." Accessed August 15, 2006, at This is the AFL-CIO http://aflcio.com/aboutus/thisistheaflcio/.

54 "Samuel Gompers and the American Federation of Labor." Digital History. Accessed September 14, 2006, at http://www.digitalhistory.uh.edu/database/article_display.cfm?HHID=228.

55 Ibid.

56 Ibid.

57 http://www.aflcio.org/aboutus/history/history/lewis.cfm

58 Ibid.

59 Ibid.

60 http://dictionary.laborlawtalk.com/Congress_of_Industrial_Organizations

61 Ibid.

62 Steven Greenhouse. "Unions Resume Debate Over Merging and Power." *New York Times*, November 18, 2004. Accessed September 14, 2006, at http://www.labornotes.org/archives/2004/12/articles/g.html

63 Ibid.

64 http://www.changetowin.org/about-us/who-we-are.html

65 http://experts.about.com/e/j/jo/John_Sweeney_(labor_leader).htm

Features:

Issues and Situations: Information from John Schnapp, "'Rightsizing' GM," *Wall Street Journal* (June 19, 2006), p. A14; Carol Hymowitz, "Mind Your Language: To Do Business Today, Consider Delayering, " *Wall Street Journal* (March 27, 2006), p. B1; "The Big Picture," *Business Week* (June 19, 2006), p. 13.

Kaffeeklatsch: Suggested by Marie G. McIntyre. "You're Boss Not Therapist, for Difficult Employee," *St. Louis Post-Dispatch* (March 19, 2006) p. E2.

Real Ethics: Information from "Bridget Jones", Blogger Fire Fury," CNN.com (July 19, 2006).

Chapter 18

1 http://www.brainyquote.com/quotes/authors/m/Margaret_j_wheatley.html

2 Nuclear Energy Institute, www.nei.org.

3 Ibid.

4 Ibid.

5 http://www.dod.mil/dfas/militarypay/newinformation/WebPayTable Version 2006updated.pdf.

6 http://www.eeoc.gov/facts/diabetes.html

7 Quote from "Today's Companies Won't Make It, and Gary Hamel Why," *Fortune* (September 4, 200), p. 386–87.

8 "The Renewal Factor: Friendly Fact, Congenial Controls," *Business Week* (September 14, 1987), p. 105.

9 Rob Cross and Lloyd Baird, "Technology Is Not Enough: Improving Performance by Building Institutional Memory," *Sloan Management Review* (spring 2000), p. 73.

10 Information from Pep: Sappal, "Integrated Inclusion Initiative," *The Wall Street Journal* (October 3, 2006), p. A2.

11 Based on discussion by Harold Koontz and Cryril O'Donnell, *Essentials of Management* (New York: McGraw-Hill, 1974), pp. 362–65; see also Cross and Baird, op.cit.

12 See John F. Love, *McDonald's: Behind the Arches* (New York: Bantam Books, 1986); and Ray Kroc and Robert Anderson, *Grinding It Out: The Making of McDonald's* (New York: St. Martin's Press, 1990).

13 Douglas McGregor, *The Human Side of Enterprise* (New York: McGraw-Hill, 1960).

14 Payton Fandray, "The Lords of Discipline, *continental* (September, 2006), pp. 97–98.

15 Example from George Anders, "Management Guru Turns Focus to Orchestras, Hospitals," *Wall Street Journal* (November 21, 2005), pp. B1, B5.

16 Information from Leon E. Wynter, "Allstate Rates Managers on Handling Diversity," *Wall Street Journal* (October 1, 1997), p. B1.

17 Information from Kathryn Kranhold, "U.S. Firms Raise Ethics Focus," *Wall Street Journal* (November 28, 2005), p. B4.

18 Information from Raju Narisetti, "For IBM, a Groundbreaking Sales Chief," *Wall Street Journal* (January 19, 1998), pp. B1, B5.

19 The "hot stove rules" are developed from R. Bruce McAfee and William Poffenberger, *Productivity Strategies: Enhancing Employee Job Performance* (Englewood Cliffs, NJ: Prentice-Hall, 1982), pp. 54–55. They are originally attributed to Douglas McGregor, "Hot Stove Rules of Discipline," in G. Strauss and L. Sayles, eds., *Personnel: The Human Problems of Management,* (Englewood Cliffs, NJ: Prentice-Hall, 1967).

20 Information from Karen Carney, "Successful Performance Measurement: A Checklist," *Harvard Management Update* (No. U9911B), 1999.

21 "Gauging the Wal-Mart Effect," *Wall Street Journal* (December 3–4, 2005), p.1 A9.

22 Eurrey results from "Too Much Work, Too Little Time, *Business Week* (July 16, 2001), p. 12.

23 http://software.seekingalpha.com/article/16814

24 Ibid.

25 http://www.latimes.com/technology/la-fi-briefs1.3sep01, 1, 3174504.story?coll=la-headlines-technology

26 http://www.thestreet.com/_googlen/newsanalysis/techgames/10306907.html?cm_ven=GOOGLEN&cm_cat=FREE&cm_ite=NA

27http://software.seekingalpha.com/article/16814

28Ibid.

29http://www.iotogo.com/contributor76_E.asp

30Seth Schiesel. "Gangs of New York." *New York Times*, October 16, 2005. Accessed February 4, 2006, at http://www.nytimes.com/2005/10/16/arts/16schi.html?ei=5088&en=a9b9949f979f4367&ex=1287115200&partner=rssnyt&emc=rss&pagewanted=print.

Features:

Insights: Information from "Daniel Yee, "Chick-Fill-A Recipe Winning Customers," *The Columbus Dispatch* (September 9, 2006), p. D1.

Issues and Situations: Information from Robert S. Kaplan and David P. Norton, "The Balanced Scorecard: Measures that Drive Performance," *Harvard Business Review* (July-August, 2005); see also Robert S. Kaplan and David P. Norton, *The Balanced Scorecard* (Cambridge, MA: Harvard Business School Press, 1996).

Kaffeeklatsch: Information from Alan Cane, "Are Virtual Offices a Benefit or Burden?" *The Irish Times* (July 14, 2006), p. 12.

Real Ethics: Paul Davidson, " 'Climate Has Changed' for Data Privacy," *USA Today* (May 12, 2006), p. B1; Ben Elgin, "The Great Firewall of China,"

Business Week (January 23, 2006), pp. 32–34; Alison Maitland, "Skype Says Text Messages Censored by Partner in China," *Financial Times* (April 19, 2006), p. 15; and, "Web Firms Criticized Over China," *CNN.com* (July 20, 2006).

Chapter 19

1 www.adageglobal.com/article?article_id=108670

2 www.missouri.edu/~news/releases/baskerswalmartstudy.html

3 Gogoi, Pallavi, and Robert Berner, "Wal-Mart Puts on a Happy Face," *Business Week Online*, April 19, 2006.

4 H. Lee Scott, "Who Pays for Health Care? A New Commitment for America," *San Francisco Chronicle* (March 16, 2006). at http://www.sfgate.com/cgi-bin/article.cgi?file=/chronicle/archive/2006/03/16/EDGO6HOO2V1.DTL (accessed april 20, 2006).

5 Jyoti Thottam. "Wal-Mart's Bank Shot." *Time* (April 17, 2006). (accessed April 20, 2006) at http://www.time.com/time/magazine/article/0,9171,1184049,00.html; Bernard Wysocki, Jr., "How Board Coalition Stymied Wal-Mart's Bid to Own a Bank," *Wall Street Journal* (October 23, 2006), pp. A1, A12.

6 "Wal-Mart Puts on a Happy Face," op. cit.

7 Ibid.

8 Ibid.

9 "China, Partner or Adversary, Comes Calling," *USA Today* (April 18, 2006) at http://www.usatoday.com/news/washington/2006-04-18-china-us_x.htm. (accessed April 20, 2006).

10 Anne Mulcahy, "How I Compete," *Business Week* (August 21/28, 2006), p. 55.

11 Gail Edmondson, "BMW's Dream Factory," *Business Week* (October 16, 2006), pp. 68–80.

12 Amy Merrick, "Asking 'What Would Ann Do?' " *Wall Street Journal* (September 16, 2006), pp. B1, B2.

13 Good overviews are available in R. Dan Reid and Nada R. Sanders, *Operations Management: An Integrated Approach*, 2nd ed. (Hoboken, NJ: John Wiley & Sons, 2006) and Roberta S. Russell and Bernard W. Taylor III, *Operations Management: Quality and Competitiveness in a Global Environment* (Hoboken, NJ: John Wiley & Sons, 2005).

14 "Survey Finds Workers Average Only Three Productive Days Per Week," www.microsoft.com/press/2005/mar 05 (retrieved October 20, 2006).

15 See Michael E. Porter, *Competitive Strategy: Techniques for Analyzing Industries and Competitors* (New York: Free Press, 1980) and *Competitive Advantage: Creating and Sustaining Superior Performance* (New York: Free Press, 1986); see also Richard A. D'Aveni, *Hyper-Competition: Managing the Dynamics of Strategic Maneuvering* (New York: Free Press, 1994).

16 Joan Woodward, *Industrial Organization: Theory and Practice* (London: Oxford University Press, 1965; republished by Oxford University Press, 1994).

17 Brian Hindo, "Everything Old Is New Again," *Business Week* (September 25, 2006), pp. 70.

18 This treatment is from James D. Thompson, *Organizations in Action* (New York: McGraw-Hill, 1967).

19 See Michael Hugos, *Essentials of Supply Chain Management*, 2nd ed. (Hoboken, NJ: John Wiley & Sons, 2006).

20 "Gauging the Wal-Mart Effect," *Wall Street Journal* (December 3–4, 2005), pp. Al, A9.

21 See Joseph M. Juran, *Quality Control Handbook*, 3rd ed. (New York: McGraw-Hill, 1979) and "The Quality Trilogy: A Universal Approach to Managing for Quality," in *Total Quality Management*, ed. H. Costin (New York: Dryden, 1994); W. Edwards Deming, *Out of Crisis* (Cambridge, MA: MIT Press, 1986) and "Deming's Quality Manifesto," *Best of Business Quarterly*, vol. 12 (winter 1990–1991), pp. 6–10. See also Howard S. Gitlow and Shelly J. Gitlow, *The Deming Guide to Quality and Competitive Position* (Englewood Cliffs, NJ: Prentice-Hall, 1987), and Juran, op cit. (1993).

22 Rosabeth Moss Kanter, "Transcending Business Boundaries: 12,000 World Managers View Change," *Harvard Business Review* (May–June 1991), pp. 151–64.

23 Dale Dauten, "Which One Would You Rather Be?" *St. Louis Dispatch* (October 8, 2006), p. C2.

24 See C. K. Prahalad, Patricia B. Ramaswamy, Jon R. Katzenbach, Chris Lederer, and Sam Hill, *Harvard Business Review on Customer Relationship Management* (Boston, MA: Harvard Business School Publishing, 1998–2001).

25 Information from "How Marriott Never Forgets a Guest," *Business Week* (February 21, 2000), p. 74.

26 For the classics see W. Edwards Deming, *Quality, Productivity, and Competitive Position* (Cambridge, MA: MIT Press, 1982) and Juran, op cit.

27 Rafael Aguay, *Dr. Deming: The American Who Taught the Japanese about Quality* (New York: Free Press, 1997); W. Edwards Deming, op cit. (1986).

28 See Edward E. Lawler III, Susan Albers Mohrman, and Gerald E. Ledford Jr., *Employee Involvement and Total Quality Management: Practices and Results in Fortune 1000 Companies* (San Francisco: Jossey-Bass, 1992).

29 Michael Hammer, *Beyond Reengineering* (New York: Harper Business, 1997).

30 Michael Hammer and James Champy, *Reengineering the Corporation: A Manifesto for Business Revolution*, rev. ed. (New York: Harper Business, 1999).

31 Hammer, *Beyond Reengineering*, op cit., p. 5; see also the discussion of processes, in Gary Hamel, *Leading the Revolution* (Boston, MA: Harvard Business School Press, 2000).

32 Thomas M. Koulopoulos, *The Workflow Imperative* (New York: Van Nostrand Reinhold, 1995); Hammer, *Beyond Reengineering*, op cit.

33 Paul Roberts, "Humane Technology—PeopleSoft," *Fast Company*, vol. 14 (1998), p. 122.

34 Ronni T. Marshak, "Workflow Business Process Reengineering," special advertising section, *Fortune* (1997).

35 A similar example is found in Hammer, *Beyond Reengineering*, op cit., pp. 9, 10.

36 Ibid., pp. 28–30.

37 Ibid., p. 29.

38 Ibid., p. 27.

39 Quotation from Hammer and Company Web site: www.hammerandco.com/WhatIsAProcessOrgFrames.html.

40 Michelle Maynard, "Toyota Shows Big 3 How It's Done," *New York Times* (January 13, 2006). at http://www.nytimes.com/2006/01/13/automobiles/13auto.html (accessed January 14, 2006).

41 M. Reza Vaghefi, "Creating Sustainable Competitive Advantage: The Toyota Philosophy and Its Effects," *Mastering Management Online* (October 2001) at

http://www.ftmastering.com/mmo/index.htm (accessed January 13, 2006).

[42] "Top 10 SUVs, Pickups and Minivans with the Best Residual Value for 2005," Edmunds.com, at http://www.edmunds.com/reviews/list/top10/103633/article.html (accessed January 14, 2006).

[43] "Making Things: The Essence and Evolution of the Toyota Production System," Toyota Motor Corporation, downloaded from http://www.toyota.com.

[44] "The 'Thinking' Production System: TPS as a Winning Strategy for Developing People in the Global Manufacturing Environment," Toyota Motor Corporation. downloaded from http://www.toyota.com.

[45] Ibid.

[46] Ibid.

[47] Maynard, op cit.

[48] *Team Project note* - Anne Mulcahy, "How I Compete," *Business Week* (August 21/28, 2006), p. 55.

Features:

Insights: Information from Christina Passariello, "Louis Vuitton Tries Modern Methods on Factory Lines," *Wall Street Journal* (October 9, 2006), pp. A1, A15.

Team Project: Anne Mulchay, "How I Complete," Business Week (August 21/28, 2006), p. 55.

Photo Credits

Chapter 1

Page 2: ©AP/Wide World Photos. **Page 6:** Courtesy Herman Miller, Inc. **Page 7:** Courtesy Monster.com. Copyright 2006, Monster, Inc. All rights reserved. www.monster.com. **Page 13:** Denis Scott/Taxi/Getty Images. **Page 17:** Tom Wagner/Corbis. **Page 18:** Courtesy Sage Publications. **Page 27:** Punit Paranjpe/Reuters/Landov LLC.

Chapter 2

Page 30: Carl D. Walsh/Aurora/Getty Images News and Sport Services. **Page 36:** Jerry Greenfield/Getty Images, Inc. **Page 39:** Photoshot/Landov LLC. **Page 42:** Time Magazine, ©Time Inc./Getty Images. **Page 43 (bottom):** Justin Sullivan/Getty Images. **Page 54:** Courtesy Tom's of Maine, Inc. **Page 49:** Courtesy Sage Publications.

Chapter 3

Page 58: ©AP/Wide World Photos. **Page 62:** ©AP/Wide World Photos. **Page 63:** ©AP/Wide World Photos. **Page 67:** Paul Barton/Corbis Stock Market. **Page 73:** Jen Petreshock/Getty Images, Inc. **Page 74:** Good to Great. ©2001 by Jim Collins. Reprinted with permission from Jim Collins. **Page 78:** ©AP/Wide World Photos.

Chapter 4

Page 82: Age Fotostock/SUPER-STOCK. **Page 86:** Courtesy Herman Miller, Inc. **Page 88:** ©AP/Wide World Photos. **Page 89:** ©AP/Wide World Photos. **Page 92:** ©AP/Wide World Photos. **Page 98:** Courtesy Harvard Business School Publishing. **Page 102:** ©AP/Wide World Photos.

Chapter 5

Page 106: Michael Fein/Bloomberg News /Landov LLC. **Page 110:** Jacques Alexandre/AgeFotostock. **Page 111:** ©AP/Wide World Photos. **Page 113:** ©AP/Wide World Photos. **Page 114:** KEVIN LEE/BLOOMBERG NEWS /Landov LLC. **Page 116:** ©AP/Wide World Photos. **Page 128:** ©AP/Wide World Photos. **Page 120:** Reprinted with permission of the American Psychological Association.

Chapter 6

Page 132: Michael Rosenfeld/Getty Images, Inc. **Page 135 (top):** ©AP/Wide World Photos. **Page 135 (center):** Tim Graham/Getty Images News and Sport Services. **Page 135 (just below center):** ©AP/Wide World Photos. **Page 135 (bottom):** Courtesy Huizenga Holdings, Inc. **Page 136 (top):** Hulton Archive/Getty Images News and Sport Services. **Page 136 (center):** ©AP/Wide World Photos. **Page 137:** Courtesy Count Me In. **Page 140:** Nic Miller/Digital Vision/Getty Images, Inc. **Page 142:** ©AP/Wide World Photos. **Page 146:** Reprinted with permission of the Academy of Management Journal. **Page 151:** William West/AFP/Getty Images News and Sport Services.

Chapter 7

Page 156: ©AP/Wide World Photos. **Page 160 (top):** ©AP/Wide World Photos. **Page 160 (bottom):** Andy Ryan/Stone/Getty Images, Inc. **Page 164:** ©AP/Wide World Photos. **Page 165:** ©AP/Wide World Photos. **Page 173:** Courtesy Springer Science and Business Media. **Page 178:** ©AP/Wide World Photos.

Chapter 8

Page 182: ©AP/Wide World Photos. **Page 186:** BLOOMBERG NEWS /Landov LLC. **Page 187:** Steve Cole/PhotoDisc/Getty Images, Inc. **Page 192:** Chad Ehlers/Getty Images, Inc. **Page 197:** Courtesy Harvard Business School Publishing. **Page 200:** ©AP/Wide World Photos.

Chapter 9

Page 204: Courtesy Mozilla Corporation. **Page 208:** ©AP/Wide World Photos. **Page 221:** Getty Images News and Sport Services. **Page 223:** Courtesy Sage Publications. **Page 225:** ©AP/Wide World Photos. **Page 228:** MIKE MERGEN/BLOOMBERG NEWS /Landov LLC.

Chapter 10

Page 234: MIKE FUENTES/Bloomberg News /Landov LLC. **Page 238:** Courtesy Siemens Corporation. **Page 241:** Beth Galton/Workbookstock/ Jupiter Images Corp. **Page 252:** Todd Davidson/Illustration Works/Getty Images. **Page 254:** Victoria Pearson/Getty Images. Reprinted with permission of Simon & Schuster. **Page 258:** STEPHEN HILGER/Bloomberg News/Landov LLC.

Chapter 11

Page 262: ©AP/Wide World Photos. **Page 265:** ©AFP. **Page 275:** Reprinted with permission of the American Psychological Association. **Page 279:** Reproduced with permission of Working Mother Media. **Page 280:** Ryuichi Sato/Getty Images, Inc. **Page 287:** Thomas Volk/Bloomberg News/Landov LLC.

Chapter 12

Page 290: ©AP/Wide World Photos. **Page 293:** ©AP/Wide World Photos. **Page 294:** ©Apple Computer, Inc. **Page 298:** Photodisc Green/Getty. **Page 305:** Ron Wurzer/Getty Images News and Sport Services. **Page 309:** Courtesy Routledge, Taylor & Francis Group. **Page 314:** MAXPPP/ Landov LLC.

Chapter 13

Page 318: ©AP/Wide World Photos. **Page 322:** ©AP/Wide World Photos. **Page 323:** Victoria Pearson/Stone/ Getty Images. **Page 327:** Courtesy W. L. Gore & Associates, Inc. **Page 334:** Reprinted from LEADERSHIP QUARTERLY, Vol. 17, Issue 2, 2006. Reproduced with permission from Elsevier. **Page 335:** PhotoDisc/Getty Images, Inc. **Page 337:** Cover art copyright c 2003 by Grove/Atlantic, Inc. Used by permission of the publisher. **Page 341:** William Thomas Cain/ Getty Images News and Sport Services.

Chapter 14

Page 344: Michael Buckner/Getty Images News and Sport Services. **Page 349:** ©AP/Wide World Photos. **Page 357:** ©AP/Wide World Photos. **Page 361:** Darren Robb/Getty Images, Inc. **Page 362 (top):** Bryan Peterson/Taxi/ Getty Images. **Page 362 (bottom):** Image supplied by John Wiley & Sons Ltd, publisher of Journal of Organizational Behavior. **Page 366:** ©AP/Wide World Photos.

Chapter 15

Page 370: Kevin Scanlon/Getty Images News and Sport Services. **Page 374:** Scott Olson/Getty Images News and Sport Services. **Page 375:** Chuck Savage/Corbis Images. **Page 376:** Getty Images News and Sport Services. **Page 384:** Reprinted with permission of the Academy of Management Journal. **Page 386:** PhotoDisc/Getty Images, Inc. **Page 390:** ©AP/Wide World Photos.

Chapter 16

Page 394: Chris Graythen/Getty Images News and Sport Services. **Page 398:** Sean Justice/Getty Images. **Page 403:** Denis Felix/Taxi/Getty Images, Inc. **Page 404:** Reprinted with permission of the Academy of Management

Journal. **Page 411:** ©AP/Wide World Photos. **Page 413:** ©AP/Wide World Photos. **Page 419:** Rusty Jarrett/Getty Images News and Sport Services.

Chapter 17

Page 422: Stan Honda/Getty Images News and Sport Services. **Page 426:** Courtesy Center for Creative Leadership. **Page 428:** Jose Luis Pelaez/Blend Images/Getty Images, Inc. **Page 431:** Getty Images News and Sport Services. **Page 433:** Getty Images News and Sport Services. **Page 446:** ©AP/Wide World Photos. **Page 441:** Reprinted with permission of the Academy of Management Journal.

Chapter 18

Page 450: Jerry Mason/Photo Researchers, Inc. **Page 453:** Courtesy

United States Army. **Page 455:** Courtesy Chick-fil-A, Inc. **Page 457:** Barros & Barros/Getty Images, Inc. **Page 462:** Stuart O' Sullivan//Getty Images. **Page 468:** REUTERS/Rockstar Games/ Landov LLC. **Page 463:** Reprinted with permission of the Academy of Management Journal.

Chapter 19

Page 472: Tim Boyle/Getty Images News and Sport Services. **Page 474:** Digital Vision/Getty Images. **Page 475:** Alexandra Boulat/VII/©AP/Wide World Photos. **Page 476:** Corbis Digital Stock. **Page 482:** Corbis Digital Stock. **Page 487:** Courtesy Harvard Business School Publishing. **Page 490:** KEN SHIMIZU/AFP/Getty Images News and Sport Services.

Organization Index

Name Index

Subject Index

SPECIAL FEATURES

REAL ETHICS

$100 Laptops
Résumé Lies
Employment Agreements
Coke's Secret Formula
Bolivia's Nationalization
Social Entrepreneurship
Left to Die
Fighting Poverty
Bankruptcy by Design
Downsized to Exhaustion
Wanted: Sales Women
Corporate Greens
Would You Volunteer?
Information Goldmine
Personality Testing
Social Loafing
Bloggers Beware
Data Privacy / Censorship
Fair Trade Fashion

RESEARCH BRIEF

Global Leadership
CSR Issues Pacesetters
Getting from Good to Great
What Really Works
Expatriate Success
Founder's Discount
Escalating Commitments
Planning by the Calendar
Female Board Members
Making Schools Work
Race Bias in Ratings
Strategic Management and Organizational Development
Charisma, Emotions, Moods
Psychological Capital
Life Satisfaction and Student Performance
Demographic Fault lines
Online Dispute Resolution
Top Managment Accountability
Sales Force Productivity

ISSUES AND SITUATIONS

Talent Wars
Ethics Training
Management Candor
Shifting Mindsets
Sweatshop Hunter
Pizzas With Passion
Lego's Wrong Turn
Camp Samsung
Being Contrarian
Microsoft's Bureaucracy
Sexual Harassment
Innovators-in-Chief
Managing the Boss
Executive Compensation
CEO Likeability
Team Building Novelties
Buzzwords / Mixed Messages
Balanced Scorecards
Lean Production

KAFFEEKLATSCH

Evidence-based Management
Day of Reckoning
Why Get an MBA
Best Jobs Going Forward
Work Hours in Europe
Gates + Buffett = Goodworks
Special Circumstances
Management Ethnography
Strategy Drivers
Social Network Analysis
Work Sabbaticals
Go Slow or Go Fast
Leadership Stereotypes
Job Disengagement
Typecasting
Dream Team Letdowns
Difficult Employees
Computer Addiction
Cost Cutting Backfires

INSIGHTS

Monster.com
Ben & Jerry's
Google
Herman Miller
Limited Brands
Count-Me-In
Motown
Kinko's
Starbucks
Dancing Deer Baking
Working Mother Media
Motorola
Southwest Airlines
Charlie Butcher
Whole Foods Market
Pixar Studios
Center for Creative Leadership
Chick-fil-A
Louis Vuitton